PERCY BYSSHE SHELLEY

*From a portrait by Amelia Curran painted in Rome in 1819 and preserved in the Shelley family until 1898*

*"I have no other likeness of him — & in so utter a desolation how invaluable to me is your picture!" Mary Shelley to Amelia Curran, August 14, 1822*

# Shelley and his Circle

being an edition of the manuscripts of

PERCY BYSSHE SHELLEY

SIR TIMOTHY SHELLEY

WILLIAM GODWIN

MARY WOLLSTONECRAFT

LEIGH HUNT

THOMAS LOVE PEACOCK

LORD BYRON

HARRIET GROVE

EDWARD JOHN TRELAWNY

HARRIET SHELLEY

MARY WOLLSTONECRAFT SHELLEY

CLAIRE CLAIRMONT

AND OTHERS

between 1773 and 1822

in

The Carl H. Pforzheimer Library

CONTRIBUTING EDITOR · VOLUME II

*The Diary of Harriet Grove*

FREDERICK L. JONES

THE CARL H. PFORZHEIMER LIBRARY

# Shelley and his Circle

## 1773–1822

EDITED BY
KENNETH NEILL CAMERON

VOLUME II

HARVARD UNIVERSITY PRESS
*Cambridge, Massachusetts*
*1961*

*Distributed in Great Britain by Oxford University Press, London*

This is the second volume of a complete edition of the manuscripts
in the Shelley and his Circle Collection (1773–1822) of The
Carl H. Pforzheimer Library, New York, N. Y.

DESIGNED BY BRUCE ROGERS

*Supplemental typography and binding design by Burton L. Stratton
Composed under the supervision of Charles W. Bowker in Monotype Caslon
Maps drawn by Liam Dunne*

*Typeset, electrotyped, printed, and bound at the Norwood, Massachusetts
plant of the Plimpton Press · Plates photolithographed by Meriden Gravure
Company · Endpaper maps printed by The American Banknote Company ·
Other maps and line drawings photoengraved by Reiman-Conway Associates*

*Library of Congress Catalog Card Number 60–5393*

PRINTED IN THE UNITED STATES OF AMERICA

*To the memory of*

## CARL H. PFORZHEIMER

*January 29, 1879*
*April 4, 1957*

# Contents

**VOLUME II**

# List of Manuscripts and Essays

## VOLUME II

### 1809

### 1810

# List of Manuscripts and Essays

# List of Manuscripts and Essays

# List of Manuscripts and Essays

# List of Manuscripts and Essays

## 1780

## 1781

## 1782

# List of Illustrations and Maps

# Shelley and his Circle

Manuscripts and Essays

1809–1811

# Shelley and his Circle : Manuscripts

## INTRODUCTION TO THE DIARY
## OF HARRIET GROVE

THE two small volumes which contain Harriet Grove's diary for 1809 and 1810 are, except for their fine, red leather binding, very much like the pocket-size memoranda and engagement books which can be found today in any stationer's shop. These books, like Harriet's, have pages with the month at the top and ruled spaces for each day of the week, and appended tables of useful information. Harriet's volumes differ only in that the information of daily usefulness in her time is no longer useful, and in the literary flavor which the 1809 volume has. Such books are not, of course, commonly used for diaries, the space allotted for each day being too restricted.[1]

How Harriet Grove used these volumes is indicated in the text and the Textual Notes. It needs only to be added here that her diary has an entry for almost every day of 1809–1810, but that the entries for December 31, 1809, and January 1–6, 1810, have been torn out. In addition, there are numerous words and lines, sometimes of considerable proportions, which she obliterated sometime after 1810. These deletions are with but rare exceptions about her cousin Percy Bysshe Shelley. Since the cancellations are in the same kind of (now) brownish ferrous ink in which the original entries were written, every effort to read them by strong light, magnification, ultra-violet light, and infra-red photography has failed, except for a few words here and there.

Harriet wrote in a very neat small hand. Except for the deleted passages, scarcely a word in her diary is unreadable. She kept within the narrow space allotted for the day, but often overflowed on the blank right-hand page for expenses, which she used only twice for its intended purpose.

Harriet Grove's diary is a valuable and fascinating document. Not only does it reveal important facts about Shelley's first love affair but it gives us a delightful glimpse at English country life among the landed gentry in the early nineteenth century and affords us an acquaintance

1. Though Harriet's volumes are almost identical in size and appearance, they differ considerably in detail, as might be expected in the products of two different publishers. (See Bibliographical Descriptions, sc 98 and sc 109.)

# The Carl H. Pforzheimer Library

with a lovely girl in her late teens in a large and intimate family. If the diary is to be read intelligently, we must first become familiar with the members of Harriet's family and with her near relations.

The Groves of Fern, Wiltshire, were an ancient family; their published pedigree[2] goes back to John de Grove of Chalfont St. Giles, who died in 1353. Their large estate known as "Fern" had been in their possession since 1583, when it was purchased by William Grove of Gray's Inn. Fern was in the southwest corner of Wiltshire, being four miles east of Shaftesbury and fifteen miles west of Salisbury. (Environs of Fern, page 503.) Harriet's grandfather, John Grove, had married twice. His second wife, Philippa, eldest daughter of Walter Long of Preshaw, Hampshire, was the mother of John's three surviving children.

One of these was Thomas Grove, Harriet's father (born in 1759), who inhabited Fern. His unmarried sister Philippa lived at Netherhampton, Wiltshire, where she was often visited by Harriet's family, partly because her house, near Salisbury, was a convenient overnight stop on journeys to Salisbury, Preshaw, Little Park, and other points. Harriet always called her Aunt Grove. She was a rather tart person and talked a great deal.

In 1782 Thomas Grove married Charlotte Pilfold, daughter of Charles Pilfold, of Sussex. The marriage resulted not only in the birth of eleven children, eight of whom survived, but in the addition of important relations for Harriet, whose mother had two sisters and at least two brothers. One of these sisters was Elizabeth, who married Timothy Shelley, of Field Place, Sussex, and was the mother of Percy Bysshe Shelley, Harriet's cousin. "Aunt Shelley" was a favorite with Harriet, who wrote her letters and always looked forward to her aunt's letters to herself and to her mother. The Groves and Shelleys felt closely drawn to each other. The other sister was Bathia, who was an intimate part of the Groves' daily life in that she married the Reverend Gilbert Jackson, D.D., rector of Donhead St. Mary, the parish church of Fern. This aunt Harriet always called Aunt Jackson. As for the uncles Pilfold,

2. In John Hutchins, *The History and Antiquities of the County of Dorset* (Westminster, 1861–1870), III, 568. Hutchins gives considerable information on the families, estates, etc., of the Grove circle. Two other works are also invaluable: Sir Richard Colt Hoare, *The History of Modern Wiltshire* (6 vols., London, 1822–1844); *Andrews' and Dury's Map of Wiltshire, 1773, A Reduced Facsimile* (Devizes, 1952).

# Shelley and his Circle : Manuscripts

they were James and Captain John Pilfold, R.N. The captain lived at Cuckfield, Sussex, about ten miles from Field Place. He became Shelley's most helpful relative in the days of his troubles with his father.

The eleven children of Thomas and Charlotte Grove, with their approximate ages as of January 1809, are as follows: Charlotte, twenty-six; Thomas, twenty-five; John, twenty-three; Emma Philippa, twenty-one; William, nineteen; Harriet, seventeen; Marianne, died in 1806; George, fifteen; Charles Henry, fourteen; Louisa, twelve; and Walter, about whom we know nothing except that he died young, before Harriet was born.[3]

With the persons, relationships, and places above in mind, the significance of Harriet's brief diary entries will be more readily understood. Before reviewing the contents of the diary, however, it is necessary to look into the previous relationship of Harriet and Shelley, whom Harriet called Bysshe, in conformity with the family practice.

Shelley and Harriet first met at Fern during the Easter holidays of 1804, when Shelley was almost twelve and Harriet almost thirteen. At that time Shelley was in his last months of attendance at Sion House Academy, operated by Dr. Greenlaw at Brentford, near London. Late in life (in 1857) Harriet's brother, Charles Henry Grove, related the circumstances of that first meeting in a letter which Hogg prints in the last chapter of his *Life of Percy Bysshe Shelley* (1858):

The first time I ever saw Bysshe was when I was at Harrow. I was nine years old; my brother George, ten. We took him [Shelley] up to Brentford, where he was at school, at Dr. Greenlaw's; a servant of my father's taking care of us all. He accompanied us to Ferne, and spent the Easter holidays there. The only circumstance I can recollect in connection with that visit was, that Bysshe, who was some few years older than we were, thought it would be good service to play carpenters, and, under his auspices, we got the carpenters' axes, and cut down some of my father's young fir-trees in the park. My father often used to remind me of that circumstance.

I did not meet Bysshe again after that till I was fifteen, the year I left the navy [as we shall see in Harriet's diary].

Shelley began corresponding with Harriet sometime in 1808. There is no evidence that he and Harriet had met since 1804, or that Harriet

3. Further information will be found in "Harriet Grove's Family and Near Relations," below.

# The Carl H. Pforzheimer Library

had ever been to Field Place. Something served to initiate the exchange of letters, which was already in vigorous progress at the beginning of 1809, and Harriet's references to "dear Field Place" lead one to think that she had visited there.

Harriet's diary for 1809 opens with a memorandum on three items concerning the last days of 1808, each of which is significant for the whole of 1809–1810. On Friday, December 30, they had driven twelve miles south to Blandford, Dorset, to attend a "pleasent [*sic*] Ball" at the Portmans' house, and on the next day had returned to Fern. This may have been an annual affair, for on January 11, 1810, they had another "most pleasent Ball" at the Portmans'. Whether in 1808 they saw their relatives, the Farquharsons, at Langton House, close at hand, Harriet does not say, but they probably did. The Portmans — Mr., Mrs., and their "beautiful children" — appear often in Harriet's diary. The second item — "I hear that Aunt Shelley gave a Ball on Friday – 30th 1808" — shows a live interest in what was going on at Field Place. She probably got the news from the third item (canceled after 1810, along with almost all others relating to Shelley), which begins, "Bysshe tells me in his Letter that . . ."

Harriet was a diligent correspondent. When her brothers and sisters were away from home, she wrote to them often. On the 4th of January she wrote to Charles, who was in the Navy, and after receiving from him "a very long letter" on the 7th, wrote him again on the 8th. On the 4th she also wrote to Aunt Shelley, and on the same day received a letter from Bysshe, to which she replied on the 7th. Several times she anticipated the day her letters would be received and when a reply might be expected. On January 9 she noted, "Bysshe will get my letter today." We find also that her twelve-year-old sister Louisa corresponded with Shelley's sister Mary. Harriet received a letter from Bysshe on the 19th and replied at once. She was looking forward eagerly to the coming of her brother John, for he had been "spending a week there at that delightful place," Field Place, and would be full of news about the Shelleys. He arrived on the 24th, probably bringing her a letter from Bysshe, from whom she heard on the same day. Another letter from Bysshe came on the 29th, and Louisa heard from Shelley's sister Mary at the same time.

[ 478 ]

# Shelley and his Circle : Manuscripts

*Introduction*                                    *Diary of Harriet Grove*

On February 3 Harriet wrote Aunt Shelley, and on the 10th was "much dissappointed [*sic*] at not hearing from" her. On February 4 there was a letter from Bysshe, to which she replied on the 9th. The 15th brought another letter from Bysshe, which she answered on the 16th. "*Dear Dear Louisa*" went back to school at Bath on the 18th; there she was apparently under the care of Mrs. Wilsonn. On the 21st Harriet "Heard from Bysshe & we shall *certainly* see him in London. *I am so glad of it.*" This letter was answered on the 23rd. Letters between the two became for a while almost daily. On March 1 Harriet received "an immense long letter," then other letters on March 3 and 8, to which she replied promptly. She also continued writing to Aunt Shelley, and to her brother Charles and sister Louisa. On March 7 it was worth noting in her diary that "My Mother heard from Dear Aunt Shelley." On the 11th she "Heard from My Dearest Aunt Shelley," to which letter she replied the next day.

The beginning of April brought excitement, for the spring trip to London was near at hand. On the 1st "We heard from John [he had returned to London on March 1] who thinks we shall see Aunt Shelley in Town which I am very glad of." She also had a letter from Bysshe, and added: "I hope this Month I shall be more fortunate *in seeing* the *person I wish* than I was at Xmas — I think I shall." On April 9 came another letter from Bysshe.

On Monday the 10th Harriet packed up for the London excursion. On Tuesday, Mr. and Mrs. Grove, Charlotte, and Harriet set out and slept the first night at Halford Bridge. On Wednesday they were in London, where they put up at John's house at 49 Lincoln's Inn Fields, which Harriet saw for the first time, and liked. A "long letter from Bysshe" was waiting for her; another came on Thursday and another on Saturday. On Sunday the 16th Bysshe and his father arrived: "the former I am very glad to see – I think Mr. Shelley appears cross ⟨——⟩ for what *reason I know* not." Harriet and Bysshe had four swift days together. On Monday they saw *Richard the Third* and the farce of *Mother Goose.* Harriet does not say that Bysshe accompanied their party, but it cannot be doubted that he did. On Tuesday "Bysshe went about Town with us." On Wednesday they "went to Clapham & saw my cousin Shelleys who I think the Nicest Girls I ever saw." These were Hellen and Mary,

# The Carl H. Pforzheimer Library

who attended Miss Fenning's School at Clapham.[4] That evening they went to the play again. The magic days came to an end on Thursday when Bysshe departed. Letter-writing was resumed at once, for Harriet wrote Bysshe on the very day he left, and again the next day, and possibly the next day also. On the 23rd Harriet received "the songs" from Bysshe, probably Shelley's own poems. On the 24th her sister Charlotte "made me a present of the Pink Dress dear Bysshe chose for us, for which I am very much obliged to them." Until the Groves left London on May 19, the cancellations in Harriet's diary are numerous. They clearly indicate that Shelley and Harriet exchanged letters every two or three days; on the 29th there was "an immense long letter from B."

Though apparently Harriet received two letters from Bysshe immediately after her return to Fern from London, there is no indication of further correspondence until June 6, three days after her return from Salisbury. There were, or appear to have been, other letters on June 13, 20, 22, 24, 27, and 29, to which Harriet replied promptly. Harriet also continued to write to Aunt Shelley, and Louisa to Mary Shelley.

Four days after the return from Salisbury, Harriet's father and his kinsman, Walter Long, discovered that "Old Fern will tumble down as the front is cracked all the way down." Harriet was "very sorry for it." Mr. Hamilton was called in, and it was soon obvious that the old house would have to be torn down and a new one erected; the initial plan was to repair old Fern, but this had to be given up. Mr. Hamilton submitted plans, which were approved. Louisa returned from her school at Bath on June 16. Two days later Harriet "Went to Lower Donhead Church & looked at the Parsonage house which we have some idea of inhabiting whilst Fern is rebuilding." The removal to the Parsonage took place on Harriet's eighteenth birthday, Monday, June 26: "Such a bustle left Dear Old Fern   Mama & Louisa went in the Pheaton [*sic*] with two family pictures before them & Charlotte & myself walked to the Parsonage Lower Donhead." (Environs of Fern, page 503.)

Though the Grove family life went on much the same, the point of view was somewhat altered. Almost every day they walked or rode the slightly less than two miles to Fern, to watch the demolition of the old house, to choose a site for the new one, then to watch the erection of

4. See sc 152 (Apr. 24, 1811).

# Shelley and his Circle : Manuscripts

the house, and always to look after the tenants and the farming, the last being the task of Mr. Grove.

Bysshe and Harriet kept up a vigorous correspondence in July. Harriet received letters on July 6, 8, 11, 13, 14(?), 15, 16, 22, 27, and 31. Her replies were often on the same day she received a letter: "Heard from Bysshe & wrote to him."

John Grove had spent a week at Field Place in January. We learn on July 12 that Bysshe's sister "Elizabeth has written a letter to John to invite him to Field Place." In July, too, Harriet began to correspond with Shelley's sister Elizabeth. On August 4 she had a letter from Elizabeth and answered it the same day. This correspondence increased; and now Harriet was writing to three people at Field Place: Aunt Shelley, Bysshe, and Elizabeth. On August 5 "our new Barouche" came. Before leaving Little Park on August 10, Harriet had two more letters from Bysshe.

At home at the Parsonage, the usual visiting, dining, and receiving of guests was resumed. "Dear John came" on September 1, full probably of news about Field Place, which was augmented by letters from Bysshe on September 3 and 5, and by "a quiz from Elizabeth." On the 6th a new and important person entered Harriet's diary, Mr. William Helyar, with whom John dined, and who himself dined with the Groves on September 10. It was to be a long time yet before Harriet came to look upon him as a future husband. In fact, her diary never gives the least indication that she ever regarded him with affection. When William Helyar came on the scene, Harriet was longing "for Mama to hear from Aunt Shelley." The letter came on September 17, and "Dear Aunt Shelley . . . says she shall always be glad to hear from me." On the 19th she had "a most affect[ionate] letter from Elizabeth."

On September 28 Aunt Jackson's husband introduced the new rector, Mr. Fletcher, to the Groves. His arrival necessitated their removal from the Parsonage. On October 3 they moved to Tollard, some five miles to the southeast, and three miles south of Fern. (Environs of Fern, page 503.) "I like this House better than [the Parsonage at] Lower Donhead" was Harriet's opinion; "Williams room is so close to mine that I hear every thing he says."

Beginning with September 6, 1809, a startling change occurs in

# The Carl H. Pforzheimer Library

Harriet's diary: for the remainder of 1809 and the whole of 1810, there are, with but three or four exceptions, no further recordings of letters from Bysshe or of letters written to him by Harriet. Unreadable cancellations referring probably to such letters occur through September 19, but thereafter there are very few cancellations in the diary. Harriet kept up a brisk correspondence with Elizabeth and Aunt Shelley, which she makes a record of in her diary, and there is plenty of evidence to prove that her interest in Bysshe had not diminished. There can be no doubt that her correspondence with Bysshe continued with the same regularity for a long time. What happened one can only conjecture, but most likely Harriet had decided to become more circumspect in making entries which might indicate the serious interest of her heart. People will occasionally pry into other people's diaries, and Harriet had probably suffered embarrassment from the quizzing of some such prying person or persons.

While at Tollard the Groves attended the church of Mr. John Helyar, uncle of William and Harry Helyar, the latter of whom lived at Sedgehill. John Helyar enters Harriet's diary on Saturday, October 7, when he called on the Groves. They attended his church the next day and were much pleased with his sermon. Thereafter they became intimately associated with the John Helyars, and Harriet wrote often of his excellent sermons. Other members of the Helyar family also from this time appear frequently in the diary. William Helyar saw the Groves at Tollard four days in a row, December 1–4, and on the last day breakfasted with them and went hunting with Harriet's father.

The diary for the first six days of January 1810 is missing. On January 8 Harriet "Wrote a long letter to Eliz$^{th}$ Shelley," and on the 9th she had a letter from "⟨dear⟩ John who has been at Field Place & been very gay there & liked his visit very much." In a letter to Charlotte, received on February 7, William "says he thinks I [Harriet] shall never be married that I do not care whether I ever do or not. He says he thinks I never liked any one so much as ⟨———⟩, that is a thing no one will *ever know* but myself." The name crossed out, could it be any other than Bysshe? On the 11th Harriet had a letter from Elizabeth Shelley. "A Deep snow" fell on the 15th and kept Aunt Grove, who "talks incessantly," from going home, and Hellen Tregonwell from coming, until the 24th. On the 22nd Aunt Grove "gave Charles a sort of a Lecture,

# Shelley and his Circle : Manuscripts

he did not swallow it very quietly." The 16th and the 23rd brought letters from Elizabeth, the last bearing with it "a part of B[ysshe']s Poem."

On March 5 Harriet received "a Parcel & letter from my Greatest Friend [7 lines are here canceled]." This could be no other than Bysshe, who probably sent books and more poetry. Harriet "Shewed the Poem," probably to Charles and Charlotte, who thought it "nonsense." Bysshe's poem was returned to him on the 10th. Two days later "My Father & Mother talk of going to Field P[lace] in our way to Town, How Happy I am for that." Harriet forwarded the Field Place idea by writing Elizabeth Shelley on the 21st "a letter which I hope may be the means of our going to Dear Field Place in our way to Town." On the same day William Helyar called at Tollard. The hoped-for letter from Elizabeth came on the 23rd: "just such a one as I wished for." The trick was turned, for Elizabeth's letter was followed on the 25th by a letter from her parents inviting the Groves to Field Place. For a brief while Harriet feared they would not go, "for which I feel the greatest sorrow as I had made up my mind for the pleasure of spending a few days at Dear Field-Place." At last, on March 27, "they say they will go to Field-Place for one day. I have written to tell E[lizabeth] of it, for it makes me so happy." The very next day she received the first of Shelley's published works: "Bysshe has sent C[harlotte] & me Zastrozzi, as it is come out." This short Gothic romance was published in London by G. Wilkie and J. Robinson, 57 Paternoster Row. Harriet was offended by Charles, who "does nothing but abuse B[ysshe's] Romance I believe he does it the more because he thinks it makes him appear a great man, but I think it makes him appear very illnatured to critisise it so *very* much." In a very short time now Harriet was to see the author himself.

The trip to London was made first a visiting excursion. Leaving Tollard on Monday, April 2, they called at Compton, stopped two nights at Netherhampton with Aunt Grove, and three nights with the Bromleys in Southampton, and got to Little Park on April 7. Here they remained with the Waddingtons for nine days. William joined them there on the 13th and decided to go to Field Place with them.

On Monday, April 16, the Groves left Little Park very early, and arrived at Field Place the same day — "⟨they⟩ are all very glad to see us. I can not tell what to make of it    very strange." This impression of strangeness persisted. "Still more odd," she wrote the next day. Harriet and her brothers William and Charles, Bysshe, and Elizabeth walked to Horsham and on the way saw the "Old House St Irvyne," a beautiful estate belonging to the Duke of Norfolk. "Had a long conversation but more perplexed than ever." In the evening they walked "to Strood by moonlight," an experience several times put into verse by Bysshe. The next day they went to Horsham again, then "left the pleasentest party in the world" to go to Cuckfield to visit with Captain Pilfold, the brother of Harriet's mother. Harriet was not pleased with the change. On the 19th they "Walked in Col. S[ergison's] Park very pretty I daresay, but my thoughts wont let me think about it."

What was the mystery that Harriet felt about her? There can be no doubt that she was ecstatically happy with Bysshe and the Shelleys. Charles Grove recollected in 1857 that "Bysshe was at that time more attached to my sister Harriet than I can express, and I recollect well the moonlight walks we four [should be five] had at Strode, and also at St. Irving's." He goes on to speak of "the dissolution [later] of an engagement between Bysshe and my sister, which had previously been permitted, both by his father and mine."[5] It seems quite clear from Harriet's diary that up to this happy meeting at Field Place there had been no kind of engagement. In all likelihood, then, what happened, and what made Harriet feel strange, was that her parents and Bysshe's parents were observing them very closely, and that at this time, seeing how happy their children were, they agreed to an informal engagement. If this is true, the general impression that the engagement had existed a considerable time before it was broken is false.

The Groves went to London on April 21, and in the Lincoln's Inn Fields house found John and "his cat perfectly well & very happy to see us." Four days later (April 25) they were joined by "Dear Aunt Shelley & my Cousins" Bysshe and Elizabeth, who remained ten days. The next morning Harriet "Walked in the Fields ⟨with dear Bysshe⟩, then went shopping & had great fun"; obviously Bysshe accompanied them shopping. They left their mothers at Mrs. Barton's; when these had got home in a dirty hackney coach, Aunt Shelley said, "she shall send for a Chain & Chain us to her." That evening and again the next

5. Quoted in Hogg, *Shelley*, II, 154–155.

day they went to the play. But there is a significant difference in the entry: "Walked out [?with] Percy." Thus suddenly Harriet shifts from Bysshe to Percy, which she continues hereafter to use. This is surely another sign of their intimacy, for lovers commonly like to use names which are not used by everyone else. That evening "P[ercy], Mama & myself sat up till the rest of the party came home & had a most delightful conversation." Again, shopping "with the Shelleys in a Hackney Coach" took up a part of another day. The 29th being a Sunday, they went to St. Paul's but were too late for the service. In the afternoon they went to Kensington Gardens, where Harriet hurt her foot. One suspects that the foot was partially an excuse for remaining indoors with Percy on Monday and Tuesday and most of Wednesday, so that while the others were out they could enjoy delicious conversation. On Tuesday evening "We all staid at home"; Harriet "played & they all danced Eliz[th] talks & is in as great spirits as ever." Several similar references to Elizabeth give us a clear impression of her as a vivacious, happy girl. On Wednesday evening (May 2) they went to the play and Harriet "liked it well enough," but obviously would have preferred a tête-à-tête with Percy. They were more fortunate on Thursday morning when "All the Party went out but me & Dearest P[ercy]." Tom Medwin of Horsham, Shelley's cousin, dined with them that day; he had probably met Harriet for the first time recently at Field Place. As for the opera in the evening, "I hate it more than ever, so does P[ercy]," for which opinion there are two obvious reasons. The next and last day, Harriet and Percy had one more morning together in the house. This was followed by "a most stupid" dinner with the Longs. Elizabeth Shelley told Harriet "something that kills me with laughing but which hinders her from coming to Tollard I am sorry to say." One would like to know what this was. On Saturday, May 5, "The Shelleys left us very sorry." There is more, but Harriet canceled it later and it is unreadable.

The remaining thirteen days in London were pleasant, but were in no way comparable to the ten days which preceded them. Moreover, for a time Harriet and her mother both had colds. The youthful musician and friend of Percy, Edward Fergus Graham,[6] came three times to give Harriet music lessons; he encouraged her to think she had a good singing

6. See SC 113 (May 20, 1810).

voice. Her two uncles Pilfold, James and Captain John, came several times to see them. On May 13 Shelley's father called; "he looks very unwell . . . Uncle [Pilfold] & him shook hands & were friends during the time he staid." He came also the next day and was "so pleasent, I am quite happy to see him so he gave me a letter from Eliz$^{th}$." It may be that Timothy Shelley's pleasantness was caused by his now looking upon Harriet as a more significant person in his life, in that she might be his future daughter-in-law. When Timothy came a third time on the 18th, to bid them good-bye, he was "in great spirits." During these days Harriet noted only one letter from Percy; on the 10th she had "heard from P[ercy]." Since she had long ago cautiously and purposefully begun to omit any reference to their correspondence, this note appears to be a slip.

The next six weeks at Tollard were the loneliest and saddest of the years 1809–1810 for Harriet. She and Charles were the only children at home, and Charles was often away visiting. Tom and Henrietta went to Cwm Elan in Wales on June 7, still further narrowing the family circle. On May 31 they heard that Louisa was ill with the whooping cough at Bath. Harriet's father and mother went to fetch her home. Upon their arrival on June 5 followed days of good hope alternating with deep anxiety. Mr. Wilkins, the surgeon, and Dr. Bearwood bled the child five times in all. Harriet "sat up with her all night" on June 17. She died on June 19 and was buried on the 25th. Aunt Jackson and Aunt Grove were a great help in this trying time.

Harriet was tremendously upset by the loss of her younger sister, and her mother sank under her sorrow. It was thought advisable that they should go away for a while. The Groves therefore went, on June 27, to Aunt Grove's at Netherhampton for six days. Then they went on July 3 to Muddiford, a seaside resort.

On July 14 occurs one of the now rare entries: "Wrote to B[ysshe] & Eliz$^{th}$ Shelley." Upon their return to Tollard on August 13, Harriet was "Much rejoiced at the return of Dear Charlotte & George." Pleasing also was the progress on the new house at Fern; the roof was being put on.

On August 30 Harriet "Wrote to Lucy Bury Percy &c." On September 17 she "Received the Poetry of Victor & Cazire, Charlotte offended & with reason as I think they have done very wrong in publishing what they have of her." This little volume of poems by Shelley and his sister Elizabeth was entitled *Original Poetry* by Victor and Cazire. It was printed at Worthing, not far from Field Place, and published by the none too reputable London bookseller, John Joseph Stockdale. It is the publisher who tells us that 1500 copies were printed, and that when he informed Shelley that one of the poems was by Monk Lewis, Shelley destroyed the whole edition. Not until 1898 was a copy discovered; and that may be the copy sent to Harriet, for in 1898 it was in the possession of one of the descendants of Harriet's brother Charles.

Charlotte did indeed have reason to be offended by one of the poems written by Elizabeth (Cazire). It is an epistle addressed to Harriet, and is a clever commentary on Charlotte's proposed visit in Cuckfield with Captain Pilfold, the object of which, as the Shelleys saw it, was to cultivate Colonel Sergison's affections. The epistle is dated April 30, 1810, and was therefore written in London while the Shelleys were visiting with the Groves. It cannot be doubted that Harriet read the poem in London and was much amused by it. To publish it, however, was quite a different thing. The relevant lines begin as follows:

> So [Charlotte] is going to [Cuckfield] you say,
> I hope that success her great efforts will pay
> That [Sergison] will see her, be dazzled outright,
> And declare he can't bear to be out of her sight.

It is possible that this epistle is connected with the mysterious entry for September 25: "My Father had a letter from M$^r$ S[helley?] which I am sorry for, as it gives more trouble." Could Harriet mean that Timothy Shelley's apology for his son's indiscretion, and comment on possible repercussions at Cuckfield, were rather calculated to disturb her relations with Percy than to do any good?

In Harriet's diary there is no further reference to Percy or to anyone at Field Place, except to a letter from Aunt Shelley to Harriet's mother. Life at Tollard continued much as heretofore, but with an increased tempo. There was constant mingling with neighbors, including the Arundells of Wardour and Ashcombe; visits to Littleton (where Tom now lived), Langton, Whatcombe (south of Blandford), Dinton (north of Fern); dancing, the reading of novels aloud, the coming and going of

# The Carl H. Pforzheimer Library

Harriet's brothers. The diary ends with an invitation to Littleton for New Year's Day, and an expectation of soon attending the annual Shaftesbury Ball.

Though Harriet's diary gives not a single hint, much had happened since those happy days in April at Field Place and in London. There is every reason to believe that Charles Grove's memory was accurate in 1857 when he wrote:

In the course of that summer [of 1810] . . . a continual correspondence was going on, as I believe there had been before, between Bysshe and my sister Harriet. But she became uneasy at the tone of his letters on speculative subjects, at first consulting my mother, and subsequently my father also on the subject. This led at last, though I cannot exactly tell how, to the dissolution of an engagement between Bysshe and my sister, which had previously been permitted, both by his father and mine.

Though Shelley was always philosophical, it is unlikely that his speculations began to alarm Harriet until he entered Oxford in October 1810 and began reading Locke, Hume, and Godwin. His opinions, which he liked to express freely and at length, did then become such as might well be most disturbing to Harriet. It is also likely that William Helyar, though he does not appear in the diary during the autumn of 1810, had become more attentive to Harriet and had for that very reason been omitted from her diary. Certain it is that when Shelley went home for the Christmas holidays, he was not altogether sure that Harriet was lost to him; but he soon knew of the man Harriet intended to marry. That Shelley suffered acutely, his letters to Hogg during the vacation are ample proof. The loss of Harriet also made his reactions against religion far more violent than they otherwise would have been. It was mainly from the Groves that the Shelleys learned how far astray Shelley's opinions had gone. In their deep concern to bring him back to orthodoxy they "persecuted" him. At home, then, Shelley had two causes of unhappiness: the loss of Harriet and the great dissatisfaction of his family with his mode of thinking. His father wanted him to quit Oxford, but Shelley refused to do so.

The first letter to Hogg in which Shelley shows that he may have lost Harriet is dated December 20. In it his anger is directed toward Christianity: "I swear on the altar of perjured love to revenge myself on the hated cause of the effect which *even now* I can scarcely help deploring." On December 26 "My unhappiness is excessive." On January 1 (sc 127) he says: "is she not gone — and yet *I* breathe *I* live"; on January 3 (sc 128): "she is no longer mine, she abhors me as a Deist, as what *she* was before. . . . Is suicide wrong? I slept with a loaded pis-tol & some poison last night but did not die." On January 6 (sc 129): "Forsake her! forsake one whom I loved! can I? never but she is gone, she is lost to me forever, forever." He encloses a five-stanza poem which is clearly inspired by his miserable condition, in that it is about his yearning for "an heart so sincere," which would truly be a gem of great price. The first stanza reads:

> Oh! take the pure gem to where southernly breezes
>     Waft repose to some bosom as faithful as fair
> In which the warm current of Love never freezes
>     As it rises unmingled with selfishness there
> Which untainted by Pride, unpolluted by care
> Might dissolve the dim ice drop, might bid it arise
> Too pure for these regions, to gleam in the skies

On January 11 (sc 132): "She is gone, she is lost to me forever    she is married, married to a clod of earth, she will become as insensible herself, all those fine capabilities will moulder."[7] The return to Oxford shortly after January 17 and the rapid series of events which led to his expulsion on March 25, 1811, were an alleviation to Shelley's unhappiness. The rift with Harriet did by no means disrupt his association with the Grove family. While he was in London after his expulsion, he was often with John and Charles in Lincoln's Inn Fields, and in July he went to Cwm Elan in Wales upon the invitation of Thomas Grove, junior, Harriet's oldest brother.

It is a mistake to think, as some do, that losing Harriet had deep and permanent effects on Shelley. As Harriet had already found someone to console her before she renounced Shelley, so Shelley had already met another Harriet who was soon to make his first love easy to forego. Indeed,

7. It is curious that Shelley should say at this date that Harriet was already "married." The news seems to be quite fresh, and obviously had reached him in a distorted form, for the fact could have been no other than that Harriet was engaged to William Helyar. It is a new element in his sorrow, which hitherto was probably related only to Harriet's breaking their engagement. (See sc 132, Jan. 11, 1811, Commentary.)

# The Carl H. Pforzheimer Library

Shelley beat his cousin to the altar. He married Harriet Westbrook in Edinburgh on August 29, 1811, whereas Harriet married William Helyar sometime later in 1811.

What kind of person was Harriet Grove? If her diary did not exist, we would know little about her except that she was a beautiful girl whom Shelley loved and who made a deep impression upon his and her cousin, Thomas Medwin. In his *Life of Percy Bysshe Shelley* (1847) Medwin said: "I still remember Miss Harriet Grove, and when I call to mind all the women I have ever seen, I know of none that surpassed, or that could compete with her. She was like one of Shakspeare's women – like some Madonna of Raphael."[8]

But fortunately the diary does exist, and from it we can readily construct her character. One of her most striking characteristics is her love for laughter, which indicates a delightful lightheartedness. She likes to laugh, to hear others laugh. This is combined with a very affectionate disposition. She loved and respected her parents and she loved her brothers and sisters, and in the restricted space in her diary she referred to them constantly as "my dear Father," "my dear Mother," "dear John," "dear dear William," "dear Aunt Shelley." For two whole years she does not mention a single instance of anger or any other lack of harmony in the family circle. Her friendliness extended to other people, whom from infants to the aged she enjoyed. There was nothing insipid or pious about Harriet's amiability. Indeed, she had a keen eye for interesting details and for character. She did not hesitate to say that she was glad a guest was going away, that an evening was tiresome, that a person was a bore. The Bennett girls, Mrs. and Miss Cooke, and Mr. Wake annoyed her more than most people. But in what she says about these and others there is no shade of vindictiveness; there is in fact usually a hint of humor. Since her small book permitted her to write only a few words each day, it was necessary to be highly selective. The incident she chose is usually vivid and significant.

It can hardly be doubted that Harriet had been away to school for several years, as her sister Louisa and Mary and Hellen Shelley were in 1809–1810. Evidently her formal education was over before she was seventeen. The diary clearly shows that Harriet had no studies to master.

8. Medwin, *Shelley*, p. 47.

# Shelley and his Circle : Manuscripts

She had already acquired the ability to play the pianoforte, to sing, to draw, and to dance, which was about all that was expected of a young girl who would probably marry soon. She did a moderate amount of reading, but this was rather for amusement than for any serious purpose. The reading was often aloud with Charlotte or others, and consisted mostly of novels.

During 1809–1810 Harriet read, in whole or part and in the order given, the following, to which must be added a few unidentified novels: Sydney Owenson's *The Novice of St. Dominick* (4 vols., 1806); Elizabeth Bennett's *The Beggar Girl and Her Benefactors* (7 vols.); Fielding's *Joseph Andrews* (2 vols., 1742); Shelley's *Zastrozzi* (1810); Milton (read to her by Charles); one of Sterne's *Sermons* (7 vols., 1760–1769); Sterne's *A Sentimental Journey* (2 vols., 1768); *St. Sebastian* (bought by Harriet's father at Muddiford); *Original Poetry* by Victor and Cazire (1810); Regina Maria Roche's *The Children of the Abbey* (4 vols., 1796); Maria Edgeworth's *Tales*;[9] Sarah Green's *The Reformist!!! A Serio-Comic-Political Novel* (22 vols., 1810); *Edmund of the Forest* (4 vols., 1797); Richardson's *Sir Charles Grandison* (7 vols., 1754); *Modern Philosophy*; and *Miss Biddy Botherim*. In August 1810 Shelley wrote Graham to send Harriet from London Scott's *The Lady of the Lake*, Locke's *Essay Concerning the Human Understanding*, and "a *Leonora* such as Elizabeth has."[10] "Now you know, dear Graham, that as this is to Harriet the sooner you send it the better." It is difficult to imagine Harriet reading Locke.

As part of her cultural life may be added the plays and operas which Harriet attended. The dramas mentioned as being seen are: James Cobb's *Paul and Virginia* (operatic farce); Shakespeare's *Richard the Third*; Thomas J. Dibdin's *Harlequin and Mother Goose, or The Golden Egg* (pantomime); Thomas J. Dibdin's *The Cabinet* (comic opera);[11] Etherege's *The Comical Revenge, or Love in a Tub* (comedy); Fielding's *An Old Man Taught Wisdom, or The Virgin Unmasked* (farce); Richard

---

9. It is impossible to know which tales: *Moral Tales for Young People* (3 vols., 1801); *Popular Tales* (3 vols., 1804); or *Tales of Fashionable Life* (9 vols., 1809–1812).

10. Quoted in White, *Shelley*, II, 455.

11. This could have been the anonymous *The Cabinet, or Much Ado About Nothing*, a farce first produced in 1806.

# The Carl H. Pforzheimer Library

Leigh's *Grieving's a Folly* (comedy); *The Devil to Pay*; John Tobin's *The Honey Moon* (comedy, with Elliston).[12] One evening Harriet's father read *The Merchant of Venice* aloud; on another Charles read *Romeo and Juliet* to her; and at Netherhampton Harriet read *Raymond and Agnes*, a melodrama by Matthew G. Lewis.

Harriet nowhere exhibits any speculative tendencies, any awareness that English political and social institutions are not all they should be, or any particular taste for poetry. One must sorrowfully conclude, then, that, beautiful, affectionate, vivacious, and intelligent though she was, marriage with Shelley would have been a sad mistake. Shelley had to have a wife who could "feel poetry and understand philosophy."[13]

In the poetry which Shelley was writing freely in 1810, his love for Harriet is often reflected. Though Harriet's influence is apparent in various poems, it will be noted that Shelley seldom wrote literally of their relationship. Most of the poems are sad; they contemplate a lasting farewell and the constancy and grief of the lovers. The precious experience of April 17, recorded by Harriet in her diary, is the inspiration for two poems. Harriet wrote: "Walked to Horsham [from Field Place] saw the Old House St. Irvyne . . . walked in the evening to Strood by moonlight." Her companions were her brothers William and Charles, Bysshe, and Elizabeth. The Groves left Field Place the next day. Before joining them in London on April 25, Shelley on the 22nd wrote and sent to Graham a poem of ten stanzas, which begins:

> How swiftly through Heaven's wide expanse
>     Bright days resplendent colors fade;
> How sweetly does the moonbeam's glance
>     With silver teint St. Irvynes glade.

Shelley solemnly warned Graham that he must by no means let his (Shelley's) family see the verses. This poem was published in Chapter VII of *St. Irvyne, or The Rosicrucian* (1811), which came out late in December 1810, under the title "Song." Stanzas 5–9 were there omitted and a new final stanza added.

The other poem commemorating the occasion is dated "April 1810,"

---

12. There was also a comic opera called *The Honey Moon*, by William Linley.

13. So Shelley told Peacock; Peacock, *Memoirs*, p. 92.

# Shelley and his Circle : Manuscripts

and was published in September 1810 as a "Song" in *Original Poetry* by Victor and Cazire. It was probably written before the other poem, and comes nearer to being a faithful transcript of their actual experience. It concludes as follows:

> The high trees that wave past the moon,
>     As I walk in their umbrage with you,
> All declare I must part with you soon,
>     All bid you a tender adieu! —
>
> Then [Harriet]! dearest farewell,
>     You and I love, may ne'er meet again;
> These woods and these meadows can tell
>     How soft and how sweet was the strain. —

The idea that they "may ne'er meet again" is, of course, fictitious. It is well to remember that when Shelley wrote this poem he was not quite eighteen.

It is Ingpen's opinion that the last poem in *Posthumous Fragments of Margaret Nicholson*, entitled "Melody to a Scene of Former Times," was also addressed to Harriet. It does indeed seem to fit the situation of Harriet's withdrawing her love from Percy, except for the date. The *Posthumous Fragments* was published near the middle of November 1810, and there is no evidence that Shelley knew of their broken engagement until shortly before he returned from Oxford to Field Place in December. Probably Harriet had by November more than once in her letters to Shelley expressed her grave concern about his radical ideas, giving him an anxiety sufficient for the purpose of composing a poem. Indeed, he had already expressed the idea of eternal separation in the poems written when he had no reason to think that it would ever occur. Certain it is that Shelley was not confronted with the actual loss of Harriet until after the publication of the "Melody to a Scene of Former Times":

> Art thou indeed forever gone,
>     Forever, ever, lost to me?
> Must this poor bosom beat alone,
>     Or beat at all, if not for thee?
> Ah! why was love to mortals given,
> To lift them to the height of Heaven,
> Or dash them to the depths of Hell?

# The Carl H. Pforzheimer Library

### HARRIET GROVE'S FAMILY AND NEAR RELATIONS

As even a brief dip into the diary will show, Harriet had numerous friends and relatives, all of whom she seems, at one time or another, to have visited. One cannot get very far among the entries without feeling the need for a guide to the ramifications of the Grove family.

*Farquharson, James* (1728–1795). The owner of Littleton and Langton House, Dorset, and father of Henrietta Grove and James John Farquharson. See Thomas Grove, junior.

*Farquharson, James John* (b. 1784). The son of James Farquharson and his successor as owner of Littleton and Langton House. He also owned Gunville House, where Thomas Grove, junior, lived for a while. He had four children, the first (Robert) being born in 1809.

*Farquharson, Robert* (b. 1809). Son of James John Farquharson.

*Grove, Charles Henry* (sometimes *Henry Charles*; 1794–1878). Harriet's youngest brother, three years her junior. After attending Harrow, he entered the Navy at an early age, but left it with pleasure in December 1809, when fifteen years old. Intending to be a physician, he lived for a while in London with his brother John, and in 1811 attended Abernethy's anatomical lectures at St. Bartholomew's Hospital. He was often with Shelley after Shelley's expulsion from Oxford, and assisted him in eloping on August 25, 1811, with Harriet Westbrook. His recollections of those hectic days in Shelley's life (printed in Hogg's *Life of Shelley*, 1858), though brief, are valuable. Charles gave up medicine, and on October 21, 1811, aged sixteen, matriculated at University College, Oxford, where he took the A.B. degree in 1815, and the M.A. in 1826.[14] Charles entered the Church and from 1826 to 1873 was rector of Berwick St. Leonard, and Sedgehill, Wilts. He died on July 14, 1878, being the last of the family to die.

*Grove, Charlotte* (b. 1783). Harriet's sister, and oldest child in the family. In January 1809 she was twenty-six years old, and almost eight and a half years senior to Harriet, to whom she was nevertheless a close and happy companion. She was attracted by Colonel Sergison of Cuckfield

14. *Alumni Oxonienses.*

# Shelley and his Circle : Manuscripts

Place, Sussex, and spent the summer of 1810 with her uncle, Captain Pilfold, at Cuckfield, probably to cultivate the colonel's acquaintance. Eventually, in May 1827, when she was thirty-four years old, she married the Reverend Richard Downer, rector of Berwick St. John, which was close to Fern and allowed her to remain within the family circle.

*Grove, Charlotte Pilfold.* Harriet's mother. She was the daughter of Charles Pilfold of Sussex. Her sister Elizabeth married Timothy Shelley and was the mother of Percy Bysshe Shelley. Her sister Bathia married the Reverend Gilbert Jackson, D.D., rector of Donhead St. Mary, the parish church of Fern, and was therefore intimately connected with the daily life of Harriet's family. Her brothers were Captain John Pilfold, R.N., of Cuckfield, Sussex, and James Pilfold. She married Thomas Grove of Fern in 1782, and was the mother of his eleven children.

*Grove, Elizabeth* (b. 1756). Harriet's aunt, and older sister of her father. In 1776 she married William Chafin Grove of Zeals, Wilts. The Chafin Groves were another important branch of the Grove family.

*Grove, Emma Philippa.* See Waddington, Emma Philippa.

*Grove, George* (1793–1838). Harriet's brother (b. September 27, 1793), two years her junior. He was fifteen and a half when Harriet's diary began. George was in the Navy for a while. He married Charlotte Eyre, daughter of Purvis Eyre, and lived in East Hays, Wilts.

*Grove, Harriet* (1791–1867). The writer of the diary. The sixth child of Thomas and Charlotte Grove of Fern, she was born on June 26, 1791. She was seventeen and a half years old when she began her diary in January 1809. Percy Bysshe Shelley (b. August 4, 1792), her cousin, was a bit more than a year younger. Late in 1811 she married William Helyar, who in 1820 inherited Coker Court, Yeovil, Somerset, from his father, William Helyar. They had four sons and four daughters. Harriet died on December 14, 1867, aged seventy-six.

*Grove, Henrietta.* Harriet's sister-in-law. She was the daughter of James Farquharson of Langton House, Dorset, and the first wife of Harriet's brother Thomas. For further details, see Thomas Grove, junior.

# The Carl H. Pforzheimer Library

*Grove, John* (1696–1769). Harriet's grandfather, of Fern. His second wife, and mother of his only surviving children, was Philippa Long, eldest daughter of Walter Long, of Preshaw, Hants. His children were Elizabeth (b. 1756), Philippa (b. 1757), and Harriet's father Thomas (b. 1759).

*Grove, John* (1784–1858). Harriet's brother (b. December 4, 1784). He was twenty-three when Harriet's diary began. John became a surgeon, and appears to have been independent financially. He lived in London, and had a house at 49 Lincoln's Inn Fields, where he had a housekeeper and cat. When the Groves made their annual trip to London in the spring, they put up at John's house; and here he was often visited by the Shelleys, especially his uncle Timothy and his cousin Percy Bysshe. He must have had some affection for Shelley, for in 1811 he made sensible and diligent efforts to bring Shelley and his irate father back into harmonious relations. In 1818 he married Jean Helen Fraser, daughter of Sir William Fraser, Bart., of Bedford Square, London. Here the Farquharsons enter the Grove family again, for Jean Helen was the granddaughter of James Farquharson, Henrietta Grove's father. By his first wife James had a daughter Elizabeth, who married Captain (later Sir) William Fraser, Bart., of Leadclune, county Inverness. Therefore James Farquharson was the father of Thomas Grove's wife Henrietta, and the grandfather of John's wife Jean Helen. John's wife was one of eleven daughters and three sons. John outlived his brother Thomas (d. 1845), and on the death of his father in 1847 inherited Fern. Upon his death in 1858 his son Thomas Grove (1823–1865) succeeded to the Grove estate, and in 1874 was created a baronet.

*Grove, Louisa* (1796–1810). Harriet's sister, the last of the children of Thomas and Charlotte Grove. She was born on March 3, 1796, and was almost five years younger than Harriet, who was devoted to her. When she was brought home from school at Bath with the whooping cough, and died on June 19, 1810, as the result of her disease and too much bleeding by the doctors, Harriet was deeply grieved. This loss of her little sister of fourteen years left Harriet with no other female companionship at home except that of her mother and her much older sister Charlotte.

[ 496 ]

# Shelley and his Circle : Manuscripts

*Grove, Marianne* (1792–1806). Harriet's sister (b. July 15, 1792). She was almost fourteen years old when she died on January 17, 1806, from burns suffered when her muslin dress caught fire. She was much loved by Harriet.

*Grove, Philippa* (b. 1757). Harriet's aunt, and sister of her father. Harriet called her Aunt Grove. She never married, and lived at Netherhampton, close to Salisbury. She was often at Fern, and the Groves were frequently at her house, which was a convenient stopping place when they journeyed to Salisbury, to the Walter Longs of Preshaw, Hants, or to the Waddingtons of Little Park, Hants. She was a great talker, and occasionally was a trifle stern with the Grove children. She was still living in 1829.

*Grove, Philippa Long*. Harriet's grandmother. The daughter of Walter Long, of Preshaw, Hants, she became (c. 1755) the second wife of John Grove, of Fern, and the mother of his three children, Elizabeth, Philippa, and Thomas.

*Grove, Thomas* (1759–1847). Harriet's father. He was the only son of John Grove of Fern. His sisters were Elizabeth and Philippa (q.v.). Thomas matriculated at University College, Oxford, on March 17, 1777, at the age of eighteen, but did not stay for a degree. Upon his father's death he inherited Fern, where he spent the remainder of his long life looking after the plantation, attending his duties as an officer in the militia and as a magistrate, in hunting, and in raising a large family. He commanded the love and respect of his children and neighbors. In 1782 he married Charlotte Pilfold, daughter of Charles Pilfold, of Sussex. They had eleven children, eight of whom survived. Thomas Grove died in 1847. His son Thomas, junior, having died in 1845, Fern was inherited by his second son John.

*Grove, Thomas*, junior (1783–1845). Harriet's brother, second child and eldest son of Thomas and Charlotte Grove. He was born on December 25, 1783. He died in 1845, two years before his father, and in consequence never possessed Fern. He was, nevertheless, well-to-do in his own right. He was the owner of the ten-thousand-acre estate Cwm Elan, near Rhayader, Radnorshire, Wales, and there his cousin Percy Bysshe Shelley visited him in July 1811 and for a few days again in June 1812. He appears, however, to have resided at Cwm Elan only in the summer

# The Carl H. Pforzheimer Library

months. In 1807 he married Henrietta Farquharson, daughter of James Farquharson, of Langton, Dorset. The Farquharson connection is an important one (John also married into that family) and requires a little explanation.

James Farquharson (1728–1795) of Gough Square, London, purchased the manor of Littleton and other estates, including Langton, in Dorset. The family home was Langton House. By his wife Ann, only daughter of the Reverend Samuel Staines, he had eight children who died before 1799, and a son, James John (b. 1784), and a daughter, Henrietta, who survived. James John, Henrietta's brother, occupied Littleton, but removed to Langton upon the death of his father. This brother had four children, the first, Robert, being born in 1809. (For more Farquharson history, see under John Grove.)

The Farquharson connection explains why Thomas Grove and his wife Henrietta were living in Gunville House, at Tarrant Gunville, a village five miles northeast of Blandford, Dorset, and six miles southeast of Fern, in 1809. The house was bought by Henrietta's brother, James John Farquharson, in 1802, from Josiah Wedgwood, the famous potter, who had owned it since 1784. In earlier times Gunville House had been "one of the grandest and most superb" in England; but it had been "entirely taken down, and its materials removed, and nothing left but some part of one of the wings or the offices, converted into a convenient dwelling house for a private family."[15] For some reason, as Harriet notes in her diary, Thomas Grove gave up Gunville (also called Eastbury in the time of its former glory) on April 1, 1810. On June 4 he took Littleton, near Blandford St. Mary, and not far from Gunville and Langton. Littleton also belonged to Henrietta's brother, and had been occupied both by him and her father. The place had once been an independent parish and manor, but was then a single house and farm.[16] Little is known of Thomas beyond Harriet's evident liking for him and his wife Henrietta, and that he had a tendency to be fat. When Harriet Shelley came to know them at Cwm Elan in June 1812, she wrote her Irish friend Miss Nugent that Thomas "is a very proud man" and "his wife is a very pleasant woman."[17]

15. Hutchins, *Dorset*, III, 456.          16. *Ibid.*, I, 167.
17. Shelley, *Complete Works*, VIII, 333.

# Shelley and his Circle: Manuscripts

Thomas' wife Henrietta died childless, and Thomas married Elizabeth Hill, daughter of C. Hill, of county Gloucester. They had one daughter, Mary, who married Rear Admiral Cospatrick Baillie Hamilton.

*Grove, Walter.* Harriet's brother. Nothing is known of him except that he died young, before Harriet was born.

*Grove, William* (b. 1790). Harriet's brother. He was born on January 21, 1790, and being nineteen in January 1809, was only a year and a half older than Harriet. This proximity in age probably accounts for his being Harriet's favorite brother, though it seems that he was also a general favorite with the family. He was in the Navy when Harriet's diary began, and in 1812 became a lieutenant. Later he married a cousin, Frances Grove, daughter of Charles Grove, M.D., of Salisbury, and sister of William Grove, of Zeals, Wilts. Little else is known of him except that he lived at Netherhampton House, Wilts, which he probably inherited from his Aunt Philippa Grove ("Aunt Grove").

*Helyar, William* (b. 1778). Married Harriet Grove late in 1811. He was the son of William Helyar, who owned two estates, one at Sedgehill, which was in the same area of Wiltshire as the Groves's estate and one near Yeovil in Somerset, about twenty-five miles away (down the road from Shaftesbury). The land at Sedgehill was partly owned by Harriet Grove's father (260 acres to Helyar's 241). Helyar (the father) built a "mansion-house" on his part of the land in 1798. In addition to this, his brother John (uncle to William Helyar, junior) was rector of the church at Tollard Royal, which the Groves attended. One would gather from references in the diary that Harriet was very fond of John and his wife. Furthermore, it appears that William Helyar, junior, lived, at least part of the time, at Sedgehill. There were thus early links between the Groves and the Helyars.

On the death of William Helyar, senior, in 1820, William Helyar, junior, as the eldest son, succeeded to the estates, both at Sedgehill and at Yeovil. In addition to his management of these estates he was Justice of the Peace for Somerset and Devon and (in 1829) he was High Sheriff of Somerset.[18]

18. Information compiled from *Burke's Landed Gentry*, 1837, 1851; Hoare, *Wiltshire*, IV, 95, 177; John Collinson, *The History and Antiquities of the County of Somerset* (Bath, 1791), II, 341; Paterson's *Roads*, 1811.

# The Carl H. Pforzheimer Library

*Jackson, Arabella*. Harriet's cousin, small daughter of her Aunt Jackson (Mrs. Gilbert Jackson), who was a sister of Harriet's mother.

*Jackson, Bathia Pilfold*. Harriet's aunt, and always called Aunt Jackson by Harriet. She was a sister of Harriet's mother Charlotte and of Shelley's mother Elizabeth (Pilfold). She married the Reverend Gilbert Jackson, D.D., rector of Donhead St. Mary, the parish church of Fern, and was therefore intimately associated with the daily life of the Grove family. She had two daughters, Arabella and Frances, and on September 12, 1809, she gave birth to another, who became Harriet's goddaughter.

*Jackson, Frances*. Harriet's cousin, the daughter of Mrs. Bathia Pilfold Jackson.

*Jackson, Mrs. Gilbert*. See Bathia Pilfold Jackson.

*Jackson, Reverend Gilbert*. Rector of Donhead St. Mary, the parish church of Fern. His wife was Bathia Pilfold, who was the sister of Harriet's mother Charlotte and of Shelley's mother Elizabeth Pilfold. They had two daughters, Arabella and Frances, and a third was born on September 12, 1809. Harriet always called him Dr. Jackson (he was a Doctor of Divinity).

*Long, Walter*. The father of Harriet's grandmother, Philippa Long Grove. His estate was Preshaw, in Hants, east of Salisbury, where the Groves visited occasionally. There was in 1809–1810 a young Walter Long who was probably a grandson of this Walter Long.

*Pilfold, Bathia*. See Bathia Pilfold Jackson.

*Pilfold, Charles*. Harriet's grandfather; father of Harriet's mother Charlotte, of Shelley's mother Elizabeth, and of Bathia (Mrs. Gilbert Jackson), and of James and Captain John Pilfold, R.N. He lived at Effingham Place, in Sussex.

*Pilfold, Charlotte*. See Charlotte Pilfold Grove.

*Pilfold, Elizabeth*. See Elizabeth Pilfold Shelley.

*Pilfold, James*. Harriet's uncle; son of Charles Pilfold.

*Pilfold, Captain John* (R.N.). Harriet's uncle; son of Charles Pilfold. He had been with Nelson in the Battle of the Nile, and had commanded

# Shelley and his Circle : Manuscripts

a frigate at Trafalgar. He was now (1809–1810) retired and living quietly with his family at Cuckfield, Sussex, about ten miles from Field Place. He was very fond of his nephew, Percy Bysshe Shelley, and gave him more help in times of need than any other relative.

*Shelley, Elizabeth* (1794–1831). Harriet's cousin and Shelley's sister (b. May 10, 1794). She was fifteen when she and Harriet began in 1809 a correspondence which lasted at least through a part of 1811. Elizabeth was a lively, fun-loving girl whose letters Harriet thought "droll."

*Shelley, Elizabeth Pilfold*. Harriet's aunt, sister of her mother, and Shelley's mother. She married Timothy Shelley of Field Place, Sussex, in October 1791. Harriet held Aunt Shelley, as she called her, in great esteem, and took much pleasure in corresponding with her. Mrs. Shelley also wrote often to her sister Charlotte, Harriet's mother.

*Shelley, Hellen*. Harriet's cousin and Shelley's sister (b. September 29, 1799). When Harriet met her and Mary Shelley at Miss Fenning's school at Clapham in April 1809, she thought them "the Nicest Girls I ever saw."

*Shelley, Mary* (1797–1884). Harriet's cousin and Shelley's sister (b. June 9, 1797). Harriet's sister Louisa corresponded with Mary.

*Shelley, Percy Bysshe* (1792–1822). Harriet's cousin (b. August 4, 1792), son of Timothy and Elizabeth Pilfold Shelley. Harriet was a little more than a year older than her cousin.

*Shelley, Timothy* (1753–1844). Harriet's uncle through his marriage with her mother's sister Elizabeth Pilfold in 1791. His estate was Field Place, near Horsham, Sussex. He was the father of Percy Bysshe, Elizabeth, and Mary Shelley.

*Shelley, Mrs. Timothy*. See Elizabeth Pilfold Shelley.

*Waddington, Emma*. Harriet's niece, the daughter of her sister, Emma Philippa Waddington.

*Waddington, Emma Philippa* (1788–1819). Harriet Grove's sister. Born on March 19, 1788, she was a trifle more than three years older than Harriet; when Harriet's diary began, she was twenty-one years old. On

# The Carl H. Pforzheimer Library

February 14, 1805, when almost seventeen, she married John Horsey Waddington. They lived at Little Park, Wickham, near Gosport, Hants, and had two small children, John and Emma. A third child was born in March 1810, and was named after his uncle George Grove, Harriet's brother, who was then in China. (Apparently there were two more sons in later years. See below under John Horsey Waddington.) There was also a George, a T., and a Madeline Waddington, who were probably the brothers and sister of John Horsey Waddington. Emma Philippa died in 1819, her husband in 1863.

*Waddington, John.* Harriet's nephew, son of her sister, Emma Philippa Waddington.

*Waddington, John Horsey* (1783–1863). Harriet's brother-in-law, husband of her sister Emma Philippa, whom he married in 1805. They lived at Little Park, Wickham, near Gosport, Hants. He died in 1863. He was the second son of George Waddington, barrister, of Ely; his mother was Caroline Horsey, daughter of Samuel Horsey, of Bury St. Edmunds. He went to Harrow, and was admitted to St. John's College, Cambridge, on June 25, 1800, aged seventeen. He resided for some time at Little Park, Wickham, Hants, and at Clay Hall, Walkern, Herts, and latterly at Langrish House, Petersfield. He had four sons and one daughter, and a brother, Henry S. Waddington.[19]

### FERN AND THE ADJACENT COUNTRY

If Harriet's diary is read with constant reference to a detailed map such as that presented here, it becomes a document wonderfully illustrative of the typical life of the landed gentry of the early nineteenth century. The family estate, Fern,[20] was of course the center of activities. Here came a constant stream of relatives and friends, to dine, to have tea, to sup, to hunt, to stay overnight or for days or even weeks. Though it was necessary to move from Fern in June 1809 while the old house

19. *Alumni Cantabrigienses.*

20. Sometimes spelled Ferne, but Fern is invariably Harriet's spelling (and that of the road guides of the period).

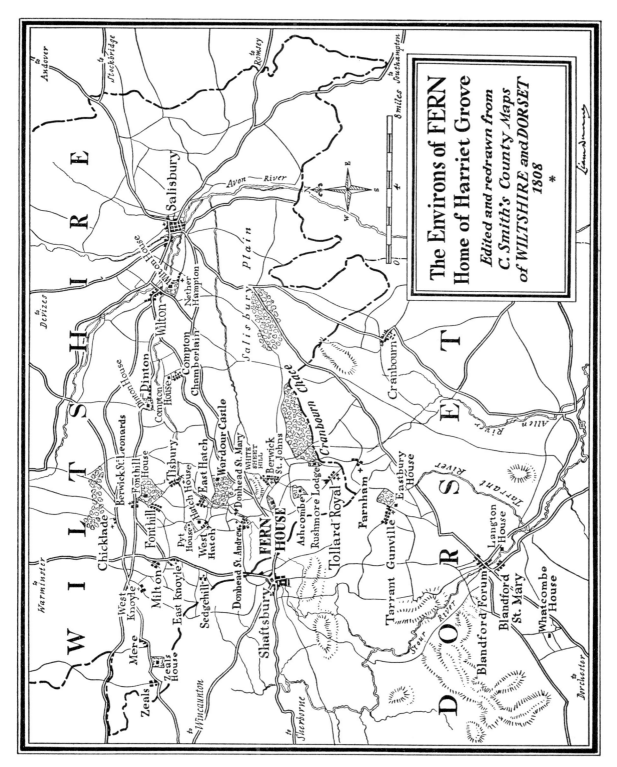

The Environs of FERN
Home of Harriet Grove

*Edited and redrawn from
C. Smith's County Maps
of WILTSHIRE and DORSET
1808*

*

was being torn down and a new one built, much to everyone's regret, Fern continued to remain the center; for from the Parsonage and later from Tollard they visited it almost every day, to supervise the farming operations and to watch the progress of the new house. The Groves themselves were always on the move in a restricted area, visiting their friends and relatives, attending occasional balls, and looking after the tenants. The whole countryside was alive with a leisurely but constant movement. The activity of the Groves was ordinarily restricted to a radius of about two miles from Fern; five miles from home was not uncommon, and fifteen miles or more were occasional. The territory was limited to the southwest corner of Wiltshire and the northeast portion of Dorset.

Fern was a farming property of considerable acreage, with a handsome family house. It was four miles east of Shaftesbury and fifteen miles west of Salisbury,[21] and the main road between these towns was about a mile north of Fern. On it was The Glove, an inn mentioned several times by Harriet; walking to it was one of her favorite outings. One mile to the east of Fern was Berwick St. John, where the Groves had many friends, especially the Misses Catherine and Frances Bennett, daughters of William Bennett, the John Stills, and the Boy family. Donhead St. Andrew (Lower Donhead) and Donhead St. Mary (Upper Donhead), one and a half miles northwest of Fern, were frequently visited in calling on Aunt Jackson and Mrs. and Miss Cooke. The Parsonage of Donhead St. Andrew the Groves lived in from June 26, 1809, until they moved south to Tollard on October 3, 1809. Directly north, and two and a half miles from Fern, was Wardour Castle, the seat of Lord Arundell, with whom the Groves were on friendly visiting terms. A little farther afield was Pitt House, the home of the Charles Bennetts; it was about four miles from Fern. Near it was Hatch House, the home of the Parkers, who were related to the Groves. Six miles from Fern in the same northwesterly direction was Sedgehill, which became particularly interesting to the Groves when their close friendship with the Reverend John Helyar and his nephew William, Harriet's future husband, developed. The Helyars were frequently at Sedgehill, and later Charles Grove was long

21. Though a few of the distances given in the introduction and notes are from road maps, most of them are from topographical maps. The distances are therefore usually minimal, not maximal.

the rector there. Zeals House, where Harriet's aunt, Mrs. William Chafin Grove, lived, was about ten miles northwest of Fern. Here on September 12, 1810, Harriet says, "Mrs. Chaffin received us in her usual form." Though this is not the limit of the Groves' wanderings to the north and northwest from Fern, they seldom went farther.

There was fully as much going on to the south and southeast of Fern, for in that direction more of the Grove relatives lived. One mile south of Fern was Ashcombe, where Mr. R. Arundell and his family lived. The Groves often visited them. Between Fern and Gunville, where Tom Grove lived for a while, the road was busy with the to-and-from visiting traffic. Gunville was at Tarrant Gunville, Cranbourn Chase, Dorset, some six miles south of Fern. Six miles southeast of Gunville was Langton House, near Blandford, the home of the Farquharsons; and within a mile west of Langton House was Littleton, Blandford St. Mary, to which Tom Grove removed from Gunville in June 1810. Gunville, Langton, and Littleton were all the property of the Farquharsons. Littleton was about twelve miles south of Fern.

Tollard Royal,[22] to which the Groves moved when they left the Parsonage on October 3, 1809, is three miles south of Fern. While at Tollard they often went to Farnham, Dorset, three miles to the southeast, where they saw their friends, the John Helyars.

The longer trips were mainly to Salisbury, fifteen miles east of Fern. Here they visited the Wyndhams, and always stopped to see Aunt Philippa Grove at Netherhampton, two miles west of Salisbury. Occasionally they went beyond Salisbury into Hampshire to visit at Presham House, the home of the Walter Longs. Harriet's grandmother was a daughter of Walter Long. The longest trip which was made with some frequency was to Little Park, Wickham, near Gosport, Hants, where Harriet's married sister, Emma Waddington, lived. This was about fifty miles from Fern. Though the journey could be made in one day, it was usually broken by an overnight stop at Aunt Grove's house in Netherhampton.

F.L.J.

22. It is not definitely known whether the Groves moved to Tollard Royal or Tollard Farnham; they are not far apart. The movements of the Groves about Tollard seem best to fit Tollard Royal.

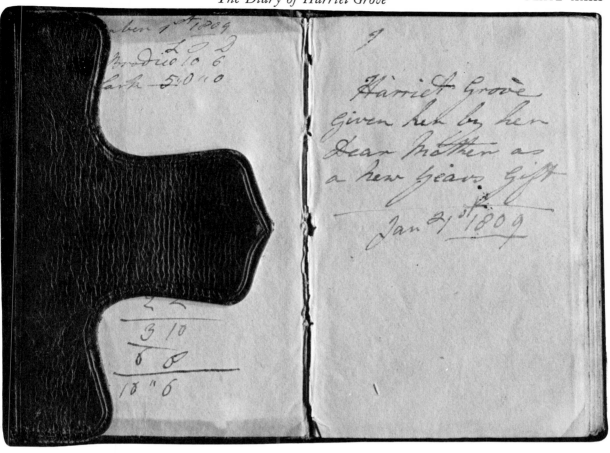

*Front endpaper (with tongue of cover folded in) and flyleaf, 1809 (SC 98)*

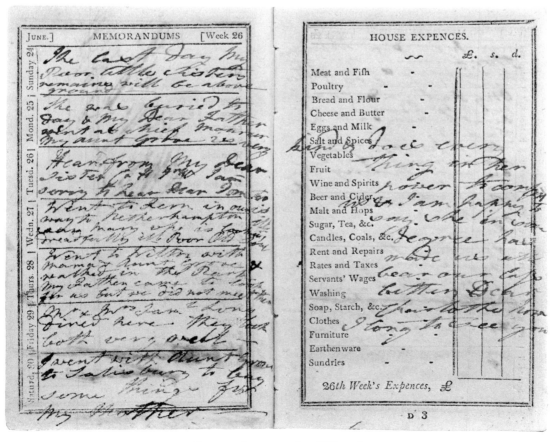

*June 24–June 30, 1810 (SC 109)*

PLATE XXIV  *The Diary of Harriet Grove*

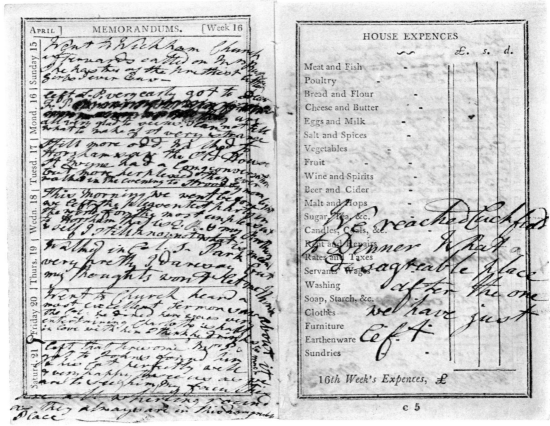

*April 15–April 21, 1810 (SC 109)*

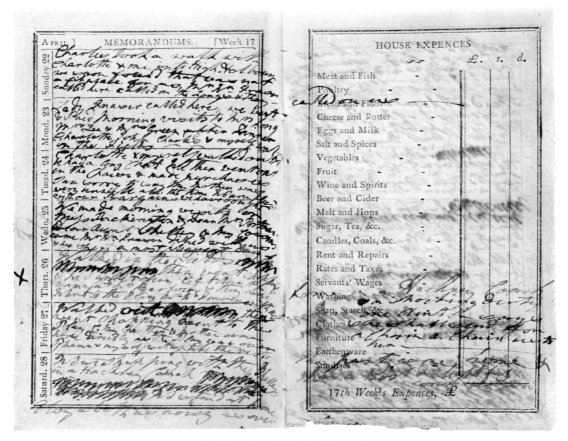

*April 22–April 28, 1810 (SC 109)*

SC 98  THE DIARY OF HARRIET GROVE FOR 1809, JANUARY 1–DECEMBER 31, 1809

MS. DIARY signed *Harriet Grove*, 99 pages in a bound volume, *The New Ladies Memorandum Book*,* 12ᵐᵒ (4.6 x 2.9 in.). Ms. entries on front and back end-papers and continuously through sigs. B–F (versos all full page entries; rectos irregularly from 1 line to full page, some blank).

PROVENANCE: Harriet Grove Helyar; Gwendolene Hussey (a grandniece) (Sotheby, Mar. 20, 1930, lot 848); Gabriel Wells (Parke-Bernet, Nov. 12, 1951, lot 472).

*THE| *New Ladies*| MEMORANDUM BOOK.| FOR |1809.| [vignette]| LONDON.| Printed for R. Baldwin,| 47, Paternoster Row.|

COLLATION: A–B⁶; C–G¹²; plus engraved title and engraved, folding frontispiece. ([F12] and G1 torn out leaving stubs.)

CONTENTS: frontispiece (recto blank); title (verso blank); Contents, p. [1]; imprint: J. Seeley, Printer, Buckingham.|, p. [1]; printed matter, pp. [1]–12; diary pages (unnumbered), sigs B–F; printed matter, pp. [1](repeated)–24; imprint: Seeley, Printer, Buckingham.|, p. 24.

Bound in red straight grain morocco, front cover extending in tongue which fits under band attached to back cover; leather-lined pocket and slit for pencil inside front cover.

The diary pages, as noted above, are unnumbered, occupying signatures B through F. The left-hand (verso) pages are reserved for the daily entries; the right-hand (recto) pages are intended for cash accounts. (Harriet Grove has used them for overflow entries.)

The diary pages are printed in red, each page in a border of double rules, leaving a narrow margin. Each verso or diary page has the running title MEMORANDUMS AND OBSERVATIONS.| [month], 1809.| [rule]| and is ruled horizontally into seven compartments. At the extreme left of each compartment, printed vertically, appear the date and day of the week, beginning with Monday (e.g., Monday 2, Tuesday 3, Wednes. 4, Thursd. 5, Friday 6, Saturday 7, Sunday 8). On the first day of the month the name of the month in capitals appears in the upper left corner of the compartment.

Each recto or accounts page has a running title on the following model: JANUARY, 1st Month, 31 Days. Week 1 [in brackets]| [rule]| Account of Cash Received || Paid| [rule]| . The remainder of the page is ruled in vertical columns of varying widths. In the first column is the date of the Monday beginning that week. When the month begins on Monday the day of the month appears in the upper left corner of the Account of Cash column. When the month begins midweek, there is a horizontal rule across the date and Account of Cash column with the date and month immediately below. (Harriet Grove used this small compartment for 1 JANUARY for a diary entry.)

The diary pages begin on a recto page which differs from all the others. It has the running title Memorandums at the beginning of the year 1809| [rule]| with the rest of the page blank (Harriet Grove did not write on this page). And since January 1, 1809, began on a Sunday, only the lower ¼ of the first verso or diary page is ruled off for an entry. The upper ¾ of this page was left blank. (Harriet Grove used it for her account of the ball on New Year's eve.)

*Harriet Grove*                                           *Diary for* 1809

SC 98    The folded engraving facing the title page is by George Corbould Scalp, and represents The Parting of Hector and Andromache. After the Table of Contents on page 1,
pages 2–3 have a long quotation from Pope's Homer's *Iliad* describing the subject of the
frontispiece engraving. Pages 5–11 are captioned "NEW SONGS, Sung at Vauxhall and
other Public Places." The music for the first group of four songs was "sold by Button
and Whitaker, St. Paul's Church Yard." The first two of these four songs were "Sung by
Mr. Fawcett, in the Comic Opera of Two Faces under a Hood," and are entitled "The
Judgment of Paris" and "A very merry hey down sort of life enough." The music for
the next group of three songs was "printed for Messrs. Clementi and Co. No. 26, Cheapside, London." Page 12, entitled "THOMSON'S DANCES for 1809," names and describes
briefly twenty-four dances, such as *My Deary O!*, *Skip Jack*, and *Boney Bewitched*, and
advises that "The above dances [are] to be had of Mess. Button and Whitaker . . . No. 75,
St. Paul's Church-Yard."

Signatures B–F contain the memoranda and accounts portion of the volume, where
Harriet made her daily entries. Beginning with sig. G, the pages are again numbered.
Pages 1–12 consist of nine short selections from literature. The pages 1–2 leaf is torn out,
making it impossible to determine the nature of the first item entitled (in the Table of
Contents) "The Husband and his two Wives." Of the other eight items, seven are poems.
Mary Robinson is the author of two of these, Miss Sydney Owenson of one; the others are
anonymous. The only surviving bit of prose is by Dr. Samuel Johnson, under the heading
"The Golden Mean." Pages 13–24 are taken up with miscellaneous items of information,
some of which are intended mainly for Londoners. They are as follows: Public Offices, &c.
in London and Westminster, With the Hours of Attendance; A List of the Most Common
Hackney Coach Fares; A Table of the Watermen's Fares; Royal Family of Great Britain;
Marketing Tables, by the Pound, Yard, Stone, &c.; Table to cast up Expences, or Wages,
By the Day, Week, Month, and Year.

*The Journal of Harriet Grove for the Years 1809–1810*, edited by Roger Ingpen
(London, privately printed, 1932) was printed in "12 copies only (not for sale) . . . at The
Curwen Press, Plaistow." Though much indebted to Ingpen's 31-page Introduction
(v–xxxv), the present edition has the advantage of fuller and more accurate information
and a text adhering strictly to the original Ms.

[Front end paper]                          [Front fly, recto]
*November 1ˢᵗ 1809*                              ⟨ ⟩
                    *£    S    D*                 *Harriet Grove*
*Sent Brodie    0    10    6*                *Given her by her*
*Sent Clark — 5    0    0*                   *Dear Mother as*
                                             *a New Years Gift*
                                                  *Janʸ 1ˢᵗ 1809*


[Front end paper] Below *Sent Clark* come further
money reckonings, totaling 10 shillings and 6
pence.

**Harriet Grove**                                    **Diary for 1809**

SC 98 [Diary pages, B1ᵛ–B2ʳ]

*We went to Mʳ Portmans on Friday &*
*went to a pleasent Ball at Blandford*
*in the Evening came home Saturday*
*31ˢᵗ of Decʳ 1808*
*I have heard that Aunt Shelley gave a*
*Ball on Friday – 30ᵗʰ 1808 –*
~~*Bysshe tells me in his Letter that*~~
*⟨———⟩ –*

Account of Cash. Received    Paid

|  | £ | s | d | £ | s | d |
|---|---|---|---|---|---|---|
| *from My Mother* | 0 | 15 | 1 | | | |
| *A pʳ of Gloves* | – | — | – | 0 | 4 | 7 |
| *Charlotte* | – | — | – | 0 | 2 | 0 |
| *Washing Bills* | — | – | 0 | 8 | 2 | |
| *Mary Dimmers* | | | | | | |
| *G Daughter* | | | | 0 | 0 | 4 |
| | | | | 0 | 15 | 1 |

## JANUARY

SUNDAY 1

*JANUARY ⟨———⟩ Colⁿ ~~staid~~ Peachy*
*dined here with my Uncle & Aunt*
*Jackson & Mʳ Wake*

MONDAY 2

*My Aunt Jackson & the rest of the*
*party left us – —*

TUESDAY 3

*⟨———⟩*

WEDNESDAY 4

*Wrote to my Aunt Shelley & Charles –*
*Mʳ & Mʳˢ Bennett & Mʳ J: Evans*
*came here —*

[Diary pages, B1ᵛ–B2ʳ] The lines without entry
date precede the entry for January 1, which is
at the bottom of the page; they were probably
written a day or two after January 1.

*pleasent* (sic); Harriet's consistent spelling of
the word.

two lines canceled. The length of a cancellation
is not indicated by the space between the
brackets except for the short passages; the

length of the longer cancellation is indicated
in a textual note if it is one Ms. line or more.
A line ordinarily has from three to five words
in it. A fraction of a line is designated by
"plus."

Account of Cash begins at the top of B2ʳ.

7 is written through *0* or *8*.

1 Jan. three lines canceled    *staid* not certain

3 Jan. three lines canceled

Diary pages, B1ᵛ–B2ʳ. Blandford is in Dorset, twelve miles south of Fern, the Groves'
family estate in southwest Wiltshire. "Aunt Shelley" was Harriet's mother's sister,
Elizabeth Pilfold, mother of Percy Bysshe Shelley, then sixteen.

Account of Cash. Harriet's older sister Charlotte at this time was twenty-six years of age.
Mary Dimmer was a nurse in the Grove household. As Harriet's diary notes, near the
beginning of the diary book for 1810, she was born in 1736 and died on December 25, 1810,
after service of twenty years with the Grove family. "G Daughter" probably means
granddaughter.

*1 Jan.* "Aunt Jackson" was Bathia Pilfold, another sister of Harriet's mother. She
was married to the Reverend Gilbert Jackson, D.D., rector of Donhead St. Mary, the
parish church of Fern.

*4 Jan.* Charles was Harriet's brother (b. 1794), three years her junior. He was in the
Navy until his release in December 1809.

**Harriet Grove**                                              **Diary for 1809**

SC 98   THURSDAY 5
~~I heard from my dear Bysshe~~ & *Louisa
heard from Mary Shelley* –

FRIDAY 6
*The Bennetts left us & Mr Evans staid
to go to the Gordons with us*

SATURDAY 7
*We had a very pleasent Dance at
Mr Gordons I have written to ~~Bysshe~~
& heard from Dear Charles, a very long
letter from him   Mr E left us*

SUNDAY 8
*Wrote to my Dear Charles the first
thing to day – Louisa has written to
Mary Shelley Charlotte wrote to Dear
Jack   we did not go to Church as it
was to Wet. My Father read Prayers*

8 Jan. *to Wet* (sic)

MONDAY 9
~~Bysshe will get my letter to day~~  *Packed
up in readiness for tomorrow* —

TUESDAY 10
*Left Fern for Little Park & arrived
here quite safe & found them all well
~~Heard from Bysshe two letters from him~~*

WEDNESDAY 11
*Wrote to Charles & John   the latter
is at Field Place   My Nephew is a
fine Child he has been innoculated
to day for the Small Pox* –

THURSDAY 12
*a Mr George Waddington came here* –
*Played with my little niece* —

FRIDAY 13
*Went to Portsmouth   George returned
with us   Dear Boy this is the last time
we shall see him*

11 Jan. *innoculated* (sic)

There were two Bennett families: William Bennett and his daughters Catherine and Frances, of Berwick St. John, one mile east of Fern; and the Charles Bennetts of Pitt House, two or three miles north of Fern.

*5 Jan.* Louisa was Harriet's younger sister (b. Mar. 3, 1796). Almost thirteen years old, she was the youngest of the Grove children. Mary Shelley was a sister of Bysshe. Born on June 9, 1797, she was now only twelve years of age.

*7 Jan.* The Gordons were neighbors of the Groves. Cary's *Roads*, 1819 (p. 109), lists "Winscombe House, J. Gordon, Esq." two miles from Shaftesbury. See also Hoare, *Wiltshire*, IV, 33.

*8 Jan.* "Dear Jack" is John Grove, Harriet's brother, twenty-three years old, who lived in London.

*10 Jan.* Little Park was the home of Harriet's sister Emma Philippa, wife of John Horsey Waddington. (Hoare, *Wiltshire*, IV, 53.) Little Park was at Wickham, near Gosport, Hampshire, about fifty miles from Fern. (Cary's *Roads*, 1819, p. 698.)

*11 Jan.* John Grove often visited Field Place, attracted mainly by Shelley's sister Elizabeth (b. 1794), then fifteen years old. "My Nephew" was John, sister Emma's young son.

*12 Jan.* George Waddington was a relative, possibly a brother, of sister Emma's husband. Harriet's "little niece" was Emma, daughter of Harriet's sister Emma.

*13 Jan.* George Grove (b. Sept. 27, 1793) was Harriet's brother, two years younger than she. George was in the Navy. Portsmouth was only a short distance southeast of Little Park.

# Shelley and his Circle : Manuscripts

**Harriet Grove**                                      *Diary for* 1809

SC 98 SATURDAY 14
*George went away early ~~Heard from~~*
*~~Bysshe~~ & Louisa heard from Mary –*

SUNDAY 15
*Wrote to ~~Bysshe~~ & Charles   Snow on*
*the ground   Packed up as we go*
*tomorrow if the snow does not prevent*
*us –*

MONDAY 16
*Left Little Park & got home quite safe*
*tho' the snow was very deep – Charlotte*
*Louisa & Susan nearly overturned in*
*Clay lane by the snow*

TUESDAY 17
*Nothing particularly happened   Miss*
*Popham did not come –*

WEDNESDAY 18
*We have not heard or seen her to day –*
*Louisa is in a great hurry to hear from*
*Mary Shelley as she expects a present*
*from her but has not heard from her*
*to day*

THURSDAY 19
*had a letter from ~~Bysshe~~ & began an*
*answer to it & wrote to my Aunt Shelley*

FRIDAY 20
*Finished my letter to ~~B~~ & wrote to*
*George —*

SATURDAY 21
*I heard from Johnny   he is coming*
*here Tuesday —*

SUNDAY 22
*Good gracious a deep snow    as M*ʳ
*Wake is here I am quite afraid he will*
*be snowed in here.*

MONDAY 23
*I hope John will be able to get here*
*tomorrow as I long to see him*

TUESDAY 24
*Dear fellow he is come to our great*
*surprise & pleasure   ~~Heard from dear~~*
*~~Bysshe~~   M*ʳ *Wake went away*

WEDNESDAY 25
*John talked a great deal about the*
*Shelleys   he has been spending a week*
*there at that delightful place.   ~~I wrote~~*
*~~to Bysshe~~ –*

THURSDAY 26
*Sent my Letter to day   M*ʳˢ *Bennett*
*called here yesterday & invited us to a*
*                                    for*
*Ball,Friday Week – heard that F & A*
*Jackson are going to School – next*
*Tuesday*

*22 Jan. he:* Harriet began to write *that,* but
canceled the *t.*

*16 Jan.* Susan was probably one of the Groves' servants.

*17 Jan.* Miss Popham was probably related to the William Wyndhams of Dinton.
Mrs. Wyndham was Laetitia Popham, daughter of Alexander Popham, one of the Masters
of Chancery. (*Burke's Landed Gentry.*)

*21 Jan.* Johnny is her brother John, who had been visiting at Field Place; hence Harriet's
special eagerness to see him.

*22 Jan.* Mr. Wake obviously was not one of Harriet's favorites. On July 2 she wrote:
"what I dislike very much that tiresome Mʳ Wake dines here"; on May 24, 1810, she
wrote him down "a great bore."

*26 Jan.* Mrs. Charles Bennett of Pitt House. "F & A Jackson" are Frances and Arabella,
daughters of Harriet's Aunt Jackson.

# The Carl H. Pforzheimer Library

SC 98   FRIDAY 27
    X   *Practiced Music before breakfast – quite*
        *a wonder – Louisa & I walked out*

SATURDAY 28
*Miss Popham came here   The Fox*
*hunters breakfasted here   Louisa & I*
*took such an immense long walk –*

SUNDAY 29
*Heard from ~~Bysshe~~ & Louisa heard*
*from Mary*

MONDAY 30
*Overturned in our way to Gunville on*
*the Top of Wind green –*

TUESDAY 31
⟨——⟩ <———> *we are none of us*
*hurt in consequence of our overturn*

FEBRUARY
WEDNESDAY I
*at Gunville – received a letter from*
*George & Charles –*

THURSDAY 2
*Came home quite safe   walked down*
*Wind green –*

31  Jan. <———> The pen went through
the paper.
5 Feb. one plus lines canceled

FRIDAY 3
*Wrote to Aunt S—y & George &*
*Charles – C– my Father & Mother*
*& John have gone to a Ball at Pitt house*

SATURDAY 4
*M^rs Bennetts Youngest Child is very*
*ill ~~I heard from Bysshe~~ they returned*
*home –*

SUNDAY 5
⟨———⟩ *M^rs Bennetts Child is very ill*
*indeed –*

MONDAY 6
*M^rs Bennetts Child is dead ——*

TUESDAY 7
*had a great many Letters ——*

WEDNESDAY 8
*Went to Church   a Fast day* ⟨———⟩ —

THURSDAY 9
⟨——⟩ ~~Bysshe~~ ⟨——⟩ *Miss Tregonwell*
*came here*

FRIDAY 10
*Charlotte's Birthday 26 – I am very*
*much dissappointed at not hearing from*
*my Aunt Shelley –*

8 Feb. two half lines canceled
10 Feb. *dissappointed* (sic)

*30 Jan.* Gunville was the residence of Harriet's older brother Thomas. It was about six miles southeast of Fern, in Tarrant Gunville, Cranbourn Chase, Dorset, and was owned by James John Farquharson, of Langton House, brother of Tom's wife Henrietta.

*3 Feb.* Aunt S—y is Aunt Shelley, Percy Bysshe Shelley's mother. C– is sister Charlotte. Pitt House is the home of the Charles Bennetts.

*9 Feb.* Hellen Ellery Tregonwell (b. 1783) was one of Harriet's dearest friends, even though Hellen was seven and a half years older. She was the daughter of Lewis-Dimoke-Grosvenor Tregonwell (1758–1832), of Cranbourn House, Cranbourn, Dorset, by his first wife.

**Harriet Grove**                                    **Diary for 1809**

SC 98   SATURDAY 11
*Emma & Waddington & their children came here – My mother heard from Aunt Shelley –*

SUNDAY 12
*Thomas left us*

MONDAY 13
*Emma calls her Grandmama a Ninny –*

TUESDAY 14
*John had a letter from Bysshe with a Valentine enclosed for M*rs *Habbersham*

WEDNESDAY 15
*I heard from Bysshe*

THURSDAY 16
*⟨——⟩ Bysshe ⟨——⟩ & Aunt Grove came here – ⟨——⟩*

FRIDAY 17
*⟨——⟩ wrote to my Dearest Aunt Shelley*

16 Feb. one line canceled

SATURDAY 18
*Dear Dear Louisa is gone back to School I miss her so much —*

SUNDAY 19
*Heard from Dear Charles*
_____

MONDAY 20
X *My Father M*r *Waddington & John returned from Bath*

TUESDAY 21
*Heard from Bysshe & we shall* certainly *see him in London   I am so glad of it –*

WEDNESDAY 22
*Took a long walk to Berry-Court, the Old Family Mansion. The Old woman that lives there is mad –*

THURSDAY 23
*Wrote to Bysshe*

FRIDAY 24
*Wrote to Louisa & Henrietta –*

17 Feb. one plus lines canceled

*11 Feb*. Harriet's sister Emma, her husband, and two small children.

*12 Feb*. Thomas was Harriet's oldest brother; born on December 25, 1783, he was twenty-five years old and heir to the family estate.

*13 Feb*. This was little Emma, daughter of Harriet's sister Emma Waddington.

*16 Feb*. Obviously Harriet wrote to Bysshe. Aunt Grove was the sister of Harriet's father. Named Philippa and born in 1757, she lived unmarried at Netherhampton, near Salisbury.

*18 Feb*. Louisa's school was at Bath, where she was evidently under the care of Mrs. Wilsonn. The entry for the 20th shows that Louisa was taken to Bath by her father, accompanied by Emma's husband and John.

*21 Feb*. Shelley was at Eton and was contemplating the Easter holidays.

*22 Feb*. Bury Court (so in *Andrews' and Dury's Map of Wiltshire*) was about half a mile northwest of Fern.

*24 Feb*. Henrietta Grove, wife of Harriet's brother Thomas. She was the daughter of James Farquharson, of Langton House, Dorset.

# The Carl H. Pforzheimer Library

## Harriet Grove

SC 98 SATURDAY 25
———————.

SUNDAY 26
⟨———⟩ ~~Bysshe~~ ———

MONDAY 27
⟨———⟩ ——

TUESDAY 28
*Sent my letter to* ⟨———⟩ *Henrietta has sent to invite us to Gunville after the Assizes* –

## MARCH
WEDNESDAY I
*Dear John left us – Received an immense long letter from* ⟨———⟩ —— *and wrote to Louisa*

THURSDAY 2
*Heard from My Dear Louisa* ~~& wrote to Bysshe~~

FRIDAY 3
*Louisa's Birthday 13* —— *A large party to Dinner – Wrote to Aunt Shelley heard from* ~~Bysshe~~ *& Charles*

SATURDAY 4
*Miss Popham left us* ———

SUNDAY 5
*Wrote to Dear Charles Heard from Dear Louisa*

26 Feb. one line canceled
27 Feb. one line canceled
9 Mar. *Tre*[gonwe]*ll   Dicthes* (sic)

MONDAY 6
*Wrote to Louisa under cover to M*ʳˢ *Wilsonn* ———

TUESDAY 7
⟨————————⟩ ~~Bysshe~~ ⟨—⟩ *My Mother heard from Dear Aunt Shelley*

WEDNESDAY 8
*The Waddingtons left us* ~~Heard from Bysshe~~

THURSDAY 9
*Charlotte & Miss Tre–ll went out a walking over hedges & Dicthes* –

FRIDAY 10
*I heard from John  M*ʳˢ *Bennett called here*

SATURDAY II
~~Wrote to dear Bysshe~~ *Dear Hellen left us* — *Heard from My Dearest Aunt Shelley* ———

SUNDAY 12
*Wrote to Aunt Shelley to day & went to S—y to Col: Breretons* ———

MONDAY 13
*Very pleasent, went to the Assize Ball (but did not dance) owing to my foot*

TUESDAY 14
*Went to the play of Paul & Virginia Liked it* ^*pretty well* ⟨———⟩

12 Mar. *S*[alisbur]*y*
14 Mar. one or two lines canceled

*4 Mar.* Miss Popham had been at Fern since January 28.
*11 Mar.* Hellen Tregonwell, who had been at Fern since February 9.
*14 Mar.* The play was an operatic farce by James Cobb.

[ 514 ]

**Harriet Grove**                                    **Diary for 1809**

SC 98   WEDNESDAY 15
*Returned home after having spent a very*
*pleasent time at Salisbury*

THURSDAY 16
*Went to Gunville;* ⟨——⟩ *Heard from*
⟨——⟩ *C–s & L–a   Got safe to Gunville*

FRIDAY 17
*Staid in doors all day   Aunt Grove is*
*here* ——

SATURDAY 18
X *Aunt Grove went away   wrote to John*
*& C–s* ——

SUNDAY 19
*Emma's   Birthday   21 — wrote   to*
*Louisa   M^{rs} Farquharson called here* —

MONDAY 20
*Came   home   from   G—e   came   down*
*Wind   green   in   the   carriage   The*
*Wad–s returned home with us* —

TUESDAY 21
⟨——⟩ *(Henrietta came here)*

WEDNESDAY 22
*Walked out for the 1^{st} time since my*
*foot was bad* ——

16 Mar. first cancellation one line   C[harle]s
& L[ouis]a
18 Mar. C[harle]s
21 Mar. two lines canceled
23 Mar. one line canceled

THURSDAY 23
⟨——⟩ *began a letter to George to send*
*to St. Helena* –

FRIDAY 24
*Heard from John & answered his letter*

SATURDAY 25
*Practised   that   beautiful   thing   Fitz-*
*Eustace — The E F–s honds came here*

SUNDAY 26
*Went   to   Church   My   Mother   heard*
*from Hellen Tregonwell* —

MONDAY 27
*The Waddingtons & Tho^s & Henrietta*
*left us   we miss the Dear Children*
*very much indeed*

TUESDAY 28
*Charlotte & myself walked up White*
*Sheet Hill where frightened by two*
*Horses running in the Park* ⟨————⟩

WEDNESDAY 29
⟨——⟩ *Charlotte   heard   from   Miss*
*Popham & Aunt C. Grove*

29 Mar. one line canceled   The month (April)
does not appear in its usual place at the top of
the space for the first day of the month. It
does appear, however, on the opposite page for
the Account of Cash.

*19 Mar.* Mrs. Farquharson was the wife of James John Farquharson, of Langton House,
Dorset.
*20 Mar.* G[unvill]e Wad[dington]s. Harriet's sister Emma Waddington and her family
had been visiting their brother Thomas Grove at Gunville. The next day Tom's wife
Henrietta also went to Fern. They all left together on Monday, the 27th.
*28 Mar.* White Sheet Hill was a short distance to the northeast of Fern.

# The Carl H. Pforzheimer Library

**Harriet Grove**                                      **Diary for 1809**

THURSDAY 30
*heard from Louisa*

FRIDAY 31
*wrote to Tit & Helen ——*

APRIL
SATURDAY 1
*Dyed My Gown. We heard from John who thinks we shall see Aunt Shelley in Town which I am very glad of – heard from Bysshe*
*I hope this Month I shall be more fortunate in seeing the person I wish than I was at Xmas — I think I Shall ——*

SUNDAY 2
*Went to Church & received the Sacrament ——*

MONDAY 3
*The Weather is rather warmer took a long walk —*

TUESDAY 4
*Wrote letter to Bysshe The Miss Benetts & Aunt Grove came here –*

1 Apr. *in Town . . . Bysshe* is in the space for Apr. 2. *I hope . . . I think I Shall* is on the Account of Cash page under date April 1. *I Shall* is written in thick large letters.

WEDNESDAY 5
*Miss Popham has sent Charlotte & me a silver Clasp for our belts*

THURSDAY 6
*The Miss Benetts of Lower Donhead dined here ——*

FRIDAY 7
*Miss Catherine Benett Dined & slept here Met Miss F Bennett going to Wardour —*

SATURDAY 8
*our party Left us Wrote to Louisa – never heard so much talking as I have since the Miss Benetts have been here as my Aunt Grove & Miss Benett are the greatest talkers in the World ——*

SUNDAY 9
*Went to Church saw the Miss Benetts Heard from Bysshe*

MONDAY 10
*Packed up, ⟨——⟩*

TUESDAY 11
*Left Fern & got to Halford Bridge –*

WEDNESDAY 12
*Got to London like Johns House – received a long letter from Bysshe*

4 Apr. *Benetts* (sic); Harriet's usual spelling of the name

10 Apr. three plus lines canceled

*31 Mar.* Louisa Grove and Hellen Tregonwell. "Tit" was a pet name for Louisa.
*4 Apr.* Catherine and Frances, daughters of William Bennett.
*6 Apr.* Donhead St. Andrew, or Lower Donhead, was a mile and a half northwest of Fern.
*7 Apr.* Wardour Castle, the seat of Lord Arundell, was two and a half miles north of Fern. (James Everard Arundell, 9th Baron Arundell of Wardour, 1763–1817.)

**Harriet Grove**                    **Diary for 1809**

SC 98

THURSDAY 13
*Had another letter from ~~B—e~~ who is at Col: Sergisons at Cuckfield M*ʳ* Bromley called here – ~~I wrote~~ ⟨——⟩*

FRIDAY 14
*Went Shopping & saw M*ʳˢ* Cook & M*ʳˢ* Ainsley*

_____

SATURDAY 15
*~~Heard from Bysshe~~ ⟨——⟩ & my Mother heard from George –*

SUNDAY 16
*~~Dear~~ Bysshe & M*ʳ* Shelley arrived here the former I am very glad to see – I think M*ʳ* Shelley appears cross ⟨——⟩ for what reason I know not ——*

MONDAY 17
*We went to the Play of Richard the third the farce of Mother Goose*

X

TUESDAY 18
*Bysshe went about Town with us to Miss Fernwoods Exhibition of Worsted & then to the Panorama of Grand Cairo ——*

WEDNESDAY 19
*⟨——⟩ went to Clapham & saw my cousin Shelleys who I think the Nicest Girls I ever saw  went to the Play of the Cabinet & the farce of Love in a Tub & the virgin unmasked*

THURSDAY 20
*~~Dear Bysshe has left us~~ ⟨——⟩ wrote to my Dear Aunt Shelley ~~& Bysshe~~*

FRIDAY 21
*~~I wrote Bysshe a good letter~~ M*ʳ* Shelley called here – he & M*ʳ* W Benett dined with us yesterday*

SATURDAY 22
*⟨——⟩ went morning visiting & shopping —*

13 Apr. *B[yssh]e;* one line canceled
15 Apr. one plus lines canceled
19 Apr. one line canceled

20 Apr. one line canceled
21 Apr. *W*[illiam]
22 Apr. two plus lines canceled

*13 Apr.* Cuckfield was about ten miles southeast of Field Place, Sussex. Here Shelley's favorite uncle, Captain John Pilfold, R.N., lived. (Warden Sergison and family will be found in *Burke's Landed Gentry*.)

*14 Apr.* Probably the Mrs. Cook who was one of the Groves' near neighbors in Wiltshire. Like the Groves, many of the country gentry visited London at this time of the year.

*16 Apr.* "Bysshe & M*ʳ* Shelley": Shelley and his father Timothy Shelley. Shelley's sister Elizabeth and his mother ("Aunt Shelley") did not come to London on this occasion, as they did in 1810.

*17 Apr.* Thomas J. Dibdin's pantomime, *Harlequin and Mother Goose; or The Golden Egg.*

*19 Apr.* The cousins were Shelley's sisters, Hellen and Mary, nine and eleven years old, who were at Miss Fenning's school at Clapham. *The Cabinet* was a comic opera by Thomas J. Dibdin; *The Comical Revenge, or Love in a Tub* was a comedy by Sir George Etherege; *An Old Man Taught Wisdom, or The Virgin Unmasked* was a farce by Henry Fielding.

SC 98    SUNDAY 23
~~Received from Bysshe~~ the songs    M^r W:
Benett & M^r Vincent dined here

MONDAY 24
Charlotte has made me a present of the
Pink Dress ~~dear~~ Bysshe chose for us
for which I am very much obliged to
them

TUESDAY 25
I heard from Dear Aunt Shelley
yesterday ⟨———⟩ ~~Bysshe~~ M^rs Cooke
& Miss P: Benett drank tea here

WEDNESDAY 26
⟨———⟩ Dined at M^rs P. Stills went
with Lady Fraser to a Rout at Lady
Glins

THURSDAY 27
⟨———⟩ Charlotte went to M^rs Goslins
rout with M^rs Long   M^r Shelley dined
with us

25 Apr. one line canceled
26 Apr. one line canceled

FRIDAY 28
Wrote to my Dearest Aunt    went to the
play of Grievinges of folly & the Devil
to pay   Waddington went with us —

SATURDAY 29
had an immense long letter from B
Dined at M^rs Longs ——

SUNDAY 30
Rode in hide Park & went to the
Foundling Chapel   heard an excellent
sermon

MAY
MONDAY 1
⟨————⟩ Heard from my Dear Aunt
S— & went to the Opera   liked it very
much ——

TUESDAY 2
Dined at M^r Knellers & were much
entertained by the odd creatures I saw
there

27 Apr. two lines canceled

23 Apr. The "songs" were probably poems by Shelley.

25–27 Apr. Mrs. Cooke, Miss Bennett, and Mrs. Stills were all probably Wiltshire neighbors. Mrs. Long was probably a relative (see note to May 3). On Lady Fraser see note to May 11 entry.

28 Apr. Richard Leigh's Grieving's a Folly, a comedy. [C. Coffey], The Devil to Pay; or the wives metamorphosed: an opera, as it is performed at the theatres (London, 1733). (Halkett and Laing.) Waddington was probably Harriet's brother-in-law, John Horsey Waddington.

30 Apr. The Foundling Hospital, in Guilford Street, was founded in 1739. (Plan of London, C1, Front Endpapers.) Handel had frequently performed his Messiah in its chapel, which was also noted for the excellent singing of the children choristers.

2 May. Cary's Roads, 1819, lists John Godfrey Kneller, Esq., as the proprietor of Donhead Hall, Ludwell, near Fern, and the estate appears on Andrews' and Dury's Map of Wiltshire (1773). See also Hoare, Wiltshire, IV, 32. Boyle's Court Guide gives his London address as 32 York Place, Portman Square.

**Harriet Grove**                                        **Diary for 1809**

SC 98    WEDNESDAY 3
⟨———⟩ *The Stills dined here   rather a
stupid Party   Charlotte flirted as usual
with W: Long*

THURSDAY 4
*Mʳ Shelley came with Col: Sergison,
the former gave me a frank for B̶ went
to a Rout at Mʳˢ Devons with Mʳˢ
Long –*

FRIDAY 5
*Dined at home – John & Papa Dined
with W. Long   heard from Dear Aunt
Shelley*

SATURDAY 6
*Wrote to Aunt S:   Dined at Mʳ Rudges
Letter from Bysshe –*

3 May. one plus lines canceled
10 May. one line canceled

SUNDAY 7
*Mʳ Shelley & a party dined here,
Waddington & Lord Hinton called in
the morning –*

MONDAY 8
⟨———⟩ *heard from Mary Shelley
Mʳ J. Wad. Lord Hinton & Coll:
Sergison Dʳ Mʳˢ & Miss Jackson
Dined here*

TUESDAY 9
*Went to the Exhibition   liked it pretty
well & to Astleys in the Evening —*

WEDNESDAY 10
*Went to the Tower   ⟨———⟩ & Sᵗ Pauls
Miss Kilderbee went with us & a
Party –*

THURSDAY 11
⟨———⟩ *Dined at Sir W: Frasers —*

11 May. one plus lines canceled

*3 May.* Possibly W[alter] Long, of Preshaw, Hants. Harriet's grandfather, John Grove, had married Philippa Long, daughter of Walter Long, of Preshaw. Cary's *Roads*, 1819, lists James Still, Esq., Clood's House, Knoyle, some two miles from the Bennetts' Pitt House.

*4 May.* Boyle's *Court Guide* for 1813 lists a C. Devon, Esq., 62 Guildford Street, Brunswick Square.

*6 May.* Boyle's *Court Guide* for 1813 lists Edward Rudge, Esq., 44 Wimpole Street.

*7 May.* John Poulett (1783–1864) was Viscount Hinton, 1788–1819, when he succeeded his father as Earl Poulett.

*8 May.* J[ohn] Wad[dington]. The Jacksons were probably relatives of Dr. Gilbert Jackson, husband of Harriet's aunt, Bathia Pilfold Jackson.

*9 May.* Astley's Amphitheatre, Westminster Bridge Road, where a variety sort of entertainment was available. Fetham, *Picture of London*, 1809 (a book for the guidance of visitors to London) notes among its amusements, exhibitions of "horsemanship and other feats of strength and agility." It also featured pantomimes, songs, and dances.

*11 May.* Sir W[illiam] Fraser, 1st Bart., of Leadclune, county Inverness. (*Boyle's Court Guide* for 1813 gives his London address as 23 Queen Square, Bloomsbury.) He had three sons (William, James John, Keith) and eleven daughters, one of whom John Grove married in 1818. The Frasers were closely connected with the Farquharsons of Langton

**Harriet Grove**                                        **Diary for 1809**

SC 98    FRIDAY 12
*Went shopping in the morning – the two M*^r* Benetts & M*^r* Barnes dined here*

SATURDAY 13
X   *Dined at M*^r* Greens & went to the Opera with M*^rs* Grey & the Kilderbee's —*

SUNDAY 14
*Walked in Kensington Gardens with M*^rs* Grey & the Kilderbees*

MONDAY 15
          *Aunt*
*Heard from ~~Bysshe~~ & Shelley M*^rs* Hamilton & Children called here the Knellers dined here – ⟨———⟩*

TUESDAY 16
*Went to Westminster Abbey with the Miss Frasers – & the Rudges dined here rather stupid*

WEDNESDAY 17
*⟨———⟩ The Bromleys came to spend the day with us went to the Play of the Honey Moon & saw Elliston*

17 May. two lines canceled
18 May. one line canceled

THURSDAY 18
*⟨———⟩ ~~Bysshe~~ the Bromleys left us, This is our last day we have to spend with Dear John*

FRIDAY 19
*⟨———⟩ M*^r* Kilderbee called upon us left Town & reached Halford Bridge – where M*^r* Benett met us*

SATURDAY 20
*Reached Salisbury & dined with Thomas at M*^rs* Gushers Lodgings*

SUNDAY 21
*Unpacked ⟨———⟩ so happy to be at Dear Fern Had Letters from Dear John ⟨———⟩*

MONDAY 22
*Dear William has made 2000£ Prize Money My Mother rode on her Horse*
           *we*
*& took a long walk with Walter Long to Wardour ——*

TUESDAY 23
*⟨———⟩ Walked to Farringdon quite tired by W. Longs nonsensical conversation*

23 May. one plus lines canceled

House, Dorset, in that Sir William's wife was Elizabeth Farquharson, half sister of James John Farquharson, of Langton. The relationship of the Frasers and the Farquharsons is made clear by the pedigree of the Farquharsons in Hutchins, *Dorset*, I, 285. (See also *Burke's Peerage*, 1833.)

*17 May. The Honey Moon*, a comedy by John Tobin. (See Allardyce Nicoll, *A History of Early Nineteenth Century Drama, 1800–1850*, London, 1930, I, 164.) Robert William Elliston (1774–1831) was one of the leading actor-managers of his day. In 1809 he was manager of the Surrey Theatre.

*19 May.* Halford Bridge was the usual overnight stopping place on the two-day journey between Fern and London.

*22 May.* William, here first mentioned in the diary, was Harriet's favorite brother. He was nineteen at this time (a year and a half older than Harriet), and was in the Navy.

**Harriet Grove**                                     **Diary for 1809**

SC 98  WEDNESDAY 24
⟨———⟩ went to Salisbury. went to
the Play there

THURSDAY 25
*Walked about the Town paying morning
visits & gossiping  went to the Ball —*

FRIDAY 26
*took a long walk in the morning, went
to Mʳˢ Whindhams rout*

SATURDAY 27
*Went to the play  we are so gay here
more so than in Town*

SUNDAY 28
*Went to the Cathedral Morning &
Evening  the Militia were there in the
the
morning & the Yeomanry in eveng*

MONDAY 29
*Staid at home this Evening  Mʳˢ
Gordon Dined with us*

TUESDAY 30
*Went to the Play bespoke by the officers
of the Yeomanry*

WEDNESDAY 31
*Mʳˢ Benett & Mʳˢ Gordon dined with
us  called on Mʳˢ Harris – ⟨———⟩*

JUNE

THURSDAY 1
*Went to a Dance at Mʳˢ Whindhams
very pleasent  Mʳ Colley was so very
entertaining  Heard from Aunt Shelley*

FRIDAY 2
*Mʳˢ Harris came with her 5 Children
went to a Dance at Col: Breretons
Mʳ Colley again the life of the party
Danced till 4 O-clock*

SATURDAY 3
*this morning we are returned to Fern
again  I am not sorry*

SUNDAY 4
*did not rise this morning till ten to
recruit after all this raking,  Wrote to
my Aunt Shelley*

MONDAY 5
*Walked by myself in the wood & garden
& wrote to John –*

TUESDAY 6
⟨———⟩ *Mʳ & Mʳˢ W: Long & Aunt
Grove came here —*

26 May. *Whindham* (sic); Harriet's usual
spelling for Wyndham.

31 May. one plus lines canceled

1 June. *Heard . . . Shelley:* on the Account of

Cash page, with an overflow from June 2. It is
difficult to determine to which date these words
belong.

6 June. one line canceled

*26 May.* Mrs. Henry Penruddocke Wyndham. Her husband (d. 1819) was M.P. for
Wilts. (See Hoare, *Wiltshire*, VI, 648–649, 815, 549, 103.)

*27 May.* "in Town": that is, in London.

*29 May.* Hoare, *Wiltshire* (IV, 33), gives John Gordon, Esq., as the proprietor of Wind-
comb Park, which, according to Cary's *Roads*, 1819, was two miles from Shaftesbury.

*6 June.* Probably the Walter Longs, of Preshaw, Hants.

# The Carl H. Pforzheimer Library

SC 98   WEDNESDAY 7
*My Father & M^r Long have found out that Old Fern will tumble down as the front is cracked all the way down   I am very sorry for it*

THURSDAY 8
*Heard from Dear Louisa   I have not heard from her a long time before —*

FRIDAY 9
*M^r & M^rs Long & Aunt Grove left us*

SATURDAY 10
*Walked out & have been reading a novel called Novice of St Dominick   like it very well —*

SUNDAY 11
*Went to Upper Donhead Church & saw all our neighbours there —*

MONDAY 12
X *M^r Hamilton came here & drew a plan for altering old Fern —*

TUESDAY 13
⟨———⟩ *Walked to the Glove   I fear we shall not walk there many times more this year —*

13 June. one plus lines canceled

WEDNESDAY 14
*Wrote ~~to B—— and~~ Charles,   We Dined at the Gordons who are very sorry to hear we are to leave Fern*

THURSDAY 15
*My Father went to Bath to fetch Louisa home. Charlotte & myself got up to make his breakfast —*

FRIDAY 16
*The two Miss Benetts called here & Louisa came home for her Holidays*

SATURDAY 17
*Went rumaging over an old Bureau & walked out with Tit. some of our neighbours dined here ———*

SUNDAY 18
*Went to Lower Donhead Church & looked at the Parsonage house which we have some idea of inhabiting whilst Fern is rebuilding*

MONDAY 19
*Saw the plan which M^r Hamilton has drawn for altering Fern & we all like it very much —*

17 June. *rumaging* (sic)

*7 June.* Harriet's affection for Fern, the family house and estate, is conspicuous throughout her diary.

*10 June.* Sydney Owenson, *The Novice of St. Dominick* (4 vols., 1806).

*13 June.* The Glove was an inn on the road from Shaftesbury to Salisbury, and about a mile north of Fern. Harriet had already been informed of the necessity of moving from Fern while the house was being rebuilt.

*15 June.* Bath, where Louisa had been in school, was thirty-odd miles from Fern. Mr. Grove got an early start.

*18 June.* The Parsonage at Lower Donhead (Donhead St. Andrew) was about two miles northwest of Fern.

# Shelley and his Circle : Manuscripts

**_Harriet Grove_**

**_Diary for 1809_**

SC 98  TUESDAY 20
⟨———⟩ *& Louisa* ⟨———⟩

WEDNESDAY 21
*Heard from John & heard we are to go to the Parsonage to remain whilst the house is done*

THURSDAY 22
⟨———⟩ ~~*from Bysshe*~~ ⟨———⟩ ——

FRIDAY 23
*Packed up as we are to leave Dear Old Fern on Monday  Walked to Lower Donhead  went through Mad Grove & Drank tea with Aunt J—*

SATURDAY 24
⟨———⟩ ~~*letter*~~ ⟨———⟩

SUNDAY 25
~~*Wrote to*~~ ⟨———⟩ *& went to Berwick Church  Mr & Mrs Boys & Miss Croom Drank tea here  This is our* last *day*

MONDAY 26
*My birthday 18 years old  Such a bustle  left Dear Old Fern  Mama & Louisa went in the Pheaton with two family pictures before them & Charlotte & myself walked to the Parsonage Lower Donhead  & very very busy unpacking*

TUESDAY 27
~~*Had letter from Bysshe*~~ *equally as busy unpacking as we were yesterday*

20 June. one and one plus lines canceled
22 June. first cancellation two plus lines
23 June. *Aunt J*[ackson]
24 June. second cancellation three lines

WEDNESDAY 28
*Walked out in the Evening to Upper Donhead & saw a little boy who was afraid to pass the Parsonage because he heard such a Hammering*

THURSDAY 29
~~*Heard & wrote to B—*~~ *Walked half way to Fern but C— & L— were afraid of a Thunder Storm ——  Mr Eason dined here*

FRIDAY 30
*Walked to Fern & were much surprised to see how much they have pulled down, it looks now in a very deplorable state*

## JULY
SATURDAY 1
*Went to Drink tea with Mrs Buttson but as she was not at home we walked in Bury wood  Mrs & Miss Cooke came & called upon us in the Evening ——*

SUNDAY 2
*Went to Church twice  made a long morning visit on Mrs Cooke  what I dislike very much that tiresome Mr Wake dines here ——*

MONDAY 3
*It rained all day  Mrs Cooke came here to gossip in the Evening —*

26 June. *Pheaton* (sic); Harriet invariably uses this spelling.
29 June. *C*[harlotte] *& L*[ouisa]

*25 June.* Berwick St. John, a mile east of Fern.
*1 July.* Mrs. and Miss Cooke appear often in the diary while the Groves lived at the Lower Donhead Parsonage. They obviously were close neighbors.

[ 523 ]

# The Carl H. Pforzheimer Library

**Harriet Grove** Diary for 1809

SC 98 TUESDAY 4
*My Mother received a letter from Aunt S— that was written 24ᵗʰ June in which she says even if we had stayed at Fern we should not have seen her*

WEDNESDAY 5
X *My Mother & Louisa called on Mʳˢ & Miss Cooke if it is fine we are to drink tea with my Aunt Jackson ——*

THURSDAY 6
*Heard from & wrote to B. Mʳˢ & Miss Cooke Dined here a very stupid evening was the result —*

FRIDAY 7
*Very wet & therefore did not go out —*

SATURDAY 8
*Received a letter from B & walked to Fern in the morning —*

SUNDAY 9
*Wrote to B a great many morning visitors Dʳ Jackson & Arabella dined with us; walked*

MONDAY 10
*Walked round Mʳˢ Cooke's Garden with her —*

TUESDAY 11
*Heard & wrote to B also heard from Dear Charles — wrote to Aunt Shelley & Henrietta & John*

4 July. *Aunt S[helley]*
13 July. *L[ouisa]*
14 July. <———>; Harriet's pen went

WEDNESDAY 12
*My Mother heard from Aunt S–, Elizabeth has written a letter to John to invite him to Field Place*

THURSDAY 13
*(———) letter from Aunt Shelley — heard from B= Made a bet with Louisa that Fern will be finished in 2 years & a half – L says it won't our bet is a Shilling ——*

FRIDAY 14
*Received <———> letter we went to Fern yesterday to fix where the New House is to stand – Louisa heard from Mary*

SATURDAY 15
*Poor Marrianne's Birthday she would have been 17 – Heard from B & Dear George his letter dated 19ᵗʰ March,*

SUNDAY 16
*Heard from Bysshe & wrote to him Charlotte & Mama went to call on Mʳˢ Benett in the morning*

MONDAY 17
*Aunt Grove came here & we all took a very pleasent walk in the Evening ——*

through the paper; one word is lost.
15 July. *Marrianne* (sic)

*12 July.* Elizabeth Shelley, Shelley's oldest sister, fifteen years of age. Harriet's brother John was in love with her; in 1811 she rejected his proposal. Harriet soon began an active correspondence with Elizabeth.

*14 July.* Louisa's letter was from Shelley's younger sister Mary.

*15 July.* Harriet's sister Marianne (1792–1806) had died from burns when her muslin dress caught fire.

## Harriet Grove

SC 98

TUESDAY 18

*M^rs & Miss Cooke dined here & we went in the Evening to Fern to fix where the New House is to stand but we did not fix*

WEDNESDAY 19

*D^r & Aunt Jackson dined here* ——

THURSDAY 20

*Walked up upon Barton Hill with Aunt Grove & Louisa, Drank tea with M^rs Cooke – In our walk met an Old Woman who amused Tit by pulling up her Petticoats to shew us her bad leg Aunt G– was much shocked*

FRIDAY 21

*Went to Fern as M^r Hamilton came to measure out the plan for the New House, we went to choose the Spot*

SATURDAY 22

*~~Heard & wrote to B—~~ Aunt Grove left us Dined at D^r Jackson's*

SUNDAY 23

*Walked to Upper Donhead very hot, Charlotte & I took a most delightful walk in the Evening* —

MONDAY 24

*Louisa & I walked together in the garden & had a most interesting conversation* ——

TUESDAY 25

*Heard from Henrietta I am happy to hear they are quite well at Cwm Elen Louisa & I went in M^rs Cookes Car intending to go to Pitt House but M^rs C– fancied there would be Thunder* —

WEDNESDAY 26

*walked upon the pavement*

THURSDAY 27

*~~Heard & wrote to B.~~ I think we have a chance of going to Field Place it makes me very happy.*

FRIDAY 28

X *This is Louisa's last day she has to stay with us, I wrote to John & sent it to Field Place where he is now* ——

SATURDAY 29

*Louisa went to school miss her very much indeed* ——

SUNDAY 30

*Went to Netherhampton staid there all night M^r I & M^rs E Long dined here*

25 *July. Elen* (sic); for Elan

25 *July.* Cwm Elan, an estate of ten thousand acres about four miles west of Rhayader, Radnorshire, South Wales, was the property of Harriet's oldest brother Thomas, who often spent his summers there. Upon the invitation of his twenty-seven-year-old cousin, Shelley spent about three weeks at Cwm Elan in July-August 1811. (See "Prelude to Shelley's Elopement," below.) In June 1812 Shelley again was there, this time with his wife (Harriet Westbrook).

Pitt House, the home of the Charles Bennetts, was a mile and a half northeast of the Parsonage.

30 *July.* At Netherhampton, two miles west of Salisbury, they spent the night with Aunt Grove, the sister of Harriet's father. The Longs who dined were doubtless relatives

# The Carl H. Pforzheimer Library

*Harriet Grove*                    *Diary for* **1809**

SC 98

MONDAY 31

⟨——⟩ *We got to Little Park* ⟨——⟩ *from B. Dear Emma knows us very well Came from Netherhampton by Romsey here, the Country is very beautiful*

## AUGUST

TUESDAY 1

*What a pleasent month this was last year – Dear little Emma talks & is very entertaining — Little John is grown a fine little fellow a M$^r$ Minchin Dined here he is a great talker*

WEDNESDAY 2

*Wrote to Bysshe – Charlotte & myself walked out & took a very long walk told little Emma to call her Aunt C– Dolly Rump*

THURSDAY 3

*Wrote to Helen & Louisa a man came with a Bear to the Gate & made it dance which amused little Emma very much*

FRIDAY 4

*Heard & wrote to Eliz Shelley I am afraid M$^r$ Shelley wont ask us to Field Place this Summer ——*

SATURDAY 5

*a very wet day our new Barouche is come, I played with dear little Emma I am still a great favorite of hers*

SUNDAY 6

*Heard from B– went to Church at Wickham & then payed morning visits but fortunately they were none of them at home except M$^r$ Garnier*

MONDAY 7

*Walked with my Mother & talked to her upon a subject that always interests me –*

TUESDAY 8

⟨——⟩ *heard from M$^{rs}$ Wilsonn & Miss Tregonwell —*

31 July. first cancellation one plus lines

who came from Preshaw, Hants, or Compton, Wilts. As the next entry shows, the Groves were on their way to visit Harriet's sister, Emma Philippa Waddington, at Little Park, Wickham, Hants.

*31 July.* The Emma here referred to is, of course, the small daughter of Harriet's sister. Little Emma had last seen the Groves on Monday, March 27.

Romsey is in Hampshire, about six miles northwest of Southampton.

*1 Aug.* Paterson's *Roads*, 1811, lists a Mr. Minchin as proprietor of Botley Grange at Botley near Wickham.

*3 Aug.* Hellen Tregonwell.

*4 Aug.* This is the first specific reference to a correspondence with Shelley's sister Elizabeth.

*6 Aug.* Cary's *Roads*, 1819, lists G. Garnier, Esq., Wickham Corner, Wickham, next-door neighbor to John Waddington, Little Park.

*7 Aug.* The subject must have been her cousin Bysshe and Field Place.

*8 Aug.* Mrs. Wilsonn lived in Bath and evidently had charge of Louisa, who was there in school.

**Harriet Grove**                                    **Diary for 1809**

SC 98    WEDNESDAY 9
~~Heard from B~~  *dined at the Garniers*
*very very stupid   they laid the first*
*stone at Fern today*

THURSDAY 10
*Went home   felt sorry to leave Emma*
*& the Dear Children ——— ~~received a~~*
~~letter from B— before I left Little Park~~
*a most tremendous Thunder storm in*
*the evening*

FRIDAY 11
⟨———⟩ – *My Mother   C– & myself*
*went to Fern in the Pheaton*

SATURDAY 12
*the Jacksons dined here upon a haunch*
*of venison* ———

SUNDAY 13
*heard the good news that M^rs Benett of*
*Pitt has a son and heir   Wrote to*
*Louisa*

MONDAY 14
*very wet so staid in all day* —

11 Aug. C[harlotte]

TUESDAY 15
~~Heard from~~ ⟨———⟩  *We have gained*
*a victory over the French by Sir A W–y*
*in the battle of Talavera de la Reyna* —

WEDNESDAY 16
*Went to Fern in the morning   they are*
*got on a great deal with the Foundation,*
~~heard from~~ ⟨———⟩.

THURSDAY 17
*Wrote to Aunt Shelley   called on the*
*Ansleys at M^rs Cookes   Lord & Lady*
*Arundell called here,   Drank Tea at*
*M^rs Cookes,   My Dear Father returned*
*home* ———

FRIDAY 18
*My Father has made me a present of a*
*Lottery Ticket which I am very much*
*obliged to him for*

SATURDAY 19
~~Wrote to~~ ⟨———⟩ ~~& heard from him~~
⟨———⟩  *the Annesleys & Gordons*
*Dined here* —

SUNDAY 20
*Wrote to Louisa   we have heard M^r*
*Fletcher the Rector of this place is dead*
*I fear we shall not reside here much*
*longer – as that is the case* —

15 Aug. *Sir A*[rthur] *W*[ellesle]*y*

*13 Aug.* Mrs. Charles Bennett of Pitt House.

*15 Aug.* The Battle of Talavera was fought on July 27 and 28. The British and Spanish
were under the command of Sir Arthur Wellesley, who defeated the French. The enemy
lost 10,000 men; the British lost 800 killed and 4000 wounded or missing. This entry in
Harriet's diary is very exceptional, in that she almost never notes current events beyond
the family circle.

*17 Aug.* James Everard Arundell (1763–1817), 9th Baron Arundell of Wardour since
1808. His mother was the daughter of John Wyndham, of Ashcombe, Wilts. In 1806 he
married a second wife, daughter of Robert Burnet Jones, of Ades, Sussex.

*20 Aug.* William Fletcher, the rector of Donhead St. Andrew, obviously did not occupy
the Parsonage. The new rector would probably wish to have the house, and the Groves

[ 527 ]

# The Carl H. Pforzheimer Library

## Harriet Grove

SC 98

**MONDAY 21**
*M*ʳ *Wake went away this morning*

**TUESDAY 22**
*C Jackson & J Gordon came here this morning to hunt with my Father we dined at the Gordons – met M*ʳ *Benett there & M*ʳ *Wake who played upon his Fiddle –*

**WEDNESDAY 23**
*Nothing particularly happened to day —*

**THURSDAY 24**
*X* ~~*Heard from & wrote to Bysshe*~~ ⟨——⟩ *heard from Emma – My Mother & Father are gone to Knoyle to pay morning visits*

**FRIDAY 25**
⟨——⟩ *The Parkers are at Field Place*

**SATURDAY 26**
*M*ʳˢ *Cooke & her Brother M*ʳ *Cooke dined here ——*

**SUNDAY 27**
~~*Heard from my Dear Bysshe*~~ *took a very pretty walk —*

**MONDAY 28**
*M*ʳˢ *& Miss Burlton M*ʳ *& M*ʳˢ *Boys & Miss Croome dined here on a Haunch of Venison Mama & Charlotte went in the morning to call on Lady A–l at Ashcombe —*

**TUESDAY 29**
~~*Wrote to Bysshe,*~~ *received a letter from* ~~*him &*~~ *John Elizabeth has sent me my Picture —— called on the Jacksons Miss Button came in so smartly dressed in Lavender Coloured Satin dress & a muslin Turband with white beads ——*

**WEDNESDAY 30**
⟨——⟩ *Lord & Lady Arundell & Miss L– A– Dined here*

**THURSDAY 31**
⟨——⟩ *Heard from John who will be here Tomorrow –*

25 Aug. three lines canceled
28 Aug. *Lady A*[rundel]*l*

30 Aug. two lines canceled
31 Aug. one plus lines canceled

would have to move. This is precisely what happened. The new rector was also called Fletcher — Nathaniel Fletcher. (Hoare, *Wiltshire*, IV, 197.)

*24 Aug.* East Knoyle was about four miles northwest of the Parsonage.

*25 Aug.* Possibly the Parkers of Hatch House, two miles northeast of the Parsonage. Shelley's uncle, Robert Parker, lived at Maidstone, Kent, and his branch of the family could be the one referred to here.

*28 Aug.* Ashcombe was a large estate belonging to the Arundell family. It was a mile south of Fern, and three miles southeast of the Parsonage.

Paterson's *Roads*, 1811, lists William Burlton, Esq., Donhead Hall, Ludwell, near Shaftesbury. In 1810 Sarah Burlton of Donhead St. Mary married Charles Cowper Bennett of Berwick St. John's, Wiltshire. (Hoare, *Wiltshire*, IV, 40, 34.)

SC 98 SEPTEMBER

FRIDAY I

*Dear John came    Charlotte & myself
drank tea* with *M*rs *C— last night & M*r
*Douglas & M*r *Butler came    Mary
Dimmer saw them go into the Church
this morning to look at M*rs *Cooke's
Door & called them the two Bishops*

SATURDAY 2

*received a letter from Emma    Dined at
M*rs *Cookes    walked to Wardour Woods*

SUNDAY 3

~~*Heard from Bysshe*~~ *walked to Upper
Donhead with John*

MONDAY 4

⟨———⟩ *M*r *W: Benett dined here*

TUESDAY 5

~~*Heard from Bysshe*~~ *Got a quiz from
Elizabeth    Went to see Tollard    we all
like it pretty well —*

4 Sept. seven plus lines canceled    *W*[illiam]
7 Sept. two plus lines canceled

WEDNESDAY 6

*John dines at M*r *W— Hilyars today
he then goes to Norton & does not return
here till Saturday    I heard from Dearest
Louisa*

THURSDAY 7

⟨———⟩ *M*r *Hamilton came here* ———

FRIDAY 8

*We went to Fern    M*rs *Cooke went
with us in her Car, it rained all the
time we were there —*

SATURDAY 9

⟨———⟩ *I long for Mama to hear from
Aunt Shelley* ———

SUNDAY 10

⟨———⟩ *Catherine    Benett    L.    Cooke
M*r *Wake & M*r *W: Helyar dined
here* ———

10 Sept. five lines canceled

*1 Sept.* Mary Dimmer was the Groves' old servant.

We find no reference to "M**rs** Cooke's Door" but on the west wall of the chantry of Donhead St. Andrew there was a monument to Captain John Cooke, who died at Trafalgar on his ship, the *Bellerophon.* (Hoare, *Wiltshire*, IV, 52.) See also entry for Oct. 1 and note for Dec. 13.

*5 Sept.* Tollard Royal was three miles south of Fern, and five miles southeast of the Parsonage. The Groves moved to Tollard on October 3.

The Reverend John Helyar, uncle of the William Helyar who married Harriet Grove, was rector of the church at Tollard Royal from 1798 to 1823. (*Burke's Landed Gentry*, 1837, 1851; Hoare, *Wiltshire*, 177.)

*6 Sept.* William Helyar, junior, was to become Harriet's husband late in 1811. For a year or more yet Harriet's affections were still centered on Shelley. Her diary never gives the slightest indication that her interest in William Helyar was growing.

William Helyar, senior, owned an estate at nearby Sedgehill and another at Yeovil in Somerset, about twenty-five miles away. Other entries indicate that the son is here referred to. He and perhaps also his brother Henry seem to have lived on the Sedgehill estate. Harriet's future husband, therefore, was a close neighbor of the Groves.

Norton was a village near Yeovil.

## Harriet Grove

SC 98    MONDAY 11
*~~This is a very pleasent thing to~~* ⟨——⟩

TUESDAY 12
⟨————⟩

WEDNESDAY 13
*M*^rs *& Miss Cooke called here before they set off for Weymouth   I heard from dear George yesterday*

THURSDAY 14
⟨————⟩ *(Aunt Jackson was brought to bed of a little girl last Tuesday 12*^th*)*

FRIDAY 15
X   *My Father & John dined at Pytt House*

SATURDAY 16
*M*^r *C. Benett breakfasted here Charlotte & myself intended to have walked to Fern but were prevented by the rain —*

SUNDAY 17
*My Mother heard from Dear Aunt Shelley who says she shall always be glad to hear from me,   John went to Netherhampton to day*

11 Sept. three lines canceled
12 Sept. nine lines canceled
14 Sept. three plus lines canceled

MONDAY 18
*John has hired an Old Woman for his Housekeeper   he says she is not quite so ugly as his last —*

TUESDAY 19
*Wrote to Dear Aunt S–y & to M*^rs *Wilsonn & Louisa & heard from Elizabeth who has written me a most affec*^t *letter,* ⟨————⟩

WEDNESDAY 20
*Answered Elizabeth Shelleys letter, dined & slept at Pytt House   Met Sir W: & Lady Parker there   the latter is looking beautiful ————*

THURSDAY 21
*We returned home after spending our time at Pyt house pleasently,   We met at Dinner there M*^r *J Kneller & his friend M*^r *Jarvis both great quizes   We called upon Aunt J– after our return home & I saw my Goddaughter that is to be ——*

FRIDAY 22
*M*^r *Eason Dined here on a Haunch of Venison   wrote to Louisa,   was much amused by the quantity of venison M*^r *E– eat –*

16 Sept. *C*[harles]
19 Sept. *Aunt S*[helle]*y*   four lines canceled

*17 Sept.* John visited Aunt Grove at Netherhampton. It is obvious that John was making the usual round of visits to friends and relatives.

*18 Sept.* The housekeeper was for John's house in London.

*20 Sept.* The Charles Bennetts of Pitt House and the Parkers of Hatch House were close neighbors.

*21 Sept.* This seems to have been the first time Harriet saw Aunt Jackson's new baby, born on September 12.

**Harriet Grove**  *Diary for* **1809**

SC 98

SATURDAY 23
*Went to Compton John went to Langton – met M^r & M^rs Long the Member & Miss Flora Long there M^rs P is quite recovered*

SUNDAY 24
*Went to Church & John came   a M^r*
  us
*Powell dined with,͏ I think Miss F Long is a pleasent Girl —*

MONDAY 25
*Came home, the Water was so high that we thought we should have been drowned ——*

TUESDAY 26
*Dear John left us   the Farmers dined here –   had a droll letter from Louisa & one from M^rs Wilsonn   Joy Joy Joy William Dear Dear William's come home   such an unexpected pleasure*

WEDNESDAY 27
*Wrote a great many letters to tell the Joyfull event of Williams arrival   heard from Eliz^th Shelley – ⟨——⟩ William is so altered I should not have known him any where*

23 Sept. *M^rs P*[enruddocke] of Compton
27 Sept. one plus lines canceled
30 Sept. *W*[illiam]

THURSDAY 28
*M^r Fletcher came with Dr Jackson & M^r Brotherton was inducted into the Church   walked to Fern   William went out a hunting  M^rs Cooke Drank tea here   We began sending some of the things to Tollard ——*

FRIDAY 29
*Went with Dear William to see Aunt Jackson   Tom was here when we came back – he wanted William to go to Gunville but we could not part with him*

SATURDAY 30
*My Father & W– went out hunting The Miss Hilyars called here   Mama had a droll letter from John —— -*

## OCTOBER

SUNDAY 1
*Received the Sacrement   Wrote to Eliz^th Shelley — M^r Wake as usual dined here,  Mary Dimmer went to Fern —— M^rs Cooke went into Church through the large Door by which means she has gained a victory over M^r Brotherton*

1 Oct. *Sacrement* (sic); sometimes spelled correctly with an *a*.

23 *Sept.* Harriet and John went in different directions. Compton, where the Longs lived, was eight miles northeast of the Parsonage. Langton, the home of the Farquharsons, was about eleven miles south of the Parsonage, slightly east of Blandford, Dorset.

Richard Godolphin Long of Rood Ashton was Member of Parliament for Wiltshire from 1806–1818. "Flora" was doubtless the Long's daughter Florentine. (*Burke's Landed Gentry*, 1898.)

26 *Sept.* William, Harriet's favorite brother, was on leave from the Navy. He was nineteen years old.

28 *Sept.* Nathaniel Fletcher was the new rector of Donhead St. Andrew of Lower Donhead. (See note to Aug. 20.) It was appropriate that Harriet's uncle, the Reverend Dr. Gilbert Jackson, rector of Donhead St. Mary, Upper Donhead, should introduce him to the Groves.

**Harriet Grove**                                    *Diary for* **1809**

SC 98  MONDAY 2
*Walked to Fern with Dear William sent almost all the things to Tollard*

TUESDAY 3
*Left Donhead & got to Tollard called on M^rs Cooke to wish her well. We are in as great a Bustle as when we left Fern —*

WEDNESDAY 4
*I like this House better than Lower Donhead — heard from Dear Louisa & Aunt Shelley Williams room is so close to mine that I hear every thing he says, Tom & a M^r Fraser called here*

THURSDAY 5
*Tom & M^r Fraser breakfasted here, & went out hunting with my Father — Henrietta M^rs F— & two Miss Frasers called here —*

FRIDAY 6
X *Wrote to Aunt Shelley & Louisa We went in the Pheaton to Sedgehill saw*

7 Oct. *Helyer* (sic)

*there M^rs Ogle & M^r & M^rs John Still* ——

SATURDAY 7
*M^r John Helyer called whilst we were at breakfast wrote in William's name to Emma I wonder if she will find it out —*

SUNDAY 8
*Went to Church M^r J: Helyar I think is a good preacher. went to Gunville after Church & found Fanny & Arabella Jackson there.*

MONDAY 9
*My Mother & I returned to Tollard to get some more Cloaths & then went to Gunville again Danced in the Evening — John came here* ——

TUESDAY 10
*We have heard poor Miss W: Arundell is dead stayed at Gunville M^r Snow & his two sons dined here — danced again this Evening*

9 Oct. *Cloaths* (sic)

*4 Oct.* Now that the Groves were at Tollard, they were only about three miles from Gunville House, Dorset, the home of Thomas and his wife Henrietta. At Fern they had been separated by six miles, at the Parsonage by eight. Tom's companion was William Fraser, son of Sir William Fraser, Bart. The Frasers appear frequently in the diary after the removal to Tollard. For their relationship with the Farquharsons of Langton, see the note to the entry for May 11.

The Groves owned "farms and lands" at Tollard. (Hoare, *Wiltshire*, IV, 171.)

*5 Oct.* Mrs. F— is probably Mrs. Farquharson, Henrietta's sister-in-law.

*6 Oct.* Sedgehill is about eight miles northwest of Tollard.

*7 Oct.* John Helyar, uncle of William Helyar, junior, was rector of the church at Tollard Royal (and also of that of Hardington near the Helyars' estate in Somerset). (See *Burke's Landed Gentry*, 1851.) John Helyar appears frequently in the diary hereafter.

*8 Oct.* Fanny and Arabella were the young daughters of Aunt Jackson.

*10 Oct.* George Snow of Langton Lodge, Langford, Dorset. (Hutchins, *Dorset*, I, 286; Paterson's *Roads*, 1811, pp. 40, 435.)

*Harriet Grove*                                    *Diary for 1809*

SC 98   WEDNESDAY 11
*Went home, & then to Fern to meet Miss Helyar who was not there – Saw Old Mary Dimmer*

THURSDAY 12
*We went to Farnham to call on M*r *J: Helyar. I did not take much fancy to her she can make herself pleasent*

FRIDAY 13
*John & William went to Gunville – M*r *Wm: Helyar & Miss C. Benett called here   heard from E– S– she has sent me some verses of Bysshe's – which I think very good*

SATURDAY 14
*Wrote to Eliz:*th *C– & myself were going Post haste to walk to Fern but Mama prevented us   John & Wm. came home. M*r *& M*rs *J. Helyar & Tom & M*r *Fraser dined here*

SUNDAY 15
*Received the Sacrament   M*r *Helyar gave us a most beautiful Sermon   C & myself walked to Fern   John & W*m *went to Langton –*

13 Oct. *C*[atherine]  *E*[lizabeth]  *S*[helley]

MONDAY 16
*M*rs *Brereton & Henrietta have both sent us an invitation to a Ball on the 25*th *when there is to be a Jubilee,   We are obliged to refuse both because we are engaged to go to Preshaw for which we are all very sorry —*

TUESDAY 17
*Charlotte had a most shocking cross letter from Aunt Grove   John & Wm. are gone there   M*r *Bingham called here   John does not return here again*

WEDNESDAY 18
*Took a very pretty walk to a Cottage near Ashcombe   Charlotte & I have made a bargain that if either of us have a prize in the lottery we are to share it between us –*

THURSDAY 19
*William says Miss Wilsonn is very ugly – The Miss Frasers & their Brother came here   I   Played at Commerce won 15 owing to M*r *W. Frasers cheating for me ——*

FRIDAY 20
*This is the day the Lottery is drawn – My Mother & the Miss Frasers went*

14 Oct. *C*[harlotte]

*11 Oct.* From this and future entries it appears that the entry for October 1, "Mary Dimmer went to Fern," means that the old servant was thereafter permanently domiciled at Fern.

*16 Oct.* Mrs. Brereton lived at Salisbury. (See the entry for June 2.) Preshaw was the home of the Walter Longs, relatives of the Groves. It was in Hampshire, southeast of Salisbury. The Jubilee of October 25, 1809, was in celebration of the beginning of the fiftieth year of George III's reign.

*17 Oct.* There is ample evidence in the diary that Aunt Grove was voluble and sharp-tongued. She is one of the few who emerge as distinct individuals.

*19 Oct.* Miss Wilsonn may be the daughter of Mrs. Wilsonn of Bath, who was probably in charge of Louisa at school.

**Harriet Grove**                                    **Diary for 1809**

SC 98 *to Fern  Charlotte & myself walked to Ashcombe ——*

SATURDAY 21
*Walked to Ashcombe  Miss J: Fraser rode on our Poney  M*r *Markland Brother of Capt M. called here  M*r *Wm. Fraser went away*

SUNDAY 22
*M*r *W. Fraser returned  went to Church, afterwards walked out with the Miss Frasers, Charlotte could not go to Church as she has got a swelled face —— I fear my Ticket is come up a blank indeed I believe we are none of us fortunes favorite*

MONDAY 23
*Left the Miss F—s at Tollard as we set off for Preshaw  Tom is to fetch them to Gunville  We arrived at Preshaw W— Long is here who is going to be married to Lady Mary Carnigie*

TUESDAY 24
*My Mother Charlotte & myself walked out  William says he shall go to Little Park*

23 Oct. *Miss* F[raser]*s* W[alter] *Carnigie* (sic); for Carnegie
26 Oct. W[illiam]

WEDNESDAY 25
*Went to Church at M*r *Ferrers  heard a most excellent Sermon on The Kings accession on the throne  We dined at Lord Northesks on Turtle  met a very pleasant party & we danced in the Evening*

THURSDAY 26
*Emma came here with little Emma they took W— back with them  We went with the Northesks to a Winchester ball & saw Lady Mildmay*

FRIDAY 27
*The Waddingtons dined here & M*r *& Miss Ferrers & her Lover M*r *Courtney The Northesks came in the Evening & we had a very pleasent Dance*

SATURDAY 28
*Left Preshaw & reached my Aunt Groves  called at Close Gate in our way were I received a letter from E— S*

SUNDAY 29
X *Heard of our Lottery Tickets  they are all Blanks but C—s who has a prize of 30 Miss Packington is here who sang to us yesterday Evening —*

28 Oct. *were* (sic) E[lizabeth] S[helley]
29 Oct. C[harlotte']*s*

23 *Oct.* For Preshaw, see note to entry for October 16. Lady Mary Carnegie, the daughter of William Carnegie, Lord Northesk, married Walter Long on February 12, 1810. (*Burke's Landed Gentry*, 1898.)

25 *Oct.* William Carnegie (1758–1831), 7th Earl of Northesk; a rear-admiral since 1804, made admiral in 1814. He married Mary, daughter of William Henry Ricketts, of Longwood, Hants.

26 *Oct.* "Here": that is, to Preshaw.

28 *Oct.* Aunt Grove's house at Netherhampton, two miles west of Salisbury.

*Harriet Grove*                                    *Diary for* 1809

SC 98 MONDAY 30

*Left Netherhampton & in our way home stopped at Fern which we were surprised to see they had got on so much with ——*

TUESDAY 31

*To our great surprise Miss Tregonwell & her Brother paid us a morning visit, Tom & H & M<sup>r</sup> Fraser also called here. William returned from Little Park*

NOVEMBER

WEDNESDAY 1

*Wrote to E- S—— M<sup>rs</sup> Farquharson has sent to invite us to Langton on Friday —*

THURSDAY 2

*Been very busy all day mending old Clothes — Received a letter from my Dear Aunt Shelley*

FRIDAY 3

*Wrote to John    went to Dinner to Langton   The Miss Frasers & their Brother are here ——*

SATURDAY 4

*Walked to Blandford with the Miss Frasers   My Mother & M<sup>rs</sup> Farquharson called on M<sup>r</sup> Portman, & in their*

*way home went to St. Mary's for Fanny & Arabella Jackson,   in the Evening played at Commerce   M<sup>r</sup> W— Fraser caused me to win the Pool ——*

SUNDAY 5

*Went to Langton Church afterwards walked to the Farm & we all exercised our lungs whilst doing so a M<sup>r</sup> Riddon came by which caused a good laugh Henrietta   Tom & Miss Tregonwell came here & a M<sup>r</sup> & M<sup>rs</sup> Ocden & their little Girl ——*

MONDAY 6

*Left Langton & returned to Tollard I think M<sup>rs</sup> Okden without exception the most affected woman I ever met with*

TUESDAY 7

*Answered my Aunt Shelleys letter & told her William would be with her on the 22<sup>d</sup>   M<sup>r</sup> Hamilton dined & slept here ——*

WEDNESDAY 8

*Went in the Pheaton to Fern & to M<sup>rs</sup> Cookes – & my Aunt Jacksons with my Mother, Charlotte & Wm – walked to Fern, my Mother & I both agree in thinking M<sup>r</sup> W<sup>m</sup> Fraser a very pleasent young man —*

31 Oct. *Tom & H*[enrietta]

1 Nov. *E*[lizabeth] *S*[helley]

*31 Oct.* St. Barbe Tregonwell (1782–1859) was Hellen Tregonwell's brother.

*4 Nov.* "In their way home": that is, back to Langton House, where by the next day there were at least thirteen guests.

*5 Nov.* The David Okedens of Turnworth, near Blandford St. Mary, Dorset, and their daughter Catherine Jane. Mrs. Okeden died on February 23, 1810. (Hutchins, *Dorset*, III, 469.)

*7 Nov.* Mr. Hamilton was building the new house at Fern.

*Harriet Grove*                                                    *Diary for* 1809

SC 98   THURSDAY 9
*Charlotte & myself walked through the Parish & were frightened by the Silly man wanting to shake hands with us Mrs & Miss Cooke came here —*

FRIDAY 10
*Mrs & Miss Cooke remained here I think Miss C– more troublesome than ever — —*

SATURDAY 11
*Mrs & Miss C– left us walked intending to call on Mrs R Arundel at Ashcombe but rain came on & prevented us*

SUNDAY 12
*Mr J Helyar came from Sedgehill & preached here heard from my dearest Aunt Shelley — Tom called here H: Tregonwell came to stay*

MONDAY 13
*We all went to Fern Dear William left us & went to Gunville he goes tomorrow to Little Park with Tom & Henrietta*

TUESDAY 14
*Helen talked to me about her dear Duffy as she calls Capt Markland wrote to Aunt Shelley – & Louisa —*

WEDNESDAY 15
*Mama & Charlotte went to call upon Mr & Mrs Fletcher the new Rector of Lower Donhead Miss Tre–ll & myself walked to Ashcombe ——*

15 Nov. *Tre*[gonwe]*ll*

THURSDAY 16
*a very hard frost the Building at Fern must now stop for the Winter wrote to William —*

FRIDAY 17
*Took a walk with Charlotte through the village it was so dirty that we were near being stuck —*

SATURDAY 18
*went out walking directly after breakfast. Shewed King Johns House to Helen Wm is to leave Little Park to day – heard & wrote to Dear William & wrote to Henrietta —*

SUNDAY 19
*Wm did not leave Little P till to day – last night We fancied the House was on fire so Charlotte Helen & myself went down stairs in our night shifts to see if it was & found it was a Tea Kettle on the fire boiling —*

MONDAY 20
*Wrote to Dear Charles whom we have not heard from for a long time & also wrote to Wm took a very pretty walk —*

TUESDAY 21
*received some Baskets that dear Wm has sent us from Little Park – Mr & Mrs Tregonwell came here —*

19 Nov. *Little P*[ark]

*12 Nov.* Mr. John Helyar often went to Sedgehill, where his brother William had his Wiltshire estate. Hellen Tregonwell's visit lasted until November 22.

*14 Nov.* In 1814 Hellen Tregonwell married Captain John Duff Markland, R.N. (1780–1848), afterwards rear-admiral.

*21 Nov.* The Tregonwells were Hellen's parents.

*Harriet Grove*                                          *Diary for* 1809

SC 98   WEDNESDAY 22
*The Tregonwells left us & we went to*
*M*ʳ *J: Stills at Berwick & met Miss*
*Helyar there who I like excessively*
*M*ʳˢ *J Stills children are the prettiest*
*I ever saw*

THURSDAY 23
X *Much entertained in the morning by*
*Miss Helyar the Stills Lady Parker*
*&c. & M*ʳˢ *John Helyar & M*ʳ *W*ᵐ *H*
*Dined here & they took Miss Helyar*
*back with them at night*

FRIDAY 24
*Returned to Tollard & heard that Dear*
*W*ᵐ *is going out to sea again immediately*
*a letter from Charles to say he is arrived*
*at Yarmouth & still dislikes his Pro-*
*fession, it is both very bad news, for I*
*am very sorry Dear Wm is going away*
*again*

SATURDAY 25
*Wrote a great many letters & walked*
*out*

SUNDAY 26
*Heard from dear W*ᵐ *which was written*
*at Field Place  M*ʳ *Helyar gave us a*
*most excellent sermon which he generally*
*does —*

23 Nov. *H*[elyar]

MONDAY 27
*Miss Catherine Benett came here yester-*
*day & left us to day which I am glad*
*of* ——

TUESDAY 28
*My Father went out hunting  a very*
*unpleasent day for Walking —*

WEDNESDAY 29
*Dear W*ᵐ *returned before Breakfast*
*Dear Fellow he leaves us again tomorrow*
*for which we are all very sorry  We all*
*dined at M*ʳ *J: H—  met the young*
*Helyars there,  Dear W*ᵐ *enjoyed him-*
*self very much  he tried to open a Piano*
*forte but could not succeed* ——

THURSDAY 30
*My Dear* ⟨——⟩ *left us* ⟨——⟩ *to day*
⟨——⟩

## DECEMBER
FRIDAY I
*The Helyars dined here all but M*ʳˢ *John*
*who was ill with a cold  We had a*
*pleasent little Dance*

SATURDAY 2
*Walked out before the House  My*
*Father hunted with M*ʳ *Chafins Hounds*
                                      *him*
*M*ʳ *W*ᵐ *Helyar returned here with*ₐ*&*
*sat some time with us —*

30 Nov. Whole entry of four lines canceled.

*24 Nov.* Charles's "Profession" at this time was the Navy, which he was shortly to quit.
*2 Dec.* The Reverend William Chafin, whose estate, Cheete, was in the vicinity of Salisbury. (Paterson's *Roads*, 1811, p. 40.) His reputation was said to rest rather upon his
sporting proclivities than his divinity. (*Wessex Worthies*, p. 68.) He was the author of
*Anecdotes and History of Cranbourn Chase.* (Allibone.) For Cranbourn Chase see Environs
of Fern, page 503.

**Harriet Grove**                                          **Diary for 1809**

SC 98    SUNDAY 3

*Heard a most beautiful sermon from*
*M*ʳ *J: H–  Miss C. H–  M*ʳ *Wm &*
*M*ʳ *J: H. & Miss Camplin came here*
*after Church ——*

MONDAY 4

*M*ʳ *William Helyar breakfasted here &*
*went hunting with my Father who had*
*a very pretty run at first close to the*
*House, they went afterwards to Fern —*

TUESDAY 5

*Heard almost from everyone of our*
*friends  Emma is to be confined again*
*either in Feb*ʸ *or March*

WEDNESDAY 6

*This day seven years ago it was Dear*
*William went to the East Indies. How*
*glad he now is returned safe  I am*
*glad he returned from thence safe but*
*most sorry he is gone again  We heard*
*from him to day  Dear fellow he arrived*
*safe on board the Orestes on Friday*
*he says the Officers on board are very*
*pleasing  he has not seen his Capt*
*yet ——*

THURSDAY 7

*Wrote to my Aunt Shelley  Charlotte*
*heard from H  S— ⟨——⟩*

3 Dec. *H*[elyar] in each case
7 Dec. three lines canceled

FRIDAY 8

*Went to M*ʳ *Boy's at Berwick  Wrote*
*to H: S:  met D*ʳ *Jackson & Col:*
*Peachy at Berwick  the latter talks*
*more than ever altho' he has lost his Wife*
*so lately*

SATURDAY 9

*left Berwick & called on my Aunt*
*Jackson in our way home  Saw & heard*
*that tiresome Col: again  heard from*
*Dear George*

SUNDAY 10

*Heard & wrote to Dear W*ᵐ *the Orestes*
*is sailed on a short cruize, a M*ʳ *Napper*
*preached here as M*ʳ *John Helyar I am*
*sorry to say has a bad cold,  M*ʳ *N–*
*dined here  he appears a sensible young*
*man*

MONDAY 11

*Wrote to Charles  M*ʳ *& M*ʳˢ *Boys*
*dined & slept here  laughed a good deal*
*at M*ʳ *B– calling his Wife my Bess –*

TUESDAY 12

*The Boy's went away  walked out for*
*an hour ——*

WEDNESDAY 13

*Dear Tom came here  Charles has*
*written word he has left the Bellerophon*
*& is coming home*

8 Dec. *H*[ellen] *S*[helley]
10 Dec. *cruize* (sic)

*6 Dec.* The *Orestes* was a small 16-gun craft which had been captured from the French.
(*The Court and City Register* for 1807, p. 141.)

*13 Dec.* The *Bellerophon*, a 74-gun warship, had recently seen action (off the Swedish
coast on June 19). In 1815 the *Bellerophon* achieved fame as the ship on board which
Napoleon surrendered. (William James, *The Naval History of Great Britain, 1793–1820*,
London, 1824, IV, 445, 446.) At Trafalgar the *Bellerophon* was commanded by Captain
John Cooke of Donhead St. Andrew. (See note for Sept. 1.)

**Harriet Grove**                                              *Diary for* **1809**

SC 98   THURSDAY 14

M*r* *Harry Helyar called here as we*
*thought to invite us to Sedgehill but no*
*such thing, the rest of the family are*
*not returned from Bath*

FRIDAY 15

*Tom & Henrietta came here  I am*
*afraid they won't go to the Shaftesbury*
*Ball with us —*

SATURDAY 16

*Heard from W: & Emma – Tom & my*
*Father went out Hunting ——*

SUNDAY 17

*Louisa & Charles came here   the latter*
*has left the Navy & is to be a ——*
*Phisician which we all like very much —*

MONDAY 18

X  *Charles began studying Greek   we are a*
*very happy party ——*

TUESDAY 19

*Wrote to Eliz:th Shelley  Mr J: Helyar,*
*& Mrs & Miss Fletcher called here*
⟨———⟩

WEDNESDAY 20

*Tom & Henrietta went away which we*
*are sorry for — Heard from Eliz:th*
*Shelley   she writes very drole Letters —*

THURSDAY 21

*Louisa heard from M: Shelley who has*
*heard that I am going to be married,*
*—— Put Beads upon our Gowns*

FRIDAY 22

*Went to the Shaftesbury ball  Had a*
*most excellent Ball   more than 20*
*Couple  Danced thro' two with Mr*
*Wm H—*

SATURDAY 23

*Returned home & in our way called on*
*Mary D— who is looking very well*

SUNDAY 24

*Heard Mr J: Helyar   I am so glad he*
*is well again   he came in & we had a*
*very agreable conversation*

MONDAY 25

*Heard a most excellent sermon from*

16 Dec. *W*[illiam]

17 Dec. *Phisician* (sic)

19 Dec. one line canceled

21 Dec. *M*[ary] *Shelley*

22 Dec. *H*[elyar]

23 Dec. *Mary D*[immer]

24 Dec. *agreable* (sic)

*14 Dec.* Harriet's parents had driven to Bath to fetch Louisa home for the Christmas
holidays. They must have returned on the 15th or 16th, for on the 16th her father went
hunting. If Harriet is right in noting Louisa's arrival on the 17th, her sister must have,
before coming to Tollard, spent the night at Aunt Jackson's or some other relative or
friend's house. Henry Helyar (b. 1784) was the brother of the William Helyar who married
Harriet Grove. He was later rector of the church at Hardington near Yeovil, Somerset.
(*Burke's Landed Gentry,* 1837.)

*17 Dec.* Charles did not, like his brother John, become a physician. He later took the
A.B. and M.A. degrees at Oxford and became a clergyman. From 1826 to 1873 he was
rector of Berwick St. Leonard, near Fern. Dying in 1878, he was the last of the Grove
family.

SC 98    *M*ʳ *J. H.   it being Xmas Day We all*
*then received the Sacrament   Charles for*
*the 1ˢᵗ time*

TUESDAY 26
*Wrote to Eliz:ᵗʰ & Wᵐ   My Father met*
*Mʳ J: H—— going to Sedgehill ——*

WEDNESDAY 27
*Walked   from   hence   to   Gunville*
*Waddington came from Little Park*

THURSDAY 28
*Mʳ W: Helyar came here   Tom was*
*in a very drole humour & made us*
*laugh*

26 Dec. *Eliz*[abe]*th* [Shelley]

30 Dec. <    > A one-inch strip is torn from
the bottom of the page, taking with it half the
entry for December 30, and all for December

FRIDAY 29
*Got up early as the Gentlemen went out*
*hunting* ——

SATURDAY 30
*Mʳˢ Portman & a party called here &*
*Mʳˢ Farquharson with <    >*

[Back end paper; in pencil]
*29ᵗʰ Octʳ   Paid Aunt*

|              | S | D |
|--------------|---|---|
| *Grove* —    | 2 | 6 |
|              | S | D |
| *Charlotte* —| 1 | 8 |

31. The next leaf is also missing. The remaining
stub indicates that there was writing on both
sides of it.

---

SC 99   WILLIAM GODWIN TO DAVID BOOTH, FEBRUARY 27, 1809

AL signed *W Godwin*, 2½ pages. Double sheet, 4ᵗᵒ (9 x 7.2 inches).
Laid paper. Watermark: [posthorn in crowned shield]| *E J F*|.
Seal: wafer, red.
Docket, page 4: *1809| Mʳ Godwin*|.

*Skinner Street, Lon-*
*don, Feb. 27, 1809.*

    *Dear sir*
    *I write this by the conveyance of Mʳ Fairly, a tradesman of Edinburgh,*
5 *& a friend of Mʳ Walter Miller, whom I have deputed, & who has kindly*
*undertaken, to collect for me, as far as his influence reaches, the debts or*
*books which, under the recommendation of Mʳ Clennel were so inauspiciously*
*sent into Scotland about a twelvemonth ago. I shall therefore take it as a*
*favour, if you will settle with him for your part of that transaction.*
10     *I was much gratified in the perusal of your letter of the 21ˢᵗ ult, though*

SC 99    *to say the truth I thought it long in coming, & began to fear that you had forgotten us. But I find in this letter the evidence of much zeal & friendship, & this is nearly as ~~grat~~ pleasing to me, though unsuccessful, as if it had been successful.*

15       *I am inclined somewhat to vary from the plan I had laid down when you were in London. I have had so little success in the attempt to establish country-connections on an extensive scale, that I am disposed to lay aside the large whole-sheet catalogue with which I furnished you, altogether; but I should be glad (as I think I told you in person) to establish an agent in*

20    *Edinburgh, <sub>for my own publications merely</sub> to whom I would allow five per cent agency, in addition to the 25 per cent at which I furnish the booksellers in London. I know not whether the <u>consignment</u> is to be objected to; but then one should know whether one has a bona fide consignée, able & alert, & not a man who would merely*

25    *leave my books to gather dust in his warehouse. M<sup>r</sup> Fairly mentions a M<sup>r</sup> Arnot, a young man who has a handsome shop in the first street in Edinburgh: but I would sooner trust your judgment than that of any man I know in that part of the world. If you think Berry the eligible man in the above points & in such other points as might occur to you, I would write to him. But perhaps*

30    *it would be better you should see him first, & sound him upon the specific proposition above-stated. Does he never come to London?*

      *M<sup>rs</sup> Godwin desires me to inform you that my health is much better; a proposition which I do not altogether believe, but I do not wish to spoil your congratulations. —— Poor Holcroft has laid for some time at the point*

35    *of death; but I <sub>am</sub> told is better. Horne Tooke too has been dying since you saw him; I hope you did not employ any evil eyes on these gentlemen.— It is also extraordinary that both our winter theatres should have been burnt down since you were here; but I am inclined to acquit you of any share in that, & there-*

40    *fore subscribe myself,*

                     *Dear sir, very truly yours*
                         *W Godwin*

      *Do not tell me what you think of the conduct of his royal highness the commander in chief.*

*Godwin to Booth*                                        *February 27, 1809*

SC 99        *M$^r$ Fairly will give you a new catalogue of our pub<   >cations,*
*including several that have been brought out for the present ca<   >l<   >gu<   >*
[Address, page 4]
*M$^r$ David Booth*
*Newburgh*
*Fife*

T HE above letter, in introducing us to its recipient, David Booth, introduces us also to some of the intricacies of the Juvenile Library. David Booth (1766–1846), who was destined to play something of a part in the Godwin-Shelley story, was a well-known character in Fifeshire in the early nineteenth century, combining the apparently incongruous professions of brewer and lexicographer. He published books on both: *The Art of Brewing* (1829) and *An Analytical Dictionary of the English Language* (1835). "Like many in this district he hailed the French Revolution as the dawn of a new era of liberty, and was a prominent Radical Reformer."[1] It was whispered in his native Newburgh that he had followed the Faustian pattern of selling himself to the devil for learning,[2] a rumor apparently aided by his Satanic appearance: not quite " 5 feet high, of very dark visage, eyes very red and watery, and presenting altogether an impish and fiendish look."[3] A few months after the date of the above letter he married Margaret Baxter,[4] daughter of another friend of Godwin's, W. T. Baxter, and in 1820 he left Scotland to come to London where he became superintendent for the press of the publications of The Society for the Diffusion of Useful Knowledge. In 1823 he published *A Letter to the Reverend T. H. Malthus, being an answer to his criticism of Mr. Godwin's work on population.* Shelley, encountering him in 1817, paid tribute to his intellectual ability: "I never met a man by whom, in the short time we exchanged ideas, I felt myself excited to so much severe

1. A. H. Millar in *The Dundee Courier*, July 8, 1922. Booth is in the *DNB*.

2. Dowden, *Shelley*, II, 174.

3. Robert Blakey, *Memoirs* (London, 1879), p. 75 (Oct. 24, 1832). On July 6, 1819, Crabb Robinson encountered Booth at Godwin's: "a singular character, not unlike Curran in person." And he adds dubiously: "A clever man, says Godwin." (*On Books*, I, 233.) Robinson notes that Charles and Mary Lamb were also present. It seems a pity that Lamb did not try out his powers of description on Booth.

4. See sc 105 (Sept. 6, 1809), Commentary.

# Shelley and his Circle : Manuscripts

SC 99   and sustained mental competition, or from whom I derived so much amusement and instruction."[5]

At the time of the above letter Godwin had known Booth for about ten years, Booth having apparently been attracted to him as a leading apostle of theoretical radicalism.[6] Booth, as we gather from the above letter, had visited Godwin in the summer or fall of 1808,[7] and they had then discussed the question of establishing an agent for the circulation of the Juvenile Library books in Edinburgh.[8]

"Mr Fairly" (line 4) – "an umbrella maker in Edinburgh, who had interested himself in Godwin's business"[9] – had recommended a Mr. Arnot; but Booth favored a Mr. Berry.[10] Booth, therefore, who is not mentioned by Godwin's biographers, was not only a close friend but was interested in Godwin's publishing business. He had apparently sold some of the books "so inauspiciously sent into Scotland" (line 7) early in 1808 on the recommendation of "Mr. Clennel,"[11] the funds for which he was to pay to "Fairly," and was assisting Godwin to re-establish his business there after the failure of the previous year.

About 1798 Godwin met a young Scotsman, John Arnot, from Edinburgh, in whom he took a considerable interest. In the following year Arnot traveled on the Continent and began writing a book on his impressions of Europe. Kegan Paul publishes a series of interesting letters

5. Shelley to William Thomas Baxter, Dec. 30, 1817.

6. William Godwin to David Booth, Oct. 14, 1799 (original letter in The Berg Collection, The New York Public Library). David Booth to William Godwin, Oct. 10, 1799. (Abinger Manuscripts, Pforzheimer Microfilm, file 23.) Booth also expresses interest in Thomas Holcroft and Mary Hays.

7. This visit can be dated by the reference to the burning down of the theaters (line 38). Drury Lane burned on February 24, 1809, Covent Garden on September 20, 1808 (both events noted in Godwin's Journal). Hence, Booth was in London prior to September 20, but not, one would gather from the tone of the letter, very much prior to it, probably in early September or August.

8. That the business concerned the Juvenile Library is clear from Godwin's comment (line 20): "for my own publications merely."

9. Paul, *Godwin*, II, 181. Pigot's *Commercial Directory* for 1820–1822 lists a John Fairley under "Umbrella Makers" at 263 High Street. Godwin records visits by Fairley in his Journal for February 27 (the visit noted in the above letter, line 4), March 2, and March 3.

10. Pigot lists two firms, Berry and Sanderson, and Berry and Dickson, under "Agents."

11. We fail to find any Clennel in the city directories of the time but *Clarke's New Law List* for 1806 and for 1814 give Lawson Mordaunt Clennel, 7 Staples Inn, London, so perhaps the Clennel of the above letter was not, as first appears, a businessman, but a lawyer. Godwin may have asked legal advice on sending his books into Scotland.

SC 99    between him and Godwin. He had earlier written a journal of his travels from Edinburgh to London and this Godwin sent to a brother of Arnot's who protested against publishing it as "subversive of all social order."[12] The last letter from Arnot is dated December 26, 1800, from Vienna, after which we hear no more of him.[13] Kegan Paul, however, prints a letter from Arnot to Peter Reid, whom he refers to simply as "a friend" whom Arnot has left behind. This reference to Reid enables us to identify Arnot's family. Peter Reid (1777–1838), a Scottish educator and medical writer, married one of the daughters of Hugo Arnot (1749–1796), a well-known Scottish historian (and father of eight children).[14] Hence, John Arnot was almost certainly a son of Hugo Arnot and Peter Reid his brother-in-law. Whether the Arnot referred to in this letter (line 26) was John Arnot or a brother we do not know but the latter seems more probable, for John does not seem to have been the type to settle down in a bookselling business. In 1800 John speaks rather condescendingly of his brother as "a good young man, as men go,"[15] and Godwin (line 26) refers to the Arnot of this letter as "a young man." One objection to this identification may be raised, namely that Godwin says "M^r Fairly mentions a M^r Arnot," which was intended to give Booth the impression that Godwin himself did not know of Arnot. But Booth, a strong-minded individual, had decided on Berry, and Godwin perhaps did not wish to put forward another candidate as of his own choosing.

It is difficult to follow these various business negotiations unless we realize that the Juvenile Library was both a publishing house and a bookshop. As the former it published books for children, some written by Godwin himself, some by other authors (including Charles Lamb). In the first book published by the Juvenile Library, *Fables, Ancient and Modern* (1805), it was stated that the Library would sell, in addition

---

12. Paul (*Godwin*, I, 342) indicates that the manuscript sent to Arnot's brother was that of his tour on the Continent but a letter from Arnot to Godwin on February 19, 1800 (*ibid.*, II, 28), makes it clear that it was the Edinburgh-to-London journal only.

13. *Ibid.*, II, 31. An account of him by Mrs. Mary Jane Godwin, which ends with his "desperate" attachment to "some German lady of rank," gives no dates but probably does not go beyond, or at least much beyond, this period (when he was in Austria). (*Ibid.*, I, 313.)

14. *DNB*. Pigot lists a James Arnot, 11 Robertson Close, under "Writers" but no Arnot under the book trades.

15. Paul, *Godwin*, II, 29.

# Shelley and his Circle : Manuscripts

SC 99   to books bearing its own imprint, "a choice Collection of School Books; also Cyphering Books, Copy Books, Copper-plate Copies, Quills, Pens, Inkstands, Slates, Black-lead Pencils, Maps, and Stationary [*sic*] of all kinds." Between 1805 and 1808, as the above letter informs us, Godwin established Juvenile Library agents in various cities. At the beginning of 1808 (line 7) he set up such an agency in Scotland. This agency, it appears, was to handle not only Juvenile Library publications but other books as well, for the "large whole-sheet catalogue" (line 18) clearly advertised more than "my own publications." By the beginning of 1809 Godwin is beginning to restrict his activities. The Juvenile Library shop at 41 Skinner Street continued to sell other books (plus stationery and maps), but the agents in other cities were to restrict themselves to books bearing the actual Library imprint. The "whole-sheet catalogue" was to be discontinued.

This catalogue must indeed have been "large." As the Juvenile Library catalogues were usually duodecimo in format (for binding in at the back of the books) a "whole-sheet catalogue" would be twenty-four pages. The most extensive of these catalogues in a Juvenile Library book in The Carl H. Pforzheimer Library is that bound in Mrs. Caroline Barnard, *The Parent's Offering; or Tales for Children* (London, 1813), which consists of twelve pages (one half sheet, duodecimo). It lists only Juvenile Library publications.

The final comments in the letter on "the conduct of his royal highness the commander in chief" is a reference to the Duke of York, whose mistress, Mrs. Mary Ann Clarke (1776–1852), had accepted bribes from Army officers to get the Duke to use his influence for their promotion.[16] Godwin had perhaps seen the account in *The Examiner* for February 26, 1809, headed "The Commander in Chief," which reported the current hearings on the matter in the House of Commons.[17]

SEE ALSO SC 105.

---

16. For a contemporary account see Elizabeth Taylor, *Authentic Memoirs of Mrs. Clarke* (London, 1809). As a result of the scandal the Duke of York was forced to resign his post as Commander in Chief and break off the affair with Mrs. Clarke (who, however, received a pension for withholding publication of the duke's love letters).

17. *The Examiner*, 1809, pp. 133–134. See also pp. 141–143 for an editorial on the subject, and pp. 137–140 for further hearings.

# The Carl H. Pforzheimer Library

SC 100    JOHN FOULKES TO WILLIAM GODWIN, MARCH 8, 1809

AUTOGRAPH BILL OF EXCHANGE signed *John Foulkes*, with *accepted| W Godwin|* in the hand of William Godwin, 1 page. Single sheet (3.3 x 7.9 inches). Laid paper. Embossed revenue stamp: [device]|
I SHILL<sup>G</sup> VI PENCE|. Imprinted revenue stamp (verso): [device]| TWELVE| PENCE| P. QUIRE|.
Endorsements.

*D448*                    £*20..0.0*                    *Elsted 8<sup>th</sup> March 1809*

                                        *11 May*
            *Two Months after date pay Messr Dawson Brooks Son &*
        *Dixon or Order Twenty Pounds value received*
5            *M<sup>r</sup> William Godwin*⎫                    *John Foulkes*
                *41 Skinner Street*  ⎬
                    *London*  ⎭

[Written vertically, across the above, in the hand of William Godwin]
    *accepted*
    *W Godwin*

[Endorsements, verso]
10    *Rf   Dawson & Co*
            *G Hann*
    *John Foulkes*
        *448*


I<small>N</small> *Kent's Directory* for 1800 we find John Foulkes, attorney, 14 Market Street, Bloomsbury.[1] In *Clarke's New Law List* for 1806 we find John Foulkes and P. W. Longdill, Holborn Court, Gray's Inn.[2] The interesting thing about this entry is that P. W. Longdill was later Shelley's attorney in the trial for the custody of his children. Shelley must have heard of Longdill from Godwin.

Dawson, Brooks, Son and Dixon, 25 Chancery Lane, appear in the

---

1. Plan of London, B1, Front Endpapers.

2. Plan of London, C1, Front Endpapers. Foulkes presumably had a house in Elsted (line 1), near Godalming in Surrey, some 35 miles from London. Godwin's lawyer friend, Thomas Turner, had a house at Binfield in Berkshire, 30 miles from London, but kept his law office in London.

**Godwin to Shield** *?April 23, 1809*

SC 100   list of bankers in *The Court and City Register* for 1807. Later, as Brooks, Son and Dixon they were Shelley's bankers.

SEE ALSO SC 61 AND SC 87.

SC 101   WILLIAM GODWIN TO WILLIAM SHIELD, ?APRIL 23, 1809

AL signed *W Godwin*, 1½ pages. Double sheet, 4$^{to}$ (10 x 8 inches). Laid paper. Watermark: COPY| 1807|.

> *Dear sir*
>
> *What I was anxious to know was how far you had spoken to the musical people, or any of those whom I suppose to be your particular connections,*
> 5  *on the subject of the Holcroft subscription. I find it partly standing, still, & that in some measure for want of the particular friends of Mr. Holcroft thoroughly understanding one another. If I found that you were so engaged in business, or otherwise prevented, as that you could not exert your better influence & your well-known kind & liberal feelings in the matter, I should think it my*
> 10  *duty to try them. I will put down some of their names on the other side, that, if you favour me with an answer to my enquiry, there may be no want of a thorough understanding in the matter.*
>
> *Believe me with great regard &*
>
> 15                   *affection yours*
>                      *W Godwin*

[Address, page 2]

*Mr. Shield*

[List, page 4]

| | |
|---|---|
| *Clementi's partners – Hyde, Collard* | *Billington* |
| *Yaniewicz* | *Cramer* |
| 20  *Crosdill* | *Salomon* |
| *M P King* | *Watts* |
| *Dr Busby* | *Dance* |
| *Stodart, Golden Square* | *Harrison* |
| *Braham* | *Swainson* |
| 25  *Incledon* | |

# The Carl H. Pforzheimer Library

SC 101    DURING the last years of his life Thomas Holcroft ran into money difficulties — the bankruptcy of a printing house in which he was interested, the failure of his play *The Vindictive Man* — and these were aggravated by a long illness.[1] He died on March 23, 1809. *The Examiner* for March 26 commented in its obituary: "He has left a young wife and six children, the oldest only nine years, totally unprovided for." On March 29 Charles Lamb wrote to Thomas Manning that "there has been a meeting of his friends and a subscription has been mentioned" for the benefit of the widow and children.[2] That the subscription was actually carried out we know because Mrs. Inchbald contributed to it.[3]

The above letter must, therefore, refer to this subscription. Godwin and Shield were doubtless at the meeting that Lamb mentions for they were among Holcroft's oldest friends and had been at his funeral.[4] Godwin was one of the few people that Holcroft sent for when he was on his deathbed,[5] and Godwin seems — to judge by the above letter — to have been in charge of the subscription.

William Shield (1748–1829), one of the leading musicians of the time, had met Holcroft in 1777 when Holcroft was an actor in a traveling

1. *Memoirs of the Late Thomas Holcroft*, Hazlitt, *Complete Works*, III, 234, 235, 236. In regard to this work we might note the following entries in Godwin's Journal: January 15, 1810: "Life of Ht [Holcroft], fin. Hazlitt calls"; January 23 and 26: "Ht revise." These entries can only mean that Godwin himself had a hand in the revision, perhaps, however, not in the total work but in a final volume — still unpublished — which contained Holcroft's diary, for it was to this that Godwin specifically objected in a letter to Mrs. Holcroft. (Paul, *Godwin*, II, 176–177; see also *The Life of Thomas Holcroft*, ed. Elbridge Colby, London, 1925, II, 315–320.) The *Memoirs*, although completed in 1810, were not published until 1816 (and the book was humorously known in the intervening years as "The Life Everlasting"). The reasons for the delay are not clear but it has been conjectured that Godwin had objections to the *Memoirs* as a whole and resisted publication. This conjecture may receive some support from Godwin's Journal entries in 1816. On May 29 and June 8 (1816) he "called" on Hazlitt (an unusual occurrence); on June 10 and July 5 Hazlitt called on him (equally unusual); on August 21, 22, and 23 Godwin read "Holcroft, Memoirs." The book was reviewed in the April *Gentleman's Magazine* (*Life of Holcroft*, II, 316) but this does not mean that it was actually in print in April, for early nineteenth-century periodicals sometimes appeared two or more months after the date imprinted on them. The May, June, and July entries may represent negotiations with Hazlitt on the work.

2. Lamb, *Letters*, II, 68.

3. Boaden, *Inchbald*, II, 147. Mrs. Inchbald informs us also that Prince Hoare gave £50 to Holcroft during his final illness. (*Ibid.*)

4. Godwin's Journal entry for April 1 runs: "Funeral of Ht, w[ith] Shield, Nicholson, Harwood, Buchan, Lamb, Thelwal, Dawe & Ralph."

5. Hazlitt, *Complete Works*, III, 237–238.

*Godwin to Shield*                    *?April 23, 1809*

SC 101  company in which Shield was playing in the band. He later put some of Holcroft's songs to music.[6]

Godwin's Journal for April 13, 1809, records a call by Shield and for April 23 a call by Godwin on Shield. When Godwin called on someone who was "not at home," he placed "na" or two strokes after the name.[7] Thus, for instance:

> March 21: "Call on Ht [Holcroft]."
> March 22: "Call on Ht$^{na}$."
> March 23: "Ht dies."

(The notation for March 22 must mean that Holcroft was too ill to see him.)

Following "Shield" in the April 23 entry Godwin put two small strokes, indicating that he was not at home. As the above letter was apparently written after a visit by Godwin in which he failed to see Shield, it was probably written on or about April 23. It certainly cannot have come early in April as it assumes that the subscription is well under way, and it can hardly be later than May as Mrs. Holcroft's desperate circumstances clearly required swift action. If by April 23 Shield had failed to contact his fellow musicians, Godwin could well feel that he was justified in a little polite prodding.

April 23 as the day of composition is indicated by other evidence also. As the letter bears neither postmark nor house address, it did not go through the mails. The absence of the house address indicates also that it did not go by private messenger and this appears to be confirmed by the placing of the name "Mr. Shield" on page 2. Occasionally one will find a letter sent by private messenger without a house address but the name is still written on page 4 so that it will be on the outside when the letter is folded. The above letter has been folded so that page 1 and page 4 (with its list of names) form the outside pages and pages 2 and 3 the inside pages. We should note also that the paper is unlike that of any other Godwin letter in our library. It is, in fact, a curious kind of paper, unusually coarse in texture and bearing a watermark which we have not seen in other paper: "COPY| 1807|."

6. *Ibid.*, pp. 79, 87. For letters between Shield and Holcroft see pp. 274–275.

7. See sc 8 (Feb. 15, 1793), Commentary.

SC 101      The indication is that Godwin sat down and wrote the letter at Shield's house when he found that he was not at home and left it for him on a desk or table unfolded with pages 2 ("Mr. Shield") and 3 up. The only visit to Shield recorded for this period was that of April 23.

Some of the musicians listed by Godwin were among the most famous of the day and can be found in the *DNB* or *Grove's Dictionary of Music and Musicians.*[8]

8. Muzio Clementi (1752–1832), pianist and composer. (Clementi was the husband of John Gisborne's sister Emma. See Gisborne, *Journals and Letters*, p. 38. He was apparently a good friend of Holcroft. See Holcroft to Godwin, Aug. 15, 1800: "I have not told you, nor can I at present tell, how nobly Clementi behaved to me; but you, and more than you, shall some day hear." Paul, *Godwin*, II, 25.)
Frederick Augustus Hyde, musician.
William Frederick Collard (1772–1860), piano manufacturer.
Felix Yaniewicz (1762–1848), violinist and composer.
John Crosdill (1751?–1825), violoncellist.
Matthew Peter King (1773–1823), composer.
Thomas Busby, composer. (In 1802 he composed the music for Holcroft's melodrama *A Tale of Mystery*.)
William and Robert Stodart, piano manufacturers, with a business in Golden Square.
John Braham (1774?–1856), tenor.
Charles Incledon (1763–1826), tenor.
Elizabeth Billington (1768–1818), singer.
Johann Baptist Cramer (1771–1858), pianist and composer; or Franz Cramer (1772–1848), his brother, violinist.
Johan Peter Salomon (1745–1815), musician. (Godwin records meeting Salomon in his Journal on January 4, 1811, at the home of John Frank Newton, the friend of Shelley's. See also Dowden, *Shelley*, I, 363; Hogg, *Shelley*, II, 134.)
William Dance (1755–1840), musician.
Samuel Harrison (1760–1812), singer.
     One further name on the list, Swainson, we find in an inscription on a facsimile of a title page of David Williams' *Letters on Political Liberty* in W. Hazlitt, *The Life of Thomas Holcroft* (London, 1925), II, between pages 198 and 199. The inscription reads: "Written by the Rev^d. David Williams and given to me, Thos. Holcroft by Mr Swainson July 2d. 1782."
     "Watts" was perhaps Richard Watts, "Music Warehouse, 87, Blackman-street," London. (*Kent's Directory* for 1810.) A "Watts" connected with music is mentioned in Holcroft's diary but he is not identified. (*The Life of Thomas Holcroft*, ed. Colby, II, 125, 135, 181, 188, 237.)

SC 102    MARY JANE GODWIN TO JOHN FLATHER, ?JUNE 9, 1809

AL signed *M. J. Godwin*, 1 page. Double sheet (4.5 x 7.1 inches). Laid paper. Watermark: [posthorn in shield, lower part]| *E J F*|. Seal: wafer, brown.

*Dear Sir,*

     *I should be obliged to you if you could call in about 5 oclock this evening.*

# Shelley and his Circle : Manuscripts

**Godwin to Flather**                                              *?June 9, 1809*

SC 102  *I think you could do a kind office in a disagreement between our friend,*
*M^r Turner, and M^r Godwin. and I hope you would have no objection.*

5  *M^r Godwin will be from home; and you and I can talk the matter over.*
*I am Dear Sir,*
*Yours obediently*
*Friday Noon.*                                                      *M. J. Godwin*

[Address, page 4]
*M^r John Flather Jun^r*

I n 1839 when Mary Shelley was editing the poetical works of Shelley
she found that she did not have a copy of *Queen Mab* and wrote to
ask their old friend, Harriet Boinville, if she could borrow her copy.
Mrs. Boinville in her reply (preserved among the Abinger Manuscripts)
agreed to lend the book and asked that it be returned to her through
"John Flather Esq^re Lincoln's Inn," who formerly, she told Mary,
lived at No. 5 Old Square.[1] When we turn to *Robson's London Directory*
for 1837 and find there listed a John Flather at 5 Lincoln's Inn, Old
Square, and at 6 Lincoln's Inn a T. Turner, we can be sure that the John
Flather of Mrs. Boinville's reply is the John Flather to whom the above
letter is addressed. Thomas Turner (line 4) was the husband of Mrs.
Boinville's daughter Cornelia (who inspired Shelley's "Stanza, Written
at Bracknell" and other lyrics), and had been a friend of Godwin's since
1803.

In the first mention of Flather in Godwin's Journal he is associated
with Turner (June 8, 1808): "T[homas] T[urner] & J. Flather sup." In
the fall of 1810 John Flather was admitted to St. John's College, Cambridge; in 1815 he received his B.A. and was admitted to the Middle
Temple; in 1818 he was called to the bar. His legal profession was that
of an "Equity Draftsman."[2]

1. Jan. 26, 1839. (Abinger Manuscripts, Pforzheimer Microfilm, file 35.) On July 14, 1841, Mary
Shelley addressed Talfourd's speech on *Queen Mab* to Mrs. Boinville via Flather. (Mary Shelley,
*Letters*, II, 150.)

2. *Alumni Cantabrigienses; Register of Admissions to the Honourable Society of the Middle Temple*,
(London, 1949), II, 435. See also *Boyle's Court Guide* for 1827. The Middle Temple records give
Flather's father as Thomas Flather of Duke Street, merchant. Mrs. Godwin addresses John Flather
as "M^r John Flather Jun^r." But she probably did not know the first name of Flather's father and
simply wanted to be sure that the letter was delivered to the son.

# The Carl H. Pforzheimer Library

*Godwin to Flather*                                    *?June* 9, 1809

SC 102    The above letter bears no date, was sent by private messenger (and hence has no postmark), and the watermark does not contain a date. It seems nevertheless possible to date the letter with a fair degree of accuracy. We might first note that the watermark occurs but four times among the letters in our library: in the above letter and in three letters by William Godwin; of these three letters two are dated 1809 and one 1810.[3]

How many quarrels Godwin and Turner had we do not know; but there is among the Abinger Manuscripts a group of letters relating to a particularly important quarrel in 1809,[4] and no other quarrel is recorded. There had apparently first been some minor disagreement in January but this was soon patched up. The real quarrel began on June 7 or 8 and is reflected in a letter from Turner to Godwin on June 8: "I can love you at a distance but if [I] cannot approach ᴧwithout paying respect the tax would make me love you less." And he closes: "Yours always but gladly so when you take of[f] your helmet." Godwin's Journal for the same day records that he wrote to Turner, presumably in reply to this letter, and that Turner called on him later in the day. Turner sent further letters on June 14, 24 ("I am a child no longer"), 26, and 29, that on June 29 breaking off relations: "We separate now because your understanding is so great it thinks it has a right to eat up mine." In the fall, the quarrel was patched up although the two were apparently no longer on the same close terms as before. They could not again, Godwin informed Turner, be "on the same intimate footing we have sometimes been . . . . dine with me every alternate Sunday; and let that be all."[5]

This, then, was probably the quarrel to which the above letter refers. Mrs. Godwin is writing to a young friend of Turner's hoping that he will intervene. As Flather has not apparently heard of the quarrel and as Mrs. Godwin refers to it rather mildly as a "disagreement" (line 3), although she was clearly worried about its future course, it is probable that the letter came at the beginning of the quarrel. It is dated "Friday Noon." On this Friday at five o'clock, Mrs. Godwin informs Flather, Godwin will be out of the house and she would like him to call so that

---

3. SC 99 (Feb. 27, 1809); SC 107 (Dec. 7, 1809); SC 110 (Jan. 24, 1810).

4. Abinger Manuscripts, Pforzheimer Microfilm, file 12.          5. *Ibid.*

SC 102   they can discuss the situation privately. The first letter from Turner to Godwin was on June 8; and in 1809 June 8 was a Thursday. On the next day, Friday, June 9, Godwin, as his Journal informs us, was dining at the house of a friend. As dinner in the Godwin circle in those days was held in the late afternoon (sometimes as early as four), Godwin would not be at home on that Friday at five o'clock. Then on June 13 the Journal records: "Flather sups." It is likely, therefore, that the above letter was written at noon on Friday, June 9, 1809, that Flather called on Mrs. Godwin on the afternoon of the same day, that he then saw Turner and four days later called on Godwin in an attempt to bring the two together. The Journal for June 15 reads: "Call on Turner, Limehouse." We might note further that between June 23 and 28, when the quarrel rose to new heights, Mrs. Godwin was out of town.[6]

6. Godwin, Journal.

SC 103   LEIGH HUNT TO MARIANNE KENT, JUNE 12, 1809

AL signed *Henry.*, 2 pages. Single sheet, 4^to (8.9 x 7.2 inches).
Wove paper.
Addition: A question mark in light blue ink near top edge center.
PROVENANCE: Marianne Hunt; Thornton Hunt.

*Monday 12^th June 1809.*

*My dearest Marian,*

*I thank you sincerely for answering me so quickly and so affectionately: when your dear head is on my bosom, I hope it will never ache again – Your*
5 *mother proposed Sunday instead of Monday for our union, & we all think it better in every respect, as you & I can then dress just as we please, and dine in Titchfield St. without any body knowing any thing of the matter, & walk home quietly to Beaufort Build^gs in the afternoon: therefore your mother says you had better come home on Thursday, as she means to tell you in her*
10 *letter today, and I am sure you will have no objection to it. We shall be married in my own parish – S^t Clement Danes, of which M^r Gurney is the rector: & M^r Hunter will go & speak to him on the subject in a day or two: M^r Hunter will also go with me to the Proctor's for a license, as he is experienced*

SC 103
15
*in these matters. In the midst of the <u>serious happiness</u> I feel on the occasion, the bustle about Proctors, & licenses, & rings, still strikes me as something approaching to the frivolous; but with regard to the clergyman, I would certainly, & I am sure you would, prefer a gentlemanly, reasonable, & sensible man for so sacred an office, to any body who comes – perhaps a careless reader, or frivolous, or drunken. As to my brother, I feel so uneasy*
20
*under deception of any kind, especially towards him, that I think it better, & so does your mother & M<sup>r</sup> Hunter, to tell him the whole affair at once, and as my sister has been invited into the country by M<sup>rs</sup> Whiting & will certainly go there, we will try if we cannot <u>keep</u> her there beyond the week: indeed she has been invited for a month, though her active little soul does not like to be*
25
*unemployed, or at least away from the bustle, so long. For my own part, I am not exactly agitated, but I have feelings that I hardly know how to define – except that I seem as if I were going to be very happy. As if! – do I say? I am sure I shall be happy, and if I know any thing of our two hearts, I am sure I shall make you happy – as happy, I trust, as you will make me. I*
30
*bless myself everyday, that I <u>know</u> you so truly. You are a lesson, which I have studied six years & got <u>soundly by heart</u>. Pray do not think this a mere pun, though really I am as little capable of writing just now as yourself. – Oh how much I shall be able to <u>say</u>! God bless you, my dear love: this is the last letter I write to you before your return, though I hope I shall receive one*
35
*in answer. Take care – great care – of yourself on the road, & come with a happy heart to the arms of*

*Your own Henry.*

*Miss Kent – at Capt. Grant's High Wycombe.*

THE above manuscript[1] was probably the last letter written by Leigh Hunt to Marianne Kent before their marriage. The circumstances in which it was written were discussed by their son, Thornton Hunt, some fifty-three years later:

1. The question mark in blue ink noted above was probably made by Thornton Hunt when considering the letter for publication. See sc 78 (July 26, 1807), Bibliographical Description and Commentary. The letter appears in part in Hunt, *Correspondence*, I, 46–47.

SC 103   Leigh Hunt was married on the 3rd of July, 1809. The marriage was to
have been somewhat sooner — on the 18th of June — and on a Monday instead
of Sunday, suggested by the bride's mother for some special reasons of the
greater privacy. The marriage, however, took place at a later date, for there was
an obstacle in the way. A licence was to have been procured, but Miss Kent
was not twenty-one years of age; and although she wanted but three months
of her majority, and the bridegroom was urged to get over the difficulty by
consenting to speak of her as being already of age, he refused. This occasioned
some change in the date.[2]

Part of Thornton Hunt's information on the changing date of the
wedding must have come from the above letter (which was in his hands),[3]
but he has compressed it almost to the point of unintelligibility. The letter
(line 5) informs us that the wedding was first scheduled for Monday,
June 19, but was changed to Sunday, June 18. The date was then changed
again, this time to Monday, July 3.

Leigh Hunt's original plan (line 7) was for the couple first to dine
together at the bride's house (2 Little Titchfield Street) and then go
"home" to 15 Beaufort Buildings, Strand, a building which housed
*The Examiner* but which contained dwelling units also.[4] He proposed
that Marianne return to London from High Wycombe on Thursday
(June 15). In the same week he intended to enlist the services of Rowland
Hunter (line 12), husband of the widowed mother of Marianne Kent.[5]

The reason, according to Thornton Hunt, for the final change of the
wedding date (to July 3), was that the bride lacked several months of
being of legal age (twenty-one). But Marianne Kent's birth date, as
recorded on her tombstone, was September 28, 1787;[6] so that she was
twenty-one on September 28 in 1808, not in 1809. Hence, either the
tombstone marking is wrong or the Kent family had informed Hunt that
she was a year younger than she actually was. Even if she had been under
twenty-one on June 18, 1809, she would still have been under twenty-one
on July 3. So either Hunt was informed of her correct age between June 18

2. *Ibid.*, p. 46. The "M$^r$ Gurney" (line 11) who was to have performed the marriage ceremony was
presumably William Gurney, whose *Sermons* were published in 1808. Hunter (see Commentary,
below) was acquainted with the Gurney family. (Hunt, *Letters*, p. 103.)

3. See fn. 1.

4. Plan of London, C2, Front Endpapers; see also sc 77 (July 12, 1807), Address.

5. See sc 77 (July 12, 1807), Commentary and fn. 3.                6. Landré, *Hunt*, I, 38 fn.

# The Carl H. Pforzheimer Library

SC 103   and July 3 or he agreed to state that she was twenty-one when he believed her to be but twenty.

Thornton Hunt does not indicate — if he knew — what part John Hunt (the "brother" — line 19)[7] played in these matters or what the "whole affair" (line 21) was that had been kept from him and was not to be disclosed. John Hunt was at the time the owner of *The Examiner* and Leigh Hunt the editor. He was aware that Leigh Hunt intended to marry Marianne Kent[8] but he may not have known that he intended to marry her so soon. As he was paying Leigh's salary, he may well have feared that the additional burden of a wife would entail extra expenditures not only for Leigh but for himself also. If he had such fears, he had justification for them. There is a manuscript letter in The Pierpont Morgan Library from Leigh Hunt to John Hunt, July 14, 1812, which lists Leigh's staggering debts and requests John's payment of them.

Marianne Hunt, in later years, became seriously alcoholic — Hunt lived in dread of her setting the house on fire — but until this time she was, as her son testifies, "an active and thrifty housewife"; and of her love for Leigh Hunt and her courage in assisting him when he was under government prosecution and in prison there can be no doubt.[9] Nor can there be any doubt, as the above letter shows, that Hunt was deeply in love with her when he married. And the following tender comment in the *Autobiography* in 1850 — left in for the later edition which appeared only after Marianne's death — shows that something of the affection survived all trials: "With this last, who completed her conquest by reading verses better than I had ever yet heard, I ultimately became wedded for life; and she reads verses better than ever to this day, especially some that shall be nameless."

7. Leigh Hunt had two other brothers, Robert and Stephen, in England, as well as John, but his relationship with John was more intimate than with the others, and such references as this simply to "my brother" are to John. A third brother, Isaac, was in North America.

8. Leigh Hunt wrote to Marianne on June 5, 1809: "My brother knows it, and approves it, all." (Hunt, *Letters*, p. 43.)

9. On her alcoholism see Blunden, *Leigh Hunt*, p. 328, and the hints by Thornton Hunt in Hunt, *Autobiography*, I, 231 fn.; Hunt, *Correspondence*, II, 164–165. For her loyalty and devotion to her husband during his imprisonment see his letters to her from prison (Hunt, *Correspondence*; Hunt, *Letters*) and one that has survived from her to her husband (Hunt, *Letters*, pp. 59–60): "Do, my love, try and rouse yourself if possible, for my sake, for the sake of our little darlings do, my life, you know, while it lasts will be devoted to you and my children, but my distress is that I cannot comfort you."

SC 104  WILLIAM GODWIN TO THOMAS WADE, AUGUST 15, 1809

AUTOGRAPH PROMISSORY NOTE signed *W Godwin*, 1 page. Single sheet (3.3 x 8.1 inches).
Laid paper. Watermark: EDMEA[D]|. Embossed revenue stamp: 1 SHILL^G VI PENCE|.

*N° 1737 M*      *No. 41, Skinner Street,*

*£ 14.7.10*    *Sept 18*

*Aug. 15, 1809*

*One month after date I promise to pay to M^r Tho^s Wade or order*
*fourteen pounds 7/10: value rec^d as per bill to Midsummer last*

*W Godwin*

5

[Endorsements, verso]
*Thomas Wade*
*Rich^d Webb*
*Rec^d R Webb*

THE London *Post Office Directory* for 1813 lists Thomas Wade, Grocer, Skinner Street, Snow Hill.[1] As Godwin was then also living on Skinner Street there can be no doubt that this was the Thomas Wade of the above note. The note is dated August 15; the groceries for which it promises payment had been purchased prior to "Midsummer" day (June 24).

SEE ALSO SC 61.

1. Plan of London, D1, Front Endpapers. *Kent's Directory* for 1800 lists a Richard Webb, "Windsor & Garden Chair-maker," Newington, Surrey. (Environs of London, page 47.)

SC 105  WILLIAM GODWIN TO DAVID BOOTH, SEPTEMBER 6, 1809

AL signed *W Godwin*, 1 page. Double sheet, 4^to (8.7 x 7.1 inches).
Laid paper. Watermark: ALLEE| 1803|.
Seal: wafer, black.
Postmarks: 1. (evening duty stamp, London): c| SE 6| ·809|; 2. (morning duty stamp, Edinburgh): SEP 9| WM| 1809|.
Docket, page 4: *M^r Godwin| 1809| Sept|.*

**Godwin to Booth**          *September 6,* **1809**

SC 105

*Skinner Street, London,*
*Sep. 6, 1809*

*My dear sir*
     *I thank you for your introduction of M^r Baxter. I dare swear he is an*
5  *honest man; & he is no fool. He has this moment laid his commands on*
*me, to inform you that he yesterday committed all that is mortal of himself &*
     *by the two-penny post*
*his daughter, to the mercy of the waves, on board the Lord Kinnaird Smack.*
     *He brought me ill news, —— that you were thinking of yourself, &*
10  *forgetting the public, that you had married a wife, & laid your Dictionary*
*on the shelf. I hope the latter part of the intelligence is not true. I am just*
*now writing, compelled by hard necessity & a concurrence of circumstances,*
*something on your subject. When it is ready I will send it you: but I feel*
*great apprehension & diffidence in treating a topic, which has seldom been*
15  *the object of my chosen attention.*
     *M^r Baxter paid me the money mentioned in your letter. I forget what.*
     *I have been ill: I am well: I am working hard, & suffering a little from*
*the effects of the exertion.*
                   *sincerely & faithfully yours*
                        *W Godwin*
20

[Address, page 4]
*M^r David Booth*
*Newburgh*
*Fife*

"M^R BAXTER" was William Thomas Baxter, "manufacturer of canvas" in Dundee, Scotland.[1] The above letter marks the beginning of his association, and that of his family, with the Godwin-Shelley circle, an association which did not end until some seventy-five years later when Miss Christy Baxter at the age of ninety-one gave an interviewer her personal reminiscences of Shelley, Mary, and Harriet.[2] Biographical material on the Baxters and Booth not used by Shelley's biographers appeared in *The Dundee Courier* for July 8, 1922:

1. *The Dundee Advertiser*, Aug. 3, 1897.        2. *Ibid.*, Sept. 7, 1897.

# Shelley and his Circle : Manuscripts

*Godwin to Booth*                                     *September 6, 1809*

SC 105     W. T. Baxter was twice married — first, to Isabella Doig, daughter of Robert Doig, manufacturer, Dundee; and second, to Mary Ann Scott, daughter of Dr. Scott. His family consisted of two sons and five daughters. These were (in order of birth) Margaret, Jessie, Elizabeth, Robert, manufacturer, Dundee, and afterwards at Lille, in France, Christina, Isabella, and John Cowley Baxter, merchant, Dundee.

The eldest daughter, Margaret, was married to David Booth (1766–1846), an eminent man of letters, and after her death Booth, in defiance of the law, married in 1814 Isabella, the youngest of his deceased wife's sisters.

The Baxter family, as has been shown, came from Tealing, and it was natural that they should have joined the Glassite Church, founded in Dundee by the Rev. John Glas, of Tealing. Booth was also a member of this congregation, but after his unlawful marriage with Isabella Baxter both he and his father-in-law were disjoined from the church.[3]

As the above letter shows (line 4), it was through Booth that Godwin became acquainted with Baxter.[4] The "wife" that Booth has just married (line 10) was Margaret Baxter. It was his second wife, Isabella, who appears in Shelley biography as the particular friend of Mary Shelley. In 1817, Booth had his wife break off this friendship with Mary.[5] Possibly his own "unlawful marriage" had made him particularly sensitive on such questions.

Booth published a Prospectus for his *Analytical Dictionary* (line 10) in 1805 and an *Introduction* to it in 1806 but the first volume of the *Dictionary* itself did not appear until 1835.[6] Hence, the reference (line 11) to the dictionary being "on the shelf." The work "something on your subject" (line 13) which Godwin was writing was either Edward Baldwin, *A New Guide to the English Tongue* (London, 1809), or Edward Baldwin, *Outlines of English Grammar* (London, 1810).

The "money mentioned in your letter" (line 16) was presumably the amount that Booth owed Godwin on the books which Godwin had referred to in his letter of February 27.

3. Article by A. H. Millar. The article is largely repeated from a previous article by the same author in the same paper on December 2, 1911. For Glas see the *DNB*.

4. Hence, Paul's (*Godwin*, II, 89) dating of an anecdote involving Godwin and Baxter as not long after Godwin's second marriage (December 1801) is incorrect.

5. Mary Shelley to W. T. Baxter, Dec. 30, 1817 (manuscript in The Carl H. Pforzheimer Library); see also Dowden, *Shelley*, II, 174–178.

6. No more volumes were published. The *DNB* sketch of Booth gives some account of the principles on which this strange dictionary was founded.

[ 559 ]

**Godwin to Wilson**                                          *October 20, 1809*

SC 105      "I have been ill" (line 17). Godwin, as we have seen,[7] had been
alarmed about his health the previous year. In the February 27 letter to
Booth he had intimated that he believed himself to be ill. He was still
under medication in 1810.[8]

SEE ALSO SC 99.

7. sc 88 (June 8, 1808).                    8. sc 112 (Apr. 5, 1810).

SC 106   WILLIAM GODWIN TO WALTER WILSON, OCTOBER 20, 1809

AL signed *W Godwin*, 1 page. Single sheet, 8$^{vo}$ (7.3 x 4.5 inches).
Wove paper. Watermark: FEL[LOWS]| 18[  ]|.
Docket, verso: *W. Godwin Oct. 20, 1809*|.

*Dear sir*

*In No. 5 of your Dissenting Churches, p. 381,*
*385,*
*&*$_\wedge$*you appear to refer*
*to some account of M$^r$ Jones of Tewkesbury which I have never met met with.*
5   *If you would point out to me the source of your information, or favour me*
*with a sight of it, you would much oblige,*

                          *Dear sir,*
                          *your most ob$^t$ serv$^t$*
*Oct. 20*                  *W Godwin*

line 4. *met met* (sic). The first *met* comes at the
end of a line.

For the record of Godwin's early years," Kegan Paul relies on an
"autobiographical fragment," which he quotes as stating that
Godwin's grandfather Edward "was destined to the profession of a
dissenting minister, and was placed at a suitable age under the reverend
Mr Samuel Jones."[1] On the death of Jones, Edward Godwin married his
widow. "A ridiculous mistake," Godwin continues (in the fragment),
"has been fallen into by some persons who have written concerning this
Samuel Jones, in supposing that he married the daughter of Mr John
Weaver, one of the ministers ejected in the reign of Charles II, who was

1. Paul, *Godwin*, I, 3. Paul makes extensive use of this fragment in the succeeding pages.

SC 106   born about the year 1632, and whose daughter may be supposed to have been about sixty at the time of Mr Jones's marriage."

Godwin's reference, the above letter informs us, is to Walter Wilson, *The History and Antiquities of Dissenting Churches . . . in London . . .*, (4 vols., London, 1808–1814). On page 381 of Volume I (1808) appears an account of Samuel Jones; on page 385 we read that Samuel Jones's widow was "the daughter of Mr. John Weaver, a worthy ejected minister, who was a considerable loser by his nonconformity."[2]

Hence, the above letter (the address page of which is missing)[3] was written to Walter Wilson. Wilson (1781–1847) was an eminent theological historian, biographer of Daniel Defoe, and one of the owners of *The Times*.

Kegan Paul dates Godwin's "autobiographical fragment" as 1800,[4] but it cannot have been written before the publication of Volume I of Wilson's work in 1808[5] and is probably later than the above letter.

2. Volumes I and II were published in 1808, Volume III in 1810, and Volume IV in 1814.

3. The letter was originally a double sheet; the second sheet of such letters was sometimes torn off for convenience in filing or mounting if it contained nothing but the address.

4. Paul, *Godwin*, I, 2.

5. Godwin specifically states (line 4) that he had not previously "met with" this "account" of Jones. Hence, the reference in the fragment must also be to Wilson.

SC 107   WILLIAM GODWIN TO BASIL MONTAGU, DECEMBER 7, 1809

AL signed *W Godwin*, 1¼ pages. Double sheet, 4$^{to}$ (9 x 7.2 inches). Laid paper. Watermark: [posthorn in crowned shield]| *EJF*|. Seal: wafer, black.

*Skinner Street,*
*Dec. 7, 1809.*

    *Dear sir*

    *The bearer, M$^r$ Samuel Girle, is one of my oldest friends. He was*
5  *bred, like myself, a nonconformist divine, but at fifty years of age, without any fault of his that I know of, his profession has left him, incumbered with a wife & six children. To maintain this family he is anxious to make every*

SC 107   *honest exertion, & I should be most happy to assist in rendering his exertions*
*effectual.*

10       *One resource that has occurred to him, has been that of taking trials in*
*short-hand, for which he deems himself competent. May I rely so much on*
*your kindness & humanity, as to request that you will give him the best*
*advice as to the way of proceeding in this cause, to which advice I know no*
*man more competent than yourself? Turn a little of your sunshine upon the*
15   *good man, & do not shrivel up his buds with the ice of discouragement.*

           *I am, Dear sir,*
              *your most obedient servant*
                 *W Godwin*

[Address, page 4]
*Basil Montagu, Esq*

Iɴ John Browne's *History of Congregationalism and Memorials of the Churches in Norfolk and Suffolk* (London, 1877), we read that "in 1780 Samuel Girle, from Daventry Academy" was minister at Lowestoft in Suffolk.[1] The minister who preceded him was William Godwin.[2]

Girle, then, was one of the few friends that dated back to the days of Godwin's ill-fated ministerial career; and he, too, was a Dissenter. Daventry Academy was one of two academies for the training of Dissenting ministers established by the William Coward fund. The other (at Hoxton) Godwin had attended.[3]

Girle seems to have achieved no prominence in the church, although his *Sermons* were published and went through three editions (1790, 1803, 1805). In 1809, as we gather from this letter, he was in difficult circumstances.

Godwin's Journal for December 7, 1809, makes no reference to Girle but a series of preceding entries indicate his endeavors to help his old friend:

1. Page 531.                  2. *Ibid.*

3. See sc 1 (May 25, 1778). Girle had perhaps learned shorthand (line 11) at Daventry. Andrew Kippis informs us that at Dr. Philip Doddridge's Dissenting academy, "Rich's short-hand was one of the first things which he expected his pupils to learn, that they might be able to transcribe his own lectures, and make extracts from the books they read and consulted, with greater ease and celerity." (*Biographia Britannica*, V, 278–279.)

SC 107        November 7: "Girles sup."
                 November 10: "Girles call."
                 November 13: "Girles at tea."
                 November 17: "Girle sups."

Basil Montagu (1770–1851), the well-known attorney and early champion of Coleridge and Wordsworth, was also one of Godwin's oldest friends. In June 1797 he and Godwin had gone on a two-week walking tour, a tour which produced a delightful series of letters between Godwin and Mary Wollstonecraft, then pregnant with Mary.[4] A few months later she was dying and Montagu was one of those in constant attendance on the grief-stricken husband.

Montagu was one of the leading advocates of the abolition of capital punishment, on which he published several works, and founded (in 1809) The Society for the Diffusion of Knowledge upon the Punishment of Death. Montagu's *Opinions of Different Authors upon the Punishment of Death* (3 vols., London, 1809–1816), appears on the Shelleys' reading list for 1816,[5] and Shelley himself wrote an essay against capital punishment, *On the Punishment of Death*, possibly in part inspired by Montagu.

In 1817 Montagu was one of Shelley's lawyers in the trial for the custody of his children.

4. Paul, *Godwin*, I, 247–269.

5. *Mary Shelley's Journal*, p. 71. The work is noted only as being read by Mary in this year, but many of the books on Mary's lists had been previously read by Shelley.

SC 108   WILLIAM GODWIN TO CHARLES BURNEY, DECEMBER 19, 1809

AN, third person, 1 page. Single sheet, 8$^{vo}$ (7.1 x 4.5 inches).
Laid paper. Watermark (trace): [posthorn in shield, lower part]| *E[JF]*|.

PROVENANCE: "Property of a Gentleman" (Sotheby, Dec. 11, 1957, lot 605).

*Skinner Str.,*
*Dec. 19, 1809.*

*M$^r$ Godwin would be happy to be favoured with D$^r$ Charles Burney's remarks as soon as possible.*

5      *The Pantheon contains twelve plates of the twelve principal Gods — it*

SC 108   *is therefore M^r Godwin's wish to have such plates as D^r Cha. Burney thinks exceptionable immediately reengraved, that the book thus corrected may not appear incomplete.*

      *A copy of the work was forwarded to D^r Burney by coach on the 5^th*

10   *instant.*

T̤HE above note[1] was addressed to the Reverend Charles Burney (1757–1817), classical scholar and educator, son of Charles Burney, the musicologist, and brother of Fanny Burney, the novelist. On January 24, 1810, Godwin wrote to him again (SC 110). The relationship of the two men and the "Pantheon" (line 5) will be discussed in the Commentary to that letter.

1. We are able to complete the watermark by comparison with SC 107 (Dec. 7, 1809) — *EJF*. If the two manuscripts are superimposed the section of the watermark on the above manuscript and the chain lines correspond exactly with the similar section of SC 107.

SC 109   THE DIARY OF HARRIET GROVE FOR 1810, JANUARY 1–DECEMBER 31, 1810

MS. DIARY signed Harriet Grove, 180 pages in a bound volume, *Silvester's Housekeeper's Pocket Book*,* 12^mo (4.5 x 2.9 in.) Ms. entries on front and back endpapers, verso of title, and continuously through sigs. B–E and first 5 leaves of sig. F (versos all full page entries; rectos irregularly from 1 line to full page, none entirely blank). (See Plates XXIII–XXIV.)

PROVENANCE: See SC 98, *The Diary of Harriet Grove for 1809.*

* *Silvester's*| HOUSEKEEPER's| 𝔓ocket 𝔅ook;| *And Ladies*| DAILY JOURNAL,| *for 1810*| [French rule]|| *NEWPORT*| *Printed & Sold by H. P. Silvester.*| *Sold also by*| *Crosby and C^o G. R. Ward, Champante and*| *Whitrow, and Muggridge, London.*| *Procter, Ludlow, Knott*| *& Lloyd Birming^m*| *& T. Wood Shrews^y*|

COLLATION: A⁶; B–F¹²; plus engraved title and engraved, folding frontispiece. (Signature B1 and a back flyleaf torn out leaving stubs.)

CONTENTS: frontispiece (recto blank); title (verso blank, used for Ms. entry); Contents, p. [3]; printed matter, pp. 4–14; [2 pages at beginning of diary missing]; diary pages (unnumbered), sigs. B–E and first 5 leaves of sig. F; summary of "expences," [F6–F7]; Memorandums at the End of the Year, 1810.| [rule]|, sig. [F8ʳ]; printed matter, pp. [124]–132; imprint: *Silvester, Printer, Newport, Salop.*| [between double rules], p. 132.

# Shelley and his Circle : Manuscripts

SC 109    Bound like SC 98, *The Diary of Harriet Grove for 1809.*

The diary pages, as noted above, are unnumbered, the pages for daily entries occupy-ing sigs. B–E and the first five leaves of F, the summary pages for accounts occupying the sixth and seventh leaves. In this volume, however, the unnumbered pages are included in the calculation of pagination, and the final printed matter begins with page 124 instead of beginning over again with page 1.

As in the Diary for 1809, the left-hand (verso) pages are reserved for the daily entries; the right-hand (recto) pages are intended for a record of "House Expences" — using, however, a different form. (Here as in the previous Diary Harriet Grove has used the right-hand pages for overflow entries.)

The pages of the Diary for 1810 are printed throughout in black, diary pages as well as the introductory and concluding printed text. Each page has a border of double rules.

Each verso or diary page has a running title on the following model: JAN. [single bracket] MEMORANDUMS [single bracket] Week 2| [rule]|| and is ruled horizontally into seven compartments. At the extreme left of each compartment, printed vertically, are the day of the week and date, beginning with Sunday. On the first day of the month the name of the month, in italic capitals, appears in the upper left corner of the compartment.

Each recto or "Expences" page has the running title: HOUSE EXPENCES.| [printer's device] £. s. d.|; below the signs for £, s, d, are ruled columns and to the left of the page a printed list of household necessities beginning: Meat and Fish| Poultry| Bread and Flour| etc. At the bottom of each is the line: 1*st* [2*d*, 3*d*, etc.] *Week's Expences,* £      |. (See Plates XXIII–XXIV.)

The frontispiece is an engraving by Bowley Salop of Hawkstone House, then belonging to Sir John Hill, Bart., off the road between Shrewsbury and Whitchurch, in Shropshire. Page [3] is entitled "Contents." Page 4 has "A Table of Expences," by the year, month, week, and day; and pages 5–8 have a "New Marketing Table, By the Pound, Yard, Stone, &c." Pages 9–14 contain a "Description of Hawkestone," which is the subject of the frontispiece engraving.

With the B gathering (the Memoranda and "House Expences" section) Harriet's daily entries begin. Following the diary entries for the year is a three-page table for entering the "Expences of Each Week in the Year"; by this means one could see at a glance the expenses by the week, month, and year. A blank page follows, with the heading "Memorandums at the End of the Year, 1810." Pages 124–132 give "Useful Receipts, &c." Among the twelve receipts are: "To Jug a Hare," "Pig's Feet and Ears Soused," "Lamb Chops in Casserole," and "To Preserve Golden Pippins." The receipts are followed by three medical remedies, including one "For a Cough, Cold, Hoarseness, and Sore Stomach," and finally by "Observations on the Weather," beginning: "If the moon change, or full, about the middle of the day, it seldom fails of producing a good deal of rain in the summer, and snow in the winter, three or four days before or after, or on the very day." At the bottom of page 132 is the colophon: "Silvester, Printer, Newport, Salop."

**Harriet Grove**  **Diary for 1810**

SC 109 [Flyleaf, recto]

*Harriet Grove*
*given her by her Mother*
*Jan$^y$ 1$^{st}$ 1810*

---

*I have got a great deal to tell my Dear*
*Louisa when she comes home next*
*Monday we shall go*
*to   F P*

[Title page, verso]

*Mary Dimmer Born April 17$^{th}$ 1736:*
*Taken from the Register at Lower*
*Donhead – She Died Dec$^{br}$ 25$^{th}$ 1810*
*sincerely regretted by the Grove Family*
*where she had lived as Nurse for more*
*than 20 years –*

## JANUARY

SUNDAY 7

X *Went to Gunville to fetch Charlotte home*
*told her the Col: had thoughts of making*
*proposals to a Miss Carter of Horsham*
*the daughter of ⟨———⟩*

[Flyleaf, recto] This note is related to the entries of Monday and Tuesday, June 4–5. The subject is denoted by F[ield] P[lace], Shelley's home, which Harriet had recently visited.

*shall go to* is written lightly in pencil.

The front end paper contains money reckonings.

[Title page, verso] See also the entry for December 26, below. The page with the entries for January 1–6 has been torn out. Some words which flowed over on the opposite "House Expences" page survive. Belonging probably to

MONDAY 8

*Wrote a long letter to Eliz$^{th}$ Shelley,*
*walked with my Mother,   received my*
*allowance from my Father* ——

TUESDAY 9

*Heard from ⟨ ⟩ar John who has*
*been at Field Place & been very gay*
*there & liked his visit very much*
*Waddington left us to day* ——

WEDNESDAY 10

*Heard from Dear Aunt Shelley &*
*Eliz$^{th}$ M$^{rs}$ Portman has invited C–*
*& me to a Ball   Tomorrow, we are*
*going – Poor Tho$^s$ Shere fell off a*
*ladder to day & is very much hurt* ——

THURSDAY 11

*Went to B— Had a most pleasant*
*Ball at Blandford   it was made up of*
*the Portman & Langton Parties ⟨———⟩*
*Old M$^r$ Snow the life of the Ball Room*

the January 1 entry is the phrase *at Gunville* — To the January 3 entry a passage of eight canceled lines probably belongs; of these only the following words can be read: ⟨   ⟩ *very which* ⟨   ⟩ *to be only a bit of red silk. I am happy to say C is better.* To the entry for January 4 probably belong three other canceled words.

7 Jan. two lines canceled

9 Jan. < > accidental ink blot

10 Jan. *C*[harlotte]

11 Jan. *B*[landford] . . . *pleasent* (sic)  two lines canceled

*7 Jan.* The "Col:" is Colonel Sergison, of Cuckfield, Sussex, whom Charlotte evidently found attractive. This topic receives further development in April and May. See also the entry for January 16.

*10 Jan.* Thomas Shere was probably one of the Groves' tenants. See also the entry for August 13.

**Harriet Grove**                                    **Diary for 1810**

SC 109   FRIDAY 12
$M^{rs}$ P– sent us as far as Thorny Down
in her chaise & four, we then went on
in the Barouche to Cranbourne   Poor
Helen very unwell

SATURDAY 13
The Portmans and Wares came   Poor
Helen ˄still very unwell   laughed at $M^{rs}$ J.
for having taken off her Under Petticoat
at the ball the other night ———

SUNDAY 14
Left Cranbourne & got to Dear Tollard
the Weather very cold

MONDAY 15
My Mother gave me a letter from Dear
$W^m$ which I ought to have had before –

TUESDAY 16
The Miss Frasers were to have come
here but sent excuses as they had colds
Louisa Charles & myself took a nice
long walk & got over Hedges to avoid
cows   heard from E. S: & the Col:
has not made proposals to Miss Carter
nor do I think from what I hear he ever
intended it

WEDNESDAY 17
Louisa bought some Poor peoples
Coloured Linen for her Pinbefores

12 Jan. $M^{rs}$ P[ortman]
16 Jan. E[lizabeth] S[helley]

THURSDAY 18
Walked out towards the Chase with my
two Dear Sisters

FRIDAY 19
Old $M^r$ Snow called here & told us
$M^r$ & $M^{rs}$ J: Helyar were going to live
at Bath   Charles took a nice long walk
with us —

SATURDAY 20
We all went to pay a morning visit on
$M^r$ J. H–   They were both at Home &
we staid an hour with them   the time
went so pleasently that it appeared much
shorter   $M^r$ Snow made a mistake about
there going to Bath as they are not going
to live there which I am glad of

SUNDAY 21
Heard from Dear $W^m$   $M^r$ Napper
Tregonwell preached here   he dined
with us with a friend of his a $M^r$ Skinner
——— they are neither very Gentlemanlike

MONDAY 22
Charlotte heard from Miss Fraser who
will be here Wednesday   She certainly
was not the Authoress of the verses
Charlotte received the other day

TUESDAY 23
tryed to Play with a Shuttle Cock Daniel
made, but could not succeed   The
Snow going away –

20 Jan. J[ohn] H[elyar]   *there going* (sic)

*12 Jan.* Harriet was visiting Hellen Tregonwell at Cranbourn, Dorset, about fourteen
miles northeast of Blandford.

*18 Jan.* Cranbourn Chase, a short distance east of Tollard.

*21 Jan.* John Tregonwell Napier (d. 1819, aged 34) was the rector at Chettle, Dorset.
(Hutchins, *Dorset*, III, 571, 572.)

*23 Jan.* Daniel was probably a servant.

**Harriet Grove**                                              **Diary for 1810**

SC 109  WEDNESDAY 24
*Miss Frasers came,  We Played all sorts of Xmas Caroles in the Evening & laughed amazingly —*

THURSDAY 25
*Walked out, then Charlotte Read the Beggar Girl to us  She Acted in the Evening to the great Entertainment of the Miss Frasers*

FRIDAY 26
*Read the Beggar girl   The Miss Frasers are got very interested in it*

SATURDAY 27
*Tom came here,   Did not make up for the interruption he made in the Beggar girl as he did nothing but talk of his grievances*

SUNDAY 28
X *We all went to Church & then took a pleasent walk, read the Beggar Girl in the Evening ——*

MONDAY 29
*So Sorry the Miss Frasers left us,   My Father & Charles walked to Fern, Wrote to Eliz:^{th} Shelley —*

TUESDAY 30
*We heard from Dear John who says M^r Shelley & Bysshe dined with him*

24 Jan. *Caroles* (sic)

*on Saturday,   heard from Dear Aunt Shelley ——*

WEDNESDAY 31
*Louisa & myself took our Drawing into the Parlour were we spent a pleasent morning together*

## FEBRUARY
THURSDAY 1
*Went a most Dirty walk to the shop met M^r J: Helyar,   coming home met some Cows which frightened us,  Louisa we lost owing to it for some time which frightened us even more than the Cows ——*

FRIDAY 2
*Louisa & I as usual sat together in the Drawing room,   it was a wet day so Charles could not go out & he came annoying us ——*

SATURDAY 3
*M^{rs} J: Helyar called here   Louisa & I were both in the Drawing room, hearing the Door bell we both ran up stairs with our Drawing apparatus*

SUNDAY 4
*Tom & M^r Fraser called here,   in the Evening Charles Louisa & myself sat in our Room talking leaving the rest of the party reading down stairs*

31 Jan. *were* (sic)

*25 Jan.* Elizabeth Bennett, *The Beggar Girl and Her Benefactors* (7 vols.).

*27 Jan.* This is one of the extremely rare passages in the diary to indicate that "grievances" existed in the happy Grove family. Sorrows and disappointment occasionally they had, but not grievances.

*30 Jan.* Shelley and his father dined with John at his house in London.

*4 Feb.* It will have been noticed long ago that William Fraser and his sisters were very frequently with Thomas Grove and the Farquharsons of Langton House, to whom they were related.

**Harriet Grove**

**Diary for 1810**

SC 109 MONDAY 5

*Dearest Louisa went to School  I miss her very much  Charles went into the world  Saw Aunt Jackson who has got all her children ill in the measles*

TUESDAY 6

*Susan returned from Bath & brought me a letter from Dear Louisa  She saw M$^{rs}$ C Grove who was dressed very smart for a Rout*

WEDNESDAY 7

*Wrote to my Dear Louisa  Charlotte heard from Wm  who says he thinks I shall never be married  that I do not care whether I ever do or not, He says he thinks I never liked any one so much as ⟨———⟩  that is a thing no one will ever know but myself/*

THURSDAY 8

*My Father went out Hunting,  So wet we none of us stirred out ——*

FRIDAY 9

*quite stupified by staying in Doors Miss Dear Louisa more than ever*

SATURDAY 10

*a Beautiful Day  M$^r$ Benett sent to invite us to Pytt House on Wednesday*

*took a long walk with Charles,  I do not quite like his sentiments  he thinks too much of appearances ——*

SUNDAY 11

*So wet could not go to Church  Tom called here, heard from & wrote to E: S:  Dear W$^m$ I heard from who is sailed for a three weeks cruize –*

MONDAY 12

*My Aunt Grove came  told us all the Gossip of Salisbury  Charles went to Gunville  he says there was a letter for M$^r$ Fraser – with an express put on it*

TUESDAY 13

*Walked out  heard from M$^{rs}$ Wilsonne Aunt Grove talked incessantly*

WEDNESDAY 14

*Aunt Grove Charlotte & myself went to Fern in the Pheaton  Charles Rode met Miss C: Benett coming here in our way  Poor Old Mary looks very ill which I was very sorry to see. My Father Rode to Hindon  is to sleep at Pytt House*

THURSDAY 15

*A Deep snow  My Father returned from Pytt house  he heard there the last Shaston Ball was very bad*

5 Feb. *in the measles* (sic)

7 Feb. The crossed-out **word** is probably *Bysshe.*

11 Feb. *E*[lizabeth] *S*[helley]

13 Feb. *Wilsonne* (sic)

14 Feb. *Pheaton* (sic)  *Miss C*[atherine] *Benett Old Mary* [Dimmer]

*6 Feb.* Susan was probably a servant. The Mrs. Grove she saw was probably Mrs. C[hafin] Grove, of Zeals, Wilts.

*10 Feb.* Mr. Charles Bennett.

*13 Feb.* Mrs. Wilsonn's letters always brought news about Louisa at school in Bath.

*14 Feb.* Hindon was about ten miles north of Tollard. Her father spent the night with the Charles Bennetts.

# The Carl H. Pforzheimer Library

SC 109    FRIDAY 16
*Walked out  Aunt Grove talks inces-*
*santly   heard from Elizabeth*

SATURDAY 17
*very cold   snow as Deep as ever,  wrote*
*a long letter to Elizabeth. Aunt Grove*
*cannot go owing to the Snow,  My*
*Father read a Play to us in the Evening*
*the Merchant of Venice* ——

SUNDAY 18
*My Mother heard of the Death of Old M$^r$*
*Hethfield who owing to his not signing*
*his will wherin he left — considerably*
*to my Mother & her Brothers & Sisters,*
*but they get nothing as he did not sign it*

MONDAY 19
*Aunt Grove cannot go away, nor Miss*
*Tregonwell come here, as the weather is*
*as bad* ——

TUESDAY 20
X  *Had a very droll Letter from Dear John,*
*the weather as bad*

WEDNESDAY 21
*Did the same as usual   walked for an*
*hour up & down on the Road, &*
*employed myself within doors as usual*

18 Feb. *Hethfield* (sic); see May 26, May 29 entries   *wherin* (sic)

THURSDAY 22
*The frost still remains   My Aunt gave*
*Charles a sort of a Lecture, he did not*
*swallow it very quietly —*

FRIDAY 23
*Tom hunted with my Father as the thaw*
*is at last come,   heard from Eliz$^{th}$ who*
*has sent a part of Bs Poem*

SATURDAY 24
*Aunt Grove left us   Miss Tregonwell*
*came   The Box of Novels came in the*
*Evening & we all began reading them,*
*Charles thinks Aunt Grove a very*
*pleasent Woman —*

SUNDAY 25
*As to Louisa I shall give her a good*
*scolding when she comes home for not*
*writing   We took a walk after Church*
*& talked of this time last year when*
*H. T. was at Fern with us & used to*
*walk out & get over Hedges   Little did*
*we think then where we should be Now*
*& that Poor Old Fern would be no more*

MONDAY 26
*Such a sight for this place   the Green*
*was filled with men who came to buy*
*M$^r$ J: H— cows which were sold by*
*Auction*

26 Feb. *J*[ohn] *H*[elyar's]

*16 Feb.* From Elizabeth Shelley.

*23 Feb.* Which of Bysshe's poems Elizabeth sent it is impossible to say. (See also
Cameron, *The Young Shelley*, pp. 306–307, and entries for Mar. 5, 8, and 10.)

*24 Feb.* In the light of the entry for February 22, Harriet's statement about Charles and
Aunt Grove would here seem to be ironical.

*25 Feb.* H[ellen] T[regonwell]. On March 9, 1809, Harriet wrote: "Charlotte & Miss
Tre[gonwe]ll went out a walking over hedges & Dicthes [sic]."

SC 109

TUESDAY 27

*M^r J: H: called here,   we took a very pleesant walk in the Park –*

WEDNESDAY 28

*A fast Day,   Dear W^m is returned to us again   We are all so happy   W^m returned in a small prize the Orestes recaptured from the French, he remains with us till Tuesday when he must join the Orestes when   it   comes   in   to Plymouth ——*

MARCH

THURSDAY 1

*Dear W^m is in his usual Spirits, he Cut Charles Hair,   C.   H.T.   & myself walked to Fern & saw Mary Dimmer*

FRIDAY 2

*Charles & W^m rode to Gunville the latter flirted as usual with his lovely Miss J: Fraser ——*

SATURDAY 3

*We Played at Commerce   as usual Dear good tempered Willy made us laugh by his great earnestness*

28 Feb. *W^m returned . . . to Plymouth*: this was written on the "House Expences" page, but not opposite the entry to which it belongs (for this space had already been used for the extended entry of February 25); it was written at the bottom of the page.

1 Mar. *C*[harles]   *H*[ellen]   *T*[regonwell]

5 Mar. *agreably* (sic)   seven lines canceled, six

SUNDAY 4

*W^m walked with us to Rushmore   We all got very Dirty particularly H: T– W^m & Charles dined at Gunville*

MONDAY 5

*Most agreably surprised by receiving a Parcel & letter from my Greatest Friend ⟨——⟩*

TUESDAY 6

*Wrote to E: S:   Tom & H: came here – H. T. slept with me   Dear W^m in such spirits said Charlotte was in love with a Capt Moustard –*

WEDNESDAY 7

*Dear W^m is gone. I hope only for a short time,   heard the delightful news that Dear Emma is safe & has got a fine Boy   Henrietta & Tom went back to G. Charlotte has received another anonymous letter with a bit of the Gentlemans Hair, fine doings indeed*

THURSDAY 8

*Shewed   the   Poem   ⟨——⟩   They ⟨——⟩ think it nonsense ⟨————⟩*

on "House Expences" page

6 Mar. *E*[lizabeth] *S*[helley]   *Tom & H*[enrietta] *H*[ellen] *T*[regonwell]

7 Mar. *G*[unville]

8 Mar. two lines canceled; then two words; third cancellation twelve lines, which take up the lower half of the "House Expences" page.

*4 Mar.* Rushmore, the home of George Pitt, was less than a mile northeast of Tollard.

*5 Mar.* The cancellation is rather good evidence that the "Greatest Friend" was Shelley. The parcel probably contained books and some of Shelley's poetry. The poem is referred to again on March 8 and 10. It appears to have been a rather long one.

# The Carl H. Pforzheimer Library

SC 109   FRIDAY 9
*We heard yesterday that Emma is doing well & the Child is to be named Geo: Grove it will please his Uncle G: G: when he returns fr China*

SATURDAY 10
*Catherine Benett came here, sent B— Poem away Walked with H: Tre, talked on various subjects*

SUNDAY 11
*M$^r$ Napier brought his love Miss Skinner with him She is pretty, but no diffidence, Heard from Dear W$^m$ who is safe arrived at Plymouth I hope we shall see him again soon*

MONDAY 12
*Miss Tre. left us, My Father & Mother talk of going to Field P— in our way to Town, How Happy I am for that*

TUESDAY 13
*Did as usual in the morning & Played at Chess with Charles in the Evening — — —*

WEDNESDAY 14
X   *Charles Benett called here C— & I*

9 Mar. G[eorge] G[rove]
10 Mar. B[ysshe's] *Poem* H[ellen] Tre[gonwell]

*were walking up & down with Books in our hands on seeing him ran in Doors. He is building a House at Sedgehill Miss B— & him are to be married in the course of the Summer*

THURSDAY 15
*M$^r$ Bingham called here heard from M$^{rs}$ Wilsonn Wrote to Dear Louisa, took a most Blowing walk on the Down with Charlotte —*

FRIDAY 16
*Walked out in the village the fool came & took hold of my hand & frightened me, My Father read aloud in the Evening one of Walkers lectures —*

SATURDAY 17
*Tom called here I do not think he looks quite so fat as he did — — —*

SUNDAY 18
*My Father & Charles rode over to Gunville where we are to dine next Thursday walked after Church*

MONDAY 19
*Took a most delightful walk to Ashcombe My Father went to Fern to receive his rents — Charles was in a most shocking gloomy humour —*

12 Mar. *Miss Tre*[gonwell] *Field P*[lace]
14 Mar. C[harlotte]

*9 Mar.* The Uncle, George Grove, was Harriet's brother, who was in the Navy.
*14 Mar.* Charles Bennett, of Lyme Regis, Dorset, son of John Bennett (d. 1808), rector of Donhead St. Andrew, married Sarah Burlton, daughter of William Burlton of Donhead St. Andrew in March 1810. (Hoare, *Wiltshire*, IV, 53, 131, 132.)
*16 Mar.* Possibly Adam Walker (1731?–1821), whose popular lectures on science at Eton influenced Shelley.

**Harriet Grove**                          **Diary for 1810**

SC 109     TUESDAY 20

*Went to Dear Fern with C– & my Father & Mother they are got on a good deal with the Building since I was last here –*

WEDNESDAY 21

*Walked to Gunville with Charlotte a most delightful day M<sup>r</sup> W<sup>m</sup> Helyar called at Tollard before we left it – I have sent E: S: a letter which I hope may be the means of our going to Dear Field Place in our way to Town*

THURSDAY 22

*The Miss Frasers & M<sup>r</sup> Far came here in the morning Charlotte & myself took a most pleasent walk in Eastbury park ——*

FRIDAY 23

*C– & I walked home from G– Received on my return a letter from E just such a one as I wished for Tom & H– came here to day after first going to Fern ——*

SATURDAY 24

*Tom & his Wife left us C: Benett came she seems to look rather grumpy ——*

SUNDAY 25

*The Shelleys have sent us word they shall be most happy to see us, but I fear*

*owing to some fancy my Mother has in her head we shall not go for which I feel the greatest sorrow as I had made up my mind for the pleasure of spending a few days at Dear Field-Place heard from dear W<sup>m</sup> who is comfortably settled on board the Scipion – walked after Church with C. Benett & Charlotte & were caught in the Rain ——*

MONDAY 26

*Miss C. Benett took leave of us & returned home but to our surprise returned again to Dinner, as her Sister was not at home to receive her*

TUESDAY 27

*⟨——⟩ at last they say they will go to Field-Place for one day. I have written to tell E– of it, for it makes me so happy*

WEDNESDAY 28

*Thank goodness C: B– has at last taken her departure. Bysshe has sent C– & me Zastrozzi as it is come out*

THURSDAY 29

*Went to Aunt Jacksons & Fern, Charles does nothing but abuse B– Romance. I believe he does it the more because he thinks it makes him appear a great man, but I think it makes him appear very illnatured to critisise it so very much*

20 Mar. *C*[harlotte]

21 Mar. *E*[lizabeth] *S*[helley]

22 Mar. *M<sup>r</sup> Far*[quharson]

23 Mar. *C*[harlotte] *G*[unville] *E*[lizabeth] *Tom & H*[enrietta]

24 Mar. *C*[atherine] *Benett*

27 Mar. one line canceled *E*[lizabeth Shelley]

28 Mar. *C*[atherine] *B*[ennett] *C*[harlotte]

29 Mar. *B*[ysshe's] *critisise* (sic)

*22 Mar.* Eastbury Park was at Gunville.

*25 Mar.* William had previously been on the brig *Orestes* (Dec. 6, 1809, entry). The *Scipion* was a large warship with 74 guns. (*The Court and City Register* for 1807, p. 136.)

*28 Mar. Zastrozzi* was a short Gothic novel, the first of Shelley's published prose works. It was published in London by G. Wilkie and J. Robinson, 57 Paternoster Row.

*Harriet Grove*                                    *Diary for* 1810

SC 109    FRIDAY 30
M*rs* Penruddocke, Hen:*ta* & Miss
Fraser called here from Gunville  M*rs* P
is more romantic than ever – M*r*
Hamilton Dined & slept here

SATURDAY 31
Packed up  they have given Charlotte
& me such a little bit of a Trunk

APRIL
SUNDAY 1
Tom called here & he told us he has
given up Gunville,  M*r* Napier dined
here & made us laugh by telling us the
Prince of Wales asked him to come & see
him & called him his little Fox hunting
friend

MONDAY 2
Left Tollard for my Aunt Grove's
called at Compton in our way  M*rs* P-
did not talk quite so much about
Napoleon

TUESDAY 3
Stayed at Netherhampton  Charlotte
read a little of Raymond & Agnes to me
which I like very much indeed –

30 Mar. Hen[riet]*ta*

WEDNESDAY 4
X left Aunt Groves & got to M*r* Bromleys
at Southampton  they both look very
well & glad to see us,  M*r* Lowdon
dined here  he looks very ill –

THURSDAY 5
We all walked upon the Key after-
wards Charles & myself walked in the
Town  Waddington came here & M*r*
Lowdon went away —

FRIDAY 6
A M*r* Hughs & M*r* Skifington Dined
here  the latter was very entertaining,
the former fancied he had been my
Fathers Tutor at Oxford

SATURDAY 7
Left Southampton & got to Little Park,
found them all well  Little G: G: a fine
little fellow,  Dear little Emma is very
much improved ——

SUNDAY 8
Played with Dear little Emma & John
walked out with Charlotte & so got
through the Day ——

2 Apr. M*rs* P[enruddocke]

*30 Mar.* The widow of Charles Penruddocke of Compton House, Compton, Wiltshire, and
her daughter Anne Henrietta. (*Burke's Landed Gentry*; Hoare, *Wiltshire*, IV, 86.)
*31 Mar.* "Packed up" for the trip to Field Place and London, which began on April 2.
*3 Apr. Raymond and Agnes* was a melodrama by Matthew G. Lewis.
*4 Apr.* The first day of travel to Netherhampton from Tollard was about sixteen miles;
the second to Southampton about seventeen miles; the third to Little Park about ten
miles; the fourth to Field Place was fifty-odd miles — a total of almost a hundred miles.
*7 Apr.* Little G[eorge] G[rove] Waddington, who was only a month old.
*8 Apr.* "& so got through the Day" is indicative of Harriet's eagerness to get to Field
Place.

**Harriet Grove**  *Diary for* 1810

SC 109  MONDAY 9
*Wrote to my Dearest Louisa  Played with Emma,  very wet & were obliged to amuse ourselves as we could*

TUESDAY 10
*Another wet day  I seldom go near Matty for which she told me to day she supposed ~~had affronted me~~ she had affronted me*

WEDNESDAY 11
*It being fine we walked out & talked of the pleasures of Tollard  afterwards Charlotte read Joseph Andrews to me —*

THURSDAY 12
*Went in the Chaise with Emma & my Niece  afterwards walked with C— Mʳ Stanhope called here  played with the dear Children, played at whist &c as usual*

FRIDAY 13
*Heard the first thing in the morning that Dear Wᵐ was here  it makes me so*

12 Apr. *C*[harlotte]
13 Apr. *F*[ield] *P*[lace]
14 Apr. *F*[ield] *P*[lace]  one plus lines canceled

*happy to see him again  I am afraid he cant go to F. P. with us*

SATURDAY 14
*A large party dined here  Dear Wᵐ says he shall go to F– P– with us which I am glad of,  How happy I feel at the idea of going there  ⟨———⟩*

SUNDAY 15
*Went to Wickham Church  afterwards called on Mʳˢ Rusham  She has two of the prettiest little girls I ever saw —*

MONDAY 16
*left L. P. very early  got to Dear F. P. ⟨———⟩ ~~they~~ are all very glad to see us. I can not tell what to make of it  very strange*

TUESDAY 17
*Still more odd,  Walked to Horsham saw the Old House St Irvyne  had a long conversation but more perplexed than ever  walked in the evening to Strood by moonlight*

16 Apr. *L*[ittle] *P*[ark  *F*[ield] *P*[lace]  one plus lines canceled

*10 Apr.* Matty may be the Madeline Waddington mentioned in the entry for July 23. She was probably the sister of John Waddington, Emma's husband.

*11 Apr. Joseph Andrews,* by Henry Fielding.

*12 Apr.* "Emma & my Niece": her sister Emma and her sister's child, little Emma.

*15 Apr.* Little Park was at Wickham. (For April 15–28 entries, see Plate XXIV.)

*16 Apr.* Harriet's remarks about her perplexity are in themselves both strange and significant. An attempt at an explanation is in the Introduction (page 484). There can be no doubt about her and Shelley's ecstatic happiness.

*17 Apr.* St. Irvyne was an estate belonging to the Duke of Norfolk. In January 1811 Shelley published a second Gothic novel entitled *St. Irvyne, or the Rosicrucian.* The origin of his title is obvious. The moonlight walk was introduced by Shelley into several of his poems. (See Introduction to the Diary of Harriet Grove, pages 492–493.)

[ 575 ]

**Harriet Grove**                    **Diary for 1810**

SC 109   WEDNESDAY 18

*This morning we went   before we left
the pleasentest party in the world for
the most unpleasent   to Horsham that
is E. B. & my Brothers & self   I still
know not what is meant   We reached
Cuckfield to Dinner   What a disagreable place after the one we have just left*

THURSDAY 19

*Walked in Col. S– Park   very pretty I
daresay but my thoughts wont let me
think about it*

FRIDAY 20

*Went to Church   heard a most excellent
Sermon   saw the Col: he dined here
was very entertaining. Charlotte is half
in love with him   I think he drinks too
much*

SATURDAY 21

*left that tiresome M$^{rs}$ P. & got to Johns
found him & his cat perfectly well &
very happy to see us as we are to see him,
My faculties are all whirling round as
they always are in this disagreable
Place ——*

18 Apr. *E*[lizabeth]   *B*[ysshe]
19 Apr. *Col. S*[ergison's]

SUNDAY 22

*Charles took a walk with Charlotte & me
into High Holborn   we soon found that
was not a fit place for us,   M$^r$ W$^m$
Fraser called here   called on the Longs
& they called on us ——*

MONDAY 23

*Lady Fraser called here,   we went
& Paid Morning visits to M$^{rs}$ Long
M$^{rs}$ Lee & M$^{rs}$ Green,   after Dinner
Charlotte John Charles & myself walked
in the Fields – –*

TUESDAY 24

*Charlotte & myself walked out & had
a long Chat   We then went out in the
Chaise & made purchases   I am sorry
to say my Mother was very unwell all
the time   We are pleased with our
Bargains we have bought*

WEDNESDAY 25

*We made morning visits on Miss
Packington & Dear M$^{rs}$ Portman.
Dear Aunt Shelley & my Cousins came
M$^r$ W$^m$ Fraser dined with us & we spent
a most pleasent day –*

21 Apr. *M$^{rs}$ P*[ilfold]

*18 Apr.* The lack of punctuation makes the first part of this entry obscure. It becomes
clear when one recognizes the clause "before we left . . . for the most unpleasent" as a
parenthetical clause which we would set off with commas or dashes. The party consisted
of Elizabeth Shelley, Bysshe, and Harriet's brothers Charles and William. Cuckfield was
ten miles southeast of Field Place. There they visited John Pilfold, brother to Harriet's
mother and soon to be a staunch friend of Shelley in his days of trouble.

*19 Apr.* Colonel Warden Sergison's estate, Butler's Green, about a mile from Cuckfield.
(Paterson's *Roads*, 1811, p. 387.)

*21 Apr.* John Grove's house was at 49 Lincoln's Inn Fields.

*22 Apr.* During this London visit the names of many Wiltshire and Dorset friends and
relatives again appear, as in 1809: William Fraser, the Longs, Mrs. Portman, etc.

*25 Apr.* Harriet's cousins were Elizabeth and Percy Bysshe Shelley.

**Harriet Grove**                                        **Diary for 1810**

SC 109    THURSDAY 26

X *Walked in the Fields with dear Bysshe*
*then went shopping & had great fun*
*left Aunt & Mama at M$^{rs}$ Bartons &*
*they came home in a Hackney Coach*
*a shocking dirty one Aunt S— says she*
*shall send for a Chain & Chain us to*
*her —— Went to the Play M$^r$ W$^m$*
*Fraser with us*

FRIDAY 27

*Walked out ⟨——⟩ Percy then went*
*shopping went to the Play C. my*
*Father & Mother came home directly*
*as the Play was over P, Mama &*
*myself sat up till the rest of the party*
*came home & had a most delightful*
*conversation*

SATURDAY 28

*Went shopping with the Shelleys in a*
*Hackney Coach ⟨——⟩ We staid at*
*home Elizabeth as noisy as ever*

SUNDAY 29

*Went to St Pauls in time to meet every*
*body coming out Two Jack Tars said*
*I was painted so Aunt S— said – Went*
*afterwards in Ken– Gardens & saw*
*the Persian Ambassador there hurt*
*my foot, a dinner party*

MONDAY 30

*Staid at home all day on account of my*
*Foot the rest of the party went to the*
*Play all but Mama & Percy*

MAY

TUESDAY 1

*Percy & I staid in doors the rest went*
*out We all staid at home in the*
*evening I played & they all danced*
*Eliz$^{th}$ talks & is in as great spirits as*
*ever*

WEDNESDAY 2

*⟨——⟩ I staid at home ⟨——⟩ my*
*foot still being bad, however I went to*
*the Play in the Evening & liked it well*
*enough —*

THURSDAY 3

*All the Party went out but me & Dearest*
*P. Tom Medwin dined here went*
*to the Opera I hate it more than ever,*
*so does P——*

FRIDAY 4

*Staid in again ⟨——⟩, Dined at M$^r$*
*Longs a most stupid ES has told me*
*something that kills me with laughing*
*but which hinders her from coming to*
*Tollard I am sorry to say —*

26 Apr. *Aunt S*[helley]

27 Apr. *C*[harlotte] *P*[ercy]

28 Apr. two lines canceled

29 Apr. *Aunt S*[helley] *Ken*[sington] *Gardens*

2 May. second cancellation one line

3 May. *Dearest P*[ercy] *so does P*[ercy]

4 May. two lines canceled *E*[lizabeth] *S*[helley]

*27 Apr.* It will be noted that from this time on Harriet calls Shelley Percy instead of Bysshe.

*28 Apr.* Harriet gives us a delightful view of Elizabeth Shelley as a high-spirited, fun-loving girl.

*3 May.* Thomas Medwin (1788–1869) was Shelley's cousin. His home was at Horsham and he and Shelley had been to Sion House Academy together. In 1847 he published his two-volume *Life of Shelley*.

**Harriet Grove**                                    *Diary for* 1810

SC 109   SATURDAY 5
⟨———⟩ *The Shelleys left us very sorry*

SUNDAY 6
*Went out to pay visits  walked in the square  staid at home in the evening ⟨———⟩*

MONDAY 7
*Graham came here & gave me my lesson in Music, much surprised by the arrival of my two Uncle Pilfolds. Uncle Jem sang to us after supper —*

TUESDAY 8
*Wrote  walked in the Fields  M^r Long M^r P & Wife & daughters dined here like Miss Flora very much  she suits me*

WEDNESDAY 9
*Went & called at M^rs Greys ⟨———⟩ came there yesterday  My Mother ill with a cold  went shopping  dined at M^r Whindhams  saw there Capt. Heath-*

5 May. seven lines canceled
8 May. M^r P[enruddocke]

*cote who is going to take the Persian Ambassador home in the Lion  My Uncles went into the City  My Mother too unwell to go out at all*

THURSDAY 10
*Went out shopping  as usual very stupid  heard from P they all went to see Plays in the evening but my Mother & me  our colds prevented us —*

FRIDAY 11
*We went to the water coloured Exhibition some figures by McFee & landscapes by Glover  very well done indeed  stayed at home  practiced a difficult piece of music for Graham*

SATURDAY 12
*I staid at home writing  Charlotte & Uncle Pilfold walked together  My Mother & Aunt Grove went together to the Exhibition  Staid at home this evening  John Charles & Uncle went to the play at half price —*

9 May. two words illegible

*7 May.* On Edward Fergus Graham, a youthful musician and protégé of Shelley's parents, see SC 113 (May 20, 1810). Though his residence was in London, he was often at Field Place.

The "two Uncle Pilfolds" were Captain John and James Pilfold. The captain, who lived at Cuckfield, Sussex, is well known to Shelley readers, but James is an obscure figure.

*8 May.* The Longs (including Flora Long) and the Penruddockes lived at Compton, Wilts. See the entries for September 23–24, 1809.

*9 May.* This is probably William Wyndham of Dinton, Wilts. See note to entry for January 17, 1809. The "Uncles" were John and James Pilfold. The *Lion* is the name of a ship.

*11 May.* John Glover (1767–1849), landscape painter, president of the Water-color Society in 1815.

**Harriet Grove**                                       *Diary for* **1810**

SC 109    SUNDAY 13

*Staid in all the morning ⟨———⟩ in the
Evening M<sup>r</sup> Shelley came here   he
looks very unwell ⟨———⟩ Uncle &
him shook hands & were friends during
the time he staid —*

MONDAY 14

*Walked to Bond street with Uncle Papa
&c, a party to dinner Brereton &
M<sup>r</sup> Helyar Aunt Grove & M<sup>r</sup> Shelley
the latter so pleasent, I am quite happy
to see him so   he gave me a letter from
Eliz<sup>th</sup> ———*

TUESDAY 15

*Went in the carriage   Graham came
& we stayed at home in the evening*

WEDNESDAY 16

               *M<sup>r</sup> W<sup>m</sup> Helyar there*
*Went in the evening to M<sup>r</sup> Longs ₍heard
very good singing by Lady Bayers &
Miss Williamson*

THURSDAY 17

*M<sup>r</sup> & M<sup>rs</sup> Green   Aunt Grove   Miss
Cluse &c dined here   Charlotte John
Charles & myself went to a M<sup>rs</sup> Jenkins
Ball   Danced & found it very pleasent*

FRIDAY 18

*Graham came   M<sup>rs</sup> Hamilton & Chil-
dren & M<sup>r</sup> Shelley   the latter in great
spirits. Graham made me try to sing,*

---

19 May. one plus lines canceled   The remainder
of this long entry, beginning with the date, is on

*he says I have a voice but I do not
believe it —*

SATURDAY 19

*We left London Friday ~~Oh~~ how sorry
am I to leave Dear John   Charlotte &
Capt P. set off together for Cuckfield
I am sorry she is gone but hope she will
like her visit — —*

    *Saturday 19<sup>th</sup> We slept at Overton
& got to Tollard to day ⟨———⟩   we
dined at Salisbury with Tom &
Henrietta who are at M<sup>r</sup> Frenche's
Lodging's, T: being out with the
Local — The last Evening we spent in
Town which was Friday M<sup>r</sup> Shelley
dined with us ⟨———⟩*

SUNDAY 20

*Went to Church   heard M<sup>r</sup> J Helyars
delightful Preaching he came here
after Church, I am sorry to say they
are going to reside at Bath*

MONDAY 21

*Went to Fern with my Mother in the
Pheaton   she begins to croak again
about the building   Mary Dimmer
pretty well   Charles & I walked out
for a little while   the only happiness
I have here*

TUESDAY 22

*Charles read to me in the morning
Milton. We walked together after Din-*

---

the "House Expences" page facing the entries
for May 20–26   four plus lines canceled

*13 May.* This entry shows that Shelley's father and Captain Pilfold did not get along
even before they disagreed about Shelley after his expulsion from Oxford.

*15 May.* On Graham see sc 113 (May 20, 1810).

*19 May.* Charlotte spent almost three months with her uncle at Cuckfield. Harriet,
Shelley, and Elizabeth thought the main attraction for her there was Colonel Sergison.
    The "Local" means the Local Militia. See June 8 entry.

SC 109   *ner, after tea we sat in my room & he read Romeo & Juliet to me –*

**WEDNESDAY 23**
*My Father & Mother went to Farnham Charles rode to Donhead I stayed at home alone after dinner walked with Charles, ⟨———⟩*

**THURSDAY 24**
*My Mother & I went in the Pheaton to Pytt house Mʳ Benett is looking better than we expected to see him, the Miss B & Mʳ Wᵐ Benett there Saw the Children Mʳˢ B gone to Bath Mʳ Wake we met there who came back with us a great bore*

**FRIDAY 25**
*Called at Wardour & Mʳˢ Cookes the last time I fear of seeing Lady A. My Aunt Jackson went to Wardour with us Miss Laura & Miss Julia were there & were glad to see us*

**SATURDAY 26**
*⟨———⟩ Charles dined at Aunt Jacksons I walked with my Father & Mother to Ashcombe Miss C Benett called here in the morning — saw in the newspaper the Death of Mʳˢ Heathfield,*

**SUNDAY 27**
X *Went to Church heard a most excellent sermon Mʳ J: Helyar came here*

*after the service & told us Mʳˢ H: had got a rash I think he has learnt to Prose, walked with Charles on the green in the evening read one of Stern's Sermons ⟨———⟩*

**MONDAY 28**
*Went to Fern to meet my Aunt Jackson & Arabella, during the time we were there a fire broke out at the Glove, owing to the timely assistance most of the Poor mans goods were saved, My Dear Father with his usual goodness went & did every thing he could & saved the Stables & outer Buildings but the Inn was entirely burnt down — but fortunately being in the day time no one was burnt I am very glad to hear poor Mʳ Westeridge will not lose much by it, tho Lord Arundell will which I am sorry for ——*

**TUESDAY 29**
*employed myself as usual in the morning Charles dined at Aunt J— Mʳˢ Heathfield is dead & left it all to my Uncles*

**WEDNESDAY 30**
*Went to Fern very hot read sentimental Journey there on our return found C Benett she stayed & walked in the evening*

23 May. one plus lines canceled
25 May. *Lady A*[rundell]
26 May. three plus lines canceled

27 May. three lines canceled
29 May. *Aunt J*[ackson's]
30 May. *C*[atherine] *Ben*[n]*ett*

*26 May.* Mr. Heathfield had died in February; see the entry for February 18.

*27 May.* Laurence Sterne, *Sermons* (7 vols., 1760–1769).

*28 May.* The Glove was one mile north of Fern, on the main road between Shaftesbury and Salisbury.

*30 May.* Laurence Sterne, *A Sentimental Journey* (2 vols., 1768).

*Harriet Grove*                                                    *Diary for* 1810

SC 109    THURSDAY 31
*Miss C B stayed here My Mother heard from M^rs H to say Dear L had the Hooping Cough & is very unwell I am in such a fright for her –*

JUNE
FRIDAY 1
*My Father & Mother went to Bath for Dearest L Miss C B went home & Charles dined at Donhead, quite alone had a letter from Dear Louisa she is better thank Goodness I am so glad for that comfort*

SATURDAY 2
*Tom called here & stayed some time Charles went to Gunville with him & so I dined alone again, & walked as I did yesterday from 5 till 8 by myself*

SUNDAY 3
*Charles & I went to Church M^r J. Helyar walked to the House with us & then went away. after dinner walked out made C– write to Percy*

MONDAY 4
*Expected my Father Mother & Dearest Louisa home but they did not come, Tom dined with us, he has taken Littleton   Charles would walk out without his Hat, all I could say to him.*

TUESDAY 5
*My Dearest Louisa is come home & looks better than I expected to see her took a solitary walk as usual ̶b̶y̶ ̶m̶y̶s̶e̶l̶f after dinner*

WEDNESDAY 6
*Dear Louisa I think is very weak but change of air will do her good My Father & Charles drank tea at Gunville Tom & Hen^t go to Cwm Elen tomorrow*

THURSDAY 7
*Dear Louisa & I dined together in the drawing room M^r Wilkins has been here & rather frightened us about her he says she must not eat meat*

FRIDAY 8
*Dear Louisa was kept in bed all day but is much better as her fever is gone*

31 May. *C[atherine] B[ennett] M^rs H[elyar] L[ouisa] Hooping (sic)*

1 June. *L[ouisa] Miss C[atherine] B[ennett]*

3 June. *C[harlotte]*

6 June. *Hen[rie]^l[ta]  Elen (sic); for Elan*

8 June. *Devises (sic)  quel (sic)*

*4 June.* Both Gunville, where Thomas had lived for some time, and Littleton, to which he was now moving, were the property of James John Farquharson, the brother of Thomas's wife Henrietta. Littleton was at Blandford St. Mary, a mile west of Langton House, where the Farquharsons lived, in Dorset.

*6 June.* Cwm Elan was Thomas Grove's estate in Wales. See note to the entry for July 25, 1809.

*7 June.* Mr. Wilkins was not a physician but a so-called surgeon (a combination of apothecary and practitioner of minor surgery). A regular doctor, Dr. Bearwood, was called in on June 12.

*8 June.* Devizes was about thirty miles northeast of Tollard.

We find the following in *The Examiner* for June 17, 1810: "WILTS LOCAL MILITIA. —A

# The Carl H. Pforzheimer Library

**Harriet Grove**                                  *Diary for* 1810

SC 109 *My Father with his troop went to Devises to quel a mutiny there amongst the local Militia  we are anxious for him to return safe ——*

SATURDAY 9
*Dear Louisa we think better,  M^rs Gordon drank tea here, Charles & myself walked till it was almost dark — Dear Louisa told me she liked me to be with her*

SUNDAY 10
*Dear Louisa is still very unwell & M^r W— bled her which rather frightened her,  My Father  returned safe from Devizes*

MONDAY 11
*M^r W— has been here & pronounces Louisa much better but thought it necessary to bleed her again,  I am so glad to hear the Dear little thing is better  I long for her to be quite well again —  She is quiet*

9 June. *Dear Louisa told . . . with her.* This last sentence is at the top of the "House Expences" page, and opposite the entry for June 3.
10 June. *M^r W*[ilkins]

TUESDAY 12
*Dear Louisa's fever as high as ever they sent for D^r Bearwood who bled her as M^r W has three times before I sat up with my Dearest Sister tonight*

WEDNESDAY 13
*Dearest Louisa is better to day & we have the greatest hopes  She was bled for the fourth time to day  My dear Father quite cryed with joy to ⟨——⟩ to think Dear Louisa was nearly out of danger*

THURSDAY 14
*Dear Louisa still continues better which makes us all so happy,  M^r W^m Benett called here in the morning & they asked him to dine  he told us John Gordons arm was wasted away almost to nothing & that they were going to send him to Town for the best advice*

FRIDAY 15
*Much the same as usual  Louisa is better thank God ——*

11 June. *M^r W*[ilkins]
12 June. *M^r W*[ilkins]

dissatisfaction has prevailed amongst a few of the non-commissioned officers and privates of the 2d Wilts Local Militia, quartered at Devizes, ever since they have been embodied, which on Wednesday se'nnight broke out into open mutiny in the person of one of the serjeants, who was committed to the guard-room. After the evening parade, a party of the regiment, with charged bayonets, forced the guard-room, and released the serjeant and two privates then under confinement; but by the assistance of nine troops of the Wiltshire Yeomanry Cavalry, and the Draycot troop of Yeomanry, whom the mayor called upon in aid of the civil power, the mutiny has been entirely quelled; two of the guilty persons tried by a Court Martial, and the ringleader severely punished. This man was sentenced to receive 300 lashes, 200 of which were inflicted on him, and the remainder remitted. The serjeant was sentenced to be broke and flogged; but in consideration of his good character, the latter part was remitted. The term of service for which the above regiment had assembled expired on Friday, when the men were dismissed, and retired peaceably to their homes."

**Harriet Grove**                                          **Diary for 1810**

SC 109   SATURDAY 16
*Dear Louisa had a slight return of fever which frightened us but it went away very soon,   M$^r$ Hamilton came & dined & went away*

SUNDAY 17
*Went to Church   Dear Louisa was worse again & M$^r$ Wilkins bled her again,   I sat up with her all night ——*
~~*I hope & pray that my Dearest Sister during her illness at least*~~ —

MONDAY 18
*We still have hopes of the recovery of my Dear little Sister*

TUESDAY 19
X *In the morning great hope but at four oclock the Dear little Angel was released from her Pain   What a lesson of Fortitude & resignation has she left us all   I hope it may please God that I never may forget it as long as I live*

WEDNESDAY 20
*My Aunt Grove & Aunt Jackson came the former stays with us till after the Dear remains are gone*

THURSDAY 21
*My Aunt Grove is so good & at times my Dear Mother is in Spirits   Aunt Jackson dined here*

FRIDAY 22
*My Dearest Louisa was put into her coffin where I hope she will ⟨——⟩*

SATURDAY 23
*how ~~solemn~~ & holy we feel   yet it is a happiness to know Dear Louisa ⟨——⟩*

SUNDAY 24
*The last day My Poor little Sisters remains will be above ground —— —*

MONDAY 25
*She was buried to day & my Dear Father went as chief Mourner   My Aunt Grove is very kind & does every thing in her power to comfort us & I am happy to say she in some degree has made us all bear our loss better   Dear Charlotte how I long to see you*

TUESDAY 26
*Heard from my Dear Sister C & H Tre$^{ll}$   I am sorry to hear Dear Tom too is ill*

WEDNESDAY 27
*Went to Fern in our way to Nether-hampton   Saw Mary who is looking dreadfully ill Poor Old Soul*

THURSDAY 28
*Went to Wilton with Mama & Aunt Grove & walked in the Park —   My Father came to look for us but we did not meet them*

FRIDAY 29
*M$^r$ & M$^{rs}$ Sam$^l$ Long dined here — they look both very well —*

22 June. two lines partly blotted out and canceled
23 June. one line canceled
26 June.   C[harlotte]  H[ellen]  Tre[gonwe]$^{ll}$:

the reading of the Ms. here is doubtful.
27 June. *Mary* [Dimmer]

*24 June*. (For June 24–30 entries, see Plate XXIII.)
*28 June*. Wilton House, the seat of the Earl of Pembroke, and the Park, were close by.

[ 583 ]

**Harriet Grove**                                    *Diary for* 1810

SC 109  SATURDAY 30
*I went with Aunt Grove to Salisbury to buy some things for my Mother –*

JULY
SUNDAY I
*Wet & a thunder storm   could not get to Church & my Father read Prayers & a Sermon in the Evening*

MONDAY 2
*My Father & Charles went to Fern & saw Aunt Jackson & all the family there —*

TUESDAY 3
*left Netherhampton for Muddiford   as we went through Ringwood I thought on Poor dear Louisa, as that is where her friend Mary Jessup lives   I cannot say much for the beauty of this Place*

WEDNESDAY 4
*We all walked on the Sands   the Tregonwells are here & very kind to us We went after dinner to see a Place Mr T has bought & talks of building on called Cairn   it is very barren but a pretty sea view*

THURSDAY 5
*I bathed this morning   Yesterday we were much surprised as Dear Wm arrived*

4 July. *Mr T*[regonwell]
6 July. *Miss Tre*[gonwe]*ll*

FRIDAY 6
*Walked before breakfast   Mrs & Miss Trell dined with us & then drank tea with their friends the Hobsons   afterwards we all walked on the Sands —*

SATURDAY 7
*Bathed   Dear Helen went with me We went to Hordell Cliff before Dinner in the Carriage with the Tregonwell Aunt Grove &c,   a most beautiful view from it ——*

SUNDAY 8
*Waked at seven by a tremendous Thunder storm,   We went after Dinner to the Lookout with the Trell & ourselves*

MONDAY 9
*The Tregonwells left us, which we are very sorry   Walked with Helen & my brothers on the sands before she went*

TUESDAY 10
*Went with my Father & Brothers to choose a Lodging for the Waddingtons who I am happy to say are coming here, Dear Wm left us ——*

WEDNESDAY 11
*It rained so could not walk out,   Charles & my Aunt had a little squabble on the subject of Mr Wm long   a very tender subject*
~~one~~ *always with my Aunt —*

7 July. *Helen* [Tregonwell]   *Tregonwell*[s]
8 July. *Tre*[gonwe]*ll*[s]

*3 July.* Muddiford was a seaside resort, near Christchurch, Hampshire, and was not very attractive to Harriet.

*9 July.* Hellen Tregonwell, Charles, and William.

# Shelley and his Circle : Manuscripts

SC 109  THURSDAY 12
*Wrote to my Aunt Shelley   went in the Carriage on the Sands,   we have taken a Hous belonging to Lady Stewart – for the Waddingtons*

FRIDAY 13
*It blew so hard we could not walk   went after Dinner to XChurch & bought Toys for Emma & John*

SATURDAY 14
*Wrote to ~~B &~~ Eliz^th Shelley   Called on M^rs Pen Whyndham who I like very much   she told us a melancholy story of the Bank at Salisbury being broke in consequence of which many are ruined –*

SUNDAY 15
*My Dear Father & Mother went with Charles to my Aunt Jacksons. Left alone with Aunt Grove,   Went to Church twice with M^rs Pen Whyndham*

MONDAY 16
*My Dear Father & Mother & the Waddingtons came   the Children are much grown   My Mother is better for her Jaunt —*

TUESDAY 17
*The Waddingtons spent the day with us, talk to Emma of our late sad loss ——*

WEDNESDAY 18
*Walked on the sands & helped to pick up shells for Emma who was delighted Received a letter from Miss Bury a friend of my dear sister L–*

THURSDAY 19
*Went to bathe. Dear little Emma accompanied me & was a little alarmed the gentlemen went to the Isle of Wight ——*

FRIDAY 20
*Walked on the Sands   a little Boy gave Emma some Shells & she made him a fine Curtesey ——*

SATURDAY 21
*Walked on the Sands, bathed &c as usual ——*

SUNDAY 22
X *My Aunt Grove Mama & myself went to Church at Xt Church   afterwards walked round it & found it very well worth seeing*

MONDAY 23
*My Dear Father very unwell in his bowels ~~left Xt Church~~ Madeline Waddington returned to Tollard with us   Emma & the Children went to Little Park —*

12 July. *Hous*[e]
14 July. *B*[ysshe]

18 July. *sister L*[ouisa]
20 July. *Curtesey* (sic)

*14 July.* The Henry Penruddocke Wyndhams lived at Salisbury.

The failure of the bank of Brickwood, Rainer and Co. in London "produced considerable loss and inconvenience" in Salisbury. The local firm of Bowles, Ogden and Co. which was "in intimate connection" with this bank had to suspend payments, and so, too, "Mr. Burrough's" bank. (Hoare, *Wiltshire*, VI, 558.)

*18 July.* This Emma was sister Emma's small daughter.

*19 July.* The "gentlemen" were her father, Charles, William, and Waddington.

*23 July.* Madeline was probably John Waddington's sister. See the entry for April 10.

*Harriet Grove*                                *Diary for* 1810

SC 109    TUESDAY 24

*M<sup>r</sup> Wilkins came to see my Dear Father who is much better we all went to see Fern which is much got on My Father is over tired by going to Fern*

WEDNESDAY 25

*Charles & Waddington went to the Salisbury Races & slept at Nether-hampton we were to have gone to Fern after dinner but the rain prevented us —*

THURSDAY 26

*Charles returned & was much pleased with the Races. My F. M. & myself went to Fern in the evening found Poor old Mary very unwell I fear she will not live over the year*

FRIDAY 27

*My Mother does all she can to keep*
           *spirits*
*up her˄but finds it very difficult some-times*

SATURDAY 28

*Rained so we could not go to Fern*
        *are*
*we˄all reading Saint Sebastian which my Father bought at Muddiford*

SUNDAY 29

*Went to Church in the morning — Charles Jackson dined & slept here heard from Charlotte who I believe we shall not see some time She is very happy where she is she says*

26 July *My F*[ather] *M*[other] *& myself* Mary [Dimmer]

MONDAY 30

*M<sup>r</sup> Hamilton came here, in the Evening wrote to dear Charlotte*

TUESDAY 31

*Went to Fern in the morning, found Mary Dimmer better, much disap-pointed the letter bag did not come as we expected to have heard from Dear George —*

## AUGUST

WEDNESDAY 1

*Went to Fern in our way to Nether-hampton & received letters from Dear Geo: who is quite well —*

THURSDAY 2

*Got to Little Park & found them all well we dined at Southampton*

FRIDAY 3

*Walked in the Garden played with Emma & John &c as usual here*

SATURDAY 4

*Wet so could not walk did much the same as usual ——*

SUNDAY 5

*Emma & the Gentlemen went to Church My Mother & I staid at home not being quite well ——*

MONDAY 6

*The Gentlemen went to Portsmouth & went on Board the Donegal to see W<sup>m</sup> M<sup>r</sup> Cook the Clergyman called here*

29 *July*. Charlotte had been at Cuckfield visiting her uncle Captain John Pilfold since May 19. She returned on August 13.

*Harriet Grove*                                          *Diary for* 1810

SC 109    TUESDAY 7
*Wrote letters & walked with my Mother*
*& Emma &cc —*

WEDNESDAY 8
⟨——⟩ *called on Lady Mary Long to*
*day they have improved Preshaw by*
*new furnishing it very well*

THURSDAY 9
*Lady Mary told us yesterday of the*
*death of Poor Lady Mildmay, which*
*I was sorry to hear altho' I know so*
*little of her & pity her friends very*
*much*

FRIDAY 10
*Packed up & played with Emma &*
*John —*

SATURDAY 11
*Left L: P: & reached Aunt Grove's to*
*Dinner   had a very wet drive in the*
*Pheaton from Little Park —*

SUNDAY 12
*Staid at Netherhampton & walked to*
*the Race Course & went to Church ——*

MONDAY 13
*Much rejoiced at the return of Dear*
*Charlotte & George   the latter is much*
*improved,   we went to Fern in our way*
*to Tollard & found the House with the*
*Roof putting on, & Thos Shere has*
*been married since we left home*

8 Aug. two plus lines canceled

TUESDAY 14
*Charlotte & myself very busy in the*
*morning   unpacking.   Mr Hamilton*
*dined here   George made us all laugh*
*he is so droll*

WEDNESDAY 15
*So Wet we could not go to Fern   George*
*went to Weymouth to see William —*

THURSDAY 16
*George returned from Weymouth but*
*without seeing Wm as his ship was*
*sailed   Charlotte & my Mother went*
*to Fern —*

FRIDAY 17
*We all went to Fern & in our way met*
*Mrs Gordon Mrs Benett & Miss*
*Partridge coming to call here   they all*
*returned to Fern with us & we shewed*
*them the House &ccc*

SATURDAY 18
*My Mother & myself called on Mrs*
*J Helyar but not being at home we*
*proceeded on to Fern —   Aunt Grove*
*came ——   George as noisy as ever*

SUNDAY 19
*Went to Church   Mr & Mrs J Helyar*
*dined here & were very pleasent —*

MONDAY 20
*Went to Fern with Aunt Grove in her*
*way home Charlotte & myself walked*
*with my Father round the Plantation*
*Mary Dimmer moved from the Kitchen*
*to the room over the Dairy*

11 Aug. L[ittle] P[ark]

*13 Aug.* For Thomas Shere, see the entry for January 10.
*15 Aug.* Weymouth was about thirty miles south of Tollard.

[ 587 ]

**Harriet Grove**            *Diary for* **1810**

SC 109    TUESDAY 21
*Went with my Mother to M$^{rs}$ Cooke
& Fern when we came back found
Helen Tregonwell here & her brother
George & Charles dined at Aunt
Jacksons*

WEDNESDAY 22
*Charlotte & I walked to the Shop
H.T. & my Mother went to Fern
M$^r$ Eason & M$^{rs}$ J. Helyar dined
here –*

THURSDAY 23
*M$^{rs}$ Farquharson dined here walked
in the Evening, George very rude —
— —*

FRIDAY 24
*Charlotte Helen & myself walked by
ourselves*

SATURDAY 25
*Helen left us in the Evening Charlotte
& myself took a pleasent walk with my
Brothers –*

SUNDAY 26
*Went to Church afterwards went to
Fern with my brothers* ⟨———⟩ *–*

MONDAY 27
*My Father & Mother went to Langton
the rest of the Party staid at home &
were very merry dancing & singing*

TUESDAY 28
*My Father & Mother returned from
Langton were they saw only M$^{rs}$
Farquharson –*

22 Aug. *H*[ellen] *T*[regonwell]
26 Aug. one plus lines canceled

WEDNESDAY 29
*Went to Fern walked with Charlotte up
White Sheet Hill where Fern House
looked very well the Miss Benetts
drank tea here & M$^r$ Hamilton came
in the Evening*

THURSDAY 30
*Wrote to Lucy Bury ~~Percy~~ &c My
Mother & Susan went to Fern —*

FRIDAY 31
*Went to Fern Charlotte & myself
walked round the Plantation & met with
a snake, which frightened us*

## SEPTEMBER
SATURDAY 1
*In our way to Fern met M$^{rs}$ J Helyar.
Aunt Jackson & Arabella met us at
Fern, & stayed there all the time we did*

SUNDAY 2
*Went to Langton to Dinner M$^r$
Hamilton Cap$^t$ Donalson M$^r$ R Parker
& M$^r$ James Fraser there*

MONDAY 3
*Charles Pony very ill so he could not go
to the Tollard Hunt we returned from
Langton*

TUESDAY 4
X *Miss Hughes & Miss Cooke came
George more noisy than ever – we
danced after tea —— Sir Arthur Paget
called here We Ladies did not see him
which as he is so Handsome perhaps
was fortunate*

28 Aug. *were* (sic)

*4 Sept.* Sir Arthur Paget (1771–1840), diplomatist; brother of Sir Henry William Paget,
1st Marquis of Anglesey. From 1807 to 1809 he was ambassador to Turkey.

## Harriet Grove

*Diary for* **1810**

SC 109    WEDNESDAY 5

*As Charlotte & I were walking in front of the House Lord Rivers rode up   I only could perceive that he had got Grey Locks   C— took him for M<sup>r</sup> Beckford of Steepleton*

THURSDAY 6

*All went to Fern but Charlotte & me, heard that W<sup>m</sup> is soon going to the East Indies again*

FRIDAY 7

*Charlotte & I walked on the Down with Daniel behind us   Dear W<sup>m</sup> is sailed for the East Indies*

SATURDAY 8

*Took a long walk with my sister Daniel & Tommy behind us   Tommy fell down two or three times & we were rude enough to laugh at him*

SUNDAY 9

*Walked after Church to the Top of Ashcombe Hill   laughed at Geo: because he said this was Monday by the Nautical day & proved it so —*

5 Sept. C[harlotte]

MONDAY 10

*Miss Hughes & Miss Cooke left us, It rained which prevented us from going to Fern ——*

TUESDAY 11

*Wet &c &c &c &c*

WEDNESDAY 12

*Went to Zeals. M<sup>rs</sup> Chaffin received us with her usual form*

THURSDAY 13

*Walked to Mere with my brothers & sister. George was nearly running over us being so riotous he nearly spoilt the Musical Clock*

FRIDAY 14

*left Zeals & met Tom & his Wife & John at Fern. Miss C. Benett also met us there –*

SATURDAY 15

*the Building at Fern completely covered in & the People supped in the House & enjoyed themselves very much —*

SUNDAY 16

*Walked to the top of Ashcombe Hill with Charlotte ⟨———⟩ —*

16 Sept. two lines canceled

*5 Sept.* George Pitt (1751–1828), 2nd Baron Rivers.

Lord Rivers and William Horace Beckford of Steepleton House, Durweston, Dorset were related. (See Hutchins, *Dorset*, I, 299.)

*7 Sept.* Daniel was probably a servant.

*8 Sept.* Tommy, apparently a small child, has not been identified.

*12 Sept.* Zeals House, where the Chafin Groves lived, was about fourteen miles northwest of Tollard.

*13 Sept.* Mere was about a mile northeast of Zeals House. Harriet's brothers and sister were Charles, George, and Charlotte.

**Harriet Grove**                                              *Diary for* **1810**

SC 109   MONDAY 17

*Received the Poetry of Victor & Cazire, Charlotte offended & with reason as I think they have done very wrong in publishing what they have of her*

TUESDAY 18

*M^rs J. Helyar went to Fern with my Mother  My sister & I walked in the Chase escorted by Tommy*

WEDNESDAY 19

*Dined at Farnham  Met M^r & M^rs Bingham & Son  M^rs J Helyar as entertaining as ever — —*

THURSDAY 20

*Went to M^rs Cookes  met the Miss Lipscombes & had a very pleasent day & a dance in the Evening*

FRIDAY 21

*Returned from Donhead & Brought the Miss L— & Miss Cooke to Fern to shew them the House  M^rs J Helyar dined with us  M^r J H. too unwell the former did nothing but make us laugh*

21 Sept. *Miss L*[ipscomb]    *M^r J*[ohn] *H*[elyar]
22 Sept. *M^rs F*[letcher]

SATURDAY 22

*Returned to M^rs Cookes  dined with the Fletchers & a dance in the Evening. M^rs F— made us laugh by telling us her Son had a swelling on his knee which was merely a puff & that she M^r & Miss F. had all had huff.*

SUNDAY 23

*After going to Church & hearing a most delightful Sermon from M^r Lipscom returned home much pleased with our visit & very sorry the Miss Lip— have left the Country as we are all much pleased with them —*

MONDAY 24

*Went to Fern in the Pheaton with George & my Mother. Henrietta & Tom dined & slept here*

TUESDAY 25

*Walked from Fern to call on the Miss Benetts at Berwick  My Father had a letter from M^r S— which I am sorry for, as it gives more trouble.*

23 Sept. *Miss Lip*[scomb]

*17 Sept. Original Poetry* by Victor and Cazire was a small volume of poetry by Shelley and his sister Elizabeth. It was printed at Worthing, Sussex, and published in London by John Joseph Stockdale. The poem that offended Charlotte was written by Elizabeth and was entitled "To Miss [Harriet Grove] From Miss [Elizabeth Shelley]." The poem, dated April 30, 1810, was written in London while the Shelleys and the Groves were visiting together at John Grove's; it concerns Charlotte's projected visit to Cuckfield and her interest in Colonel Sergison.

*18 Sept.* Cranbourn Chase, slightly to the east of Tollard.

*19 Sept.* Farnham was a small village in Dorset just across the county line from Tollard Royal.

*25 Sept.* M^r S— must be M^r Shelley, Percy Bysshe Shelley's father. The letter possibly may have related to the poem which offended Charlotte. Harriet may mean that Timothy Shelley's apology for his son did more harm than good.

[ 590 ]

*Harriet Grove*                                    *Diary for* 1810

SC 109   WEDNESDAY 26
*Went to Fern   met M^rs Cooke & party*
*there walked with Miss Lipscombe*
*round the plantation*

THURSDAY 27
*as usual went to Fern   walked round*
*by the Glove & the White Cottage with*
*my Sister,   met M^r & M^rs R Arundell*
*in their Gig in our way home*

FRIDAY 28
*Walked from Fern to Wardour with*
*Charlotte ——*

SATURDAY 29
*Walked at Fern &c as usual   in the*
*evening my Father & John entered into*
*an argument*

SUNDAY 30
*Walked in the Chase after Church with*
*my Sister & Brothers,   John went to*
*Gunville –*

## OCTOBER
MONDAY I
*Charlotte & myself did not go to Fern*
*which we were glad of, John returned*
*from Gunville*

TUESDAY 2
*Went to Fern   M^r Hamilton there*
*my brothers returned so late from shoot-*
*ing that we began to be frightened*
*M^r Eason dined here*

WEDNESDAY 3
X *called at the Cottage in our way to Fern*
*the Shepherds daughter was in less pain*

THURSDAY 4
*Called on Lord & Lady Arundell at*
*Wardour. We saw her pretty little girl*
*& she shewed us her drawings   we met*
*M^r & M^rs Benett there*

FRIDAY 5
*Charlotte & myself stayed at home &*
*laughed very much making a Comb*
*Bonnet ——*

SATURDAY 6
*Went to Fern & my Mother very nearly*
*left us behind there*

SUNDAY 7
*After Church John & Charles left us*
*We were all most sorry to part with*
*them ——*

MONDAY 8
*in our way to Fern met Lord & Lady*
*Arundell coming here   they returned*
*& went to Fern with us*

TUESDAY 9
*Went to Pyt house   called in our way*
*on M^rs Cooke,   M^rs Burton & M^r &*
*M^rs Charles Benett met us & M^r Bowles*
*who was very entertaining.*

*27 Sept.* The R. Arundells lived at Ashcombe, which the Groves passed on their way
between Fern and Tollard.

*7 Oct.* Charles lived in London with his brother John for more than a year.

*Harriet Grove*           *Diary for* **1810**

SC 109    WEDNESDAY 10
*Lady Parker & M^rs Still &c called on us, Lord & Lady & M^r Arundell & the Gordons dined here, & we spent a very pleasent day*

THURSDAY 11
*Went to a fête Champetre at M^rs Peter Stills, saw M^rs & Miss Dobson Lady Parker &c & her little Girl thought M^rs D– a very pleasent woman, returned to Tollard by 5 Oclock*

FRIDAY 12
*Went to Fern & were agreably surprised by seeing Miss Popham M^rs Warre & M^rs Whindham Miss Popham returned with us to Tollard —*

SATURDAY 13
*Went to Dinton with my Sister & Miss Popham, on our arrival found only M^rs Warre there as M^rs Whindham was gone to London to her Father who was very ill Spent a very pleasent day with M^rs Warre who I think very pleasent Saw her three Children & all the little Whindhams who are very fine*

SUNDAY 14
*M^rs Warre set off at 9 Oclock, My Sister & myself left Dinton at eleven, found M^r J: Helyar here on our arrival –*

MONDAY 15
*My Mother went to Fern & brought Miss Hughes & Miss Lipscomb here ——*

TUESDAY 16
*Charlotte & myself went as far as Ashcombe in our way to Fern & then returned as it rained which wetted us through before we got home*

WEDNESDAY 17
*It rained the whole day so we were obliged to stay in doors all day in the evening we went on with the Children of the Abbey –*

THURSDAY 18
*My Mother & Miss Hughes went to Fern My Sister Miss Lipscum & myself walked out between the showers –*

FRIDAY 19
*Went to the Gordons in our way took Miss H– & Miss L. to M^rs Cookes – Aunt Jackson & Arabella dined at the Gordons*

SATURDAY 20
*Rained all the morning read M^rs Edgeworths Tales M^r & M^rs Benett came to dinner in the Evening. looked at some drawings in a sketch book —*

19 Oct. *Miss H*[ughes] *& Miss L*[ipscomb]

*10 Oct.* William George Parker of the Royal Navy married Elizabeth Still of East Knoyle, Wiltshire in 1808. (*Burke's Landed Gentry.*)

*13 Oct.* William Wyndham (1767–1841) and his family lived at Dinton House, Dinton, ten miles northeast of Tollard.

*17 Oct.* Regina Maria Roche, *The Children of the Abbey* (4 vols., 1796), a novel.

*20 Oct.* Since Maria Edgeworth published three different series of *Tales*, it is not possible to identify those read by Harriet. Most likely are the recent and then incomplete *Tales of Fashionable Life* (9 vols., 1809–1812).

*Harriet Grove*                                          *Diary for* 1810

SC 109  SUNDAY 21
*Returned to Tollard   My Mother heard from Aunt S.   It rained very hard the whole way home ——*

MONDAY 22
*Drew an Old woman   M<sup>r</sup> J Helyar called here   went on in the Evening with the Children of the Abbey*

TUESDAY 23
*Did not go to Fern as my Mother thought it would rain,   went on in the evening with our Novel ——*

WEDNESDAY 24
*George went to Littleton & we went to Fern where we met M<sup>rs</sup> C & the Miss Benetts   we shewed them the House & then walked to Berwick with them*

THURSDAY 25
*George returned from Littleton to hunt with my Father,   we called on M<sup>rs</sup> J. Helyar ——*

FRIDAY 26
*Rode one of my Fathers Horses to Fern, met M<sup>rs</sup> Cooke & party there   Geo: returned to Donhead with them*

SATURDAY 27
*My Father & George went out hunting & met their friend M<sup>r</sup> Adams,   heard from John –*

21 Oct. *Aunt S*[helley]
24 Oct. *M<sup>rs</sup> C*[ooke]
28 Oct. five lines canceled

SUNDAY 28
*Very Wet & my Father read Prayers at home ⟨——⟩*

MONDAY 29
*Tom & Henrietta came here   both grown fat & looking very well*

TUESDAY 30
*Henrietta & Mama went to Fern, Charlotte & I walked our hour –*

WEDNESDAY 31
*My Mother & Hen<sup>t</sup> went to Rushmore the latter delighted with that place ——*

## NOVEMBER
THURSDAY 1
X *My Mother & Henrietta went to Hanley to call on M<sup>rs</sup> Adams & M<sup>rs</sup> Mills who where neither of them at home   Lady Arundell sent us an invitation to come to Wardour*

FRIDAY 2
*M<sup>r</sup> Adams was to have dined here but sent word his wife had family pains ——*

SATURDAY 3
*staid in all day on account of the weather ——*

SUNDAY 4
*Went to Church   M<sup>r</sup> J. H so ill he could scarcely go through the service   M<sup>r</sup> Adams dined here*

1 Nov. *Han*[d]*ley   M<sup>rs</sup> Mills:* the name is uncertain   *who where* (sic)
4 Nov. *M<sup>r</sup> J*[ohn] *H*[elyar]

*1 Nov.* Handley was to the east of Tollard and a short distance northeast of Farnham, Dorset.

# The Carl H. Pforzheimer Library

SC 109   MONDAY 5
*My Brother & Sister left us & George went with them*

TUESDAY 6
*We went to Wardour where we met M$^r$ & M$^{rs}$ R Arundell M$^r$ & M$^{rs}$ Dotter & Miss Benson My Father & Mother slept in the State Bedroom Lady Arundell was kind enough to invite C. & me to stay some time with her —*

WEDNESDAY 7
*After Breakfast we left W. & went to M$^r$ Longs Rood Ashton & found the House more comfortable than Wardour*

THURSDAY 8
*Rained the whole day so C. read out a Novel to us which was a very stupid one*

FRIDAY 9
*Came home which we are none of us sorry for, tho' we spent a very pleasent day at M$^r$ Longs*

SATURDAY 10
*a most shocking wet day read the Reformist in the Evening —*

SUNDAY 11
*George returned from Littleton, M$^r$ J Helyar preached & to our great*
          *is*
*surprise$_\wedge$as well as ever he was —*

6 Nov. *C*[harlotte]
7 Nov. *W*[ardour]

MONDAY 12
*My Father & George went out hunting & in the Evening we read our Novel as usual*

TUESDAY 13
*Went to Fern to meet my Aunt & Miss Pakington George went to M$^{rs}$ Cookes*

WEDNESDAY 14
*Rained the whole day so my Father & Brother could not go out hunting —*

THURSDAY 15
*Walked &c as usual*

FRIDAY 16
*Went on with our stupid novel we are reading, called Edmund of the forest ——*

SATURDAY 17
*Took a walk with my Sister & we fancied we heard a great noise like the falling of armour ——*

SUNDAY 18
*M$^r$ & M$^{rs}$ J Helyar called here, & they told us the Helyars were arrived at Sedghill ——*

MONDAY 19
*Tom called here & gave us a long account of M$^r$ Farquharson's Lady who he has seen at Cadstock*

TUESDAY 20
*Sent letters to W$^m$ in India, M$^r$ & M$^{rs}$ Gordon came here whom we are very glad to see —*

8 Nov. *C*[harlotte]

*5 Nov.* The brother and sister[-in-law] were Tom and Henrietta.

*10 Nov.* Sarah Green, *The Reformist!!! A Serio-Comic-Political Novel* (2 vols., 1810).

*16 Nov. Edmund of the Forest* (4 vols., 1797), no author discoverable.

     The William Helyars had a house and grounds at Sedgehill. See the entry for September 6, 1809.

**Harriet Grove**                                    **Diary for 1810**

SC 109   WEDNESDAY 21
*Arabella Charlotte & I played Battle-*
*dore & Shuttlecock & in the Evening*
*Chess —*

THURSDAY 22
*M^r & M^rs Gordon left us   George went*
*to M^rs Cookes for the last time as*
*M^rs C goes to Town Tomorrow*

FRIDAY 23
*Went to Fern  Mary Dimmer was a*
*little better,  in the Evening we read*
*Sir Charles Grandison -  George much*
*amused by Charlotte rapping out the*
*d—m—n—s*

SATURDAY 24
*Began to learn one of Shakespeares*
*speeches & C & I took it in our heads*
*to Sing & fancy we have voices —*
*M^r Easton breakfasted here*

SUNDAY 25
*M^r & M^rs J: Helyar dined here, & were*
*very pleasent  They have invited us to*
*come & see them when we go to Bath*
*which we shall certainly do —*

MONDAY 26
*Play at Chess with Ch⟨  ⟩.  she beat*
*me which I cannot but say I was dis-*
*pleased at*

24 Nov. C[harlotte]
26 Nov. Ch⟨ ⟩. possibly Ch[uck.] for
Charlotte. The word is compressed and con-

TUESDAY 27
*We practised our singing & my Father*
*was greatly pleased to hear his Daughters*
*sing so finely*

WEDNESDAY 28
X *My Fathers birth day  I wish he may*
*see many many happy returns of this*
*day ——George nearly killed us with*
*laughing he was so droll*

THURSDAY 29
*Went to Littleton where I never was*
*before  think it a very nice House*

FRIDAY 30
*Charlotte & I walked in the Fields*
*going to Blandford  M^rs Farquharson*
*& M^r & Miss Marsh dined here,*
*beat C. at Chess*

DECEMBER
SATURDAY 1
*We were alone  Charlotte beat me at*
*Chess,  we acted in the Evening Brutus*
*& Cassius —*

SUNDAY 2
*Went to Church at Langton & called*
*on M^rs Kirbey who was confined to her*
*room with a Cold*

tracted; the *y* of *Play* on the line above comes
down into it.
30 Nov. C[harlotte]

*23 Nov.* Samuel Richardson, *Sir Charles Grandison* (7 vols., 1754).
*29 Nov.* Her brother Thomas had moved to Littleton House near Blandford St. Mary in
June 1810.

# The Carl H. Pforzheimer Library

*Harriet Grove*                                    *Diary for* **1810**

SC 109   MONDAY 3
*M$^r$ & M$^{rs}$ J Basturd & M$^r$ Snow dined here   I think M$^{rs}$ J: B: rather pretty beat C. at Chess*

TUESDAY 4
*The Gentlemen went out Hunting with the Fox Hounds, We Ladies called on M$^{rs}$ Portman & saw her & her beautiful Children —— beat Geo: at Chess*

WEDNESDAY 5
*We all went to the Convent at Spetsbury, the Rev$^d$ Mother & Sister Placider the dirtiest Creatures I ever saw Sister Mary Barbara very clean & pretty & she sold us some work bags &c M$^{rs}$ Farquharson made me a present of a work basket*

THURSDAY 6
*M$^r$ & M$^{rs}$ Pleydell & there two daughters & M$^r$ & M$^{rs}$ Baker dined here — L. P. I think looks ill*

FRIDAY 7
*We went Langton where we met M$^r$ Ford who dined here –   He was at Cambridge with J: Waddington*

3 Dec. *Basturd* (sic)
6 Dec. *there* (sic)
7 Dec. *went* [to] *Langton   J*[ohn] *Waddington*

SATURDAY 8
*Returned to Tollard to our great surprise Miss C. Benett came in just before dinner, she told us Old M$^r$ Helyar was nearly blind, ——*

SUNDAY 9
*C. Benett Charlotte & myself took a walk   I stumbled over a style to their great amusement but did not hurt myself*

MONDAY 10
*very Wet & Miss Benett sent a Hack Chaise for her Sister, the Box came from Town & we began Modern Philosophy*

TUESDAY 11
*Heard from L. B.   M$^r$ Easton dined here & we entertained him with our Novel in the Evening ——*

WEDNESDAY 12
*We all played Battledore it being wet M$^r$ Easton made us all laugh*

THURSDAY 13
*M$^r$ & M$^{rs}$ Adams called here   C. & I escaped seeing them by walking out — Geo: laughed a good deal at Miss Biddy Botherim*

11 Dec. *L*[ucy] *B*[?ury]. See entry for August 30.
13 Dec. *C*[harlotte]

*3 Dec.* The Reverend J. Bastard lived at West Lodge, some three miles from Langton. (Cary's *Roads*, 1819, p. 850. See also Hutchins, *Dorset*, I, 272, III, 523.)
*4 Dec.* The Portmans lived at Blandford.
*5 Dec.* The convent was a short distance south of Blandford. According to Hutchins' *Dorset* (III, 519) a "society of religious ladies of the order of St. Augustine" had been set up at Spettisbury House shortly before Harriet Grove's visit. There were thirty-three women in the community. The "superior" was a "Mrs Stoner, of Stoner in Oxfordshire."
*6 Dec.* Edmund Morton Pleydell of Whatcombe House near Blandford. (Paterson's *Roads*, 1811, p. 40.) The Pleydells had six daughters, one of them called Louisa. (Hutchins, *Dorset*, I, 199.) Paterson gives a Peter William Baker of Ranston in the same neighborhood.
*8 Dec.* "Old M$^r$ Helyar" was the father of William Helyar.
*13 Dec. Miss Biddy Botherim* was a novel.

[ 596 ]

*Harriet Grove*                                                    *Diary for* 1810

SC 109    FRIDAY 14
*It rained as usual   we played Battle-dore & read Miss Botherim*

SATURDAY 15
*I am sorry to hear the King is not well & a Regency is determined on   We finished our Novel, which we liked very much* ——

SUNDAY 16
*Heard a very good Sermon on the subject of receiving the Sacrement* —— *Wrote a letter to Aunt Jackson* ——

MONDAY 17
*Played at Battledore with my Mother & made her laugh* ——

TUESDAY 18
*Went to Whatcombe   met M^r & M^rs Hodges & two daughters   in the Eve-ning we danced & began to learn a Cotillion & had a great deal of laughing*

WEDNESDAY 19
*We walked out   the two Miss Hodges & C & E Pleydell walked through some water   the rest of the party more prudent   We danced again this Eve-ning* ——

THURSDAY 20
*A very wet day & we made a great noise playing all sorts of games & danced the morning with our Cotillon to a*

*famous band   In the Evening Charlotte & I acted & did all sorts of things to make them laugh*

FRIDAY 21
*Left Whatcombe for which we are all very sorry   went to Littleton in our way home   found M^r Hamilton here, who told us Fern was very much got on*

SATURDAY 22
*Sat. Geo: learnt the Cotillon steps, & we read a novel* ——

SUNDAY 23
*Dear George left us for Little Park   we miss him very much   went to Church & did the same as usual* –

MONDAY 24
*Very Wet,   read our Novel in the Eve-ning as usual* ——

TUESDAY 25
*Went to Church being Xmas day,   heard a most excellent Sermon,   bought pocket Book for next year* – *Drank Toms health who is 27 to day*

WEDNESDAY 26
*Betty told us the 1^st thing to day that poor Old Mary Dimmer died yesterday morning,   Poor Old Woman   she is now happy for there never was a better woman* – *& we shall all regret her as long as we live* ——

16 Dec. *Sacrement* (sic)
20 Dec. *Cotill[i]on*
21 Dec. The entry for the 21st runs through the

space for the 22nd. After this a heavy black line was drawn; and beneath it the brief entry for Saturday the 22nd was written.

*18 Dec.* Whatcombe was south of Blandford, Dorset. It was the residence of the Pleydells.
*19 Dec.* "C & E" stand for Cornelia and Emma Pleydell. (See Hutchins, *Dorset*, I, 199.)
*21 Dec.* "found M^r Hamilton here" means at Tollard.
*26 Dec.* See Harriet's note about Mary Dimmer immediately preceding the entries for January. Betty was probably either a servant or a tenant.

[ 597 ]

**Godwin to Burney**  *January 24, 1810*

SC 109 THURSDAY 27

X *Jhon Gordon breakfasted here, & told us there is to be a Shaftesbury Ball soon which we are very glad of —*

FRIDAY 28

*My Brothers came  joyful event, George more noisy than ever, Hen^{tta} sent us an invitation for the 1^{st} of Jan^{ry} — 1811 —*

SATURDAY 29

*a most severe frost — John went out a shooting  had three shots & killed every time,  in the evening had a great deal of laughing teaching my Brothers the rigadoon step ——*

SUNDAY 30

*Went to Church & received the Sacrement. John Gordon came to dinner George more noisy than ever*

MONDAY 31

*I wish my Father would give us our allowance  John Gordon left us this morning  I gave him some Country*

27 Dec. *Jhon* (sic)
31 Dec. *Tamborine* (sic)
[Back fly, verso] *Clarck* (sic)  All the April items

*28 Dec.* "My Brothers came": George, John, William, and probably Charles.

*Dances for the Band at Shaftesbury. We danced in the Evening Daniel played the Violin & W^m the Tamborine to us. We are very much afraid the snow will prevent us from going to Littleton Tomorrow —*

[Back fly, verso]

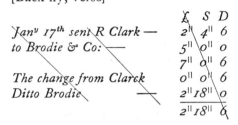

|  | X | S | D |
|---|---|---|---|
| *Jan^y 17^th sent R Clark —* | 2 | 4 | 6 |
| *to Brodie & Co:* | 5 | 0 | 0 |
|  | 7 | 0 | 6 |
| *The change from Clarck* | 0 | 0 | 6 |
| *Ditto Brodie* | 2 | 18 | 0 |
|  | 2 | 18 | 6 |

|  | S | D |
|---|---|---|
| *April 5th Paid for p^r of Habit Gloves* | 3 | 0 — |
| *9 Paid Washing —* | 7 | 7 — |
| *9 Do: Scissors —* | 3 | 9 — |
| *10 Paid for Boxes & c* | 2 | 0 — |
| *14 Paid Washing —* | 4 | 6½ — |
| *14 Paid p^r of Clogs —* | 8 | 6 |

|  | S | D |
|---|---|---|
| *April 23 – Paper* | 0 | 6 |

except the last relate to the visit to Little Park in April 1810; the purchase of paper on April 23 was made in London.

SC 110 WILLIAM GODWIN TO CHARLES BURNEY, JANUARY 24, 1810

AL signed *W Godwin*, 1 page. Double sheet, 4^{to} (9 x 7.2 inches). Laid paper. Watermark: [posthorn in crowned shield]| *EJF*|. Seal: wafer, black. Postmarks: 1. (receiving house stamp, London): Ludgate Hill| 2 py [P] Paid|; 2. (delivery stamp, London): 4 o'Clock Even.| JA[N] 24| 1810| TWO PENNY PAID|.

**Godwin to Burney**          *January 24, 1810*

SC 110

                  *Skinner Street,*
                  *Jan. 24, 1810.*

  *Dear sir*

  *I am happy to inform you that I have been able to clothe four of the*
5 *gods [Venus, Apollo, Mercury & Mars] for the precise sum of twelve guineas,*
*which, considering the high price of all sorts of apparel at present, I hope*
*you will allow to be a good bargain. Seriously, if by this small sacrifice I shall*
*be in any degree advanced in the good opinion & kindness of a man of your*
*eminent talents & learning, I shall hold my money to have been well spent.*

10 *In the course of a fortnight (three weeks at farthest) the books with the*
*altered plates will be ready for delivery, & copies shall immediately be*
*forwarded to you. If you wish for any sooner, with the plates omitted, do me*
*the favour to let me know.*

  *I have heard nothing lately from the Master of the Rolls in Ireland.*
15 *I fear this is owing to the ill state of his health.*

  *I am, sir, with great esteem,*
     *your obliged & most obedient servant*
       *W Godwin*

[Address, page 4]
*The rev. D^r Charles Burney*
20 *Greenwich*
  *Paid*

THE above letter (the second to Charles Burney in our library)[1] is addressed to Dr. Burney's private school at Greenwich (Environs of London, page 47) where Godwin's son William was a pupil. "William, I think, is decidedly improved. Mr. Burney writes this concerning him, 'My pupil left me in good looks, and with an excellent character.'"[2]

  Godwin's previous communication to Burney (sc 108) illuminates the enigmatic comments on clothing the gods (line 4) and the "books with the altered plates" (line 10). Both refer to Godwin's book (written

1. See sc 108 (Dec. 19, 1809).

2. William Godwin to Mary Jane Godwin, July 9, 1817, Paul, *Godwin*, II, 251. (See also pp. 257–258.)

# The Carl H. Pforzheimer Library

SC 110   under the pseudonym "Edward Baldwin") *The Pantheon, or Ancient History of the Gods of Greece and Rome . . . with Engravings of the Principal Gods. . . . Second Edition . . . Printed for M. J. Godwin at the Juvenile Library*, London, 1809.[3] Godwin's Journal for March 21, 1810, reads: "Pantheon, 3 pp. (Ceyx)"; and for March 27: "Pantheon, Index." These entries indicate that Godwin revised the work (first published in 1806) between March 21 and March 27.[4] The "three weeks at farthest" of the above letter (line 10), it would seem, got somewhat stretched.

As Burney was to receive "copies" and not a copy of the book, it had presumably been ordered for use at his school.[5] One might surmise further that Burney had objected to nude engravings of four of the gods as unsuitable for school use and that Godwin had agreed to have the plates re-engraved with clothing for the gods.[6]

Burney's objections, however, were mild compared to those of the Home Office. Among the State Papers is a report from an agent of Lord Sidmouth (of *Masque of Anarchy* fame) on the subversive effects of the Juvenile Library on the educational system, which in view of the above letter has a special interest. It reads in part as follows:

> Godwin's Library was carried on for some time in Hanway Yard, Oxford Street, without any name either at the shop or on the several publications published for it. The business has since been removed to Skinner Street, Snow Hill, for the last three or four years; for some time also it was called the Juvenile Library; no name appeared.

3. For the 3rd edition see the list of Juvenile Library publications at end of Volume II of Caroline Barnard, *The Parent's Offering; or Tales for Children*, Juvenile Library (London, 1813).

4. "Ceyx" is presumably a reference to the legend of Ceyx and Alcyone. Ceyx, however, does not appear in the index to the 2nd edition.

5. *The British Critic* for April 1807 (quoted in *The Parent's Offering*) considered the book "a very convenient as well as agreeable manual, for introducing younger readers to a knowledge of Ancient Mythology," and as "in all respects a proper book for the use of Schools." The Juvenile Library in its first publication, *Fables, Ancient and Modern* (1805), advertised: "N.B. Schools supplied. Letters from any part of the United Kingdom (post paid) will be duly attended to."

6. The gods mentioned (line 5) are unclothed in the 2nd edition (1809). Godwin, before meeting with Burney's objection, had apparently thought his illustrations suitable for school use. The book (first published in 1807) is dedicated to the Reverend Matthew Raine, Headmaster of Charterhouse (attended by Godwin's stepson, Charles Clairmont), and the Preface contains the comment: "It has long been a complaint, that books detailing the History of the Heathen Gods abounded with ideas and pictures by no means proper to be presented to the juvenile mind. Particular attention has been given to that article in the composition of this volume. It is expressly written for the use of young persons of both sexes. . . ."

SC 110     At length Mr. J. Godwin was written on the door-post in very small letters; within a very few months it appeared boldly in large letters over the door; still it is very little known that the proprietor is *Godwin*, the author of *Political Justice*. There appears to be a regular system through all his publications to supersede all other elementary books, and to make his library the resort of preparatory schools, that in time the principles of democracy and Theo-philan-thropy may take place universally.

In order to allure schools of a moderate and a lower class, he holds out the temptation of an allowance of threepence in every shilling for such books as are published by him. He publishes books with the name of Edward Baldwin, Esq., which are said to be his own writing.

One of these, *Baldwin's Mythology*, has been introduced at the *Charter House*. It is an insidious and dangerous publication. The preface is calculated to mislead well-disposed persons, who may perhaps be too indolent or misjudging to read through the whole work; it professes to exalt the purity and show the superiority of Christianity over the heathen morality taught in the Grecian and Roman mythology, and then through the whole work improperly excites the curiosity of young persons to read the grossest stories on the subject, and artfully hints the wisdom of the morality of the heathen world. The principal works he has published are a Grecian, a Roman, and an English History, all three of the size of Goldsmith's abridgments. In these, every democratic sentiment is printed in italics that they may not fail to present themselves to a child's notice . . . .

Godwin has also among his list Mylius's *English Dictionary*, which has been inadvertently introduced into *Christ's Hospital*.[7]

The "Master of the Rolls in Ireland" (line 14) was John Philpot Curran, who had been appointed to that office in 1806.

7. Quoted in MacCarthy, *Shelley*, pp. 161–163. "Mr. J. Godwin" must have been a misreading of "M. J. [Mary Jane] Godwin." See sc 42 (July 28, 1802), Commentary and fn. 9.

SC 111   WILLIAM GODWIN TO JOSEPH GODWIN, JANUARY 25, 1810

AUTOGRAPH PROMISSORY NOTE signed *W Godwin*, 1 page. Single sheet (3.6 x 8.9 inches).
Wove paper. Watermark: E WILDING| 1805|. Embossed revenue stamp: [device]| I SHILL^G VI PENCE|.
Endorsements.

SC 111                              due 25/28 mar
        £26..13..2                                        No. 41, Skinner Street,
                                                              Jan. 25, 1810
                Two months after date I promise to pay to M<sup>r</sup> Jo. Godwin or
5                   order twenty three pounds thirteen shillings & two pence:
                    value rec<sup>d</sup>

                                                          W Godwin

        [Endorsements, verso]
                Jo<sup>s</sup> Godwin–
                Rec<sup>d</sup> for
10                    Hains & Co
                  Tho<sup>s</sup> Bassett
                      23–13–2


THE above is William Godwin's second note to his brother Joseph. Godwin's Journal for January 25, 1810, records: "Jo G calls."
SEE ALSO SC 61 AND SC 93.


SC 112   WILLIAM GODWIN TO ROBERT HALL, APRIL 5, 1810

AUTOGRAPH PROMISSORY NOTE signed *W Godwin*, 1 page. Single sheet (3.6 x 9 inches).
Laid paper. Embossed revenue stamp: [device]| 1 SHILL<sup>G</sup> VI PENCE|.
Endorsements.

        5 W                          8 June
                                                          No. 41, Skinner Street,
        £7.2.7
                                                              April 5, 1810
5           Two months after date I promise to pay to M<sup>r</sup> Rob<sup>r</sup> Hall or order
                seven pounds 2/7: value rec<sup>d</sup> as per bill
                                                          W Godwin

        [Endorsements, verso]

**Godwin to Hall**                                    *April 5, 1810*

SC 112          *Rob^t Hall*

10

$$R^d\ 11\quad 2\quad 7$$
$$\underline{\qquad\quad 9\quad 7}$$
$$10\quad 13\quad -$$

*Down*

*Jn Fisher*

*H 184*

15          *E Carlile*

G ODWIN, as we have seen, became worried about his health in the spring of 1808, complaining to Dr. Edward Ash of fainting spells.[1] Ash apparently prescribed medication (purchased from Robert Hall, apothecary and surgeon). Godwin seems to have improved for in August he informed Curran that his health had been "indifferent" but was "better."[2] In his letter to David Booth the following February he was again worried;[3] and apparently with justification. In September he noted cryptically (again to Booth) "I have been ill: I am well."[4] The "ill" period must have come between February and September.

The above note[5] shows that the "I am well" of September 1809 was also overly optimistic, for Godwin was again purchasing medicine from Hall in April 1810. Nor was he yet out of the woods. On July 19, 1811, Crabb Robinson recorded that Godwin was ill: "I believe a return of his alarming complaint" (which must refer to the fainting spells).[6]

SEE ALSO SC 61 AND SC 88.

1. SC 88 (June 8, 1808), Commentary.

2. SC 91 (Aug. 19, 1808).

3. SC 99 (Feb. 27, 1809), line 33.

4. SC 105 (Sept. 6, 1809), line 17.

5. The tradesmen to whom Hall passed the note are identifiable from *Kent's Directory* for 1800: J. S. Fisher, "Linen-draper," 3 Holborn Bridge (Hall's shop was on Holborn Hill); E. Carlile, "Wholesale Haberdasher," 11 Bow Lane, Cheapside. (Plan of London, D2, Front Endpapers.) Bow Lane comes between Queen Street and Bread Street.

6. *On Books*, I, 39. On July 31 Robinson noted that Godwin still looked ill.

# The Carl H. Pforzheimer Library

## PERCY BYSSHE SHELLEY

*(August 4, 1792–July 8, 1822)*

### PRINCIPAL WORKS

1810–1811   The Necessity of Atheism

1812   An Address to the Irish People

1812   A Letter to Lord Ellenborough

1812–1813   Queen Mab

1814   A Refutation of Deism

1815   Alastor

1817   A Proposal for Putting Reform to the Vote

1817   Address to the People on the Death of the Princess Charlotte

1817   The Revolt of Islam

1818   Julian and Maddalo

1818   Lines Written among the Euganean Hills

1818–1819   Prometheus Unbound

1819   The Cenci

1819   The Masque of Anarchy

1819–1820   A Philosophical View of Reform

1820   Letter to Maria Gisborne

1820   The Witch of Atlas

1820   Œdipus Tyrannus

1821   Epipsychidion

1821   A Defence of Poetry

1821   Adonais

1821   Hellas

1822   Charles the First

1822   The Triumph of Life

### EARLY LIFE

THE family connections of Mr. Shelley," wrote Leigh Hunt in his *Autobiography*, "belonged to a small party in the House of Commons, itself belonging to another party. They were Whig Aristocrats, voting in the interests of the Duke of Norfolk."[1] The family, however, had been neither aristocrats nor Whigs until the rise of Shelley's grandfather, Sir Bysshe Shelley. Sir Bysshe, born in Newark, New Jersey, in 1752, established the family fortunes by two marriages and made a political alliance with the Duke of Norfolk whereby his son Timothy, father of the poet, became a Member of Parliament. To this seat Timothy's son was intended to succeed. Politics, the Duke informed young Percy Bysshe, "are the proper career for a young man of ability and of your station in life."[2] But the "young man," born in a year in which Godwin was writing *Political Justice* and the French Revolution was rising to its

1. Hunt, *Autobiography*, II, 28.

2. Hogg, *Shelley*, I, 129. Hogg does not name the "duke" who gave Shelley this advice but the context shows that it was Norfolk.

# Shelley and his Circle : Manuscripts

*Percy Bysshe Shelley* **1792–1822**

heights, had other plans. He had soon passed beyond the Whigs into republicanism and beyond republicanism into Godwinian egalitarianism. He wished not to sit in Parliament but to reform it, and ultimately to do away with it.

The influence of Shelley's grandfather upon him is an interesting and puzzling question. That the influence is there is certain. Sir Bysshe, his grandson informs us, was "a complete Atheist."[3] His talk was largely of politics and liberally flavored, one would gather, with denunciations of "bigots" and "tyrants."[4] He was a flamboyant and dominating character, living in a small house in Horsham instead of in his castle, Castle Goring, and mingling in a democratic way — perhaps a relic of his American birth and American mother — with the town folk "in the tap-room of the Swan Inn."[5] But the influence must have been rather indirect than direct for we hear of little contact between grandfather and grandson beyond a story that the grandfather paid for the printing of the grandson's first volume of verses.

Of Sir Bysshe's son Timothy, later Sir Timothy, *The Gentleman's Magazine* wrote that he "possessed, in a high degree, the best qualities of the English country gentleman"; and we have a picture of him by a visitor to the family estates (at Field Place near Horsham in Sussex) as "clad in his yeoman-like garb and tanned leather gaiters."[6] His letters are in accord with the picture. They reveal a man of solid common sense, with a good head for practical detail and the management of affairs, but with little imagination or capacity for abstract reasoning. "Never read a book, Johnnie," he told his second son, "and you will be a rich man."[7] The advice, however, was given only in the bitterness of the disasters attending the first son, disasters which Timothy attributed in large part to reading. Timothy himself had read books — he was an M.A. of Oxford University — and had at first taken a good deal of pride in the talented Percy Bysshe. "My son here," he told Henry Slatter, bookseller of Oxford, "has a literary turn; he is already an author, and do pray indulge

3. Shelley to Elizabeth Hitchener, Jan. 26, 1812.

4. Shelley to Sir Bysshe Shelley, Oct. 13, 1811.

5. [Joseph Gibbons Merle], "A Newspaper Editor's Reminiscences," *Fraser's Magazine*, XXIII (June 1841), 702. See also Medwin, *Shelley*, p. 11.

6. Quoted in White, *Shelley*, I, 14, 12.  7. Quoted, *ibid.*, p. 12.

# The Carl H. Pforzheimer Library

him in his printing freaks."[8] Father and son, although never deeply intimate, were fond of each other; Shelley's sisters tell of his standing vigil anxiously outside his father's door when the good squire was down with an attack of the gout.

Of Shelley's mother surprisingly little is known. Although she is said to have been a gifted letter writer (her sister, wife of John Grove of Fern, Wiltshire, was a painter), her letters do not seem to have survived. From Shelley's accounts of her in his letters she seems to have been an intelligent and liberal-minded woman who had the confidence of her son and who was strongly devoted to him. "Mrs. Shelley often spoke to me of her son," wrote a later visitor to Field Place, "her heart yearned after him with all the fondness of a mother's love."[9] Yet, in all the years of his exile from home, and in his personal troubles — the suicide of Harriet, the deaths of his children — there is no record of Shelley's writing to his mother or receiving a letter from her.

Although Shelley never fulfilled the ambition of his father that he succeed him in Parliament he was brought up in the expectation that he would do so. He was, that is to say, brought up in the Whig creed, and the Whig creed, during these years of war with France, was a surprisingly liberal one: sympathy for the principles of the American and French revolutions; the extension of the franchise (out of a population of 11,000,000 only 11,000 had the vote); the abolition of the rotten boroughs (300 out of 513 members owed their seats to individual "proprietors"); the championing of the cause of the Irish (who were represented by Protestants in an English parliament); a faith that the "mighty changes of the rising world" (to quote Thomas Erskine) would bring about "a happy and glorious consummation."[10] An imaginative youngster imbibing these ideas had not far to step to get to republicanism and Tom Paine or from republicanism to Godwinian egalitarianism. And the young Shelley made both steps.

The seeds of religious dissent were present at Field Place also. "Indeed, his religious opinions were also very lax," wrote Shelley's

8. Henry Slatter to Robert Montgomery, Dec. 13, 1833, Robert Montgomery, *Poetical Works* (London, 1854), p. 442.

9. Captain Kennedy, quoted in Hogg, *Shelley*, II, 152.

10. *Hansard*, XXXIII (1797–1798), 661.

# The Carl H. Pforzheimer Library

cousin, Thomas Medwin, of Timothy, ". . . he possessed no true devotion himself, and inculcated none to his son and heir."[11] He subscribed to a book of Unitarian sermons, signing himself: "A friend to religious liberty."[12]

Shelley's subsequent views were not, therefore, as is often stated, the result of a rebellion against a conservative home. On the contrary the basis for them was laid in that home. Radical views on political subjects and deistic views in religion are present in his earliest works, in the novel *Zastrozzi* and the book of verses, *Original Poetry*, both written before he went to Oxford or had studied *Political Justice*.

His first taste of some of the consequences that might follow such views came when he was little more than an Eton schoolboy. He and his cousin, Harriet Grove, had long been attracted to each other, and had reached an "understanding" approved by both families. The understanding was broken off, we are informed by Harriet's brother Charles, because of "the tone of his letters on speculative subjects," letters which Harriet showed to her father.[13]

At Oxford Shelley met Thomas Jefferson Hogg, son of a northern landowner, who later became his biographer, and who has left us a vivid picture of their first meeting:

At the commencement of Michaelmas term, that is, at the end of October in the year 1810, I happened one day to sit next to a freshman at dinner: it was his first appearance in hall. His figure was slight, and his aspect remarkably youthful, even at our table, where all were very young. He seemed thoughtful and absent. He ate little, and had no acquaintance with anyone. I know not how it was that we fell into conversation, for such familiarity was unusual, and, strange to say, much reserve prevailed in a society where there could not possibly be occasion for any. We have often endeavoured in vain to recollect in what manner our discourse began, and especially by what transition it passed to a subject sufficiently remote from all the associations we were able to trace. The stranger had expressed an enthusiastic admiration for poetical and imaginative works of the German school. I dissented from his criticisms. He upheld the originality of the German writings. I asserted their want of nature.

'What modern literature', said he, 'will you compare to theirs?'

I named the Italian. This roused all his impetuosity; and few, as I soon discovered, were more impetuous in argumentative conversation. So eager was

11. Medwin, *Shelley*, p. 13.                     12. Dowden, *Shelley*, I, 5 fn.
13. Charles Grove to Hellen Shelley, Feb. 16, 1857, Hogg, *Shelley*, II, 155.

# The Carl H. Pforzheimer Library

our dispute that when the servants came to clear the tables, we were not aware that we had been left alone.[14]

Hogg, like Shelley, had questioned the tenets of orthodox religion. From his own and Hogg's writings on the subject Shelley put together and had printed a little pamphlet entitled *The Necessity of Atheism*, by which they did not mean that atheism was necessarily true but that certain arguments logically ("of necessity") seemed to point toward it. These they modestly requested their theological betters to answer. The sequel is also told by Hogg:

It was a fine spring morning on Lady Day, in the year 1811, when I went to Shelley's rooms: he was absent; but before I had collected our books he rushed in. He was terribly agitated. I anxiously inquired what had happened.

'I am expelled,' he said, as soon as he had recovered himself a little, 'I am expelled! I was sent for suddenly a few minutes ago; I went to the common room, where I found our master and two or three of the fellows. The master produced a copy of the little syllabus, and asked me if I were the author of it. He spoke in a rude, abrupt, and insolent tone. I begged to be informed for what purpose he put the question. No answer was given; but the master loudly and angrily repeated, "Are you the author of this book?" If I can judge from your manner, I said, you are resolved to punish me, if I should acknowledge that it is my work. If you can prove that it is, produce your evidence; it is neither just nor lawful to interrogate me in such a case and for such a purpose. Such proceedings would become a court of inquisitors, but not free men in a free country. "Do you choose to deny that this is your composition?" the master reiterated in the same rude and angry voice.' Shelley complained much of his violent and ungentlemanlike deportment, saying, 'I have experienced tyranny and injustice before, and I well know what vulgar violence is; but I never met with such unworthy treatment. I told him calmly, but firmly, that I was determined not to answer any questions respecting the publication on the table. He immediately repeated his demand; I persisted in my refusal; and he said furiously, "Then you are expelled; and I desire you will quit the college early to-morrow morning at the latest." One of the fellows took up two papers and handed one of them to me; here it is.' He produced a regular sentence of expulsion, drawn up in due form, under the seal of the college.

Shelley was full of spirit and courage, frank and fearless; but he was likewise shy, unpresuming, and eminently sensitive. I have been with him in many trying situations of his after-life, but I never saw him so deeply shocked and so cruelly agitated as on this occasion. A nice sense of honour shrinks from the

14. Hogg, *Shelley*, I, 46.

# Shelley and his Circle : Manuscripts

most distant touch of disgrace — even from the insults of those men whose contumely can bring no shame. He sat on the sofa, repeating, with convulsive vehemence, the words, 'Expelled, expelled!' his head shaking with emotion, and his whole frame quivering.[15]

As does not seem to have been noted, Shelley could not answer the Master's question because he had not alone written the pamphlet. Hogg had written part of it. And to answer would have been to implicate his friend. Immediately on hearing the news from Shelley, Hogg also went before the college dons and also was expelled.

The angry and troubled air of men, assembled to commit injustice according to established forms, was then new to me; but a native instinct told me, as soon as I entered the room, that it was an affair of party; that whatever could conciliate the favour of patrons was to be done without scruple; and whatever could tend to impede preferment was to be brushed away without remorse.

The next day Shelley and Hogg left for London on the stagecoach and a long period of negotiations between Shelley and his father began, Timothy Shelley being upset almost to the point of distraction by the disgrace of expulsion. Even as these negotiations were going on, however, a more serious crisis was in the making. Shelley had become interested in a school friend of his sister Hellen's, Harriet Westbrook, the daughter of a wealthy coffee house owner; in August they eloped to Scotland.

With this elopement a new chapter in Shelley's life opens, and with it we end the second volume of this edition, the letters and other documents presented (including the diary of Harriet Grove) illustrating the germinal period in Shelley's life and thought: his early literary plans; his developing ideas on religion, politics, philosophy, society; the writing of *The Necessity of Atheism*; Hogg's misrepresentations of the relationship between himself and Elizabeth Shelley and between Shelley and Harriet Grove; the domestic crisis following the expulsion; the development of the romance with Harriet Westbrook.

Following the elopement Shelley went to Ireland to assist in the movement for Catholic Emancipation and the severing of the Act of

---

15. *Ibid.*, pp. 168–169. Hogg's account is colored by his concept of Shelley and needs to be compared with others (as given, for instance, in Edmund Blunden's "Shelley Is Expelled," *On Shelley*, Oxford University Press, 1938). But there is, as usual, a certain core of truth in Hogg's narrative and it has the virtue of dramatic vividness.

# The Carl H. Pforzheimer Library

Union between Great Britain and Ireland (a union which Byron referred to as "the union of the shark with his prey").[16] He there addressed a large public meeting at which Daniel O'Connell was the principal speaker, published *An Address to the Irish People*, and established contacts with various Irish nationalists. These experiences moved him from an obsessive anticlericalism toward social reform. The first product of the change, *A Letter to Lord Ellenborough* (1812), was a vigorous plea for freedom of the press. The second, his poem *Queen Mab* (1812–1813), surveyed the social evils of the past and present and depicted a "gradual renovation"[17] in the future (not, as is usually stated, a sudden change to the millennium; Shelley, no more than did Godwin, believed in social miracles).

It was while writing *Queen Mab* that Shelley first became acquainted with Godwin (in October 1812). It was nearly two years later (July 28, 1814) that he eloped with Godwin's daughter Mary; and it was more than two years after this elopement that Harriet Shelley committed suicide (November 8, 1816). (Harriet's pathetic suicide letter we shall present in a later volume.) The following March (1817), although he and Mary were then married, he was deprived by law of the custody of his children by Harriet (Charles and Ianthe), and the following year he left England for Italy.

In Italy his life was comparatively uneventful. After a year and more of wandering, during which he and Mary lost two children, Clara and William, and a third, Percy Florence, was born, they settled in Pisa. There they were joined by Byron, Trelawny, Jane and Edward Williams, and others to make a brilliant intellectual circle, Byron writing on *Don Juan*, Shelley writing *Epipsychidion*, *Adonais*, and *Hellas*. It was as a result of his efforts to have Byron establish a new journal — *The Liberal* — to battle the Tory *Quarterly* that Shelley met his death. He had brought Leigh Hunt to Italy to assist in the scheme and while returning from an editorial conference with Hunt and Byron was drowned in the Bay of Spezzia (July 8, 1822) along with Edward Williams. He was twenty-nine years of age. No other English poet had by so early an age produced such a body of work. Had Shakespeare died at twenty-nine, he would have

16. *Hansard*, XXII (1812), 651.

17. *Queen Mab*, VIII, 143. In a later volume of this edition we shall present a copy of *Queen Mab* annotated by Shelley to form the manuscript for another poem based on *Queen Mab*.

# Shelley and his Circle : Manuscripts

been known only as one of the most promising Elizabethans, inferior to Marlowe or Jonson, but somewhat above Greene and Lyly.

## POET AND THINKER

The letters of Shelley which we present in this volume are, it must be remembered, the letters of a very young man. When he wrote the first of them (sc 113) he was still an Eton schoolboy, and when he wrote the last (sc 176) he had just turned nineteen.

Most people on attaining maturity look back on their adolescence with filtering vision; and there is a general tendency to depict youth not as it is but as one would like it to be. For Shelley, however, no such comfortable illusion is possible; many of his youthful letters have survived in manuscript with all their romantic schemings and enthusiasms intact. We cannot, of course, take such letters as representative of Shelley (although critics unfriendly to him have done so) but, on the other hand, we have to recognize that through their general juvenile patterns there are discernible the seeds of the mind that was to produce *Prometheus Unbound* and *The Cenci, A Defence of Poetry* and *A Philosophical View of Reform.*

It is precisely this latter point that Hogg and some other biographers omit. Hogg, deft though he is at humorous, semifictional narrative, has little understanding of Shelley's thought or poetry. His tone is that of a biographer of a minor eccentric rather than of a major poet.

Although in the nineteenth century such Shelley admirers as George Bernard Shaw, Thomas Hardy, H. Buxton Forman, H. S. Salt, and William Michael Rossetti regarded Shelley as an intellectual poet, the concept of him as a pure lyricist later grew to dominate the scene and fed the complaints of the "new critics" (who attack Shelley because he fails to write in the style of John Donne). Now it is true, of course, that Shelley wrote lyrics, in fact, some of the finest lyrics in the language, including "To a Skylark" and "Ode to the West Wind." But to describe him as a "lyric poet" and leave it at that would be like describing Shakespeare as a sonneteer. Shelley was not primarily a lyric poet but a philosophical poet — as Carl Grabo pointed out more than two decades ago in *The Magic Plant: The Growth of Shelley's Thought*:

# The Carl H. Pforzheimer Library

*Percy Bysshe Shelley*                                    1792–1822

An overstress of emotion has been the curse of Shelleyan criticism. Shelley the thinker is distorted and obscured in the haze of emotional speculation. He is thereby wholly falsified, for if ever a man lived the intellectual life and was less the victim of unreason and blind emotion it was Shelley. He thought passionately. For him a beautiful idea was as exciting as is a beautiful woman or the thought of an illicit amour to some of his critics. Impassioned thinkers constitute but a small part of the human race, the part of greatest importance to be sure, but misunderstood, derided, hated, and crucified by the rest of mankind. It will be incomprehensible to many people that Shelley was not chiefly preoccupied with clouds, skylarks, and beautiful dream maidens; that he spent vastly more time and thought upon questions of practical politics, and upon the problems of good and evil, and of free will and determinism. Shelley's was a poetic mind but also a philosophic mind, realizing that ideal of poet-philosopher which he most admired in the great minds of the past.[18]

Both Shelley's range as a "poet-philosopher" and the "modern" applicability of his thought are greater than is commonly supposed. This underestimation is due partly to that "overstress of emotion" which characterizes the textbook and anthology accounts and partly to a neglect of Shelley's prose works.

Central to his thinking, as to that of Hunt and Godwin, is the humanitarianism of the period, a humanitarianism the spirit of which is concentrated in the two famous lines in *Julian and Maddalo* —

> Me — who am as a nerve o'er which do creep
> The else unfelt oppressions of this earth —

and which found expression in his philosophy of love. This philosophy anticipates in some respects such modern psychological theories as Freud's on the libido; for Shelley conceives of love as a unifying force with widely variant manifestations, biological, psychological, and social — sexual love, romantic love, friendship, love of humanity, love of nature:

Man is in his wildest state a social being: a certain degree of civilization and refinement ever produces the want of sympathies still more intimate and complete; and the gratification of the senses is no longer all that is sought in sexual connexion. It soon becomes a very small part of that profound and complicated sentiment, which we call Love, which is rather the universal thirst for a communion not merely of the senses, but of our whole nature, intellectual, imaginative and sensitive; and which, when individualised, becomes an imperious

18. Grabo, *The Magic Plant*, p. vii.

necessity, only to be satisfied by the complete or partial, actual or supposed, fulfilment of its claims. This want grows more powerful in proportion to the developement which our nature recieves [*sic*] from civilization; for man never ceases to be a social being. The sexual impulse, which is only one, and often a small part of those claims, serves, from its obvious and external nature, as a kind of type or expression of the rest, as common basis, an acknowledged and visible link. Still it is a claim which even derives a strength not its own from the accessory circumstances which surround it, and one which our nature thirsts to satisfy.[19]

This is an extraordinary passage to have been written in the early nineteenth century. Shelley does not make the dichotomy customary at least since the troubadours, and first openly challenged in the present century by D. H. Lawrence, among others, between the biological and romantic aspects of love. The "sexual impulse" is "a type or expression of the rest." In another passage he speaks of the sexual act as "the act which ought always to be the link and type of the highest emotions of our nature."[20] If Shelley differs from some modern psychologists in regarding the biological aspect of love as subordinate to the total love pattern, others (for instance, Erich Fromm) are turning toward this concept.

Love, for Shelley, however, extends beyond sexual and even beyond all individual personal relationships:

> *Thou* demandest what is love? It is that powerful attraction towards all that we conceive, or fear, or hope beyond ourselves, when we find within our own thoughts the chasm of an insufficient void, and seek to awaken in all things that are, a community with what we experience within ourselves . . . This is Love. This is the bond and the sanction which connects not only man with man, but with every thing which exists.[21]

> That Light whose smile kindles the Universe,
> That Beauty in which all things work and move,
> That Benediction which the eclipsing Curse
> Of birth can quench not, that sustaining Love
> Which through the web of being blindly wove
> By man and beast and earth and air and sea,
> Burns bright or dim, as each are mirrors of

19. *A Discourse on the Manners of the Antient Greeks Relative to the Subject of Love*, Notopoulos, *Platonism*, pp. 408-409.

20. *Ibid.*, p. 410.                    21. *On Love*, Shelley, *Complete Works*, VI, 201.

# The Carl H. Pforzheimer Library

> The fire for which all thirst; now beams on me,
> Consuming the last clouds of cold mortality.[22]

The "eclipsing Curse of birth" is death; the great counter to death is love, love which is part of the "web of being," both in man and in nature.

This philosophy of love did not blind Shelley to present evils. On the contrary, it gave him more insight by holding up a vision of the possible as against the actual. His general views on these matters, his social philosophy, received their most complete expression in his long prose work, *A Philosophical View of Reform.* Like Godwin — and Rousseau — he did not believe that evil was inherent in humanity but that it arose from corrigible social causes. Like Godwin — and Condorcet — he believed that this evil had been diminishing, that society had been progressing, and that it would progress further. He did not, however, view this progress, as did Godwin, primarily as the result of "reason." History, he believed, had been dominated by a struggle between despotism and liberty; in this struggle, liberty, although many times defeated, had always arisen again, and arisen stronger than before. There had been a clear line of progress since "the dissolution of the Roman Empire": the Italian city states, the Puritan revolution in England, the American revolution:

> The system of government in the United States of America was the first practical illustration of the new philosophy. Sufficiently remote, it will be confessed, from the accuracy of ideal excellence is that representative system which will soon cover the extent of that vast Continent. But it is scarcely less remote from the insolent and contaminating tyrannies under which, with some limitation of these terms as regards England, Europe groaned at the period of the successful rebellion of America. America holds forth the victorious example of an immensely populous, and as far as the external arts of life are concerned, a highly civilized community administered according to republican forms.[23]

Following the American revolution came the French, an even greater upheaval:

> The just and successful Revolt of America corresponded with a state of public opinion in Europe of which it was the first result. The French Revolution was the second.

22. *Adonais*, lines 478–486.

23. *A Philosophical View of Reform*, Shelley, *Complete Works*, VII, 10–11.

# Shelley and his Circle : Manuscripts

*Percy Bysshe Shelley*                                                1792–1822

Connected with these political upheavals were social and economic phenomena of a new and complex kind (thrown into relief by the economic crisis following the Napoleonic wars):

The mechanical sciences attained to a degree of perfection which, though obscurely foreseen by Lord Bacon, it had been accounted madness to have prophesied in a preceding age. Commerce was pursued with a perpetually increasing vigour, and the same area of the Earth was perpetually compelled to furnish more and more subsistence. The means and sources of knowledge were thus increased together with knowledge itself, and the instruments of knowledge. The benefit of this increase of the powers of man became, in consequence of the inartificial forms into which society came to be distributed, an instrument of his additional evil. The capabilities of happiness were increased, and applied to the augmentation of misery. Modern society is thus a[n] engine assumed to be for useful purposes, whose force is by a system of subtle mechanism augmented to the highest pitch, but which, instead of grinding corn or raising water acts against itself and is perpetually wearing away or breaking to pieces the wheels of which it is composed.

Following the French Revolution, liberty had again been restricted — by Napoleon, first, then by Castlereagh and Metternich with their Quadruple Alliance. But now, in his own day, a new rise of liberty was beginning, in Germany, Spain (1819), Italy (1820), and Greece (1821).

We find the same concepts also in the poetry; for instance, in the Chorus to liberty in *Hellas*:

> From age to age, from man to man,
>   It lived; and lit from land to land
>   Florence, Albion, Switzerland.
> Then night fell; and, as from night,
> Re-assuming fiery flight,
> From the West swift Freedom came,
>   Against the course of heaven and doom,
> A second sun array'd in flame,
>   To burn, to kindle, to illume.
> From far Atlantis its young beams
> Chased the shadows and the dreams.
> France, with all her sanguine steams,
>   Hid, but quench'd it not; again
>   Through clouds its shafts of glory rain
>   From utmost Germany to Spain.

# The Carl H. Pforzheimer Library

The new resurgence of liberty would surpass the American and French revolutions even as they had surpassed the Puritan revolution (a prediction partially fulfilled in 1830 and 1848). In time the (continuing) expansion of liberty would result in the egalitarian society envisaged by Godwin:

> Thrones, altars, judgment-seats, and prisons; wherein
> And beside which, by wretched men were borne
> Sceptres, tiaras, swords, and chains, and tomes
> Of reasoned wrong, glozed on by ignorance,
> Were like those monstrous and barbaric shapes,
> The ghosts of a no more remembered fame . . . .
> The loathsome mask has fallen, the Man remains, —
> Sceptreless, free, uncircumscribed, — but man:
> Equal, unclassed, tribeless and nationless,
> Exempt from awe, worship, degree, the King
> Over himself.[24]

This evolutionary vision of history provided the inspiration for Shelley's first major poem, *Queen Mab*, and supplied the frame on which was hung the lengthy narrative of *The Revolt of Islam*. It animated alike his masterpiece, *Prometheus Unbound*, and the three great odes, "Ode to Liberty," "Ode to Naples," and "Ode to the West Wind."

Shelley, like his own favorite philosophical poets, Dante and Milton, was ever consumed by the mysteries of Man's relations to the universe; and these, too, he converted into poetry, in "Hymn to Intellectual Beauty" —

> The awful shadow of some unseen Power
>    Floats tho' unseen among us —

in *The Triumph of Life*, in "Mont Blanc," in "The Cloud," in *The Sensitive Plant*, in *Adonais*:

> The One remains, the many change and pass;
> Heaven's light forever shines, Earth's shadows fly;
> Life, like a dome of many-coloured glass,
> Stains the white radiance of Eternity,
> Until Death tramples it to fragments.

24. *Prometheus Unbound*, III, iv, 164-169; 193-197.

# Shelley and his Circle : Manuscripts

In other poems, *Alastor*, *Julian and Maddalo*, *Epipsychidion*, he searched into his own mind and life, hoping there to find truths for other men also —

> Mind from its object differs most in this:
> Evil from good; misery from happiness;
> The baser from the nobler; the impure
> And frail, from what is clear and must endure.
> If you divide suffering and dross, you may
> Diminish till it is consumed away;
> If you divide pleasure and love and thought,
> Each part exceeds the whole.

As is insufficiently recognized he produced narrative verse with an extraordinary range of effects and styles, from the intensity of the final passage of *Epipsychidion* or the Madman's soliloquy in *Julian and Maddalo* to the supple ease of the *Letter to Maria Gisborne* with its realistic vignettes:

> But what see you beside? A shabby stand
> Of Hackney-coaches — a brick house or wall
> Fencing some lonely court, white with the scrawl
> Of our unhappy politics; — or worse —
> A wretched woman reeling by, whose curse
> Mixed with the watchman's, partner of her trade,
> You must accept in place of serenade.

In the year 1819 Shelley tried a new medium, the drama. His play *The Cenci*, declared by Leigh Hunt to be "the greatest dramatic production of the day," failed to find a producer (although as a book it went into a second edition). In the present century, however, it has begun to come into its own and has been produced in Europe (Paris, Moscow, Prague), in the United States, and in London:

Although the performance lasted three solid hours, with only one short break, the audience listened with rapt attention from start to finish, and, exhausted as it must have been by the effort required to grasp Shelley's magnificent imagery, it would not leave until everybody had been called again and again, and Miss Thorndike, looking positively worn out after playing the long trying part of Beatrice, had come forward to make a speech.[25]

25. *The Graphic*, Nov. 18, 1922, quoted in Kenneth N. Cameron and Horst Frenz, "The Stage History of Shelley's *The Cenci*," *PMLA*, LX (December 1945), 1085.

# The Carl H. Pforzheimer Library

*Percy Bysshe Shelley*                                            1792–1822

In 1821 Shelley attempted still another field, that of literary philosophy. Although not a professional critic, as were Hunt and Hazlitt, he had previously written some criticism (in reviews and prefaces), but with *A Defence of Poetry* he entered the realm of Wordsworth's Preface to *Lyrical Ballads* and Coleridge's *Biographia Litereria* — the analysis not so much of individual works as of the nature of literature itself. This analysis he continued also in his Prefaces, for instance, in that to *Prometheus Unbound*, where, perhaps most concisely, he discusses the relationship of literature to history:

The peculiar style of intense and comprehensive imagery which distinguishes the modern literature of England, has not been, as a general power, the product of the imitation of any particular writer. The mass of capabilities remains at every period materially the same; the circumstances which awaken it to action perpetually change. If England were divided into forty republics, each equal in population and extent to Athens, there is no reason to suppose but that, under institutions not more perfect than those of Athens, each would produce philosophers and poets equal to those who (if we except Shakespeare) have never been surpassed. We owe the great writers of the golden age of our literature to that fervid awakening of the public mind which shook to dust the oldest and most oppressive form of the Christian religion. We owe Milton to the progress and development of the same spirit: the sacred Milton was, let it ever be remembered, a republican, and a bold inquirer into morals and religion. The great writers of our own age are, we have reason to suppose, the companions and forerunners of some unimagined change in our social condition, or the opinions which cement it.

The range of Shelley's prose is essentially the same as that of the poetry: social philosophy, history, metaphysics, ethics, narrative. One large group revolves around social and political subjects: another parliamentary reform essay in addition to *A Philosophical View of Reform*: three works of protest against social injustice: *A Letter to Lord Ellenborough* (a plea for freedom of the press); a defense of the prosecuted radical publisher, Richard Carlile, in the form of an open letter to *The Examiner; Address to the People on the Death of the Princess Charlotte*, which protested the execution of three workmen who had been incited to Luddite violence by the government labor spy known as Oliver (a work of extraordinary vigor of style):

So soon as it was plainly seen that the demands of the people for a free representation must be conceded if some intimidation and prejudice were not conjured up, a conspiracy of the most horrible atrocity was laid in train. It is impossible to know how far the higher members of the government are involved in the guilt of their infernal agents. It is impossible to know how numerous or how active they have been, or by what false hopes they are yet inflaming the untutored multitude to put their necks under the axe and into the halter. But thus much is known, that so soon as the whole nation lifted up its voice for parliamentary reform, spies were sent forth. These were selected from the most worthless and infamous of mankind, and dispersed among the multitude of famished and illiterate labourers. It was their business if they found no discontent to create it. It was their business to find victims, no matter whether right or wrong. It was their business to produce upon the public an impression, that if any attempt to attain national freedom, or to diminish the burthens of debt and taxation under which we groan, were successful, the starving multitude would rush in, and confound all orders and distinctions, and institutions and laws, in common ruin. The inference with which they were required to arm the ministers was, that despotic power ought to be eternal.[26]

Another group of works deals with philosophical questions: *A Refutation of Deism; On a Future State; On the Devil and Devils; On Life*:

Life and the world, or whatever we call that which we are and feel, is an astonishing thing. The mist of familiarity obscures from us the wonder of our being. We are struck with admiration at some of its transient modifications, but it is itself the great miracle. What are changes of empires, the wreck of dynasties, with the opinions which supported them; what is the birth and the extinction of religious and of political systems, to life? . . . We are born, and our birth is unremembered, and our infancy remembered but in fragments; we live on, and in living we lose the apprehension of life.[27]

In *Speculations on Metaphysics* he ventures into the problems of the identity and analysis of the self:

If it were possible that a person should give a faithful history of his being, from the earliest epochs of his recollection, a picture would be presented such as the world has never contemplated before. A mirror would be held up to all men in which they might behold their own recollections, and, in dim perspective, their shadowy hopes and fears, — all that they dare not, or that daring and desiring, they could not expose to the open eyes of day. But thought can with difficulty visit the intricate and winding chambers which it inhabits. It is like a river whose rapid and perpetual stream flows outwards; — like one in dread

26. Shelley, *Complete Works*, VI, 79–80.        27. *Ibid.*, pp. 193–194.

who speeds through the recesses of some haunted pile, and dares not look behind.[28]

Still another group of works discusses ethical and religious questions: *Essay on Christianity; Speculations on Morals; A Discourse on the Manners of the Antient Greeks Relative to the Subject of Love,* which contains one of Shelley's most eloquent passages on the social status of women:

Among the antient Greeks the male sex, one half of the human race, recieved [*sic*] the highest cultivation and refinement; whilst the other, so far as intellect is concerned, were educated as slaves . . . The gradations in the history of man present us with a slow improvement in this respect. The Roman women held a higher consideration in society, and were esteemed almost as the equal partners with their husbands in the regulation of domestic economy and the education of their children. The practices and customs of modern Europe are essentially different from and incomparably less pernicious than either, however remote from what an enlightened mind cannot fail to desire as the future destiny of human beings.[29]

The notorious homosexuality of the ancient Athenians, he believed, was not primarily psychological but was the consequence of the social subordination of women: "Among the Greeks these feelings, being thus deprived of their natural object, sought a compensation and a substitute."

In reading Shelley's prose, even more than in reading his poetry, one feels that of all the great English poets of the past (not excluding Blake or Byron) he was the most modern in his social thinking. It has been said that he was neglected by his age; but as Newman White pointed out, it was not so much that his age neglected him as that it was afraid of him. In Shelley's day as in ours there were those who wished to have certain problems regarded as settled and others as taboo; but Shelley regarded little as settled and nothing as taboo. He questioned everything: political and parental authority, marriage and divorce laws, Christian theology, the relation of sex to love, the nature of the self. Such questioning was profoundly disturbing to a still largely feudal society which tolerated rotten boroughs, approved of paternal absolutism, had virtually no divorce procedures, nodded benignly at romantic love but considered sex unmentionable, barred from the government, the universities, and the professions all except members of the Established Church, and

28. *Ibid.,* VII, 64.   29. Notopoulos, *Platonism,* p. 409.

preferred to keep psychological analysis on a purely sentimental level. Shelley's questions were all the more disturbing because he reached out beyond the immediate issue. The limitations of the franchise led him to consider the uses of government in general; the marriage and divorce laws provoked inquiries into the nature of marriage; and everything drove his mind to the problem of the meaning of history, until, as George Bernard Shaw commented, we find him "anticipating also the modern view that sociological problems are being slowly worked out independently of the conscious interference of man."[30] It was this desire to seek out regardless of consequence the final value and nature of things that led Shelley to anticipate later trends of interest and thought. The things that he refused to consider as settled are, after all, still with us — and still unsettled. His thinking does not, of course, always run along the same lines as ours, but it is surprising how frequently it does; and his suggestions — even when he is wrong — are often startling in their individual insights. Furthermore, he was able to express his philosophy not only in the reasoned analysis of prose but also, and primarily, in the imaginative synthesis of poetry.

K.N.C.

30. *Note Book of the Shelley Society* (London, 1888), p. 31.

SC 113   P. B. SHELLEY TO EDWARD FERGUS GRAHAM, MAY 20, 1810

AL signed *P B Shelley*, 4 pages. Double sheet, 4^to (8.8 x 7.1 inches). Laid paper. Watermark: c WILMOTT| 1808|. Seal (trace only): ?wax, red. Postmarks: 1. (mileage stamp): ETON| 26|; 2. (morning duty stamp, London): c| 21 MY 21| 1810|.

PROVENANCE: John Davies (Puttick, Sept. 9, 1851, lot 232); Mr. Marlow; H. Buxton Forman; Harry B. Smith. *De Ricci 7* (p. 88).

—— *May 20, 1810.*

*My dear Graham* –

    *It is never my custom to make new friends whom I cannot own to my old ones, and though I may be very far gone in Romance, I am not yet so*
5 *far, over head and ears in heroics, but that I have knowledge enough of the*

**Shelley to Graham**                                                        *May 20, 1810*

SC 113    *world, to percieve that no disinterested motive can lead a man to enter into*
*a friendship with another with whose temper, capacity and talents he is most*
*certainly ignorant. If he takes me for any one whose character I have drawn*
*in Zastrozzi he is mistaken quite ——*

10    *The words as far as I can recollect after the crayons, were –*
*"I beg leave, Sir, to take this opportunity of offering my thanks for your*
*very great civility" I am &c – —— Now if there was any thing in this*
*sentence, merely expressive of my gratitude for his politeness as one gentle-*
*man to another; if there was any thing I say which could authorize the*

15    *very sentimental and unexpected answer, I am willing to confess myself to*
*blame —— Believe me most thankful for your advice concerning it, & that I*
*take it unreservedly, for however cautious I may be in contracting new friend-*
*ships, it shall never be said but that I am faithful to my old ones. How am to*
*answer him, will you tell me that too – – . . I am certainly always the sport*

20    *of ex<        >dinary and unprecedente< > circumstances! I wonder if*
*every one that writes a romance draws such a train of eccentric events after*
*him — –*
*The crayons will do very well,   will you pay Merle for them —   I wish you*
*would come to Eton, but do not put yourself out of your way, and we will*

25    *settle.*

*Adieu   Yours faithfully*
*P B Shelley ——*

*I act unlike every other mortal enough in all conscience, without seeking for*
*more Quixotish adventures —— such as contracting heroic sentiments –*

30    *Heavens! if I had <u>condescended</u> as he calls it what a long letter I should*
*have had! by to-day's Post —*

[Address, page 4]
*Edward Fergus Graham Esq*
*(29) Vine Street*
*Piccadilly*

35    *London*

line 5. *in:* Shelley apparently started to write *a,*   line 6. *percieve* (sic)
then elongated and dotted it.            line 7. *with whose* (sic)

# Shelley and his Circle : Manuscripts

**Shelley to Graham**                                        **May 20, 1810**

SC 113

line 11. "*I beg . . . civility.*" Shelley has begun each line in the manuscript with quotes: "*I beg,* "opportunity, "*for your.*

line 13. *gentleman:* The second *e* is dotted (as also in *sentimental* below). Nevertheless, it is clearly an *e* and not an *i*. Shelley does not always seem to have dotted his *i*'s with each word but with a group of words and sometimes in his haste did not note which were *i*'s and which *e*'s.

line 18. am [I] *to*

line 19. The second dash is written through a half-formed letter.

line 20. *ex<traor>dinary*

line 21. *a train:* Shelley apparently began to write *an.*

line 33. Shelley places the (*29*) in the lower left corner of the address space opposite *London.*

THE above was one of a small group of letters by Shelley to his boyhood friend, Edward Fergus Graham (?1787–?1852), that were sold in London in 1851, perhaps by Graham himself or members of his family.[1] At the time of writing the letter Shelley was only seventeen and in his final year at Eton. He entered Oxford in the fall.

Graham, "the son of a person in the army, had, when very young, displayed great musical talent, and had by chance attracted the notice of the father of [Percy] Bysshe Shelley. Mr. Timothy Shelley undertook to provide for the education of Graham, and took him into his house, where he was treated as a member of the family."[2] William Michael Rossetti remembered him as visiting his father in about 1845. "He was a musician, and I suppose a teacher of music."[3] That Rossetti was correct is shown by the fact that the London *Post Office Directory* for 1843 lists an Edward Graham, a "teacher of singing."[4] A death notice of an

1. A verse letter from Shelley to Graham in The Berg Collection of The New York Public Library bears the notation: "Percy Bysshe Shelley to Mr. Graham. This came from the Graham family." Hence, the Graham family preserved manuscripts. As the above letter was first put on the market in 1851 and Graham apparently did not die until 1852 (see Commentary, below), it may be that he himself arranged the sale of 1851 (noted in de Ricci, p. 86).

2. [Joseph Gibbons Merle], "A Newspaper Editor's Reminiscences," *Fraser's Magazine*, XXIII (June 1841), 700. On Merle, see Commentary, below. Merle's source was probably Graham himself. That Graham was, as is apparently implied, brought up at Field Place and there "treated as a member of the family" seems doubtful. Certainly Shelley's letters to him do not indicate so intimate a relationship.

3. Quoted in Shelley, *Complete Works*, VIII, xxiv.

4. His address is given as 21 Dover Street. He is listed also in 1849, 1851, and 1852 (at 160 Albany Street, as a "professor of singing"). But he is not in the next directory available to us, namely 1860. As a young man Graham was a pupil of Joseph Woelfl (1772–1812), a well-known Austrian musician then living in England. Woelfl is listed among the celebrities in a contemporary tourist guidebook to London. (J. Feltham, *The Picture of London for 1809,* pp. 254–256.) See *Grove's Dictionary of Music and Musicians.* If Timothy Shelley paid for Graham's instruction by so famous a teacher as Woelfl he must have had considerable regard for him.

# The Carl H. Pforzheimer Library

SC 113  Edward Graham at Worth Hall, Sussex, appeared in *The Gentleman's Magazine* for June 1852.[5] As Worth was only a few miles from the Shelley family estate at Field Place and was the site of another Shelley estate,[6] we can presume that this death notice was indeed that of Shelley's friend.

The identity of the "Merle" mentioned in the above letter (line 23) has long been a puzzle to Shelley scholars. Newman I. White has argued that he was Joseph Gibbons Merle, who later became editor of *The Globe* and *Galignani's Messenger*.[7] At the time of the above letter he was a young clerk at Ackerman's art and music store. Some thirty-two years later he described his first meeting with Shelley in Graham's rooms in London:

Shelley had been frequently described to me by his admiring friend Graham as a very superior being — as a poet, as a philosopher. Shelley, I knew, had already published several effusions which had attracted considerable notice; I was the poor parent of one solitary production, and that a string of wretched verses in an ephemeral publication. My pride dreaded humiliation; and such was the effect of the contrast which I had made in my own mind between Shelley and myself, that when Graham, who received me at the door of the house in which he lodged, opened the door of the room on the first floor, where Shelley was waiting for me, my legs trembled with nervous agitation. But short indeed was the suffering inflicted upon me by the terrors of my imagination, and the absurd pride with which I had in vain endeavoured to arm myself. The impressive eye of the young poet beamed upon me in all the radiance imparted by his benevolent heart; he grasped my hand with the fervour of old acquaintance, and in a second we were friends.

I have no *technica memoria* to assist me in a description of our first interview. I remember, however, that we passed three hours in free and unrestrained conversation. Shelley discoursed much of literature, and urged me to persevere in my poetical wanderings.[8]

It was Merle's dread of "humiliation" which led to the writing of the above letter. Shelley had taken advantage of the fact that Merle

5. Shelley, *Complete Works*, VIII, xxiii–xxiv.

6. Mark Antony Lower, *A Compendious History of Sussex* (London, 1870), II, 274; Ingpen, *Shelley in England*, pp. 2, 3.

7. White, *Shelley*, I, 48–50, 574–575. Merle is listed in Boase, *Modern English Biography*. The *CBEL* notes that he edited *The Globe* from 1825 to 1830. In 1817–1818 he edited *The White Dwarf*. As this periodical was a Tory answer to the Radical *Black Dwarf*, Merle and Shelley must have been diametrically opposed in their social and political views.

8. *Fraser's Magazine*, XXIII (June 1841), 701.

SC 113 worked in a store that sold art supplies to have him purchase some crayons (to be given as a present to Harriet Grove).[9] Merle had apparently felt that the young aristocrat had been condescending (line 30) in his reply and had complained to Graham. Graham had written to Shelley; and the above letter is Shelley's answer. Shelley denies that he has "*condescended*." He has done no more than write an ordinary note of thanks (line 13).

Merle knew that Shelley had published several "effusions." Of these, we gather from the above letter (lines 4, 9, 21), the one that most impressed Merle was the "romance" *Zastrozzi.* The "character" (line 8) with whom Shelley is denying personal identity is probably Verezzi, a gloomy, romantic figure who is put upon and fooled by everyone.

9. That the crayons were for Harriet Grove is clear from Shelley's next letter to Graham, May 29, 1810: "I had a letter from Harriet this morning in which she tells me the crayons do very well." Harriet's skill as an artist received recognition in *Original Poetry* by Victor and Cazire ("From Miss —— to Miss ——," lines 33–38).

SC 114 ELIZABETH SHELLEY, *COLD COLD IS THE BLAST*, JULY AND AUGUST 1810

MS. (transcribed by P. B. Shelley), 3¾ pages. Double sheet, 4^to (9.3 x 7.3 inches). Wove paper. Watermark: 1808|. Octagonal embossed stamp: [crown]| BATH|.

PROVENANCE: Thomas Jefferson Hogg; John Ewer Jefferson Hogg (Sotheby, July 27, 1922, lot 335).

> Cold cold is the blast when December is howling
>  Cold are the damps on a dying mans brow
> Stern are the seas when the wild waves are rolling
>  And sad the grave where a loved one lies low
> 5 But colder is scorn from the being who loved thee
> More stern is the sneer from the friend who has proved thee
> More sad are the tears when these sorrows have moved thee
>  Which mixed with groans, anguish & wild madness flow.

**Shelley, Cold cold is the blast**                    *July and August* 1810

SC 114   *And ah! poor Louisa has felt all this horror*
10         *Full long the fallen victim contended with fate*
          *Till a destitute outcast abandoned to sorrow*
             *She sought her babe's food at her ruiner's gate*
          *Another had charmed the remorseless betrayer*
          *He turned callous aside from her moans & her prayer*
15        *She said nothing but wringing the wet from her hair*
             *Crossed the dark mountain side tho the hour it was late*

          *'Twas on the dark summit of huge Penmanmawr*
             *That the form of the wasted Louisa reclined,*
          *She shrieked to the ravens that croaked from afar*
20           *And she sighed to the gusts of the wild sweeping wind*
                        *clouds*
          *I call not yon ~~rocks~~ where the thunder peals rattle*
          *I call not yon rocks where the elements battle*
             *But thee perjured Henry I call thee unkind*

25        *Then she wreathed in her hair the wild flowers of the mountain*
             *And deliriously laughing a garland entwined*
          *She bedewed it with tears, then she hung oer the fountain*
             *And laving it, cast it a prey to the wind*
          *"Ah! go" she exclaimed "where the tempest is yelling*
30        *'Tis unkind to be cast on the sea that is swelling*
          *But I left a pityless outcast my dwelling*
             *My garments are torn so they say is my mind"*

          *Not long lived Louisa – but over her grave*
             *Waved the desolate form of a storm-blasted yew*
35        *Around it no demons or ghosts dare to rave*
             *But spirits of Peace steep her slumbers in dew*
          *Then stay thy swift steps mid the dark mountain heather*
          *Tho chill blow the wind & severe be the weather,*
          *For perfidy traveller cannot bereave her*
40           *Of the tears to the tombs of the innocent due*

[ 626 ]

**Shelley, Cold cold is the blast**                    *July and August* 1810

SC 114  *Ah sweet is the moonbeam that sleeps on yon fountain*
  *And sweet the mild rush of the soft sighing breeze*
*And sweet is the glimpse of yon dimly seen mountain*
  *'Neath the verdant arcades of yon shadowy trees*
45  *But sweeter than all ——*

     *P e n m a n m a w r*

*And ah! she may envy the heart stricked quarry*
  *Who bids to the scenery of childhood farewell*
*She may envy the bosom all bleeding & gory*
50    *She may envy the sound of the drear passing knell*
*Not so deep are his woes on his death couch reposing*
*When on the last vision his dim eyes are closing*
*As the outcast—*

 *Those notes were so soft & so sad that ah! never*
55    *May the sound cease to vibrate on memory's ear*

line 6. In order to fit the line in, Shelley has curved and cramped *proved* downward and written *thee* below it and up to the right edge of the paper. He has similarly crowded the final word or words of other lines.

line 18. *Louisa: L* is written through another letter, possibly *H*.

line 32. *my* is written through *her*.

line 37. *mountain* is badly cramped.

line 46. *Penmanmawr* is written in very large and black unjoined letters about .8 of an inch below line 45, which is the final line of poetry on page 3. It appears to be in Shelley's hand. Shelley does occasionally write words in unjoined letters. See SC 124, line 68.

line 47. *stricked* (sic). Hogg (*Shelley*, I, 126) reads "shocked."

line 52. *When:* probable reading

COLLATION (excluding incidentals of punctuation).
COLD, COLD IS THE BLAST, *ORIGINAL POETRY* BY VICTOR AND CAZIRE (WORTHING, 1810).

line 9. poor ——— has

line 14. turned laughing

line 17. the wild height of the dark Penmanmawr,

line 18. wasted ——— reclined;

line 22. yon rocks

line 23. yon clouds

line 24. But thee, cruel ———

line 27. o'er

line 28. leaving it

line 29. exclaimed, "when the

line 33. lived ———

line 36. peace

AH! SWEET IS THE MOONBEAM, *ORIGINAL POETRY.*

line 45. all was thy tone of affection,

*Shelley, Cold cold is the blast*        *July and August* 1810

SC 114    STERN, STERN IS THE VOICE, *ORIGINAL POETRY.*

line 47. he may     heart-stricken
line 48. the friend of affection farewell,
line 49. He may     and gory,
line 50. He may
line 51. deep is his grief

line 53. outcast whose love-raptured senses are losing,
line 54. Those tones
line 55. Can     Memory's

ELIZABETH SHELLEY, some two years younger than her brother, joined him in some of his early literary enterprises. They wrote a play together and collaborated on a volume of verse: *Original Poetry* by Victor (Shelley) and Cazire (Elizabeth), published in 1810. It has become a commonplace of Shelley criticism to dismiss this volume, in the words of an early reviewer, as "downright scribble," but one has to remember that they are, after all, juvenile verses. Of the two sets of poems, although Shelley's have a wilder sweep of imagination, Elizabeth's exhibit more technical dexterity. In fact, the couplets of the first two poems in the volume, which are by Elizabeth, are handled with an informality and skill remarkable for a girl of fifteen.[1]

But Elizabeth did not follow up this early promise. What we know of the rest of her life is the result almost entirely of her associations with her brother. His letters of 1810 and 1811 published in this volume show her efforts to avoid an involvement with her brother's "mad friend," Thomas Jefferson Hogg. In 1814, on Shelley's last visit to Field Place, she welcomed him, and a visitor noted that she and her brother were as alike as twins.[2] As early as 1811 Shelley had been troubled about her growing conservatism, which he attributed to their father's influence; in 1816 he evolved a scheme to put her beyond her father's reach by taking her and their sister Hellen to Ireland.[3] It was in connection with this scheme that the brother and sister apparently met for the last time.[4] Following this we hear no more of Elizabeth — there is no record of

1. For a brief sample see "Introduction to the Diary of Harriet Grove," above, p. 487.

2. Hogg, *Shelley*, II, 153.

3. Dowden, *Shelley*, I, 478; White, *Shelley*, I, 372.

4. *Mary Shelley's Journal*, p. 17. Mary's entry for October 1, which is incorrectly given in the printed texts, reads, in part: "we all walk to Hackney MJC & Mary call at M^rs Hugford see Eliza Helen & Anne." MJC is Mary Jane Clairmont. (Abinger Manuscripts, Pforzheimer Microfilm, reel 1.)

**_Shelley, Cold cold is the blast_**                    **_July and August_ 1810**

SC 114  Shelley's writing to her or hearing from her — until a cryptic comment by Mary Shelley in December 1831: "Shelley's eldest sister, Elizabeth, has just died — of a decline — but this will not soften their hearts."[5] She died unmarried, at the age of thirty-seven, nine years after her brother, and was buried in the graveyard of Warnham Church.

The above manuscript consists of one complete poem and parts of two others. Although Hogg appears to have been unaware of it, they had all been published in 1810 in _Original Poetry_.

The complete poem comprises lines 1–40, five eight-line stanzas. It is in _Original Poetry_ with the general title "Song," and is dated "July, 1810." Lines 41–45 above are the opening lines of "Ah! sweet is the moonbeam" in _Original Poetry_, which is dated "August, 1810." The whole poem is in sixteen lines (four four-line stanzas). Lines 47–53 are from the second stanza of a third poem, "Stern, stern is the voice." And lines 54–55 are the first two lines of the third and final stanza of the same poem. This poem is twenty lines in length (two eight-line and one — the last — four-line stanzas). It also is dated "August, 1810." Shelley has left a somewhat longer space between lines 40 and 41 above than he has between the previous stanzas, and the large "Penmanmawr" is apparently intended to separate the third poem from the second.

These poems were published by Hogg in his life of Shelley as one continuous poem and in an inexact text. Subsequent editors have not been able to correct the text as they have not had access to the manuscript (which remained in the Hogg family until it was acquired for this library).

In publishing the poems Hogg commented: "Bysshe wrote down these verses for me at Oxford from memory. I was to have a complete and more correct copy of them some day. They were the composition of his sister Elizabeth, and he valued them highly as well as their author . . . ."[6] During the Christmas vacation Shelley (at Field Place) included a poem

---

5. Mary Shelley to E. J. Trelawny, December 1831, Mary Shelley, _Letters_, II, 51. Elizabeth Shelley was born on May 10, 1794, and died on December 17, 1831. It seems that her life was spent almost entirely within the confines of Field Place. "Decline" in Victorian England often referred to tuberculosis. Shelley was diagnosed as tubercular in 1815 (Mary Shelley's "Note on Alastor," Shelley, _Complete Works_, I, 198) and his son Charles died of tuberculosis at the age of eleven. (Ingpen, _Shelley in England_, pp. 513–514.) The comment on "soften their hearts" is a reference to the financial difficulties Mary and her son were having with the Shelley family.

6. Hogg, _Shelley_, I, 126.

SC 114　by Elizabeth in a letter to Hogg on January 11 (1811) with the comment: "These are Eliza's she has written many more, & I will shew you at some future time the whole of the composition."[7] From this one would gather that this January 11 poem was the first of Elizabeth's that Hogg had seen. Hence, the above verses cannot have been written down for Hogg before the Christmas vacation but between Shelley's return to Oxford on about January 26 and his leaving Oxford for good on March 26. Hogg's statement that they were written down not at Field Place but at Oxford is supported by the fact that they are not on the paper Shelley normally used at Field Place[8] but are on the same paper as two letters written at Oxford.[9]

Although Hogg states that these "verses" were by Elizabeth his statement has been overlooked by Shelley's editors. The editors of *Complete Works*, for instance, simply repeat Garnett's tentative attributions (which give all three to Shelley).[10]

Newman I. White in his biography of Shelley notes Hogg's attribution of "Stern, stern is the voice" to Elizabeth, and seems inclined to accept it, but fails to note that Hogg quotes also from "Ah! sweet is the moonbeam"; and he does not comment on "Cold cold is the blast."[11]

One reason for attributing "Stern, stern is the voice" and "Ah! sweet is the moonbeam" to Shelley is that they are apparently addressed to Harriet Grove. But when they are read in the light of Elizabeth's authorship they appear to be pleas from a sister on behalf of a brother. "Ah! sweet is the moonbeam," for instance, concludes:

> And thou dearest friend in his bosom for ever
> 　　Must reign unalloyed by the fast rolling year,
> He loves thee, and dearest one never, Oh! never
> 　　Canst thou cease to be loved by a heart so sincere.

In a letter to Elizabeth on May 25, 1811 (sc 162), Hogg speaks of having seen "specimens" of her poetry and quotes phrases from "Cold cold is the blast." Shelley in a letter to Hogg of ?July 21, 1811 (sc 171)

7. sc 132 (Jan. 11, 1811), line 84.

8. See sc 123 (?Dec. 10, 1810–?Jan. 22, 1811), Commentary.

9. sc 119 (*ca.* Nov. 17, 1810); sc 121 (Nov. 30, 1810). The 1808 watermark is the same in all three but is distinctly different from the 1808 in sc 113 (May 20, 1810), written at Field Place.

10. Shelley, *Complete Works*, I, 413.　　　　　11. White, *Shelley*, I, 583.

SC 114  comments: "it was E's poetry that first attracted your attention, charmed, & now has bewitched you!" This, coupled with Hogg's statements, leaves no doubt that Shelley had informed Hogg that these poems were by Elizabeth. And there seems no reason to believe that he was not telling the truth. If he had not been, Hogg could, for all he knew, easily have found him out, for in December 1810 Shelley was interested in bringing Hogg and Elizabeth together. After quoting the poems Hogg comments: "I was to undertake to fall in love with her; if I did not I had no business to go to Field Place, and he would never forgive me. I promised to do my best . . . ."[12] It is rather curious that Shelley wrote the poems down at all, for, as they were already in print in *Original Poetry*, one would think that he would simply have handed Hogg a copy of that volume. Possibly he did not have a copy or possibly he did not wish Hogg to see his juvenile poems. Stockdale, the publisher of *Original Poetry*, informs us that although Shelley had 1480 copies printed he ordered them all destroyed on Stockdale's discovering that one poem was plagiarized from Monk Lewis.[13] Hogg was apparently kept in ignorance of the existence of the book (although he did know about the Margaret Nicholson volume).[14]

Hogg states that Shelley copied down these lines "from memory." That he did not copy them from *Original Poetry* is clear from the Collation above. But if he was able to remember these lines, including one complete poem, why was he not able to recall something of the missing lines also? Perhaps he did know the three poems by heart but was giving Hogg only some general samples. One would presume from Hogg's comment that the manuscript was written in his presence.

Of the verses themselves they are, like everything else in *Original Poetry*, juvenile. It is curious to note that Shelley used the names of Elizabeth's betrayed heroine and villain, Louisa and Henry, in a long narrative poem in the Esdaile copybook.[15] When Elizabeth's poem appeared in *Original Poetry* the names were left blank, perhaps to suggest that the story was true and contemporary.

12. Hogg, *Shelley*, I, 126–127.          13. See Cameron, *The Young Shelley*, pp. 305–306.
14. sc 3 (Aug. 9, 1786–1794), Commentary.

15. Dowden, *Shelley*, I, 347. Except for the names, however, there seems to be no similarity between the two works — at least so far as one can judge from Dowden's brief summary of "Henry and Louisa."

SC 115   WILLIAM GODWIN TO JOHN POCOCK, JULY 4, 1810

AUTOGRAPH PROMISSORY NOTE signed *W Godwin*, 1 page. Single sheet (3.6 x 9 inches).
Wove paper. Watermark: E WILDING| 1801|. Embossed revenue stamp: [device]| I SHILL^G VI PENCE|.
Endorsements.

*Due Jany 7ᵗʰ 1811*

*£27– –*                           *No. 41, Skinner Street,*
                                        *July 4, 1810*

       *Six months after date I promise to pay to Mʳ John Pocock or order*

5           *twenty-seven pounds:   value recᵈ*

                                  *W Godwin*

[Endorsements, verso]

*31          1456*
*John Pocock*
    *Rf Mew & Co*
10    *J Williams*

WE FIND in *Kent's Directory* for 1823 John Pocock, coal merchant, 11 Staple Inn, Holborn, but a few blocks from Godwin's house. In the same neighborhood we find Mew and Co., linen drapers, 301 High Holborn.[1]

Godwin's Journal, curiously enough, records him as being out of London from July 1 to July 5, 1810. As Godwin often wrote the entries a week or more after their dates it may be that he made a mistake in the Journal and had actually returned on July 4; or it may be that he predated his note July 4.[2]

SEE ALSO SC 61.

1. Plan of London, C1, Front Endpapers. Staple Inn was just west of Southampton Buildings.
2. See SC 24 (Nov. 28, 1799), fn. 11.

SC 116   P. B. SHELLEY TO J. J. STOCKDALE, SEPTEMBER 6, 1810

AL signed *Percy B. Shelley*, 1¾ pages. Double sheet, 4ᵗᵒ (8.8 x 7.1 inches).
Wove paper. Watermark: C WILMOTT| 1808|.
Seal: wax, red: [shield, lower part]|.

# Shelley and his Circle : Manuscripts

***Shelley to Stockdale***                 ***September 6, 1810***

Frank, by Timothy Shelley.
Postmarks: 1. (mileage stamp): HORSHAM| 41|; 2. (morning duty franking stamp,
London): FREE| 7 SE 7| 1810|.
Docket, page 4, in the same hand as SC 148: *Shelley| 6 Sept. 1810|.*
PROVENANCE: Hodgson (Apr. 22, 1937, lot 556). *De Ricci 9* (p. 261).

*Field Place*
*Sept<sup>r</sup> 6. 1810.—*

*Sir /*

    *I have to return you my thankful acknowlegdement for the receipt of*
5  *the books, which arrived as soon as I had any reason to expect, the superfluity*
*shall be balanced as soon as I pay for some books which I shall trouble you*
*to bind for me ——*
*I enclose you the title page of the Poems which as you will see, you have*
*mistaken on account of the illegibility of my hand-writing — I have had*
10  *the last proof-impression from my Printer this morning & I suppose the*
*execution of the work will not be long delayed — As soon as it possibly can,*
*it shall reach you, & believe me, Sir, grateful for the interest you take in it ——*
    *I am, Sir*
        *your obedient humble Ser<sup>t</sup>*
15         *Percy B. Shelley*
[Frank and address, page 4, in the hand of Timothy Shelley]
*Horsham, September Six*
        *1810*
*M<sup>r</sup> Stockdale Bookseller,*
*41 Pall Mall*
20  *London*
*T.Shelley.*

line 4. *acknowlegdement* (sic)

How and when Shelley's letters to his early publisher, John Joseph
Stockdale, first came on the market does not appear to be known.
They were apparently in the hands of Shelley's Victorian editor, Richard

SC 116   Herne Shepherd, in the 1870's.[1] Since then several have turned up at various sales. This library possesses two, the above letter and one of April 11, 1811 (sc 148).

Stockdale (1770–1847) published Shelley's and Elizabeth Shelley's juvenile volume, *Original Poetry*, and his second horror novel, *St. Irvyne: or, The Rosicrucian*, both in 1810. During the Christmas vacation of 1810–11 Shelley suggested Stockdale as a possible publisher for Hogg's novel *Leonora*. Stockdale became alarmed at the antireligious sentiments of the novel, made inquiries about Hogg, found that he was considered antireligious in his home county, and wrote to Timothy Shelley that Hogg was "the master spirit" leading his son "astray."[2] It was in connection with these and other matters that Shelley wrote his letters to Stockdale, a correspondence which began with the above letter.

Following this exposé of Hogg's views Shelley broke off relations with Stockdale, sending him a bitterly recriminatory letter on January 28, 1811, and after that writing him only the letter of April 11, which inquires about the sale of *St. Irvyne*.

In 1826–1827 these letters from Shelley to Stockdale were published under rather unusual circumstances. In 1826 Stockdale brought out *Memoirs of Harriet Wilson* (republished in 1955), which gave detailed accounts of the love affairs of Harriet Wilson with men high in English public life.[3] Stockdale was attacked for this publication, the truth of which was denied. He then chose a curious way of defending himself. He began in December (1826) the publication of a weekly periodical ironically entitled *Stockdale's Budget of "all that is Good, and Noble and Amiable, in the Country,"* in which he presented scandalous stories of contemporaries of British society to show that *Harriet Wilson* was not exaggerated. Wedged in among these juicy items there appeared a series of articles on Stockdale's acquaintance with Shelley, in the course of which he reprinted the letters. At first these articles seem completely incongruous but soon the tone of Stockdale's comments makes his motive clear: to establish his own respectability by presenting himself as the would-be rescuer of a youthful atheist.

1. De Ricci, p. 261.
2. *Stockdale's Budget*, 1827, Jan. 3, p. 26, Jan. 10, p. 34.
3. See the *DNB* under "Harriette Wilson."

SC 116     The "Poems" referred to in the above letter (line 8) was *Original Poetry*. Stockdale stated that he received 1480 copies of this work from the printers on September 17.[4] On September 18 an advertisement for it appeared in *The Morning Chronicle*. It would appear from this letter, however (line 8), that there must have been an earlier advertisement. As Stockdale did not print the volume, Shelley cannot be complaining that he has made a mistake on the actual title page. (The printing was done by C. and W. Phillips at Worthing.) Hence, Shelley must mean that he had sent Stockdale a handwritten draft of the title page to use in an advertisement and that this advertisement contained a mistake due to Stockdale's misreading of Shelley's handwriting. Shelley is now (line 8) sending him a proof of the title page so that Stockdale can correct the advertisement.

The books (line 4) which Stockdale had sent to Shelley cannot have been copies of *Original Poetry*, for it did not come from the printer until September 17. As Stockdale was a bookseller as well as publisher they were presumably some books which Shelley had ordered from him.

Timothy Shelley, as a Member of Parliament, had the privilege of franking letters, and Shelley naturally availed himself of this privilege in order to avoid paying postage. A franking signature, it might be noted, was not in itself sufficient. By an act of 1784, a Member of Parliament had not only to sign the letter on the outside but also to write in the date, the post town, his own address, and the address to which the letter was to be delivered. So far as Timothy was concerned, "Horsham" served both for the post town and his own address. A franked letter was stamped with a special stamp containing a crown and the word "FREE."[5]

4. *Stockdale's Budget*, Dec. 13, 1826, p. 1.

5. Alcock and Holland, pp. 185–189. The crown was added first in 1799. See illustration in "Postmarks and the Dating of Manuscripts," below, p. 919.

SC 117   JAMES LIND TO M. E. SHERWILL, OCTOBER 21, 1810

AL signed *James Lind.*, 2¼ pages. Double sheet, 4to (9.1 x 7.2 inches). Laid paper. Watermark: J FURNESS & CO| 1807|. Seal: wax, red: [?wreath]|.

# The Carl H. Pforzheimer Library

SC 117                              *Windsor Sunday 21 Oct<sup>r</sup> 1810.*

*Dear Sir——*

*I enclosed return your sketch of your armorial bearings; and a very correct Plate of mine, the only thing particular in mine is, that there are*

5 *three Colours in the Wreath; for a discription of them see the <u>Genealogy of</u>* *<u>the family of Lind</u>, of which Lucy has a copy. But what I have sent I imagine will be sufficient for the Seal-cutter.*

*As to my self I am in Statu quo, and the Dean and Canons have not as yet passed their Sentence on Vickary   He has been fined £15.0.0 by the Civil*

10 *power.*

*I am sorry for your being obliged to pass a Month at Colnbrook, which for a Soldier is no very hard Duty in the present times. My friend Col: Smollet made himself Master of Italian, and became an excellent Draftsman* when quartered there.

15 ⌄*He was killed at the Hilder. His Death was a national loss; for he was a most accomplished Soldier, and amiable young man.*

*I thank you for your information respecting the use of the Stramonium. I find that some people use the Root and stalks near the root, cutt small, and had found great relief by Smoking them.*

20 *I shall look at your ugly Clock at Hansons and hope to hear of its performing well, which is all you wish of it, I suppose.*

*I beg my best wishes, to my Dear Lucy, and am sorry at our not seeing Her so soon as we expected at Windsor. Dorothea is not yet returned from Church so cannot untill She returns inform you respecting Princess Amelia*

25 *or send you any Windsor News*

*This bad day makes my very unwell, so beg you will excuse this incorrect Scrawl. from your ever faithful, and affectionate Father in Law*

*James Lind.*

[Page 3]

*My Seal is cut by a Chinese of which I shall endeavour to make a good*

30 *impression on this Letter.——*

[Address, page 4]

*To*
*Captain M. E. Sherwill*
*K. O. Stafford Militia*
*Kew.*

[ 636 ]

SC 117    line 5. *discription* (sic)

line 9. *Vickary* comes at the end of a line; hence the omission of the period (as often in Shelley's letters also).

line 16. *young man* ends the final paragraph on page 1; page 2 begins *I thank*. Lind anticipates this by using *I thank* as a catchword at the end of page 1.

line 18. *cutt* (sic)

line 25. *News* ends a line. See line 9 above.

line 26. *my very* (sic)

J AMES LIND (1736–1812), the main facts of whose life will be found in the *Dictionary of National Biography*, was a scientist and physician. As a scientist he published three papers for the Royal Society. As a physician he wrote an account of "the Fever of 1762 at Bengal," and became one of the physicians to King George III at Windsor. He took a sympathetic interest in the students at nearby Eton and used to tell with relish "many particulars of the rebellion at Eton, some laughable anecdotes of the boys destroying the whipping-post and then selling it to one another."[1] On one Eton schoolboy in particular he was to have a lasting influence.

Among the biographical scraps that Mary Shelley in later years wrote about her husband is the following:

He became intimate, also, at Eton, with a man whom he never mentioned, except in terms of the tenderest respect. This was Dr. Lind, a name well known among the professors of medical science. 'This man,' he has often said, 'is exactly what an old man ought to be. Free, calm-spirited, full of benevolence, and even of youthful ardour; his eye seemed to burn with supernatural spirit beneath his brow, shaded by his venerable white locks; he was tall, vigorous, and healthy in his body; tempered, as it had ever been, by his amiable mind. I owe to that man far, ah! far more than I owe to my father; he loved me, and I shall never forget our long talks, where he breathed the spirit of the kindest tolerance and the purest wisdom!'[2]

Four years after Lind's death Shelley commemorated their friendship in the story of Laon and the hermit in *The Revolt of Islam*:

That hoary man had spent his livelong age
    In converse with the dead, who leave the stamp

1. Mary Delany, quoted in Hughes, *Nascent Mind*, p. 27.

2. Quoted in Hogg, *Shelley*, I, 35.

SC 117
> Of ever-burning thoughts on many a page,
>     When they are gone into the senseless damp
>     Of graves;–his spirit thus became a lamp
> Of splendour, like to those on which it fed.[3]

It was probably from Lind that Shelley first borrowed Godwin's *Political Justice*;[4] and it was Lind who turned Shelley to chemistry and strengthened that general interest in science stimulated by Adam Walker at Sion House and Eton, an interest which was to find creative expression in his poetry from *Queen Mab* to *Hellas*.

The above letter — written in the very month in which Shelley was entering Oxford — is to Lind's son-in-law Captain Markham Edes Sherwill. Sherwill, too, was a man of cultural tastes. A friend of Sir Walter Scott's, he tried to interest Scott — unsuccessfully — in the poetry of John Clare;[5] and in later years he befriended another unfortunate poet, Charles Caleb Colton, an eccentric and dissipated divine (author of the once widely read book of aphorisms, *Lacon*), whose poems he edited and who committed suicide at Sherwill's house at Fontainebleau.[6]

---

3. *The Revolt of Islam*, IV, viii. The Laon and hermit episode runs from III, xvii to IV, xxxii. Mary Shelley, in the passage quoted above, goes on to give a story by Shelley to the effect that once when he was ill with a high fever his father wished to have him put in an asylum but Dr. Lind prevented this. The Laon and hermit episode seems to be in part an idealized retelling of this story.

    Medwin (*Shelley*, p. 33) suggested that the character of the aged counselor, Zonoras, in *Prince Athanase* (lines 125 ff.) was also based on Lind. The suggestion is plausible.

4. Hogg, *Shelley*, I, 313–314; Cameron, *The Young Shelley*, p. 322. According to Hogg (*Shelley*, I, 92–93) Lind used to treat his schoolboy friend to a long and rounded curse upon the king, which Shelley once repeated to Hogg and which he applied also to his own father. (For a possible reflection of these episodes by Godwin in *Mandeville* see Brown, *Godwin*, p. 324.) That Lind ever so cursed the king has been doubted because of his loyalty to the king and his gentle disposition (Dowden, *Shelley*, I, 32–33 fn.; *Letters about Shelley*, p. 132; Hughes, *Nascent Mind*, p. 27), but the anecdote may have some truth in it. Shelley repeated the curse to Hogg and while he might have exaggerated it he probably did not invent it. What Lind said in public and what he said at tea with his youthful republican admirer may not have been identical. His attitude toward his royal, insane patient could well have been ambivalent.

5. J. W. and Anne Tibble, *John Clare, a Life* (London, 1932), pp. 114, 149. See also pp. 157, 373.

6. See the lengthy obituary notice (written by Sherwill?) in *The Gentleman's Magazine*, CII (June 1832), 564–566. Two books of poems by Colton were edited by Sherwill. The first was *Thoughts in Rhyme* (Paris, 1832), the preface of which is signed "Markham Sherwill, Fontainebleau, September, 1832." The second book, listed in the British Museum catalogue, was *Modern Antiquity and Other Poems* (1835). The British Museum catalogue lists Captain Markham Sherwill also as the author of *Ascent of Captain M. Sherwill (accompanied by Dr. E. Clark) to the Summit of Mont Blanc . . . in*

**Shelley to Roe**                    *?ca. November 17, 1810*

SC 117     The book to which Lind refers (line 5) shows his interest both in printing and in genealogy. He had a private press with wooden type set up at Windsor and on it he printed, among other works, *The Genealogy of the Families of Lind and the Montgomeries of Smithton* by Sir Robert Douglas. The Princess Amelia whom he mentions (line 24) was the favorite daughter of George III. With her death on November 2, 1810, the king's insanity became permanent.

*Letters Addressed to a Friend* (London, 1826). The Library of Congress catalogue lists as his *A Brief Historical Sketch of the Valley of Chamouni* . . . (Paris, 1832). The British Museum catalogue also lists James Lind Sherwill, *A Geographical and Statistical Report of the Dinagepore District* (1863). James Lind Sherwill was perhaps the son of Markham Sherwill and Lucy Lind Sherwill (line 22).

Markham Sherwill was not an army officer (and does not appear in the *Army Lists*) but an officer in the militia (as the address indicates). We find him in the British War Office's *List of Officers of the Militia of the United Kingdom* (London, 1809) as a Captain in "The (King's Own) Stafford Militia" (hence the K. O. of line 33). The "Col: Smollet" (line 12) who was killed at the Hilder was a regular army officer. He was Lieutenant Colonel Alexander Smollet whose name appears in the *Army Lists* for 1799 but not for 1800. The Hilder action took place in 1799.


SC 118     P. B. SHELLEY TO JAMES ROE, ?CA. NOVEMBER 10, 1810

AL signed *P. B Shelley*, 1 page. Single sheet (3.5 x 7.2 inches). Laid paper.

PROVENANCE: Sotheby (June 25, 1923, lot 676). *De Ricci 16A* (p. 226).


*Dear Roe*
    *Can you send me that poetical scrap, I left with you as I have some ideas about finishing it to day*
                                        *yours    P. B Shelley*

[Address, page 2]
5            —— *Roe Esqʳ*


SC 119     P. B. SHELLEY TO JAMES ROE, ?CA. NOVEMBER 17, 1810

AL signed *Percy Shelley.___*, 1 page. Double sheet, 12ᵐᵒ (6.5 x 4.5 inches). Wove paper. Watermark: 1808|.

PROVENANCE: Sotheby (June 25, 1932, lot 675). *De Ricci 16B* (p. 226).

# The Carl H. Pforzheimer Library

*Shelley to Roe*              *?ca. November 17, 1810*

SC 119   *Dear Roe*
     *At ½ past 4 or 5. oClock there will be wine & Poetry in my room ——*
*Will you honor me with your Co.*

                                    *Your devd Ser*

5                                         *Percy Shelley.*

    *½ 2 oClock*
    [Address, page 4]
         —— *Roe Esq^r*
         *Trinity College*

ONE gets the impression from Hogg that he was Shelley's only friend at Oxford and that Shelley was little known in the university. From other sources, however, we find that, brief though his stay was, he made a mark on the undergraduate literary life of Oxford and had several other friends. Among these, the above notes inform us, was James Roe of Trinity College. According to *Alumni Oxonienses* Roe was the son of James Roe, gentleman farmer of the town of Pembroke in Wales, and entered Trinity College, Oxford, in 1809, one year before Shelley.[1] How Shelley became acquainted with him we do not know, but he must, to judge from the tenor of Shelley's notes, have had literary interests.

The two notes to Roe are typical Oxford undergraduate intracollege notes. It is curious that they survived, for such notes are usually destroyed shortly after their receipt.

The notes are undated but it seems likely that they revolve around the composition and publication of *Posthumous Fragments of Margaret Nicholson*. The reference in SC 119 to "Poetry" — with a capital P — is probably not just to poetry in general but to the publication of this volume and a "wine" party held on the occasion. Shelley referred to his previous (Victor and Cazire) volume, published before he entered Oxford, simply as "our Poetry." He did not normally drink wine at Oxford or later,[2] so that the "wine" may refer to some special occasion. As the

1. Roe took his B.A. in 1815. We find a James Roe at 4 Gray's Inn Square in *Clarke's New Law List* for 1825.

2. Hogg, *Shelley*, I, 87; II, 82. "Temperance," as is not always noted, was later as much a part of Shelley's dietary views as vegetarianism. Hogg (*Shelley*, II, 82) states that at Oxford Shelley sometimes drank negus (spiced and sweetened wine diluted with water).

# Shelley and his Circle : Manuscripts

**Shelley, Death! where is thy Victory!**            *?November 17–*
*?December 8, 1810*

SC 119   *Posthumous Fragments* was advertised as "Just Published" on November 17,[3] SC 119 was probably written about that date.

What the "poetical scrap" of SC 118 was we do not know, but as the Margaret Nicholson volume was Shelley's only major poetical enterprise at Oxford, the reference is most likely to a poem intended for it. If this is correct, then the first note precedes the second (hence, our above order), and as Shelley wanted to "finish" it "today" this may indicate that he was preparing the volume for the press, which would perhaps have been around November 10. This date would fit also with the fact that it would have taken Shelley some time to know Roe well enough to discuss his poetry with him. The term had opened on October 10.

The sending of notes from one college to another was (and is) a regular feature of Oxford undergraduate life. Normally these notes are given to the porter of the writer's college and delivered by hand. This, as the address "Trinity College" shows, was the case with the second note. But it cannot have been the case with the first because it bears no college address. Furthermore, the folds and blotting show that it was hastily written and folded (roughly down the middle lengthwise and then crosswise). The probability is that Shelley went to Trinity, found that Roe was not in, and wrote the note on the spot and left it for him.

3. In *The Oxford University and City Herald*, quoted in MacCarthy, *Shelley*, p. 39.

SC 120   P. B. SHELLEY, *DEATH! WHERE IS THY VICTORY!* ?NOVEMBER 17–?DECEMBER 8, 1810

HOLOGRAPH MANUSCRIPT, 2 pages. Single sheet, 4^{to} (9.9 x 8 inches). Laid paper. Watermark: J WHATMAN|.

PROVENANCE: Thomas Jefferson Hogg; John Ewer Jefferson Hogg (Sotheby, July 27, 1922, lot 333).

> *Death! where is thy Victory!*
> *To triumph whilst I die*
>         *ebon wing*
> *To triumph whilst thine* ~~hand of fate~~
> *Enfolds my shuddering soul*

5

*Shelley, Death! where is thy Victory!*   *?November 17–*
*?December 8, 1810*

SC 120

Oh! death where is thy sting
Not when the tides of murder roll
When nations groan that Kings may bask in bliss
Death! canst thou boast a victory such as this

10

 When in his hour, of pomp & power
  Thy blow the mightiest murderer gave
  Mid nature's cries, the sacrifize
   Of millions to glut the grave
When sunk the tyrant desolation's slave

15

Or Freedom's life blood streamed upon thy shrine
Stern tyrant couldst thou boast a victory such as mine

To know in dissolution's void
    *bubbles sank*
 That mortals ~~hopes & fears~~ away

20

That every thing but Love destroyed
 Must perish with it's kindred clay
  Perish Ambitions crown
  Perish her sceptered sway
From Death's pale front fade Pride's fastidious frown

25

In Death's damp vault the lurid fires decay
That Envy lights at heaven-born virtues beam
  That all the cares subside
  Which lurk beneath the tide
  Of life's unquiet stream

30

  Yes this is victory
And on yon rock whose dark form glooms the sky
To strech these pale limbs when the soul is fled
To baffle the lean passions of their prey
To sleep within the palace of the dead! —

35

Oh! not the King around whose dazzling throne
His countless courtiers mock the words they say
Triumphs amid the bud of glory blown

*Shelley, Death! where is thy Victory!*    *?November 17–*
*?December 8, 1810*

SC 120

As I, in this cold bed & faint expiring groan

40
                     *grandeur*
Tremble ye proud whose ~~bosoms~~ mocks the woe

Which props thy column of unnatural state

    Ye, the plainings faint & low

                    *soul*
~~Which~~ from misery's tortured ~~breast~~ that flow

45
      Shall usher to your fate. .

Tremble ye conquerors at whose fell command

The war-fiend riots oer a peaceful land

    Ye, desolations gory throng

    Shall bear from victory along

50
      To that mysterious strand

line 2. *ium* of *triumph* here and in line 4 is compressed into a short wavy line. The manuscript gives evidence of hasty composition.

line 11. *mig* of *mightiest* is compressed.

line 12. *sacrifize* (sic)

line 19. *away* is written through *decay.*

line 32. *strech* (sic)

line 36. The *i* of *courtiers* is elongated and at first the reading seems to be *countless countless.*

Shelley, writing rapidly, carried over the appearance of the first word into the second. The Esdaile Ms. (see below) gives *courtiers* and Hogg independently came to the same reading.

line 39. The final *r* of *grandeur* is elongated.

line 40. The *s* of *mocks* is in darker ink, as is *grandeur* (line 39).

line 50. This is the last line on page 2 and comes at the bottom of the page.

COLLATION (excluding incidentals of punctuation).

TO DEATH, SHELLEY, *COMPLETE WORKS*, III, 73–74 (ESDAILE COPYBOOK).

line 1. victory?

line 6. O Death!

line 7. where the

line 9. could'st thou

line 11. Thy slave

line 12. Nature's    sacrifice,

line 13. myriads

line 14. sensualism's slave;

line 16. stern despot,    Victory

line 19. That earthly hopes and fears decay;

line 21. with its

line 23. its sceptred

line 24. fades

line 26. Which Envy    Virtue's

line 31. some rock,

line 32. stretch

line 35. the wretch,

line 40. ye Kings, whose luxury

line 41. That props the

line 42. curses deep tho'

line 44. breast

line 47. happy land!

line 48. Desolation's

line 49. Victory

line 50. Death's mysterious. (Following this line the editor in Shelley, *Complete Works*, places a line of dots so that presumably there is some indication in the Esdaile copybook that the poem is incomplete.)

# The Carl H. Pforzheimer Library

***Shelley, Death! where is thy Victory!***         *?November 17–*
                                                     *?December 8, 1810*

SC 120     THE above manuscript was one of four which, Hogg indicates,[1] were
given to him by Shelley at Oxford. Three of them are now in
The Carl H. Pforzheimer Library[2] and until their purchase had remained
in the hands of the Hogg family. The whereabouts of the fourth manuscript, a verse dialogue between Death and a Mortal, does not seem to
be known. It appears, however, that Hogg presented it in 1834 to the
Norfolk antiquary, Dawson Turner (whom we have previously noted
as having purchased some of Godwin's manuscripts).[3] Such, at least,
seems to be the implication of a letter to Dawson Turner, dated May 30,
1834, which Hogg, without explanation, throws into his text before
presenting the Death and a Mortal dialogue: "I now send you a poem,
or rather a rough draft of part of a poem, by his hand . . . ." The manuscript was presumably included in the following notation in the Dawson
Turner sale at Puttick and Simpson in 1859: "Shelley, P. B., 2 A. L. s.
and 8 pages 4to. of Aut. Poems, etc. 1810–1815."

These four were, interestingly enough, the only literary manuscripts
that Shelley ever gave to Hogg[4] (although in the text of some of his letters
in 1810 and 1811 he included poems); and they were all given during the
few months of their friendship at Oxford. After this, Shelley ceased to
take Hogg into his confidence in regard to his literary work. No fragment
of *Queen Mab* or *Alastor* or *The Revolt of Islam* went to Hogg; nor did
any parts of the great works of the Italian period. A gulf in ideas and
literary taste later developed, a gulf which goes far to explain Hogg's
blind spots in his biography.

Hogg introduces the above poem, "Death! where is thy Victory?"
abruptly with the sentence: "The following unfinished verses were
written at Oxford; they have never been published."[5] The manuscript
bears no date but in the Esdaile copybook the poem is dated 1810. If it
was written in 1810, at Oxford, it must have been written between
October 10, 1810, when the Oxford term began, and about December 8

1. Hogg, *Shelley*, I, 122–126.
2. sc 114 ("Cold cold is the blast"), sc 123 ("The Wandering Jew"), the above manuscript.
3. sc 59 (*Fleetwood*), Commentary, p. 335.
4. Unless we include also a translation from Aristotle's *Ethics* (sc 124).
5. Hogg, *Shelley*, I, 124.

**Shelley, Death! where is thy Victory!**          *?November* **17–**
                                                  *?December* **8, 1810**

SC 120   when Shelley left for the Christmas vacation.[6] But it seems possible to narrow the date still further. The poem does not appear in *Posthumous Fragments of Margaret Nicholson* ("Just Published" on November 17);[7] yet its subject matter – denouncing war and monarchy – is so much in line with some of the Margaret Nicholson poems that had it been in existence Shelley would almost certainly have included it.

In addition to the above transcript (given to Hogg) Shelley must have had at least one more. In a letter of December 11, 1811, to his friend Elizabeth Hitchener he wrote: "I think I shall also make a selection of my younger poems for publication."[8] This "selection" was made for the Esdaile copybook (see Collation above). Hence, the transcription for the Esdaile copybook took place a year or more later than the composition of the poem, and it cannot have been made from the above manuscript because Shelley had already given it to Hogg.

As to the literary significance of the poem (which may have received its initial inspiration from Pope's "The Dying Christian to his Soul"[9]) it would possess little were it not the juvenile work of a developing major poet. It helps to mark Shelley's transition from the Gothic horrors of the Victor and Cazire volume, with its loose, careless style, to the social radicalism of *Queen Mab*, with its compact intensity. The verse form and flow, in fact, are — except for the rhyme — very similar to *Queen Mab*. The poem reveals something also of Shelley's unfolding lyrical talents. "Lean passions" (line 33) and "life's unquiet stream" (line 29) are better than anything he had done previously. "Life's unquiet stream" perhaps evolved into "life's unquiet dream" in the "Hymn to Intellectual Beauty." As with *Queen Mab* or the opening poem of the Margaret Nicholson volume, the political references are probably less abstract than might at first appear. The "mightiest murderer" (line 11), for instance, is almost certainly George III.

---

6. He did not return to Oxford until late in January 1811.

7. MacCarthy, *Shelley*, p. 39.

8. The letter is undated but bears a London postmark of December 14 and a Keswick postmark, so that December 11 is probably the correct date as mail normally took three days to go from Keswick to London.

9. The final lines of which are derived from I Corinthians, xv.55.

**Shelley to Graham**                                    *November 30, 1810*

SC 121   P. B. SHELLEY TO EDWARD FERGUS GRAHAM, NOVEMBER 30, 1810

AL signed *P B Shelley*, 2¾ pages. Double sheet, 4^to (9.1 x 7.2 inches).
Wove paper. Watermark: 1808|. Octagonal impressed stamp: [crown]| BATH|.
Seal (torn).
Postmarks: 1. (dated mileage stamp)*:* [o]XFO[RD]| [30] NO 30 |[1810]| [57]|;
2. (morning duty stamp, London)*:* B| 1 DE 1| [1]810|.
PROVENANCE: John Davies (Puttick, Sept. 9, 1851, lot 236); H. Buxton Forman
(Anderson, Mar. 15, 1920, lot 630). *De Ricci 15* (p. 91).

*Oxford   Nov. 30   1810*

*My dear Graham*

    *I enclose a 5 £ note which is all I can immediately spare; I shall see
you in a fortnight; Whenever you mention <u>money</u> make it <u>visible</u>, as since*

5   *having looked over your letter I can find nothing like it; —      The part of
the Epithaliamium which you mention, (ie from the end of Satan's triumph
— is the production of a friends <u>Mistress</u>; it had been concluded there but
she thought it abrupt & added this; it is omitted in numbers of the copies, —
that which I sent to my Mother of course did not contain it — I shall possibly*

10  *send you the abuse to day, but I am afraid that they will not insert it — But
you mistake, the Epithaliamium will make it sell like wildfire, and as the
<u>Nephew</u> is kept a profound secret, there can arise no danger from the indel-
icacy of the Aunt —— It sells wonderfully here, & is become the fashionable
subject of discussion —— What particular subject do you mean, I cannot*

15  *make out I confess. — Of course to my Father Peg is a profound secret, he
is better & recovering very fast.- ——      How is the King & what is thought
of Political affairs.*

    *Will you tell me what I owe you*

                     *Yours affec^t*
20                       *P B <u>Shelley</u>*

[Address, page 4]
*Edward Graham Esq^r*
*No. 29 Vine Street*
*Piccadilly*
*London*

line 6. *Epithaliamium* (sic)                    pressure by the pen and stands out in thick
line 12. *Nephew* is written with emphatic     black lines. The underline is also thick and black.

**Shelley to Graham**                                          *November* 30, 1810

SC 121   $\mathbf{S}$INCE EDWARD GRAHAM lived in London (whereas Shelley, in these years, was at Eton, Field Place, or Oxford), Shelley made use of him to handle literary matters. As early as April 1, 1810, in anticipation of the publication of *Zastrozzi*, he blandly exhorted Graham to *"pouch the reviewers — £*10 will be sufficient I should suppose." Later in April he commissioned him to send out copies of *Zastrozzi*. On August 11 he enclosed £3 for books for Harriet Grove.[1] Late in September he wrote: "You have not done what I told you. The *Morning Chronicle* at least has not inserted it. I shall expect to hear a full account of all your proceedings."[2] *The Morning Chronicle* for September 18 carried an advertisement for *Original Poetry* by Victor and Cazire.

The above letter continues the game, this time in connection with the next volume of poetry, "Peg" (line 15) — *Posthumous Fragments of Margaret Nicholson*, "edited" by John Fitzvictor (son of "Victor" and "nephew" to Margaret Nicholson). Shelley sends Graham £5 (line 3), which again is probably connected with some form of advertising, and intended later to send him some "abuse" (line 10). One might guess that Shelley had Graham insert advertisements in the *Chronicle*, and perhaps also in other papers, after which Shelley would write an abusive letter on the work advertised in order to arouse interest in it. This is in line with his youthful pranks of this period (as in the Advertisement to the *Posthumous Fragments* itself).

"Fragment supposed to be an Epithalamium of Francis Ravaillac and Charlotte Cordé" (line 6) is the second poem in the *Posthumous Fragments*. The section that had alarmed Graham must have been the torrid love-making of lines 82–102. Satan's "triumph" ends at line 68. The claim that lines 69–102 were written by a "friends *Mistress*" (line 7) may be mere schoolboy fantasy or it may mean that Elizabeth Shelley wrote some of the final lines, thus collaborating as she had in *Original Poetry*. Shelley could conceivably have thought of her as Hogg's "mistress" (in the Petrarchan sense).[3]

1. White, *Shelley*, II, 454–455.

2. Dated in Shelley, *Complete Works* (VIII, 15), as "Friday, [?September], 1810." This may be Friday, September 19. In the letter Shelley asks "What think you of our Poetry? What is said of it?" *Original Poetry* was published on September 18 (*ibid.*, p. 14 fn.).

3. See "Shelley, Hogg, and Elizabeth Shelley," below.

**Godwin to Taylor**                                        **?December 6, 1810**

SC 121      The illness of George III (line 16) was officially taken note of in a bulletin by his physicians on October 29, and it was soon reported that the illness was mental in nature. *The Morning Chronicle* noted that he had "sunk, under the agitation of his mind, into a state of inability to perform the functions of his high office."[4] Both Houses of Parliament adjourned from November 1 until November 15.

The above manuscript reveals a frequent habit of Shelley's in letter writing. The date and return address (line 1) have blotted in folding; the rest of the page has not; hence the date and return address were added after page 1 was written.

4. Quoted in *The Examiner*, Nov. 4, 1810, p. 693. *The Examiner* comments (p. 692): "The disorder which has again attacked his MAJESTY naturally supersedes the common objects of anxiety in the public mind."

SC 122      WILLIAM GODWIN TO JOHN TAYLOR, ?DECEMBER 6, 1810

AL signed *W Godwin*, 1 page. Single sheet (5.4 x 9.7 inches).
Laid paper.
Docket, page 1: *1810| John Taylor Esq. opera|*.
PROVENANCE: A. E. Newton (Parke-Bernet, May 14–16, 1941, lot 138).

> *My dear sir*
> *I did myself the pleasure of calling this evening to ask you whether you would do me the favour to eat mutton to-morrow at my house with a very pretty woman, a very wise man, &c. But why should I hope? My hour*
> 5  *is the unfashionable hour of four, & my invitation is out of all rule & etiquette.*
> *your obliged servant*
> *W Godwin*

*Thursday*

THE above letter[1] is unaddressed and is dated only "Thursday," but the docketing "1810| John Taylor Esq. opera|" gives us a clue to the date, recipient, and place of delivery. Turning to Godwin's Journal

1. The letter is mounted in a copy of Edward Baldwin [i.e., William Godwin], *History of Rome* (London, 1844). Inserted in the book is a letter to A. Edward Newton from C. S. Wainwright, Commercial Agent for Canadian National Railways, Los Angeles, November 7, 1921, stating that the book came from "Sir P. F. Shelley's Library." It was perhaps purchased at the sale of books from the library of Lord Abinger (7th Baron Abinger) at Rownhams, near Southampton, in February 1920. (For information on this sale, see catalogue of The Library of Jerome Kern, The Anderson Galleries, January 1929, lot no. 1112.) Godwin's letter was perhaps mounted in the book by Newton.

**Shelley, The Wandering Jew**  *?December 10, 1810– ?January 22, 1811*

SC 122  for 1810 we find that on one Thursday and one only in that year is there a notation of a "J. Taylor." This is in the entry for Thursday, December 6: "... theatre, Spoiled Child. adv. [i.e., present] Cooper, Dawe & J. Taylor."

In the Theatre Division of The New York Public Library we find programs for Covent Garden for November 29 and December 19, 1810, both of which announce a double bill for those evenings: a farce, *The Spoil'd Child*, and an opera, *Gustavus Vasa*. We may presume that the bill for December 6 also included the opera.

Godwin and John Taylor, then, were apparently both at Covent Garden on the night of Thursday, December 6, 1810, to see *Gustavus Vasa* and Godwin sent the above letter to Taylor, perhaps by an usher.

The only John Taylor associated with Godwin in the biographies is John Taylor of Norwich, from whom Godwin borrowed money. And at first one would assume that this was the John Taylor of the above note. But Godwin's other letters to John Taylor of Norwich do not have the playful tone of the above letter, and as he lived not in London but in Norwich he would be less likely to be at Covent Garden than would a Londoner. The Abinger Manuscripts show that Godwin was acquainted with another John Taylor, newspaper editor (first of *The Morning Post* and then of *The Sun*), playwright (*Monsieur Tonson*), and author (*Records of My Life*). He wrote to Godwin as early as 1795 praising "your ingenious and interesting work," *Caleb Williams*. In 1823 he wrote to Mrs. Godwin in a manner which shows a long-standing acquaintanceship.[2] Most probably this was the John Taylor (1757–1832) to whom Godwin wrote the above letter.

2. Abinger Manuscripts, Pforzheimer Microfilm, files 27 and 43.

SC 123  P. B. SHELLEY, FRAGMENT OF *THE WANDERING JEW*, ?DECEMBER 10, 1810–?JANUARY 22, 1811

HOLOGRAPH MANUSCRIPT, 3½ pages. Double sheet, 4$^{to}$ (8.7 x 7 inches). Laid paper. Watermark: c WILMOTT| 1810|. Title in the hand of T. J. Hogg.

# The Carl H. Pforzheimer Library

**Shelley, *The Wandering Jew***  ***?December 10, 1810–***
***?January 22, 1811***

PROVENANCE: Thomas Jefferson Hogg; John Ewer Jefferson Hogg (Sotheby, July 27, 1922, lot 334).

*The Wandering Jew ——*

*did the Elephant trample on me in vain the iron hoof of the wrathful steed*
*The mine big with destructive power burst upon me, & hurld me high in*
*the air. I fell down upon heap of smoking limbs but was only sing^d   The*
5 *Giants steel club rebounded from my body. The executioners hand could not*
*strangle me, nor w^d the hungry Lion in the Circus devour me   I cohabited*
*with poisonous snakes I pinched the red crest of the Dragon the serpent stung*
*but cd. not kill me. The Dragon tormented but cd. not devour me. I now*
*provoked the fury of Tyrants I said to Nero thou art a bloodhound said to*
10 *Christern thou art a bloodhound, said to Muley Ismail thou art a blood*
*hound: The tyrants invented cruel torments but c^d not kill me. Ha! not to*
*be able to die not to be able to die! not to be permitted to rest after the toils*
*of life, to be doomed for ever to be imprisoned in this Clay formed Dungen*
*to be forever clogged with this worthless body its' load of Diseases & infirmities*
15 *to be condemned to hold for milleniums that yawning monster Time that*
*hungry hyena ever bearing children, ever devouring again her offspring. Ha!*
*not to be permitted to die! Awful avenger in Heaven, hast thou in thine*
*armoury of wrath a punishment more dreadful! Then let it Thunder upon*
*me. command an hurricane to sweep me down to the foot of Carmel that I*
20 *there may lie extended. May pant writhe & die*

*And Ahasuerus dropped down Night covered his bristly eyelids. The*
*Angel bore me back to the cavern Sleep here said the Angel, sleep in peace,*
*the wrath of thy Judge is appeased, when thou shalt awake he will be arrived*
*he whose blod thou sawest flow upon Golgotha   whose mercy is extended*
25 *even to thee*

line 1. The title is cramped between the first line and the top edge of the paper, running through the *t* of *Elephant* and the *t, p*, and *l* of *trample*. It was perhaps written in when Hogg was preparing to have the manuscript copied for publication in his life of Shelley (1858).

line 4. *heap* (sic)

line 10. *Mulei* is a possible reading. The word is blotted but a short *y* seems visible through the blot. There is no dot for an *i*. ("Mulei" is the *German Museum* reading; see Collation.)

line 13. *Dungen*: the final *n* fades off in an indeterminate scrawl which may be intended as *on*. Shelley in many places in the manuscript contracts his final letters, particularly *ed, g*, or *y*.

line 15. Below the *T* of *Time* is a crossed-out

## Shelley, *The Wandering Jew*

*?December* **10**, **1810–**
*?January* **22**, **1811**

SC 123    letter, apparently the beginning of a word or words to be added between the lines. (*La Belle Assemblée* reads "*Sameness* and *Time*"; see Collation.)

line 17. *avenger* is the final word on the last line of page 2; *aven* is written large, then *ger* goes into a small blotted scrawl that overflows the right margin across the fold into page 3. Shelley must have written with the sheet open.

line 19. *hurricane:* the *n* has a long first loop and looks like an *h.*

line 20. *pant* and *die* are blotted; the *h* of *writhe* is written small and looks rather like an *e.* The words appear to have been written with a kind of dramatic violence.

line 24. *blod* (sic)

COLLATION (excluding punctuation, spelling, capitalization and contractions).

BELLE: THE WANDERING JEW, *LA BELLE ASSEMBLÉE; OR, BELL'S COURT AND FASHIONABLE MAGAZINE,* VI (1809), 20.

MAB: PERCY BYSSHE SHELLEY, *QUEEN MAB; A PHILOSOPHICAL POEM; WITH NOTES* (LONDON, 1813), PP. 188–189, NOTE TO "VII. — PAGE 88. AHASUERUS, RISE!"

MUSEUM: THE WANDERING JEW, BY SCHUBART, *GERMAN MUSEUM, OR MONTHLY REPOSITORY OF THE LITERATURE OF GERMANY, THE NORTH AND THE CONTINENT IN GENERAL,* III (1801), 424–426. (Identical with BELLE except as indicated.)

line 2. BELLE: upon me

line 3. MUSEUM: powder

line 3. BELLE: under me

line 3. BELLE: into the air

line 4. BELLE: heaps of
　　MAB: fell on heaps of

line 4. BELLE: and was

line 5. BELLE: giant's
　　MAB: giant's

line 6. BELLE: me; the tiger's tooth could not hurt me; nor
　　MAB: me, the tyger's tooth could not pierce me; nor

line 7. BELLE: and pinched
　　MAB: and pinched

line 7. MUSEUM: dark-red crest

line 8. MAB: destroy me. The dragon

line 8. BELLE: could not destroy me.
　　MAB: dared not to devour me.

line 9. MAB: I said
　　MUSEUM: tyrants; said

line 10. BELLE: Christiern
　　MAB: Christiern

line 10. MAB: I said

line 10. MUSEUM: Mulei

line 11. BELLE: but did
　　MAB: but did

line 13. BELLE: to be imprisoned for ever in the
　　MAB: to be imprisoned for ever

line 15. BELLE: behold

line 15. BELLE: monster, *Sameness* and *Time*
　　MAB: monster Sameness, and Time

line 15. MUSEUM: that lascivious and hungry hyena

line 16. BELLE: children, and ever
　　MAB: children, and ever

line 16. BELLE: offsprings

line 17. MUSEUM: [*Museum* text repeats phrase "not to be permitted to die."]

line 17. BELLE: thy

line 19. BELLE: a hurricane
　　MAB: a hurricane

line 20. MUSEUM: extended, pant

line 20. BELLE: and writhe
　　MAB: and writhe

line 21. MAB: [The *Queen Mab* text omits the final paragraph.]

line 21. MUSEUM: Ahasverus

line 21. BELLE: an angel

line 22. BELLE: carried him

line 22. BELLE: Angel to Ahasuerus, "Sleep
　　MUSEUM: Angel to Ahasverus

line 24. BELLE: Golgotha, and whose

line 24. BELLE: also extended to thee

# The Carl H. Pforzheimer Library

**Shelley, The Wandering Jew**          *?December 10, 1810–*
*?January 22, 1811*

SC 123    THE legend of the Wandering Jew exerted a never-ending fascination upon Shelley. During the winter of 1809–10, when he was but seventeen, he wrote a narrative poem in four cantos on the subject. It was the theme of a hopeless seeking for death that especially attracted him in the legend, a theme which occurs in his first novel, *Zastrozzi* (1810). In 1813, the Wandering Jew, Ahasuerus, and his story appear in *Queen Mab* and its Notes. The following year the theme is again treated in Shelley's fragmentary romance, *The Assassins*. In 1815 it is woven into the verse of *Alastor*. In 1821 Ahasuerus appears in *Hellas* to warn the Turkish emperor of his downfall. Here he is no longer, as in the earlier works, a victim of divine persecution but a mystic and philosopher.

## TEXTS

One does not work long with Shelley's early writings on the Wandering Jew without feeling that he has strayed into a kind of Alice-in-Wonderland world in which nothing is what it seems. The text and even the authorship of the 1809–10 poem, *The Wandering Jew*, have provided exasperating puzzles since the beginnings of Shelley scholarship; and the problems which emerge from the above innocent-appearing manuscript are almost equally complex.

Let us attempt to clear some ground by noting first that there are three *prose* versions of the Wandering Jew story: (1) the above manuscript; (2) a footnote in the 1809–10 poem, *The Wandering Jew*; (3) a Note to *Queen Mab*.

The Note to *Queen Mab* contains a good deal more of the story than does either the above fragment or the footnote in *The Wandering Jew*. It is fairly close to the text of the fragment (as the Collation shows) but quite different from that of the *Wandering Jew* footnote. For instance, in the sentences immediately prior to those with which the above fragment begins, the *Queen Mab* Note reads: "From cloud-encircled cliffs did I precipitate myself into the ocean; but the foaming billows cast me upon the shore and the burning arrow of existence pierced my cold heart again." The *Wandering Jew* footnote for what is apparently the parallel of this passage reads: "I cast myself from the overhanging summit of

**Shelley, The Wandering Jew**  ?December 10, 1810–
?January 22, 1811

SC 123  the gigantic Teneriffe into the wide weltering ocean. The clouds which hung upon its base below, bore up my odious weight; the foaming billows, swoln by the fury of the northern blast, opened to receive me, and, burying [me] in a vast abyss, at length dashed my almost inanimate frame against the crags."

Clearly we are here dealing with two different versions of the story. What were the origins of these versions? How are they related to the above manuscript? Let us begin with Shelley's own comments.

To the footnote in the 1809–10 poem, *The Wandering Jew*, Shelley adds: "I have endeavoured to deviate as little as possible from the extreme sublimity of idea which the *style* of the German author, of which this is a translation, so forcibly impresses."[1] The implication in this comment is that this version is a translation by Shelley. But Shelley did not know German at this time.[2] Medwin, who apparently wrote part of this poem in collaboration with Shelley, and hence should know, seems to imply that it was done by his (Medwin's) German master[3] (but from what original we do not know).

To the *Queen Mab* Note on the Wandering Jew Shelley adds: "This fragment is the translation of part of some German work, whose title I have vainly endeavoured to discover. I picked it up, dirty and torn, some years ago, in Lincoln's-Inn Fields." This *Queen Mab* Note was probably written between the summer of 1811 and the spring of 1813.[4]

Hence, in the *Wandering Jew* footnote Shelley gave an original translation, and in the *Queen Mab* Note a translation taken from a fragment which he claimed he had found in Lincoln's Inn Fields.

The problem was further complicated by Medwin. In 1823 in the preface to his poem *Ahasuerus*, Medwin wrote as follows:

In one of the daily rides I was accustomed to take in the spring of 1822, at Pisa, with Lord Byron and Mr. Shelley, a juvenile production [*Queen Mab*] of the latter, published without his consent, happened to become the subject of conversation; in the course of which, Lord Byron asked Mr. Shelley why he

---

1. Shelley, *Complete Works*, IV, 376 fn.    2. Hogg, *Shelley*, I, 122.

3. Medwin, *Shelley*, p. 489 (Appendix).

4. It was in this period that Shelley was working on the Notes to *Queen Mab* (or the essays which later became the Notes). See Cameron, *The Young Shelley*, pp. 400–402.

**Shelley, The Wandering Jew**

*?December* **10**, **1810–**
*?January* **22**, **1811**

SC 123    had prefaced his note on the Wandering Jew, attached to the poem above alluded to, with an assurance that it was accidentally picked up in Lincoln's-inn-fields; his reply was, "ask M., he best can answer the inquiry."

Though I perfectly remembered the circumstance of having given the note in question to Mr. Shelley, some fifteen years ago, I had a very vague recollection of what it contained, nor at this distance of time can I trace its origin. Whether it was translated by a German master who at that time attended me, from his own language, or was partly his composition, and partly mine, or what its real history is, I am at this moment entirely ignorant.[5]

In 1847 he wrote: "Mrs. Shelley is strangely misinformed as to the history of the fragment, which I, not Shelley, picked up in Lincoln's-Inn-Fields (as mentioned in my preface to *Ahasuerus*), and which was not found till some of the cantos had been written."[6] He does not mention the note to the poem, *The Wandering Jew*, but assumes that the two notes are the same.

When Hogg printed his version in 1858 he voiced skepticism of both Shelley's and Medwin's stories (a skepticism apparently shared by Byron):

Before Shelley came to Oxford he composed a tale, or a fragment of a tale, on the subject of the Wandering Jew, giving to him, however, the name of a Persian, not of a Jew – Ahasuerus, Artaxerxes. This no learned, accurate German would have done. That he found the composition in the streets of London is an integral portion of the fiction. . . . Somebody or other, determined not to be left behind in the race, declares that he found it himself, if I mistake not, and presented it to Shelley. Was not this worthy gentleman also present at Gnossus when the tablets of Dictys were brought to light by the earthquake? A portion of the fragment has been printed in the notes to *Queen Mab*. I have amongst Shelley's papers a fragment of the fragment, in his handwriting. It is one leaf only, and it appears to be the last, the conclusion of the story.[7]

Hogg apparently regarded the fragment as an original composition of Shelley's. A few years after the publication of his life of Shelley, however, it was shown to be a translation of a German poem by Christian Friedrich Daniel Schubart and it was discovered that an English transla-

5. Medwin, *Shelley*, p. 489 (Appendix).

6. Medwin, *Shelley*, p. 42. Mary Shelley in her edition of Shelley's poems in 1839 had repeated Shelley's claim to have found the "fragment."

7. Hogg, *Shelley*, I, 122.

**Shelley, The Wandering Jew** *?December 10, 1810–*<br>*?January 22, 1811*

SC 123  tion had appeared in a periodical called *German Museum* in 1801.[8] This *German Museum* version was presumed to be the probable source for Shelley's *Queen Mab* version until 1940 when Newman I. White announced a further discovery:

> The translation was "a scrap of paper" picked up in Lincoln's Inn Fields by either Shelley or Medwin. It was from *La Belle Assemblée, or Bell's Court and Fashionable Magazine*, for January 1809, pp. 19–20, and not the *Germanic Museum* for 1801, as Dowden and others have supposed. A close textual comparison of these two translations with Schubart's original shows that the 1809 translation is copied from the 1801 translation. There are several slight verbal variations in the two, and Shelley's version agrees in these with the 1809 version. . . . An inaccurate paraphrase of part of it appears as a footnote in Shelley's *The Wandering Jew*.[9]

White's position, then, is that "Shelley's version" (by which he means that in the *Queen Mab* Note) comes from the *Belle Assemblée* text and that the version in the poem on the Wandering Jew is a "paraphrase" of this same text. There is, however, no single "version" by Shelley. There are two versions (in print), that in the Note to *Queen Mab* and that in Hogg's *Life of Percy Bysshe Shelley* (taken from the above manuscript). And the version in the poem on the Wandering Jew is not a "paraphrase" of the *Belle Assemblée* text but a separate work.

That White was correct in stating that the text of the *Queen Mab* Note is closer to *La Belle Assemblée* than to the *German Museum* is shown by a comparison of the texts, especially in the opening paragraph[10] (missing from the above manuscript, which begins *in medias res*). There

8. *The Complete Poetical Works of Shelley*, ed. William Michael Rossetti (London, 1881), I, 434–435; Dowden, *Shelley*, I, 44 fn. For the *German Museum* see Textual Notes above. The *German Museum* version is signed P.W., presumably by the translator. It is followed by another translation from Schubart, "Jupiter," also signed P.W.

9. White, *Shelley*, I, 580–581. White mistakenly gives the title as *Germanic Museum*. The full title is *German Museum, or Monthly Repository of the Literature of Germany, the North and the Continent in General*. According to William S. Ward's *Index and Finding List*, it was published from January 1800 to June 1801.

10. For instance, the third sentence ends and the fourth begins as follows in the *Queen Mab* Note: ". . . the unfeeling wretch drove Him away with brutality. The Saviour of mankind staggered. . . ." *La Belle Assemblée* has the same wording; but *German Museum* reads: ". . . drove him away with spiteful brutality: and the Saviour staggered. . . ."

# The Carl H. Pforzheimer Library

SC 123   are, however, differences between the *Belle Assemblée* and *Queen Mab* texts. In line 3, for example, *Belle* reads *under me*, *Mab* reads *upon me*; in line 4 *Belle* reads *fell down upon*, *Mab* reads *fell on*; in line 6 *Belle* reads *hurt*, *Mab* reads *pierce*; in line 8 where *Belle* reads *destroy*, *Mab* reads *devour*; in line 15 *Belle* reads *behold*, *Mab* reads *hold*. These differences can hardly have arisen from faulty transcription alone. Shelley, therefore, cannot have copied his *Queen Mab* Note directly from *La Belle Assemblée*. On the other hand the *Belle* and *Mab* texts are sufficiently close to indicate some form of ultimate relationship.

If we turn now to the above manuscript we find that it, too, is closer to *La Belle Assemblée* than to the *German Museum*. For instance, our manuscript follows *La Belle Assemblée* in reading *red crest* (line 7), not *dark-red crest*, and in omitting *German Museum's lascivious and* (line 15). But the text of our manuscript could no more be derived from either the *German Museum* or *La Belle Assemblée* than could the *Mab* text, for it shares the above-noted readings — *under, I, pierce, devour, hold* — with the *Mab* text and differs in them from both *La Belle Assemblée* and the *German Museum*. In the final paragraph (omitted in *Queen Mab*) the manuscript reads *bore me*, the *Belle* and *Museum* texts read *carried him*; the manuscript reads *Whose*, they read *and whose*; the manuscript reads *even to*, they read *to*. The manuscript differs from them also in the omission of *the tiger's tooth could not hurt me* (line 6) and *Sameness and* (line 15).

The above manuscript, as the Collation shows, differs also in several readings from the *Queen Mab* Note. The *Queen Mab* Note includes *the tyger's tooth could not pierce me* and *Sameness, and*. In line 4 the manuscript reads *down upon*, *Mab* reads *on* (*Belle* and *Museum* both read *down upon*); in line 8 the manuscript reads *kill*, *Mab* reads *destroy* (*Belle* and *Museum* both read *kill*); in line 8 also the manuscript reads *cd.*, *Mab* reads *dared* (*Belle* and *Museum* both read *could*). In line 11 the manuscript reads *c$^d$*, *Mab* reads *did* (*Belle* and *Museum* read *did*). The manuscript differs from *Mab* in the placing of *for ever* (line 13). The manuscript text and the *Mab* text, therefore, were not derived directly from the same basic text for these, too, are not the kind of deviations that can be ascribed solely to carelessness in transcription. We seem, then, to

SC 123  be confronted not with one but two unknown direct sources, one for the above manuscript and one for the *Queen Mab* Note.

What the *Queen Mab* Note text was or how Shelley got hold of it remains a mystery. He never makes it clear when he picked it up. Medwin, although writing of the *Queen Mab* Note (1811–1813), placed the episode "some fifteen years" prior to 1823, which would put it in 1808 or 1809. And if anything was picked up it was probably in this period, for it was then and then only that Medwin and Shelley were working together on the Wandering Jew legend. Medwin, however, informs us that "the fragment" "was not found till some of the cantos had been written." And for two friends to be working on a poem on the Wandering Jew and then to find by chance a fragment of a poem on it blowing around in Lincoln's Inn Fields seems to border on the miraculous. If there had been any such dramatic discovery either during or before composition it would surely have been commented on by the youthful authors in *The Wandering Jew*. Furthermore, Shelley's contention in the Note to *Queen Mab* that he did not know the "title" of the "fragment" that he claimed to have picked up can hardly be true, for that Note was published in 1813 and Shelley had given the same material under the title *The Wandering Jew* in 1809–10.

But although the "picking up" story is highly dubious, Shelley's contention that he did not know the author may be true. If he had seen either the *German Museum* or *La Belle Assemblée* he would have known the author, for both name Schubart.[11] That he had not seen either periodical may be indicated also in his reference to the work as a "fragment," "part of some German work." Both periodicals present the work as complete, which, in fact, it is — a short poem on one aspect of the life of the Wandering Jew.

### DATING AND COMPOSITION

That the above manuscript was the one in the possession of Hogg is shown not only by textual comparison but also by its provenance and

11. *La Belle Assemblée* adds the following note under the title: "Our Readers are acquainted with the uses to which Mr. Lewis, in his Novel of the Monk, has converted the ancient legend of the Wandering Jew. — The original story was the invention of the celebrated Schubart, and is as follows."

**Shelley, The Wandering Jew** *?December 10, 1810–
?January 22, 1811*

SC 123   by its correspondence with Hogg's description of his manuscript (quoted above). When or how Hogg received it from Shelley he does not say, but he places it immediately after a letter of Shelley's announcing his return to Oxford following the Christmas vacation and along with poems given to him at Oxford.[12]

Other evidence also places the manuscript in this period. It bears no date but the watermark is c WILMOTT| 1810| and the sheet is 8.7 by 7 inches. Examination of the letters in our collection reveals Shelley using this paper for two letters only, both of them to Hogg and both from Field Place: January 3, 1811 (sc 128), and January 6, 1811 (sc 129). Examination of the Shelley letters in The Berg Collection of The New York Public Library discloses two other letters on this paper: one to Janetta Phillips, and a verse letter to Graham, both of which are undated but which can be dated from other evidence as May 1811. Both were written at Field Place. Of twenty-two Shelley letters between May 20, 1810, and June 5, 1811, in our collection, fifteen are on Wilmott paper of various sizes and dates of watermarks. After that date there are no more of our Shelley letters on Wilmott paper. It would appear, furthermore, that this Wilmott paper was from a stock at Field Place, for of these fifteen letters only one was not written at Field Place, namely the first, May 20, 1810, which was written at Eton. When Shelley wrote to Hogg from Field Place on January 17 (sc 135) the paper was Wilmott; when he wrote to Timothy Shelley from Oxford on February 17 (sc 140) the paper was not Wilmott. A letter to Graham from Oxford on February 14, 1811, now in The Berg Collection, is not on Wilmott paper but the verse letter written from Field Place in May is. And several of the Timothy Shelley letters from Field Place in our collection are on Wilmott paper. The indication is that the above manuscript was written at Field Place.

The letter to Hogg from Field Place on January 3, 1811, is of special interest. It is not only written on Wilmott paper, identical in watermark and chain lines with that of the *Wandering Jew* manuscript, but it contains phrases almost identical with those in the manuscript. In the

12. Hogg, *Shelley*, I, 120–126; sc 135 (Jan. 17, 1811), sc 114 ("Cold cold is the blast"), sc 120 ("Death! where is thy Victory!"). See also sc 124 (?Dec. 10, 1810–?Jan. 22, 1811), Commentary.

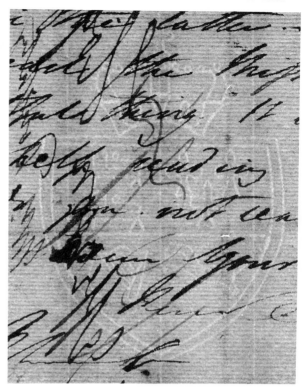

*Royal coat of arms, quartered, in crowned shield (SC 171)*

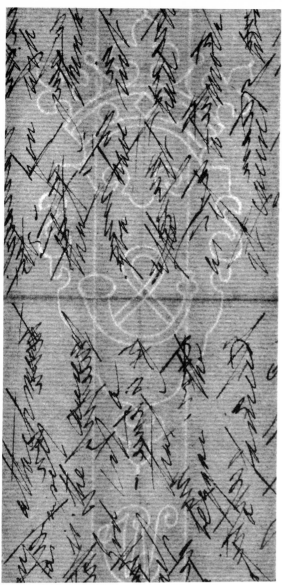

*Posthorn in crowned shield, with*
*Wilmott cipher (SC 133)*

*Shelley crest (SC 145)*      *Elizabeth Shelley's*
*initials (SC 132)*

*Shelley coat of arms with crest*
*(SC 150)*

*Fleur-de-lis/1798/c&n/(SC 35)*

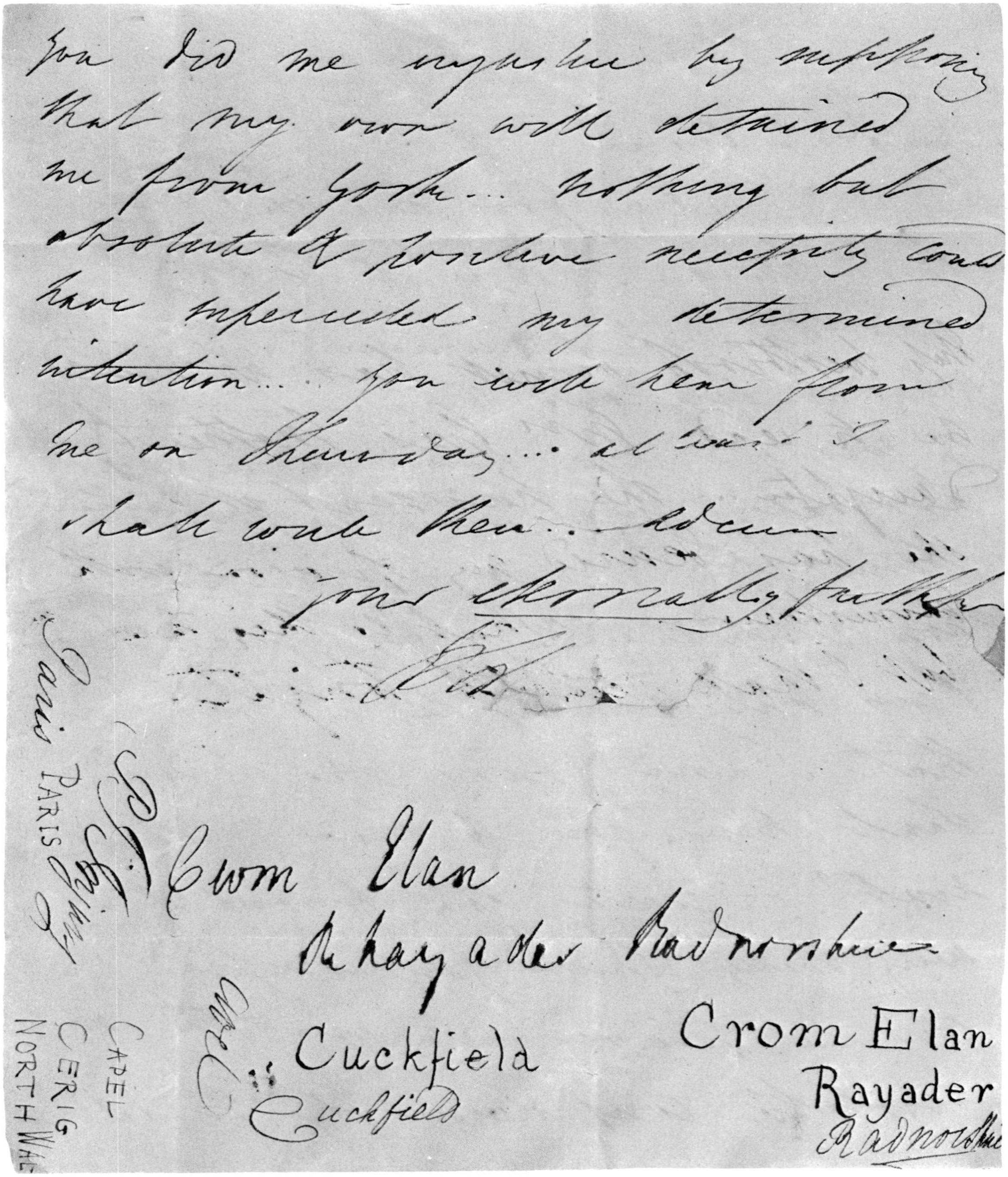

PLATE XXVI

*P. B. Shelley to T. J. Hogg, July ?15, 1811 (SC 169), page 2 (with notations by T. J. Hogg, and blottings)*

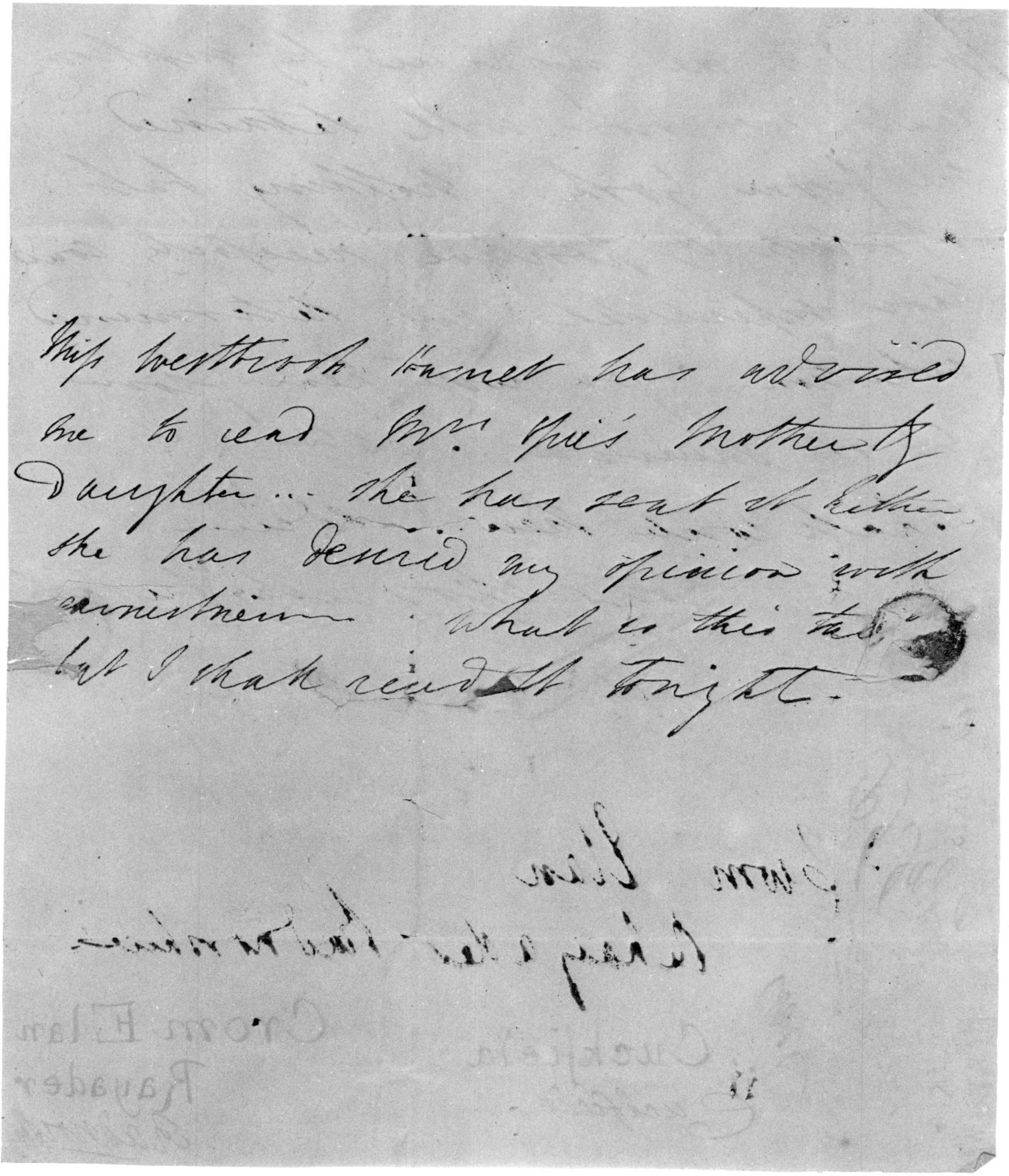

PLATE XXVII

Miss Westbrook Harriet has advised
me to read Mrs Opie's Mother &
Daughter... she has sent it hither
she has desired my opinion with
earnestness. What is this that,
but I shall read it tonight.

*P. B. Shelley to T. J. Hogg, July ?15, 1811 (SC 169), page 3 (with blottings)*

PLATE XXVIII

*Watermarks*

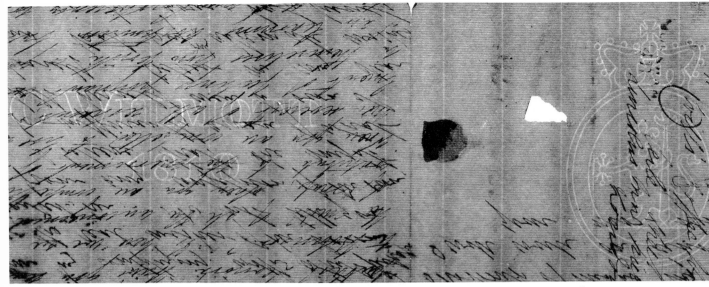

C WILMOTT/1810/(*countermark*), *lion rampant in crowned oval (watermark)*(*SC 126*)

BUDGEN & WILMOTT/1809/(*SC 130*)

HALL & TAPLIN/1804/(*SC 50*)

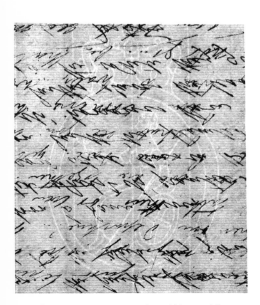

*Britannia in crowned oval*/(*SC 166*)

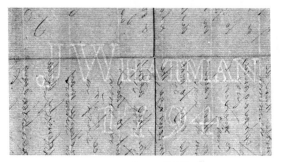

J WHATMAN/1794/(*SC 28*)

**Shelley, Aristotle's Ethics**   *?December 10, 1810–*
*?January 22, 1811*

SC 123   letter (sc 128, line 35) Shelley writes: "Has vengeance in its armoury of wrath a punishment more dreadful!" In the manuscript (line 17) he writes: "hast thou in thine armoury of wrath a punishment more dreadful!" In the letter (line 14) he writes: "For the immoral 'never to be able to die, never to escape from some shrine as chilling as the clay-formed dungeon which now its inhabits is the future punishment which I believe in." In the manuscript (line 13) he writes: "not to be able to die . . . to be doomed for ever to be imprisoned in this *Clay formed* Dungen."

Thus the probability is that the manuscript was written at Field Place during the Christmas vacation — about December 10, 1810, to about January 22, 1811.[13] As the manuscript has not been folded for transmission through the mails it was probably given to Hogg by Shelley at Oxford between about January 26, when Shelley returned to Oxford, and March 26, 1811, when he and Hogg left Oxford.

The manuscript may originally have contained an initial sheet giving the first section of the text. The *Belle Assemblée* text totals 114 lines; the final section of it covered by the manuscript totals 44 lines. As the manuscript contains three pages and four lines of writing, this would indicate that there was another double sheet, four pages, which contained the first portion of the text.

13. Shelley had arrived at Field Place by December 10 because he inscribed a copy of *St. Irvyne* (now in The Berg Collection of The New York Public Library) to his uncle, Robert Parker, from there on that date. He informed Hogg in a letter of *ca.* January 23 that he would be back at Oxford on January 24 or 25; on January 17 (sc 135) he stated that he would be in London on "Tuesday" (i.e., Jan. 22).

SC 124   P. B. SHELLEY, TRANSLATION FROM ARISTOTLE'S *ETHICS*, ?DECEMBER 10, 1810–?JANUARY 22, 1811

HOLOGRAPH MANUSCRIPT, 4 pages. Double sheet, folio (12.7 x 7.9 inches). Laid paper. Watermark: [Britannia in crowned oval]|; countermark: ABBEY MILL| 1809|.

PROVENANCE: Thomas Jefferson Hogg; Major R. J. Jefferson Hogg (Sotheby, June 30, 1948, lot 65A).

SC 124                    <u>8 Chapter</u>   *Ari*                              *F.P*

Cha

stat⟨ ⟩

*It is a question whether a man ought to love himself ~~or~~ more than another;*

5    *for they who love themselves best are blamed, & are called, as if by an oppro-*
*brious title ~~the~~ lovers of themselves. . It is evident that the wicked man does*
he does this the more
*every thing for his own sake, ~~he~~ in proportion as he is more abandoned, ~~It~~*
*Men reproach him as one who does nothing except for his own sake— But*

10    *the virtuous man thro' a love of virtue & in proportion as he is more virtuous*
*he acts the more for the sake of virtue & of his friend, & neglects his own*
*interests; but facts, contradict this reasoning & with justice, for men say*
*that you ought most to love the person who is most friendly, but he is most*
*friendly who wishes well to his friend for his sake, & would wish so, <u>even</u>*

15    *altho' no one sh^d know it; —— But – these properties & every other by which*
*the friendly person is distinguished are chiefly found existing in a man towards*
arising
*himself, for it has been proved that every friendly office ~~passes~~ from a man's*
passes
20    *self to others; & every opinion agrees with this reasoning, as friends have*
*one soul, every thing is common,   Equality is friendship; "the knee nearest*
*the leg." all these are most applicable to a man's self, for a man is most*
*friendly to himself. therefore ought to love himself best both sides of the*
*question wearing the appearance of truth we are justly in doubt to which*

25    *we ought to incline. We must distinguish & define these opinions that we*
*may see how far, & in what respects each side is true . . the case w^d soon be*
*plain if we understood what each party means by self-love . . . for the one*
*party uses it as a term of reproach for those who give themselves the greater*
*share of wealth, of honour, & of bodily pleasure. the vulgar busy themselves*

30    *in the acquisition of these things, considering them as the chief good, wherefore*
*they become objects of contention, such is the nature of the vulgar.— Thus*
*from the baseness of the vulgar this apellation has become ignominious. .*
*It may justly be considered as a term of reproach to men who are <u>thus</u> lovers*
*of themselves, it is evident that it is the custom of the vulgar to call those lovers*

**Shelley, Aristotle's Ethics**  ?*December 10, 1810–*
?*January 22, 1811*

SC 124 *of themselves who ~~claim~~ procure for themselves these things —— But if any
one sh^d always strive to act virtuously, if he eminently sh^d arrogate to himself
~~wisdom that~~ whatever is consistent with wisdom virtue & honour, no one
would call such a one, selfish, nor w^d reproach him; but such a person w^d
appear to be very selfish, for he claims to himself what is most honorable,*

40 *most profitable, & gratifies X the nobler propensities of his nature, & is
entirely subservient to them. –*

---

*X gratifies ~~the a being~~ a being who is far superior to himself, & is entirely
subservient to her,*

---

*X And as a ~~city~~ the supreme power of the city evidently is most essentially*

45 *"The city" & every thing else is an adjunct to it; thus it is with human
nature. & he who loves such a being & ~~is grat~~ gratifies him he is most selfish*
          in pro
*— a man is called powerful or weak ~~who is or is not able to govern his~~ mind
in proportion as his mind does or does not govern as ~~with person~~ this consti-*
                                      as the greatest
50 *tutes the essence of a man. these men appear to ~~have acted~~ have done those
things most willingly which they have done in unison with reason. . It is
evident that is ~~man~~ the essence of a man, & that the virtuous man values this
most. Wherefore he is most selfish, but, this species of self-love is different*

55 *from that which is used as a term of reproach, & differs as much from it, as*
     a life
*~~living~~ according to reason differs from a life according to passion. . A desire
of what is honorable from that of what appears profitable all men praise as
honour, those who labor more than others in the performance of virtue, if all*

60 *were to contend in integrity & endeavour to act most honorably all necessaries
w^d be common & the greatest good w^d be in the power of each individual –
if such is the nature of virtue. therefore the virtuous man ought to be selfish
for by acting honorably he will reap advantage himself & ~~a pr~~ profit others.
but the wicked ought not to be selfish for he will injure himself & his neighbours*

65 *following his evil inclinations. for ~~the acts~~ what the wicked does is different
from what he ought to do, but the virtuous does what he ought, for the mind
always selects What is best for itself–  The virtuous man obeys his mind.*

**Shelley, Aristotle's Ethics**  ***?December* 10, 1810–**
***?January* 22, 1811**

SC 124  *it is a true saying that the good man, should perform man things for his*
*friends & country even if it ~~shd be ordered~~ death shd. be demanded – he will*

70  *reject wealth & honor & every advantage which is the object of contention,*
*whilst he carefully procures for himself virtue, every one wd prefer the enjoy-*
*ment of great happiness for a short while, to that of trifling Obt for a long*
*time. . to live a happy life for one year ~~to a life of one day to~~ to live under*

75  *the dominion of chance for many years — one great & noble action to many*
*trifling*

line 1. *Ari:* probable reading

line 2. *Cha:* probable reading; written in large elaborate curling lines.

line 3. *stat⟨ ⟩:* probable reading; in very small letters immediately below the (thick) underline of *8 Chapter*. The illegible letter may be *m* followed by a dash.

line 8. *It:* probable reading

line 19. *passes* is actually placed above the line between *to* and *others. to* is the first word of the line in the manuscript but as the double *f* of *office* came down in front of it, there was no space to insert *passes* above the line in front of *to* as the sense requires.

line 24. the cross lines for the second *t* of *truth,* the *t* of *justly,* the final *t* of *doubt* follow the words and have the appearance of dashes. These and other indications show that Shelley was writing rapidly.

line 28. *using* converted into *uses.*

line 29. *honour* ends in a scrawl but *honour* and not *honor* seems intended; so, too, in lines 37

and 59; in line 70 the spelling is clearly *honor.*

line 32. *apellation* (sic)

line 35. ~~*claim:*~~ the final *m* is incomplete. Shelley apparently changed his mind before he had completed the word.

line 37. ~~*wisdom that:*~~ probable reading

line 50. ~~*greatest:*~~ probable reading

line 68. *good man, should perform:* Unlike the haste shown in the rest of the manuscript these words appear to have been written with unusual slowness; the *o* and *d* of *good,* the *m* of *man,* all the letters of *should,* and *p* and *er* of *person* are written as separate, unjoined units. Perhaps Shelley was looking at the text that he was translating or copying, instead of at the paper, and writing mechanically as he looked.

line 68. *man* (sic): *man*[y].

line 72. *Obt* (sic): The usual contraction for obedient in the close of a letter; here stands for *obedience.*

line 76. *trifling* is the final word on the last line of page 4.

**T**HEY are very dull people here', Shelley said to me one evening soon after his arrival [at Oxford], with a long-drawn sigh, after musing awhile; 'a little man sent for me this morning, and told me in an almost inaudible whisper that I must read: "you must read", he said many times in his small voice. I answered that I had no objection. He persisted; so, to satisfy him, for he did not appear to believe me, I told him I had some books in my pocket, and I began to take them out. He stared at me, and said that was not exactly what he meant: "you must read *Prometheus Vinctus,* and Demosthenes *de Coronâ,* and Euclid."

**Shelley, Aristotle's Ethics**     *?December 10, 1810–*
*?January 22, 1811*

SC 124   "Must I read Euclid?" I asked sorrowfully. "Yes, certainly; and when you have read the Greek works I have mentioned, you must begin Aristotle's Ethics, and then you may go on to his other treatises. It is of the utmost importance to be well acquainted with Aristotle." This he repeated so often that I was quite tired, and at last I said, "Must I care about Aristotle? what if I do not mind Aristotle?" I then left him, for he seemed to be in great perplexity.'

Notwithstanding the slight he had thus cast upon the great master of the science, that has so long been the staple of Oxford, he was not blind to the value of the science itself. He took to the scholastic logic very kindly, seized its distinctions with his accustomed quickness, felt a keen interest in the study, and patiently endured the exposition of those minute discriminations, which the tyro is apt to contemn as vain and trifling.[1]

Later, Hogg further informs us in discussing the origin of *The Necessity of Atheism*, he and Shelley "made a very careful analysis" of the works of Locke and Hume "as was customary with those who read the *Ethics* and the other treatises of Aristotle for their degrees."[2]

The "little man" of Hogg's anecdote was no doubt one of Shelley's tutors at University College (perhaps the Dean, George Rowley) who was making the customary assignment of readings and translations for the term. In spite of Shelley's initial balking at this assignment it is clear (from Hogg's second paragraph) that he became interested in Aristotle and the Aristotelian logic.

Aristotle was, of course, not an influence on Shelley of the same order as Plato, nor can one point to a single direct effect of the *Ethics* parallel to that of one other work also assigned by Shelley's tutor at their first interview, namely Aeschylus' *Prometheus Bound*, but nevertheless Shelley learned from Aristotle. The influence of the *Ethics* is present in the *Speculations on Morals*, although blended with that of Hume and others, and Aristotle is listed among those to be treated in a planned essay on "progressive excellence."[3] In the *Discourse on the Manners of the Antient Greeks Relative to the Subject of Love*, written in Italy in 1818, Shelley praises Aristotle's contributions to thought, particularly in ethics:

1. Hogg, *Shelley*, I, 70.     2. *Ibid.*, p. 163.
3. Shelley, *Complete Works*, VII, 72.

[ 663 ]

# The Carl H. Pforzheimer Library

**Shelley, Aristotle's Ethics**

*?December* **10**, **1810**–
*?January* **22**, **1811**

In physical knowledge Aristotle and Theophrastus had already — no doubt assisted by the labours of those of their predecessors whom they criticise — made [advances] worthy of the maturity of science. . . . Metaphysics, the science of man's intimate nature, and logic, or the grammar and elementary principles of that science, recieved [*sic*] from the latter philosophers of the Periclean age a firm basis. All our more exact philosophy is built upon the labours of these great men, and many of the words which we employ in metaphysical distinctions were invented by them to give accuracy and system to their reasonings. The science of morals, or the voluntary conduct of men in relation to themselves or others, dates from this epoch. How inexpressibly bolder and more pure were the doctrines of those great men, in comparison with the timid maxims which prevail in the writings of the most esteemed modern moralists.[4]

In his last great work, the unfinished *Triumph of Life*, Shelley indicates, however, that he did not regard Aristotle as a final authority but as a great pioneer whose scholasticism was supplanted by the science-minded Bacon:

> The other long outlived both woes and wars,
> Throned in the thoughts of men, and still had kept
> The jealous key of Truth's eternal doors,
>
> If Bacon's eagle spirit had not leapt
> Like lightning out of darkness — he compelled
> The Proteus shape of Nature, as it slept
>
> To wake, and lead him to the caves that held
> The treasure of the secrets of its reign.[5]

Of Shelley's early studies in Aristotle only two traces remain, the above manuscript and a letter to Hogg of May 9, 1811 (sc 158): "What constitutes real virtue   motive or consequence.? surely the former. in proportion as a man is selfish so far has he receded from the motive which constitutes virtue; I have left the proof to Aristotle . ." It has been suggested that this comment indicated that Shelley enclosed the above translation from Aristotle within this letter, but that it was not so

---

4. Text in Notopoulos, *Platonism*, pp. 405–406.

5. *The Triumph of Life*, lines 266–273. Shelley had just commented on Aristotle's pupil Alexander the Great; hence, "the other" for Aristotle. For a possible echo from Bacon in the passage see William O. Scott, "Shelley's Admiration for Bacon," *PMLA*, LXXIII (June 1958), 229.

*Shelley, Aristotle's Ethics*                    *?December* 10, 1810–
                                                 *?January* 22, 1811

SC 124    enclosed — or, indeed, enclosed in any letter — is shown by the fact that it bears none of the characteristic folding marks of a sheet folded within a letter.[6] Furthermore, Shelley has written "Single Sheet" on the outside of this particular letter, indicating that there was no other sheet folded within it. Shelley's reference in the letter is intended to be taken by Hogg either as a general reference to their discussions on Aristotle a few months previously at Oxford, or, more likely, to specific discussions on the above manuscript, for example (line 6): "the wicked man does every thing for his own sake . . . But the virtuous man thro' a love of virtue & in proportion as he is more virtuous he acts the more for the sake of virtue & of his friend, & neglects his own interests . . ."

The question of selfishness and virtue was, as Shelley's letters of the Christmas vacation of 1810–11 show, a frequent subject of discussion between the two friends. Shelley feared that Hogg's system of "perfectibility" in love had elements of "self" in it.[7] It might have been as a result of these arguments that Shelley gave Hogg the above translation from Aristotle, a translation perhaps originally done routinely for his tutor.[8]

The initials "F.P" in the heading show that the manuscript was written at Field Place; Hogg's comments on Shelley's study of Aristotle at Oxford indicate the Oxford period as the time of composition. Most probably, therefore, the translation was made at Field Place during the Christmas vacation of 1810–11 (*ca.* December 10 to *ca.* January 22),[9] and

6. This translation from Aristotle was at first thought to be an original work by Shelley. (Walter Sidney Scott, ed. *Shelley at Oxford*, [London], 1944, p. 48.) The discovery that it was a translation was presented in two articles in 1946: Kenneth Neill Cameron, "Shelley and Aristotle," *Notes and Queries*, CXC (Feb. 23, 1946), 80; Carlos Baker, "Shelley's Translation from Aristotle," *MLN*, LXI (June 1946), 405–406. Baker suggested that the manuscript had been enclosed in the letter in May (incorrectly dated May 13 in the standard editions).

7. See sc 127 (Jan. 1, 1811), and Commentary.

8. The editor of *Notes and Queries*, *loc. cit.*, suggested that the translation was perhaps done for Shelley's tutor. This suggestion is supported by the interview with the tutor given by Hogg and quoted above.

9. See sc 123 (?Dec. 10, 1810–?Jan. 22, 1811) and sc 136 (Jan. ?19–21, 1811), Commentaries. It is theoretically possible, of course, that it was done while Shelley was at Field Place during the spring and summer of 1811 prior to his elopement with Harriet Westbrook on August 25. But this is unlikely. Shelley would have no special motive for making such a translation at that time, and he gave no manuscripts to Hogg following their period of friendship at Oxford.

[ 665 ]

# The Carl H. Pforzheimer Library

SC 124      then given to Hogg at Oxford following Shelley's return. It was apparently at this time also that Shelley gave Hogg other literary manuscripts.[10]

The section of the *Ethics* which Shelley thus presented to Hogg comprises about the first three quarters of Chapter Eight of Book Nine. As with some of the other manuscripts given to Hogg, this one seems at first to be incomplete — ending without punctuation at the end of a page —[11] and yet it probably is complete, for the final word comes at the end of a sentence and of a train of thought. Shelley was perhaps trying to give the impression of a fragment of a larger work. And if this is so then the above manuscript must have been copied especially for Hogg and was not a first draft for Shelley's tutor. The manuscript gives a sense of rapidity of writing, the thought constantly running ahead of the words, which also makes one suspect that it was not a first-time translation from the original. It may be that Shelley had translated the passage for his tutor and either knew it well or had his first draft beside him as he wrote. (See line 68 in the Textual Notes.)

In Book Eight Aristotle begins his discussion of friendship, a topic that would have a special interest for Shelley and Hogg. He presents it as one of the most important sources of happiness: "For without friends no one would choose to live, though he had all other goods." In Book Nine he continues the discussion and brings up in Chapter Four the apparently paradoxical argument that friendship is based on self-love. In Chapter Eight of Book Nine (from which the above excerpt is taken) he defines self-love. His argument runs as follows: (a) it is thought that a good man should not act from love of self; (b) but what a man feels toward his friend he also feels toward himself; (c) there is a difference between sensuous love and intellectual or moral love; (d) intellectual and moral self-love is good for it makes one perform good deeds in order to make oneself worthy of such love; (e) hence, this kind of love felt for a friend is good also. The final section of the chapter, which is not in Shelley's manuscript, runs as follows (in a modern translation):[12]

10. See SC 114 (July-August 1810); SC 120 (?Nov. 17–?Dec. 8, 1810); SC 123 (?Dec. 10, 1810–?Jan. 22, 1811).

11. See also SC 120 (?Nov. 17–?Dec. 8, 1810) and Commentary.

12. *The Works of Aristotle*, ed. W. D. Ross, IX, *Ethica Nicomachea*, trans. W. D. Ross (Oxford, 1925).

## Shelley, Aristotle's Ethics

*?December 10, 1810–*
*?January 22, 1811*

SC 124   Now those who die for others doubtless attain this result; it is therefore a great prize that they choose for themselves. They will throw away wealth too on condition that their friends will gain more; for while a man's friend gains wealth he himself achieves nobility; he is therefore assigning the greater good to himself. The same too is true of honour and office; all these things he will sacrifice to his friend; for this is noble and laudable for himself. Rightly then is he thought to be good, since he chooses nobility before all else. But he may even give up actions to his friend; it may be nobler to become the cause of his friend's acting than to act himself. In all the actions, therefore, that men are praised for, the good man is seen to assign to himself the greater share in what is noble. In this sense, then, as has been said, a man should be a lover of self; but in the sense in which most men are so, he ought not.

Shelley's translation is the earliest of his extant Greek translations (his *Symposium* is still used today; for instance, in the Everyman edition). It is interesting to compare his style with that of the leading English translator of the time, the famed and eccentric scholar (rumored worshiper of Jupiter) Thomas Taylor. Shelley's style is noticeably more direct and simple than Taylor's. For instance, where Shelley writes (line 5), "for they who love themselves best are blamed," Taylor writes, "For those are reprehended who love themselves transcendently."[13] For line 40, of which Shelley gives a variant version, Taylor writes: "for he distributes to himself things which are most beautiful and good, is gratified in his most principal part [intellect,] and in all things is obedient to it." A modern translation renders the final phrase: "gratifies the most authoritative element in himself." The phrase "the knee nearest the leg" (line 21) Taylor gives as "the knee is near to the leg." A modern translation (by W. D. Ross) notes that the phrase literally means "the knee is nearer than the shin," and gives as an equivalent "charity begins at home."

13. [The Works of Aristotle] *Translated from the Greek by Thomas Taylor* (London, 1806–1812), [VII], *The Rhetoric, Poetic and Nicomachean Ethics of Aristotle* (London, 1811), 556–557.

# The Carl H. Pforzheimer Library

## SHELLEY, HOGG, AND ELIZABETH SHELLEY:
### HOGG'S CENSORSHIP OF SHELLEY'S LETTERS

The first period of the relationship of Hogg and Shelley extended from their initial meeting at University College, Oxford, in October 1810 until Shelley's elopement with Harriet Westbrook late in August 1811. During this first period the personal (as distinct from the intellectual) interest in their letters centers around Hogg and Elizabeth Shelley, with a secondary emphasis on Shelley's dissolving romance with Harriet Grove.

On both subjects distortions have crept into Shelley biography because of changes made in the texts of these letters by Hogg. Nor has it really been possible in the past to correct these distortions, as the following facts indicate. Hogg published forty-four letters for this period[1] in his life of Shelley (changing the text as he saw fit). In 1910 partial corrections in five of these letters, made by Lady Jane Shelley, were published.[2] In 1943 and 1944 four letters in full and seven in part out of these forty-four were published from the manuscripts.[3] In the present volume we publish thirty-four of these forty-four letters from the manuscripts plus collations with Hogg's texts.

1. Presumably these are all that are still extant.

2. By André Koszul in *La Jeunesse de Shelley* (Paris, 1910), pp. 405–418, and subsequently by Roger Ingpen in his edition of Shelley's letters (1914) and in Shelley, *Complete Works*, VIII (1926). On Lady Shelley see "The Provenance of Shelley and his Circle Manuscripts," below, p. 892 and fn. 30. Lady Shelley did not record all of Hogg's changes. For instance, in the letter of December 20, 1810 (now with the Abinger Manuscripts) in the second to last paragraph "shall ever" should read "can," "toleration" should read "religion," "of intolerance" should read "of Xt's." (Shelley, *Complete Works*, VIII, 26.)

3. In *The Athenians* (London, 1943), *Shelley at Oxford* ([London], 1944), and *Harriet and Mary* (London, 1944), edited by the Reverend Walter Sidney Scott (the husband of a grandniece of T. J. Hogg), and republished in *New Shelley Letters* (Yale University Press, 1949). Scott published a total of twenty-nine letters from Shelley to Hogg either in whole or in part. He did not have available to him material previously purchased by The Carl H. Pforzheimer Library from the Hogg family (see "The Provenance of Shelley and his Circle Manuscripts," below, pp. 904–907) nor some letters which Lady Shelley failed to return to the Hogg family and which were among the Abinger Manuscripts.

Although Scott's texts are a welcome advance over Hogg they leave much to be desired. He frequently misreads Shelley's hand, omits words as illegible which can be read (sometimes quite easily), makes silent changes in spelling, punctuation, and capitalization, and seldom indicates Shelley's cancellations (which are often most revealing). His customary statement following the presentation of part of a letter — "The rest of the above letter is printed accurately in Hogg's 'Life of Shelley'" — usually only means that Hogg's changes are somewhat less extreme in the omitted portion. One manuscript by Hogg he attributes to Shelley (no. 11 in *New Shelley Letters*).

# Shelley and his Circle : Manuscripts

## *Hogg's Censorship of Shelley's Letters*

The changes made by Hogg have two main purposes: to cover up his youthful antireligious radicalism; to disguise his pursuit of Elizabeth Shelley. Of these, the second requires particular emphasis because it has resulted in false pictures of Hogg himself, the relationship of Hogg, Shelley, and Elizabeth Shelley, and that of Shelley and Harriet Grove.

Hogg's picture of himself in his *The Life of Percy Bysshe Shelley* as the rational, sophisticated young man of the world trying to direct the eccentric footsteps of his poet friend has generally been taken at its face value. And so, too, with his picture of Shelley obsessedly striving to arrange a match between his sister Elizabeth and the semireluctant Hogg. The manuscripts of these letters, however, show Hogg as a young man of violent and unstable passions who was more dependent on Shelley than Shelley was on him. They also show that while it is true that Shelley was at first interested in promoting such a match, the real initiative came from Hogg and in time assumed such recklessness — including a wild trip from York to Field Place[4] — that Shelley began to throw cold water on the whole affair. Hogg was able to distort these facts by simply transferring his own interest in Elizabeth Shelley to Shelley's in Harriet Grove, as, for instance, when he changed Shelley's question "Let me now ask you what reason is there for despair, even supposing your love to be incurable," into "Let me now ask you, what reason *was* there *then* for despair, even supposing *my* love to *have been* incurable."[5]

By noting the pattern of changes in the thirty-four letters at our disposal it is possible to deduce some of the changes in the other ten letters also. And if these changes are placed beside those in the intellectual content, we are able to see the full nature of the distortions not only in the letters but also in the narrative of Hogg's life of Shelley. Hogg was co-author of *The Necessity of Atheism* — the atheistical arguments were his, the anticlerical arguments were Shelley's — and sole author of an antireligious novel *Leonora* (which he represented as Shelley's). Hogg's antireligious views were similar to Shelley's; his character was, in spite of a surface reticence, equally volatile.

In considering these facts, however, one must be careful not to

4. See sc 168 (July ?6–18, 1811), Commentary.
5. From the first letter of the series, sc 125 (Dec. 23, 1810), line 19. Our italics.

# The Carl H. Pforzheimer Library

## *Shelley, Hogg, and Elizabeth Shelley*

exaggerate. Hogg and Shelley were both very young men at this time. In December 1810 when the correspondence opens, they were but eighteen, and although well developed intellectually, were immature emotionally. Each had led the sheltered existence of the upper-class English boy of the time and had little knowledge of the world. And although the emotions involved in the Elizabeth Shelley affair were certainly strong and genuine there hangs over it an air of fictional intrigue. It was, in fact, when Hogg wished to penetrate beyond this convention that Shelley began to back out. To read these letters with a literalist attitude is to read into them sophistications not intended.

Hogg's reasons for making the changes in the letters are not difficult to perceive. He was sixty-five when he was writing his life of Shelley — the letters do not appear in his "Shelley at Oxford" articles of 1832–1833 —[6] and had become a High Church Tory. He had no intention of making a disclosure of his youthful romantic passionings and antireligious radicalism. The honorable course would have been to have stated in his preface that certain passages, mainly of a personal nature, were omitted from the letters, and then to have omitted them. But there was just enough of the opportunist in Hogg to prevent him from taking this course. The letters seemed too good for him to omit anything; a declaration that material was omitted would arouse unwelcome curiosity. Instead, he would quietly make changes. One can see clearly enough how Hogg must have reasoned, and appreciate something of the dilemma which he faced; but one cannot excuse him. The changes resulted in distortions of Shelley's character beyond Hogg's already shallow concept of him; they misrepresented a series of events and relationships and misled succeeding biographers. The interesting fact is, however, that Hogg preserved the letters. He must have realized that in doing so there was always danger of their being published after his death, and revealing his chicanery. Perhaps he felt that after a long enough lapse of time the true story might be told.

The changes in these letters are symptomatic of Hogg's method in his life of Shelley as a whole. He felt free to select and slant his material at will, more in the manner of a novelist than of a biographer. "*Our* Book

6. In *The New Monthly Magazine*, reprinted in Thomas Jefferson Hogg, *Shelley at Oxford*, with an Introduction by R. A. Streatfeild (London, 1904).

*must* be *amusing*," he wrote to Lady Jane Shelley.[7] And such, indeed, was his objective: to write an "amusing" book. The result is a highly readable caricature, somewhat in a *Pickwick Papers* style, which has, unfortunately, often been taken for a portrait. By a proper reading between the lines, it can be made to throw much light, especially psychological, upon the young Shelley. But how false a picture an uncritical reading can convey is shown in the following letters.

K.N.C.

7. Sept. 10, 1857, Grylls, *Mary Shelley*, p. 290.

SC 125    P. B. SHELLEY TO T. J. HOGG, DECEMBER 23, 1810

AL signed *P.B.S.*, 4 pages. Double sheet, folio (12.8 x 7.9 inches).
Laid paper. Watermark: [lion rampant in crowned oval]|; countermark:
c wilmott| 1807|.

PROVENANCE: Thomas Jefferson Hogg; Major R. J. Jefferson Hogg (Sotheby, June 30, 1948, lot 1). *De Ricci 19* (p. 120).

*Field Place    Dec. 23    1810*

*My dear Friend*

     *The first desire which I felt on receiving your letters was instantly to come to London, to sympathise in the sorrows of a friend if they are beyond*
5    *alleviation. – That I cannot do this week    on Sunday or Monday next I will come, if you still remain in Town. — Why will you add to the never dying remorse which my egotising folly has occasioned, for which so long as its fatal effects remain never can I forgive myself, by acusing yourself of a feeling as criminal which I can but regard as another Trait of that amiability*
10    *which has marked your character since first I had the happiness of your friendship. – Where exists the moral wrong of seeking the society of one whom you loved, what offence to reason, to virtue was there in desiring the communication of a correspondence in order that both yourself & my sister might see if by coincidence of intellect you were willing to enter into a closer,*
15    *an eternal union — No — it is no offence to reason or to virtue, it is obeying its most imperious dictates, it is complying with the designs of the Author of our Nature can this be immorality – Can it selfishness or interested*

SC 125   *ambition to seek the happiness of the object of attachment, I think your own*
         *judgement, your own reason must answer in the negative –. Let me now ask*
  20   *you what reason is there for despair, even supposing your love to be incurable*
         *— My sister's disposition is in all probability divested of the enthusiasm*
         *by which yours is characterised, can therefore her's be prophetic, even*
         *supposing that she may not be susceptible of that feeling which arises from*
         *an admiration of virtue, when abstracted from identity – I have attempted*
  25   *again to plead your cause but unsuccessfully. she said — "even supposing*
         *I take your representation of your friends qualities & sentiments in which*
         *as you coincide in & admire I may fairly imagine to be exaggerated altho'*
         *you may not be aware of the exaggeration, what right have I admitting that*
         *he is so superior to enter into a correspondence which must end in delusive*
  30   *dissapointment when he finds how really inferior I am to the being which*
         *his heated imagination had pictured" —     This was unanswerable, particu-*
         *larly as the prejudiced description of a brother who loves his sister as I do,*
         *may, indeed must have given to you an erroneously exalted idea of the*
         *superiority of her mental attainments.—     I have said that the measures*
  35   *which you pursued are not uncongenial to the strictest morality. You must*
         *see that they militate wi< > the recieved opinions of the world, < >hat*
         *therefore do they offend but < >rejudice & superstition that superstitiou< >*
         *bigotry inspired by the system upo< > which at present the world acts of*
         *< >lieving all that we are told as incontrovertible facts. . I hope that what*
  40   *I have said will induce you to allow me still to Remain your friend,   I hope*
         *that you will have an opportunity of seeing, of conversing with her; how sorry*
         *I am that I cannot invite you here. – I will tell you the reason when we meet*
         *— Believe me my dear Friend when I assert that I shall ever continue so to*
         *you. – I have reason to lament deeply the sorrows with which fate has marked*
  45   *my life: I am not so deeply debased by it, however; that the exertions for the*
         *happiness of my friend shall supersede considerations of narrower & selfish*
         *interest; but that his woes shall claim a sigh before one repining thought arise*
         *at my own lot. — I know the cause of all your dissapoin< >nt worldly*
         *prejudice. mine < > the same; I know also its or< >n — bigotry*
  50   *Adeiu. Write ag< > beleive me your most sincere < >end:     adeiu*
                             *P.B.S.*

*Shelley to Hogg*                                           *December 23, 1810*

SC 125  line 8. *acusing* (sic)

line 17. *Can it* [be]

line 25. "*even* . . . . : Shelley places quotes at the beginning of each line in quoting his sister's remarks.

line 30. *dissapointment* (sic)

line 36. *wi<th>*; long, irregular hole in paper (pp. 3–4) here and below

line 36. *recieved* (sic)

line 36. *<w>hat*

line 37. *<p>rejudice*

line 37. *superstitiou<s>*

line 38. *upo<n>*

line 39. *<be>lieving*

line 40. *Remain: Re* is written through *re.*

line 48. *dissapoin<tme>nt*

line 49. *mine <is>*

line 49. *or<igi>n*

line 50. *Adeiu* (sic)

line 50. *ag<ain>*

line 50. *beleive* (sic)

line 50. *sincere:* Shelley apparently wrote *sincerely* but changed the final *l* into an *e* and blotted out a following letter.

line 50. *<fri>end*

COLLATION (selected passages).

T. J. HOGG, *THE LIFE OF PERCY BYSSHE SHELLEY*, I, 145–147. (Hogg's changes indicated by italics.)

line 4. *that* a friend might sympathise in those sorrows, *which* are beyond alleviation

line 8. by accusing yourself of a feeling, as *intrusive,*

line 11. the society of one, whom *I* loved?

line 12. the communication of a *lengthened* correspondence, in order that both, *she* and *myself*, might see, if by coincidence of intellect *we* were willing to enter into a closer, an eternal union?

line 20. what reason *was* there *then* for despair, even supposing *my* love to *have been* incurable? *Her* disposition was in all probability divested of the enthusiasm by which *mine* is characterised

line 24. *My sister* attempted *sometimes* to plead *my* cause, but unsuccessfully. She said: — "Even supposing I take your representation of your *brother's* qualities

line 29: to enter into an *intimacy,*

line 32. the prejudiced description of a *sister,* who loves *her brother* as *she does, might,* indeed must, have given to *her* an erroneously exalted idea of the superiority of *my* mental attainments. *You* have said, that the *philosophy,* which *I* pursued, *is* not uncongenial *with* the strictest morality;

SHORTLY after the commencement of the Michaelmas term on October 10, 1810, Shelley, then a freshman, met Thomas Jefferson Hogg, who had entered Oxford the previous February,[1] in the dining hall of their college, University College. The term ended on about December 8.

1. White, *Shelley*, I, 586; Edmund Blunden, "Shelley is Expelled," *On Shelley* (Oxford University Press, 1938), pp. 2–5; Scott, *Hogg*, p. 22. Hogg (*Shelley*, I, 46) states that he met Shelley "at the commencement of the Michaelmas term, that is, at the end of October." And he also notes that it was Shelley's "first appearance in hall" (i.e., for dinner). But "the Michaelmas term" in 1810 began not "at the end of October" but on October 10; and it is unlikely that Shelley would not be "in hall" until the end of the month. Hogg, relying on his memory, twenty-two years later — the statement first appeared in his 1832 articles on Shelley at Oxford — is probably inaccurate. The two probably met on about October 10.

[ 673 ]

# The Carl H. Pforzheimer Library

SC 125    Shelley had returned to Field Place by December 10.[2] Hogg, whose home
was less accessible — the northern village of Norton, fifteen miles from
Durham — stayed at Oxford and then, on the invitation of friends at
Lincoln's Inn, went to London.[3] On December 20 Shelley received a letter
or letters from him giving his London address and answered him on the
same day.

During their eight weeks together at Oxford the two had become
fast friends and had had long discussions, some recorded by Hogg, on a
variety of topics, including Shelley's sister Elizabeth and his cousin
Harriet Grove. Shelley's correspondence with Harriet Grove had been
broken off by the Grove family in the fall of 1810, shortly before Shelley
entered Oxford, because of his growing antireligious sentiments. Shelley,
however, was still interested in his cousin, incensed over the "bigotry"
which had terminated the correspondence, and still hopeful of resuming
his relationship with her. All this, as we can gather from the subsequent
letters, he must have told Hogg at Oxford, and apparently told with
some vehemence. At the same time he had given Hogg a glowing picture
of his sister Elizabeth, his collaborator on *Original Poetry* — some samples
of which he later presented to Hogg (sc 114) — emphasizing her intellectual gifts and expressing the hope that she and Hogg might make a
match, in fact, an "eternal union" (line 15), though one unblest by the
agencies of the church which had "injured" him by breaking up his
romance with his cousin.

What Shelley had not anticipated was the intensity of Hogg's
reactions to his portrait of Elizabeth. Putting the above letter together
with those of December 26 and 28 (sc 126), it appears that Hogg wrote
a letter to Elizabeth, that Elizabeth refused to enter into correspondence
with him, and that he then retreated into "despair" (line 20) and
remorse.

By the time of the writing of the above letter Shelley had received
Hogg's letters telling of his "sorrows." Hogg, after having written to
Elizabeth and having been rebuffed, had written once more declaring
his love and his despair to be alike "incurable" (line 20), and Shelley

2. He inscribed a copy of *St. Irvyne* (now in The Berg Collection of The New York Public Library)
to his uncle, Robert Parker, "Field Place, Dec. 10, 1810."

3. Scott, *Hogg*, pp. 12, 27–28.

# Shelley and his Circle : Manuscripts

SC 125    had expostulated with Elizabeth, but in vain. He attempted to solace
Hogg by taking the blame on himself, his "egotising folly" (line 7),
which had made him feel that the "eternal union" (line 15) might come
to pass. But he seems somewhat alarmed by the violence of Hogg's
emotions, feeling perhaps that they were not exclusively engendered by
Elizabeth's intellectual attainments, and informing Hogg that after all
there was a problem of "the recieved opinions of the world" (line 36),
opinions which might be obtuse to the morality of Hogg's "measures"
(line 34).

To this letter Hogg, as we can gather from Shelley's of December 26,
replied expressing his gratitude for Shelley's assistance and his remorse
at having transgressed the bounds of "delicacy." This December 26
letter is known only in Hogg's printed text but by changing some of
his first-person pronouns back into the second person, and so on, we can
see what Shelley probably wrote:

Come, I must be severe with [you], I must irritate the wound which I wish
to heal.

Supposing the object of [your] affections does not regard [you], how have
you transgressed against its dictates; in what have you offended? . . . Circumstances have operated in such a manner, that the attainment of the object of
[your] heart [is] impossible, whether on account of extraneous influences, or
from a feeling which possessed her mind, which told her *not* to deceive [you], not
to give [you] the possibility of disappointment. . . . It is with reluctance to my
own feelings that I have entered into this cold disquisition, when [my] heart
sympathizes so deeply in [your] affliction.

In the above manuscript there is but one actual reference to Harriet
Grove, namely in the final comments on "sorrows" and "worldly
prejudice." And so, too, in the December 26 letter — a final reference
to "sorrows" and "that which injured me" (i.e., Christianity).

The situation as disclosed in these letters is the reverse of that
depicted by Hogg in his life of Shelley. It is not Shelley who is distraught
or dependent but Hogg.

The above letter is unaddressed. Presumably it was folded within an
address sheet.

SEE ALSO "SHELLEY, HOGG, AND ELIZABETH SHELLEY."

**Shelley to Hogg**                                    *December 28, 1810*

SC 126    P. B. SHELLEY TO T. J. HOGG, DECEMBER 28, 1810

AL unsigned, 2½ pages. Double sheet, folio (12.7 x 8.1 inches).
Laid paper. Watermark: [lion rampant in crowned oval]|; countermark:
c WILMOTT| 1810|.
Seal: wafer, red.
Postmarks: 1. (mileage stamp)*:* HORSHAM| 41|; 2. (morning duty stamp, London)*:*
E| 29DE2[9]| 1810|.
Notation, page 3, in the hand of T. J. Hogg: *on Sunday*|.

PROVENANCE: Thomas Jefferson Hogg; Major R. J. Jefferson Hogg (Sotheby,
June 30, 1948, lot 2). *De Ricci 21* (p. 121).

*Dec. 28. 1810. F P*

*My dear Friend*

    *The encomia of one incapable of flattery is indeed flattering. — Your*
*discrimination of that Chapter is more just than the praises which you bestow*
5  *on so unconnected a thing as the Romance taken collectively — I wish you*
*very much to publish Leonora   Have you sent it to Robinson? — Oh here*
*we are in the midst of all the uncongenial jollities of Xmass, when you are*
*compelled to contribute to the merriment of others. When you are compelled*
*to live under this – severest of all restraints, concealment of feelings poignant*
10  *enough in themselves how terrible is your lot. I am learning Abstraction, but*
*I fear that my proficiency will be but trifling — I cannot dare not to speak*
*of myself. — Why do you still continue to despond, to say that you* <u>must</u>
*despair — may I ask how can this despair be authorized, when it is rational*
*to suppose that at some future time mutual knowlegde would awaken a*
15  *reciprocality of feeling — Your letter to my sister arrived in a moment of a*
*when she could least bear any additional excitement of feelings; I have*
*succeeded now in calming her mind, but at first she knew not how to act,*
*indeccision & a fear of injuring another by complying with what perhaps*
*were the real wishes of her bosom distracted her — I do not tell you this from*
20  *any confession of her own, for I believe that she might not be sufficiently*
*aware of what she felt herself even to own it to herself. — Believe me my dear*
*friend that my* <sub>only</sub> *ultimate wishes* <u>now</u>*, are for your happiness and that of my*
*Sisters. At present a thousand barriers oppose any more intimate connexion,*
25  *barriers which altho unnatural & fettering to the virtuous mind, are never-*

**Shelley to Hogg**                    *December 28, 1810*

SC 126    *theless unconquerable: —     I will if possible come to London on Monday,*
*certainly some time next week,   I shall come about 6 o/Clock will remain*
*with you until that time the next morning when I will tell you my reasons for*
*wishing to return. Adeu. Excuse the shortness of this as the S^{vt} waits. I will*

30        *write on Sunday*

                              *Your most sincerely*

[Address, page 4]

*T. Jefferson Hogg Esq^r*

*Wills' Coffee House*

*Serle Street*

35        *Lincolns Inn Fields*

*London*

line 1. *F P* (Field Place) is written with a thinner pen and lighter touch than the rest of the letter. It was almost certainly not written at the same time as the date or salutation, both of which are especially dark, probably indicating a freshly dipped pen.

line 14. *knowlegde* (sic)

line 15. *reciprocality* (sic)

line 18. *indeccision* (sic): Shelley appears to have inserted the second *c* later.

line 18. *injuring:* The *ing* is compressed, as often in Shelley, the final *g* being atrophied into a simple downward curved line. So, too, with *wishing*, line 29. These compressed forms will be transcribed *ing*.

line 24. *Sisters* (sic): sister's

line 29. *Adeu* (sic)

line 31. *Your* (sic)

COLLATION (selected passages).

T. J. HOGG, *THE LIFE OF PERCY BYSSHE SHELLEY*, I, 151–152. (Hogg's changes indicated by italics.)

line 5. I wish you very much to publish *a tale; send one to a publisher.*

line 12. Why do you still continue to *say, Do not despond,* that you must *not* despair?

line 13. *I admit that* this despair *would be unauthorised,*

line 15. Your letter arrived *at* a moment when *I* could least bear any additional excitement of feelings. I have succeeded now in calming *my* mind, but at first *I* knew not how to act;

line 19. the real wishes of *my* bosom, distracted *me.* I do not tell you this *by way of* confession of *my own state,* for I believe that *I may* not be sufficiently aware of what *I* feel *myself,* even to own it to *myself.*

line 24. more intimate connexion, *any union with another,* which, although unnatural and fettering. . . .

IN A letter of December 20 Shelley had informed Hogg that *St. Irvyne* had "come out," and that he could get a copy from Stockdale. As there is no mention of Hogg's reaction to the novel in Shelley's letter of December 26, presumably Shelley received a letter from Hogg on

# The Carl H. Pforzheimer Library

SC 126  December 27 or 28. In this letter Hogg apparently praised Shelley's novel and further bemoaned his own "despair" at the rebuff by Elizabeth. Shelley commiserates with him and points out the unfortunate existence of proprieties. He is both discouraging Hogg and at the same time, and with diabolic intent, teasing him: "the real wishes of her bosom" (line 19).

On December 20 Shelley advised Hogg to take a book which he had written to "Wilkie and Robinson . . . he publishes Godwin's works." This book, as appears from the above letter (line 6), was Hogg's novel *Leonora*.[1] From the other letters in this series and from comments by Henry Slatter, bookseller of Oxford, we can tell that the novel was of an antireligious nature,[2] and hence likely to be published by publishers of Godwin, who was considered not only a political radical but also an atheist. (This reference to Godwin, we might note, calls for a re-examination of Shelley's statement in his first letter to Godwin that he had believed him enrolled among the "honourable dead.")[3]

SEE ALSO "SHELLEY, HOGG, AND ELIZABETH SHELLEY."

1. Partly as a result of Hogg's changes in the letters, *Leonora* was for a long time regarded as the joint product of Shelley and Hogg. It was first argued to be by Hogg alone in Frederick L. Jones, "Shelley's Leonora," *Modern Philology*, XXXII (May 1935), 392–393. See also W. S. Scott, ed. *Shelley at Oxford* (London, 1944), p. 19.

2. Henry Slatter to Robert Montgomery, Dec. 18, 1833, Robert Montgomery, "Oxford: or Alma Mater," *Poetical Works*, London, 1854, p. 442. The letter was first quoted in the 3rd (1833) and succeeding editions of "Oxford," issued as a separate poem. Slatter believed *Leonora* to be the joint product of Shelley and Hogg. It is possible that Shelley had some share in the work but if so it must have been of a minor nature, for the letters make clear that he regarded it as Hogg's novel, speaking, for instance, in a letter of January 3, 1811 (sc 128, line 50) of "y$^r$ heroine."

3. In his December 20, 1810, letter he also comments: "It is not William Godwin, who lives in Holborn; it is *John*, no relation to the other." Shelley clearly seems to have believed Godwin to have been alive as of December 20, 1810, and it would be strange if one so interested in Godwin's works had thought otherwise. The problem is complicated, however, by the fact that on January 7, 1812, four days after his first letter to Godwin, he comments to Elizabeth Hitchener: "Godwin yet lives: if Government, at one time, could have destroyed any man, Godwin would have ceased to be." This statement to Elizabeth Hitchener seems at first to imply that Shelley had not realized until recently that Godwin was still alive; but it only seems to mean this because we tend to take it in conjunction with the previous statements to Godwin: "I had enrolled your name in the list of the honourable dead," "the inconceivable emotions with which I learned your existence and your dwelling." The statement to Elizabeth Hitchener is simply an exclamatory statement. Paine, Shelley is saying — as the full context shows — is dead, but Godwin and Burdett are still alive (which was general knowledge). The statement on January 3 to Godwin, then, does not mean that Shelley had until recently believed him to be dead but only that when he had first heard of him as a boy he had believed him to be already among the immortals. Shelley had known of Godwin's continuing existence for a year or more, and Hogg at least seems to have had some intimation of his address. William Godwin lived on Skinner Street, Snow Hill, which was near Holborn.

SC 127    P. B. SHELLEY TO T. J. HOGG, JANUARY 1, 1811

AL unsigned, 3¾ pages. Double sheet, folio (12.7 x 8.1 inches).
Laid paper. Watermark: [lion rampant in crowned oval]|; countermark:
C WILMOTT| 1810|.
Seal: wafer, black.
Postmarks: 1. (mileage stamp): HORSHAM 41|; 2. (morning duty stamp, London):
E| 2 JA 2| 1811|.
Notation, page 4: [?] *Coffe House* 6| 6

PROVENANCE: Thomas Jefferson Hogg; Major R. J. Jefferson Hogg (Sotheby,
June 30, 1948, lot 3). *De Ricci 22* (p. 121).

*My dear Friend*

   *I cannot come to London before next week. I am but just returned to*
*F.P. from an inefficient effort.. Why do you my happy friend tell me of*
*perfection in love, is she not gone – and yet I breathe I live. but adeiu to*
5  *egotism I am sick to Death at the name of self. Oh your Theory cost me much*
*reflexion, I have not ceased to think of it since your letter came, which was*
*put into my hands at the moment of departure on Sunday Mor. – Is it not*
*however founded on that hateful principle – Is it self which you propose to*
*raise to a state of superiority by your system of eternal perfectibility in love:*
10  *No. – were this frame rendered eternal, were the particles which compose it*
*both as to intellect & matter indestructible, and then! to undergo torments*
*such as now we should shudder to think of even in a dream, to undergo this*
*I say for the extension of happiness to those for whom we feel vivid preference;*
*then would I love adore idolize your Theory wild unfounded as it might be;*
15  *but no. I can concieve neither of these to be correct – Considering matters in*
*a Philosophical light, it evidently appears (if it is not treason to speak thus*
*cooly on a subject so deliriously extatic) that we were not destined for misery.*
*– What then shall happiness arise from. Can we hesitate? Love! dear love,*
*and tho every mental faculty is bewildered by the agony, which is in this life*
20  *its' too constant attendant, still is not that very agony to be preferred to the*
*most Thrilling sensualities of Epicurism. — I have wandered in the snow*
*for I am cold we< > – & mad – pardon me, pardon my delirious egotism*
   *this really shall be the last* ~~Yet she~~ *My sister is well, I fear < > is*
*not quite happy, but is much more cheerful than some days ago.*    *I hope*
25  *you will publish Leonora. I shall then give a copy to Eliza unless you forbid*

**Shelley to Hogg**                                    *January 1, 1811*

SC 127    *it, I would do it not only to tell her what your ideas are on the subject of*
          *Religion, but that she should see you in* <u>*every*</u> *point of view —    You will*
          *not examine her character; but mortality is not Godhead amiable as it may*
          *some times be — I am at treason however. I will check my volubility. Do*
30        *not direct y^r next letter to F.P. only to Horsham. —    To-morrow I will*
          *write more connectedly    Yours sincerely*

          [Address, page 4]
          *T. Jefferson Hogg Esq^r*
          *Will's Coffee House*
          *Serle Street*
35        *Lincolns Inn Fields*
          *London*

line 4. *adeiu* (sic)

line 15. *concieve* (sic)

line 17. *extatic* (sic)

line 22. *we*< >: The paper is slightly torn near the edge on a fold. Following the *e* is a short straight line, probably a dash. Hogg, perhaps transcribing before the tear, gives *wet*. The straight line is too low to be the cross of a final *t*.

line 23. Following *Yet* is the seal tear. Part of the paper, however, still adheres to the seal and on this paper *she* can be read. Both *Yet* and *she*

are crossed out with thick, violent strokes.

line 23. *fear* <*she*>

line 25. *unless . . . Do not:* This passage (11 lines) occupies the top half of page 4. Then comes the address, written vertically, and then below the address the final three lines *direct y^r . . . . sincerely.*

line 36. *London* is written very small and cramped between the line above and the address fold; perhaps Shelley forgot it and added it after the letter was folded.

COLLATION (selected passages).
T. J. HOGG, *THE LIFE OF PERCY BYSSHE SHELLEY*, I, 154. (Hogg's changes indicated by italics.)

line 23. My sister is well; I fear she is not quite happy *on my account*, but is much more cheerful than *she was* some days ago. I hope you will publish a *tale;*

line 26. I would do it not only to *show* her what your ideas are on the subject of *works of imagination, and to interest her,* but that she should see

*her brother's friend* in *a new* point of view. *When you examine her character, you will find humanity,* not *divinity,* amiable as *the former* may sometimes be: *however, I, a brother, must not write treason against my sister; so* I will check my volubility.

S HELLEY had promised in his letter of December 28 to write to Hogg "on Sunday" and hoped to see him in London "on Monday," which was New Year's Eve. The above letter was postmarked in London on

SC 127 January 2. If it was written (as it probably was) on the day on which it was posted in Horsham, its date is January 1, for it took one day for mail to go from Horsham to London.[1]

Shelley had, he now informs Hogg, been unable to keep his promise to see him in London on New Year's Eve, and had apparently not written to him "on Sunday." On Sunday morning, in fact, he had left Field Place for some unstated destination and had received a letter from Hogg just as he was leaving (line 6).

In this letter, Hogg had proposed a theory of "eternal perfectibility in love" (line 9). From the above letter and the next (sc 128, January 3), we can gather something of its nature. It was "sensual" and "Epicurean," embodied a pessimistic view of human destiny, and had atheistic overtones. By "perfectibility," Hogg, using the word in the accepted Godwinian sense, did not mean being "perfect," but advancing towards perfection — through a series of love affairs. Shelley's objection to the theory is that it places the emphasis on the "self" and not on the beloved. Love he regards — and here we can see in its early stages what later became one of his central doctrines — not as an egocentric but as an expansive force. Love directed inward to the "self" is not love but sensuality. Love, real love, is a turning outward to the beloved (and, as he later developed the concept, beyond the beloved toward humanity). Hogg's argument has clearly troubled him, but in this letter, written hastily after his return, he does not go deeply into it.

Where had Shelley been? Why had he not written to Hogg "on Sunday" or visited him in London on the next day? His implication in this letter (line 2 — "I am but just returned to F.P. from an inefficient effort") combined with the statement in his January 6 letter that he "followed her"[2] is that he had been to see Harriet Grove at Fern and had been rebuffed. But Shelley does not quite say this; he merely hints it. And there were obstacles in the way of a trip to Fern from Horsham. In the first place it is unlikely that his father would have given permission as the "understanding" with Harriet had long been broken off; and he

1. The mail coach left Horsham for London at 7 p.m. and would arrive early the next morning; the letter would then be stamped with a morning duty stamp. (See "Postmarks and the Dating of Manuscripts," below, pp. 918–919.)

2. sc 129 (Jan. 6, 1811), line 29.

SC 127    could hardly have made a secret journey by himself as Fern was some eighty miles away and not on a main coach route.

If he really went to Fern (or its neighborhood) he most likely went from London (via the main coach route to Shaftesbury). His letter of December 28 indicates that he had received permission to go to London. His cousin, Charles Grove, brother of Harriet Grove, informs us: "During the Christmas vacation of that year, [1810] and in January 1811, I spent part of it with Bysshe at Field Place . . . ."[3] Grove does not say so but it may be that Shelley went to stay with him in London and that they returned together to Field Place. And if Shelley did make such a trip to London, it is possible that Charles Grove arranged a meeting in the vicinity of Fern with Harriet. But more likely the "followed her" of the January 6 letter is a rhetorical exaggeration of a trip to London where his cousins gave him the news which sent him into the moody depths of this and the following letter.

The comment "I am at treason" (line 29) probably refers to a "satirical poem" which he informed Hogg he was writing on December 20, and which may be the same as the so far undiscovered *A Poetical Essay on the Existing State of Things* announced in the *Oxford University and City Herald* on March 9.[4]

3. Charles Grove to Hellen Shelley, Feb. 16, 1857, quoted in Hogg, *Shelley*, II, 155.

4. For some discussion of this work see Cameron, *The Young Shelley*, p. 50. Hogg's tampering with the text here — "I, a brother, must not write treason against my sister" — changes Shelley's meaning entirely. Lady Shelley leaves this unaltered. (Shelley, *Complete Works*, VIII, 32; "The Provenance of Shelley and his Circle Manuscripts," below, p. 905.)

SC 128    P. B. SHELLEY TO T. J. HOGG, JANUARY 3, 1811

AL signed *PBS*, 7 pages. 2 double sheets, 4$^{to}$ (8.7 x 7.2 inches).

Laid paper. Watermark, both sheets: c WILMOTT| 1810|.

Seal: wax, black: *ES* [in oval]|.

Postmarks: 1. (mileage stamp): HORSHAM| 41|; 2. (morning duty stamp, London): E| 4 JA 4| 1811|.

Notation, page 8: *2 . . 9 . . 1*

PROVENANCE: Thomas Jefferson Hogg; Major R. J. Jefferson Hogg (Sotheby, June 30, 1948, lot 4). *De Ricci 23* (p. 121).

**Shelley to Hogg**                                   *January 3, 1811*

SC 128                                               *F.P. Dec. 3. 181*

*My dear Friend*

*Before we doubt or believe the existence of any thing it is necessary that*
*we should have a <u>tolerably</u> clear idea of what it is –     The word "God" has*
5  *been will continue to be the source of numberless errors until it is erased from*
*the nomenclature of Philosophy. – it does not imply "the Soul of the Universe*
*the intelligent & <u>necessarily</u> beneficent actuating principle" – This <u>I</u>*
*believe in; I may not be able to adduce proofs, but I think that the leaf of a*
*tree, the meanest insect on w$^h$ we trample are in themselves arguments more*
10 *conclusive than any which can be adduced that some vast intellect animates*
*Infinity –   If we disbelieve <u>this</u>, the strongest argument in support of the*
*existence of a future state instantly becomes annihilated. I confess that I*
*think Pope's "all are but parts of one tremendous whole" something more*
*than Poetry, it has ever been my favourite theory. For the immoral "never*
15 *to be able to die, never to escape from some shrine as chilling as the clay-*
*formed dungeon which now its inhabits is the future punishment which I*
*believe in. Love, love <u>infinite in extent</u>, eternal in duration, yet (allowing*
*your theory in that point) perfectible should be the reward; but can we suppose*
*that this reward will arise spontaneously as a necessary appendage to our*
20 *nature, or that our nature itself could be without a cause, a First Cause, a*
*God, – when do we see effects arise without some causes, what causes are*
*there without correspondent effects? –   Yet here I swear, and as I break my*
*oath may Infinity Eternity blast me, here I swear that never will I forgive*
                                                                    *revenge.*
25 *Christianity! it is the only point on which I allow myself to encourage it;*
*every moment shall be devoted to my object which I can spare, & let me hope*
*that it will not be a blow which spends itself & leaves the wretch at rest but*
*lasting long revenge! I am convinced too that it is of great disservice to society*
*that it encourages prejudice which strikes at the root of the dearest the tenderest*
30 *of its ties. Oh how I wish I <u>were</u> the Antichrist, that it were <u>mine</u> to crush the*
*Demon, to hurl him to his native Hell never to rise again –   I expect to*
*gratify some of this insatiable feeling in Poetry. You shall see, you shall*
*hear. – but it has injured me, she is no longer mine, she abhors me as a Deist,*
*as what <u>she</u> was before. Oh! Christianity when I pardon this last this severest*

SC 128   *of thy persecutitions may God (if there be a God) blast me! Has vengeance in its armoury of wrath a punishment more dreadful!   Yet forgive me   I have done, & were it not for your great desire to know <u>why</u> I consider myself as the victim of severer anguish that I could have entered into this brief recital –*

*I am afraid there is selfishness in the passion of Love for I cannot avoid*

40   *feeling every instant as if my soul was bursting. but I <u>will</u> feel no more! it is selfish I would feel for others, but for myself oh! how much rather would I expire in the struggle. Yet that were relief – Is suicide wrong? I slept with a loaded pis-tol & some poison last night but did not die. – I could not come on Monday my sister w<sup>d</sup> not part with me, but I must I will see you soon. –*

45   *My sister is now comparatively happy, she has felt deeply, had it not been for her, had it not been for a sense of what I owed to her to you I should have bid you a final farewell some time ago. But can the dead feel. dawns any daybeam on the night of dissolution?*

*Pray publish Leonora. demand 100 £ for it from Robinson, he will give it*

50   *in the event. It is divine, is delightful   not that I like y<sup>r</sup> heroine, but the poor Mary is a character worthy of Heaven. I adore it. Adieu my dear friend*

                *Your sincere PBS.*

*Wedgewood has written I'll send his letter   'tis too long to answer*

*I cont : con   I continue     I contrive to dissapate Eliza's melancholy by*

55   *keeping her as much as possible employed in Poetry, you shall see some tomorrow*

*I can't tell when I <u>can</u> come to Town. I wish it very much*

[Address, page 4]

*T. Jefferson Hogg Esq<sup>r</sup>*

*Will's Coffee House*

60   *Serle Street*

*Lincolns Inn Fields*

*London*

line 1. Written with thick, dark strokes; has blotted off on the last line of the page in folding.

line 21. *without some:* w written over another letter, probably *f.*

line 33. *injured me:* under *me,* which comes near the bottom of page 4, is written *My,* upside down; Shelley apparently first began his letter here and then turned the sheet over.

line 33. *Deist, as what <u>she</u>:* These words are in thick, heavy strokes as is the underlining of *she.*

line 35. *persecutitions* (sic): [persecutions]. Shelley appears to have been writing rapidly.

SC 128    line 36. *punishment:* e appears to have been written through an *a*.

line 36. *more:* Shelley apparently began to follow *punishment* with *of* and wrote the *m* of *more* through the *of*.

line 37. *great:* The initial *g* is written through a *d*. Shelley apparently started to write *desire* and changed to *great desire*.

line 40. *instant:* The final *t* is written through *ce*.

line 45. *had:* blotted or scratched out

line 53. *answer* is the final word on page 7 and comes about three quarters of the way down the page, leaving the final quarter blank. Then *I cont . . . very much* is written on page 8, *I cont . . . employed in* above the address (written vertically), the rest below. Lines 54–57 must have been written after the letter had been folded as Shelley would normally have used the blank final quarter of page 7 for them.

line 54. *dissapate* (sic)

COLLATION (selected passages).

T. J. HOGG, *THE LIFE OF PERCY BYSSHE SHELLEY*, I, 155–157. (Hogg's changes indicated by italics.)

line 4. The word "God," *a vague word*, has been,

line 6. *Does it not* imply "the soul of the universe, the intelligent and necessarily *beneficient*, actuating principle." This *it is impossible not to* believe in,

line 9. arguments more conclusive than any which can be *advanced*,

line 23. never will I forgive *intolerance!*

line 30. Oh! how I wish I were the *avenger!* — that it were mine to crush the demon; to hurl

him to his native hell, never to rise again, *and thus to establish for ever perfect and universal toleration.*

line 33. she abhors me as a *sceptic*, as what she was before! Oh, *bigotry!* When I pardon this last, this severest of thy persecutions, may *Heaven* (if there be *wrath in Heaven*) blast me!

line 49. Pray publish *your tale;* demand one hundred pounds for it *from any publisher;*

THE above letter[1] shows conclusively that Shelley prior to his expulsion from Oxford was a deist and not an atheist. He begins here to question some of the roots of Hogg's theory of "perfectibility in love."

1. The conflict between the date, in Shelley's hand, on the heading, "F.P. Dec. 3· 181 ," and that of the London postmark, January 4, 1811, has caused some dispute as to the date of composition. W. S. Scott in *New Shelley Letters*, for instance, misread the date as December 8, 1810, and placed this as the first letter from Shelley to Hogg from Field Place.

The place-and-date line (see Textual Notes) was written just before the letter was folded and seems to have been written very hastily. At first sight the "3" following "Dec." does look like an eight but examination shows that it is a 3 which has blotted. The top loop goes from left to right and not from right to left, which is the usual way of making an eight (as here in the 8 of "181 "). The dot after the "3" may mean that Shelley intended to follow it with a zero but not being sure of the date did not complete it. We often find confusion in Shelley's datings at the end or beginning of a year. The fact, however, that he here leaves out the year (not indicating whether it is 1810 or 1811) suggests also some affectation — as though he were saying with an ironical flourish that he neither knew nor cared what date or year it was.

December 3, however, could not possibly be the date of composition: (a) the letter is addressed to Hogg at Lincoln's Inn Fields and Shelley did not know that Hogg was at that address until December 20, as his letter of that date states; (b) the letter continues the arguments of the letter of January 1 in answer to one received from Hogg on December 30. Hence, the date of composition must be deduced from the postmark (January 4), i.e., January 3. (See SC 127, Jan. 1, 1811, fn. 1.)

# The Carl H. Pforzheimer Library

SC 128    The self-centered and sensual element that troubles him in that theory,
he believes, rests upon Hogg's rejection of a God and immortality. He
agrees that the specific God of Christianity is nonexistent but he thinks
that Hogg uses the word in too sweeping a sense, that he is denying the
existence of any spiritual substance whatsoever in nature — a "Soul of
the Universe" (line 6). With this atheistical argument Shelley will not
agree. He cannot "adduce proofs," but he believes in such a "Soul" and,
consequently, he hints, in a "future state" (line 12). In this future state
there may be rewards and punishment. The "immoral" (line 14) will
live forever in the body ("the clay-formed dungeon");[2] the good will
exist eternally in love. He disagrees with Hogg's theory of perfectibility
of sensual love but he believes that "eternal" love will be "perfectible"
(line 17). He wants to reassure Hogg that he at least shares his antichris-
tian views. But that he is still very much feeling his way comes out in
the conclusion (line 47): "can the dead feel."

Although his letters are not available, Hogg has, one would gather
from Shelley's reply, worked his way through to a materialist philosophy
akin to that of Diderot or d'Holbach, a rather extraordinary feat for a
young student in the early nineteenth century.

The reason for Shelley's bitterness about Christianity is, as before,
his disappointment over Harriet Grove. He had perhaps heard, shortly
before writing the above letter and that of January 1 (sc 127), that
Harriet's engagement (to Helyar) was certain, for these letters with their
pistols and poisons (line 43) and walks in the snow[3] reveal a more extreme
agitation than do previous letters.

Little is said of Elizabeth but Shelley is perhaps again teasing Hogg.
The "ES" of the seal (see Plate xxv) was presumably made in the wax by
her ring. That she was consulted on this is most unlikely, but Hogg
could so take it if he wished. And in the letter itself Shelley speaks no
more of her retreat from Hogg, only of her "melancholy" (line 54), a
result presumably of her having "felt deeply" (line 45).

2. For this and other parallels with the "Wandering Jew" fragment see sc 123 (?Dec. 10, 1810–?Jan.
22, 1811). The preceding quotation (line 13) is from Pope's *Essay on Man*, I, 267, with the mis-
quoting of "tremendous" for "stupendous."

3. sc 127 (Jan. 1, 1811), line 21.

SC 128     "Mary" (line 51), one might conjecture by analogy with Hogg's published novel, *Memoirs of Prince Alexy Haimatoff*, was one of his sentimental women characters, the heroine, Leonora, one of his young ladies of fashion.[4]

One result of the antireligious speculations of Hogg and Shelley was the writing of letters to various well-known men, posing questions and asking for answers. One thus favored was "Wedgewood" (line 53), who was probably connected with the famed pottery family and may have been Josiah the younger, benefactor of Coleridge and a man of general intellectual interests.[5]

4. See the London, 1952, edition of *Alexy Haimatoff*, an edition which also contains a review by Shelley.

5. On the Wedgwoods see Eliza Meteyard, *A Group of Englishmen (1795–1815) being records of the younger Wedgwoods and their friends . . .* (London, 1871).

SC 129    P. B. SHELLEY TO T. J. HOGG, JANUARY 6, 1811; P. B. SHELLEY, *OH! TAKE THE PURE GEM TO WHERE SOUTHERNLY BREEZES*

AL signed *Percy Shelley*, including poem, 11¼ pages. 3 double sheets, 4$^{to}$ (8.7 x 7.1 inches).
Laid paper. Watermarks: sheets 1 and 3: c wilmott| 1810|; sheet 2: [posthorn in crowned shield]| cw|. Gilt edges.
Seal: wafer.
Frank, by Timothy Shelley.
Postmarks: 1. (mileage stamp): horsham| 41|; 2. (morning duty franking stamp, London): free| 7 ja 7| 1811|.

provenance: Thomas Jefferson Hogg; Major R. J. Jefferson Hogg (Sotheby, June 30, 1948, lot 5). *De Ricci 24* (p. 121).

*My dear Friend*

    *Dare I request <u>one</u> favor. for <u>myself</u> for my own interest not the keenest anguish which the most unrelenting Tyrant could invent should force me to request from you so great a sacrifise. – It is a beloved sister's happiness which*
5    *forces me to this. I saw her when she recieved your letter of yesterday. I saw*

[ 687 ]

SC 129    *the conflict of her soul, she said nothing but re-directed it, & sent it instantly*
*to the Post. Believe me I feel for you more than I will <u>allow</u> myself to perceive*
*for any dissapointments which I have undergone. Write to me whatever you*
*wish to say to Eliza you may say in that, and she might by a brother's wish*
10    *what in the other case I dared not even to recommend. What would I not give*
*up to see you, to see my Sister happy. I know the means by which it can be*
*effected, but consider what a Female sacrifises when she returns the attachment*
*of one whose faith she supposes inviolable ever. To add to the agony which*
*is indescribable, which is only to be felt will she not encounter the opprobrium*
15    *of the world, and what is more severe (generally speaking) the dereliction &*
*contempt of those who before had avowed themselves most attached to her.*
*— <u>I</u> do not encourage the remotest suspicion, I am convinced of your Truth*
*as I am of my own existence, still is not <u>Natural</u> in Eliza even altho She*
                the
20    *may return ~~your~~ most enthusiastic prepossessions arising from the conscious-*
*ness of your intellectual superiority, ignorant as she is of your <u>every</u> opinion,*
*<u>every</u> sensation (for <u>unlimited</u> confidence is requisite for the existence of*
*mutual love) to have some doubts, some fears, Besides when in her Natural*
*character, her spirits are good her conversation animated, & almost in*
25    *consequence ignorant of the refinements in Love, w<sup>ch</sup> can only be attained by*
*solitary reflexion. — Forsake her! forsake one whom I loved! can I? never*
*but she is gone, she is lost to me forever, forever. There is a mystery which I*
*dare not to clear up, it is the only point on which I will be reserved to you. —*
*I have tried the methods you recommend I followed her, I would have*
30    *followed her to the end of the earth but —   .   If you value the little happiness*
*which yet remains, ~~if~~ do not mention again to me sorrows which if you could*
*share in, would wound an heart which it now shall be my endeavour to heal*
*from those which it has already received. I will crush Christianity! I will at*
*least attempt it. to fail even in so useful an attempt were glorious I enclose*
35    *some Poetry*

    *Oh! take the pure gem to where southernly breezes*
      *Waft repose to some bosom as faithful as fair*
    *In which the warm current of Love never freezes*
      *As it rises unmingled with selfishness there*

SC 129
        *Which untainted by Pride, unpolluted by care*
         *Might dissolve the dim ice drop, might bid it arise*
        *Too pure for these regions, to gleam in the skies*

        *Or where the stern warrior his country defending*
         *Dares fearless the dark-rolling battle to pour*
45               *Or*
        *~~Where~~ oer the fell corpse of a dread Tyrant bending*
         *Where Patriotism red with his guilt-reeking gore*
        *Plants Liberty's flag on the slave-peopled shore*
        *With Victory's cry, with the shout of the free*
50     *Let it fly taintless spirit to mingle with thee*

        *For I found the pure gem when the day-beam returning*
         *Ineffectual gleams on the snow-covered plain*
        *When to others the wished-for arrival of morning*
         *Brings relief to long visions of soul racking pain*
55     *But regret is an insult – to grieve is in vain*
           *Say*
        *And why should we grieve that a spirit so fair*
        *Seeks Heaven to mix with its kindred there*

        *But still 'twas some Spirit of kindness descending*
60        *To share in the load of mortality's woe*
        *Who over thy lowly built sepulchre bending*
         *Bade sympathy's tenderest tear-drop to flow*
        *Not for thee soft compassion celestials did know*
        *But if Angels can weep, sure Man may repine*
65     *May weep in mute grief oer thy low laid shrine*

        *And did I then say for the Altar of Glory*
         *That the earliest the loveliest flowers I'd entwine*
        *Tho' with millions of blood-reeking victims 'tis gory*
         *Tho' the tears of the widow polluted its shine*
70     *Tho' around the orphans, the fatherless pine.*
        *Oh! fame all thy glories I'd yield for a tear*
        *To shed on the grave of an heart so sincere.*

[ 689 ]

**Shelley to Hogg**                                        *January 6, 1811*

SC 129   *I am very cold this morning, so you must excuse bad writing as I have been*
         *most of the night pacing a Church yard: I must now engage in scenes of*
75       *strong interest, You see the subject of the foregoing. I send because I think*
         *it may amuse you –.   Your letter has just arrived. I will send Wedgewood*
         *to University when I can collect him; – If it amuses you, you can answer*
         *him, if not I will. I consider your argument against the non-existence of a*
         *Deity. Do you allow that some* Supernatural *power actuates the organiza-*
80       *tion of physical causes, it is evident so far as this, that if* power, *wisdom*
                                              continual
         *are employed in the͜arrangement of these affairs that this power &c is*
                                    comprehension
         *something out of the* common *of Man as he now exists; at least if we allow*
85       *that the soul is* not *matter. Then* even *admitting that this actuating principle*
         *is such as I have described, admitting it to be finite, there must be* something
         *beyond this which influences* it's *actions and all this series advancing as if*
                                                                              can
         *it does in one instance, it* must *to infinity, must at last terminate, if it* can
90       *terminate in the existence which may be called a Deity; and* if *this Deity*
         *thus influences the actions of the Spirits (if I may be allowed the expression)*
         *which take care of minor events (supposing your Theory to be true) why is*
         *it* not *the soul of the Universe, in what is it* not *analagous to the Soul of Man?*
         *Why* too *is* not *Gravitation the soul of a Clock, I entertain no doubt of the*
95       *fact, altho it possesses no capabilities of variation; if the principle of life,*
         *and (that of reason put out of the question as in the cases of dogs, horses &*
         *oysters) be* soul, *then Gravitation is as much the Soul of a Clock, as animation*
         *is that of an oyster  <     >  I think we may not inaptly define* Soul *as the*
              supreme
100      *most͜superior and distinguished abstract appendage to the Nature of any*
         *thing. But I will write again. My head is rather dizzy to day on account of*
         *not taking rest, & a slight attack of Typhus*
                        *adiu   I will write soon*
                              *Your sincerest*
105                           *Percy Shelley*

[Frank with address, page 12, in the hand of Timothy Shelley]

# Shelley and his Circle : Manuscripts

**Shelley to Hogg**                                          *January 6, 1811*

SC 129    *Horsham, January Six*
          *T. Jeff^n Hogg Esq^r*
          *University College*
          *Oxford*
110       *T. Shelley*

line 1. Opposite this line and in the top margin are complex circular letters; see Commentary.

line 4. *sacrifise* (sic)

line 5. *recieved* (sic): Shelley in this period has trouble with *ei* and *ie* and sometimes writes through them to make them indistinguishable. So too with other spelling uncertainties. The *ie* here, however, is clear.

line 7. *perceive:* probable reading

line 8. *dissapointments* (sic)

line 18. *is* [it] *not*

line 30. *but* — . (sic)

line 36. There is a line drawn vertically down the middle of the poetry to join the rule below line 73.

line 57. The line under *And* was perhaps intended to cancel it.

line 65. *grief* is written through some other word, possibly *woe*.

line 69. *shine* [shrine], cramped into margin.

line 75. *I send* [it]

line 98. < >: Seal tear, but nothing is apparently missing as Shelley, anticipating the seal, has not written to the outer edge for the lines above and below.

line 103. *adiu* (sic): Shelley in these letters to Hogg sometimes writes, in haste, *adiu* or *adeu*.

COLLATION (selected passages).
T. J. HOGG, *THE LIFE OF PERCY BYSSHE SHELLEY*, 1, 158–159. (Hogg's changes indicated by italics.)

line 2. Dare I request one favour for myself — for my own *sake?* not the keenest anguish

line 4. so great a sacrifice *of friendship.*

line 5. *She* saw *me* when *I* received your letter of yesterday. *She* saw the conflict of *my* soul. *At first* she said nothing; *and then she exclaimed,* "*Re-direct* it, and *send* it instantly to the post!" Believe me, I feel *far more* than I will allow myself to *express, for the cruel* disappointments which I have undergone. Write to me whatever you wish to say; *you may say what you will on other subjects; but on that I dare not even read what you would write. Forget her?* What would I not *have given up to have been thus happy? I thought I knew* the means by which it *might have been* effected. *Yet I* consider what a female sacrifices when she returns the attachment *even* of one whose faith she supposes inviolable. *Hard is* the agony which is indescribable,

line 17. I *was* convinced of *her* truth, as I *was* of my own existence. Still *was it* not natural in *her*, even although she *might* return the most enthusiastic prepossessions arising from the consciousness of intellectual *sympathy*, ignorant, as she *was*, of *some of my opinions, of my sensations*

COLLATION (excluding incidentals of punctuation).
ON AN ICICLE THAT CLUNG TO THE GRASS OF A GRAVE, SHELLEY, *COMPLETE WORKS*, III, 88–89 (ESDAILE COPYBOOK).

line 36. Southerly
line 38. of love
line 39. Circulates freely and shamelessly there,
line 40. by crime,
line 41. icedrop

line 46. tyrant
line 47. patriotism
line 49. victory's
line 50. Spirit
line 51. daybeam

[ 691 ]

# The Carl H. Pforzheimer Library

SC 129   line 53. longed-for

line 54. long   night-dreams          soul-racking

line 56. And why

line 58. to meet with its own kindred

line 59. Yet 'twas some Angel

line 60. Mortality's

line 61. lowly-built

line 62. teardrop

line 63. And consigned the rich gift to the sisters of snow.

line 64. *angels*   I may

line 65. And shed tear drops tho' frozen to ice on thy shrine.

line 66. altar of glory,

line 67. of flowers

line 68. Though           'twas gory,

line 69. Though the

line 70. Though around it

line 71. Fame,

line 72. a heart

HOGG, now back at Oxford, has written again to Elizabeth Shelley. Elizabeth on being given the letter silently readdressed it and gave it back to the servant who had brought it (line 6). That there was any "conflict of soul" involved in this process is most unlikely, but Shelley, still interested in bedeviling Hogg, chooses so to interpret it. (All this is lost in Hogg's mutilated version.)

Then, following his usual pattern of alternating between Hogg-Elizabeth and Shelley-Harriet, Shelley turns to the latter pair (beginning with line 26, "Forsake her . . ."). The comment "there is a mystery which I dare not to clear up," coming immediately after the lament "she is lost to me forever, forever," probably means simply that Harriet is engaged. Shelley is trying to weave romantic insinuations to mystify Hogg.[1]

The comment on the poem (line 75), "You see the subject of the foregoing," implies that it deals with something already discussed with Hogg, apparently the loss of Harriet Grove plus suicide fantasies similar to those of the previous letter. The Esdaile manuscript version of the poem, as we note in the Collation heading, contains a title, "On an Icicle that Clung to the Grass of a Grave,"[2] and this gives us something of a clue to its meaning. The grave is (in fantasy) Shelley's, the gem (line 36) is an icicle frozen from an angelic tear on the grave, the "spirit so fair" (line 57), the "heart so sincere" (line 72) who is being mourned (by celestial rather than earthly mourners) is Shelley; and the poem may be

1. See sc 132 (Jan. 11, 1811), Commentary.

2. On the Esdaile copybook, see fn. 4 and "The Provenance of Shelley and his Circle Manuscripts," below, p. 898.

SC 129  taken as one of the first of Shelley's long series of self-dramatizations in the romantic manner which culminates in *Adonais*.[3] The comment in the first stanza on the Love which is ever warm and "untainted by Pride" is perhaps a reflection on the colder love of Harriet Grove which bowed to family "Pride."

As Shelley was just beginning to put the Esdaile copybook together in December 1811, the Esdaile version must be later than that in the above letter. And this is shown also by the superiority of some of the readings, for example (Collation, line 63), "sisters of snow."[4]

Following the poem, the letter reverts to the theme of the existence of God, which had arisen from Hogg's letter received on Sunday, December 30, when Shelley was leaving for his "inefficient effort." As Hogg is clearly arguing against the existence of God and Shelley for it, Shelley's phrase "your argument against the non-existence of a Deity" must be incorrect. He must mean "your arguments against the existence of a deity," or "your arguments for the non-existence of a deity." Shelley's counter-argument (on causation) is similar to that in the preceding letter.

Wedgwood's letter (line 76) Shelley is forwarding to himself at University College, Oxford.

The top margin of the above letter contains elaborate circular doodles of interlocking capital letters, apparently P's and B's. These were probably done by Hogg because they resemble the PBS italic monogram on the manuscript of his poem "It heeds not the tempest," dated January 10, 1811 (SC 131), and were apparently done after the

---

3. Some self-portraiture, although not direct, is probably inherent in the characters of Zastrozzi and Verezzi in *Zastrozzi*. It is more direct in that of Ginotti in *St. Irvyne*, especially in Ginotti's account of his youth at the beginning of Chapter X.

4. Ingpen, in presenting the above poem from the Esdaile copybook, dated it "1811" (Shelley, *Complete Works*, III, 88) but in a note (*ibid.*, VIII, 37) he comments: "In an autograph manuscript copy of Shelley's this poem is named 'On an Icicle that clung to the grass of a grave,' and is dated (perhaps incorrectly) 1809." Ingpen does not state that the "autograph manuscript" is that in the Esdaile copy book but it probably was, for he did not have access to the above manuscript (which remained in the hands of the Hogg family), and no other manuscript is known.

The Esdaile copybook is just what the name implies. It consists of copies of poems previously written but revised in late 1811, 1812, and 1813 for intended publication. The above poem, then, may have been originally composed in 1809, revised at the time of the above letter and revised again for the copybook; or it may have been composed between January 1 and 6, 1811 (the date of the above letter) and revised for the copybook.

SC 129   letter was written. (They intrude upon the first line of writing; if they had been there before Shelley began his letter he would normally have begun farther down the page in order to avoid running through them.) It would seem as though Hogg had both this letter and his own manuscript before him at the same time and tried first to work out a PBS monogram on the above letter and then completed it on his own manuscript.

SC 130   LEIGH HUNT TO MESSRS. BUTTON AND WHITAKER, JANUARY 8, 1811

AL signed *Leigh Hunt.*, 1 page. Double sheet, 4<sup>to</sup> (8.9 x 7.1 inches). Wove paper. Watermark: BUDGEN & WILMOTT| 1809|. (See Plate XXVIII.) Seal: wafer, brown. Docket, page 4: *Leigh Hunt| Jan<sup>y</sup> 1810.|*.

*Trinity College – Cambridge,*
*8<sup>th</sup> Jan<sup>y</sup> 1811.*

*Dear Sirs,*

    *I beg you to accept my sincerest acknowledgments for your very acceptable*
5   *present of the numbers of Handel already published, which was sent round to me from Beckenham to Carburton Street just before I set off on a visit to this place. The spirit, in which this present has been made, saves me, at this present moment, from the mortification of making you both an apology on a subject, which has from day to day been at my tongue's end, and from day*
10   *to day been ~~put off~~ kept silent in the hope of doing away the <u>necessity</u> of that apology. If I exercise your patience a little longer on this head, be persuaded that my own anxiety is by no means at rest upon it in the mean while. With regard to the little poems which I had the pleasure of writing for you, the information that they had succeeded with the public would have been a quite*
15   *sufficient return for them at any time; but as it is, I cannot think my debt discharged to you even on this score, as I shortly hope to prove to you in a better manner than I can in prose.*

      *Your obliged & obed<sup>t</sup> serv<sup>t</sup>*

        *Leigh Hunt.*

[Address, page 4]

*Hunt to Button and Whitaker*                    *January 8, 1811*

SC 130   *Mess^rs Button & Whitaker,*
         *Saint Paul's Church Yard,*
         *London.*
         *Private.*
         *By favour of M^r Hunter.*

IN THE year 1807, according to *Grove's Dictionary of Music and Musicians*, S. J. Button, a bookseller of 24 Paternoster Row,[1] went into partnership with John Whitaker (1776–1847), a popular song writer, to found a music publishing business at 75 St. Paul's Churchyard. (The London *Post Office Directory* for 1813 lists the business as "Music Repository.") Button was an old friend of Rowland Hunter,[2] bookseller at 72 St. Paul's Churchyard and stepfather to Leigh Hunt's wife Marianne. It was doubtless through Hunter that Hunt got to know Button and Whitaker, with both of whom for a time he was quite intimate.[3] In 1808 and 1809 the firm published three songs, the words by Hunt, the music by Whitaker: "Silent Kisses," "Love and the Aeolian Harp," and "Mary, Mary, List Awake."[4] It is to these songs that Hunt refers (line 13).

In the year 1815 these songs became the occasion for a curious lawsuit. An Irish publisher called Hime pirated the songs, and, when Whitaker brought suit, countered by claiming that one of them, "Silent Kisses," was obscene and hence not subject to copyright protection. We excerpt the following from *The Examiner's* report of the case:

Mr. Serjeant JOY desired the witness to read the last verse of the song called "*Silent Kisses*," which he did. The words were: —

"Yes, when our lips move, yet have nothing to say,
"And our eyes in each other's warm beam fade away

1. The London *Post Office Directory* for 1800 lists a William Button, bookseller, 24 Paternoster Row; so that either *Grove's* is mistaken in the initials or there were two booksellers named Button at that address.

2. Leigh Hunt to Mrs. Rowland Hunter, Sept. 13, 1808, Hunt, *Letters*, p. 34.

3. Hunt's early letters contain frequent references to Button and Whitaker. Marianne Kent stayed with the Buttons for a time. (Hunt, *Letters*, p. 34.)

4. Hunt, *First Editions*, pp. 28, 343, 356; Landré, *Hunt*, II, 485–486. Hunt quotes "Love and the Aeolian Harp" in a letter to Marianne Kent on October 19, 1808, as "a new song" just set to music by Whitaker. In the case of Whitaker versus Hime (see below) it was testified that the three songs had been engraved in 1808 and 1809. (*The Examiner*, June 4, 1815, p. 366.)

SC 130

"'Tis then my heart springs up, and trembles to thee,
"As the arrow still trembles when fixed in the tree.
"Oh! Never let ear rob a part of our blisses;
"Oh! all for the heart be our – Silent Kisses." . . .

*Sir John Stevenson* deposed, that Mr. Whitaker (whom he only knew by his works) was a Composer of great celebrity, whose compositions he had no doubt would sell well — they were perhaps of a class, he said, to meet a better sale than Haydn's. Mr. Whitaker was a remarkably original composer. Any Composer would suffer immensely, and there would be an end to the exertions of genius, if piracy could be permitted with impunity. Sir John being asked, whether he did not think the verse read a little tawdry? replied, "I own it is a little warm." — "That's a new name for tawdry," said the Counsel: "Don't you think it hot, Sir John?" "That," he answered, "depends on the constitution of the person reading it."[5]

The judge did not view Hime's defense with sympathy; the plaintiff was awarded £50 damages. In the next issue of *The Examiner* Hunt commented:

We conclude then by informing Mr. Joy and his coadjutor, for their own benefit and for that of the persons whom *they*, and not ourselves, would injure, by exciting them to look for scandalous meanings where none are intended, that all the obscenities to be found in the song in question, come from their own wretched imagination, — are spots from their own vitiated sight.[6]

5. *The Examiner*, June 4, 1815, pp. 366–367.

6. *Ibid.*, June 11, 1815, p. 383. See also Landré, *Hunt*, II, 487–488.

SC 131   T. J. HOGG, *IT HEEDS NOT THE TEMPESTS*, JANUARY 10, 1811

HOLOGRAPH MANUSCRIPT, 1¾ pages. Single sheet, folio (12.7 x 7.9 inches). Laid paper. Watermark: *KENT*| 1809|.

PROVENANCE: Thomas Jefferson Hogg; Major R. J. Jefferson Hogg (Sotheby, June 30, 1948, lot 104).

*It heeds not the tempests It heeds not their scowling*

         oak
*The ~~Lord~~ of the forest sublime on the rock*

*It heeds not the winds w^ch around it are howling*

5      *Unmoved it defies their impetuous shock*

SC 131  *With tortuous roots it clings close to the correi*
  *Whilst its leaves by the blast of stern Autumn are shriven*
 *Its summit envelopped in mists ~~grey~~ chilling hoary*
  *The oak shoots its branches athwart the wide heaven*
10  *From the rocks at its base the dark Ivy ascending*
     bark
  *To the moss-covered ~~trunk~~ it progressive adheres*
 *In sinuous folds around the trunk bending*
  *Thus shrouded a Pillar of verdure appears*
15  *Next every firm limb entwining embracing*
  *Its fibres prolonging umbrageous extends*
 *Here with its dark cluster the foliage gracing*
   long shoots  deep tresses
 *Whilst there its ~~veined leaf~~ in a ~~ringlet~~ depends*

20  *The leaves of the forest when Autumn is waning*
  *Fall a prey to the keen frost deciduous fade*
 *But the leaf of the Ivy eternal remaining*
  *Will for ever encompass the oak with its shade*
     roar
25  *Ah heardst thou the ~~sound~~ tis the oak of the mountain*
     ~waters
  *As headlong its borne to the ~~valley~~ below*
    as the swift back
 *Ah heardst thou the sound ~~tis the deep rocky~~*
30
     to the fountain
 *~~Receives the huge trunk~~*
  *From the deep rocky bason ~~the~~ streams ~~waters~~ eddying flow*
   Wind
 *did the force of the ~~blast~~ each tempest collecting*
35
     towered in gaunt pride
  *Oer whelm the huge trunk w^{ch} ~~for ages has stood~~*
 *did the red flame of heaven its vengeance directing*
  *Hurl headlong the Oak w^h its rage long defied*
 *The evening was silent each Zephr reposing*
40  *The tremulous Spire of the Poplar was still*
 *With petal unmoved every flower was closing*
  *The Sun's last pale beam had expired on the hill*

**Hogg, It heeds not the tempests**                              *January* 10, 1811

SC 131

45  The *Ivy* *insidious* ~~every~~ <sup>each</sup> juice had been draining
         2        1

The moisture imbibing the Sap drew away

Each dew drop from heaven on its own leaves detaining

Had thus hurried the oak to a speedy decay

                *Fond Youth*
50  ~~My friend~~ to the tale of the Ivy attending

                     <sup>oak</sup>
From the ~~king~~ of the Forest this lesson derive

Had some hand stripped the ivy w<sup>ch</sup> round it was bending

              <sup>Oak</sup>
55  The ~~king~~ of the Forest had now been alive

Strip the first shoots of passion thy need then is sorest

When ~~flattering~~ loves proffers eternal bliss to the mind

Believe not – remember the Oak of the Forest

In seemed in perennial verdure enshrined

                         <sup>must</sup>
60          <sup>not</sup>        <sup>how soon wouldst</sup>
~~Ah~~ *hadst* thou its vigor ~~yet still must~~ thou perish
        2        1

With Adversity's storms thou knowst not to contend

65  Nor knowst thou superior to others to flourish

                    <sup>first</sup>
Ah Strip the ~~shoots of the~~ Ivy w<sup>ch</sup> round thee w<sup>d</sup> bend

              Jany 10 — 1811

                Univ. Coll

70               PBS                    PBS

line 6. *correi* (sic): corrie (a circular hollow on the side of a mountain)

line 8. *envelopped* (sic)

line 8. *hoary: athwart* of line 9 has been written through *hoary* but presumably Hogg intended it to stand, for otherwise there would be no rhyme for *correi*. Hogg has cramped the end of these (and other) lines into the right edge so that the ends of the lines overlap with each other.

line 16. *prolonging: ing* is written through *ed*

line 16. *extends* (sic)

line 19. *depends* (sic)

line 22. *But: B* is written through *Th.*

line 24. *roar:* probable reading

line 25. *thet: e* is written through *a*

line 25. *mountain: m* is written through *f*

line 28. *the swift:* Hogg in making changes here presumably forgot to delete *the.*

line 32. *bason: NED* gives bason as an alternate form of basin. Shelley uses it also; see sc 171 (July ?21, 1811), line 8.

line 35. *gaunt pride:* probable reading; cramped downward into edge

[ 698 ]

SC 131

line 41. *flower:* What appears to be a *t* has been added following the *r*; perhaps Hogg intended *floweret.*

line 47. *detaining: de* is written through *con*

line 56. *Strip:* Hogg has omitted the *t* but placed a cross line over the *r*. There is a large *x* in the left margin opposite *Strip.*

line 57. *eternal: al* is written through *ity*

line 59. *In* (sic)

line 62. *hadst thou:* Hogg's intention here is not clear. "Thou hat not" does not make sense.

line 70. *PBS PBS:* intertwined italic monograms at bottom of page, the second set larger than the first. See sc 129 (Jan. 6, 1811), Textual Notes and Commentary.

SHELLEY's letter to Hogg of January 12 (sc 133) opens with a comment upon the above poem:

Your letter with the extremely beautiful enclosed poetry came this morning – It is really admirable, it touches the heart, but I must be allowed to offer *one* critique upon it – You will be surprised to hear that I think it unfinished; you have not said that "the ivy after it had destroyed the oak, as if to mock the miseries w^ch it caused twined around a pine which stood near" – it is true therefore but does not comprehend the whole truth. –

The meaning of both Shelley's comment and Hogg's poem is to be found in the previous correspondence with its theme of unrequited love — Shelley's for Harriet Grove, Hogg's for Elizabeth Shelley — and especially in the January 6 letter (sc 129) with its gloom and death fantasies. Hogg, in reply, writes the above poem on an oak which had survived storms and lightnings but was destroyed by an ivy vine which sapped its strength. The insidious ivy, the conclusion informs us with unadorned directness, is "passion" which the "Fond Youth" (first written "My friend") should strip from himself if he wishes to survive. Shelley takes the reference personally and replies, in effect, that not only has Harriet Grove — the ivy — "destroyed" him — the oak — but has now, to "mock" his "miseries," turned to another — a mere "pine" (Harriet's future husband, William Helyar).[1]

The above manuscript cannot have been that sent to Shelley as it has not been folded for transmission as a letter. Furthermore, it was found among the Hogg family papers. Both its date and its condition indicate that it was a first draft (retained by Hogg), from which a copy was made and sent to Shelley on the same day.

1. In the January 11 letter (sc 132) the metaphor is varied and he becomes (line 31) a "clod of earth."

# The Carl H. Pforzheimer Library

SC 132   P. B. SHELLEY TO T. J. HOGG, JANUARY 11, 1811; ?ELIZABETH SHELLEY, *YES! THE ARMS OF BRITANNIA*

AL signed *P B S–*, including transcription of poem by ?Elizabeth Shelley, 7 pages. 1 double sheet, 2 single sheets, folio (12.6 x 8 inches). Laid paper. Watermark, double sheet: [lion rampant in crowned oval]|; countermark, double sheet: C WILMOTT| 1810|; watermarks, single sheets: C WILMOTT| 1810|. Seal: wax, red: *ES* [in oval]|. (See Plate xxv.) Frank, by Timothy Shelley. Postmarks: 1. (mileage stamp): HORSHAM| 41|; 2. (morning duty franking stamp, London): FREE| 12 JA 12| 1811|.

PROVENANCE: Thomas Jefferson Hogg; Major R. J. Jefferson Hogg (Sotheby, June 30, 1948, lot 6). *De Ricci 25* (p. 121).

*Field Place – Friday*

*My dear Friend.*

    *I will not now consider y* *argument w^ch arrived this morning. I wait till tomorrow; it coincides exactly with Eliza's sentiments on the subject to*
5   *whom I read it, indeed it has converted her, altho' from my having a great deal to do to day I cannot listen to so full an ex^n of her sentiments on the subject as I w^d wish to send you. I shall write to you to morrow on the subject, when if you clear up some doubts which yet remain, dissipate some hopes relative to the perfectibility of man – generally considered as well as individually,*
10  *I will willingly submit to the System which at present I cannot but strongly reprobate. How can I find words to express my thanks for y^r mild, y^r generous conduct with regard to my Sister; with susceptibilities such as your own; yet to promise what I ought not to have required, what nothing but a dear Sisters peace could have induced me to demand. – Pardon me; believe that the first*
15  *wish of my heart is that against w^ch I seem to be acting in opposition – when y^r letter came and my Sister* <u>*instantly*</u> *returned it, what arguments did I leave unused to induce her to recall the Servant who took it.. She was deaf to every solicitation. "Reason, Virtue, Justice forbade it, as* <u>*yet*</u> *she was uninfluenced by passion, as yet she w^d follow the dictates of that Reason which*
20  *was unimpaired by awakened susceptibilities, he w^d be dissapointed in me, most* <u>*bitterly*</u> *so. I will not read it." I, even I a brother did not see the force of her Reasoning, I submitted, submitted to what I knew must inflict a most cruel pang.*

**_Shelley to Hogg_**                    **_January 11, 1811_**

SC I 32  *Religion! this is thy remote influence. — What can I say on the subject of*
25     *yr. letter to Eliza, is it not dictated by the most generous of human Motives,*
        *& yet I have not shewn it to her. Need I explain the reason? —— It is the*
        *only thing on which I will make the least cloud of mystery, it is the only*
        *point on which I will be a solitary being – to be solitary, to be reserved in*
        *communicating pain sureely cannot be criminal, it cannot be contrary to the*
30     *most strict duties of friendship. She is gone, she is lost to me forever   she is*
        *married, married to a clod of earth, she will become as insensible herself,*
        *all those fine capabilities will moulder. Let us speak no more on the subject,*
        *do not deprive me of the little remains of peace which yet linger. That which*
        *arises from endeavours to make others happy. The poetry w^h I sent you*
35     *alluded not to subject of my nonsensical ravings. —— I hope that you are*
        *now publishing Leonora. Lundi w^d do it as well as any one; if even he will*
        *not publish it, he will print it, & I will engage to dispose of 500 Copies. –*
        *Stockdale is acquainted with y^r family – Hinc illae lachrymae — I attempted*
        *to Deistify my father; mirabile dictu! he for a time listened to my arguments;*
40     *he allowed the impossibility (considered abstractedly) of any preternatural*
        *interferences of providence he allowed the impossibility of witches ghosts*
        *miracles. – But when I came to apply the truths on which we agreed so*
        *harmoniously, he started at the bare idea of Xt never having existed, &*
        *silenced me with an equine argument   ""in effect these words " I believe because*
45     *I do believe" – My Mo^th fancies me in the High road to Pandemonium, she*
        *fancies I want to make a deistical coterie of all my little sisters. – You must*
        *be very solitary at Oxford, I wish I could come there now . . but for reasons*
        *w^ch I will tell you at meeting it is delayed for a fortnight — I have a Poem,*
        *with M^r Lundi which I shall certainly publish. There is some of Eliza's in it:*
50     *I will write to morrow I have something to add to it & if Lundi has any*
        *idea (when he speaks to you of publishing it w^th my name will you tell him*
        *to leave it alone till I come . .*

        *Yes! the arms of Britannia victorious are bearing*
            *Fame, Triumph & Glory wherever they spead*
55       *Her Lion his crest oer the nations is rearing;*
            *Ruin follows! it tramples the dying & dead*

SC 132

                                                   -bed-

*Thy countrymen fall, the ~~complaint-breathing sigh~~*

                      blood-reeking bed

60       *Of the battle-slain sends a complaint-breathing sigh*

      *It is mixed with the shoutings of Victory!*

*Old Ocean to shrieks of Despair is resounding*

      *It washes the terror-struck nations with gore*

*Wild horror the fear-palsied Earth is astounding*

65       *And murmurs of fate fright the dread-convulsed shore*

*The Andes in Sympathy start at the roar*

      *Vast Aetna alarmed leans his flame-glowing brow*

      *And hugh Teneriffe stoops with his pinnacled snow.*

*The ice-mountains echo. the Baltic, the Ocean*

70       *Where Cold sits enthroned on his column of snow*

*E'en Spitzbergen perceives the terrific commotion*

      *The roar floats on the whirlwinds of sleet as they blow*

      <     >d *tinges the streams as half frozen they flow*

        <     >e *meteors of war lurid flame thro' the air*

75       *They mix their bright gleam with the red Polar glare.*

    *X*       *X*       *X*       *X*       *X*       *X*       *X*

*All are Bretheren, – the*         *African bending*

      *To the stroke of the hard hearted Englishmans rod*

*The courtier at Luxury's Palace attending*

80 *The Senator trembling at Tyranny's nod*

*Each nation w^(ch) kneels at the footstool of God*

*All are Bretheen; then banish Distinction afar*

*Let concord & Love hear the miseries of War.*

*These are Eliza's. she has written many more, & I will shew you at*

85 *some future time the whole of the composition. I like it very much . if a*

*Brother may be allowed to praise a sister. I will write to morrow*

                             *y^(r)'s. with affection*

                                  *P B S –*

*Can you read this?*

**Shelley to Hogg**                                    *January 11, 1811*

SC 132  [Frank with address, page 8, in the hand of Timothy Shelley]
90  *Horsham, January Eleven*        *1811*
    *T. Jeff^n Hogg Esq^r*
    *University College*
    *Oxford*
    *T:Shelley.*

line 6. *ex^n:* Hogg gives *exposition.* Cf. sc 133 (Jan. 12, 1811), line 33.

line 18. Shelley put opening quotations at the beginning of each line of his paraphrase of his sister's comments: *it; by; the dictates; was; susceptibilities; -pointed; so.*

line 20. *dissapointed* (sic)

line 29. *sureely* (sic)

line 30. *forever* is the last word on the line; the following *she* is shaky and badly blotted.

line 33. *deprive me: de* written through *pre.*

line 35. *to subject* (sic)

line 51. *to you* [ ) ]

line 54. *spead* (sic)

line 70. *column:* probable reading

line 73. *<Bloo>d*

line 77. *the*          *African:* blank in Ms.

line 82. *Bretheen* (sic)

COLLATION (selected passages).
T. J. HOGG, *THE LIFE OF PERCY BYSSHE SHELLEY*, 1, 105–106, 162–165. (Hogg's changes indicated by italics.)

line 3. I will not now consider your *little Essay,*

line 5. indeed it has *convinced* her,

line 11. How can I find words to express my thanks for *such* generous conduct with regard to my sister *with talents and attainments,* such as *you possess,* to promise what I ought not *perhaps* to have required, what nothing but a dear sister's *intellectual improvement* could have induced me to demand. What can I say on the subject of your letter *concerning Elizabeth?* is it not dictated by the most generous *and disinterested* of human motives? I have not shown it to her *yet, I need not* explain the reason. *On this point you know all. There* is only *one affair, of* which I will make the least cloud of mystery; it is the only point on which I will be a solitary being!

line 35. I hope that you are now publishing *one of your tales.* L—— would do it, as well as any one; *if you do not choose to publish a book at Oxford, you can print it there;* and I will engage to dispose of five hundred copies. S—— *professes to be* acquainted with your family; hinc illae lacrymae! I attempted to *enlighten* my father,

line 40. He allowed the *utter incredibility* of witches, ghosts, *legendary* miracles. But when I came to apply the truths, on which we *had* agreed so harmoniously, he started at the bare idea of *some facts generally believed,* never having existed,

line 45. she fancies I want to make a deistical coterie of all my little sisters: *how laughable!* You must be

SHELLEY's request to Hogg on January 6 (sc 129) — "write to me whatever you wish to say to Eliza you may say in that" – certainly produced results. Hogg, ignoring this advice, either sent Elizabeth another letter, via Shelley, which Shelley felt it unwise to give to her (line 26)

SC 132   or, more likely, had sent Shelley a copy of his previous letter to her. He also sent an "argument" (line 3), presumably on the usual topics of his "arguments" at this time, namely God and love. And he must have sent a letter to Shelley, for Shelley replies to some comments which Hogg has made on the poem included in the January 6 letter (line 34).

Shelley is himself still unconvinced by Hogg's "argument," its "System" – presumably the old argument on an ascending ladder of sensual love – he "cannot but strongly reprobate" (line 10). But, although he himself found it rather strong meat, it coincided (line 4) "exactly with Eliza's sentiments on the subject."

Although he read the "argument" to his sister, Shelley did not give Hogg's letter to her; and he is strangely vague on his motives: "Need I explain the reason? —— It is the only thing on which I will make the least cloud of mystery" (line 26). If we take this in conjunction with the comment on the Harriet Grove affair in the January 6 letter – "There is a mystery which I dare not to clear up" – and with the fact that in the present letter he follows the comment with a switch to Harriet Grove – "she is lost to me forever she is married" – it seems probable that Hogg's letter to Elizabeth Shelley had some reference to Harriet Grove. One might conjecture that Shelley had not informed Hogg of Harriet's engagement but had placed the whole blame for the break-up of the affair on the religious intolerance of her family (with the unwilling Harriet being severed from her beloved) and Hogg had written to Elizabeth perhaps requesting her intervention on behalf of her brother. The phrase "she is married" (line 30) has given the commentators some trouble, for Harriet was not married until the autumn; it has even been suggested that it be amended to "she married!"[1] But, as the manuscript shows, "she is married" is what Shelley wrote, and there is no reason to doubt that it was what he intended. He is trying to impress Hogg by exaggerating the engagement into a marriage (with overtones of his stoicism under the blow: "Let us speak no more on the subject" – line 32).

Shelley next turns to Hogg's letter to him. Hogg, taking the hint from the comment in the January 6 letter (line 75) on the verses included in it — "You see the subject of the foregoing" — had apparently inter-

---

1. The emendation, first suggested by Peacock, was accepted by the editors of Shelley, *Complete Works*, and others.

SC 132   preted them as suicide fantasies, and this Shelley denies. The verses which he now encloses (attacking the war and British colonial policy) he attributes to Elizabeth. It is possible, however, that they were by Shelley himself for they appear in the Esdaile copybook (under the title *Fragment of a Poem, the original of which was suggested by the Cowardly and Infamous Bombardment of Copenhagen*)[2] and this book was to be published as Shelley's. We know of no poems by Elizabeth that were to appear in it; and the other poems we have by Elizabeth show no such political radicalism as is manifested here. They are either sentimental narratives or lyrics or light conversation pieces.[3] Shelley may have attributed the verses to Elizabeth in order to stimulate Hogg's interest. Once again the letter is sealed with Elizabeth's seal.

The "Poem" (line 48) with "Mr. Lundi" (John Munday of Munday and Slatter, Oxford booksellers and publishers) was probably, once more, the *Poetical Essay on the Existing State of Things*.

2. Shelley, *Complete Works*, III, 316–317; VIII, 40–41 fn.

3. See sc 114 ("Cold cold is the blast"), and *Original Poetry* by Victor and Cazire.

SC 133   P. B. SHELLEY TO T. J. HOGG, JANUARY 12, 1811

AL signed *PBS*, 11¼ pages. 3 double sheets, 4[to] (8.7 x 7 inches). Laid paper. Watermark: [posthorn in crowned shield]| cw|. Gilt edges.   (See Plate xxv.)
Seal: wafer.
Postmarks: 1. (mileage stamp): HORSHAM| 41|; 2. (morning duty stamp, London): E| 15 JA 15| 1811|.
PROVENANCE: Thomas Jefferson Hogg; Major R. J. Jefferson Hogg (Sotheby, June 30, 1948, lot 70). *De Ricci 27* (p. 122).

*Field Place   Jan. 12. 1811.*

*My dear Friend*

*Your letter with the extremely beautiful enclosed poetry came this morning – It is really admirable, it touches the heart, but I must be allowed to offer one critique upon it – You will be surprised to hear that I think it unfinished; you have not said that "the ivy after it had destroyed the oak, as*

# The Carl H. Pforzheimer Library

SC 133   *if to mock the miseries w^ch it caused twined around a pine which stood near"*
*— it is true therefore but does not comprehend the whole truth. — As to the*
*stuff w^ch I sent you, I write all my poetry of that kind from the feelings of the*

10   *moment — if therefore it neither has allusion to the sentiments which rationally*
*might be supposed to possess me, or to those w^ch which my situation might*
*awaken me, it is another proof of that egotizing variability whilst I shudder*
*when I reflect how much I am in it's power. To you, to I dare represent myself*
*as I am; wretched to the last degree — sometimes one gleam of hope, one faint*

15   *solitary gleam dares to illume the darkened prospect before me . . but it has*
*vanished. I fear it will never return   My sister will I fear never return the*
*attachment which would once again bid me be happy. Yes! in this alone is*
*my feeble anticipation of peace placed!. But what am I? —. am I not the most*
*degraded of deceived enthusiasts, do I not deceive myself — I never never can*

20   *feel peace again, What necessity is there for continuing in existence. —   But*
*God! Eternity! Love! my dear friend I am yet a sceptic on these subjects*
*w^d that I cd. believe them to be as are represented w^d that I c^d totally disbelieve*
*them: But no! that w^d be selfish. I still have firmness enough to resist this last*
*this most horrible of errors. —.   Is my despair the result of the hot sickly love*

25   *which enflames the admirers of Sterne or Moore. — it is the conviction of*
*unmerited unkindness, the conviction that s^d a future world exist the object*
*as myself*
*of my attachment w^d be as miserable is the cause of it. — I here take God*
*(if a God exists) to witness that I wish torments which beggar the futile*

30   *description of a fancied Hell would fall upon me; provided Thereby I could*
*attain that happiness for what I love, which I fear can never be. — The question*
*is what do I love?.   it is almost unnecessary to answer. Do I love the person,*
*the embodied identity (if I may be allowed the ex^n) No! I love what is superior*
*what is excellent, or what I concieve to be so, & wish, ardently wish to be*

35   *convinced of the existence of a God that so superior a spirit should derive*
*happiness from my exertions — Amato for Love is Heaven, & Heaven is Love.*
*Oh! that it twere. You think so too, — yet you disbelieve the Existence of an*
*eternal omnipresent spirit Am I not mad.? alas I am, but I pour my ravings*
*in the ear of a friend who will pardon them. — Stay! I have an idea, I think*

40   *Ill can prove the existence of a Deity. A first cause . . I will ask a Materialist*

[ 706 ]

SC 133    *how came this universe at first. He will answer by chance. – What chance?*
*I will answer in the words of Spinosa – "An* <u>infinite</u> *number of atoms had*
*been ~~falling~~ floating* <u>from</u> *all eternity in Space till at last one of them for-*
*tuitously diverged from it's track which dragging with it another formed the*
45    *principle of Gravitation & in consequence the universe" – What cause*
*produced this change, this chance? surely some, for where do we know that*
*causes arise without their correspondent effects; at least we must here, in so*
*abstract a subject reason analogically. Was not this then a* <u>cause</u>, *was it not*
*a* <u>first</u> *cause. – was not this first cause a Deity. now nothing remains but to*
50    *prove that this Deity has a care, or rather that it's only employment consists*
*in regulating the present & future happiness of it's creation, – our ideas ~~are~~*
*of ~~if~~ infinite space &ᶜ are scarcely to be called ideas for we cannot either*
*comprehend or explain them; therefore the Deity must be judged by us from*
*attributes analogical to our Situation. Oh! that this Deity were the Soul of*
55    *the Universe, the Spirit of universal imperishable love. – Indeed I believe it;*
*—— but now to yʳ argument of the necessity of Xtianity ~~You say since w~~*
*I am not sure that your argument was not* <u>intended</u> *to prove its inutility –*
*if it was not you allow, you say that Love is the only rational source of*
*happiness,* <u>one</u> *Man is capable of it; why not all? The cullibity of man*
60    *praeterite, I allow, but because men are & have been cullible, I see no reason*
*why they sʰᵈ always continue so, – Have there not been fluctuations in the*
*opinions of mankind; and as the* <u>stuff</u> *which soul is made of must be in every*
                                                                                system
*one the same, would not an extended ~~profu~~ of rational & morall̶ unprejudiced*
65    *education render each individual capable of experiencing that degree of*
*happiness to which each ought to aspire, more for other than self. Hideous!*
*hated trait of Xtianity Oh! Xt how I hate thy influence; they all are bad*
*enough. – but do we not now see Superstitition decaying, is not its influence*
*weakened. except where Faber Rowland Hill & several other of the Armaged-*
70    *don-Heroes maintain their posts with all the obstinacy of cabalistical*
*dogmatism. How I pity them, how I despise, hate them.*
*Stockdale knows Mʳ Dayrell, pray publish Leonora, I am beyond measure*
*anxious for her appearance   Adieu.*
*Excuse my mad arguments, they are none at all, for I am rather confused,*

**Shelley to Hogg**                          *January* 12, 1811

SC 133   *& I fear in consequence of a fever they will not allow me to come on the 26.*
*but I will Adeu.*

*Your affectionate friend*
*PBS*

[Address, page 12, in red ink]
*T. Jefferson Hogg Esq^{re}*
80   *University College*
*Oxford*

*You can enclose*
*to T S.*

line 10. *moment* is the final word on the first page and Shelley has curved it down and compressed it, something which he frequently does at the end of a line.

line 12. ~~*me:*~~ Although a line runs through the word, Shelley perhaps intended to underline and not cancel it.

line 15. *solitary:* Shelley apparently began to write *solitarily,* got as far as the second *l* and then converted it into a *y.*

line 22. *as* [they] *are*

line 33. *ex^n:* Hogg gives "expression." Cf. SC 132, line 6, where Hogg gives *ex^n* as "exposition."

line 34. *concieve* (sic)

line 36. ~~*Amato:*~~ The final *o* is not certain.

line 37. *twere* (sic)

line 50. *employment:* The second *m* appears to be written through a *d.*

line 64. *profu:* probable reading; [?profusion]

line 66. *other* (sic)

line 75. *& I:* The seal still adhering blocks out the center of the *I.*

line 76. *Adeu* (sic)

line 80. *You can enclose| to T S.* is written on page 12 perpendicular to the address on an edge that would be tucked in as a flap. These two lines are in black ink and have blotted in the folding.

COLLATION (selected passages).

T. J. HOGG, *THE LIFE OF PERCY BYSSHE SHELLEY,* 1, 167-170. (Hogg's changes indicated by italics.)

line 16. My sister will, I fear, never return the attachment which would once again bid me be *calm.*

line 20. But *Heaven!* Eternity! Love!

line 35. convinced of the existence of a *Deity,* that so superior a spirit *might* derive *some degree of* happiness from my *feeble* exertions:

line 37. you disbelieve *not* the existence of an eternal, omnipresent Spirit.

line 57. I am not sure that your argument *does not tend* to prove its *unreality.*

line 66. Hideous, hated *traits* of *Superstition.* Oh! *Bigots,* how I *abhor your* influence; they are all bad enough, — but do we not see *Fanaticism* decaying?

line 70. the obstinacy of *long-established* dogmatism?

line 72. *S.* knows Mr. *D. would* publish *your tale.*

THIS letter continues the subjects and discussions of the previous Shelley-to-Hogg letters: Elizabeth Shelley, the nature of God, love, Harriet Grove, and the horrors of Christianity. Shelley is still arguing for the existence of God (line 45): "What cause produced this change,

SC 133   this chance?"[1] God is still to Shelley, as in the January 3 letter, a spirit of universal love — to which Hogg apparently replies with a steady, undeviating skepticism. Under this pressure, Shelley's deism is beginning to buckle: "w$^d$ that I cd. believe . . ." (line 22); "if a God exists" (line 29).

Hogg's skepticism applied also to social matters. Man had been "cullible" (line 60; i.e., gullible); he would always be "cullible." Hence, there was little hope for progress. Shelley rejects this, and rejects also Hogg's argument (line 56) that Christianity is "necessary" (apparently an ironical argument).[2] He sees only evil in the activities of such popular divines as George Stanley Faber (line 69) and Rowland Hill.[3]

Shelley's "despair" (line 24), he implies, results from the loss of Harriet Grove. We might note, however, that on the day preceding the letter he had asked Stockdale to send a copy of *St. Irvyne* to another Harriet (the first reference to Harriet Westbrook in Shelley's correspondence). The "enclosed poetry" by Hogg (line 3) was doubtless that of sc 131 (January 10, 1811). "Moore" (line 25) is not Thomas Moore but John Moore (1730–1802), a minor novelist. "Dayrell" (line 72) was a minister known to Hogg. On December 18 Shelley had written to Stockdale requesting him to send a copy of *St. Irvyne* to Hogg at "Rev. [John] Dayrell's, Lynnington Dayrell, Buckingham."

The final comment, "you can enclose to TS," means that Timothy Shelley had agreed to allow Hogg to make use of his franking privileges. In this connection we might note the red ink of the address and the discrepancy between the date of the letter (January 12) and the date of the London postmark (January 15). As it took one day for mail to come

1. The preceding argument on the atoms, which is attributed to Spinoza, is, of course, an echo of Lucretius' "fortuitous concourse of atoms." Shelley may have been misled by the article "Atheist" in *Nicholson's Encyclopedia* (with which he was acquainted): "He attributes everything to a fortuitous concourse of atoms . . . in the year 1619, Spinoza was burned to death [!] for having avowed his adherence to the opinion of atheism." On Nicholson see sc 69 (?Sept. 11, 1805).

2. See sc 135 (Jan. 17, 1811), Commentary.

3. Faber (1773–1854), a well-known theological writer of the time, lived at Durham and was acquainted with the Hogg family. See sc 154 (Apr. 26, 1811). Rowland Hill (1744–1833 — not to be confused with the Rowland Hill of post-office fame) is listed in a tourist guide book of the time as one of the wonders of London churchdom, "remarkable for a very vehement kind of eloquence . . . followed by the most crowded audiences, chiefly composed of the lower classes of society." (J. Feltham, *The Picture of London for 1803*, p. 233.)

SC 133    from Horsham to London, the letter must have been mailed on January 14. The red ink may indicate that it was not addressed at the time at which it was written, and hence, probably not until January 14. The comment "you can enclose to TS," however, as we note, is in black ink and was blotted in folding; so that the letter must have been folded immediately after being written. And if it was folded it must have been sealed also because so thick a letter (three double sheets) would not have remained folded unless it had been sealed. The probable explanation is that the letter was sealed by Shelley[4] on the 12th and left for Timothy Shelley to frank and address (part of the franking process)[5] but this Timothy failed to do. He had perhaps already left for London, where he was later in the month, for the letter of January 11 (sc 132) is franked but that of January 14 (sc 134) is not. Shelley may have thought that the letter had been franked and posted, but discovering on the 14th that it had not been, addressed it himself and sent it to the post.

4. See sc 132 (Jan. 11, 1811).                    5. See sc 116 (Sept. 6, 1810), Commentary.

SC 134    P. B. SHELLEY TO T. J. HOGG, JANUARY 14, 1811

AL signed *P. B S.*, 3 pages. Double sheet, 4$^{to}$ (8.7 x 7.1 inches).    (See Plates XXIX–XXXII.)
Laid paper. Watermark: [posthorn in crowned shield]| cw|. Gilt edges.
Seal: wafer, red.
Postmarks: 1. (mileage stamp): Horsham| 41|; 2. (morning duty stamp, London): E| 15 JA 15| 1811|.
PROVENANCE: Thomas Jefferson Hogg; John Ewer Jefferson Hogg (Sotheby, July 27, 1922, lot 326). *De Ricci 28* (p. 122).

*My dear Friend*

*Your letter & that of Wedgewoods came to day, y$^{rs}$ is excellent — & I think will fully (in his own mind) convince M$^r$ W. – I enclosed 5 sheets of paper full this morning & sent them to the Coach with yours . . I sate up all*
5    *night to finish them; they attack Xtiantity's very basis which at some future time I will tell you, & I have attempted to prove from the existence of God the futility of the Superstition upon w$^{ch}$ he founds his whole scheme ——.    I was sorry to see that you even remotely suspected me of being offended with you. How I wish that I c$^d$ persuade you that it is impossible. I am really*

**Shelley to Hogg**                    *January 14, 1811*

SC 134   *sleepy can you suppose that I sh* *be so apathetic as ever to sleep again till*
            *my last slumber but it is so, & I shall take a walk to S* *Leonard's Forest to*
            *dissipate it. Adieu. You shall hear from me tomorrow*

                                      *Yr sincere friend*
                                         *P. B S.*

15   *Stockdale has behaved infamously to you, he has abused the confidence you*
            *reposed in him in sending L & has made very free with y* *character with my*
            *Father. I shall call on S– in my way & explain. — May I expect to see*
            *Leonora printed*

            [Address, page 4]
            *T. Jefferson Hogg Esq* *re*
20   *University Coll:*
            *Oxford*

line 5. *Xtiantity's* (sic)

line 15. *infamously:* The seal tear has removed
the tops of the *f*, *m*, and *u* but the paper is still
adhering to the seal and the letters can be made
out; *sly* can be seen through the seal.

line 16. *L⟨?a⟩*. The letter has been folded without
blotting (perhaps because of Shelley's sleepiness,
line 10) and consequently the inside pages are
smeared. (See Plates XXX–XXXI.)

COLLATION (selected passages).
T. J. HOGG, *THE LIFE OF PERCY BYSSHE SHELLEY*, I, 170–171. (Hogg's changes indicated
by italics.)

line 5. they attack *his hypothesis in its* very
basis, which, at some future time, I will *explain
to* you; and I have attempted to prove, from the
existence of *a Deity and of Revelation*, the futility
line 15. *S——* has behaved infamously to *me:*
he has abused the confidence *I* reposed in him

in sending *him my work;* and *he* has made very
free with your character, *of which he knows
nothing*, with my father. I shall call on S——
in my way, *that he may* explain. May I expect
to see *your Tale* printed?

I N HIS January 3 letter (SC 128)[1] Shelley informed Hogg that he would
send Wedgwood's "long" argument on to him; on January 6 (SC 129)[2]
he said that he would forward it to University College when he had it
"collected" (which probably means that he had lost part of it). Hogg
has now received the argument, answered it, and returned it to Shelley
along with his own reply; Shelley has sent the reply on to the beleaguered
Mr. Wedgwood with an additional five sheets of his own.

It was perhaps this dispute with Wedgwood which led to the composi-

1. Line 53.                           2. Line 77.

SC 134 tion of *The Necessity of Atheism*, for this pamphlet was almost certainly written at about the same time.[3] In *The Necessity of Atheism*, Shelley embodied both his own anticlerical arguments and Hogg's atheistical arguments.[4] At the time of the composition of the pamphlet he was still a deist; and the request in its Advertisement for further illumination was seriously intended. Shelley had opposed atheism not only in these letters to Hogg but in *Zastrozzi* and *St. Irvyne*,[5] and did not become an atheist until several months later (a process doubtless assisted by his expulsion).[6]

Hogg, ignoring Shelley's advice of December 20, had sent the manuscript of *Leonora* (line 16) to Stockdale, who, discerning its anti-religious tendencies, wrote to Timothy Shelley that his son was being led astray by Hogg, an accusation which produced vigorous letters of protest from both Hogg and Shelley.[7]

St. Leonard's Forest (line 11), in the vicinity of Horsham, was according to the tale inhabited both by a "famous DRAGON, or serpent," "reputed to be nine feete or rather more, in length" and the "horrible decapitated spectre" of "former squire Paulett."[8] Doubtless these legends made it especially attractive to Shelley.

3. See Cameron, *The Young Shelley*, pp. 330–331. It was probably written between about January 11 and 25.

4. *Ibid.*, pp. 328–331; Frederick L. Jones, "Hogg and *The Necessity of Atheism*," *PMLA*, LII (June 1937), 423–426.

5. *Zastrozzi, Complete Works*, V, 47–48, 52, 100; *St. Irvyne, ibid.*, pp. 176–177, 199. A good deal of the sentiment against atheism in these novels is obscured by their anticlerical horror-mongering. The "atheism" of Zastrozzi or Nempere (Ginotti) is designed to make the flesh creep, not to produce converts.

6. The expulsion took place on March 25. On April 24 Shelley wrote to Hogg that he considered himself among the "bigots in Atheism" (sc 154, line 17). An atheistic point of view, however, did not appear in his works until 1813 and 1814 in *Queen Mab* and *A Refutation of Deism*.

7. Hogg to Stockdale, Jan. 21, 1821, *Stockdale's Budget*, Jan. 10, 1827; Shelley to Stockdale, Jan. 28, 1811.

8. [Howard Dudley], *The History and Antiquities of Horsham* (London, 1836), pp. 45–49.

SC 135 P. B. SHELLEY TO T. J. HOGG, JANUARY 17, 1811

AL unsigned, 1¾ pages. Double sheet, 4^{to} (8.7 x 7 inches).
Wove paper. Watermark: CHARLES WILMOTT| 1809|. Gilt edges.
Seal: (torn).
Postmarks: 1. (mileage stamp): HORSHAM| 41|; 2. (morning duty stamp, London): E| 19 JA 19| 1811|.

*Shelley to Hogg*                                                          *January* 17, 1811

SC 135  PROVENANCE: Thomas Jefferson Hogg; Major R. J. Jefferson Hogg (Sotheby, June 30, 1948, lot 9). *De Ricci 30* (p. 122).

                                        *Field Place      Jan 17 1810*

*My dear Friend,*

    *I shall be with you as soon as possble next week, you really were at Hungerford whether you knew it or not. You tell me nothing about Leonora,*
5   *I hope she gets on in the press  I am anxious for her appearance, Stockdale certainly behaved in a vile manner to you, no other Bookseller w^d have violated the confidence reposed in him. I will talk to him in London where I shall be on Tuesday. Can I do any thing for you there. —— You notice the peculiarity of "my Sister" in my letters.     It certainly arose independent*
10  *of consideration, and I am happy to hear that it is so. —  Your systematic cudgel for Xtianity is excellent, I tried it again with my Father who told me that 30 years ago he had read Locke but this made no impression – the "equus et res" is all that I can boast of; the "pater" is swallowed up in the first article of the Catalogue. —  You tell me nothing of Leonora. I am all*
15  *anxiety about her. I am forced hastily to bid you adieu –*

[Address, page 4]
*T. Jefferson Hogg Esq^r*
*University College*
*Oxford*

line 1. *1810* (sic)

line 3. *possble* (sic)

line 7. *confidence: secrecy* has been written first and *confidence* has been written through it.

line 15. The *u* of *adieu* trails off in a long line and the signature is omitted.

COLLATION (selected passages).
T. J. HOGG, *THE LIFE OF PERCY BYSSHE SHELLEY*, I, 190–191. (Hogg's changes indicated by italics.)

line 4. You tell me nothing about *the tale which you promised me.* I hope *it* gets on in the press, I am anxious for *its* appearance. S—— certainly behaved in a vile manner to *me;*

line 10. Your systematic cudgel for *blockheads* is excellent. I tried it *on* with my father,

line 14. You tell me nothing of *the tale;* I am all anxiety about *it.*

O N JANUARY 16 Shelley wrote briefly in reply to Hogg's commiserations on his loss of Harriet Grove (the truth about which Hogg still did not seem to know) and intimated that part of his "mortification" was due

# The Carl H. Pforzheimer Library

SC 135  to jealousy (i.e., of Helyar). Then on the next day he wrote the above letter (misdated "1810").

Shelley has had another discussion on religion with his father following that recorded on January 11. Having failed to make an impression with his own arguments he uses some of Hogg's, a "systematic cudgel for Xtianity" (line 10), which was perhaps the same as the "argument of the necessity of Xtianity" received on January 11.[1] The "cudgel" perhaps worked its way into *The Necessity of Atheism* although we must remember that the *Necessity* is not directed so much against Christianity as against the concept of God in general. It was probably as a result of Stockdale's disclosures[2] that Timothy became anxious about his son's religious views and had these discussions with him.

During the vacation Hogg went on a walking tour from Oxford to Stonehenge and other places and had evidently written describing his trip. In his biography of Shelley he records passing through Hungerford (line 14).[3]

We may note how in this letter (and others) Hogg's changes in the text tone down both his and Shelley's antireligious views and obscure the name and authorship of *Leonora*.

1. See sc 133 (Jan. 12, 1811), line 56.      2. See sc 134 (Jan. 14, 1811).
3. Hogg, *Shelley*, I, 114.

SC 136  P. B. SHELLEY TO T. J. HOGG, JANUARY ?19–?21, 1811

AL unsigned, 3¾ pages. Double sheet, 4ᵗᵒ (8.7 x 7.1 inches).
Wove paper. Watermark: CHARLES WILMOTT| 1809|. Gilt edges.

PROVENANCE: Thomas Jefferson Hogg; Major R. J. Jefferson Hogg (Sotheby, June 30, 1948, lot 10). *De Ricci 31* (p. 122).

*My dear Friend*

*You are all over the Country. I shall be at Oxford on Friday or Saturday evening, I will write to you from London. My father's prophetic prepossession in your favour is become as high as before it was to your prejudice. Whence*
5  *it arises or from what cause I am inadequate to say. I can merely state the fact; he came from London full of your praises . . – your family, & that of*

**Shelley to Hogg**                                    *January ?19–?21, 1811*

SC 136  *M$^r$ Hogg at Stockton upon Tees. – Your principles are* <u>*now*</u> *as divine as*
*before they were diabolical. I tell you this with extreme satisfaction, & to sum*
*up the whole he has desired me to make his Compt$^s$ to you, to invite you to*
10  *make Field Place y$^r$ head quarters for the Easter Vacation. — I hope you*
*will accept of it. — I fancy he has been talking in Town to a M$^r$ OCallaghan*
*who is acquainted with your family   however that may be I hope you have*
*no other arrangement for Easter which can interfere with granting me the*
*pleasure of introducing you personally here — You have very well drawn*
15  *your line of distinction between instinctive & rational motives of action, the*
<u>*former*</u> *are not in our own power, yet we may doubt if even these are* <u>*purely*</u>
*selfish, as congeniality sympathy unaccountable attractions of intellect w$^c$*
*arise independent frequently of any considerations of y$^r$ own insterest,*
*operating violently in contradiction to it, & bringing on wretchedness which*
                                                                        *which*
20  *your reason plainly foresees, yet although y$^r$ judgement dissapproves of you*
*take no pains to obviate. – All this is not selfish. – And surely the operations*
*of reason of judgement in a man whose judgement is fully convinced of the*
                            *any*
25  *baseness of* ~~*that*~~ *motive* ~~*mu*~~ *can never be consonant with it. —*
        *Adeiu*

                                        *Your affectionate*

line 13. *arrangement:* The second *a* has been
formed by a dash across the top of an *n.* As
both this dash and some of the dots over the
*i's* are in a darker ink Shelley must have checked
the letter over.

line 21. *reason:* The first letter is a *p* changed
to an *r.*
line 21. *dissapproves* (sic)
line 26. *Adeiu* (sic)

ALTHOUGH the above letter is undated, its general period is established
as January 1811 by the fact that it is related to the letters of
January 11–17. And its place within this period can be fairly definitely
determined. Shelley states (line 2) that he intends to be back at Oxford
"on Friday or Saturday evening." As he addressed a letter from Oxford
on Monday, January 28, the contents of which indicate that he had
arrived there but shortly before, "Friday or Saturday evening" must
refer to Friday, January 25, and Saturday, January 26,[1] so that he must

1. See also sc 133 (Jan. 12, 1811), line 75.

SC 136   have intended the above letter to be delivered in Oxford later than Saturday, January 19 (otherwise his "Friday or Saturday" would be ambiguous).

Shelley informs Hogg (line 3) that he will write to him from London (clearly within a few days). In the letter of Thursday, January 17 (sc 135), he states that he will be in London "on Tuesday." This must be Tuesday, January 22. If Shelley stuck to this plan, the above letter must be earlier than January 22 because it was not written in London but (to judge from the contents) at Field Place.

These indications of initial and terminal dates are supported by the fact that of the letters between January 11 and 17, the above letter is most closely related to that of January 17. It is on the same paper, and no other letter in the vacation series in our library is on this paper. (The only other letter in our library on this paper is Shelley to Hogg, May 21, 1811, sc 161). Both the above letter and that of January 17 mention Hogg's vacation tour and Shelley's approaching return to Oxford.

The above letter is not only undated, it is also unaddressed. But (as the Provenance shows) Hogg received it. Hence, it must have either had a separate address sheet or been placed inside another letter. If it was enclosed in another letter this would most likely have been that of January 17. But an examination of the fold lines of both letters and the blottings on the January 17 letter[2] show that it was not so enclosed, so that it was probably folded within a separate address sheet which Hogg did not preserve.

Hogg in printing the letter removed the name "M^r. OCallaghan" and substituted for it "some of the northern Members of Parliament" (his only major change). The only Member of Parliament named O'Callaghan in the 1807–1812 Parliament was James O'Callaghan.[3] He represented Tregony in Cornwall but may have come from the north.[4]

2. Page 2 of the January 17 letter (sc 135) has blotted on page 3. Hence there was no letter enclosed between these pages. The folding lines of the above letter do not correspond to those of sc 135, and show that when folded it was too large to fit within sc 135.

3. Robert Beatson, *A Chronological Register of Both Houses of the British Parliament, 1708–1807* (London, 1807), III, 394.

4. In the days of "rotten boroughs" and the buying of parliamentary seats, a man's seat was not necessarily his place of residence.

**Godwin to Druce**                                    *January 26, 1811*

SC 136     It has not previously been noted that Shelley must have been in London from Tuesday, January 22, until either Friday or Saturday, January 25 or 26. "During the Christmas vacation of that year [1810], and in January 1811," wrote Charles Grove in 1857, "I spent part of it with Bysshe at Field Place, and when we returned to London, his sister Mary sent a letter of introduction with a present to her schoolfellow, Miss Westbrook, which Bysshe and I were to take to her. I recollect we did so, calling at Mr. Westbrook's house."[5] Shelley, as we have seen, was probably in London from December 30 to January 1, and it may have been then that Charles Grove accompanied him back to Field Place. But it cannot have been then that he called on Harriet Westbrook, for Grove states that the visit took place "when we returned to London." As Shelley was not in London again until January 22, it must have been during this latter period (January 22–25) that Shelley made his first visit to his future wife. On January 11, he had requested Stockdale to send her a copy of *St. Irvyne*, perhaps in anticipation of this visit.

5. Hogg, *Shelley*, II, 155.


SC 137   WILLIAM GODWIN TO J. DRUCE, JANUARY 26, 1811

AUTOGRAPH PROMISSORY NOTE signed *W Godwin*, 1 page. Single sheet (3.4 x 8 inches).
Laid paper. Embossed revenue stamp: [device]| 1 SHILLING VI PENCE|.
Endorsement.

*£ 10.10.4*                                    *No. 41, Skinner Street,*
                                               *Jan. 26, 1811*
        *Two months after date I promise to pay to Mr James Druce or order*
           *ten pounds 10/4: value recd as per bill to Saturday last*
5                                              *W Godwin*

[Endorsement, verso]
    *Recd Josh Druce*
        *for*
    *James Druce*

———————————

# The Carl H. Pforzheimer Library

*Godwin to Warner*                                            *January 30, 1811*

SC 137    PIGOT's *Metropolitan Directory* for 1828–1829 yields a James Druce, butcher, 74 Fleet Market. That this was the firm of the James Druce of the above promissory note is apparent from the fact that Fleet Market ("removed about 1829–1830, for the formation of Farrington Street")[1] was within a few blocks of Godwin's house on Skinner Street.[2]

SEE ALSO SC 61.

1. Harben, *Dictionary of London*. Plan of London, D1, Front Endpapers.
2. In the same vicinity we also find a Joseph Druce, butcher, 9 Bell Yard, Temple Bar.

SC 138    WILLIAM GODWIN TO J. WARNER, JANUARY 30, 1811

AUTOGRAPH PROMISSORY NOTE signed *W Godwin*, 1 page. Single sheet (3.4 x 8 inches).
Laid paper. Watermark: [posthorn in crowned shield, upper part]|. Embossed revenue stamp: [device]| 1 SHILLᴳ VI PENCE|.
Endorsements.

*May 3rd*

                                               *No. 41, Skinner Street,*
*£21 . . 9 . . 6*                               *Jan. 30, 1811*

        *Three months after date I promise to pay to Mr Jos. Warner or*
5         *order twenty-one pounds 9/6: value recd to Christmas last*
                                             *W Godwin*

                                                 *2304*

[Endorsements, verso]
*Josʰ Warner*
*Wᵐ Williams*
10   *Recd for*
     *Thoˢ Morgan & Co*
      *Jnᵒᵒ Price*

A PREVIOUS note from Godwin to the grocery firm of Jacob and Joseph Warner and Co. (SC 68, August 5, 1805) was also passed on to William Williams, baker, of Somers Town. The London *Post Office Directory* for 1813 gives Thomas Morgan and Co., merchants, 7 Oat Lane, Cheapside.

SEE ALSO SC 61.

[ 718 ]

SC 139   P. B. SHELLEY TO TIMOTHY SHELLEY, FEBRUARY 6, 1811

AL signed *P B Shelley.*, 10 pages. 3 double sheets, 4<sup>to</sup> (8.8 x 7.2 inches).
All wove paper. Watermark, on all sheets: L TOVIL| 1808|. Octagonal embossed
stamp, on all sheets: BATH| [leaves]|.
Seal: wax, red: [?crest]|.
Postmarks: 1. (dated mileage stamp): OXFORD| 8 FE 8| 1811| 57|; 2. (morning duty
franking stamp, London): FREE| 9 FE 9| 1811|.
Forwarding address.

PROVENANCE: Sir Timothy Shelley; William Whitton; Charles Withall; John A.
Spoor; W. T. H. Howe; Audrey Wedderburn Auslander. *De Ricci 34* (p. 248).

*Unv: Coll: Ox. Feb. 6. 1810*

My dear Father,

Your very excellent exposition on the subject of Religion pleases me
very much. I have seldom seen ideas of Orthodoxy so clearly defined. – You
5   have proved to my complete satisfaction, that those who do not think at all,
a species which contains by far the major part of even civilized society ought
to be restrained by the bonds of prejudicative religion, by which I mean that
it is best that they should follow the religion of their fathers whatsoever it may
be. – not having sufficient pinciple to discharge their duties without leaning
10   on some support; a slight support being better than none at all . . So much
for the beings who ought to take things upon trust; . . But after a rational
being, or rather a being posessing capabilities for superadded rationability,
has, proceeding to perfectibility passed that point, before which he could not
~~not~~ or cared not to reason, after which he both did reason, & took interest in
15   the inferences which he drew from that reason . . Do you then deny him to
use that reason in the very point which is most momentous to his present, to
his future happiness, in the very point which as being of greater importance,
demands a superior energization of that most distinguishing faculty of
Man . . You cannot deny him that which is, ~~the~~ or ought to be the essence
20   of his being, you cannot deny it him without taking away that essentia, and
leaving him not an "animal rationale" but "irratinale" retaining no
distinguishing characteristic of "Man" but "animal bipes, implume
risibile" – I then have passed that point, because I do reason on the
subject, I do take interest in that reasoning, & from that reasoning I have
25   adduced to my own, I think I cd. to your private satisfaction, that the

[ 719 ]

SC 139   *testimony of the twelve Apostles is insufficent to establish the truth of their doctrine, not to mention how much <u>weaker</u> the evidence must become, when filtered thro' so many gradations of history, so many ages.*

*Supposing twelve men, were to make an affidavit before you that they had*
30   *seen in Africa, a vast snake three miles long. suppose they swore that this snake eat nothing but Elephants, & that you knew from all the laws of nature, that enough Elephants c<sup>d</sup> not exist to sustain the snake . . w<sup>d</sup> you believe them? The case is the same, . . it is clearly therefore proved that we cannot if we consider it believe facts inconsistent with the general laws of Nature,*
35   *that there is no evidence sufficent, or rather that <u>evidence</u> is insufficient to prove such facts. I c<sup>d</sup> give you a methodical proof if you desire it, or think this to be inconclusive . . As to Locke Newton &<sup>c</sup> being Xtians. I will relate an anecdote of the latter. At Cambridge he kept Chickens and making a Box for them, he formed a large hole for the Hen to gou̶ out of, smaller ones*
40   *for the chicken . . What an inconsistency for a Genius who was searching into the mechanism of the Universe . . Lockes Xtianity cannot <u>now</u> appear so surprising, particularly if we mention . . Voltaire, Lord Kames, M<sup>r</sup> Hume, Rousseau, D<sup>r</sup> Adam Smith, D<sup>r</sup> Franklin, et <u>mille</u> alios, all of whom were Deists, the life of all of whom was characterised by the strictest morality;*
45   *all of whom whilst they lived were the subjects of panygeric, were the directors of literature & morality. — <u>Truth</u> whatever it may be has never been known to be prejudical to the best interests of mankind, nor was there ever a period of greater tranquillity in which the name of Religion was not even mentioned, Gibbon's History of the decline & fall of the Roman empire, proves this truth*
50   *satisfactorily — Thus far, my dear Father have I thought it necessary to explain to you my sentiments to explain to you upon what they are founded, as far as the imperfect medium of a letter will allow. – At some leisure moment may I request to hear your objections (, if any yet remain) to my private sentiments —— "Religion fetters a reasoning mind with the very bonds*
55   *which restrain the unthinking one from mischief" this is my great objection to it. — The coming of Xt was called ευαγγελλιον, or good tidings, it is hard to believe how those tidings <u>could</u> be <u>good</u> which are to condemn more than half of the world to the Devil. for as S<sup>t</sup> Athanasius says, "He who does*

**Shelley to Shelley**                                           **February 6, 1811**

SC 139  *not believe sh^d go into etenal fire"* — *As if belief were voluntary, or an action*
60  *not a passion (as it is) of the mind. — I will now conclude this letter, as*
*knowing your dislike to long scrawls, I fear I must have tired you. Believe me,*
*whatever may be my sentiments yr^s most dutiful*

*affect . . P B Shelley.*

[Address, page 12]
*T. Shelley Esq^r M.P.*
65  *Miller's Hotel*
*Wes^tr Bridge*
*London*

[Forwarding address]
*Horsham*
*Sussex*

Shelley's handwriting to his father is, compared to his hasty scrawls to Hogg, neat and clear. So, too, with the signature.

line 9. *pinciple* (sic)

line 12. *posessing* (sic)

line 18. *demands:* Shelley first wrote *demanded*, then wrote an *s* through the *e* and canceled the final *d*.

line 20. *essentia:* Shelley apparently first wrote *essensia* and then put a *t* through the *s*.

line 21. *"irratinale"* (sic)

line 25. *I cd.* (sic)

line 26. *insufficent* (sic)

line 34. *consider:* Under *der* is a short line which trails off. Shelley perhaps intended to underline the word.

line 35. *sufficent* (sic)

line 36. *methodical proof:* There is a faint line under *al* to *pr* which may be intended as underlining.

line 39. *gou:* probable reading, possibly *goou*

with *ou* compressed. Shelley perhaps started to run *go* into *out*. In his letters to Hogg in this period he frequently runs words together.

line 40. *chicken:* The *n* comes up in a final curl which may represent the beginning of an *s*.

line 44. *was: as* is written through *ere*.

line 45. *panygeric* (sic)

line 47. *prejudical* (sic)

line 51. *upon* is written through a partially erased *their.*

line 51. *are:* Through the *e* is written the initial stroke for a *t* or *f*. Perhaps Shelley began to run *are* into *founded*. See *gou,* line 39, above.

line 53. *objections (,if* (sic): The comma comes after the parenthesis, but it would seem that Shelley first wrote the comma and then, as a second thought, the parenthesis, and inadvertently placed it slightly in front of the comma.

line 56. ευαργελλιον (sic): ευαγγελιον

line 59. *etenal* (sic)

THE above letter[1] reflects the alarums and excursions of the Christmas vacation which led to *The Necessity of Atheism.*
Stockdale, as we have seen, sniffed out the heresies in Hogg's

1. Shelley misdates the letter 1810 for 1811.

# The Carl H. Pforzheimer Library

SC 139   *Leonora,* made inquiries about him, and gave "delicate hints" to Timothy of the dangers besetting his son. But Stockdale then found out — probably from Shelley himself in London on his way to Oxford — the much more serious information that a "Metaphysical Essay in support of Atheism" had been written and was about to be "promulgate[d] throughout the university."[2] He wrote in haste to Timothy. On January 30 (1811) Timothy replied: "I am so surprised on the receipt of your letter this morning that I cannot comprehend the meaning of the language you use. I shall be in London next week, and will then call on you."[3]

Thus when Timothy wrote the letter to which the above is an answer, he had, almost certainly, heard that something was afoot. *The Necessity of Atheism* had, in fact, been written and was about to appear.[4] On the very day on which the above letter was passing through London on its way to Horsham the following advertisement appeared in *The Oxford University and City Herald:*

*Speedily will be published,*
To be had of the Booksellers of London and Oxford,
THE
## NECESSITY OF ATHEISM.
"Quod clara et perspicua demonstratione caveat pro vero habere, mens omnino nequit humanae." — Bacon de Augment. Scient.[5]

Shelley, therefore, when he penned the above letter, knew that *The Necessity of Atheism* was about to be published.

Timothy's letter is apparently no longer in existence. Possibly it discussed the impending promulgation of the "Metaphysical Essay in support of Atheism," but, if it did, Shelley's reply gives no hint of it. One gets the impression that it was mainly an exposition of Christian theology. Perhaps Timothy did not seriously believe Stockdale's story and either did not mention the pamphlet or mentioned it only in passing. At any rate Shelley ignored it and concentrated solely on the theological arguments.

But if the pamphlet itself was ignored, its contents were not. Timothy would have been surprised had he known that the arguments

2. *Stockdale's Budget,* Jan. 3, 1827, p. 26.

3. *Ibid.,* Jan. 10, 1827, p. 34. See also the issue of January 17, 1827, p. 42.

4. See Cameron, *The Young Shelley,* pp. 330–331.       5. MacCarthy, *Shelley,* p. 108.

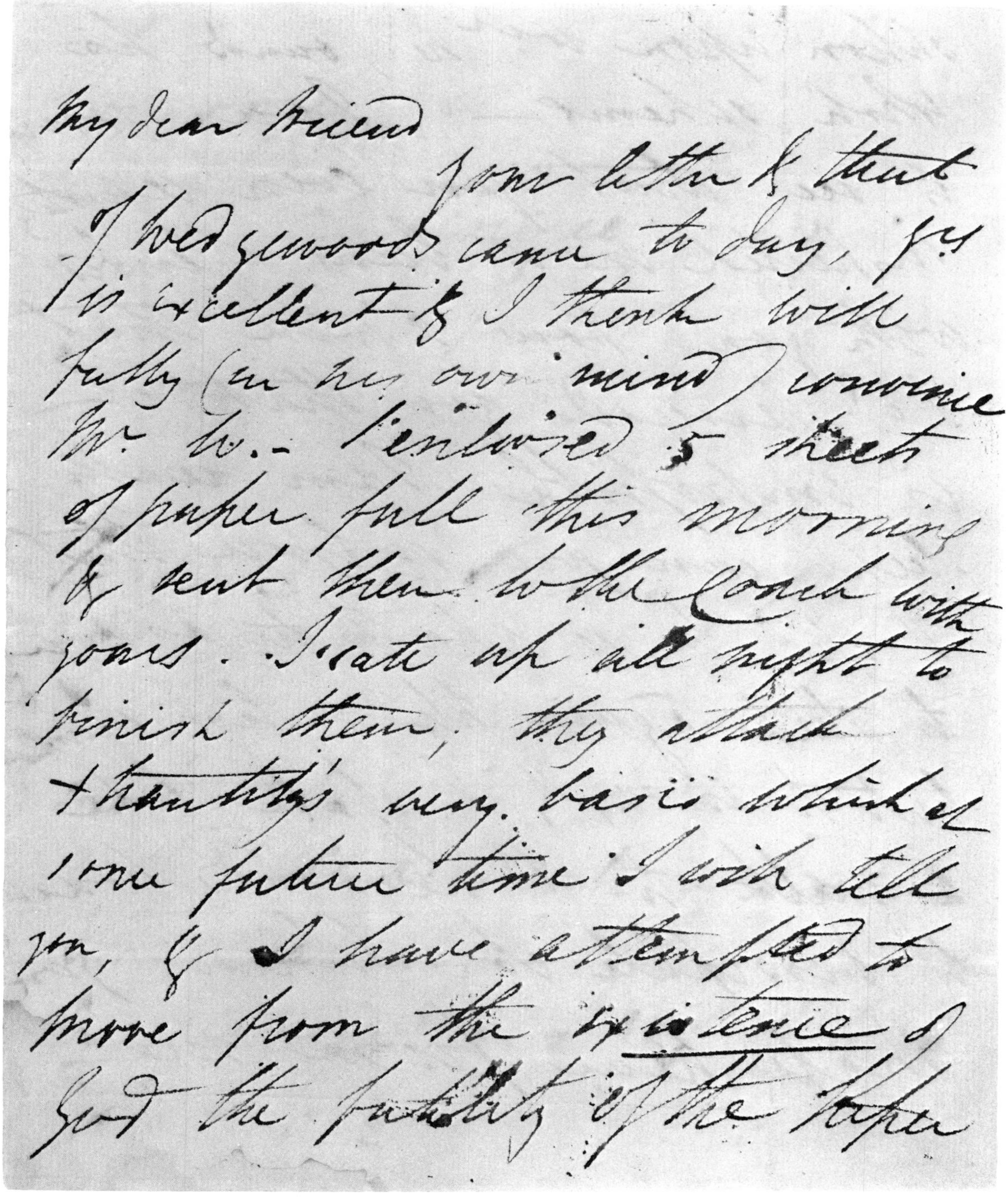

PLATE XXIX

My dear friend
                    Your letter & that
of Wedgewood came to day, yrs
is excellent & I think will
fully (in his own mind) convince
Mr W. — I enclosed 5 sheets
of paper full this morning
& sent them to the Coach with
yours. I sate up all night to
finish them, they attack
+ xxxxxx very basis which at
some future time I wish tell
you, & I have attempted to
prove from the existence of
God the futility of the hopes

*P. B. Shelley to T. J. Hogg, January 14, 1811 (SC 134), page 1*

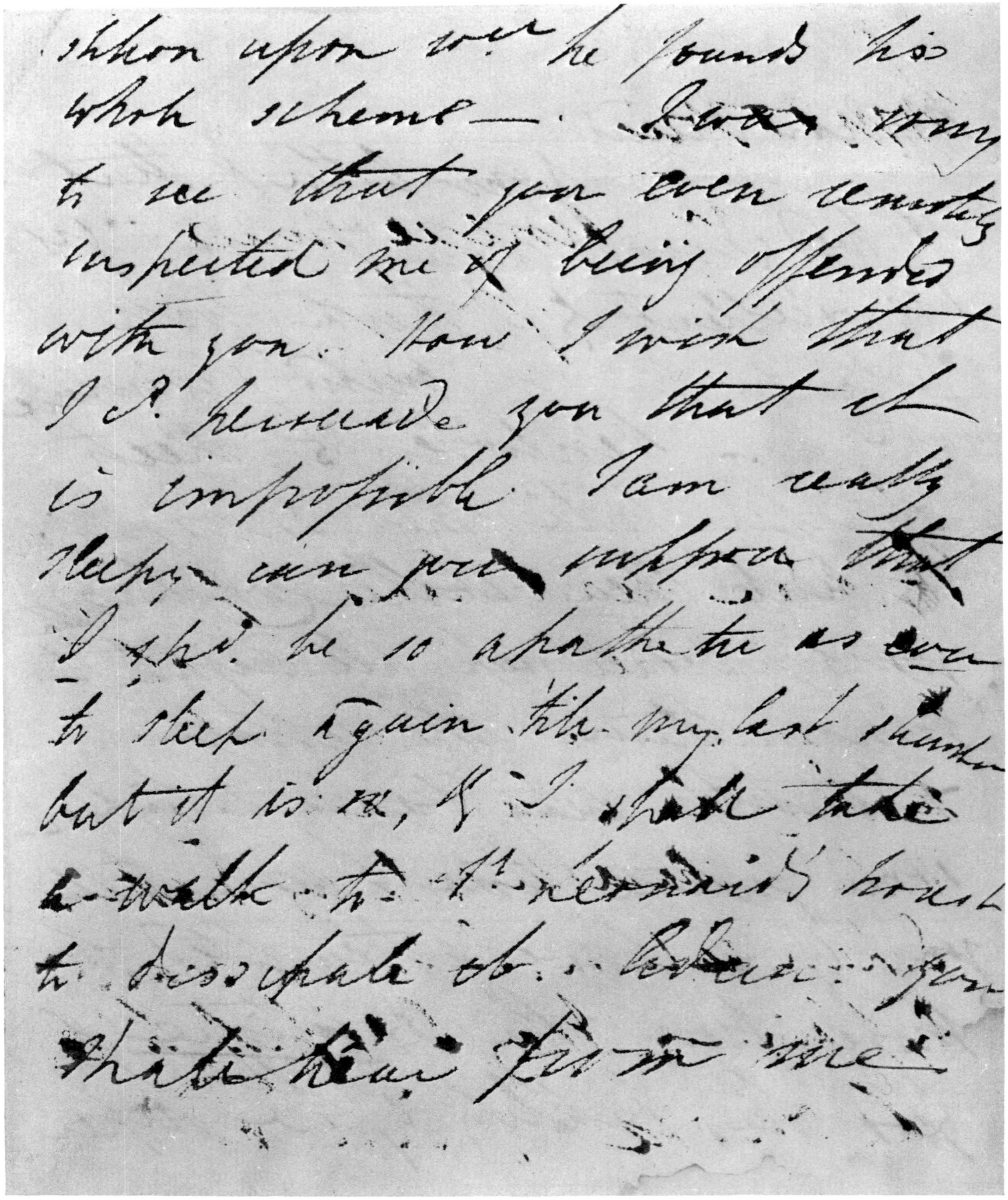

PLATE XXX

*P. B. Shelley to T. J. Hogg, January 14, 1811 (SC 134), page 2*

PLATE XXXI

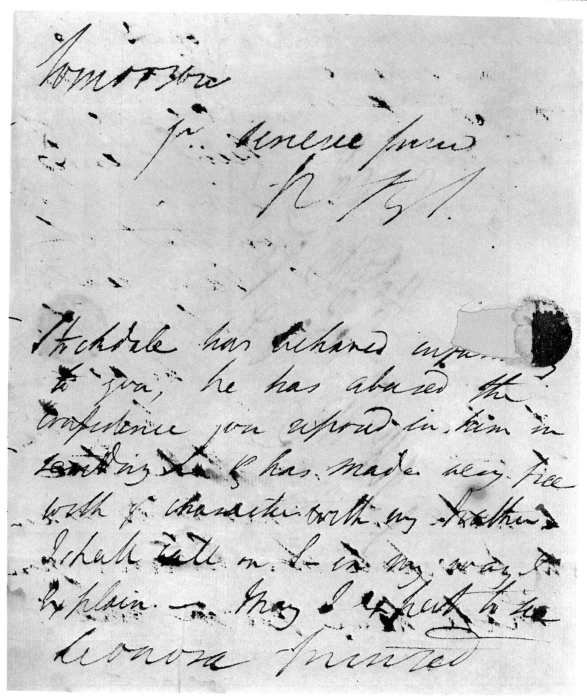

*P. B. Shelley to T. J. Hogg, January 14, 1811 (SC 134), page 3*

PLATE XXXII

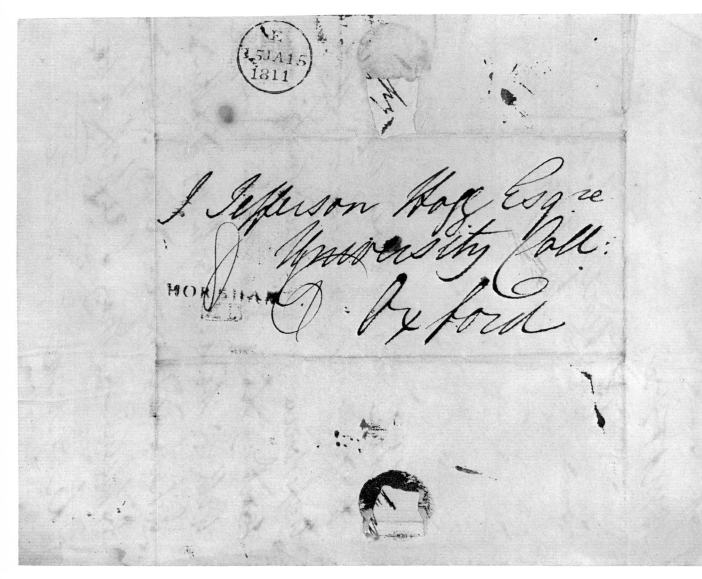

*P. B. Shelley to T. J. Hogg, January 14, 1811 (SC 134), address page*

SC 139    his son was using in his letter were those he had already used in *The Necessity of Atheism*. The argument on miracles (line 23), for instance, appears in the *Necessity*:

> The testimony that the Deity convinces the senses of men of his existence can only be admitted by us, if our mind considers it less probable that these men should have been deceived than that the Deity should have appeared to them . . . our reason can never admit the testimony of men, who not only declare that they were eye-witnesses of miracles but that the Deity was irrational, for he commanded that he should be believed, he proposed the highest rewards for faith, eternal punishments for disbelief.

The source for both passages was David Hume's *Essay on Miracles*. The letter, in fact, echoes Hume's language:

> Our evidence, then, for the truth of the *Christian* religion, is less than the evidence for the truth of our senses; because even in the first authors of our religion, it was no greater; and it is evident it must diminish in passing from them to their disciples; nor can anyone be so certain of the truth of their testimony, as of the immediate object of his senses.[6]

One other argument in the letter also comes from the *Necessity*, namely (line 59): "As if belief were voluntary, or an action not a passion (as it is) of the mind." In the *Necessity* this appears as: "we can only command voluntary actions, belief is not an act of volition, the mind is even passive . . . ." Belief or lack of belief, Shelley is arguing, cannot in itself be a sin (and hence punishable) because belief is arrived at not by the will but by the reason. It is an intellectual, not a moral, question.

All of these arguments, as in the previous correspondence with Hogg, are deistic rather than atheistic. Shelley does not advance the central atheistic argument of the *Necessity* — presumably Hogg's — that "it is easier to suppose that the Universe has existed from all eternity, than to conceive a being capable of creating it," an argument also derived from Hume.

In addition to the Humean arguments on miracles and faith Shelley makes free use of the language of the Aristotelian tradition then still current at Oxford. Timothy would be familiar with this language — e.g. (line 21), "animal rationale" and (line 12), "a being posessing *capabilities for superadded rationability*" — and Shelley perhaps felt that it would

6. From the opening paragraph of Hume's *Essay on Miracles*.

SC 139   tend to quiet his fears. (In the next clause Shelley slides into Godwinian phraseology with "proceeding to perfectibility," but Timothy would not be expected to recognize this.) As Shelley states in his next letter to Timothy (sc 140), he can refute the "learned Doctors" by "the very rules of reasoning which their *own systems* of logic teach me." The definition of man as "an unfeathered biped" (line 22) derives ultimately from Plato's *Politicus.*

The discrepancy between Shelley's date of February 6 and the Oxford postmark date of February 8 was perhaps due to a failure to post the letter immediately. That February 6 was the date on which the letter was completed is shown by the fact that the date heading has blotted at the bottom of page 1 in folding. Hence, the date heading was (as seems to have been customary with Shelley at this time) written after the body of the letter; and the letter was then folded immediately.

The above letter and the following letter are, so far as is known, the only extant letters by Shelley to his father from Oxford. The ironical tone of the opening of the above letter gives one the impression that Shelley was sharing it with Hogg. The irony he hoped would pass over Timothy's head.

SC 140   P. B. SHELLEY TO TIMOTHY SHELLEY, FEBRUARY 17, 1811

AL signed *Percy B Shelley.*, 2¾ pages. Double sheet, 4<sup>to</sup> (9.1 x 7.2 inches).
Wove paper. Watermark: [Prince of Wales feathers]| MJL| 1808|.
Seal: wafer, red.
Postmarks: 1. (dated mileage stamp): o[XF]OR[D]| 17FE17| 1811| 57|; 2. (morning duty franking stamp, London): FREE| 18 FE 18| 1811|.

PROVENANCE: Sir Timothy Shelley; William Whitton; Charles Withall (Sotheby, June 22, 1918, lot 713). *De Ricci 37* (p. 248).

*My dear Father /*

*    I suppose that by this time you are at Horsham, I dress in black for the late M<sup>rs</sup> Sidney, her death was certainly a necessary consequence of her complaint. M<sup>r</sup> Rolleston's logic lectures yet continue, as to divinity it is a*
5   *study which I have* <u>*very*</u> *minutely investigated, in order to detect to my own satisfaction "the impudent & inconsistent falsehoods of priestcraft, – I am*

SC 140    *in consequence perfectly prepared to meet any examination on the subject;*
*It is needless to observe that in the Schools Colleges &c which are all on the*
*principle of Inquisisstorial Orthodoxy with respect to matters of belief I shall*
10    *perfectly coincide with the opinions of the learned doctors, although by the*
*very rules of reasoning which their <u>own systems</u> of logic teach me I c<sup>d</sup> refute*
*their errors. – I shall not therefore publickly come under the act "De heretico*
*comburendo" –*

     *I have not yet finished Parthenon, I hope I shall make it a Poem, such*
15    *as you w<sup>d</sup> advise me to subject to M<sup>r</sup> Dallaway's critisism. – St. Irvyne sells*
*fast at Oxford.*

     *I am My dear Father*

                         *your very dutiful affect< >*
                         <u>*Percy B Shelley.*</u>

20    *Oxford – Feb. 17. 1811.*

     [Address, page 4]
     *T. Shelley Esq<sup>r</sup>*
     *Field Place*
     *Horsham*
     <u>*MP*</u>   *Sussex*

line 3. *Sidney:* The *d* is written through the second loop of an *n*; the first loop has been converted into an *i* by having a dot placed above it.

line 9. *Inquisisstorial* (sic)
line 12. *publickly:* The *k* is written through an *l* or a *t*.
line 15. *critisism* (sic)

O N FEBRUARY 13 Shelley sent a copy of *The Necessity of Atheism* to Graham to be used for an advertisement in *The Globe.* On February 17 he wrote the above letter to Timothy, perhaps having received a reply to his letter of February 6 (sc 139).

From the January 11 letter to Hogg (sc 132) we gather that Timothy was trying to keep an open mind (by admitting the "impossibility . . . of any preternatural interferences") but was shocked by his son's denial of the basis of the Christian religion. The discussion recorded in the January 17 letter (sc 135) was apparently on a more abstract ground (reminding Timothy of his long-forgotten reading in Locke). From the

SC 140　February 6 letter one would gather that Timothy had argued that Locke and Newton were Christians, and restated his belief in the importance of faith. In the above letter Shelley, perhaps sensing his father's alarm, skirts these and other thorny questions and tries to reassure him. Timothy was, like many Whigs, opposed to Catholicism ("priestcraft") and Shelley, in this letter, tries to represent his own antireligious sentiments as going little further than this. He assures his father that he will not come into public conflict with the authorities on these subjects, that he is attending lectures, that he is busy with a poem on an innocuous subject — the *Parthenon*, which Timothy was encouraging him to submit for the Newdigate prize —[1] that he is dutifully in mourning for one of the family.[2]

Matthew Rolleston (line 4) was one of the more brilliant younger dons at University College. In 1805, the year of his matriculation, he published the *The Anti-Corsican, a poem in three cantos*, and he had the distinction of winning the Newdigate twice in succession, in 1807 and 1808.[3]

1. The subject for the Sir Roger Newdigate prize for English verse at Oxford in 1811 was "ancient ruins." The prize was won by Richard Burdon of Oriel. See SC 171 (July ?21, 1811). According to Hogg (*Shelley*, I, 189), it was Timothy who proposed that Shelley enter for the Newdigate and "induced a distinguished scholar . . . the Rev. Edward Dallaway, Vicar of Leatherhead, secretary to the Earl Marshal, and the historian of the county of Sussex" to assist him.

2. Mrs. Sidney was Henrietta Frances Shelley-Sidney, who had died on February 5, 1811, wife of John Shelley-Sidney, the son of Bysshe Shelley by his second wife, Elizabeth Jane Sidney. As Timothy was Bysshe's son by his first wife, Mary Catherine Mitchell, John Shelley-Sidney was Timothy's half brother.

3. See *Alumni Oxonienses* and *Oxford University Historical Register*, 1888, p. 398. His Newdigate poem of 1807, *Moses . . . conducting the Children of Israel from Egypt . . .* , went through at least four editions, his Newdigate poem of 1808, *Mahomet*, was, according to the British Museum catalogue, reprinted in 1810.

SC 141　P. B. SHELLEY, RECEIPT TO JOHN SLATTER, MARCH 12, 1811

AUTOGRAPH RECEIPT signed *Percy B: Shelley*, 1 page. Single sheet (2.9 x 10 inches). Laid paper.

PROVENANCE: Sir Timothy Shelley; William Whitton; Charles Withall. *De Ricci*, p. 254.

*Received of M^r Slatter, on March 12. 1811 the sum of 10 £.*

*Percy B: Shelley*

# Shelley and his Circle : Manuscripts

SC 142   P. B. SHELLEY, RECEIPT TO JOHN SLATTER, MARCH 23, 1811

AUTOGRAPH RECEIPT signed *Percy B: Shelley*, 1 page. Single sheet (3 x 9.5 inches). Laid paper. Watermark: [Britannia in crowned oval, upper part]|.

PROVENANCE: Sir Timothy Shelley; William Whitton; Charles Withall.

*Received of M*ʳ *Slatter on March 23. 1811 the sum of 10 £.*

*Percy B: Shelley*

WHEN Timothy Shelley accompanied his son to Oxford, he stayed for several days at the lodgings where he himself had lived when an undergraduate of University College. The house was occupied by John Slatter, "Plumber and Glazier," son of his former landlord. John Slatter's brother, Henry Slatter, Timothy discovered, had entered into partnership with Joseph Munday, Oxford bookseller and printer. Whereupon Timothy proudly took his "young man" to see Henry Slatter and asked the bookseller to encourage his "printing freaks." [1] As a consequence *Posthumous Fragments of Margaret Nicholson* was published by Munday in November (1810). Shelley, during the Christmas vacation correspondence with Hogg, suggested Munday as a publisher for *Leonora*.

Shelley was also interested in another work which he thought the firm might publish, "a large historical and poetical work relative to Sweden" by one John Brown.[2] He was, in fact, so persuasive that Munday and Slatter advanced him £200 and went security for an additional £400.[3] Shelley, Henry Slatter informs us, placed "a part of the manuscript in the printer's hands, with promise of sending the remainder," "new type was laid down and paper bought" and printing was actually begun.[4] But it was interrupted by Shelley's expulsion. The debt remained unpaid.

1. Henry Slatter to Robert Montgomery, Dec. 18, 1833, quoted in Robert Montgomery, *Oxford or Alma Mater* (London, 1833, and succeeding editions). Slatter and Munday seem to have been in partnership since at least January 1807, for in that month they issued the first number of the *Oxford Review*. (Charles H. Timperley, *Encyclopedia of Literary and Typographical Anecdote*, London, 1842, p. 910 fn.)

2. Slatter to Montgomery.

3. Henry Slatter to Sir Timothy Shelley, Aug. 13, 1831, quoted in Ingpen, *Shelley in England*, Appendix I, pp. 630–631.

4. Slatter to Montgomery. See also Ingpen, *Shelley in England*, p. 147.

# The Carl H. Pforzheimer Library

SC 142      At the time of the expulsion, Slatter further relates, Shelley "went to the house where his father had lodged when he brought him to Oxford, and obtained the loan of twenty pounds to pay his traveling expenses to London." This £20 was put up by his brother, John Slatter. On coming to London some time after the expulsion Slatter called at Shelley's lodgings but he was not in. Shelley then (April 16, 1811) sent him the following note: "Directly I get my affairs a little settled, I will send you the £20 you were so kind as to lend me. – I have not yet heard from Munday, suppose I shall soon. Directly the trunks come I will send Mr. B's writings."

On January 9, 1823, following Shelley's death, John Slatter wrote to Timothy Shelley requesting him to "settle my account against your son," a request that Timothy refused, noting that Shelley had had "an ample allowance" and that he had himself asked Slatter to advise Shelley against "any irregularities" when he had stayed with him.[5]

The mention by Henry Slatter of the £20 that Shelley got from his brother, the admission of a £20 debt by Shelley to John Slatter, and the fact that the above checks to "M$^r$ Slatter" total £20 indicate that these checks represent the £20 that Shelley borrowed from John Slatter. But if so, Henry Slatter's contention that Shelley borrowed the money following his expulsion must be wrong, for the expulsion took place on March 25 and these checks are dated respectively March 12 and March 23. Henry Slatter, we must remember, was writing nearly twenty-three years later.

For what purpose, then, did Shelley borrow the £20? The most likely explanation is that it was connected with his dealings with John Brown and his "political work relative to Sweden."

Brown seems to have been a rather mysterious character. Henry Slatter did not know much about him. "Your Son while at College," he informed Sir Timothy, "became acquainted with a person of the name of Brown but who was living at Oxford under the assumed name of Bird."[6] Dowden, making enquiries at Oxford, obtained further information. "Mr. Browne, better known at Oxford under his assumed name of 'Bird,' had been an officer in the Royal Navy." There he had suffered

---

5. Ingpen, *Shelley in England*, p. 629.          6. *Ibid.*, p. 631.

SC 142    "heavy oppression." Shelley had been interested in "Browne" or "Bird" since the spring of 1810 and in addition to the £600 for the book on Sweden had lent him £150.[7] If we put all this information together there can be no doubt but that the mysterious "Browne" or "Bird," who flits through the biographies, is the person who is listed in Allibone and the British Museum catalogue as "John Brown of Great Yarmouth," author of treatises on the British Navy — one of them dealing in part with "The Prosecution for Libel instituted against the Author by Admiral Montague" — and of *The Northern Courts; containing Original Memoirs of the Sovereigns of Sweden and Denmark, since 1776* (2 vols., London, 1818).[8] In the Preface to this latter work Brown informs us that it "was originally intended to be a miscellany" with the sketches of the reigns of the sovereigns relegated to an appendix and that "eleven or twelve sheets were printed ere that plan was abandoned." This would correspond with Slatter's statement that "the printing of the work, however, was not far proceeded with." And, as we can gather from Shelley's note in April to John Slatter, he was having the manuscript shipped to him from Oxford in his trunk. If, therefore, Shelley was interested enough in Brown to have raised £600 for publishing his book, to have lent him an additional £150, and to have his manuscript in his possession, it may be that the two loans of £10 each from John Slatter also went to Brown. As the manuscript was in the press when Shelley left Oxford, he must have been having dealings with Brown during the period of March 12–23 covered by the above notes, and we do not know of any other special financial matter beyond the scope of his "ample" allowance that he was engaged in at this time.

Both the above receipts appear to be on the same make of paper; the chain lines correspond. Slatter sent them to Timothy Shelley in 1823.

---

7. Dowden, *Shelley*, I, 108. Dowden also notes (I, 110 fn.) that "Bird" and Shelley paid a guinea apiece to the defense fund for Peter Finnerty, the Irish radical journalist, as listed in *The Oxford University and City Herald*, March 2, 1811.

8. In 1806 Brown published *The Mysteries of Neutralization; or, the British Navy vindicated from the charges of injustice and oppression towards neutral flags;* in 1807 he published another naval tract entitled *Veluti in Speculum* which had to do with his prosecution for alleged misconduct when agent for a ship called *The Silenus*. Outside of these publications little seems to be known of him. *The Northern Courts* was published by Archibald Constable in Edinburgh and Rest Fenner, Paternoster Row, in London.

SC 142 Timothy turned them over to Whitton,[9] and they were sold with the Whitton papers in 1918.[10]

9. On January 15, 1823, Whitton wrote to Henry Slatter: "Sir Tim Shelley declines making any payment to you on account of it and any further application to him or me on the subject will be considered an intrusion." (Ingpen, *Shelley in England*, Appendix 1, p. 630.)

10. See "The Provenance of Shelley and his Circle Manuscripts," below, p. 902. sc 142 is pasted in a copy of a facsimile edition (London, *ca.* 1870) of Shelley's *Posthumous Fragments of Margaret Nicholson*, which bears the bookplates of Henry Francis Redhead Yorke, Harry B. Smith, and Willis Vicary.

SC 143 TIMOTHY SHELLEY TO T. J. HOGG, MARCH 27, 1811

AL signed *T:Shelley.*, 1 page. Double sheet, 4^to (8.9 x 7.2 inches).
Laid paper. Watermark (Wilmott cipher): [posthorn in crowned shield]| *CW*|.
Seal: wafer, red.
Frank, by Timothy Shelley.
Postmarks: 1. (mileage stamp): HORSHAM| 41|; 2. (morning duty franking stamp, London): FREE| 28 MA 28| 1811|; 3. (dated mileage stamp): OX[F]O[R]D| 29MA[29]| 1811| 57|; 4. (morning duty franking stamp, London): FREE| 30 [MA 30]| 1811|. Forwarding address.

PROVENANCE: Thomas Jefferson Hogg; Major R. J. Jefferson Hogg (Sotheby, June 30, 1948, lot 66).

*Field Place*
*27^th March 1811*

*Sir*
*The invitation my Son wrote me word that you would accept to spend the*
5 *Easter Vacation at Field Place, I am sorry to say the late occurrence at Univ: Coll. must of Necessity preclude me that pleasure, as I shall have to bear up against the affliction that such a business has occasion'd.*
*I am y^r very Hbl: Serv^t.*
*T:Shelley.*

[Frank, with address, page 4]
10 *Horsham, March Twenty Seven*
*1811*
*T. J. Hogg Esqr.*
*Univ. Coll.*
*Oxford* ·
15 *T:Shelley*

[ 730 ]

# Shelley and his Circle : Manuscripts

*Shelley to Hogg*                                    *March 27, 1811*

SC 143    [Forwarding address]
*No29*
*M<sup>r</sup> Grahms Vine Street*
*Piccadily*
*London*

$S$HELLEY and Hogg were expelled from Oxford on March 25. As mail normally took two days to go from Oxford to Horsham, the above letter (March 27) shows that Timothy must have been informed immediately by the authorities of University College of the expulsion. He had, then, been so informed, before he received a letter from his son, dated March 29, giving an account of the "late violent tyrannical proceedings of Oxford."

Timothy's letter, as we can tell from the postmarks, passed through London on its way to Oxford on March 28, was mailed back to London on March 29 and arrived there on the morning of March 30.[1] (All these postal peregrinations, as the stamps show, were free because of Timothy Shelley's franking privileges as a Member of Parliament.)

Shelley and Hogg had left Oxford for London on March 26. The readdressing of the letter shows that Shelley had left Edward Fergus Graham's address with the porter at University College as the forwarding address for both himself and Hogg. Hogg received the letter in London on March 30, the day after Shelley wrote to inform his father of the "proceedings."

It is interesting to note that Timothy's first reaction is to place the blame on Hogg. The invitation so cordially extended in January[2] is summarily withdrawn. For this change we can probably thank Stockdale and his story that Hogg was "the master spirit . . . lead[ing] him [Shelley] astray."[3] Nor did Timothy change his mind. Several months later Shelley's friend, Joseph Gibbons Merle, visiting Field Place, found that Timothy was still agitatedly blaming Shelley's "acquaintances" for his

1. See "Postmarks and the Dating of Manuscripts," below, pp. 922, 918–920.

2. sc 136 (Jan. ?19–?21, 1811), line 9.

3. Quoted in *Stockdale's Budget*, Jan. 3, 1827, p. 26.

SC 143    misfortunes.[4] Timothy's reactions during these months, it must, however, be recognized, are those of a man upset to the point of distraction. Overwhelmed by the disgrace of the expulsion he hits out blindly; and Hogg is his first target. He cannot bring himself to believe — at least consciously — that his son is at fault; the blame must lie elsewhere. The degree of his agitation is clearly visible in the above letter. He began to say "The invitation . . . has been withdrawn" or words to that effect, but halfway through got off on a new construction.

The primary cause of Timothy's agitation was not Shelley's anti-religious views. As Shelley's letter of February 6 (sc 139) shows, he was acquainted with those views, and although he did not agree with them, he does not seem to have raised any strenuous objections. The agitation stemmed rather from the social disgrace of the expulsion. Timothy as a Whig and the scion of a *nouveau riche* family was particularly sensitive on such matters — and doubtless terrified at the prospect of breaking the news to the redoubtable Sir Bysshe.

4. [Joseph Gibbons Merle], "A Newspaper Editor's Reminiscences," *Fraser's Magazine*, XXIII (June 1841), 705.

SC 144    TIMOTHY SHELLEY TO JOHN HOGG, APRIL 5, 1811

AL signed *T:Shelley.*, 2¼ pages. 1 double sheet, 4$^{to}$ (8.8 x 7.2 inches); 1 single sheet [address sheet], folio (7.6 x 12 inches).
Laid paper. Watermarks: double sheet (Whatman cipher)*:* [posthorn in crowned shield]| *JWJ*|; single sheet*:* [Britannia in crowned oval]|.
Seal (Shelley family crest and coat of arms): wax, black*:* [griffin's head surmounting coat of arms]|.
Frank, by Timothy Shelley.
Postmark: (evening duty franking stamp, London)*:* FREE| 5 AP 5| 1811|.

PROVENANCE: Thomas Jefferson Hogg; Major R. J. Jefferson Hogg (Sotheby, June 30, 1948, lot 67).

*House of Commons*
*Sir*                                              *5$^{th}$ Apr. 1811*
*I have the honor to address ~~you~~ you upon the Subject of the Unfortunate Affair that has happend to my Son & yours at University College Oxford.*
5    *I have undeavour'd to part them by directing my Son to return home, & also*

**Shelley to Hogg**                                              *April 5, 1811*

SC 144    *giving the same advice to your Son, & back'd by that opinion by Men of*
*Rank & Influence. All is without Effect, therefore I would suggest to you to*
*come to London, & try our joint endeavours. for that purpose. I have not*
*seen your Son, nor have I as yet seen my own, but I must so do very soon.*

10             *They are at N⁰ 15 Poland St. Oxford Road. Have the goodness to address*
*me, Miller's Hotel Westr Bridge. I am at a loss now to know whom I address*
*not being able to get the direction. Thise Youngsters must be parted & the*
*Fathers must exert themselves. The favor of yr Answer will oblige, Should I*
*be in the Country when you come up I can very soon be here.*

15                             *I have the Honor*
*to be, Sir, yr very Obedt.*
*Hbl: Servt.*
*T:Shelley.*

*Sir James Graham tells me there are several of the name Therefore into*
20  *whosever hands this comes, will have the goodness to find out the right person.*
*[Frank, with address, address sheet]*
*London, April Five 1811*
*—— Hogg Esqr*
*Stockton*
*on Tees*
25  *T:Shelley.*

line 4. *happend* (sic)

line 5. *undeavour'd* (sic): the *un* begins a line and comes immediately below the *Un* of *University* and this may have unconsciously directed Timothy's pen.

line 6. *opinion: op* written through another letter or letters.

line 12. *Thise* (sic): Timothy Shelley apparently

first wrote *this* intending to write *This youngster* (i.e., his own son). The final *e* stands slightly apart from the *s*. Then he forgot to remove the dot over the *i* or change the *i* to an *e*. The letter gives indication of haste and distraction.

line 13. *Should: S* is written through the *f* of a partly erased *If*.

IT has been assumed that Timothy Shelley rushed up to London immediately after receiving his son's letter of March 29,[1] but the above letter of April 5 is the first indication we have of his actually being

1. Ingpen, *Shelley in England*, pp. 215–216; White, *Shelley*, I, 122.

SC 144  in London and it gives the impression that he had but recently arrived. It is addressed from the House of Commons, where Timothy had been inquiring about the Hogg family among his parliamentary acquaintances, and this he would be most likely to do shortly after coming to town. He probably first went to Edward Fergus Graham's and there received the Poland Street address (line 10). Then he spoke to various "Men of Rank & Influence" (line 6), a category presumably including the Duke of Norfolk, Whitton, and Sir James Graham (line 19).[2] He either wrote to or had a message delivered to his son and Hogg advising them to return to their respective homes. Then he penned the above letter to John Hogg.

Not knowing Mr. Hogg's address, Timothy left the final page of his double sheet blank, presumably intending later to fill in the address. It was perhaps at this point that he encountered Sir James Graham, who told him there were several Hogg families in the Stockton region. Fearing his letter might reach the wrong person he apparently decided to wrap it in an address sheet and leave its final page blank for a forwarding address if one proved necessary.

2. There were two men of this name in Parliament in 1811, both of them from the north of England and hence likely to have information on the Hogg family, Sir James Graham (1753-1825) of Edmund Castle, Cumberland, and Sir James Graham of Netherby, Cumberland (d. 1824). Of the two, Sir James of Netherby seems more likely to have been Timothy's informant. He had been at Oxford and his son was at Oxford (1810-1812) when Shelley was there. (See *Alumni Oxonienses*. On Sir James of Edmund Castle see *Burke's Landed Gentry* and *Alumni Cantabrigienses*.)

The association of various Grahams with the Shelleys is curious. Sir Bysshe was apparently interested in a famed medical quack of the time, Dr. James Graham (1745-1794; *DNB*), and Timothy assisted with the musical education of Edward Fergus Graham. (See SC 113, May 20, 1810, Commentary.)

SC 145  TIMOTHY SHELLEY TO JOHN HOGG, APRIL 6, 1811

AL signed *T:Shelley.*, 2 pages. Double sheet, 4^{to} (9 x 7.3 inches).
Wove paper.
Seal (Shelley family crest): wax, black: [griffin's head surmounting coronet]|.
(See Plate xxv.)
Frank, by Timothy Shelley.
Postmark: (evening duty, franking stamp, London): FREE| 6 AP [6]| 1811|.

PROVENANCE: Thomas Jefferson Hogg; Major R. J. Jefferson Hogg (Sotheby, June 30, 1948, lot 69).

**Shelley to Hogg**                                              **April 6, 1811**

SC 145
                                                    *Millers Hotel*
                                                    *West^r Bridge*
*Sir*                                                    *6^th Ap^l 1811*
*Since I wrote yesterday, I find I did not address the letter right, yet it may*
5   *reach you, however as I am just come from M^r Wharton, who told me that*
*you liv'd at Norton near Stockton; I have only to urge you to get your Young*
*Man home. -&- They want to get into professions together, if possible they*
*must be parted, for such Monstrous Opinions that occupy their thot^s, are*
*by no means in their favor. I hope you have rec^d my letter of yesterday — &*
10  *will take immediate means of acting as you think proper. This is a most*
*deplorable Case & I fear we shall have much trouble to root it out. Paleys*
*Natural Theology, I shall recommend my Young Man to read, it is extremely*
*Applicable,; I shall read it with him. a Father so employ'd must impress*
*his Mind more sensibly than a Stranger. I shall exhort him to divest himself*
15  *of all prejudice already imbib'd f^m his false reasoning, & to bring a willing*
*Mind to a work so essential to his own & his Family's happyness.*

*I understand you have more Children, God grant they may turn out*
*well, & this Young Man see his Error.*
                                    *I remain y^r Obed^t*
                                    *& Afflicted fellow sufferer*
20                                              *T:Shelley.*

*[Frank, with address, page 4]*
*London, April Six 1811*
*John Hogg Esqr*
*Norton*
25  *Stockton*
*Tees*
*T:Shelley.*

Sɪʀ JAMES GRAHAM[1] knew only that Hogg's family lived in the vicinity
of the town of Stockton and not that they were at the nearby village
of Norton. Timothy, afraid that his letter would not reach Mr. Hogg,
made further inquiries and learned the exact address from "M^r Wharton"

1. See sc 144 (Apr. 5, 1811).

*Clarke to Hogg*          *April* **6, 1811**

SC 145    (line 5; presumably Richard Wharton, Member of Parliament from Durham).[2] Timothy's agitation is apparent in both this and the preceding letter.

When Timothy finally saw his son on April 7 he began immediately with the threatened indoctrination *via* "Paley" (line 11):

He felt in several pockets, and at last drew out a sheet of letter-paper, and began to read.

Bysshe, leaning forward, listened with profound attention. 'I have heard this argument before,' he said; and, by-and-by, turning to me, he said again: 'I have heard this argument before.'

'They are Paley's arguments,' I said.

'Yes!' the reader observed, with much complacency, turning towards me, 'you are right, sir,' and he folded up the paper, and put it into his pocket; 'they are Palley's arguments; I copied them out of Palley's book this morning . . .[3]

Shelley's aversion to Paley — "For my part I had rather be damned with Plato and Lord Bacon, then go to Heaven with Paley and Malthus"[4] — probably dates from this time.[5] Prior to this — in his deist period — he had been sympathetic to some of the ideas of Paley.[6] Timothy's sincere but heavy-handed efforts produced the opposite effect to what he had intended.

2. Robert Beatson, *A Chronological Register of Both Houses of the British Parliament, (1708–1807)* (London, 1807), II, 101. Wharton was elected in 1807; the next election was 1812.

3. Hogg, *Shelley*, I, 184. "Palley" is supposed to represent Timothy's pronunciation of Paley.

4. Preface to *Prometheus Unbound*. See also Claire Clairmont's Journal, Nov. 8, 1820, White, *Shelley*, II, 602. Shelley is apparently echoing Cicero (*Tusculanæ disputationes*): "I would rather be wrong with Plato than right with such men as these [the Pythagoreans]."

5. In December 1811 he wrote sarcastically of Paley to Elizabeth Hitchener; he refuted arguments of Paley's in *A Refutation of Deism* (1814).

6. Hughes, *Nascent Mind*, pp. 64–65.

SC 146    ROBERT CLARKE TO JOHN HOGG, APRIL 6, 1811

AL signed *R Clarke*, 2 pages. Double sheet, 4$^{to}$ (9.8 x 7.8 inches).
Laid paper. Watermark: [posthorn in crowned shield]|.
Seal: wafer, green.
Postmark: (mileage stamp): ELL[ES]MERE| 181|.
Notation: in shorthand in pencil near upper edge of page 4.

PROVENANCE: Thomas Jefferson Hogg; Major R. J. Jefferson Hogg (Sotheby, June 30, 1948, lot 72).

**Clarke to Hogg**                                   **April 6, 1811**

SC 146

*Ellesmere 6. Apl 1811*

*My dear Sir*

    *J$^{no}$ Brewster came to me this morning: I have had the whole history from him, and the reason of all this strange Conduct in your son and Shelley, is*
5 *what I supposed, a desire to be singular. – There is no striking Impiety in the Pamphlet: but it goes to shew that, because a supreme Power cannot be seen, such a power may be doubted to exist. It is a foolish performance so far as Argument goes; but written in good Language. These two young Men gave up associating with any body else some months since: never dined in*
10 *College: dressed differently from all others, and did every thing in their power to shew singularity: As much as to say "We are superior to everybody." – They have been writing Novels. Shelly has published his, and your son has not. — Shelly is son to the Member for Shoreham, and it is probable that he will be taken home as soon as his father knows where he is. – He has*
15 *always been odd, I find, and suspected of Insanity: but of great Acquirements: so is your son. I mean, as to the latter, he is of high repute in College. —*

    *You need not be anxious, at all, I think, about any criminal prosecution: the Pamphlet is not of the kind to merit such a proceeding, I should apprehend.*
20 *– It will blow over, I have no doubt, and Jefferson may be admitted into any of the Inns of Court. He cannot return to either of the Universities without a disavowal of his opinions: At his time of life that is not to be expected. — I wo$^d$ recommend your writing to him again to come home: let me know what he says, if he do not comply with your request, and I will soon be at his elbow,*
25 *if I find any good can be done. —*

    *Excuse haste, as I steal away to write ——*

                          *Most faithfully your's*
                              *R Clarke*

[Address, page 4]

    <        >
30    <     >*ton*
    <     >*kton upon Tees*

line 12. *Shelly* (sic)            line 27. *your's* (sic)
line 13. *Shelly* (sic)

## Clarke to Hogg

*April 6, 1811*

SC 146   JOHN HOGG, on receiving the news of his son's expulsion, put matters in the hands of Robert Clarke, the writer of the above letter.[1] Clarke was a lawyer at Stockton and the agent for the estates of the Earl of Bridgewater at Ellesmere in Shropshire.[2]

Clarke, in turn, got in touch with John Brewster, whose father, the Reverend John Brewster, had been vicar of Stockton and was the author of several books including a four-volume *Parochial History of Stockton-upon-Tees* (1796).[3] A later edition of this book (*ca.* 1840) contained an article by John Hogg, brother of Thomas Jefferson Hogg. As John Brewster was an undergraduate of University College, Oxford, from 1810 to 1813,[4] his account of the events surrounding the expulsion was an eye-witness account and reflects something of the view of the student body of the college. It is rather similar to that given by C. J. Ridley, then a Junior Fellow of the college: "The aforesaid two had made themselves as conspicuous as possible by a great singularity of dress, and by walking up and down the centre of the quadrangle as if proud of their anticipated fate."[5] Shelley, for his part, had no high opinion of Brewster

1. A photostatic copy of the shorthand notation on page 4 of the manuscript (see Bibliographical Description) was sent to Mr. William J. Carlton of Andover, Hants., a leading authority on the shorthand of the period. Mr. Carlton was kind enough to reply to our request:

> The first three words of the shorthand note are clearly written and I have no doubt that they may be transcribed "The promised land." The remainder is not so clear and I can only say that the fourth word on the top line appears to be "like" or "look"; the next word is probably "as" or "is"; the last but one has the consonantal outline "s t n" (which might represent "stone" or "Satan"); and the last word appears to have the consonantal outline "b r r" or "p r r" ("barrier"?).

The similarity between this shorthand note and others on some of our manuscripts by T. J. Hogg makes it likely that this note, too, was by Hogg. One might guess — in view of the contents of the letter — that the general reference is to the expulsion (Oxford perhaps being the "promised land").

2. *Alumni Oxonienses* gives him as son of Thomas Clarke of Durham Castle, Durham, and as attending Christ Church, taking his B.A. in 1776. *Clarke's New Law List* for 1806 and for 1814 lists him as a Stockton attorney. Ingpen (*Shelley in England*, p. 220) is incorrect in stating that Clarke was "on the spot in London." He was, as the above letter shows, at Ellesmere. He came to London from Ellesmere at Mr. Hogg's request.

3. See Allibone and *Alumni Oxonienses*.

4. *Alumni Oxonienses*. Apparently Brewster had taken the day off to travel from Stockton to Ellesmere — during his Easter vacation — to give the story to Clarke. One might surmise that Mr. Hogg got in touch with the Reverend John Brewster as soon as he heard of the expulsion, knowing that his son was also at University College. Clarke's opening comment without explanation — "Jnᵒ Brewster came to me this morning" — indicates that the visit had been expected.

5. Dowden, *Shelley*, I, 123–124.

PLATE XXXIII

My Dear Boy    Miller Hotel
                5th April 1811

I am unwilling to decide &
act on the Information you
gave me on Sunday as the Ultimate
Determination of your Mind; the
Disgrace which hangs over you
is most Serious, & though I have
felt as a Father & Sympathiz'd in
the Misfortune which your Cri-
-minal opinions, & improper Acts
have begot; yet you must know
that I have a Duty to perform
to my own Character as well as
to your young Brother & Sisters;
Above all, my feelings as a
Christain require from me a decided
& firm Conduct towards you.
If you shall require aid or assis-
-tance from me, or any Protection

*Timothy Shelley to P. B. Shelley, April 9, 1811 (SC 147), page 1*

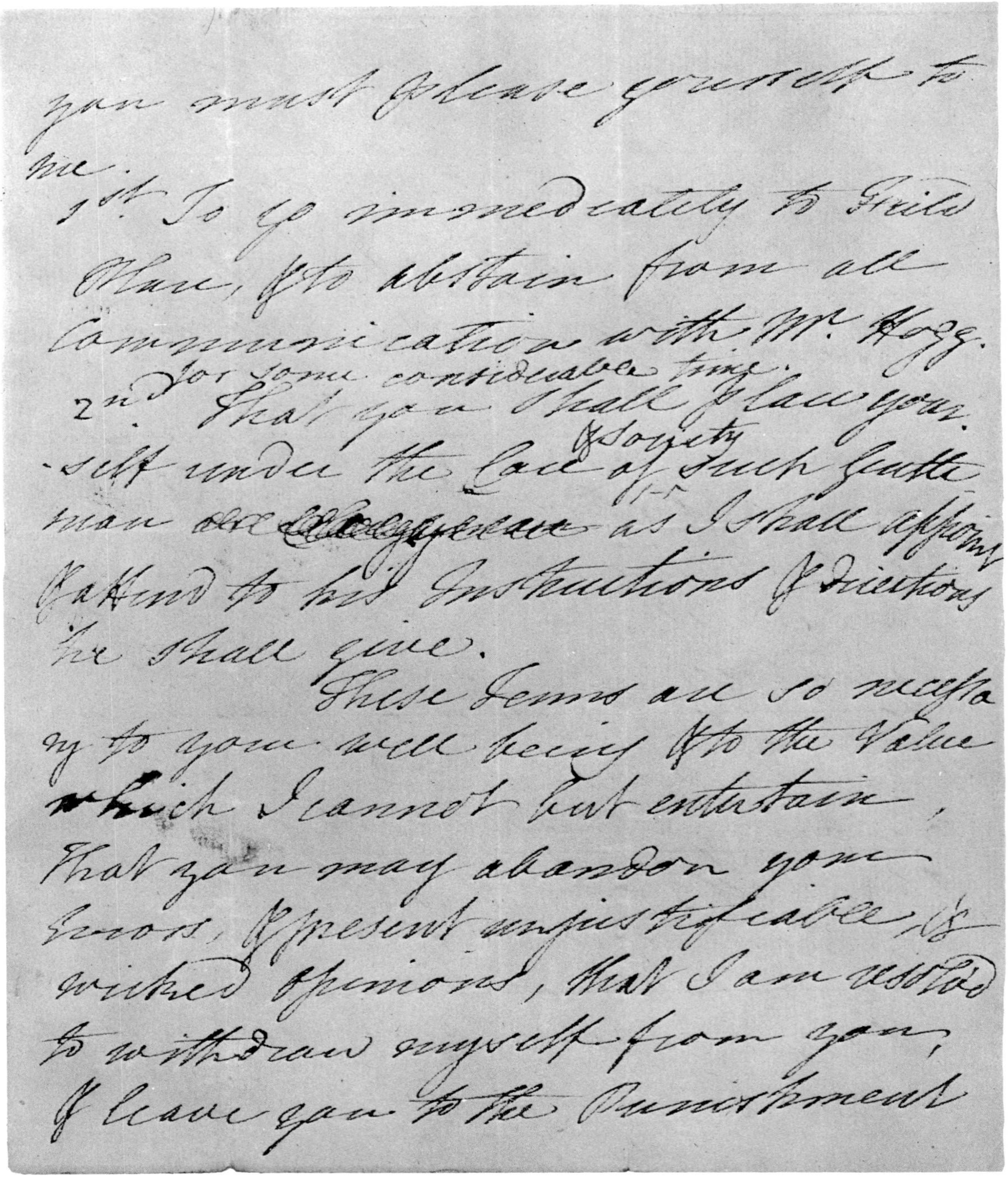

PLATE XXXIV

you must [please yourself to
me.
1st To go immediately to Field
Place, & to abstain from all
communication with Mr Hogg.
for some considerable time.
2nd That you shall place your-
self under the care & Society of such Gentle
man as I shall appoint
& attend to his Instructions & directions
he shall give.
These terms are so necessa
ry to your well being & to the Value
which I cannot but entertain,
that you may abandon your
error, & present unjustifiable &
wicked opinions, that I am resolved
to withdraw myself from you,
& leave you to the Punishment

*Timothy Shelley to P. B. Shelley, April 9, 1811 (SC 147), page 2*

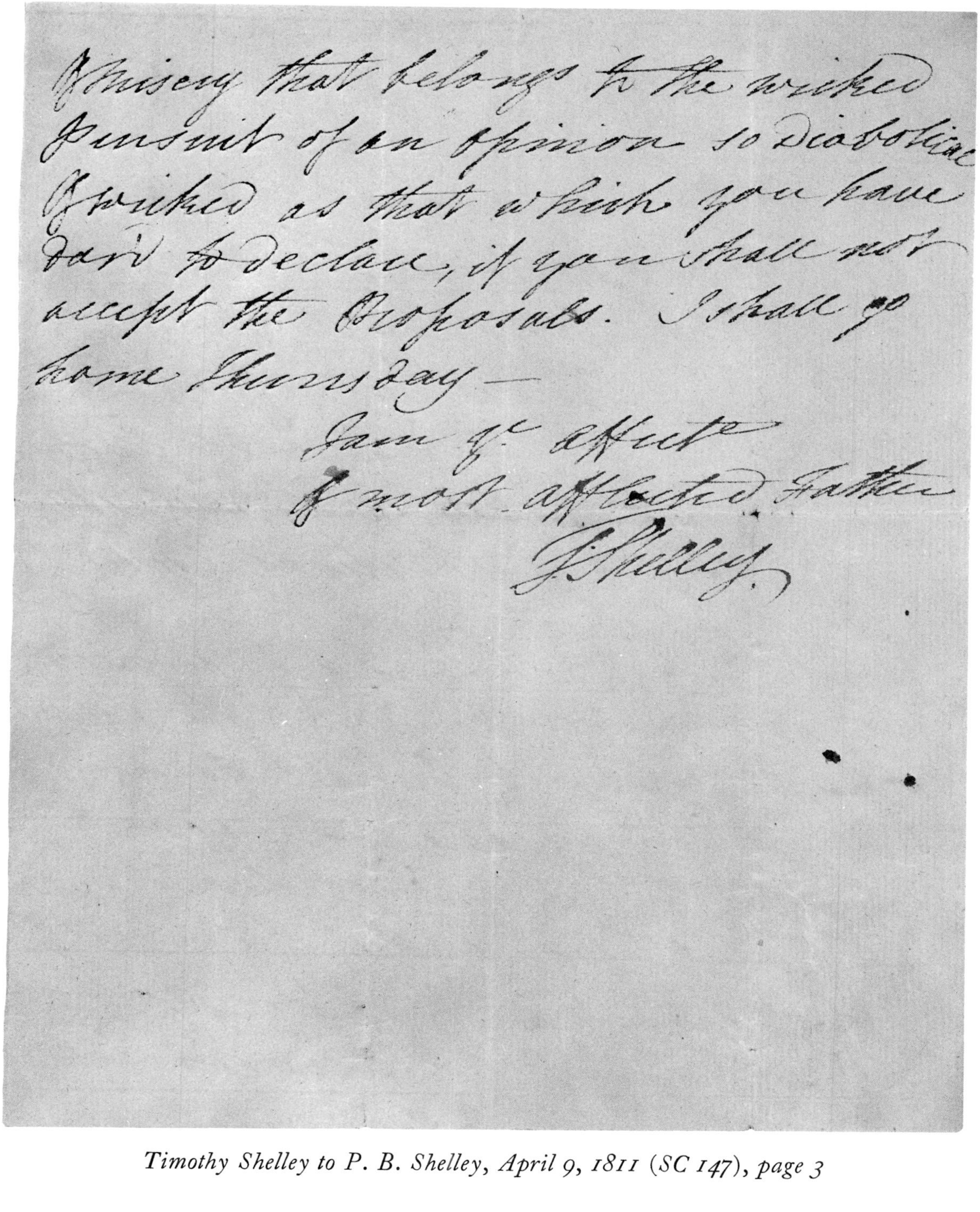

PLATE XXXV

& Misery that belongs to the wicked
Pensuit of an opinion so diabolical
& wicked as that which you have
dar'd to declare, if you shall not
accept the Proposals. I shall go
home Thursday —

        I am yr affecte
      & most afflicted Father
         T Shelley.

*Timothy Shelley to P. B. Shelley, April 9, 1811 (SC 147), page 3*

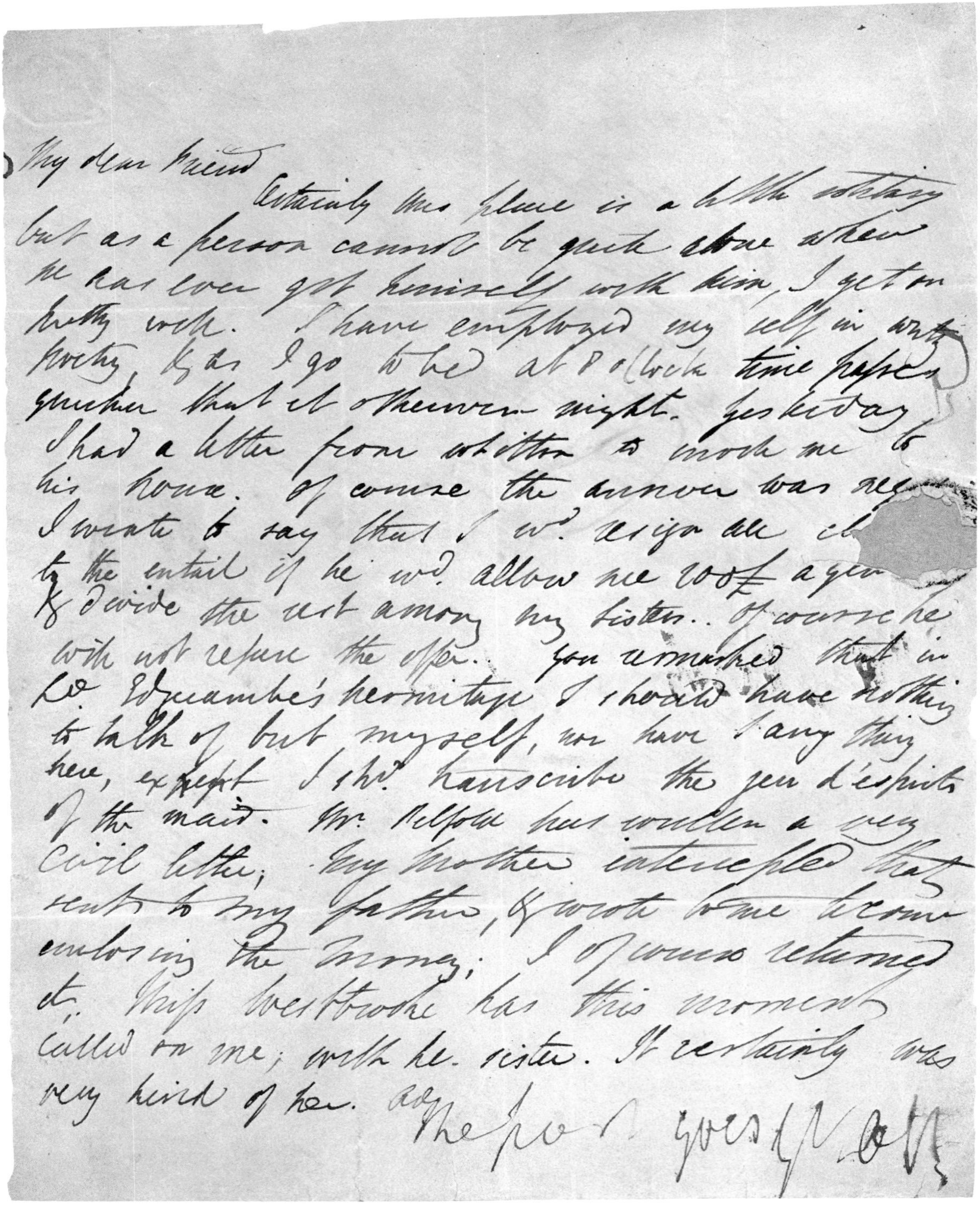

PLATE XXXVI

My dear Friend
          Certainly Mrs Place is a little solitary
but as a person cannot be quite alone when
he has ever got himself with him, I get on
pretty well. I have employed my self in writing
poetry, & as I go to bed at 8 oclock time passes
quicker than it otherwise might. Yesterday
I had a letter from Whitton to invite me to
his house. Of course the answer was ——
I wrote to say that I wd. resign all claim
to the entail if he wd. allow me 100£ a year
& divide the rest among my sisters.. Of course he
with not refuse the offer.. You remarked that in
Ld. Edgcumbe's hermitage I should have nothing
to talk of but myself, nor have I any thing
here, except I shd. transcribe the jeu d'esprits
of the maid. Mr. Telford has written a very
civil letter; my mother intercepted that
sent to my father, & wrote to me & come
enclosing the money; I of course returned
it. Miss Westbroke has this moment
called on me; with her sister. It certainly was
very kind of her. Ad.
                    the post goes & I

*P. B. Shelley to T. J. Hogg, April 18, 1811 (SC 151), page 1*

SC 146   (later vicar of, respectively, Greatham and Laughton). "Yʳ Brewster,"
he informed Hogg, "is worse than stupid. he is provoking."[6]

The novels (line 12) which Shelley and Hogg had been writing were,
respectively, *St. Irvyne* (published in November or December 1810) and
*Leonora.*[7]

The contrast between the liberal attitude of Clarke and the inflexibility of Timothy Shelley and Whitton is most striking. If Clarke had
had the management of Shelley as well as of Hogg the episode would
certainly have been resolved with less friction. John Hogg had, in fact,
as the above letter shows, not intended to go to London at all but to have
Clarke go alone. It was perhaps Timothy Shelley's letters, received at
about the same time as this from Clarke, that made him change his plans
and go to London himself.

6. SC 152 (Apr. 24, 1811), line 6.

7. *St. Irvyne,* one would gather, made something of a stir in Oxford undergraduate circles. Charles
Kirkpatrick Sharpe, then at Christ Church, wrote to a friend on March 15, 1811, some ten days
before the expulsion: "Our Apollo next came out with a prose pamphlet in praise of atheism, which
I have not as yet seen; and there appeared a monstrous romance in one volume called 'St. Irvyne,
or the Rosicrucian.' Here is another pearl of great price! All the heroes are confirmed robbers and
causeless murderers, while the heroines glide *en chemise* through the streets of Geneva, tap at the
palazzo doors of their sweethearts, and being denied admittance leave no cards, but run home to
their warm beds and kill themselves." (Dowden, *Shelley,* I, 125.)


SC 147   TIMOTHY SHELLEY TO P. B. SHELLEY, APRIL 9, 1811

AL signed *T:Shelley.*, 2½ pages. Double sheet, 4ᵗᵒ (8.8 x 7.2 inches).   (See Plates
XXXIII–XXXV.)
Laid paper. Watermark (Whatman cipher): [posthorn in crowned shield]| JWJ|.
Gilt edges.

PROVENANCE: Thomas Jefferson Hogg; Major R. J. Jefferson Hogg (Sotheby,
June 30, 1948, lot 68).

*Millers Hotel*
*My Dear Boy*                                                           *9ᵗʰ April 1811*
*on Sunday*
*I am unwilling to receive & Act on the Information you gave me yesterday*
5   *as the Ultimate determination of your Mind; The Disgrace which hangs over*
*you is most Serious, & though I have felt as a Father & Sympathiz'd in the*

# The Carl H. Pforzheimer Library

**Shelley to Shelley**                                           *April 9, 1811*

SC 147 *Misfortune which your Criminal opinions, & improper Acts have begot;*
*yet you must know that I have a Duty to perform to my own Character as well*
*as to your Young Brother & Sisters; Above all, as my feelings as a Christian*

10 *require of me a decided & firm Conduct towards you.* ^from^

    *If you shall require aid or assistance from me, or any Protection you*
*must please yourself to me.*

    *1ˢᵗ To go immediately to Field Place, & to abstain from all Communica-*

15 *tion with Mʳ Hogg.*
*for some considerable time.*

    *2ⁿᵈ That you shall place yourself under the Care of, ^& Society^ such Gentleman*
*or Clergyman as I shall appoint & attend to his Instructions & directions*

20 *he shall give.*

    *These Terms are so necessary to your well being & to the Value which*
*I cannot but entertain, That you may abandon your Errors, & present*
*unjustifiable, & wicked Opinions, that I am resolv'd to withdraw myself*
*from you, & leave you to the Punishment & Misery that belongs to the wicked*

25 *pursuit of an opinion so Diabolical & wicked as that which you have dar'd*
*to declare, if you shall not accept the Proposals. I shall go home Thurrsday*

———

       *I am yʳ affectᵉ*
      *& most afflicted Father*
        *T:Shelley.*

line 2. The *9* is written through some other number, apparently an *8*, and was formed by developing the lower loop of the *8*. See line 4, *yesterday* for *Sunday*. April 9 was a Tuesday in 1811.

line 18. *Gentleman* (sic): The caret before *such* is misplaced.
line 26. *Thurrsday* (sic)

Two days after Shelley wrote his belated report [his letter of March 29 on the expulsion]," Newman I. White comments, "we find Mr. Timothy Shelley at his regular London lodgings, Miller's Hotel, over Westminster Bridge. Since he could hardly have received Shelley's letter before March 30, he must have left Field Place at once in order to

[ 740 ]

SC 147   reach London, locate the boys through Graham (for Shelley's letter bore no address), and arrange an interview for March 31."[1]

But Timothy apparently did not, as we have seen, leave immediately for London. And no interview took place between Shelley and his father on Sunday, March 31. The belief that it did is based on Hogg's dating of the above letter as April 5,[2] an error followed by later editors and biographers.

Hogg's error was natural enough because the first figure of the date does at first appear to be a five, but examination shows that although Timothy first began some other number (perhaps an eight) he then wrote a nine over it. The cross of the *t* of *th* above this nine gives it the appearance of a large five. But that the date could not be April 5 is shown by the fact that in his letter to John Hogg of April 5 Timothy states that he has not yet seen his son and in his letter of April 6 he mentions no such meeting, as he would certainly have done had it taken place. Hence, the first meeting between Shelley and his father was on Sunday, April 7, and the above letter was written on Tuesday, April 9. As Timothy had evidently had a consultation with Whitton prior to writing the letter,[3] one might suspect that the propositions contained in it were Whitton's rather than Timothy's. On the same day Timothy wrote to Whitton: "You observe how they are now determined and what materials they are made of — I shall and will be firm. . . ."[4] But even as Timothy was thus stressing his firmness he was, as the above letter shows, beginning to

1. White, *Shelley*, I, 122; see also Ingpen, *Shelley in England*, pp. 215–216, and Peck, *Shelley*, I, 115.

2. Hogg, *Shelley*, I, 187. As the letter has neither address nor postmark it must have been sent by messenger (from Miller's Hotel, near Westminster Bridge, to Poland Street, near Oxford Street; Plan of London, C 3, B 1, Front Endpapers). The presence of the letter among the Hogg family papers indicates that Shelley turned it over to Hogg (as he did with others also; see Hogg, *Shelley*, I, 189).

3. Ingpen, *Shelley in England*, p. 226.

4. Ingpen (*ibid.*) misdates Timothy Shelley's letter of April 9 to Whitton as April 8. Examination of the manuscript in the Yale University Library shows that the date — in Timothy Shelley's hand — is April 9. The letter bears two postmarks, that (undated) of the receiving house, Bridge Street, Lambeth (just across Westminster Bridge and presumably near Miller's Hotel), and that of the (Westminster) central post office: "10 AP‖ 8 oClock Morn‖ Two Penny Paid‖." This means that the letter went out of the Westminster post office on the 8 a.m. "walk" and hence was probably written in the evening of April 9. As the date on this letter to Whitton was written correctly the first time, it is probable that the above letter to Shelley — with its hesitation on the date — was written earlier in the day.

# The Carl H. Pforzheimer Library

SC 147    waver. He added the qualification "for some considerable time" (line 16) to his first demand and deleted "or Clergyman" (line 19) from his second.

SC 148    P. B. SHELLEY TO J. J. STOCKDALE, APRIL 11, 1811

AL signed *P. B. Shelley.*, 1 page. Double sheet, 8ᵛᵒ (7 x 4.5 inches).
Wove paper.
Seal: wafer, gray.
Postmarks: 1. (receiving house stamp, London): [?Two Py] [   ]| Unpaid| [   ]|;
2. (delivery stamp, Westminster): 4 o'Clock| 11.AP| 1811 EV.| [   ]|.
Docket, page 4, in same hand as that on sc 116: *Shelley| April 1811|*.

PROVENANCE: George D. Smith (Anderson, Jan. 20, 1921, lot 279); Major W. Van R. Whitall (American Art, Feb. 14, 1927, lot 1126); W. T. H. Howe; Audrey Wedderburn Auslander. *De Ricci 44* (p. 263).

*Sir.*

*Will you have the goodness to inform me of the number of copies which you have sold of 'Sᵗ Irvyne'. Circumstances may occur, which will oblige me, in case of their event to wish for my accounts suddenly, perhaps you*
5   *had better make them out now —*

                   *Sir*
             *Yʳ obᵗ humbˡ Svʳ*
               *P. B. Shelley.*
      *15 Poland Sᵗ Oxford Sᵗ*

[Address, page 4]
10   *Mʳ Stockdale*
   *41*      *Pall Mall*

Aᴸᴛʜᴏᴜɢʜ by the time *St. Irvyne* was published, Shelley was absorbed in his new social and philosophical interests, and would not even condescend to read proof, he still felt the book would have a good sale. "As to the method of publishing it," he wrote to Stockdale on November 14, 1810, "I think as it is a thing which almost mechanically sells to circulating libraries, etc., I would wish it to be published on my *own* account." This same optimism underlies the above letter. Shelley apparently expected that the novel would by April have realized a profit.

# Shelley and his Circle: Manuscripts

SC 148     There was, however, no money to be had from Stockdale. *St. Irvyne* did not sell, and Stockdale was left with a considerable "remainder," which in 1822 (apparently hoping to profit from the publicity attending Shelley's death), he brought out with a new title page.[1] His loss on the volume by 1826 he calculated to have been £300 (plus interest).[2]

The anticipated "circumstances" (line 3) which might require a sudden rendition of "accounts" were doubtless related to the preceding ominous letter from Timothy with its threat of financial abandonment – "I am resolv'd to withdraw myself from you."

1. Forman, *Shelley Library*, p. 15; Wise, *Shelley Library*, p. 33; Sylva Norman, *Flight of the Skylark* (University of Oklahoma Press, 1954), p. 17.

2. *Stockdale's Budget*, Jan. 3, 1827, p. 26.

SC 149     P. B. SHELLEY TO JOHN HOGG, APRIL ?12, 1811

AL signed *P. B. Shelley.*, 2 pages. Double sheet, 4^to (8.8 x 7.1 inches). Wove paper. Watermark: BATH| 1810|. Embossed stamp: [crown]| BATH|. Seal: wafer, yellow.

PROVENANCE: Thomas Jefferson Hogg; Major R. J. Jefferson Hogg (Sotheby, June 30, 1948, lot 11). *De Ricci 43* (p. 138).

*Sir/*

*I accompanied, (at his desire) M^r Jefferson Hogg to M^r Clark who was entrusted with certain propositions to be offered to my friend . . I was there extremely surprised; no less hurt than surprised to find that my father in his*
5 *interview with Mr. C. had either unadvisedly or intentionally let fall expressions which conveyed an idea that Mr. J. H. was the "original corruptor" of my principles. That on this subject, (notwithstanding his long experience) M^r T. Shelley must know less than his son, will be conceded; & I feel it but justice in consequence of your feelings, so natural, which M^r C. communi-*
10 *cated, positively to deny the assertion; I feel this tribute which I have paid to the just sense of honor you entertain, to be due to you as a gentleman, I hope my motives stand excused to your candour. Myself & my friend have offered concessions, painful indeed they are, but such as on mature considera-tion we find due to our high sense of filial duty.*

[ 743 ]

**Shelley to Hogg**                                   *April ?12, 1811*

SC 149   *Permit me to request your indulgence for the liberty I have taken in thus*
*addressing you, to remain*

> *Y$^r$ obedient h$^{le}$ Ser$^t$*
> *P. B. Shelley.*

*15 Poland Street*
20   *Oxford S$^t$*

[Address, page 4]
*John Hogg Esq$^r$*
*&$^c$ &$^c$ &$^c$*

line 9. *justice in: to* apparently changed to *in*
line 9. *feelings:* Shelley began with an *o*, then
added *f* to it but failed to cancel the *o*.
line 21. The address is smeared as though by
water. *The Gentleman's Magazine*, LXXXI

(April 1811), 312, notes "rain and wind" in
London on April 12.
line 22. The *&$^c$*'s are large and elaborate with
long curling tails.

A CHRONOLOGY of the main events of the period between the expulsion
from Oxford and Hogg's departure from London will be of assistance in understanding the significance of the above letter and the other
letters in the sequence.

|  |  |
|---|---|
| March 25. | Morning; Shelley and Hogg expelled.[1] |
| March 26. | Morning; Shelley and Hogg leave for London. |
| March 26. | Evening; they stay at a London coffee house for the night; visit the Groves. |
| March 27. | 4 a.m. Shelley visits Medwin.[2] Shelley and Hogg find lodgings at 15 Poland Street. Timothy Shelley writes to Hogg (sc 143). |
| March 29. | Shelley writes to his father announcing the expulsion. |
| April 3–5. | John Hogg, father of Thomas Jefferson Hogg, writes to his friend and legal adviser, Robert Clarke, agent to the Earl of Bridgewater at Ellesmere.[3] |
| April 4–5. | Timothy Shelley arrives in London. |
| April 5. | Timothy Shelley writes to John Hogg (sc 144). |

1. The dates and events following are, unless otherwise noted, derived from Hogg, *Shelley*, I, 172–
198, Ingpen, *Shelley in England*, pp. 213–240, the manuscripts and photostats in our library, and
the manuscripts of Timothy Shelley's letters to Whitton in the Yale University Library.

2. Medwin, *Shelley*, pp. 87–88.

3. As Clarke replied on April 6 (from Ellesmere) John Hogg must have written to him (from Norton)
at least one and probably two days prior to this date.

**Shelley to Hogg**                                    *April ?12, 1811*

SC 149       April 6.      Timothy writes again to John Hogg (sc 145). Clarke, at Ellesmere, writes to John Hogg (sc 146).

April 7.      Shelley and T. J. Hogg meet with Timothy Shelley at Miller's Hotel, London.

April 8–9.    John Hogg arrives in London.

April 9.      Timothy Shelley writes to his son (sc 147) and to his lawyer, William Whitton, asking his advice. John Hogg calls on Timothy Shelley.

April 10.     Shelley writes to his father objecting to the interference of a Mr. Hurst, a trustee of some Shelley estates.[4]

April 10–11.  Clarke arrives in London[5] and has an interview with Timothy Shelley.

April 11.     Timothy Shelley writes to Whitton putting the whole matter

4. Shelley believed that his father had requested Hurst to see him; but on April 11 Timothy Shelley wrote to Whitton as follows (text from original manuscript in the Yale University Library and quoted by permission):

> *I desir'd M$^r$ Hurst after I saw you to take no part in the business whatever — by a Note left for him & in person, as I accidentally saw him. Allow me to say I have acted upon the Principle you had the goodness to suggest, & I shall & will act up to it in every circumstance from Conviction of its rectitude, nor shall I answer the Note. I will thank you from henceforth to be the only person I shall apply to in this business. From every Idea of doing what is right . . . I have given no Authority to M$^r$ Hurst but the contrary —*

If we place this letter beside the following remark in a letter of April 12 from Robert Parker to Timothy Shelley — "he [P. B. Shelley] expressed great satisfaction at finding you did not send Mr. Hurst to him" — it appears that it was Whitton who was behind Hurst's intervention. (Ingpen, *Shelley in England*, p. 229.)

5. On April 11, Timothy Shelley wrote as follows to Whitton (text from original manuscript in the Yale University Library):

> *M$^r$ Clark agent to the Earl of Bridgewater, & the Friend of M$^r$ Hogg, whom I have now seen — will send you a letter from M$^r$ Faber Rector of Redmarshal n$^r$ Stockton upon Tees which will open more to your View.*
>
> *At any time you wish to see M$^r$ Hogg or send him a line address it to him at the undermentioned Gentleman's —*
>
> *I will My D$^r$ Sir now leave this Young Lunatic to your management as I shall go home.*
> > *Believe me y$^{rs}$*
> > *most Truly*
> > > *T: Shelley*
>
> *11 Ap$^l$ 1811*
> *M$^r$ Clark No 38 New Bond Street*
> > *42*

Clarke, therefore, must have been in London by April 11; and it is difficult to see how he could have arrived before April 10 because he informed John Hogg (from Ellesmere) on April 6 that he would not go to London until he had a reply from him. The reply can hardly have come from Norton (in the vicinity of Durham) before April 9 or 10 and it would then have taken him a day to get to London from Ellesmere.

SC 149

in his hands, and returns to Field Place. Shelley's cousin, John Grove, writes to Timothy Shelley that he has had "several conversations" with Shelley and that if Hogg would leave "you will find Bysshe inclined to agree to most of your proposals." Hogg has an interview with his father. Whitton writes to Sir Bysshe decrying Shelley's "impiety and effrontery."

| | |
|---|---|
| April 12. | Timothy Shelley's brother-in-law, Robert Parker, calls on Shelley and finds in him "a pretty strong desire to be reconciled to his family." |
| April 12–13. | Shelley and Hogg submit "proposals" to John Hogg, who accepts them.[6] |
| April 13. | Shelley mails the "proposals" to his father. |
| April 14. | Timothy Shelley receives the "proposals," and rejects them in a letter to Whitton and a letter to Clarke (sc 150). |
| April 15. | Sir Bysshe writes to Whitton urging "unconditional submission." Clarke writes to Timothy Shelley stating that Mr. Hogg has accepted the "proposals." |
| April 16. | 9 p.m. T. J. Hogg and Clarke leave London for Ellesmere. Timothy Shelley informs Whitton of "the Separation."[7] From this point on Shelley is alone in the lodgings in Poland Street. |

Where in this sequence does the above letter fit? As it bears no street address or postmark it must have been sent by private messenger. It was later than April 10–11 because it mentions Timothy Shelley's interview with Clarke. It was written to Mr. Hogg while he was still in London. We do not know when Mr. Hogg left London but it seems likely that it was on or about the same day as his son and Clarke left (April 16). Timothy refers to him as in London on April 14 but does not mention him on April 16 or later. Hence, the terminal date can be set at April 16.

On April 14 Timothy Shelley received the "proposals," which must have been mailed from London on April 13, by which time Mr. Hogg had

6. The "proposals" were not seen by Timothy on April 11; they were received at Field Place on April 14. Hence, they must have been drawn up on April 12–13.

7. Timothy Shelley to William Whitton, April 16, 1811 (from original manuscript in the Yale University Library):

> *The enclos'd will inform you of the Separation of these Youngsters. My Son will be left, as it were, in Solitary Confinement. I wish something could be done with the Apostate.*

Ingpen (*Shelley in England*, p. 240) dates this letter wrongly as April 14.

SC 149  approved of them. The "concessions" of the above letter (line 13) are presumably the same as these "proposals." They had not at the time of the writing of this letter, however, been accepted by Mr. Hogg, and they had not been seen by Timothy Shelley when he left London on April 11. Taking all these factors together we can date the above letter with fair certainty as April 12.

Timothy Shelley, as we have seen, had had his suspicions of Hogg's evil influence aroused by Stockdale in December. In January, after obtaining more information on Hogg's family, he felt that his suspicions were unfounded and invited Hogg to spend the Easter vacation at Field Place. But the news of the expulsion again turned him against Hogg and he canceled the invitation (sc 143). The interview of April 7 had not changed his mind, and he may have expressed his feelings to John Grove. Nor did Shelley's disclaimers affect him. When Joseph Gibbons Merle visited at Field Place, probably in May or June, he found that Timothy still believed Hogg was at the root of his son's "corruption" and that Shelley was still denying it.[8] There was, moreover, in spite of the above letter, some justification for Timothy Shelley's suspicions. The letters between Shelley and Hogg during the Christmas vacation show Hogg arguing in favor of atheism and Shelley resisting it.

8. Quoted in Cameron, *The Young Shelley*, pp. 87–88. Merle does not specifically mention Hogg but the implication is clear. The exact date of his visit to Field Place we do not know but it appears to have been shortly after Shelley's return there in May.

SC 150  TIMOTHY SHELLEY TO ROBERT CLARKE, APRIL 14, 1811

AL signed *T:Shelley.*, 3 pages. Double sheet, single sheet [address sheet], 4^{to} (8.7 x 7.1 inches).
Laid paper. Watermarks: double sheet (Whatman cipher): [posthorn in crowned shield]| *JWJ*|; single sheet (Wilmott cipher): [posthorn in crowned shield, lower part]| *CW*|. Gilt edges.
Seal (Shelley family crest and coat of arms): wax, red: [griffin's head surmounting coat of arms]|.  (See Plate xxv.)
Frank, by Timothy Shelley.
Postmarks: 1.(mileage stamp): HORSHAM| 41|; 2. (morning duty franking stamp, London): FREE| 15 AP 15| 1811|.
Docket, address sheet: *Re*| *P.B.S.*|.

# The Carl H. Pforzheimer Library

*Sir*

    *This morning I rec^d a letter from my Son, who said He & M^r Hogg jun^r had submitted proposals to M^r Hogg who had done them the Honor ~~to~~ of expressing his approbation of them with the Condition of mine.*

5     *I found I c^d do no more with either of them, & as the letter came from M^r Faber, whose Character must be mild & benevolent indeed – Yet I consider'd it right to give my business into M^r Whittons hands to guard my Honor & Character in case of any prosecutions in the Courts– and to direct my Son to do what was right in the first instance, so he will now–*

10     *M^r Hogg must be deciev'd if He agrees to the Proposals, indeed what right have these Opiniated Youngsters to do any such thing— Undutyfull & disrespectful to a degree. —*

    *viz*

    *The Parties feel it their Duty to <u>Demand</u> an unrestrain'd Correspond-*
15     *ence ——*

    *When M^r T. J. Hogg enters at the Inns of Court, or commences any other Profession, that M^r P. B. Shelley may be permitted to select that intention in Life which may be consonant with his Intentions to which he may Judge his Abilities adequate – Surely Sir M^r Hogg*
20     *never c^d agree to such Insolence ——*

    *I beg my Compt^s to M^r Hogg and hope he will be firm & decided with these misguided youngsters –*

                        *I am, Sir y^r.*
                        *very Hbl: Serv^t.*
25                             *T:Shelley.*

*Field Place*
    *14^th Ap^l 1811*
*Desire M^r Hogg Jun^r to inform you of our conversation &c. last Sunday. You say the Persons name is Clark where you lodge*
30   *M^r Clark with*
    *M^r Hogg*

**Shelley to Clarke**                                        *April 14, 1811*

SC 150  [Frank, with address, address sheet]
     *Horsham, April Fourteen   1811*
     *M^r Clark*
     *N^o 38 New Bond Street*

35     *42*
     *London*
     *T: Shelley.*

line 3. Some illegible letters have been smeared out above *Hogg;* they were perhaps intended as further identification of Mr. Hogg. That they were inserted later is shown by the fact that there is a dot under the *r* of *jun^r* (in the line above) that comes down into these smeared letters but has not itself smeared.

line 10. *deciev'd* (sic): a common misspelling also in Shelley's letters.

line 16. *T. J.* appears to be *J. J.* but *J* and *T* are often indistinguishable in the script of the period. Timothy either intended *T. J.* or copied mechanically from the letter of Shelley's that he was following (line 2).

THE letter and proposals which so aroused Timothy's wrath, and from which he quotes (line 14), must have been mailed from London on April 13 as Timothy received them on April 14. The letter which "came from M^r Faber" (line 5) is not — as Timothy's vague wording might seem to imply — the letter from his son, which was being forwarded by Faber, but a separate letter, a "very long letter to Mr. Hogg" from Faber himself. This letter Clarke had read to Timothy and was to forward to Whitton.[1]

On April 15 Clarke replied to Timothy's letter, confirming that Mr. Hogg had agreed to the proposals and had "refrained from stating objections to a correspondence between the young men, because it did not appear to him that it could be prevented from being carried on through the medium of a third person."[2]

In addition to Robert Clarke, Mr. Hogg was also apparently being advised by "Faber." The Reverend George Stanley Faber, although a local vicar and a friend of the Hogg family, was a nationally known divine. He was also a fellow alumnus with Shelley and Hogg of University College, and author of more than forty theological works.[3] He had

1. See SC 149 (Apr. ?12, 1811), fn. 5, and Ingpen, *Shelley in England*, p. 236.
2. Quoted in Ingpen, *Shelley in England*, p. 239.
3. On Faber see the *DNB*, Allibone, and the British Museum catalogue. He was vicar at Stockton from 1805 to 1808.

SC 150 received rather rough epistolary treatment at the hands of the youthful atheists, but, with true Christian benevolence, had urged a course of forgiveness and moderation, which, however, was not looked upon with much favor by the opposite side.

The above letter, in fact, brings out once more the divergence between the attitude of Mr. Hogg and his advisers and that of Timothy, Sir Bysshe, and Whitton. Mr. Hogg, Clarke, and Faber were all of the opinion that the young men could be brought to reason by sympathetic guidance; Timothy, Whitton, and Sir Bysshe were all — as Sir Bysshe put it — for "unconditional Submission." On the copy of Shelley's letter and proposals which Timothy sent on to Whitton he wrote: "Fine fellows these to presume to offer proposals."[4]

In spite of his attempted inflexibility, however, Timothy is clearly distraught. He confuses the letter from his son and the letter from Faber (line 5). He leaves his thoughts hanging in the air, for instance (line 9), "so he will now–." In copying the proposals from his son's letter, he writes "intention" (line 18) for "situation."[5]

The comment "You say the Persons name is Clark where you lodge" is addressed to Clarke and not to Mr. Hogg. The London *Post Office Directory* for 1813 lists a W. Clarke, "Bookseller, Stationer &c." at 38 New Bond Street. Robert Clarke, then, must have been lodging with a relative. We may note that 38 New Bond Street was just around the corner from John Westbrook's coffee house, "The Mount," at 78 Grosvenor Street. (Plan of London, B2, Front Endpapers.) Mr. Hogg was apparently (line 29) also staying with W. Clarke.

4. Ingpen, *Shelley in England*, p. 233.

5. *Ibid.* "*Demand*" (line 14) was not underlined or capitalized in Shelley's letter.

SC 151 P. B. SHELLEY TO T. J. HOGG, APRIL 18, 1811

AL unsigned, 1 page. Single sheet, 4$^{to}$ (9 x 7.1 inches). (See Plate xxxvi.) Wove paper. Octagonal embossed stamp: [crown]| BATH|.
Seal: wafer, dark red.
Postmark: (evening duty stamp, London): A| AP 18 ·811|.

PROVENANCE: Thomas Jefferson Hogg; Major R. J. Jefferson Hogg (Sotheby, June 30, 1948, lot 12). *De Ricci 48* (p. 123).

**Shelley to Hogg**                                   *April 18, 1811*

SC 151  *My dear Friend*

*Certainly this place is a little solitary but as a person cannot be quite*
*alone when he has even got himself with him, I get on pretty well. I have*
*employed my self in writing poetry, & as I go to bed at 8 oClock time passes*
5  *quicker that it otherwise might. Yesterday I had a letter from Whitton to*
*invite me to his house. Of course the answer was neg<    > I wrote to say*
*that I w^d resign all clai< > to the entail if he w^d allow me 200£ a yea< >*
*& divide the rest among my Sisters . . Of course he will not refuse the offer . .*
*You remarked that in L^d Edgecumbe's hermitage I should have nothing to*
10  *talk of but myself, nor have I any thing here, except I sh^d transcribe the jeu*
*d'esprits of the maid. M^r Pilfold has written a very civil letter; My Mother*
*intercepted that sent to my father, & wrote to me to come enclosing the Money;*
*I of course returned it. Miss Westbrooke has this moment called on me; with*
*her sister. It certainly was very kind of her. Ad*

15                                              *The post goes yr aff*

[Address, page 2|
                  *Esq^r*
*T. Jefferson Hogg*
*R. Clarke's Esq^r*
*Ellesmere*
20  *Shropshire*

Some of the periods and dots on the *i*'s in this letter, although apparently in the same ink, are uniformly darker than the others and appear to have been added as a body following the completion of the letter. The periods apparently so added are those following *well*, line 3, *house*, line 6, *maid*, line 11, *sister*, line 14, *her*, line 14.

line 5. *that* (sic)

line 6. *neg<ative>* : seal tear

line 7. *clai<m>* : The *ai* can be seen on a section of the paper adhering to the remainder of the seal. So, too, with the upper part of *ea* in *yea<r>*, line 7.

line 10. *except* is written through *expect*.

line 14. *Ad[ieu]*

line 15. *y[ou]r[s] aff[ectionately]*. The final *f* drops down into a kind of abortive *y*. The complimentary close is written in a large hasty scrawl. As it has blotted in folding, the letter must have been folded immediately. The address, however, is written in a normal hand and in full.

SHELLEY, as we have seen, had called on Harriet Westbrook during the Christmas vacation, probably late in January.[1] We do not have any record of a meeting between the two following this January visit,

1. See sc 136 (Jan. ?19–?21, 1811), Commentary.

SC 151    but the above letter indicates that there must have been at least one such meeting. Eliza Westbrook ("Miss Westbrooke," line 13) and Harriet ("her sister") would hardly call on Shelley on April 18 as a result of his single visit in January.[2] And the reference "Miss Westbrooke" and "her sister" is clearly to people that Shelley and Hogg had recently discussed. Yet Shelley and Harriet can hardly have met at 15 Poland Street, for Hogg had not seen Harriet when he left London on April 16;[3] presumably, then, Shelley had called at the Westbrooks' house in Chapel Street. Furthermore, he must either have been there or at least have written to Harriet shortly before writing the above letter, for it can hardly be accidental that the visit took place immediately after Hogg's departure.

On the day preceding this visit Shelley had written to Whitton:

*As common report, & tolerably good authority informs me that part of Sir Bysshe Shelley's property is entailed upon me; I am willing by signature to resign all pretensions to such property, in case my father will divide it equally with my & My Mother sisters,& allow me now 100£ per an: as an annuity which will only amount to 2000£.: perhaps less.*[4]

Shelley is not, in this letter to Whitton or in the above letter, it should be emphasized, offering to give up the whole of the family estates but only "that part of Sir Bysshe's property" which was entailed upon him, i.e., some £80,000 out of a total estate of some £200,000. He would still inherit the remaining £120,000.[5] His object was, as later at the

2. "Miss Westbrooke," in accordance with customary English usage, probably refers to the elder sister, for Shelley normally follows this usage. See sc 152 (Apr. 24, 1811), line 70, sc 153 (?Apr. 25, 1811), line 26; sc 157 (May 8, 1811), line 42; but see also sc 153 (?Apr. 25, 1811), line 33. Harriet, home for the Easter holidays, was perhaps bringing Shelley money from his sisters. (Peacock, *Memoirs*, p. 64.)

3. Hogg states that he saw Harriet "for the first time" in Edinburgh after the elopement. (Hogg, *Shelley*, I, 253.) Nor had he seen Eliza. (*Ibid.*, p. 274.) It is possible that Eliza and Harriet had called at Poland Street when Hogg was out but Shelley and he seem at this time to have been almost inseparable.

4. Text from photoduplicate of manuscript in a folio volume of such duplicates which came from the library of Sir Buckston Browne. The manuscript is now in the Bodleian Library. The letter is endorsed "reced at 10 o Clock on 18" (i.e., 10 a.m.). It is followed by another letter by Shelley, dated (but not in Shelley's hand) "18 Ap? 1811," which shows that Whitton had replied immediately, asking Shelley to dine with him. Shelley, as he tells Hogg (line 6), declined. Hence, Shelley first wrote the letter offering to relinquish the entail and then that declining Whitton's invitation and not vice versa as the above letter seems to imply.

5. On the Shelley estate see White, *Shelley*, I, 394–395.

SC 151   settlement of 1815, to trade part of the estate for a fixed income. Shelley had not, as he tells Hogg (line 7), asked Whitton for £200 a year but £100. Presumably he was ashamed to tell Hogg — who tended to twit him on his impracticality — how little he had asked for. His father finally agreed to £200.[6]

The reference to "L<sup>d</sup> Edgecumbe's hermitage" (line 9) is puzzling. Hogg prints it as "Lord Mount Edgecombe's hermitage," as though the reference were to the estates (in Cornwall) of Richard Edgecumbe, 2nd Earl of Mount Edgecumbe; but we know of no connection between him and the Shelley family nor of any possible significance to the reference. A more probable explanation is that Shelley confused Lord Edgecumbe and Lord Egerton. On April 24 (sc 152, line 63) he speaks of Hogg as "the Hermit" (on the Bridgewater estates) and of possibly visiting him there. The Earl of Bridgewater was John William Egerton (1753–1849). Hogg, editing the letter some forty-six years later, perhaps did not recall the reference or remember the family name of the earl.

The letter bears no receiving house stamp but a Central Post Office (Inland Mail) stamp only. It must, therefore, have been collected by a postman ringing his bell on his return trip to the Central Post Office (a normal daily procedure for Inland Mail carriers).[7] As this street collection, however, was between 5:00 and 6:00 p.m. Shelley's comment "The post goes" may mean that the visit of the Westbrook sisters took place between these times. There is, however, some indication that they may have actually come earlier in the afternoon and Shelley used the approaching mail collection as an excuse to close the letter. The final lines are scrawled off in a hurry but the address is in Shelley's normal hand, and the periods and the dots on the *i*'s were apparently filled in later. Shelley possibly, after finishing the letter with a hasty flourish — excited by the appearance of his visitors —[8] folded it (as the blots indicate) but did not seal or address it. Then when the visitors had gone he may have opened it, checked it over, added the dots and periods, folded it again, and addressed it.

6. See sc 159 (May 14, 1811), line 11. See also sc 152 (Apr. 24, 1811); sc 155 (Apr. 29, 1811); sc 156 (May 8, 1811); sc 157 (May 8, 1811); sc 174 (Aug. 3, 1811); *Complete Works*, X, 416.

7. See "Postmarks and the Dating of Manuscripts," below, pp. 920–921.

8. As is perhaps indicated also in the slip "expect" for "except" (Textual Notes, line 10).

# The Carl H. Pforzheimer Library

SC 152  P. B. SHELLEY TO T. J. HOGG, APRIL 24, 1811

AL signed *P. BS.*, 3½ pages. Double sheet, folio (11.9 x 7.4 inches).
Laid paper. Watermark: [Britannia in crowned oval]|; countermark: GR| 1806|.
Seal: wafer, blue.
Postmark: (evening duty stamp, London): C·| AP 24| ·811|.

PROVENANCE: Thomas Jefferson Hogg; Major R. J. Jefferson Hogg (Sotheby,
June 30, 1948, lot 14). *De Ricci 50* (p. 123).

*Wednesday*

*My dear Friend*

    *You have with wonderful sagacity (no doubt) refuted an argument of
mine whose very existence I had forgotten.* ⟨ ⟩ *Something singularly concieted*
5  *no doubt by the remarks you make on it. Fine flowery language you say—
Well. I can't help it   you see me in my weakest moments, all I can tell you
of it is that I certainly was not laughing as you conjecture   this circumstance
may go against me, I do not know that it will however, as I have by no means
a* precise *idea of what the subject of this composition was. ——   The*
10  *Galilean is not a favorite of mine. So far from owing him any thanks for his
favors, I cannot avoid confessing that I owe a secret grudge to his carpentership the reflecting part of the community, that part in whose happiness we have
so strong an interest, certainly do not require his morality which when there is
no* vice *fetters* vertue: – *There we agree . . let this horrid Galilean rule the*
15  *canaille then . . I give them up, I will no more mix politics & virtue they are
incompatible. ——   My little friend Harriet W. is gone to her prison house . .
she is quite well in health, at least so she says, tho she looks very much otherwise I saw her yesterday, I went with her sister to Miss H's. & walked about
Clapham Common with them for two hours. the youngest is a most amiable*
20  *girl, the eldest is really concieted but very condescending; I took the* sacrament
*with her on Sunday; — .   You say I talk philosophically of her kindness
in calling on me., She is very charitable & good. I shall always think of it
with gratitude, because I certainly did not deserve; it & she exposed herself
to much possible odium. – It is perhaps scarcely doing her a kindness, it is*
25  *perhaps inducing positive unhappiness to point out to her a road which she
is inclined so nobly to follow; A road which leads to perfection, the attainment
of which perhaps does not repay the difficulties of the progress. What do* you

[ 754 ]

SC 152  *think of this; If trains of thought development of mental energies influence*
*in any degree a future state, if this is even possible, if it stands on at all*
30    *securer ground than mere hypothesis, then is it not a service .. Where am I*
*gotten. – perhaps into another ridiculous argument; .. I will not proceed,*
*for I shall forget all I have said, & cannot in justice animadvert upon any*
*of your critiques. – ——      I called on John Grove this morning. I met my*
*father in the passage, & politely enquired after his health, he looked as black*
35    *as a thunder cloud & said .. "Your most humble Servant!" I made a low*
*bow & wishing him a very good morning passed on. He is very irate about*
*my proposals. I cannot resign any thing till I am 21    I cannot do any*
*thing, therefore I have 3 more years to consider of the matter you mentioned. –*
*I shall go down to F.P. soon. I wait for M$^r$ Pilfold's arrival, with whom I*
40    *shall depart – He is resolved (the old fellow) that I shall not stay at F.P.*
*If I please, as I shall do, for some time I will .. this resolution of mine was*
*hinted to him .. "Oh then I shall take his sister away, before he comes". ——*
*But I shall follow her, as her retirement cannot be a secret .. This will probably*
*lead me to wander about for some time; You will hear from me however*
45    *wherever I am, if all these things are useless you will see me at York, or at*
*Ellesmere if you still remain there . . . The scenery excites mournful ideas.*
*I am sorry to hear it, I hoped that it w$^d$ have had a contrary effect. May I*
*indulge the idea that York is as stupid as Oxford. And yet you did not wander*
*alone amid the mountains .. I think I shall live at the foot of Snowdon ..*
50    *Suppose we both go there directly. – Do not be surprised if you see me at*
*Ellesmere .. Yes do for it would be strange thing. —— I am now nearly*
*recovered. Strange. Florian could not see the conclusions from his own*
*reasoning, — How can the hope of a higher reward, stimulating an action*
*make it virtuous if the essence of virtue is disinterestedness, as all who know*
55    *any thing of virtue must allow, as he does allow ⸪ How inconsistent is this*
*religion! how apt to pervert the judgement, finally the heart of the most*
*amiably intentioned who confide in it ⸪ I wish I was with you in the moun-*
*tains cd. not we live there? Direct to Poland S$^t$ 15 I write tomorrow to York.*
*Your affectionate friend*
60                                      *P. BS.*

**Shelley to Hogg**                                    *April 24, 1811*

SC 152   *Y*ʳ *Brewster is worse than stupid. he is provoking. Have you really* <u>*no one*</u>
*to associate with, not even a peasant a child of nature, a spider? — And this*
*from the Hermit, the Philosopher? . . . Oh you are right to laugh at me . . I*
*finished the little poem one of whose stanzas you said was pretty. – It is on*

65   *the whole a most stupid thing as you will confess when I some day inflict a*
*perusal of it on your innocent ears. —— Yet I have nothing else to amuse*
*myself with & if it does not injure others, & you cannot avoid it I do not*
*see much harm in being mad. —* <u>*You*</u> *even vindicate it in some almost*
*inspired stanzas which I found among my transcriptions to day . .*

70   *Adieu. I am going to Miss W's to dinner, Her father is out. I will write*
*tomorrow . .*

[Address, page 4]

*T. Jefferson Hogg Esq*ʳ

*R. Clarkes' Esq*ʳ

*Ellesmere*

75   *Shropshire*

line 4. ⟨ ⟩: one or two letters canceled

line 4. *concieted* (sic): see line 20.

line 11. *carpentership* concludes a line (as does *otherwise*, line 17). Often if Shelley ends a sentence at the end of a line he omits punctuation.

line 22. *on me.*: This period (and others) is in darker ink and was apparently added later.

line 23. *deserve; it &:* Shelley seems to have fumbled here; the semicolon makes no sense; the *it* seems to have started out to be something else; the ampersand is written over a letter.

line 23. *exposed:* probable reading. Shelley began with some other letters, then wrote over and smeared them.

line 29. It is difficult to say whether Shelley intends his underlining to cover *at all* or only *all*. His underlinings are often short strokes.

line 31. *gotten:* Shelley first wrote *gottn;* then he changed the second *t* into an *e* and inserted another *t;* the period and dash come under the final *n*.

line 51. *do* can be clearly made out on the paper adhering to the seal, as can the upper part of *I am*.

line 51. [a] *strange thing*

line 52. *Florian:* probable reading; the initial letter is blotted; Hogg reads *Florian,* perhaps remembering the reference.

line 54. *who:* Shelley began with some other letter, perhaps a *t*, and canceled it.

line 61. Lines 61–71 are written on page 4 on either side of the address.

COLLATION (selected passages).

T. J. HOGG, *THE LIFE OF PERCY BYSSHE SHELLEY*, I, 344–345. (Hogg's changes indicated by italics.)

line 9. "The Galilean is not a favourite of mine," *a French author writes. The French write audaciously — rashly.* "So far from owing him any thanks for his favours, I cannot avoid confessing that I owe a secret grudge to his carpentership — *charpenterie*. . . ."

[ 756 ]

SC 152 THAT the "argument" of Shelley's (line 3) which Hogg was refuting was a written argument is shown by Shelley's reference to it (line 9) as a "composition." The word "composition" seems to imply a separate work and not a letter — an anticlerical work, in "flowery" language (line 5), which could be taken as sardonic. But no "composition" by Shelley of this nature in the months preceding the above letter seems to have survived among the Hogg family papers. Hogg apparently took Shelley's manuscripts with him from Oxford to London and then to Ellesmere.

The pronouns referring to Harriet and Eliza Westbrook are somewhat tangled, but the emphasis is on Harriet. The sense seems to run as follows: Shelley and Eliza went to visit Harriet at Miss Hawkes's school at Clapham. (Environs of London, page 47.) Then comes a parenthetic reference to Eliza as "concieted" and "condescending" (line 20). The "her" with whom the sacrament was taken would seem by the semicolon and other evidence (see below) to refer to Eliza. But the next "her" and the "she" who is "charitable & good" (line 21) refer to Harriet, as Shelley returns to his main theme. Hogg was certainly aware that it was Harriet in whom Shelley was interested, for, although there are references to both sisters in the letters of the next few months, it is Shelley's "love" for Harriet that he "jokes" about.[1]

When did Harriet return to school, and what was the Sunday on which Shelley took the sacrament? Both dates have been obscured by Hogg's dating (followed by Ingpen) of a letter of April 20 as April 28. According to Sotheby's catalogue of the sale of the Hogg family letters on June 30, 1948, the postmark on this particular letter (beginning "I am now at Grove's") is April 20. As the letter was written in London and postmarked in London (for it is a dated postmark), the postmark probably indicates the date of composition. And this is borne out by Shelley's comment in the letter: "Yesterday, she [Harriet] was better, to-day her father compelled her to go to Clapham." Since the above letter (April 24) mentions visiting Harriet at Clapham (line 19) it must be later than this comment unless she went to Clapham (to boarding school), returned home, and then went back to school on April 23,[2] which

1. sc 174 (Aug. 3, 1811).

2. The above letter is postmarked April 24 in London. As it was also written in London, it was probably written on the same day. "Yesterday" (line 18), therefore, was probably April 23.

SC 152    seems an unlikely procedure. The probability is that Harriet returned to school on Saturday, April 20; and Shelley took the sacrament (in London) on Sunday, April 21. As Harriet was then at Clapham, the "her" with whom he took the sacrament must have been Eliza (who was perhaps trying to weed out his heretical views). Then, on Tuesday, April 23, he went with Eliza to Clapham to see Harriet.

The school attended by Harriet Westbrook (and Hellen and Mary Shelley) was on the north side of Clapham Common. A guidebook of 1801 refers to it as "Mrs. Fenning's boarding school for young ladies." "After passing the Church is a white house, with a court and grass-plat in front, fenced against the road by a balustrade." The school was taken over by a Miss Hawkes, and a town plan of 1815 records it under her name.[3]

The comment on "Florian" (line 52) is presumably a reference to one of the works of John B. Florian (Florian-Jolly), perhaps to *An Elementary Course of the Sciences and Philosophy* (2 volumes, London, 1806).

3. Michael Burgess, *The Chronicles of Clapham* (London, [1929]), pp. 41, 82. Burgess is quoting James Edwards, *Companion from London to Brighthelmston*, 1801. See also MacCarthy, *Shelley*, p. xv, and Dowden, *Shelley*, I, 140. MacCarthy's description is derived from a granddaughter of Mrs. Fenning's. Shelley indicated in a letter to Graham on April 23, 1810, that the school was close to Clapham Church. It was first on the south side of the Common and was moved to the north side in 1791. (Letter from Edmund V. Corbett, Borough Librarian, Metropolitan Borough of Wandsworth.)

SC 153    P. B. SHELLEY TO T. J. HOGG, APRIL ?25, 1811

AL unsigned, 4 pages. Double sheet, 4$^{to}$ (9 x 7.3 inches). Wove paper. Gilt edges.

PROVENANCE: Thomas Jefferson Hogg; Major R. J. Jefferson Hogg (Sotheby, June 30, 1948, lot 17). *De Ricci 51* (p. 123).

*My dear Friend*

     *Your two letters were delivered to me. — Believe me that I will not so soon give up for lost a being whom I considered so amiable. — I will not yet decide. Yet your criterion is to the point, & terribly just. — If <u>unequivocal</u>*
5    *traces of her having yielded to the guidance of the <u>first</u> motives can be found; are we then to despair .. But I quit the subject the experiment <u>shall</u> be made .. I abide by the result, I anxiously eagerly anticipate the moment of trial ..*

**Shelley to Hogg**                                      **April ?25, 1811**

SC 153

<sup></sup>

10   *Moment! ought it not rather to be years, or rather ought <u>years</u> even decide <sup>to</sup>*
*upon a question so important ——*
*You sent me some beautiful verses . . . But I am not accustomed to be flattered,*
*& you will make me either vain <u>past</u> bearing, or confused past recovery if*
*you talk so of my weak essays of procedure on the "steep ascent" of per-*
*fectibility Why! how dare I attempt to climb a mountain when I have no*
15   *guide to point out the path, but a few faint sparks which at intervals illumine*
*the gloom; to these even am I not more indebted to <u>you</u> than to myself.?*
*Certainly a Xtian <u>may</u> be amiable, she <u>may</u> be so, but then she does not*
*understand, has neglected to investigate the religion which retiring, modest*
*prejudice leads her to profess . . —.     But one who certainly <u>never has</u>*
20   *investigated the matter, seen the slight grounds upon which the existence of a*
*God rests; surely the glaring inconsistencies of Xtianity must strike her,*
*surely she can find Benefits enough to return thanks to a Creator for, without*
*having recourse to his <u>Son</u>, & the Holy G^t Otherwise by your criterion of*
*amiability that being would deserve our most fervent attachment who wor-*
25   *shipped all the Roman Pantheon, (old or new) . . I write tomorrow . . I am now*
*called to Miss Westbrook. I was too hasty in my telling my first unfavourable*
*impression she is a very lever girl, tho' <u>rather</u> affected . . — No! I don't know*
*that she is. — I have been with her to Clapham, I will tell you an anecdote. —*
*Harriet Westbrook has returned thither as I mentioned, they will not speak*
30   *to her, her school fellows will not even reply to her questions, she is called an*
*<u>abandoned</u> wretch, & universally hated which she remunerates with the*
*calmest contempt. My third sister Hellen, is the only exception, she in spite*
*of the <u>infamy will</u> speak to Miss W. because she cannot see how she has*
*done wrong . . . There are some hopes of this dear little girl, she would be a*
35   *divine little scion of infidelity if I could get hold of her . . I think my lessons*
*here must have taken effect —— I write tomorrow.*

line 22. *a Creator: a* is written through *God*, which has been slightly erased.

line 27. *[c]lever:* There is no initial *c*. There is a dot in front of *l* which is perhaps supposed to represent *c*.

line 29. *thither:* Shelley apparently first wrote *there.*

line 30. *school: sch* is written through some other letters. Shelley's writing often falters when he discusses Harriet. See sc 152, Textual Notes, line 23.

line 36. The dash after *effect* is extremely dark and thick.

# The Carl H. Pforzheimer Library

## Shelley to Hogg

**April ?25, 1811**

SC 153   COLLATION (selected passages).
T. J. HOGG, *THE LIFE OF PERCY BYSSHE SHELLEY*, I, 400. (Hogg's changes indicated by italics.)

line 17. Certainly a *saint* may be amiable;
line 20. the slight grounds upon which *these dogmas rest*, — surely the glaring inconsistencies of *every system of mythology* must strike her?

Surely she can find benefits enough to return thanks to *her* Creator for, without having recourse to *the mythological personages of superstition?*

THE above manuscript is unaddressed[1] and undated,[2] but it is clearly to Hogg, and the date can be determined by other evidence. Harriet went to Clapham on April 20; Shelley and Eliza visited her on April 23. The comment in the above letter, "I have been with her [Eliza] to Clapham," must refer to this visit of April 23, which was Shelley's first, and, so far as we know, only visit there with Eliza. Hence, this letter must have been written shortly after April 23. It might be argued from this reference that it was written before the April 24 letter in which the visit to Clapham is also mentioned and in more detail. But this is not necessarily so. Shelley often in these letters to Hogg repeats things that he had said in previous letters. And here he has a motive for repetition as he is rather relishing the romantic implications of these happenings.

The indications are, in fact, that the letter was written on April 25, coming between SC 152 (April 24) and SC 154 (April 26). (a) In the April 24 letter Shelley promises to "write tomorrow" (line 58). (b) The two themes of "amiability" and "despair" are begun in the above letter (line 3) and developed in the April 26 letter. And the repeated phrase "I write tomorrow" seems to promise a further development of the ideas of this letter. (Shelley had just been "called to Miss Westbrook," line 25, and, hence, was short of time.)

The fact that the letter was among Hogg's papers (see Provenance)

1. There is a trace of a red wax seal on page 4 which could have come from an address sheet. See below, fn. 3.

2. Ingpen in his edition of Shelley's letters dated it "about May 1, 1811," but in his later editing of the letters for the *Complete Works* he changed this to "?April 25, 1811." He does not give his reasons for either date. The "about May 1" conjecture, however, he must have based on the comment (line 29), "Harriet Westbrook has returned thither [to school at Clapham]," for he thought (mistakenly) that she had returned there on April 27. (See SC 152, Apr. 24, 1811, Commentary.)

SC 153  shows that he received it. But as it is unaddressed Shelley must have folded it inside an address sheet or another letter.[3]

What is the subject which called forth the discussion on "despair" and "amiability?" One's first impression is that it was Harriet Grove, that Harriet is the "being" (line 3) whom he will not give up for "lost." But if we note the changes that Hogg made in the text of the April 26 letter, it becomes clear that the "being" is Elizabeth Shelley. Both letters are, in fact, replies to Hogg's apparently agitated answer to Shelley's comments on April 20: "My sister does not come to town, nor will she ever, at least I can see no chance of it. I will not deceive myself; she is lost, lost to everything; Intolerance has tainted her — she talks cant and twaddle."[4] Hogg apparently wrote back to say that this statement — with its suggestion that Hogg had better give up hope — had reduced him to "despair," but that surely she was not hopeless, was she not "amiable" (i.e., liberal-minded and open to reason)? Shelley replies that she may be amiable but she certainly gives no evidence of independent thinking. He will answer further "tomorrow."

Shelley's own interests were, in fact, shifting to Harriet Westbrook, whose "persecution" at school (line 29), although overdramatized, did have some foundation in fact. A Mrs. Fields, who was also a pupil at the school, recalled in a letter in 1860 that Harriet had had a letter (presumably from Shelley) torn up by the head mistress and that she had been expelled. Southey had heard a similar story. From a letter by Harriet herself we gather that the reason for the persecution was her friendship for an "atheist": "You may conceive with what horror I first heard that

3. Shelley would normally fold one letter within another only if he had forgotten to mail the first of the two; but we know of no example of his having done so with any letters to Hogg; usually he mailed them shortly after he wrote them. On the other hand address sheets were customarily used if there was no blank space available on the letter itself (as is the case with the above letter; see Bibliographical Description).

One minor point of bibliographical interest may be noted. The folds on the above letter indicate that it was not folded within a sheet the same size as itself. Had it been so folded it would have the usual letter folds. As it is, the letter has been folded vertically in three and then doubled over to make a small packet about 4.4 by 3 inches. Furthermore, the trace of a seal (fn. 1) may show that not all the face of the letter was protected, as it would have been if it had been in a sheet the same size as itself or in a larger sheet. The indication is that it was folded within a smaller sheet and made a bulging packet. (Hogg apparently did not preserve address sheets.)

4. Shelley, *Complete Works*, VIII, 77. On the date see SC 152, Commentary.

SC 153   Percy was an Atheist; at least, so it was given out at *Clapham.*"[5] Shelley
does not mention any of this to Hogg. Perhaps he was trying to give the
impression that the "persecution" was the result of Harriet's romantic
interest in him, her boldness in calling on him, which, he suggested in the
April 24 letter might (line 23) have exposed her "to much possible
odium."

5. Dowden, *Shelley,* I, 149; Harriet Shelley to Catherine Nugent, Shelley, *Complete Works,* VIII,
295; see also Shelley to Elizabeth Hitchener, Oct. 27, 1811, and Eliza Westbrook to Shelley, June 11,
1811 (Ingpen, *Shelley in England,* pp. 276–277).

SC 154   P. B. SHELLEY TO T. J. HOGG, APRIL 26, 1811

AL signed *P B Shelley,* 5½ pages. Double sheet, folio (11.9 x 7.4 inches); single
sheet, folio (11.9 x 7.7 inches).
Laid paper. Watermark, double sheet: [Britannia in crowned oval]|; counter-
mark, double sheet: GR| 1806|; watermark, single sheet: GR| 1805|.
Seal: wafer, light green.
Postmark: (evening duty stamp, London): c.| AP 26|· 811|.
Notation, page 6: *Apr 28*

PROVENANCE: Thomas Jefferson Hogg; Major R. J. Jefferson Hogg (Sotheby,
June 30, 1948, lot 15). *De Ricci 52* (p. 123).

*My dear Friend*
        *You indulge despair;* why *do you so . . I will not philosophize, it is
perhaps a poor way of administering comfort to say that you* ought *not to
be in need of it . . I fear the despair which springs from dissapointed hope,*
5   *is a passion a passion too which is least of all reducible to reason . . But it is a
passion it* is *independent of volition, it is the necessary effect of a cause which*
must *I fear continue to operate – wherefore then do I ask* why *you indulge
despair. — And what shall I tell you, which can make you happier, which
can alleviate even solitude & regret . . Shall I tell you the truth; . . oh you are*
10  *too well aware of that or you would not talk of despair – Shall I say the time
may come when happiness shall dawn upon a night of wretchedness . . . Why
should I be a false prophet if I said this, I do not know, except on the general
principle that the evils in this world powerfully overbalance its pleasures.
How then could I be justified in saying this – I will tell you to cease to think .*

SC 154   *to cease to feel I will tell you to be any thing but what you are; & I fear you*
*must obey the command before I can talk of hope .. —   I find there can be*
*bigots in Atheism as well as Religion,   I perhaps may be classed with the*
*former, I have read your letter attentively — Yet all Xtians do judge of us in*
*the way which you reprehend, faith is one of the highest moral virtues, the*
20   *foundation indeed upon which all others must rest, & Christians think that*
*he who has neglected to cultivate this, has not performed one third of the*
*moral duties, as Bp. Warburton dogmatically asserts. — The Xtians then,*
*by this very faith without which they c^d not be Xtians think the most virtuous*
*Atheist must have neglected one third of the moral duties .. If then a Xtian,*
25   *the most amiable of them, regards the best Atheist as far from being virtuous,*
*has not an Atheist reason to suspect the amiability of a system which incul-*
*cates so glaringly uncharitable opinions; — can a being amiable to a high*
*degree possessed of course of judgement without which amiability would be*
*in a poor way, hold such opinions as these? Supposing even they were*
30   *supported by reason they ought to be suspected, as leading to a conclusion ad*
*absurdum, since however they combine irrationality & absurdity with effects*
*on the mind most opposite to retiring amiability are they not to be more than*
*suspected. Take Christianity lop off all the disgusting excrescencies, or*
*rather adjuncts retain virtuous precepts, qualify selfish dogmas, (I would*
35   *even allow as much irrationality as amiability could swallow but uncombined*
*with immorality & self-conceitedness,) do all this, & I will say it is a system*
*which can do no harm, & indeed is highly requisite for the vulgar . . . But*
*perhaps it is best for the latter that they should have it as their fathers gave*
*it them, that the amiable the enquiring should reject it altogether. —— Yet*
40   *I will allow that it may be consistent with amiability when amiability does*
*not know the deformity of the wretch which it really is as we behold it. —*
*I cannot judge of Christianity by the flowers which are scattered here &*
*there .. You omit the mention of the weeds, which grow so high that few*
*botanists can see the flowers; & those who do gather the latter, are frequently*
45   *I fear tainted with the pestilential vapor of the former. The argument of*
*supremacy is really amiable, without that I should give up the remotest*
*possibility of success .. Yet that applies but to the existence of a Creator, that*
*is inconsequential, the enquirer here the amiable enquirer does not pause*

[ 763 ]

SC 154   *at the world lest she should be left supreme, she advances one step higher not*
50      *being aware, or not chusing to be aware of the infinity of the staircase which*
        *she ascends. — This is irrational but it is not unamiable, it does not involve*
        *the hateful consequences of selfishness, self-conceitedess, & the subserviency*
        *of faith to the volition of the believer, which are necessary to the existence of*
        *"a spurious system of Theology" — A Deist I will allow may be more*
55      *amiable than an Atheist, altho' in one instance reason is allowed to sleep,*
        *that amiability may watch .. Yet my dear friend this is not Christianity nor*
        *can that system stand excused on this ground as its very principle revolts*
        *against the dear modesty which suggests a dereliction of the reason in the*
        *other instance. I again assert, nor perhaps are you prepared to deny, much*
60      *as your amiable motive might prompt you to wish it that Religion is the*
        *child of cold Prejudice & selfish fear; Love of God Xt or the H.G. (all the*
        *same) certainly springs from the latter motive, is this Love. You know too*
        *well it is not, here I appeal to your own heart to your own feelings .. At that*
        *tribunal I feel that I am securre, I once could tolerate Christ .. he then merely*
65      *injured me .. he merely deprved me of all that I cared for, touching myself,*
        *on Earth, but now he has done more and I cannot forgive .. – Eloisa sai< >*
        *"I have hated myself that I migh< > love thee, Abelard!" .. when I hear a*
        *Christian prepared to say so, as her sincere sentiments, I then will allow*
        *that in a few instances, the virtue of Religion is seperable from the vice – She*
70      *is not lost for ever! how I hope that may be true, but I fear I can never ascer-*
        *tain, I can never influence an amelioration, as she does not any longer*
        *permit an Atheist to correspond with her. She talks of Duty to her Father.,*
        *And this is yours   Religion   You will excuse my raving my dear friend,*
        *I know you will not be severe upon my hatred of a cause which can produce*
75      *such an effect as this – — You talk of the dead .. Do we not exist after the*
        *tomb .. It is a natural question my friend, when there is nothing in life yet*
        *it is one of which you have never told me your opinion ..*
        *You shall hear from me again soon .. I send some verses. — I heard from Faber*
        *yesterday. All that he said was. —— My letters are arrived. G. S. Faber. ——*
80          *My dear friend Y$^r$ Affectionate*
                                        *P B Shelley*
        *15 Poland S$^t$*

# The Carl H. Pforzheimer Library

*Shelley to Hogg*                                    *April 26, 1811*

SC 154 [Address, page 6]

  *T. Jefferson Hogg Esq^re*
  *Post Office*

85  *York*

  *to be left until called for. —*

line 4. *dissapointed* (sic)

line 38. *that they* is crowded in between *latter* and *should* and was apparently written later.

line 50. *or not:* r is written over *f*.

line 52. *self-conceitedess* (sic)

line 64. *securre* (sic): The word is cramped at the end of a line.

line 65. *deprved* (sic)

line 66. *sai<d>*

line 67. *migh<t>*

line 69. *seperable* (sic)

line 81. *Shelley:* The signature trails off at the end. The second *l* is abortive and the *ey* is compressed.

COLLATION (selected passages).

T. J. HOGG, *THE LIFE OF PERCY BYSSHE SHELLEY*, 1, 358. (Hogg's changes indicated by italics.)

line 2. *I* indulge despair. Why do *I* so? I will not philosophise; it is, perhaps, a poor way of administering comfort *to myself* to say, that *I* ought not to be in need of it.

line 7. Wherefore, then, do *you* ask, Why *I* indulge despair?

line 14. *You* will tell *me* to cease to think, to cease to feel; *you* will tell *me* to be anything but what *I am;* and I fear *I* must obey the command before I can talk of hope.

line 16. I find there can be bigots in *philosophy* as well as *in* religion;

line 18. Yet all *religionists* do judge of *philosophers* in the way which you reprehend;

line 20. and *religionists* think,

line 22. The *religionists*, then, by this very Faith, without which they could not be *religionists*, think the most virtuous *philosopher* must have neglected one third of the moral duties. If, then, a *religionist*, the most amiable of them, regards the best *philosopher* as far from being virtuous, has not a *philosopher*

line 33. Take *any system of religion*, lop off

line 41. the deformity of the wretch*ed errors, and that they* really *are* as we behold *them*. I cannot judge of *a system* by the flowers

line 54. A *religionist*, I will allow, may be more amiable than a *philosopher*,

line 56. this is not *Intolerance*, nor can that *odious* system

line 60. religion is *too often* the child of cold prejudice and selfish fear. Love of *a Deity, of Allah, Bramah (it is* all the same), certainly springs from the latter motive;

line 64. I once could *almost* tolerate *intolerance,* — *it* then merely injured me *once; it* merely deprived me

line 67. When I hear a *religionist* prepared to say so,

line 71. she does not any longer permit *a "philosopher"* to correspond with her.

line 76. yet it is one *on* which you have never told me *any solid grounds for* your *opinions.*

SHELLEY, in the above letter,[1] takes up again the "despair" and "amiability" themes begun in the previous one. He is especially interested in answering Hogg's arguments on amiability, which Hogg had

1. On the Notation see SC 155 Apr. 29, 1811), Commentary.

[ 765 ]

SC 154    used to show that all was not hopeless with Elizabeth: even if she had Christian tendencies she might still be "amiable." But Shelley will have none of this. No Christian, he points out, advancing with obvious dialectical glee to the attack, can be "amiable" because Christians believe that lack of faith is a sin. Hogg can, if he so wishes, find this stated in Bishop Warburton (line 22), surely a sufficiently high authority.[2] (Shelley is reverting to the argument which he inserted in *The Necessity of Atheism*: since "belief is not an act of volition" but of reason it is illogical to attach "a degree of criminality to disbelief."[3] A deist can be "amiable" (line 54) because a deist, although believing in a creative God, arrives at his conclusions through reason and not dogma. A deist does not regard unbelief as sinful. But a Christian! Hogg — the implication runs — can expect neither pity nor understanding.

In the conclusion the argument shifts — typically — to Harriet Grove. Hogg — perhaps alarmed at the growing intimacy with Harriet Westbrook disclosed in the April 20[4] letter — had apparently asked about Harriet Grove. Shelley's reply shows no real interest in effecting a reconciliation.

The letters which Shelley had sent to the Reverend George Stanley Faber (line 78) perhaps contained further anticlerical arguments.[5]

2. William Warburton (1698–1779), the well-known scholar and divine, editor of Shakespeare and intimate of Pope. Shelley is perhaps referring to his *Doctrine of Grace*, 1762.

3. That this was one of Shelley's and not Hogg's contributions to *The Necessity of Atheism* is indicated by Shelley's letters of the time. See SC 139 (Feb. 6, 1811), Commentary.

4. Dated April 28 by Hogg; see SC 152 (Apr. 24, 1811), Commentary.

5. See SC 150 (Apr. 14, 1811).

SC 155    P. B. SHELLEY TO T. J. HOGG, APRIL 29, 1811

AL signed *P*, 2½ pages. Double sheet, 4[to] (9 x 7.2 inches).
Wove paper. Watermark: IVY MILL| 1810|. Octagonal embossed stamp: [crown]| BATH|. Gilt edges.
Seal (trace only:) wafer, red.
Postmark: (evening duty stamp, London): B·| AP 29| ·811|.
Notation, page 4: *May 1st*

PROVENANCE: Thomas Jefferson Hogg; Major R. J. Jefferson Hogg (Sotheby, June 30, 1948, lot 16). *De Ricci 54* (p. 123).

**Shelley to Hogg**                                    *April 29, 1811*

SC 155                                        *15 Poland S^t*

*My dear Friend ..*

  *Father's as fierce as a lion again. — The other day he was in Town ..*
*John Grove saw him, succeeded in flattering him into a promise that he w^d*
5 *allow me 200 £ per.an, & leave me, to <u>misery</u>. Now he has left town, &*
*written to disanull all that he before promised. – Nemus is flattering like*
*a courtier, & will I conjecture bring him about again. – He wants me to go*
*to Oxford to apologise to Griffiths &^ec — No ·· of course ·· ——*
*I suppose you are now at York. I wish I could come & join you, particularly*
10 *as I fear you think too much on subjects which are better for oblivion than*
*memory. Write some thing, will you make a novel, engage in some pursuit*
*which <u>can</u> interest you. I wish you would allow <u>me</u> to be your D^r Willis, I*
*would <u>not</u> as I thrreatned in the Piazza, confine you in a dark room; no I*
*would advise a regimen the very opposite to that which I then recommended. —*
15 *You say the scenery of Wales is <u>too</u> beautiful. Yet why not allow that to*
*interest you, why not cultivate the taste for Poetry which it is useless to deny*
*that you possess. — Indeed I wish to come to York. I <u>shall</u> as soon as I can;*
*not that I mean the strain detains me, as I am nearly well, but I want to*
*settle pecuniary matters .. I am quite well off in that now Remember it is idle*
20 *to talk of <u>money</u> between us, & little as it may do for politics, with us you*
*must allow that possession of <u>bullion chattells</u> &c is common; — Tell me*
*then if you want cash, as I have nearly drained you, & all delicacy, like*
*Sisters stripping before each other is out of the question ——. Our beautiful*
*Lady tells me that the post is ready. So adeiu.*
25        *Your affec P*
*I will write when <u>I hear from you</u> ... <u>this goes to York.</u>*
[Address, page 4]
*T. Jefferson Hogg Esq^re*
*Post Office*
*York*
30 *To be left until called for*

---

line 1. The heading is written in a large scrawl (about .7 of an inch high) across the top of the page. It must have been written after the letter was completed as it has blotted in the folding.

line 5. *to misery: to* is written over *the.*

line 6. *disanull* (sic): The second *l*, as often in Shelley, is much shorter than the first.

line 13. *thrreatned* (sic)

SC 155   line 24. *adeiu* (sic)                           line 26. *you: y* and part of *o* are on the paper
         line 25. The *P* goes off into a long hooked curve   adhering to the seal.
         to indicate the following initials.

O N ABOUT April 21 William Whitton, the Shelley family lawyer, sent on to Timothy copies of Shelley's letters to him and noted the difficulties he was encountering: "The Gent is very angry and has thought proper to lecture me on the occasion."[1] It was only after Timothy saw Shelley's letters, with their cool "proposals" to "relinquish his Fortune" and "abandon his Parents,"[2] that he began to harden his heart against his son. On Tuesday, April 23, he came to London and saw Whitton either on that or the next day (on the Thursday he was tied up with parliamentary committee meetings).[3] It was doubtless this interview with Whitton, who took a harsh, uncompromising attitude towards Shelley, that had made Timothy "fierce as a lion" (line 3). John Grove ("Nemus" — line 6 — is Latin for a grove) brought him around but when he got back to Field Place he hardened his heart again, perhaps under the influence of the unbending Sir Bysshe: "No terms but unconditional Submission can be admitted now."[4] It was perhaps Whitton who suggested (line 8) that Shelley should be made to "apologise to Griffiths" (Dr. James Griffith, Master of University College).[5]

Shelley is still trying to divert Hogg (then about to go from Ellesmere to be apprenticed to a conveyancer at York) from his obsession with Elizabeth — "subjects which are better for oblivion than memory" (line 10) — even implying jocosely that there is something of madness in his passion. (Dr. Francis Willis, line 12, was a physician in attendance on George III during his madness.)[6]

1. Ingpen, *Shelley in England*, p. 252. Ingpen does not give the date of Whitton's letter but Timothy answered it on April 22 (*ibid.*, p. 253) and would presumably answer so important a communication immediately.

2. *Ibid.*, p. 254; see also White, *Shelley*, I, 131.          3. Ingpen, *Shelley in England*, p. 255.

4. Sir Bysshe Shelley to William Whitton, Apr. 15, 1811, *ibid.*, p. 237.

5. On Griffith see White, *Shelley*, I, 76, 113, 618; Blunden, *Shelley*, p. 49.

6. For Willis see the *DNB*. The Piazza (line 13) was an open arcade in Covent Garden (Plan of London, C2, Front Endpapers) designed by Inigo Jones after the piazza in Leghorn. Byron comments in *Beppo* (v):

   For bating Covent Garden, I can hit on
   No place that's called "Piazza" in Great Britain.

SC 155      That the Notation (see also sc 154, April 26, 1811) was added at the
York Post Office is indicated by the fact that it must have been written
while the letter was still folded (unfolded, "May" is above the address,
"1st" below it, but when folded they come together). The custom must
have been to date on arrival a letter addressed only to the post office.
The Notation shows also that the letter took two days to go from London
to York; so, too, with sc 154.

SC 156  P. B. SHELLEY TO T. J. HOGG, MAY 8, 1811

AL unsigned, 3½ pages. Double sheet, folio (15.8 x 10.2 inches).
Laid paper. Watermark: [fleur-de-lis]|; countermark: 1808|.
Seal: wafer, brown.
Postmarks: 1. (receiving house stamp, London): BOND S[T]|; 2. (evening duty
stamp, London): A·| MA 8| ·811|; 3. Star stamp.
Endorsement, page 4, in the hand of T. J. Hogg.

PROVENANCE: Thomas Jefferson Hogg; Major R. J. Jefferson Hogg (Sotheby,
June 30, 1948, lot 18). *De Ricci 55* (p. 124).

*My dear Friend*
       *Again I write to you from S.B. — I have received very few of your
letters they have been sent to Portland S$^t$, & I cannot recover them there is
one to day from Yoxford, are you there? — You have reason, you have a*
5   *right to be surprised that I am not at Field Place, that I did not instantly
fly thither in spite of every thing I will explain as soon as possible; you will
hear that I am there in the course of a few days —— The estate is entirely
entailed on me, totally out of the power of the enemy, he is yet angry beyond
measure; pacification is remote; but I will be at peace vi et armis; I will*
10  *enter his dominions preserving a quaker like carelessness of opposition,
I shall manage a l'Amerique & seat myself quietly in his mansion turning
a deaf ear to any declamatory objections –. A few days ago I had a polite
note from M$^r$ Hunt Editor of the Examiner to invite me to break-fast. –
I complied, I dined with him on Sunday . . . he is a Deist despising J.C.*
15  *&c – & yet having a high veneration for the Deity, the consequence of our
acquaintance was a long argument, but he certainly means the same as an
Atheist,  they differ but in name . . He will not allow this; with him God is*

**Shelley to Hogg** **May 8, 1811**

SC 156  *neither omnipotent, omnipresent, nor identical, he destroys too all those*
*predicates in non, against which we entered our Protest, he says that God is*
20  *comprehensible, not doubting but an adequate exertion of reason (which,*
*he says, is by no means to be despaired of) would lead us from a contempla-*
*tion of his works to a definite knowledge of his attributes, which are by no*
*means limited .. Now here is a new God for you — In practise such a Deist*
*is this is an Atheist, as he believes that this Creator is by no means perfect,*
25  *but composed of good & evil like man, produces that mixture of these principles*
*which is evident. —— Hunt is a man of cultivated mind, & certainly exalted*
*notions; — I do not entirely despair of rescuing him from out of this dam-*
*nable heresy from Reason – Mʳˢ Hunt is a most sensible woman, she is by no*
*means a Xtian, & rather Atheistically given; — It is a curious fact that they*
30  *were married when they were both Wesleyan Methodists & subsequently*
*converted each other .. Solitude is most horrible; in despite of the αφιλαυτια*
*which perhaps vanity has a great share in, but certainly not with my own*
*good will I cannot endure the horror the evil which comes to self in solitude ..*
*I spend most of my time at Miss Westbrooks, I was a great deal too hasty*
35  *in critisizing her character; – how often have we to alter the impressions*
*which first sight or first any thing produces; I really now consider her as*
*amiable, not perhaps in a high degree; but perhaps she is; –. I most probably*
*now am prejudiced for you cannot breathe you cannot exists if no parts of*
*loveliness appear in co-existent beings. I think were I compelled to associate*
40  *with Shakespeare's Caliban with any wretch, with the exception of Lord*
*Courtney, my father, Bᵖ Warburton or the vile female who destroyed Mary*
*that I should find something to admire; .. what strange being I am, how*
*inconsistent; in spite of all my basted hatred of self – – this moment thinking*
*I could so far overcome Natures law as to exist in complete seclusion, the*
45  *next starting from a moment of solitude starting from my own company as it*
*were that of a fiend, seeking any thing rather than a continued communion*
*with self . . . Unravel this mystery . . . but no. I tell you to find the clue*
*which even the bewildered explorer of the cavern cannot reach . . . I long for*
*the moment to see my Sister you shall then hear from me even oftener. I lost*
50  *three letters which I had written to you in my carelessness .. Adieu my dear*
*Friend, believe me ever attentive to you and Eliza. —*

SC 156    *I wish that vile family despotism the viler despotism of religion did not stand between the happiness of the two beings which excuse the φιλαυτια would constutute mine.*

55       *Adiu*                         *Y^r eternal friend*

*6 South. Build.*

[Address, page *4*]

*Single Sheet*

*T. Jefferson Hogg Esq^re*

*M^r Doughty's*

60    *Coney Street*

*York*

[Endorsement, page 4, in the hand of T. J. Hogg]

*a —*

*reced May*

*10    1811*

65    *T J Jefferson*

*T Jefferson Hogg*

line 24. *is this* (sic)

line 35. *critisizing* (sic)

line 43. *basted: boasted*

line 54. *constutute* (sic)

line 55. *Adiu* (sic)

COLLATION (selected passages).

T. J. HOGG, *THE LIFE OF PERCY BYSSHE SHELLEY*, 1, 368–371. (Hogg's changes indicated by italics.)

line 12. I had a polite note from *a man of letters, to whom I had been named,*

line 14. despising *superstition,* &c., &c., yet having a high veneration for the Deity, *as he affirmed. And, in* consequence, a long argument *arose between him and some of his acquaintance; that a Deist* certainly means the same as an Atheist;

line 17. with him *the Deity* is neither

line 19. against which *they* entered *their* protest.

line 22. which are *not unlimited.* Now, here is a new *kind of* God for you!

line 23. In practice, such a Deist as this, is, *as they told him,* an Atheist;

line 25. that mixture of these principles which is evident *everywhere. He* is a man

line 27. *and his friends* do not entirely despair

line 28. *His wife* is a most sensible woman; she is by no means a *bigot, but* rather *Deistically given.*

line 49. my *sisters;* you

line 50. Adieu! My dear friend, believe me ever attentive to *your happiness.*

line 52. the viler despotism of *society, could never* stand between the happiness of two beings. Excuse the φιλαυτια, *it* would constitute mine.

# The Carl H. Pforzheimer Library

SC 156    THIS letter records the first meeting between Shelley and Leigh Hunt, a meeting which Hogg obliterated from Shelley biography (Collation, line 12) by deleting Hunt's name and substituting for it "a man of letters, to whom I had been named."

This early period of acquaintanceship — their real friendship did not begin until late in 1816 — is noted by Hunt in his *Autobiography*:

> I first saw Shelley during the early period of the *Examiner*, before its indictment on account of the Regent; but it was only for a few short visits, which did not produce intimacy. He was then a youth, not come to his full growth; very gentlemanly, earnestly gazing at every object that interested him, and quoting the Greek dramatists. Not long afterwards he married his first wife; and he subsequently wrote to me while I was in prison, as I have before mentioned.[1]

According to Thornton Hunt this first meeting between Shelley and Leigh Hunt came as the result of Shelley's submitting a "manuscript poem" to Rowland Hunter, the publisher. The poem "proved by no means suited" to Hunter and Hunter sent him to "seek the counsel of Leigh Hunt,"[2] presumably thinking that *The Examiner* might be a more suitable medium of publication (for a work doubtless of a radical cast). Thornton Hunt does not give the dates of Shelley's encounters with Hunter but they must have taken place between the time of his arrival in London at the end of March and his first meeting with Hunt, which the above letter establishes as Sunday, May 5, 1811.

Shelley, however, had been in contact with Hunt before this. On March 2, 1811, he addressed a letter to him from Oxford informing him that his father was a Member of Parliament and "on attaining 21 I shall, in all probability, fill his vacant seat." He urged Hunt to form a coalition of liberals and reformers to defeat the Tories. Enclosed in the letter were a proposal for a meeting, at which such a coalition might be started, and "an address to the public." When, therefore, Shelley followed Hunter's

---

1. Hunt, *Autobiography*, II, 27–28.

2. *Ibid.*, II, 27. Rowland Hunter married the widowed mother of Mrs. Leigh Hunt, Mrs. Thomas Kent. He was "the nephew and successor of [Joseph] Johnson, the well-known bookseller in St. Paul's Churchyard" (friend and publisher of Mary Wollstonecraft). (*Ibid.*, I, 231 fn.) We do not know what the poem was that Shelley submitted to Hunter. Perhaps it was the mysterious *Poetical Essay on the Existing State of Things* advertised as "just published" in *The Oxford University and City Herald* on March 9, 1811, but of which no copy has been found.

SC 156    advice and wrote to Hunt, Hunt doubtless recalled this letter and invited the young poet to dinner.

Hunt had perhaps expected the conversation to turn on politics and poetry, but, as the above letter shows, it must have been mainly on religion, a topic probably developing out of an account by Shelley of his expulsion.[3] Shelley, it should be noted, now considers himself no longer a deist but an atheist[4] and is arguing against the case for a creative deity that he had supported in his earlier letters to Hogg.

Hogg has expressed surprise that Shelley has not left for Field Place. The reason for the delay is doubtless to be found in the comment "I spend most of my time at Miss Westbrooks" (line 34), a comment which shows that Shelley's interest in Harriet and Eliza ("Miss Westbrook") had changed in the brief period between their visit on April 18 (sc 151) and this letter (May 8) from a casual acquaintanceship into intimacy. Shelley must have been a very lonely young man after Hogg left London, as is, indeed, revealed in his obsession with solitude (lines 31 and 45). The comment, "I cannot endure the horror the evil which comes to *self* in solitude," we might note, anticipates something of *Alastor, or The Spirit of Solitude*, composed more than three years later. In fact, "starting from a moment of solitude starting from my own company as it were that of a fiend" (line 45) may have woven itself into the lines (on the solitary hero of *Alastor*):

> Startled by his own thoughts, he looked around.
> There was no fair fiend near him, not a sight
> Or sound of awe but in his own deep mind.[5]

The reference to a letter from Hogg coming from Yoxford (line 4) is puzzling. Hogg had been at Ellesmere and had left Ellesmere to go to York. If Shelley's statement is correct one can only suppose that for

---

3. Shelley was rather fond of giving such accounts. Three of them have been preserved, to Godwin, to Southey, and to Peacock. (See Edmund Blunden, "Shelley is Expelled," *On Shelley*, Oxford University Press, 1938, pp. 16–19.)

4. See also sc 154 (Apr. 26, 1811): "I find there can be bigots in Atheism as well as Religion, I perhaps may be classed with the former."

5. Lines 296–298. The same theme is indicated in the above letter in "αφιλαυτια" (line 31 — hatred of oneself) and "φιλαυτια" (line 53 — love of oneself). See also sc 158 (May 9, 1811), line 41, and sc 172 (July ?22, 1811), line 8, "philautian." See also Peck, *Shelley*, I, 426–427; White, *Shelley*, I, 195.

SC 156    some reason Hogg went to Yoxford before going to York. But Yoxford is a village on the east coast of Suffolk, equally remote from both York and Ellesmere. Did Shelley perhaps misread or pretend to misread Hogg's heading or a postmark?

Hogg claimed that his letters were "not so long or so numerous as his" (Shelley's),[6] but one would gather from Shelley's comments here that they were quite frequent and sometimes also quite long. A fair number of them seem to have gone to Portland Street (line 3).

Shelley's entry into the "dominions" of "the enemy" (i.e., Timothy Shelley) was almost as triumphant as he here anticipates.[7] "Vi et armis" (by force of arms) is from Horace.

Of Shelley's "wretches" (line 40), Bishop Warburton was the famed eighteenth-century scholar,[8] "Lord Courtney" was the third Viscount Courtenay of Powderham Castle, Devon (1768–1835). He was apparently not active in either political or religious affairs, but he had extensive estates in Ireland and seems to have been particularly harsh in their administration, and he had a reputation for dissolute living,[9] both characteristics calculated to excite Shelley's wrath. As to the "vile female who destroyed Mary" (line 41), we have only Dowden's (undocumented) note that "Mary was an unhappy girl known to Hogg, who had embodied part of her story in his unpublished novel 'Leonora.'"[10]

The comment (line 2), "Again I write to you from S.B." (i.e., "6 South. Build.," line 56), is probably a reference back to a letter of April 20,[11] "I am now at Grove's," addressed from Lincoln's Inn Fields.

6. Hogg, *Shelley*, I, 245.                    7. See sc 159 (May 14, 1811), Commentary.

8. See sc 154 (Apr. 26, 1811).

9. According to *The Gentleman's Magazine*, n.s. IV (1835), 670, Powderham Castle was entirely kept up by the revenue from the Irish estates. In the early 1820's extensive rioting in southern Ireland was precipitated by ill treatment of the laborers on these estates and a parliamentary enquiry was conducted on the subject. (*The Letters of King George IV, 1812–1830*, ed. A. Aspinall, Cambridge University Press, 1938, III, 300; *The Diary and Correspondence of Charles Abbot, Lord Colchester*, ed. Colchester, London, 1861, III, 328–329.) In 1831 Courtenay was declared Earl of Devon by the House of Lords, apparently a questionable decision. Thomas Christopher Banks, the genealogist, was sufficiently angered by it to write *A Letter to the Right Honorable the Lord Brougham and Vaux...* (London, 1831) on the subject, from which (e.g., pp. 22–23) we gather that Courtenay's reputation was somewhat unsavory.

10. Dowden, *Shelley*, I, 155–156 fn. See also sc 128 (Jan. 3, 1811), line 51, and *Shelley, Complete Works*, III, 318.

11. See sc 152, Commentary.

**Shelley to Hogg**                                   *May 8, 1811*

SC 156 John Grove had a house at 49 Lincoln's Inn Fields. One block from Lincoln's Inn Fields is the Southampton Buildings. Perhaps one of the Groves had a room or an office there. Number 6 is not listed in *Boyle's Court Guide* (1820), which may mean that it was an office.

The paper of this letter (see also SC 158) is a fine quality large folio. Presumably it was supplied by the Groves.

The Bond Street Inland Mail receiving house stamp shows that the letter was posted in London. As New Bond Street (the receiving house was at 25 New Bond Street) was between Southampton Buildings and the Westbrooks' house on Chapel Street, Shelley perhaps posted this letter on his way between these two points. The following letter (SC 157) also bears a London postmark of May 8, but of the two, the above was written earlier because Shelley has not yet recovered Hogg's letters (line 3) and in the following letter (line 1) states that he has.[12]

12. The Star stamp on this letter is of rare occurrence. Alcock and Holland write of this kind of stamp as follows: "Another group of stamps consists of varieties, usually in red, of a four pointed star. These are known from the 1790s to 1840, and Hendy states that they were used at the Inland Office of the London G.P.O. On letters of 1796 we have seen a small solid star, but there is no indication of its purpose . . . Hendy shows another stamp consisting of a solid star of the same shape as Fig. 1813 but with a circular frame. This variety and Fig. 1813 he states were used at the Inland Office of the London G.P.O. on letters wrongly charged." Figure 1813 corresponds to the Star stamp on the above letter.

SC 157 P. B. SHELLEY TO T. J. HOGG, MAY 8, 1811; P. B. SHELLEY, *WHY IS IT SAID THOU CANST BUT LIVE*

AL unsigned, including poem, 5 pages. Double sheet, single sheet, 4$^{to}$ (8.8 x 7.2 inches).
Wove paper.
Seal: wafer.
Postmarks: 1. illegible [possibly BOND ST.]; 2. (evening duty stamp, London): [?c]·| MA 8| ·811|.

PROVENANCE: Thomas Jefferson Hogg; Major R. J. Jefferson Hogg (Sotheby, June 30, 1948, lot 19). *De Ricci 61* (p. 36).

*I found this moment all your lettres they were in G. Portland S$^t$ – I blush when I write the directions to you. — How salacious a street! – So* <u>*you*</u> *are in Solitude, I wish I could be with you, I wish you cd. manage to*

**Shelley to Hogg**                    **May 8, 1811**

SC I 57   *come to Town. — 200£ per an .. is really enough .. more than I can want ..*

5   *besides what is money to me, what does it matter if even I cannot purchase*
*sufficient genteel clothes .. I still have a shabby great coat, & those whose good*
*opinion constitutes my happiness would not regard me the better or the worse*
*for this or any other consequence of poverty – 50£ per an. w<sup>d</sup> be quite enough ..*
*Why you will be a grandee .. when Heaven takes y<sup>r</sup> father you will be in*

10   *possession of immense wealth .., the sixth of 3000£ per an .. that perhaps*
*convertible from 3 into 5 per cent property — I should not know how to act*
*with such a store. — But no. I would not possess above half of it. – Yet well*
*do I see why you would not reject it; – you think it would possibly add* <sub>to</sub>

15   *the happiness of some being to whom you cherish some remote hope of approxi-*
*mation, union .. the indissoluble sacred union of love*

        *Why is it said thou canst but live*
          *In a youthful breast & fair*
        *Since thou eternal life canst gagive*

20           *Canst bloom forever there*

                         *possesses*
        *Since withering pain no power ⟨     ⟩*
          *Nor Age to blanch thy vermeil hue*
        *Since time's dread victor death confesses*

25           *Tho bathed with his poison dew*
        *Still thou retainst unchanging bloom*
        *Fixed tranquil even in the tomb. —*
        *And oh! when on the blest reviving*
          *The day star dawns of love*

30         *Each energy of soul surviving*
          *More vivid soars above ——*
        *Hast thou ne'er felt a rapturous thrill*
          *Like June's warm breath athwart thee fly*
        *Oer each idea then to steal*

35           *When other passions die*
        *Felt it in some wild noonday dream*
        *When sitting by the lonely stream*

**Shelley to Hogg**                                          *May 8, 1811*

SC I 57

> *Where Silence says mine is the dell*
> *And not a murmur from the plain*
40 *And not an echo from the 〈      〉 fell*
> *Disputes her silent reign*

*Excuse this strange momentary mania, I am now at Miss Westbrooke's*
*she is reading Voltaires Philosophique Dictionnaire. I am writing to you.*
*But I broke off a page ago . . . Have you hope, can you have hope, then*
45 *indeed are you fitted for an Orlando Speroso (if there is such an Italian word)*
*I have* faint *hopes I have some it is true just enough to keep body & soul*
*together; but you – . . I almost despair . . . you have not only to conquer all*
*the hateful prejudices of religion, not only to conquer duty to father,* duty
*indeed of all kind . . but I see in the back ground a monster more terrific . .*
50 *Have you forgotten the tremendous Gregory: the opinion of the world, its*
*myriads of hateful champions, its ten thousands of votaries who deserved a*
*better fate, yet compulsatorily were plunged into this – – I tremble when*
*I think of it . . . Yet* marriage *is hateful, detestable, – a kind of ineffable*
*sickening disgust seizes my mind when I think of this most despotic most*
55 *unrequired fetter which prejudice has forged to confine it's energies . . . Yet this*
*is Xtianity . . & Xt* must *perish before this can fall; I do < > now even*
*speak of Xt as Xt* is *but as the world have made him; for antimatrimonialism*
*is as necessarily connected with infidelity as if Religion & marriage began*
*their course together; – How can we think well of the world. Surely these*
60 *moralists think young men are like young puppies (as perhaps generaliter*
*they are) not endowed with vision till a certain age.*

[Address, page 6]

*T. Jefferson Hogg Esq*^re
*M*^rs *Doughtys*
*Coney Street*
65 *York*

---

line 1. *lettres* (sic)

line 22. 〈        〉: scratched and blotted out

line 40. 〈    〉: The canceled word, of which
about four letters were written, perhaps began
with *P.*

line 56. <*?not*> *now:* seal tear; *now* is on the
paper adhering to the seal.

line 57. *as the: as* is visible below the paper
adhering to the seal and *the* on it.

## Shelley to Hogg

SC 157   COLLATION (selected passages).
T. J. HOGG, *THE LIFE OF PERCY BYSSHE SHELLEY*, 1, 365–367. (Hogg's changes indicated by italics.)

line 9. When heaven takes your father you will *probably* be in possession — *as his eldest son* — of some £3000 per annum,

line 47. *I* have not only to conquer all the hateful prejudices of *superstition*,

line 53. Yet marriage, *Godwin says*, is hateful, detestable.

line 55. This is *the fruit of superstition*, and *superstition* must perish before this can fall! *For men never* speak *of the author of religion* as *of what he really was*, but as *being what* the world have made him. Anti-matrimonialism is as necessarily connected with *scepticism* as if

THIS letter (in Hogg's text) has been placed out of sequence by Shelley's editors. Hogg dated it "Post-mark, May 2, 1811."[1] Ingpen, in his edition of the letters, suggested "May ?12," in which he was followed by de Ricci. In the *Complete Works* Ingpen changed this to "May ?18." The (London) postmark, however — which Ingpen had not seen as the manuscript was not available to him — reads "May 8." As we have seen the letter was written later in the day, following Shelley's discovery of Hogg's misdirected letters. (The letters had gone to Great Portland Street in mistake for nearby Poland Street.[2])

The letter, furthermore, was written in whole or in part at the Westbrooks' (line 42), 23 Chapel Street. The paper it is written on is much inferior to that usually used by Shelley and stands in particular contrast to that of sc 156 and sc 158, both of which were probably on the Groves' paper.

Putting sc 156 and the above letter together we might speculate on the following sequence of events. Shelley first wrote the preceding letter (sc 156) at Southampton Buildings, then left for Poland Street, discovered that Hogg's letters had been at Great Portland Street (or Portland Street), and either began the above letter at Poland Street or at the Westbrooks': "I found this moment all your lettres." If he began it at his Poland Street lodgings then he must have broken off in the middle (lines 42, 44) and left for the Westbrooks', taking the letter with him. On the way he would pass the Bond Street receiving house for the Inland Mail in New Bond

1. Hogg, *Shelley*, I, 214.

2. Great Portland Street is but two blocks from Poland Street; a small street called simply Portland runs into Poland Street. (Plan of London, B1, Front Endpapers.) The "salacious" street is neither of these but Coney Street (line 64). (On "coney" see the *NED*.)

SC 157 Street where the preceding letter (sc 156) was posted. On his way back from the Westbrooks' to Poland Street he perhaps posted the above letter at the same receiving house.[3]

Among Hogg's letters there must have been one answering Shelley's of April 29 (sc 155), in which Shelley stated that he might get £200 a year in the settlement with his father. Hogg had apparently replied that that was not sufficient, and Shelley is here (line 4) arguing that it is. Hogg has replied also to Shelley's letters of April 25 and 26 (sc 153 and sc 154) on Elizabeth. Shelley again tries to discourage him: Elizabeth is corrupted by religion, duty to her father, and deference to convention.[4]

At the same time Shelley is not opposed to love, with its "indissoluble sacred union" (line 16), and he inserts a little poem on the subject. Love is not for youth alone, the elderly — it is implied — need not despair, for love is eternal, beyond time and death. One might perhaps presume from the theme and its conjunction with Eliza Westbrook in the following sentence (line 42) that it was written to Eliza (who at twenty-nine probably looked to the nineteen-year-old poet as sufficiently middle-aged to require reassurances).[5]

The "indissoluble sacred union" however, does not include marriage. Hogg, we may note,[6] attributes Shelley's comments to Godwin. Shelley must have discussed with him the famous antimatrimonial arguments of *Political Justice*, e.g.: "Marriage is law, and the worst of all laws . . . an affair of property, and the worst of all properties. So long as two human beings are forbidden by positive institution to follow the dictates of their own mind, prejudice is alive and vigorous."[7]

3. For these various peregrinations see Plan of London, C1, B1, B2, A2, Front Endpapers.

4. "The tremendous Gregory: the opinion of the world" (line 50) is presumably a reference to the demands for moral and doctrinal orthodoxy of Pope Gregory I.

5. The poem does not appear in the Esdaile copybook; the above is the unique manuscript. Hogg misread *but* in the first line as *not* and thus obscures the poem's meaning (Hogg, *Shelley*, I, 214). We must not be misled by Shelley's later dislike of Eliza into failing to see his early regard for her; for example, see sc 156 (May 8), line 34.

6. Collation, line 53.

7. Godwin, *Political Justice*, 1st ed., II, 850. Godwin tamed the passage down somewhat in the later editions. (See Godwin, *Political Justice*, Priestley ed., II, 507–510, III, 219–220.) Shelley follows Godwin's views in *Queen Mab* (Note to V, 189). See also sc 169 (July 15, 1811), Commentary.

# The Carl H. Pforzheimer Library

**Shelley to Hogg**                                    *May 9, 1811*

SC 158   P. B. SHELLEY TO T. J. HOGG, MAY 9, 1811

AL signed *P* ⟨   ⟩, 3¾ pages. Double sheet, folio (15.8 x 10.2 inches).
Laid paper. Watermark: [fleur-de-lis]|; countermark: 1808|.
Seal: wax, red.
Postmark: (evening duty stamp, London)*:* A·| MA 9| ·811|.

PROVENANCE: Thomas Jefferson Hogg; Major R. J. Jefferson Hogg (Sotheby,
June 30, 1948, lot 20). *De Ricci 56* (p. 124).

*Have you forgotten it. have you forgotten that "laws were not made for*
*men of honor" – ? Your memory may fail, it is human . . . but the infernal*
*conclusion you have drawn, which I see you cannot will not admit is too*
*much. There are some points on which reasoning is inefficient to convince*
5   *the mind, no one could persuade me of that tortoise & Achilles business even*
*altho'they might say that I must believe it, because they had proved it, & I*
*c^d find no flaw in their reasoning. I could not endure the bare idea of marriage*
*even if I had no arguments in favor of my dislike . . but I think that I have.*
*I shall begin a la Faber, how far I proceed thus you have to judge: – Your*
10   *first assertion on which stands all the rest, does not profess to be founded on*
*proof but the long established opinion, uncontroverted, undisputed except by*
*occasional characters of brilliancy or darkness . . "that it is a duty to comply*
*with the established laws of y^r country" . . . This I deny . . Then virtue does*
*not exist . . or if it does, exists in so indefinite a manner, Protean like so*
15   *changes its appearance with every varying climate that what a crime in*
*England becomes not merely venial, perhaps praiseworthy at Algiers that*
*each petty river, each chain of mountains, an arm of the sea constitutes a line*
*of distinction between two different kind of duties, to both of which it is*
*requisite that virtue should adapt itself . . . What constitutes real virtue*
20   *motive or consequence.? surely the former. in proportion as a man is selfish*
*so far has he receded from the motive which constitutes virtue; I have left the*
*proof to Aristotle . . shall we take Godwin's criterion, expediency . . oh*
*surely not. — Any very satisfactory general reform is I fear impracticable,*
*human nature taken in the mass, if we compare it with instances of individual*
25   *virtue is corrupt beyond all hope. for these laws are necessary, these are not*
*men of honor, they are not beings capable of exalted notions of virtue, they*
*cannot feel the passions of soft tenderness the object of whose regard is distinct*

[ 780 ]

**Shelley to Hogg**            **May 9, 1811**

SC 158   *from selfish desire; – is it right that of these the world should be composed?*
*certainly not, were the evil to be obviated —— but it is not to be obviated, all*
30   *essays of benevolent reformists have failed. — Any step however small towards*
*such obviation is however good, as it tends to produce that, which tho impos.*
*yet were it poss. w^d be desirable. On this plan then do I recommend anti-*
*matriomonialism. it is a feeling which (as we take it, & as it is now the sub^t*
*of discussion) can at once be experienced by minds which at least adore virtue*
35   *it is then of general application & if every one loved then every one would be*
*happy .. this is impossible, but certain it is that the more ~~the~~ who love, the*
*more are blest. Shall then the world step forward, that world which wallows*
*in selfishness & every hateful passion, the consequence of an abuse of reason,*
*shall that world give laws to souls who smile superior to its palsying influence,*
40   *who let the tempest of prejudice rave unheeded happy in the consciousness*
*of the αφιλαυτια of motive. Oh no —— can you compare Eloisa & a ruffian ..*
        *self*
*Eloisa who sacrifised all for another, McHeath who sacrifised every other for*
*himself. These motives are wide apart as the Antipodes, wide as the characters*
45   *themselves, wide as virtue & vice .. take then your criterion & measure by*
*that . . . For Gods' sake if you want more argument read the marriage*
*service before you think of allowing an amiable beloved female to submit to*
*such degradation —. But you are convinced before, but I do not admire the*
*source of conviction – It is knight-like. I am no admirer of knights their*
50   *obedience was not founded on reason; & if we were errands you should have*
*the tilting all to yourself — Now my <   > friend what can you want with*
*600£ per an.   surely you, with any amiable being could easily live on half:*
*believe me, these are very secondary considerations; — There stay, I am*
*wandering but is the Antigone immoral. Did she wrong when she acted in*
55   *direct in noble violation of the laws of a prejudiced society. You will I know*
*have the candor to acknowlegde that y^r premise will not stand & I now most*
*perfectly agree with you that political affairs are quite distinct from morality,*
*that they cannot be united —— Tomorrow I go to Field Place; direct hence-*
*forward there till you here again as if they have removed Eliza, I shall follow*
60   *my letters will then be more interesting, as they will be filled with what is*
*equally so to us .. Heaven defend us from a dissapointment —— The Misses*

# The Carl H. Pforzheimer Library

SC 158   *Westbrooke are now very well, I have arranged a correspondence with them, when I will impart more of the character of the eldest Believe me y<sup>r</sup> most affectionate P⟨ ⟩———*

65   *Direct until further orders to Captain Pilfold*
*Cuckfield*
*Sussex*
[Address, page 4]
*Single Sheet*
*T. Jefferson Hogg Esq<sup>re</sup>*
70   *M<sup>rs</sup> Doughty's*
*Coney Street*
*York*

line 14. *does: d* is written through *ex.*
line 15. *what* [is] *a crime*
line 32. *antimatriomonialism* (sic)
line 36. *who* is written through another word or beginning of a word, possibly *the.*
line 43. *sacrifised* (sic)
line 50. *errands* (sic)
line 51. *tilting:* seal tear. *til* is visible through the seal.
line 51. *my* ⟨ ⟩: seal tear
line 56. *acknowlegde* (sic)

line 59. *here* (sic)
line 60. *then be . . . affectionate P* ⟨ ⟩: written vertically on page 4 opposite the address. Shelley's underlining is very thick and has blotted in the folding. *P* ⟨ ⟩ looks at first as though it had been crossed out but this is due to a blotted imprint from the *ff* of *affectionate.*
line 61. *dissapointment* (sic)
line 64. *affectionate P* ⟨ ⟩———: *P* ⟨?*BS*⟩
line 65. *Direct . . . Sussex* is written below the address and upside down on either side of the seal.

COLLATION (selected passages).
T. J. HOGG, *THE LIFE OF PERCY BYSSHE SHELLEY*, 1, 415. (Hogg's changes indicated by italics.)

line 61. equally so to *both.* Heaven defend *me* from a disappointment!

HOGG dates this letter "Cuckfield, August 9, 1811." Ingpen, following a suggestion by W. M. Rossetti, dates it "Cuckfield, [?May 13, 1811]." Hogg must have misread the postmark, taking the sorting table initial A as the designation of month. The A of MA is slightly blurred but quite decipherable, and the postmark is unquestionably May 9. Furthermore, the letter must have been written in London and not in

SC 158   Cuckfield because it bears only a London postmark. As the paper is the same as that of sc 156[1] presumably it was written at the Groves'.

Shelley, perceiving the need for at least one ally in his battle with Field Place, secured the support of his uncle, Captain John Pilfold, a formidable old sea dog, veteran of Trafalgar, then retired at Cuckfield in Sussex[2] (thirty-nine miles from London and about fifteen miles from Field Place).[3] Apparently Shelley's first plan was to go directly to Field Place accompanied by the captain. On April 24 (sc 152) he informed Hogg: "I wait for M[r] Pilfold's arrival, with whom I shall depart." But he then decided to go first to Cuckfield and (line 65) gives Hogg his address there. Hogg, perhaps reading the letter carelessly (some forty-six years later), may have thought that it had been written at Cuckfield.

Hogg's mistakes in regard to date and place have obscured the date of Shelley's departure from London for Field Place (via Cuckfield). Shelley's biographers and editors have presumed that the comment "Tomorrow I go to Field Place" (line 58) referred to Shelley's leaving Cuckfield for Field Place. But it refers, in fact, to his leaving London. And once we ascertain the correct date of the letter the date of Shelley's leaving London is set as May 10. Shelley, therefore, was in London from March 26 (the day following his expulsion from Oxford) until May 10. It was during this period that his interest in Harriet Westbrook began to kindle and his philosophical views developed from deism to atheism.

The substance of the above letter is a continuation of the anti-matrimonial theme of the previous letter (sc 157), which Shelley now views as part of the general question of legal authority, in opposition to Hogg's contention (line 12) "that it is a duty to comply with the established laws of y[r] country." (Hogg, although radical in religion, was conservative in politics.) Shelley's argument here he later developed more fully in his fragmentary *Speculations on Morals*:

Some usurper of supernatural energy might subdue the whole globe to his power; he might possess new and unheard of resources for induing his punishments with the most terrible attributes of pain. The torments of his victims

1. May 8, 1811, Commentary; see also sc 157 (May 8, 1811), Commentary.

2. For Pilfold, see "Harriet Grove's Family and Near Relations," above, pp. 500–501.

3. Paterson's *Roads* (1811), pp. 17, 34, 387; *Laurie and Whittle's New Traveller's Companion* (London, 1810), map 2.

SC 158   might be intense in their degree, and protracted to an infinite duration. Still the "will of the lawgiver" would afford no surer criterion as to what actions were right or wrong. It would only increase the possible virtue of those who refuse to become the instruments of his [tyranny].

MacHeath (line 43) was the philandering hero of Gay's *The Beggar's Opera*. Shelley, in expressing disapproval of him, indicates that, although he is against marriage, he is not in favor of promiscuity (as he was again to point out to Hogg in his review of *Memoirs of Prince Alexy Haimatoff* some three years later).

The "correspondence" (line 62) which Shelley had "arranged" with the Westbrooks went, as he failed to mention to Hogg, not to Field Place but to Cuckfield.[4] Shelley did not want his family to know of his growing intimacy with Harriet.

4. The only extant letter in the correspondence is one from Eliza Westbrook to Shelley on June 11 addressed to "Capt. Pilfold's, R.N.|Cuckfield, Sussex." (Ingpen, *Shelley in England*, pp. 276–277.) Shelley also received a letter from Eliza on May 19. (Shelley to Hogg, May 19, 1811, Shelley, *Complete Works*, VIII, 95.)

SC 159   P. B. SHELLEY TO T. J. HOGG, MAY 14, 1811

AL unsigned, 3¼ pages. Double sheet, 4$^{to}$ (8.7 x 7.1 inches).
Laid paper. Watermark: BUDGEN & WILMOTT| 1808|.
Seal (Shelley family crest): wax, black: [griffin's head surmounting coronet]|.
Frank, by Timothy Shelley.
Postmarks: 1. (mileage stamp): HORSHAM| 41|; 2. (morning duty franking stamp, London): [F]RE[E]| 16 [  ] 16| 1811|.

PROVENANCE: Thomas Jefferson Hogg; Major R. J. Jefferson Hogg (Sotheby, June 30, 1948, lot 21). *De Ricci 57* (p. 124).

*enclose to T. Shelley Esq$^r$ M.P.*
*Field Place May 14. 1811.*

*My dear Friend*
    *I now write to you from hence. I have at <u>last</u> reached the place of my*
5  *destination; – I know you will anxiously await this . . On my arrival I found my sister ill, she has been confined with a scarlet fever, the ignorance of these country physicians has I think prolonged her confinement, she is now much better, but scarcely able to articulate from a sore throat, you shall hear more*

SC I 59    *when I write again. I must acknowlegde that some emotions of pleasure were*

10    *mingled with those of pain when I found that illness had prevented her writing to me. – I have come to terms with my father, I call them very good ones, I am to possess 200£ per an . . I shall live very well upon it, even after the legal opinion which you enclosed . . I am also to do as I please with respect to the choice of abode; I need not mention what it will be. – When do you*

15    *come to London, at what time    a year, six months, four months? Faber will be written to today    you may depend upon the exertion of my palavering energies; –. It would be a strange I do know a stranger composition than would be the melange which you spoke of. Try . . compose it, I am sure I could not The Confessions of Rousseau are the only things of the kind that*

20    *have appeared, & they are either a disgrace to the confessor or a string of falsehoods . . probably the latter. But the world would say that ours were the latter, nor could I blame them for such an opinion as probable truth is to be the judge of testimony, & singularity must be improbable or it would not be singularity . . nor do I think that it has often come under the observation of the*

25    *world, that two young men should hold such arguments come to such conclusions, & take such singular criterions for reasoning . . . Is not the latter strangest. — — How goes on Leonora; I have heard nothing of her, I cannot get an answer from Munday: –   Do they tremble . . I thought the Abingdon printer was too stupid, & I defy a zealot to say it does not support Xt. If*

30    *an Author's own assertion in his own book make be taken as an avowal of his intentions it does support Xt . . You could not do more. Mine is not printable, it is as bad as la Necessite & would certainly be prosecuted . . all danger about prosecution is over . . It was never more than a hum – . I will tell you a peice of the most consummate hypocrisy I ever heard of – . A relation*

35    *of mine was walking with my Uncle, (who by the bye has settled matters admirably for me) . . says this Xtian . . "to tell you the truth I am an Atheist," – . . "Ah Ah" thought the Capᵗ "old birds are not to be caught with chaff" "are you indeed? was the cold reply & no more was got out of him . . I tell you this as the Capᵗ told it <    > Is this irrational being really convinced*

40    *<    > what we attained by the use of reason? <    > he is he is a disgrace to reason, & I am sorry that the cause has gained weakness by the accession of weakness . . But he is nothing no est professes no ism but superbism &*

**Shelley to Hogg**                                        **May 14, 1811**

SC 159  *irrationalism. — He ̶h̶a̶s̶ forbidden my intercourse with my sister, but the*
       *Cap^t brought him to reason, he prevents it however as much as possible,*

45     *which is very little . .      My Mother is quite rational . . she says, "I think*
       *prayer & thanksgiving is of no use. If a man is a good man, atheist or Xtian*
       *he will do very well in whatever future state awaits us." This I call liberality.*
       *You shall hear from me soon again, — I write to Faber: – I know you will*
       *excuse a longer letter as I am going to read to Eliza*

50                                              *Your ever affectionate friend*

       [Frank, with address, page 4, in the hand of Timothy Shelley]

       *Horsham, May Fifteen*

                       *1811*

       *T. J^n Hogg Esqr*
       *M^rs Doughty's*

55     *Coney Street*
       *York*
       *T:Shelley*

line 1. The blotting shows that this line was written immediately before the letter was folded.

line 9. *acknowlegde* (sic)

line 30. *make* (sic)

line 32. *la Necessite* (sic): probable reading. The first word is smeared and the second is cramped downward into the right margin.

line 34. *peice* (sic)

line 38. *indeed? was* (sic)

line 39. *<to me>*: seal tear

line 40. *<by>*: seal tear

line 40. *<If>*: seal tear

line 43. ̶h̶a̶s̶: Shelley perhaps intended to substitute *had* for *has*.

line 45. Shelley places quotation marks before *think* and *If* (line 46), as they begin lines, but not before *Xtian* (line 46) and *future*, although they also begin lines.

line 51. *Fif* is written through some other letters, perhaps *Six*.

COLLATION (selected passages).

T. J. HOGG, *THE LIFE OF PERCY BYSSHE SHELLEY*, I, 372–373. (Hogg's changes indicated by italics.)

line 27. How goes on *your tale?* I have heard nothing of *it. As for mine* I cannot get an answer from *L——*.

line 29. and I defy a zealot to say it does not support *orthodoxy.*

line 31. it does support *orthodoxy. I* could not do more, *and yet they say* Mine is not printable; it is as bad as *Rousseau*

line 36. says this *Wiseacre*, "to tell you the truth, I am a *Sceptic.*"

line 40. what *men have* attained

line 46. If a man is a good man, *philosopher*, or Christian,

# Shelley and his Circle : Manuscripts

*Shelley to Hogg*                                           *May 14, 1811*

SC 159   SHELLEY, as we have seen, planned to leave London on May 10 with
Captain Pilfold to go to Cuckfield. On May 14 he wrote the above letter to Hogg from Field Place. (It was addressed and franked by Timothy[1]
on May 15 and passed through the London Post Office on May 16.)
The period between May 10 and May 14 was occupied by negotiations
between Cuckfield and Field Place. "I have settled matters tolerably,"
Shelley informed his friend Edward Graham, "£200 per an .. free agency
&c. he looks rather blue today but the Capt. keeps him in tol. order."[2]

Shelley had, in fact, with Pilfold's help, gained all his demands.
Timothy had surrendered. "To go immediately to Field Place," to
"abstain from all communication with Mr. Hogg.," to be placed under
the guidance of a tutor appointed by Timothy, such had been Timothy's
stern terms on April 9 (sc 147). Shelley had countered with a demand for
£200 a year, "unrestrained correspondence" with Hogg, and freedom
in selecting his future profession.[3] He had not returned "immediately"
to Field Place; he came back at his leisure a month later. He had been
granted the £200 (line 12). He not only gained the right of "unrestrained
correspondence" with Hogg but turned the letters over to Timothy to
frank and told Hogg to "enclose" (line 1) to Timothy so that Hogg
might take advantage of the frank also. He was placed under no tutor.
He had the right to choose his place of "abode" (line 13) and hints that
it will be with Hogg in London.

One would gather from this letter that Hogg had proposed that
Shelley and he write a confessional account of the intellectual adventures
which had led to their expulsion. Shelley had written a new work, apparently a novel (line 31), sufficiently anticlerical to risk prosecution[4] (which
was no longer a danger in regard to *The Necessity of Atheism*).[5]

1. As were also the letters of January 6, January 11, and other letters.

2. Shelley, *Complete Works*, X, 416.

3. P. B. Shelley to Timothy Shelley, [Apr. ?13, 1811], *ibid.*, VIII, 62. See also Ingpen, *Shelley in England*, pp. 217, 232–233; Shelley to Hogg, sc 151 (April 18, 1811).

4. Possibly it was the same as the now lost novel *Hubert Cauvin* on which Shelley was working in January 1812 and of which he claimed to have written two hundred pages. (See Shelley to Elizabeth Hitchener, Jan. 2, Jan. 7, 1812, and Dowden, *Shelley*, I, 199.) Shelley had informed Stockdale as early as December 18, 1810, that he was working on a new novel of a radical character. (See sc 146, Apr. 6, 1811.) For the Abingdon printer (line 28) see Ingpen, *Shelley in England*, p. 147.

5. On April 13, 1811, Whitton wrote to C. and W. Phillips, printers of *The Necessity of Atheism*: "I have been informed that a prosecution is intended against you." (Ingpen, *Shelley in England*,

# The Carl H. Pforzheimer Library

*Shelley to Hogg*                              *May 14, 1811*

SC 159       The "relation" who informed Captain Pilfold that he was an
"atheist," was, as the comments show, Timothy Shelley. Timothy was
certainly no atheist but he did consider himself something of a liberal in
religious matters. He once subscribed for two copies of some Unitarian
sermons under the title of "A friend to religious liberty."[6]

The above letter, as we have noted, was addressed and franked by
Timothy Shelley. A further examination of the manuscript raises a question as to whether it was not also read by him. Only a section of the seal
remains but there is sufficient to show that it was the same as that used
by Timothy on two letters in our library, one to John Hogg, April 6, 1811
(sc 145), and one to William Whitton, January 23, 1815, and that it does
not appear on any of Shelley's letters in our library. As the letter to
John Hogg was written at Miller's Hotel in London, the seal must have
been one that Timothy carried on his person. So the probability is that
Timothy sealed this letter. If he did not seal it in Shelley's presence he
could also have read it.

In view of this possibility two other questions arise. Did Timothy
seal all the letters to Hogg that he franked? Was it part of the agreement
that Timothy should supervise the correspondence after the return to
Field Place? The answer to both questions seems to be no. The letters
of January 11 and 12, 1811 (sc 132 and sc 133), franked by Timothy,
were, as we have seen, almost certainly sealed by Shelley. That Timothy
did not supervise the correspondence is indicated by the fact that the
letter of June 4 (sc 164) was addressed by Shelley and not franked by
Timothy. Furthermore, if there had been such an agreement some warn-
ings about it would appear in Shelley's letters.

Nor, to take the other side of the picture, does the initial note
"enclose to T. Shelley Esq[r] M.P." mean that Hogg's letters were to be
read by Timothy Shelley. If Hogg so addressed his letters they would be
delivered under Timothy Shelley's frank and Shelley would not have to
pay a postal fee. Hogg had presumably so addressed his letters in December and January. Shelley is simply informing him it is still all right to do so.

p. 194 fn.) Timothy took the threat seriously (*ibid.*, p. 231) but Mr. Hogg's representative, R.
Clarke, did not (*New Shelley Letters*, pp. 28–29).

6. Dowden, *Shelley*, I, 5 fn. Unitarianism was then the creed of advanced liberalism. See also Medwin,
*Shelley*, p. 13.

SC 159      Hence, it is most unlikely that Timothy was generally given an opportunity to read the letters that he franked. But the evidence of the seal on the above letter cannot be discounted. And to this one can add the internal evidence of the letter itself. There would really be little point in Shelley's making the extended derogatory remarks of lines 34–45 about Timothy for Hogg's benefit. There is nothing quite comparable to them in his other letters to Hogg. Once one realizes, however, that Timothy might have been given the opportunity of reading the letter the impression grows that the remarks were intended for his eyes. They are similar to the insults of the verse letter to Graham of about the same date.[7] Shelley perhaps simply folded the letter[8] and left it for Timothy to seal, daring him, as it were, also to read it.

7. On the dating of this letter see Cameron, *The Young Shelley*, pp. 292, 343.

8. See Textual Notes, line 1.

SC 160    P. B. SHELLEY TO T. J. HOGG, MAY 17, 1811; P. B. SHELLEY, *TO THE MOONBEAM*

AL unsigned, including poem, 4½ pages. Double sheet, 4[to] (8.8 x 7.2 inches); single sheet, 4[to] (8.7 x 7 inches).

Double sheet, wove paper. Single sheet, laid paper. Watermarks: double sheet: CHARLES WILMOTT| 1809|; single sheet (Wilmott cipher): [posthorn in crowned shield]| *CW*|.

Seal: wafer, pink.

PROVENANCE: Thomas Jefferson Hogg; Major R. J. Jefferson Hogg (Sotheby, June 30, 1948, lot 22). *De Ricci 60* (p. 124).

*Field Place May 17 1811*

*My dearest Friend*

    *Your letters have never reached me, these sallies of imagination are not noticed by vulgar postmen, but you know my direction now. ——     Eliza*

5  *is quite recovered in health I mean, nor do I think her Xtianity of the most inerasible nature. It is indeed so little that she confesses the world to be the only reason of her yet retaining the mummeries; X[t] is not the Son of God, the world is eternal, there all is agreed, & in the speculative points of Religion she is atheistical as the most determined Xtomogue could desire . . . But*

# The Carl H. Pforzheimer Library

**Shelley to Hogg**                                     **May 17, 1811**

SC 160 *what is this speculation   a dry inactive knowlegde of what really is, unin-*
*fluencing the conduct, I had supposed that the annihilation of X$^t$ would*
*involve the fall of the world's opinion .. But the world's opinion must be*
*destroyed, after which Religion is of little consequence even if it does exist,*
*which is indeed not very probable, as there can then be no temptations to self*
15 *deception – – The opinion of the world, the loss of which is attended with*
*much inconvenience, with the loss of reputation which is by some considered*
*as synonymous with virtue; this is the supporter of prejudice . . . Eliza is*
*no more a Xtian than I am, but she regards as a sacred criterion the opinion*
*of the world, the discanonization of this saint of hers is impossible, until*
20 *some more worthy of devotion is pointed out; but where eyes are shut nothing*
*can be seen .. She asks: Am I wrong to regard the opinion of the world, what*
*would compensate to me for the loss of it? Good Heaven what a question ..*
*Is it not answerable by a word; if you were here by a look . . . I too have lost*
*her confidence, that confidence once so unbounded – but it is to be regained ..*
25 *Behold me then enthusiastic quixotic, resolved, convinced that things shall*
*be as I order it, that all my plans shall succeed that   but I shall anticipate*
*all your castle buildings .. so adeiu to the subject .. Why will you not send*
*me some poetry; I wish to see it directly ..*

*— To The Moonbeam*

30      *Moonbeam, leave the shadowy vale*
           *To bathe this burning brow*
       *Moonbeam, why art thou so pale*
       *As thou walkest oer the dewy dale*
           *Where humble wild flowers grow*
35           *Is it to mimic me?*
           *But that can never be*
           *For thine orb is bright*
           *And the clouds are light*
       *That at intervals shadow the star studded night*

40      *Now all is deathy still on Earth*
           *Natures tired frame reposes*
       *And ere the golden mornings birth*

**Shelley to Hogg**                                              **May 17, 1811**

SC 160

It's radiant hues discloses
Flies forth its balmy breath,
45   But mine is the midnight of death
And natures morn
To my bosom forlorn
Brings but a gloomier night, implants a deadlier thorn

Wretch! suppress the glare of madness
50      Struggling in thine haggard eye
For the keenest throb of sadness
Pale despairs most sickening sigh
Is but to mimic me
And this must ever be
55      When the twilight of care
And the night of despair
Seem in my breast but joys to the pangs that walk there

Here is raphsody .. now I think that after this you ought to send me poetry ...
Pray which of the Miss W's do _you_ like .. they are both very amiable, I do
60   not know which is favoured with your preference. As to your manner; call
it _manner_ if you will, perhaps it is proper thus to express, a thing which I
thought was inexpressible call it so then, for I do not know other name .—
How gets on your onion-loving Deist, pray what is there in onions & red
herrings which can make her less amiable .. she is not very handsome either
65   Oh that is all imagination —— I have written to Faber, I wrote the moment
yʳ letter came & make no doubt but he will think me a very good young man.
—— I Cannot so deeply see into the inferences of actions as to come to the
odd conclusion which you observe on, in the matter of Miss W. Where we
have _facts_, they are superior to all the reasoning in the world. I should like
70   <    > hear your Faberesation

Your ever affectionate

line 1. The bar of the 7 curves down in the middle, which makes it look somewhat like a "y"; a similar tendency appears in other sevens by Shelley, for instance, that in sc 135 (Jan. 17, 1811), line 1.

line 5. _recovered_ is the last word on the line. Shelley frequently considers ending on the margin as a kind of punctuation. So, too, with _inexpressible_, line 62.

## *Shelley to Hogg*                                        *May 17, 1811*

SC 160  line 5. *the* written through *mo*
line 6. *inerasible* (sic)
line 10. *knowlegde* (sic)
line 27. *adeiu* (sic)
line 58. *raphsody* (sic)

line 69. *the reasoning: the* can be made out from the paper adhering to the seal; so, too, with *hear*, line 70.

line 70. <to> *hear*: see above, line 69.

COLLATION (selected passages).
T. J. HOGG, *THE LIFE OF PERCY BYSSHE SHELLEY*, I, 376–377. (Hogg's changes indicated by italics.)

line 5. (Hogg omits from "I mean" to "nature," line 6).

line 6. *It is most true that the mass of mankind are Christians only in name; their religion has no reality.* So little, indeed, that *they almost* confess the world to be the only reason *for their* yet retaining *their* mummeries. Christ is not the Son of God: the world is eternal, *their practice would seem to declare.* There *almost* all *are* agreed, and in the speculative points of religion *they seem to be as* Atheistical as the most determined *Materialist* could desire.

line 11. *One would suppose* that the annihilation of *superstition* would involve the fall of the world's opinion; but *if* the world's opinion *were* destroyed, *superstition would be* of little consequence,

line 17. *Certain members of my family are* no more Christians than *Epicurus himself was;* but *they regard* as a sacred criterion the opinion of the world; the discanonisation of this saint of *theirs* is impossible until some*thing* more worthy of devotion is pointed out;

line 21. *They would ask, are we* wrong to regard the opinion of the world; what would compensate *us* for the loss of it?

line 23. word? *So I have but little of their* confidence: *the* confidence *of my sister even is diminished,*

line 25. *But enough of this! In letters,* behold me enthusiastic,

line 70. Your *letter to F—.*

COLLATION (excluding incidentals of punctuation).
TO THE MOONBEAM, SHELLEY, *COMPLETE WORKS*, III, 71–72 (ESDAILE COPYBOOK).

line 32. Moonbeam cool, why
line 33. glidest along the midnight vale,
line 34. dewy flowerets grow?
line 37. thy path
line 39. star-studded
line 42. Yet in the
line 43. uncloses
line 44. her balmy

line 45. Death,
line 46. Nature's morn,
line 49. Suppress
line 52. Despair's
line 54. can ever
line 55. darkness of
line 56. death of
line 57. wake there.

The above letter is unaddressed and unpostmarked; yet it has been folded and sealed. As its provenance shows that Hogg received it, it must have gone through the mails inside an address sheet, or, less likely, another letter.[1] Curiously enough, however, the outside sheet is

1. We know of no instance in which Shelley placed one letter inside another, but address sheets were fairly common.

SC 160    blank and hence could have been used for the address. Perhaps Shelley sealed it and then presented it to his father for franking, and his father placed it inside another sheet before franking and addressing it.

For a second time one or more of Hogg's letters have been undelivered (line 3),[2] this time apparently as a result of some humorous twist to the Cuckfield address, a "sally of imagination" (line 3) indulged in by Hogg. Hogg had been informed of the Cuckfield address on May 9 (sc 158) and of the transition to Field Place — "you know my direction now" — on May 14 (sc 159).

After some conversation with Elizabeth, Shelley is now able to give Hogg a brighter picture. She is not irrevocably lost to enlightenment. She even has atheistic tendencies. The only enemy is convention and this Hogg could dissipate by a "look" (line 23).

One would normally assume — as Hogg was supposed to — that the poem (lines 29–57) was of recent composition, but it appears also in the Esdaile copybook (see Collation) and is there dated "September 23, 1809."[3] Hence, although Shelley seems to be hinting a source of inspiration in the "Miss W's" (line 59), it was a product of the early period of his romance with Harriet Grove.

The last three lines of each stanza, especially the final line (e.g., line 39) with its curious compressed, leaping rhythm, anticipate (metrically) some of Shelley's later lyrics, for instance, the Chorus of Spirits in the fourth act of *Prometheus Unbound:*

> And our singing shall build
> In the void's loose field
> A world for the Spirit of Wisdom to wield;
> We will take our plan
> From the new world of man,
> And our work shall be called the Promethean.

---

2. See sc 157 (May 8, 1811) and Commentary. Ingpen assumed that there was only one batch of lost letters and hence dated this May 8 letter wrongly as "May ?18," presuming that it followed the above letter. (Shelley, *Complete Works*, VIII, 92 fn.) Shelley received a letter from Hogg at Cuckfield on May 19. (*Ibid.*, p. 94.)

3. *Ibid.*, III, 316. See also sc 166 (June 18–19, 1811), Commentary. In spite of the date, however, the Esdaile copybook text almost certainly represents a later revision than that of the above manuscript. (See "The Provenance of Shelley and his Circle Manuscripts," below, p. 898.)

4. Lines 153–158.

# The Carl H. Pforzheimer Library

## Shelley to Hogg

**May 21, 1811**

SC 161  P. B. SHELLEY TO T. J. HOGG, MAY 21, 1811

AL signed *P B Sheley*, 2½ pages. Double sheet, 4^{to} (8.7 x 7 inches).
Wove paper. Watermark: CHARLES WILMOTT| 1809|. Gilt edges.
Seal: wax, red: *PL* [in oval]|.
Postmarks: 1. (mileage stamp): HORSHAM| 41|; 2. (morning duty stamp, London):
E| 22MY22| 1811|.

PROVENANCE: Thomas Jefferson Hogg; Major R. J. Jefferson Hogg (Sotheby,
June 30, 1948, lot 23). *De Ricci 63* (p. 124).

*My dearest Friend*

*She is quite <u>well</u>, she is pe fect in <u>health</u>;–. now thats enough, you have*
*no fever to sympathize in: but who can minister to a <u>mind</u> diseased .. She is*
*very gay, very lively; I did not shew her y^r letter, because I think it is barbarous*
5 *to diminish what the possessor considers as a pleasure, altho' I have always*
*considered that volatitility of character evinces no capabilities for great*
*affections. It is a kind of self satisfaction in trivial things that is constantly*
*exerting itself, it is a species of continual awakened pride . . . But it is*
*not constitutional, it <u>used</u> not however to be the character of my sister . . .*
10 *serious contemplative, affectionate; enthusiastically alive to the wildest*
*schemes, despising the world . . . Now .. apathetic to all except the*
*trivial amusements, & despicable intercourses of restrained conversation;*
*bowing before that hellish Idol: the <u>world</u>, appealing to it's unjust decisions*
*in cases which demands a trial at the highher Tribunal of conscience: – Yet*
15 *<u>I</u> do not despair what she <u>once was</u>, she has a power to be again .. but will*
*that power ever be exerted .. I do not hesitate to say that I think she is not*
*worthy <u>of you</u>, <u>once</u> she was, once the fondest warmest wish which ever I*
*cherished was the <u>eternal</u> union of two beings who appeared to me made for*
*each other .. But she is now <u>not</u> what she was, she is not the singular angelic*
20 *being whom you adored & I loved; I mourn her as <u>no more</u>, I consider the*
*sister whose happiness is mine as dead .. Yet have I not hopes of a resuscita-*
*tion. Certainly or I would not tear your heart with the narration. But it is*
*necessary that you should be informed of the real state of the case ..*
*Think no more, for she has murdered thought; yes think, devote yourself*
25 *with ardor, . . . on me yes on me descends the whole weight of your*
*affliction. What right had I day after day to expatiate, to magnify the*

***Shelley to Hogg***                                    ***May 21, 1811***

SC 161   *excellence of a being who might Change, who has changed . .   What right*
*had I to introduce you to the destroyer   !   Ad eu. I leave Field Place*
*tonight . . but return on Friday*

30                                                    *Your eternally affection<        >*
                                                                *P B Sheley*

[Address, page 4]

*T. Jefferson Hogg Esq^{re}*
*M^{rs} Doughty's*
*Coney Street*
35   *York*

line 2. *pe fect* (sic)

line 4. *her: he* followed by a short dash presumably intended for an *r.*

line 6. *volatitility:* probable reading; the third *i* is written through a *y.*

line 14. *demands* (sic)

line 14. *highher* (sic)

line 28. *Ad eu:* probable reading. The *Ad* blotted; Shelley perhaps lifted his pen, skipped the *i,* left a short space to get away from the blot, and ended with *eu* (or possibly *iu;* see sc 160, line 27).

line 31. *Sheley* (sic). There is no second *l;* but there appears to be an abortive *e* following the *l.* The *y* is only partly formed and ends in a scrawl. *Sheley* is apparently a semideliberate contraction. After the signature was written the letter was immediately folded and made a large blot on the opposite page (page 2). The last lines appear to have been written in haste.

COLLATION (selected passages).

T. J. HOGG, *THE LIFE OF PERCY BYSSHE SHELLEY,* 1, 379-381. (Hogg's changes indicated by italics.)

line 2. *we* have

line 4. letter; *it was too grave; and* I think

line 16. that I think she is not worthy *of us*

line 18. *to witness the eternal perfectibility of a being, who appeared to me made for perfection.* But

line 20. whom *I loved, whom I adored:*

line 22. I would not tear *my* heart with the narration.

line 24. *I will* think no more *of her,* for she has murdered thought. Yes; *I will* think, *and* devote *myself* with ardour!

line 25. on me, descends the whole weight of *my* affliction!

line 26. to expatiate *upon to another,* to magnify *to myself* the excellence of a being who might change

line 27. What right had I *to seek* to introduce you

Hogg had clearly viewed with some alarm Shelley's letter of May 14 (sc 159) which announced Elizabeth's scarlet fever. He wrote a letter to Shelley, to which the above is an answer. And he wrote also to Elizabeth, which epistle, however, Shelley coolly took upon himself not to show to its intended recipient (line 4) because he thought it would

# The Carl H. Pforzheimer Library

SC 161    "diminish" her "pleasure." Presumably Hogg's letter was too ardent and Shelley realized that it would annoy Elizabeth. His censorship, however, did not discourage Hogg, who apparently on receipt of the above letter set about to pen another to Elizabeth (SC 162).

Once more we can see Shelley's elaborate teasing of Hogg, first raising, then dashing his hopes, and writing always in a tone just touching on the mock-heroic (line 27): "What right had *I* to introduce you to the destroyer!"[1] As we have seen, Hogg in his biography invariably represents himself as manipulating Shelley.[2] Apparently he did not perceive the subtle ways in which Shelley was playing on his feelings and motives.

We might note the MY on the London Inland Mail postmark for May. The London Inland Mail postmark for May in SC 156, SC 157, and SC 158 is MA. SC 5 (May 11-12, 1787) bears a Dublin MY stamp and a London Inland Mail MA stamp. SC 67 (May 13, 1805) bears a Penny Post MY stamp.

We might note also that Shelley's letters stamped MA were mailed in London, and the one stamped MY (the above letter) was mailed at Horsham and passed through London. (The month on the franking stamp on SC 159 is illegible.) There may, therefore, have been a difference between the Inland Mail stamp for letters mailed in London and those coming into London for mailing out (in the case of the above letter, to York).

The problem is complicated by a use of MA sometimes for March, for instance, on the franking stamp of SC 143 (March 27, 1811).[3]

Further investigation on this matter is indicated. Meantime, those attempting to date letters in May or March in these years on the basis of postmarks alone should keep the possibility of confusion in mind.

1. The mock heroics are here embellished by two quotations from *Macbeth;* "Canst thou not Minister to a minde diseas'd?" (line 3; V.iii.50); "Macbeth doth murther Sleep" (line 24; II.i.47).

2. See, for instance, Humbert Wolfe's comments on Hogg's picture of himself trying to guide Shelley's "faltering and wayward steps." (Hogg, *Shelley,* I, viii.)

3. We note two MA stamps in Alcock and Holland, one a franking stamp of 1794 (fig. 833) the other a Penny Post stamp of 1794 (fig. 117), but the authors do not state whether the MA stands for March or May. MR appears in Penny Post stamps on three Godwin letters in these years (SC 48, Mar. 10, 1803; SC 49, Mar. 14, 1803; SC 76, Mar. 7, 1807); MY appears on one (May 13, 1805). Alcock and Holland give two General Post paid stamps with MR for March (figs. 680 and 682, 1799 and 1794 respectively) and one unpaid (fig. 24, 1798).

**Hogg to Shelley**                                    *May 25, 1811*

SC 162   T. J. HOGG TO ELIZABETH SHELLEY, MAY 25, 1811

AL (draft) signed *T Jefferson Hogg*, 3 pages. Double sheet, 4$^{to}$ (9.9 x 8 inches). Laid paper. Watermark: [fleur-de-lis]|.
Seal (Hogg family crest and coat of arms): wax, red: [oak tree| shield with boars' heads]|.

PROVENANCE: Thomas Jefferson Hogg; Major R. J. Jefferson Hogg (Sotheby, July 26, 1948, lot 269).

*Amen*
        *It is unne*
                        of the nature of the conv$^n$ w$^{ch}$
        It is unnecessary to inform you ~~that~~ the anecdotes of my friend & some
5  ~~elegant~~ specimens of poetry produced in my mind I cannot apologize for it
~~for~~ conviction at least is involuntary. — I ~~cannot be mistaken for~~ All perception of pleasure or pain is ~~of a~~ compound ~~nature~~ resulting from the relative
natures of the perceiver & the object perceived the variety of tastes is infinitely
diversified If ~~from~~ an anecdote apparently trifling developed a trait of
10  character w$^{ch}$ irdicated the highest degree of amiability the perception cannot
be false I am not deceived but differ from the generality of mankind in my
opinions of what constitutes the amiable If the tale of the sorrows of Louisa
afforded the most exquisite pleasure & deeply affected my heart more so than
any poem w$^{ch}$ I ever read with one exception (Gertrude). Am I mistaken if
                        feelings
15  I infer that the ~~heart~~ w$^{ch}$ dictated the tale the genius w$^{ch}$ clothed it in language
                                                            were of a
~~so~~ adapted to the subject with such elegance such precision? No sure the
        (         )
superior I had better,
20  inference is just But my feelings ~~differ~~ my ideas of the plaintive the elegant
                                differ from those of the
the simple but insinuating in thoughts & language. —— The poem may not
generality of mankind
25  square exactly with the rules of Criticism but it is a false <u>taste</u> only to prefer
                                        dark
the hand w$^{ch}$ clothed the Cambrian hills with the ~~wild~~ mountain heather to
        divides
that w$^{ch}$ ~~arranges~~ them into formal parterres of roses & carnations/ But I
                                what is more repugnant to your feelings
30  will pause to avoid dry disquisition or the appearance of flattery. You know
the favor w$^{ch}$ I presumed to request but you do not know my gratitude for the
gentle manner in w$^{ch}$ it was denied I cannot express it. — ~~The feeling is so~~

**Hogg to Shelley**                                    ***May 25, 1811***

SC 162 ~~delightful I w^d gladly encrease it. — I am firmly convinced that your reasons~~

35  ~~are~~ I fondly cherished the hope of seeing you under the most favorable

but
circumstances ~~at Easter when~~ this hope w^ch had for some time afforded me

was
not only consolation but the highest gratification ~~w^ch~~ destroyed in one moment

40  by the most unforseen the most unexpected incident w^ch I suppose never

before was the fate of anyone. Judge of my disappointment! —— I often

reflect upon your reasons for denying a favor w^ch w^d crown me with happiness

at the expense of a trifling exertion. – I am persuaded that if you had no

higher motive than the Xtian rule of doing as you w^d be done by – you w^d

45  ~~without~~ confer this greatest of obligations you w^d for a moment forget your

natural superiority & consider yourself in my situation. But some powerful

motive induces you to act otherwise. – I am firmly convinced of the existence

What As I am not possessed
of penetrate^n adequate to the discovery ~~of its nature~~

50  of some cogent reason. ~~But~~ I cannot discover ~~what~~ it is – do I request too

much in begging to learn the nature of ~~it~~. The most sanguinary government

informs the criminal of the reasons of his condemnation — Punishment is

at all times painful yet it is an alleviation to know the justice of the sentence.

well aware
55  I am ~~convinced~~ of the justice of mine. It is however more satisfactory to a

comprehend
being possessed of a shadow of reason to ~~know~~ the precise application of

the general truth
justice in his case than to know that his judge is inflexibly just Our cases

60  are not parallel if you receive bare justice you must be possessed of perfect

happiness. I fear without a large portion of mercy my lot w^d be most wretched.

—— I cannot I must confess discover the precise reason. You cannot suppose

imagine
I am so vain so conceited ~~to~~ as to ~~conceive~~ that a correspondence carries with

65  it the shadow of an engagement of the most remote nature .. No impossible

feel most acutely
—— I hope I ~~am convinced~~ of my own inferiority in every point. – You

cannot imagine that if now I w^d gladly resign my existence sh^d you command

w^d
70  it I ~~shd~~ refuse for a moment when the duty of Gratitude was so infinitely

with w^ch I might have been blessed.
increased to restore ever every letter shd you request it. —— No if when I am

SC 162  *dead some kind gentle spirit who survives me w^d inscribe on my grave that*

                                                      *some*
75      *I had gathered gleaned a scattered smiles how calm w^d be my sleep —— time*

        *& the weeds w^d respect my epitaph & w^d not deface or overshadow my tomb.*

                                    *slowly*
        *The moon & stars as they glided through the cloudless sky w^d shine with*
        *unusual lustre when they viewed a spot consecrated by such an inscription*

80      *—— Perhaps the opinion of mankind is valuable to me it appears vain &*

        *trifling — but I admit it is valuable estimable inestimable how does this favor*

        *interfere with the acquisition of it — Intuition will not inform the busy*

        *world I need not speak of the improbability the impossibility of any other*

                                              *be to*                        *direct*
85      *mode of information — If I request too great a favor to receive immediate*

        *information perhaps you will be instruct me through the medium of our*

                                        *once*              *ever bow in s the silent obedience of*
        *common friend your brother. — I did hoped I cd submit without the least*
        *submission*
90      *regret to your commands. that I cd not only hate but torture myself to procure*

        *the most trifling gratification for one I adore. This is my general sentiments*

        *& ever shall remain such but there are moments when the spirit is borne down*

                              *time*                    *If my request is exorbitant*
        *very very low it at such a period as this I write. — Grant me at least your*

95      *one favor believe me eternally immutably yours —— ——*

        [Page 4]

        *York May 25. 1811*
        *T Jefferson Hogg*

---

line 3. *conv^n:* contraction for *conviction.* See line 6.

line 6. *A* written over *a*

line 19. ⟨?*said supreme*⟩: cramped into right edge

line 20. *better:* probable reading. Lines 17, 19, 20 may possibly read: *were of a superior I had better said supreme.*

                                                      *be to*
line 85. There is a long hooked line around *great a favor* and another line from it leading to the space between *information* and *perhaps.*
                              *be to*
These lines indicate that *great a favor* is to follow *information.* Hogg intended the sequence

to run as follows: *If I request too to receive*
        *direct*              *be to*
*immediate information great a favor perhaps*

line 94. *it at* (sic)

line 96. Written 4.5 inches up from fold and parallel to fold; *York* begins 1 inch from bottom edge.

line 97. Written on outer edge opposite fold; initial *J* begins 3.1 inches in from bottom edge. The signature is followed by the seal which is in the corner where the bottom and outer edges meet. The signature is written upside down to line 96.

# The Carl H. Pforzheimer Library

*Hogg to Shelley*                                        *May 25, 1811*

SC 162     THE above manuscript is a draft of a letter from Thomas Jefferson Hogg to Elizabeth Shelley, no doubt the letter received by Shelley at Cuckfield on May 31 and sent on by him to Elizabeth.[1] That it is by Hogg is shown by the signature and the handwriting. That it is to Elizabeth Shelley is clear from the content. That it is a draft and not a final copy is shown by its cancellations and interlineations. Hogg kept drafts also of two letters to Mrs. Shelley and a poem which he sent to Shelley.[2]

Taken together the signature, folding lines, date, and seal on page 4 present something of a puzzle. As the seal bears the imprint of the Hogg family crest and coat of arms[3] the document was presumably sealed by Hogg. The folding lines (verified by the position of the seal) are those normal for a letter folded for mailing.[4] But the document bears no address and no postmark. The indication is that it was mailed; if so it must have been folded within a letter or a separate address sheet.

Shelley, writing to Hogg on May 31 from Cuckfield (sc 163) comments: "Your letter is dispatched to my Sister." This can hardly refer to the above manuscript for Hogg would not intend a rather messy draft without either salutation or complimentary-close-with-signature for Elizabeth.[5] It must refer to a final draft. This final draft had perhaps been addressed to Elizabeth Shelley care of P. B. Shelley. Hogg would not wish this letter to reach Elizabeth in an opened state. On the other hand he might wish Shelley to know of its contents.[6] It may be, then,

---

1. See sc 163 (May 31, 1811), sc 164 (June 4, 1811).

2. sc 168 (July ?6–18, 1811); sc 177 (Aug. 22, 1811); sc 131 (Jan. 10, 1811).

3. The full crest and coat of arms are not legible. See *New Shelley Letters*, p. 44 fn., and William Fordyce, *History and Antiquities of the County Palatine of Durham* . . . (Newcastle-upon-Tyne, [1857]), II, 206.

4. We might note also that some of the crossed-out lines on page 3 (line 71, "with w$^{ch}$ I might have been blessed," to line 95, "eternally immutably yours —— ——") have blotted on page 2. Hence, the letter was folded immediately. If it was simply a literary composition there would normally have been no need for immediate folding but if Hogg had a post to catch there might have been.

5. Furthermore, the time elapsed seems too long, for if Hogg mailed the above draft on May 25 Shelley would have received it by May 27 or 28.

6. That Shelley did see the letter may be indicated in his comments in a letter of *ca.* July 21 (sc 171, lines 31–35): "and it was E's poetry that first attracted your attention, charmed, & now has bewitched you! . . unless you were influenced by the vague unconnected prejudiced praises which *I would* at times speak of E . . . ," which sounds like a reference to the opening sentence of the above letter.

SC 162  that he enclosed the above draft in a letter or address sheet to Shelley
for his advice and suggestions and that Shelley returned it to him.[7]

Hogg's object in writing the letter — after the sad fate of his
previous one — was to persuade Elizabeth to see him. He had expected
to see her at Easter (line 37) when Shelley invited him to Field Place;
but this invitation had been canceled by Timothy Shelley (sc 143). His
interest had been particularly aroused by "some specimens of poetry"
(line 5) by her. These "specimens," as the reference to Louisa and the
Cambrian Hills shows, were those which Shelley wrote out for Hogg at
Oxford (sc 114). Hogg had been much moved by the sad plight of Louisa
— only Campbell's *Gertrude of Wyoming* had moved him more[8] — and
by her death in the Cambrian Hills[9] among the "dark mountain heather"
(line 26) — a phrase directly quoted from Elizabeth's poem.[10]

7. If this was the case Hogg did not waste time; he could not have received his draft back until
May 29; if Shelley had the final version in his hands by May 31, Hogg must have copied it and
mailed it back immediately

8. The popularity of Campbell's bathetic narrative *Gertrude of Wyoming* was such that Hogg intends
his comment as high praise. Gertrude — like Louisa — dies tragically.

9. Louisa (sc 114, line 17) died on "the dark summit of huge Penmanmawr," one of the Cambrian
Mountains.

10. sc 114 (July-August 1810), line 37.


SC 163  P. B. SHELLEY TO T. J. HOGG, MAY 31, 1811

AL unsigned, ½ page. Single sheet, 4^to (9.1 x 7.4 inches).
Laid paper. Watermark: 1810|.
Seal: wafer, red.
Postmarks: 1. (mileage stamp): CUCKFIELD| 44|; 2. (morning duty stamp, Lon-
don): B| 1 JU 1| 1811|.

PROVENANCE: Thomas Jefferson Hogg; Major R. J. Jefferson Hogg (Sotheby,
June 30, 1948, lot 28).

*My dear Friend*
*Your letter is dispatched to my Sister . . . I shall be there on Sunday;*
*you shall I hope have a favorable answer; If my interest has weight, if she*
*yet regards me as a friend & brother she cannot refuse . . . But no . . . this*
5      < > *coercion . . you shall hear on Sunday*

# The Carl H. Pforzheimer Library

SC 163    [Address, page 2]

*T. J. Hogg Esq^r*
*M^{rs} Doughty's*
*Coney Street*
*York*

line 5. <    > covered by seal
line 5. *on:* visible on the paper adhering to the
seal; so, too, with the *8* of *1810* in the watermark.

COLLATION (selected passages).
T. J. HOGG, *THE LIFE OF PERCY BYSSHE SHELLEY*, I, 410. (Hogg's changes indicated by
italics.)

line 2. *I have despatched a letter* to my sister,      line 3. *I hope I shall* have a favourable answer.
*inclosing your last letter to me.*      line 3. If *her* interest *in me* has weight;

HOGG (followed by Ingpen) dated this letter "July 1." The London
morning duty postmark,[1] "1 JU 1," however, stands for June and
not July, which is represented by JY or JUL.[2] The letter must have been
written on May 31, and went from Cuckfield to London with the morning
mail on June 1. Hogg similarly misdated a June 4 letter (sc 164) as July 4.
(His dating a third letter "June 2" is correct, as is shown by its context.)[3]
The result of these misdatings — not to mention Hogg's changes in text
— has been to obscure the sequence of events and motives. The correct order is: May 31 (the above letter), June 2 (*de Ricci 65*), June 4
(sc 164).

     Shelley received Hogg's letter to Elizabeth at Cuckfield on Friday,

1. The stamp has the single rim used by the Inland Mail for morning duty. See Alcock and Holland,
p. 21; Robinson, *British Post Office*, p. 204. The mail coach passed through Cuckfield for London at
midnight. (Paterson's *Roads*, 1811, p. 526.)

2. Alcock and Holland, figs. 30, 31, 146, 516, 565, 567, and 850 show JY, figs. 510, 688, 768, and 836
show JUL.

3. The manuscript of this June 2 letter is now among the Abinger Manuscripts. Examination of it
shows that the address page and the conclusion of the text are missing. As Hogg gives a conclusion,
however, apparently the letter was complete when he transcribed it, and he either took the date
from the conclusion of the letter or this time correctly read the postmark. The fact that the letter
is among the Abinger Manuscripts shows that it was one of those inspected by Lady Shelley (see
"The Provenance of Shelley and his Circle Manuscripts," below, p. 905). Perhaps she lost or mis-
laid one page.

**Shelley to Hogg**                                                                    *June 4, 1811*

SC 163   May 31 and "dispatched" it to her.[4] He expected to be back at Field
Place on Sunday, June 2, and to know her answer then.

    The blotting shows that the letter was folded immediately after it
was written.

> 4. See SC 162 (May 25, 1811). Presumably Hogg addressed the letter to Field Place, and it was brought
> to Shelley at Cuckfield (some fifteen miles away). Shelley apparently sent it back to Field Place by
> messenger ("dispatched").

SC 164   P. B. SHELLEY TO T. J. HOGG, JUNE 4, 1811

AL unsigned, 3 pages. Double sheet, 4^to (8.7 x 7 inches).
Wove paper. Watermark: CHARLES WILMOTT| 1809|. Gilt edges.
Seal: wafer, red.
Postmarks: 1. (mileage stamp): HORSHAM| 41|; 2. (morning duty stamp, London):
E| [5] JU 5| 1811|.

PROVENANCE: Thomas Jefferson Hogg; Major R. J. Jefferson Hogg (Sotheby,
June 30, 1948, lot 29). *De Ricci 76* (p. 126).

*My dearest Friend*

    *I am surprised — — — for the sake of every thing for which we live listen
to reason. . . .    If you will not listen to me, see the Chapter in Locke which
Faber ought to have read & profited by . . .    What is enthusiasm, whether*
5 *in religion, politics or morality, all equally inexcusably fatuitous; yours is
in the latter; you seek the happiness of another, under an idea that she is most
aimiable, even admitting the last, is it not wrong when you see that you can
not contribute to her happiness, to render yourself unfit to do so to another.
But I do not admit it, it is false; & surely who is the best judge; you who never*
10 *beheld her   never heard her converse, & in addition to this confessedly &
strongly prejudiced prejudiced like Religions votaries who reason whilst
they can, & when that ceases to be possible, they feel from this last there is no
appeal   surely you do not mean to imitate these, who I ask is the better
judge? or you, as you must be the last of these, or I dispassionate cool,*
15 *certainly cool you cannot deny that, probably dispassionate, since little as
you may be disposed to credit my feelings concerning αφιλαυτια I have here no
interest to act otherwise than I say. . . .    How then do you still persist! . .
I own it, it was the fondest wish of my heart, & bitterly was I dissapointed*

[ 803 ]

**Shelley to Hogg**                                              *June 4, 1811*

SC 164  *at its annihilation . .     I own it . .     I desired, eagerly desired to see you &*
20      *my sister irrecoverably united where you have no priest but love: I pictured*
        *to myself Elysium in beholding my only perfect friend daring the vain*
        *world, smiling at its silly forms, setting an example of perfection to an*
        *universe . . .     I do not estimate as you know from relation-ship, I am cool*
        *I hope . . .     I should now grieve to see <u>you</u> sacrifised; when there <u>may</u>*
25      *ex<    > a perfect being, nothing under w<    >h I consider as worthy of*
        *you . . .     I do not flatter I do not temporize     I am as severe with you as*
        *I <u>can</u> be; I own I cannot bear to see you sacrifising yourself and every one*
        *who really estimates you . .*

                        *I write tomorrow*
30                              *Your ever affectionate*

[Address, page 4]
*T. Jefferson Hogg Esq<sup>r</sup>*
*M<sup>rs</sup> Doughty's*
*Coney St.*
<u>*York*</u>

line 7. *aimiable* (sic)

line 18. *dissapointed* (sic)

line 21. Following *in* is a slanted line, perhaps the stroke of a letter (at the end of the line).

line 24. *sacrifised:* sacrifise is given in the *NED* as an alternate form.

line 25. *ex<ist>*

line 25. *w<hic>h*

line 29. Lines 29–30 are in a finer and lighter stroke than the body of the letter. Shelley apparently added these lines some time after completing the body of the letter for they have blotted on page 2 in the folding, but the heavier and darker writing above them has not.

COLLATION (selected passages).
T. J. HOGG, *THE LIFE OF PERCY BYSSHE SHELLEY*, 1, 410–411. (Hogg's changes indicated by italics.)

line 9. But do I not admit *this? And yet* it seems false.

line 9. *Who,* surely, is the *better* judge? you — who never beheld her, never heard her converse, and, in addition to this — *or I, who* — *still I am* confessedly strongly prejudiced,

line 14. *I, as I must be like one of these* or *you,* dispassionate, cool; — cool you cannot *but be,*

line 17. How, then, do *I* still persist *in* ——.

line 19. I own it: I desired, eagerly desired to see *myself* and *her irrevocably* united *by the rites of*

the Church, *but where the high* priest *would have been* Love; I pictured to myself Elysium in beholding my only perfect *one* daring the vain world

line 24. I should now grieve to see *myself* sacrificed, when there may exist a *less imperfect* being, *and I might be perhaps* considered as *not wholly unworthy* of her. *You* do not flatter; *you* do not temporise; *you are* as severe with *me* as *you* can be. I own I cannot bear, *you tell me,* to see you sacrificing yourself, and every one who really *esteems* you.

[ 804 ]

# Shelley and his Circle : Manuscripts

SC 164    Hogg (followed by Shelley's editors) dated this letter July 4, once again misreading a JU (June) postmark for July.[1] The postmark (Inland Mail, London), however, is unquestionably June 5.

Hogg refuses to be discouraged by Elizabeth's rebuffs and Shelley is writing — rather exasperatedly — to discourage him further (line 17): "How then do you still persist!"

Hogg's (typical)[2] change of "you & my sister" (line 19) to "myself and her" has led to speculation that Shelley was contemplating an incestuous union with his sister, and from speculation to controversy. "A very grave conjecture might be, and has been built upon its terms," wrote W. M. Rossetti in his *Memoir of Shelley*, "but I suspect that, owing to Hogg's slovenly editorship, there is a serious misprint in it, and shall leave it without further comment."[3] Dowden, reading these remarks, assured Rossetti that there was "no misprint in the letter" and that Shelley was "simply" saying that "he would have wished Hogg and Elizabeth united without marriage and would wish to act in like manner when the time should come."[4] Dowden's theory was attacked by a reviewer, and Dowden answered: "The reviewer speaks of my skating here 'over thin ice.' No; I tread on solid ground, and Mr. Rossetti, whose candour the reviewer commends in rejecting the odious theory, is by my side."[5]

The correct text, printed above, shows that the controversy was needless, and the incident provides an example of the importance of determining a text before theorizing. One might wonder, in passing, how Dowden was able to assure Rossetti that there was "no misprint in the letter" when he had not seen the manuscript.[6]

1. See sc 163 (May 31, 1811), Commentary.

2. See "Shelley, Hogg and Elizabeth Shelley," above.

3. (London, 1886), p. 28, fn.          4. *Ibid.*, p. iii.

5. Quoted in Shelley, *Complete Works*, VIII, 120 fn.

6. The statement sounds as though it came from Lady Shelley (with whom Dowden was in touch). That Dowden had not seen the manuscript is clear from his comment; for the printed text had been tampered with. So far as is known the manuscript remained in the Hogg family until its sale in 1948. (See Provenance.) There is no indication that it was among those borrowed by Lady Shelley. (See "The Provenance of Shelley and his Circle Manuscripts," below, p. 905.) Dowden's strained interpretation of the passage as printed by Hogg, however, comes so close to the truth that one wonders if he had not received some information on the subject. Lady Shelley may, at some point, have received an interpretation of the passage from Hogg.

# The Carl H. Pforzheimer Library

SC 165 P. B. SHELLEY TO T. J. HOGG, JUNE 16, 1811

AL signed *PBS*, 5 pages. Double sheet, folio (11.9 x 7.3 inches); single sheet, folio (11.9 x 7.8 inches).
Laid paper. Watermark, double sheet: [Britannia in crowned oval]; counter-mark, double sheet: GR| 1806|; watermark, single sheet: GR| 1806|.
Seal: wax, red: *PL* [in oval]|.
Frank, by Timothy Shelley.
Postmarks: 1. (mileage stamp): HORSHAM| [41]|; 2. (morning duty franking stamp, London): FREE| 18 JU 18| 1811|.

PROVENANCE: Thomas Jefferson Hogg; Major R. J. Jefferson Hogg (Sotheby, June 30, 1948, lot 24). *De Ricci 68* (p. 125).

*My dear Friend.*
*I wish I thought as you do; but I cannot, it is all in vain . . .   Unwilling as I am conviction stares in my face & mocks my lingering credulity . . oh! that you were here! That artifice the most subtle of which degraded beings*
5   *are capable has been used I doubt not, but altho' this tallies with the wishes of the artificers, a very different cause from their machinations effected it. — A change, a great & important change has taken place in my sister. Every little action which formerly used to be so eloquent, every look which was wont to be so expressive of openness now are enlisted in the service of prejudice . .*
10   *All is studied   art has superceded, not combined with Nature. & it is in vain that either you or I decieve ourselves longer. Your letter came this morning, I burnt that one of mine, I shuddered even to look at a page of it, the flames destroyed it   Your letter came . . the experiment you recommend has been tried within these few days repeatedly but without the slightest effect.*
15   *Scorn, the most virulent, neglect & affected pity for my madness is all that I can obtain in reply. "You & y^r mad friend Hogg! Those whom I have seen, who have seen me, may have some little excuse for their folly" —   This is all that I could hear, nothing else she would say . . .   Then, far from being in the least affected by all I can say of you . .   Her spirits are uncommonly*
20   *lively, I sometimes attempt the same liveliness to see if congeniality even in folly would effect any thing; . . No . .   even this is in vain, she is then, & then only constrainedly silent . . . Oh my friend who is likeliest to be right, he who muses at a distance on the abstract idea of perfection annexing it to*

**Shelley to Hogg**                                    *June 16, 1811*

SC 165  *a being whom one present cannot attribute it to . . . one too who is passion-*
25      *ately prejudiced to that side of the question* ~~to which~~ *the truth of which he has*
*not admitted or rather rejected, (delictum ⟨    ⟩) I shall see you in July, I*
*am invited to Wales, but I shall go to York . . . what shall we do? how I long*
*again for your conversation . . .    The ideas* here *rise in solitude, they*
*pass thro' a mind as solitary; unheeded gloomy retrospection introduces them;*
30      *anticipation even gloomier bids them depart to make way for others; these*
*roll on, still, still will they urge thier course, 'till Death closes all! . . . Where-*
*fore should we linger, unhappiness dissapointment enthusiasm & subsequent*
*apathy follow our steps, w^d it not be a general good to all human beings that*
*I should make haste away – – – So you stay . . . stay to make thousands*
35      *happy.* One *is unworthy of you . . . & all my wishes are closed, since I see*
*that union impossible & unjust which once was my fondest vision. For*
*myself, I knew what an unstable decietfull thing Love was, but still did I*
*wish to involve you in the pleasing delusion . . . . the mist dissipates . . the*
*light is strong is clear . . I am not blind, are you? Will you be? It is neither*
40      *to your own, nor to the beings happiness which you desire that you should*
*longer continue so . . .    Where is* she *whom* you *adore . . . alas! where is*
*virtue, where is perfection? . . .    where you cannot reach . . . is there*
*another existence. No. then you never can reach it . . . Is there another*
*existence Yes . . . then you shall live there, rendering, & rendered happy.*
45      *Perhaps the flowers think like this, perhaps they moralize upon thier state,*
*have thier attachments, theier pursuits of virtue, adore despond, hope, despise*
*. . . Alas! then do we like they perish, or do they like us live for ever!*
*But am I not a* Philosopher? *do I not pursue virtue for virtue's sake . . . why*
*then do I wander wildly, why do I write madly: why has sleep forsaken me,*
50      *why are you & my sister forever present to my mind? except when selfishness*
*bids me start at what I am now to what I once was . . .    Adeiu . . . I am*
*going to take the sacrament . . . In spite of my melancholy reflexions the*
*idea rather amuses me. You shall hear from me soon again. I write very*
*often, but have not always courage to send my letters . . . Believe me*
55                              *Your's ever affect*
                                    PBS

# The Carl H. Pforzheimer Library

[Frank with address, page 6, in the hand of Timothy Shelley]

SC 165  *Horsham, June Sixteen*
                    *1811*

*T. J. Hogg Esq.ʳ*
60    *Mʳˢ Doughty's*
      *Coney Street*
      *York*
      *T. Shelley*

line 3. *lingering:* The first *n* is written through a *g*.

line 8. *formerly:* Shelley began to follow the *e* with a long upstroke, perhaps for an *l*, and changed it to an *r*.

line 10. *superceded* (sic)

line 11. *decieve* (sic)

line 16. Shelley places quotes at the beginning of each line of his sister's remarks: "*whom*; "*me*; "*for*.

line 26. (*delictum* ⟨?*est*⟩): probable reading. The writing is very faint as the pen was apparently in need of dipping. Hogg read *deliberately*, but this does not seem possible.

line 31 *thier* (sic)

line 32. *dissapointment* (sic)

line 37. *decietfull* (sic)

line 45. *thier . . . thier . . . theier* (sic). The *i*'s and *e*'s are clearly formed.

line 51. *Adeiu* (sic): *Ad* is on paper adhering to seal.

COLLATION (selected passages).
T. J. HOGG, *THE LIFE OF PERCY BYSSHE SHELLEY*, I, 401–404. (Hogg's changes indicated by italics.)

line 10. It is in vain that *you try to persuade me to* deceive *myself* longer.

line 16. "You and your mad friend! Those, whom I have seen, *and* who have seen me, *make but* little excuse for *your* folly." Then, far from being in the least affected by all I can say of *my vexation,*

line 23. the abstract idea of perfection, *that I once dreamed,* annexing it.

line 36. For myself, I *know* what an unstable, deceitful thing Love *is;* but still did I wish to involve *myself* in the pleasing delusion.

line 39. I am not blind, *nor* are you; — *shall I* be? It is neither to *my* own, nor to the being's happiness which *I desired,* that *I* should longer continue so! Where is she whom *I adored?*

line 42. Where *I* cannot reach. Is there another existence? No! Then *I* can never reach it. Is there another existence? Yes! Then *I* shall

line 52. the idea rather amuses *and soothes* me.

T͟HERE is, so far as is known, no extant letter between that of June 4 (sc 164) and this of June 16.[1] Shelley apparently wrote some but

1. June 16 was a Sunday in 1811, which may explain why the London postmark is two days later than the date of the letter (given in the frank) instead of the usual one day. That the letter was written on the day on which it was franked is indicated by the reference (line 52) to the sacrament and by the opening sentence of the next letter (sc 166).

SC 165  did not mail them (line 53). He also wrote one to Elizabeth on behalf of Hogg but later burned it.[2]

One problem in attempting to assess the Shelley-Hogg correspondence is that we have only one side of it. Hogg preserved Shelley's letters but Shelley apparently did not preserve Hogg's. (Shelley, in fact, seldom preserved any letters.) We can, however, reconstruct something of Hogg's letters from Shelley's replies. The one to which the above was a reply was apparently somewhat frenzied. Hogg seems to have been driven almost to distraction by Elizabeth's refusal to have anything to do with him. Shelley is trying both to calm Hogg and to discourage him: Elizabeth has changed; she will not yield; Hogg should seek someone else. He clearly has no real intention of inviting Hogg to Field Place in spite of the carelessly thrown in "oh! that you were here!" (line 3) which Hogg immediately seized on. He expects that he will next see Hogg at York, where he will go instead of Wales.[3]

Hogg's changes — particularly in the pronouns — have once again obscured the picture, and one gets the impression that the letter deals with Shelley's love for Elizabeth or for Harriet Grove instead of Hogg's for Elizabeth.

2. "Your letter came this morning, I burnt that one of mine" (line 11) may refer to the comment in the June 2 letter: "I wrote to entreat that she would answer your letter kindly; I wrote very long. *This is* the answer." (Text from Abinger Manuscripts, Pforzheimer Microfilm, file 25. Hogg's text, we might note, reads: "I wrote to entreat that she would receive my letter kindly.") Hogg had apparently asked to see the letter to Elizabeth (which, if Shelley is telling the truth, must have been returned to him).

3. Shelley states that he received two invitations to Wales, one from his cousin, Charles Grove, one from Mr. Westbrook. See SC 167 (June 20, 1811) and Commentary.

SC 166  P. B. SHELLEY TO T. J. HOGG, JUNE 18–19, 1811; P. B. SHELLEY, *SWEET STAR! WHICH GLEAMING OER THE DARKSOME SCENE*; *HOPES THAT SWELL IN YOUTHFUL BREASTS*

AL unsigned, including two (or possibly three) poems, 4 pages. Double sheet, folio (11.9 x 7.3 inches).
Laid paper. Watermark: [Britannia in crowned oval]|; countermark: GR| 1806|. (See Plate XXVIII).

PROVENANCE: Thomas Jefferson Hogg; Major R. J. Jefferson Hogg (Sotheby, June 30, 1948, lot 27); Alan D. N. Smith (Sotheby, June 19, 1951, lot 493). *De Ricci 74* (p. 125).

# The Carl H. Pforzheimer Library

SC 166   *I wrote to you on Sunday . . . Reason have you to say that I was violent . . .*
*I was Mad! you know that very little sets my horrid spirits in motion; I*
*drank a glass or two of wine at my Mothers instigation, then began raving . .*
*She to quiet me gave me Pens Ink & Paper. I wrote to you . . .  She is (Eliza)*

5   *indeed unworthy of you. . . .  Do not rest much on her Poetry . .  Miss*
*Philipps betrayed twice the genius . . greater amiablity – if to affect the*
*feelings is the proof of an excess of the latter, surely you cannot deny it. . . .*
*You are so prejudiced on this head . . .*
*I am a perfect hermite, not a being to speak with, I sometimes exchange a*

10   *word with my Mother on the subject of the weather, upon which she is*
*irresistibly eloquent     otherwise all deep silence! . . . I wander about this*
*place, walking all over the grounds with no particular object in view . . I*
*cannot write except now & then to you . . . sometimes to Miss Westbrook*
*My hand begins to hurry, & I am tired & ennuied . . .  The only thing*

15   *that has interested me, if I except your letters has been one Novel . .  It is*
*Miss Owenson's Missionary an Indian tale. will you read it, it is really a*
*divine thing . . Luxima the Indian is an Angel . . What pity that we cannot*
*incorporate these creations of Fancy, the very thought of them thrills the soul*
*. . . Since I have read this book I have read no other . . . but I have thought*

20   *strangely . . .*
*I transcribe for you a strange melange of maddened stuff which I wrote by*
*the midmight moon last night.*

     *Sweet star! which gleaming oer the darksome scene*
     *Thro' fleecy clouds of silvery radiance flighng'st*

25      *Spanglets of light on evening's shadowy viel*
     *Which shrouds the day beam from the waveless lake*
     *Lighting the hour of sacred love, more sweet*
     *Than the expiring morn-star's paly fires*
     *Sweet star! when wearied nature sinks to sleep*

30      *And all is hushed, – all save the voice of love,*
     *Whose broken murmurings swell the balmy blast*
     *Of soft Favonius, which at intervals*
     *Sighs in the ear of stillness. — art thou ought but love*

SC 166

35

40

45

50

55

60

*Lulling the slaves of interest to repose*
*With that mild pitying gaze . . oh! I cd. look*
*On thy dear beam 'till every bond of sense*
*Became unnerved. . . . .*

*Hopes that swell in youthful breasts*
    *Live they thro' the waste of time? . . .*
*Love's rose an host of thorns invests*
    *Cold ungenial is the clime*
        *Where its' honours blow*
*Youth says . . the purple flowers are mine*
    *Which die the while they glow*

*Dear the boon to Fancy given*
    *Retracted whilst it's granted! — — —*
*Sweet the rose which lives in Heaven*
    *Altho' on Earth 'tis planted*
        *Where its' honours blow*
*Where by Earth's slaves the leaves are riven*
    *Which die the while they glow. . . .*

            *X   X   X   X*

*Age cannot love destroy*
    *But perfidy can blast the flower*
    *E'en when in most unwary hour*
    *It blooms in Fancy's bower*
*Age cannot love destroy*
    *But Perfidy can rend the shrine*
    *In which its vermeil splendors shine*

            *X   X   X*

*Ohe! jam satis dementiae I hear you exclaim. I have been thinking of Death*
*& Heaven for four days . . What is the latter? . . shall we set off . . . Is*
*there a future life; whom should we injure by departing? should we not*

## *Shelley to Hogg*                                    *June 18–19, 1811*

SC 166   *benefit some . . .     I was thinking last night when from the summer house*
    65   *I saw the moon, just behind one of the chimneys if she were alone to witness*
         *our departure? . . But I do not talk thus, or even think thus when we are*
         *together . . .   how is that    I scarce dare. yet now I dare . . .     I shall*
         *see you in three weeks. I am coming to York in my Way to Wales, where*
         *possibly I shall not go . . . be that as it may . . you shall see me . . . I intend*
    70   *to pedestrianize.*
         *The Post fellow wants the letter.*
         *Adeiu. Beleeve me your Most*
                 *affectionate . .*

    75
                                                   *You will*
                                                   *hear on*
                                                   *Monday.*

line 6. *amiablity* (sic)

line 14. *tired.* Shelley has left the loop of the *d* half formed, as though to indicate his "tiredness" and "ennui."

line 25. *viel* (sic)

line 35. *gaze* is written over another word or part of a word, perhaps *love.*

line 39. Hogg reads "Leave they this." (Hogg, *Shelley*, I, 232.) But *Leave* is not a possible reading. Above the (unclear) *o* of *thro'* is a dot which is apparently accidental or was carelessly added

later but which Hogg took as a dot for an *i*; hence his *this* reading. See Collation (with the Esdaile copybook), line 39.

line 50. *Where* is written through *Youth.* See line 43. Shelley was apparently copying a written text.

line 72. *Adeiu* (sic)

line 72. *Beleeve* (sic)

line 74. Lines 74–76 are written vertically in the lower right corner.

COLLATION (selected passages).
T. J. HOGG, *THE LIFE OF PERCY BYSSHE SHELLEY*, I, 396. (Hogg's changes indicated by italics.)

line 1. Reason have you to say that I was *unreasonable.*

line 4. Eliza*beth* is, indeed, *an* unworthy *companion of the Muses. I* do not rest much on her poetry *now.*

line 7. *I am sure* you cannot deny *that* you are *unprejudiced* on this head.

COLLATION (excluding incidentals of punctuation).
[LOVE'S ROSE]| *1810*, SHELLEY, *COMPLETE WORKS*, III, 75 (ESDAILE COPYBOOK).

line 38. Hopes, that bud

line 39. Live not thro'

line 40. a host

line 41. And ungenial

line 42. its blossoms

line 44. That fade

line 46. while 'tis

line 47. that breathes in

line 50. While by the frosts its

line 51. That fade

# Shelley and his Circle: Manuscripts

**Shelley to Hogg** June 18–19, 1811

SC 166 THIS letter is undated and unaddressed.[1] Hogg leaves it undated but places it immediately following the letter of Sunday, June 2. Shelley's editors (followed by de Ricci) date it "about June 27."[2] The internal evidence, however, shows that it must come between the letters of June 16 (sc 165) and June 20 (sc 167). Dating it, in fact, turns out to provide an interesting exercise in showing that the interlockings of such evidence can sometimes provide a fairly firm structure. The general association of the letter with those of June 16 and 20 is indicated by two facts: all three letters mention the scheme of going to York instead of to Wales; the above letter and the June 20 letter both state that Shelley expects to be in York in three weeks and both mention his recent reading of *The Missionary*.[3]

A more exact sequencing is made possible by two further facts. (a) The above letter states "I wrote to you on Sunday." Shelley wrote only three letters to Hogg on Sundays in June 1811: June 2, 16, 23.[4] The "on Sunday" reference cannot be to the June 2 letter because Shelley also states in the above letter that he intends to be in York in three weeks, and although Shelley did intend to be in York about three weeks from June 20 he did not intend to be there in three weeks from June 2. Nor can the reference be to the Sunday, June 23, letter because that letter was almost certainly the last one written to Hogg from Field Place; in it Shelley discusses Hogg's projected trip to Field Place — a great event — and intimates that he will see him in a few days. If there had been another letter following that of June 23 it would certainly mention this trip of Hogg's, but no other letter does, including the above

1. The letter was presumably folded inside an address sheet. Hogg does not seem to have kept the address sheets to Shelley's letters. The letter is blotted on page 4 and the blots show that it was folded in such a way as to make page 1 the outer page (normally, a double-sheet letter was folded with page 4 as the outer page because the address was written on that page). As the folds are the normal letter folds, the letter was probably folded inside a sheet about the same size as itself. The blotting indicates that it was folded hastily, as the "Post fellow" (line 71) waited.

2. *Shelley, Complete Works*, VIII, 117; so, too, in Ingpen's separate editions of the letters.

3. Line 16 and sc 167 (June 20, 1811), line 56. Sydney Owenson, *The Missionary, An Indian Tale* (London, 1811), 3 vols. In 1812 Miss Owenson married Sir Thomas Charles Morgan and thereafter was known to English literature as Lady Morgan. For some account of the book and its influence upon Shelley (especially on *Alastor*) see Hughes, *Nascent Mind*, pp. 90–92; White, *Shelley*, I, 195, 700–701.

4. June 9 and 30 were also Sundays but apparently Hogg kept all Shelley's letters to him and there is none for either of those dates.

# The Carl H. Pforzheimer Library

SC 166 letter. Hence, the "Sunday" reference in the above letter must be to Sunday, June 16.

(b) But although the letter was, as the above facts indicate, written later than June 16 it was, almost certainly, written before June 20, for whereas the above letter simply notes (line 68) "I am coming to York in my Way to Wales," the June 20 letter elaborates (sc 167, line 2): "I shall be with you in three weeks . . . possibly less – take lodgings for me at York, if possible, at M^rs Doughty's. It is best to be before-hand as lodgings may be scarce . . ."

The above letter, then, must have been written between June 16 and June 20 (a Thursday). It was, furthermore, not written on Monday, June 17, for if it had been written on a Monday Shelley would not have commented in his postscript, "You will hear on Monday"; nor would he have said (line 1), "I wrote to you on Sunday" but, rather, "I wrote to you yesterday." The letter, therefore, was almost certainly written on either Tuesday, June 18, or Wednesday, June 19.

In its content the letter pursues a familiar strain. Once again Shelley is trying to discourage Hogg. Elizabeth is "unworthy" of him. Not even her poetry, apparently admired by Hogg, is of much consequence. She has not half the genius of Janetta Philipps (in the publication of whose *Poems* Shelley was taking considerable interest at this time).[5]

In regard to the poetry included Shelley seems to be giving Hogg the impression that it was written "by the midnight moon last night" (line 21).[6] But this cannot be true for all of it. No other text is known for the first poem (lines 23–37), but the poem on "love's rose" (lines 38–60) appears in the Esdaile copybook and is there dated 1810.[7] Hence, in regard to these lines, at least, Shelley is apparently trying to pass off — as he did before[8] — old poetry as new in order to give it a contemporary romantic flavor.

5. Shelley wrote two letters to Miss Philipps (May 16, 1811, and [May] 1811), from which it appears that he had seen the poems in manuscript and had offered to pay for their publication. This offer was apparently turned down for the book was published by subscription. The subscription list in the *Poems* (Oxford, 1811), however, shows that Shelley was active in its promotion.

6. The word "melange" (line 21) seems to imply that all of the poems were composed together "last night."

7. See Collation (with Esdaile copybook), above, and Shelley, *Complete Works*, III, 75, 317. "1810" is the title of the poem in the copybook. The title "Love's Rose" was supplied by W. M. Rossetti.

8. See sc 160 (May 17, 1811), Commentary.

SC 166     It is not clear whether the second set of verses comprises one poem or two on a similar theme. Shelley's editors have presumed that it comprises one, although Shelley did not include the third stanza in the Esdaile copybook version[9] and it is written in different stanzaic form. (Hogg omits the row of X's, line 52.) The first two stanzas deal with the theme of love fading as the result of the ravages of "the waste of time" but living on in the "Fancy."[10] The third brings in a new thought, namely that "perfidy" can destroy love both in reality and in the imagination ("Fancy's bower") even although time ("age") cannot. It may be that this third stanza — with its possible reference to the "perfidy" of Harriet Grove — was added later (perhaps even by the "midnight moon"). Apparently it was not in the manuscript that Shelley used when he was compiling the Esdaile copybook (from the fall of 1811 into 1813).

Shelley intended (line 70, "pedestrianize") to walk to Wales. "My excursion," he informed Elizabeth Hitchener on June 25, "will be on foot for the purpose of better remarking the manners, and dispositions of the peasantry." It seems unlikely, however, that he carried out this intention. Rhayader was 181 miles from London, part of it through the Welsh mountains, and if Shelley had made such a trip on foot we would have heard something of it in his letters, but he makes no further reference to it. Furthermore, the approximate times of his leaving London and arriving at Rhayader apparently make such a walking trip impossible. The interesting thing, however, is that he did consider it. Such trips were not unusual at the time (as witness Keats's tour in Scotland).

"Ohe! jam satis dementiae" (line 61), possibly a quotation from a classical writer, may be rendered: "Oh! that is enough of foolishness."

9. Shelley, *Complete Works*, III, 317. He did, however, include a third (unpublished) stanza. (*Ibid.*)
10. The word "honours" in these verses (lines 42 and 49) seems to be used in a curious sense.

SC 167  P. B. SHELLEY TO T. J. HOGG, JUNE 20, 1811

AL unsigned, 5½ pages. Double sheet and single sheet, folio (11.9 x 7.2 inches). Laid paper. Watermark, double sheet: [Britannia in crowned oval]|; countermark, double sheet: GR| 1806|; watermark, single sheet: GR|1806|. Seal: wax, red: *PL* [in oval]|.

# The Carl H. Pforzheimer Library

**Shelley to Hogg**                                          **June 20, 1811**

SC 167  Postmarks: 1. (mileage stamp): HORSHAM| 41|; 2. (morning duty stamp, London): E| 21JU21| 1811|.

PROVENANCE: Thomas Jefferson Hogg; Major R. J. Jefferson Hogg (Sotheby, June 30, 1948, lot 25). *De Ricci 71* (p. 125).

*My dearest Friend*
*I shall be with you in three weeks . . . possibly less. – take lodgings for me*
*at York, if possible, at M^rs Doughty's. It is best to be before-hand as lodgings*
5 *may be scarce . . . What pleasure is even the anticipation of u^nestrained*
*converse . . I shall leave Field Place in a fortnight Old Westbrook has invited*
*me to accompany him & his daughters to a house they have at Aberystwythe*
*in Wales . . I shall stay about a week with him in Town when I shall come*
*to see you . . . Get lodgings —*
10 *How I wish that I could think exactly like you, that I could effectually imitate*
*your sentiments sentiments which inspire language that acts almost like*
*magic. When I read your letters, I think exactly completely like you, I wonder*
*am shocked at my own depravity in doubting what then appears so evident . . .*
*yet how evident! I lay down your letter, I look around me, I consider, I*
15 *behold the true state of the case . . Machinations have indeed succeeded, but*
*they are the machinations of wordly interest; It is true, it is true, I am on the*
*spot, I observe it. I am not only cool, but most violently prejudiced to that*
*opinion against which now conviction presses . . . Yet how is this? Fallen*
*as she is, I almost think that I could participate in her views . . that I could*
20 *adjust the glittering tinsel ornaments of anticipated matriimonialism, that*
*I could like a fashionable brother, act as a jackall for husbands . . Yet no!*
*this were too much, any thing but this, any thing but this last this only severe*
*trial of prejudiced attachment But yet I could watch her steps and even in*
*this degraded state could I essay to minister to her happiness, even when*
25 *she became bound to some fool, in a bond fit only for a Jewess, even then I*
*could rack my phiz into a smile to please her . . But this must not be . . .*
*you are not thus to be sacrifised, & much as I wish to think like you, yet I*
*think it were imbecile to model my opinion upon your's in that only point,*
*where there are many chances for my being right, where were I the least*
30 *enlightened of men, many chances for your being wrong, being what you*

[ 816 ]

SC 167  *are . . .     On every other point I believe that my opinion is your's . . .*
*wholly unreservedly your's. It is a sacrifise which I acknowlegde as due to*
*your superiority where we have opportunities of having an equal view of the*
*contested subject. —— but here! . . . do you not see . . you are under the*
35  *influence of a tyrannic passion, which you acknowledge, increases rapidly*
*under all it's disadvantages —— Surely a man under violent passion is not*
*a judge of the merits of it's object . . . particularly when these merits are*
*principally founded on two poems, confessedly not the subjects of universal*
*approbation, founded on the testimony of a brother ardently prejudiced . . .*
40  *He, then the sport of unreflecting sensation, alive to enthusiasm the most*
*irrational, he than whom the gale that blows was not more variable, in any*
*thing but friendship; — on the testimony of whom, who seized on some*
*detached noble sentiments, & then ascribed to her whose they were, perfection,*
*divinity, all the properties which the wildest religious ascribes to the god whom*
45  *he adores . . .     Had I then, been sacrifising at the altar of the Indian*
*Camdeo, the god of mystic love; and are you become an unreflecting votary*
*at it's shrine . . Consider . . . Consider. Matrimony is the word dear to*
*you, does it vibrate in unison with the hidden strings of rapture, awaken*
*divine anticipation . . . Is it not the most horrible of all the means which*
50  *the world has had recourse to, to bind the noble to itself – Yet this is the*
*subject of her constant & pointed panygeric it is in vain that I seek to talk*
*to her, it is in vain that I represent, or rather endeavour to represent the*
*futility of the worlds opinion "This then is the honorable advice of a brother"*
*. . "It is the disinterested representation of a friend" to which answer*
55  *followed a sneer, & an affected sportiveness of gaiety that admitted of no*
*reply . . . —— Have you read a new Novel, the Missionary by Miss*
*Owenson. It is a divine thing, Luxima the Indian Priestess, were it possible*
*to embody such a character, is perfect . . .     The Missionary has been my*
*companion for some time. I advise you to read it.*
60  ~~*I am*~~ *How much I admire your sentiments about Leonora!. You give up*
*the world, you resign it, & all its vanities . . you are right & so do I . .*
*Political or literary ambition is vice. Nothing but one thing is virtue. Adeu*
                                          *Your eternal friend–*

**Shelley to Hogg**                                    *June 20, 1811*

SC 167    *Yet I almost regret Leonora, how I wish you could get the MSS, but perhaps*
65        *it is not prudent.*

[Address, page 6]
*T. J. Hogg Esq^r*
*M^rs Doughtys*
*Coney S^t*
*York*

line 5. *unestained:* Shelley, presumably after completing the word, added the *r* above the *n*. In his general speed of writing he occasionally omits letters but this is the only case so far in which he has added one previously omitted. He does not seem generally to have read over these letters to Hogg after he wrote them. The blotting shows that they were usually folded immediately after composition.

line 17. *but:* Shelley apparently began with some other word and wrote *but* through it.

line 23. *steps* is written through some other word.

line 29. *are* is apparently written through *is*.

line 32. *sacrifise* is given as an alternate form in the *NED*.

line 32. *acknowlegde* (sic)

line 51. *panygeric* (sic); *panygeric* ends a line.

line 51. *to, that,* and *endeavour* can be completed from the paper adhering to the seal.

line 53. Shelley places quotes at the beginning of each line in quoting his sister's remark (before *the* and *brother*).

line 60. *I am:* Probable reading; letters partly obscured by wax from the sealing.

line 62. *Adeu* (sic)

line 64. Written across the writing on page 5 in a wavy line following the spaces between words and lines. Sometimes in letters of the period we find whole pages containing writing first horizontal and then vertical. The object was to save postage by getting more on a page — but it makes for difficult reading.

COLLATION (selected passages).
T. J. HOGG, *THE LIFE OF PERCY BYSSHE SHELLEY*, I, 406–408. (Hogg's changes indicated by italics.)

line 27. *I am* not thus to be sacrificed;

line 34. the influence of a *tyrannical preconception,* which you acknowledge increases *somewhat* under all *these* disadvantages? Surely a man under *a misguiding preconception*

line 44. the *Deity,* whom he adores.

line 47. *But I* consider, *I remember: there is one point of sympathy between you.* Matrimony, *I know,* is *a* word dear to you;

line 54. To which, *unanswered,* followed a sneer,

line 60. How much I admire *the* sentiments *in your tale!*

line 61. You are right, and so do *it!*

line 64. Yet I *should* almost regret *your tale!* How I wish you could *send me* the MSS.; but perhaps it *would* not *be* prudent; *it might miscarry.*

---

THE story of Shelley's various invitations to Wales becomes more complex as his letters proceed. On June 16 he informed Hogg: "I am invited to Wales, but I shall go to York."[1] A few days later he

1. SC 165 (June 16, 1811), line 26.

SC 167  wrote: "I am coming to York in my Way to Wales, where possibly I shall not go . . ."[2] In the above letter (line 6) he gives Hogg the further information that he has been invited to Aberystwyth in Wales by "Old Westbrook," and his plan seems to have involved the following stages: (a) to spend a week with the Westbrooks in London (line 8, "in Town"); (b) to go from London to York for a visit with Hogg; (c) to return to London and from there "accompany" the Westbrooks to Aberystwyth. Shelley implies to Hogg that the previously mentioned invitation was that from the Westbrooks. But although he did go to Wales he did not go to Aberystwyth; he went to visit his cousin, Thomas Grove, at Cwm Elan near Rhayader, some thirty miles from Aberystwyth (straight down the same coach road).[3] Hogg, on receiving a letter from Rhayader some weeks later, was clearly puzzled. He had apparently presumed all along that Shelley was with the Westbrooks at Aberystwyth.[4]

Shelley is apparently trying to befuddle Hogg and weave romantic insinuations. The invitation to Wales mentioned in the June 16 letter was almost certainly from the Groves and not the Westbrooks, because although Shelley had received the Groves' invitation before he left London on May 10[5] he had probably received the Westbrooks' invitation just prior to writing the above letter[6] for it is not mentioned in a letter to Shelley from Eliza Westbrook on June 11.[7] It may, in fact, have been that invitation which precipitated the writing of the above letter (coming so close to the preceding one). It may be that Shelley, in answer to Eliza, told her he was going to be in the vicinity of Rhayader and Eliza replied that as Aberystwyth was on the same road as Rhayader, he could perhaps combine the two visits.

Whatever the plans were they were upset by two events. Timothy Shelley found out something of Shelley's intentions and he ended up at the Groves'.[8] While at the Groves' he received a letter from Harriet

2. sc 166 (June 18–19), line 68.          3. Paterson's *Roads*, 1811.

4. See sc 170 (July ?18, 1811), line 8.

5. Charles Grove to Hellen Shelley, Feb. 16, 1857, Hogg, *Shelley*, II, 156.

6. The above letter, written at Field Place, bears a London morning duty receiving stamp of June 21; hence, it was written on June 20.

7. Ingpen, *Shelley in England*, pp. 276–277.          8. See sc 170 (July ?18, 1811), line 2.

SC 167    Westbrook which changed his plans about York (if he had ever seriously considered York), and sent him in a rush to London.

      The meaning of the above letter is, once more, distorted by Hogg's changes from its theme of Hogg and Elizabeth to Shelley and Elizabeth. Shelley is continuing his discouragement of Hogg's pursuit of his sister. The description of Hogg as "a man under violent passion" (line 36) indicates that Hogg's letters — unfortunately not preserved — must have been extremely agitated.

      "Camdeo, the god of mystic love" (line 46), is from the book Shelley later mentions (line 56), *The Missionary* by Sydney Owenson.[9]

      The "one thing" which is "virtue" (line 62) is probably the selfless, ideal love which was already beginning to crystallize as the core of Shelley's moral philosophy. He is hinting, as he had before, that Hogg's love for Elizabeth is self-seeking.

9. Shelley, *Complete Works*, VIII, 112 fn. See also sc 166, fn. 3.

SC 168    T. J. HOGG TO MRS. TIMOTHY SHELLEY, JULY ?6–18, 1811

AL (draft) unsigned, 4 pages. Double sheet, 4^to (9.7 x 8.1 inches).
Laid paper. Watermark: *TW&BB|*.

PROVENANCE: Thomas Jefferson Hogg; Major R. J. Jefferson Hogg (Sotheby, July 26, 1948, lot 280).

*expedition c^d not be felt.* ——

                                          *be*
     *As you were so obliging as to ~~express so some degree of~~ interested in*
    *health*
5   *my ~~welfare~~ I take the liberty of writing to you. I certainly did not feel any*
                                                   *done so*
  *ill effects from the fatigue that on such an+ I w^d certainly have ~~indulged~~*
  *~~myself in that pleasure sooner~~ had it been in my power. —— I can never*
  *sufficiently express my gratitude for your kindness — any kindness shewn*
                                        *valuable*
10   *to my friend ~~&~~, or myself is ten times more ~~kind~~ on account of the perhaps*
  *indelible stigma w^ch the liberality of Oxford was pleased to fix upon us. ~~The~~*
  *~~punishment of Cain was intolerable when the earth was almost desolate~~*
  *~~Surely never was punishment so severe exacted for so trifling an offense~~*
15   *~~Perhaps the whole of human malice c^d not have suggested a greater injury.~~*

**Hogg to Shelley**                                    *July ?6–18, 1811*

SC 168

> upon moral virtue
> For a bare speculation⌃for carrying perhaps a little too far some of the
> arguments of Locke for the amusement of a rainy morning without a moments
> warning without even the mockery of a false trial to enrol publickly two young
>
> 20          the bane of society & enemies of mankind                    essayed
> men amongst those wretches⌃who as the last effusion of depravity⌃to banish
> all restraint                                                    by
> ⌃all virtue & consequently all happiness from earth⌃publicly denied the
>                                              ever
> 25          Is surely a heavy punishmt for so venial an offence
> existence of a deity. —— ~~Perhaps no crime⌃deserved such a punishment wch~~
> To preclude for ever their access to those sources of knowledge
> ~~in addition   to it⌃precluding for ever those advantages (   ) the attainmt~~
> wch are open to all ōrs wch are only to be found at Oxford — Wd alone have been too severe a penalty    a loss
> 30  ~~of knowledge wch cd be found only at Oxford & wch they who inflicted it best~~
> wch was best known to be irreparable by those who inflicted it
> ~~knew that the loss was irreparable wd prevent any laudable ambition any inter-~~
> ~~course in society wd so cause perpetual discord & distrust in the families &~~
>                                      still                      It is easy entirely to destroy
> 35  ~~wch perhaps might sever ties if possible⌃more sacred. It is impossible ever to~~
>                  ~~is all that is necessary~~
>          ~~reputation An unfounded assertion~~
> ~~retrieve it up an opportunity of evincing by actions how w incorrect the general~~
> ~~censure is can rarely occur — And what actions when the mind is base will not~~
> 40  ~~admit of two constructions?~~ — Words even the most solemn ~~profession~~ prot-
> estations are in the power of any one - & what ~~form of~~ words can ~~be of any~~
>                  are uttered
> avail wch ~~is used~~ by a person ~~classe~~ branded indiscriminately as an Atheist.
> In addition a great degree of plausability nay even ~~the~~ a kind of magic power
> 45  named sophistry wch can mislead the judgment or even the senses generally
>                                                  feel
> forms part of the character of that class. — I severely ~~felt~~ the evil resulting
> from this opinion when an amiable precaution refused the favor of a few
> moments conversation even when sought at the ~~price of a considerable~~ risque of
> 50  violent & lasting displeasure in case my friends had discovered my absence. -
>                                                  afflict me deeply
> I had hoped to ~~convince~~ to remove some prejudices wch ~~are the source of misery~~
> ~~to me.~~ I had hoped to prove that I am not ~~altog~~ entirely depraved & abandoned
> & ~~that~~ to convince that if I had presumed to hope that my hopes were ~~consistent~~
> 55  ~~with~~ respectful & honorable In this I was cruelly disappointed. — The refusal
> was so decided I cd not venture then to hope for mercy        so decided as almost

SC 168   *to exceed justice & compell me to return immediately — Perfect neglect*

<s>I certainly am</s>

60   *perfect indifference must produce the keenest anguish – but to be hated*
<s>much affected o with this disappointmt</s> .

*but I pause.* ‡

*despised as unprincipled abandoned I must confess that I am perfectly*
*at a loss how to act – yet every difficulty is an additional stimulus if it is*
*possible to find addional motives. —— I cannot refrain from presuming*
65   *upon your kindness it was unusual unmerited so is the favor wᶜʰ I ask*
—— <s>If I obtain your advice I am so</s> *The cause is animating inspiring to*
*any exertion to whatever is barely possible I am equal. Danger of difficulties*
*I am unconscious of their existence . If I have your advice I shᵈ even presume*
*to hope but I ask too much – perhaps when you are at leisure a line a word*
70   <s>were it to tell me she is well & happy</s> *wᵈ not be <s>to</s> refused. — Surely my*
*transgression is not very great Surely to admire to love what is admirable &*
*amiable is natural —— irresistibly natural. — <s>If</s> the expression of such*
<s>love ⟨ ⟩</s> *passions may be sometimes culpable. but not when dictated by the*
*most correct honor —— At least nature feeling reason the general opinion of*
75   *mankind do not condemn it — if a thousand cruel difficulties present them-*
*selves it cannot be incorrect to recͤ the advice of ōrs how to surmount them*

*at least*

*it cannot but be kind to give it —. — That such are my sentiments you‸have*
*penetration to discover even when I am disgraced by the name of Atheist. ——*

*to*

80   *I must confess I was amused by the recital of the strange reports‸wᶜʰ my*
*visit in Sussex gave rise. <s>An</s> The truly consistent character of an Atheistical*
*Clergyman was introduced desseminating his doctrines & large bundles of*
*printed & mss blasphemies — In the accident wʰ <s>so</s> has added so much to*
85   *my zeal & so amply <s>ref</s> rewarded my risque & exertions it was stated that*
*this truly reverend divine was seen looking through the windows of Warnham*
*Church in a treasonable manner nay so lively so inventive is the human*
*imagination when once prejudiced that even the innocent oil the ⟨ ⟩ wᶜʰ*
*covered my head was perverted to revolutionary & regicidical purposes*

[Beginning at the bottom of page 4]

90   *But surely human tyranny never went to greater lengths when the whole*
*interest of a University was turned to blast every prospect of public advancemt*

## Hogg to Shelley                    *July ?6–18, 1811*

SC 168    *or domestic happiness. — What cd more effectually check the career of*
*laudable ambition than this public infamy? — What was more calculated*
*to sow the seeds of domestic dissention to disturb radically the peace of*
95    *families to create discord amongst relations perhaps to sever bonds if poss.*
*more sacred! —— An unfounded report is able to destroy the reputation of*
*an individual: How can he retrieve it? – An oppurtunity of evincing by*
unfounded
*actions how ~~incorrect~~ the general censure is can rarely occur And what*
100    *actions when the mind is once prejudic will not admit of two interpretations?*
*I confess I know none wd to God I did. ——‡ But surely what is effected*
*by injustice & oppression cannot be of long duration. There is & ever has*
*been a principle of natural equity in the constitution of things wch will not*
*allow truth & honor to be overwhelmed. I am conscious of no merit but*
105    *inflexible integrity is in the power of every one & it is hard to suffer as a*
now
*criminal – Is it impossible that eventually what appears ~~evil~~ hostile may<sub>∧</sub>*
*prove advantageous kindness under discouraging circumstances is a species*
*of generosity wch claim a higher degree of gratitude everything is valuable wch*
110    *tends to increase such an obligation*

The first line was apparently added later and is intended to follow the + on line 7, *the fatigue that on such an expedition cd not be felt.* Hogg means that his desire to meet Elizabeth kept him from feeling fatigue on his long journey from York to Field Place.

line 23. *by . . . denied* (sic)

line 29. *ōrs:* others. The line over *ōrs* indicates a contraction.

line 37. ~~*assertion:*~~ probable reading

line 44. *plausabity* (sic)

line 52. ~~*misery:*~~ probable reading

line 54. ~~*consistent:*~~ The *ful* of *respectful* has been added later. Hogg first wrote *consistent with respect and honor.* Then he added the *able* to *honor* and *ful* to *respect; ful* is cramped below the line.

line 61. *pause.*——‡: The cross corresponds to that on line 101; apparently lines 101–110 (beginning with *But surely*) are supposed to be inserted here. Hogg has no caret after *abandoned*

but the sense requires that *but I pause* follow *abandoned.* Then Hogg perhaps substituted *But surely what . . .* (line 101) for *but I pause* and failed to cancel it. Lines 101–110 (beginning with *But surely*) apparently are intended to be interpolated between *abandoned* and *I must confess.*

line 64. *addiōnal* (sic). The stroke over *ōn* is intended to indicate a contraction. Hogg's haste in writing this draft is clear here and elsewhere.

line 76. *rēcē:* receive

line 89. *my head:* probable reading. This line is wedged between two other lines, the writing of which is upside down to it. See line 90 below.

line 90. The passage, lines 90–110, beginning at the bottom of page 4 here runs into the lines coming down from the top of the page and the two passages are interlineated.

line 97. *oppurtunity* (sic)

line 100. *prejudic:* cramped into the edge of the paper at the left-hand edge.

# The Carl H. Pforzheimer Library

SC 168   THE above manuscript is a draft of a letter by Hogg similar to SC 162 (May 25, 1811), which was written to Elizabeth Shelley. It has been asserted that this draft, too, was intended for Elizabeth.[1] Its content and tone, however, show that this cannot be true and that it was to someone else, someone in contact with her and to be addressed with respect (line 68): "If I have your advice I sh$^d$ even presume to hope but I ask too much – perhaps when you are at leisure a word ~~were it to tell me she is well & happy~~ w$^d$ not be ~~to~~ refused."

The explanation is doubtless to be found in the following comments by Shelley to Hogg in his letters from Cwm Elan in July: "I have heard from the Westbrooks & from my Mother. — The latter cannot yet have rece[i]ved your's, as epistolary communications take some time in going to ~~York~~ Sussex from York via Rhayader." "Your letter was sent to my Mother last post day, I am well assured she will do nothing prejudicial to our interests . . . there is one altitude . . . to which I think *she* cannot soar. Intolerance." "Your letter is sent to my Mother, who is very much interested for you . . ."[2]

Hogg, therefore, had written a letter to Mrs. Shelley, had sent it to Shelley at Cwm Elan, and Shelley had forwarded it to Field Place. If we combine this fact with the content and date of the above manuscript there can be little doubt that we are dealing with a draft of this letter to Mrs. Shelley.[3]

The manuscript throws new light both on Mrs. Shelley (always a somewhat enigmatic figure) and on the relations of Elizabeth, Hogg, and Shelley. It gives further weight, for instance, to Shelley's comments on his mother's tolerance.

Hogg presumes, in this draft, that Mrs. Shelley has considerable interest in his cause. He asserts that Elizabeth refused to see him because of his atheistical views; and he explains the circumstances of the expulsion in terms which indicate that he realized Mrs. Shelley would be sympathetic to the recital. He would certainly not have written to Timothy Shelley with fine sarcasm about the "indelible stigma w$^{ch}$ the

---

1. Frederick L. Jones, "Hogg's Peep at Elizabeth Shelley," *Philological Quarterly*, XXIX (October 1950), 424.

2. SC 171 (July ?21), SC 172 (July ?22), SC 173 (July ?27–29).

3. See also SC 162. On the date see Commentary, below.

Holbrook

Warnham

Hunger Hill

Slinfold

Field Place

Warnham Church

Hawksbourne

Moated House

Roughey Street

Warnham Pond

Earthings

Broadbridge Mill

HORSHAM

St Leonards Forest

New Lodge

Itchingfield

Summerham Farm

Westons

Tower Hill

Chesworth

Coolhurst

Muntham

Denne Park

Plummer's Plain

Southland

Monk's Gate

Sedgwick Farm

Cripplegate

Cold Staple

Nuthurst Farm

Nuthurst

Warnham Church

Field Place

Map of the Country
Four Miles Around Horsham
and other Illustrations
from *The History and Antiquities of Horsham*, 1836
Edited and redrawn.

Miles 0    1    2    3    4    5

[ 825 ]

**Hogg to Shelley**                                    *July ?6–18, 1811*

SC 168  liberality of Oxford was pleased to fix upon us" (line 12) or to hint (line 35) that love has "bonds" "more sacred" than those of family ties. Mrs. Shelley was no atheist or revolutionary — as the jibes at the French materialists (line 21)[4] indicate — but she was certainly considered by Hogg to be a woman of intelligence and liberal views. If her attitude towards the expulsion had not been very different from that of her husband, Hogg would not have dwelt on such themes as "without even the mockery of a false trial" (line 19) or "too severe a penalty" (line 29). He clearly anticipates a reaction of indignation and sympathy.

On the other hand it becomes apparent that Elizabeth did not share her mother's views. Hogg, as he points out, had made a long journey — three days and nights on a coach — and had risked the "violent & lasting displeasure" (line 50) of his family[5] — to see Elizabeth, but she refused him even "the favor of a few moments conversation" (line 48), and he had to content himself with peeping at her through the windows of Warnham Church (line 84). Hogg was right in believing this to be extraordinary behavior, for he was, after all, an eligible young man (from a well-to-do family) and was apparently considered as such by Mrs. Shelley. One would expect that Elizabeth might at least have consented to see him. Certainly, she was not being held back by her mother. Her refusal implies an unusual motivation. The explanation which Hogg gives, namely her prejudice against him on religious grounds, is supported by Shelley's laments on her narrow viewpoint and submission to convention[6] (probably under her father's influence).

As to Hogg's character, we see in this letter not only his impetuosity — a three-day journey in the hope of a few moments' conversation — and his flair for the sardonic, but — in his excoriation of the Oxford authorities — something of that youthful radicalism which had attracted

4. Hogg's comments on the "wretches" (line 21) echo the usual Tory attacks of the time on the French materialists (some of whom he had himself read with approval at Oxford). He is trying to disguise his own atheism from Mrs. Shelley and imply that he and Shelley were not convinced of the truth of atheist doctrine. His implication (line 17) that *The Necessity of Atheism* did not propagate atheism but simply raised the question of its validity is correct (although a good deal more thought went into its production than is implied in — line 18 — "for the amusement of a rainy morning").

5. Hogg must mean "family" and not merely "friends" but does not wish to imply that his family would object to his associating with the Shelleys.

6. See, for instance, sc 165 (June 16, 1811).

# The Carl H. Pforzheimer Library

SC 168   Shelley to him. Hogg is indignant, bitter, and unyielding. One has the feeling that it was just as well that he was handled by the tactful Mr. Robert Clarke and did not have a Whitton and a Timothy Shelley to contend with.

The above manuscript also provides information on Hogg's visit to Field Place, a visit unknown to Shelley's earlier biographers.[7] The plan for the visit was outlined by Shelley in a letter of June 23 to Hogg:

> Come, then, my dear friend: happy, *most* happy shall I be if you will share my little study; happy that you come on an errand so likely to soothe me, and restore my peace. There are two rooms in this house, which I have taken exclusively to myself; my sister *will* not enter them, and no one else *shall:* these you shall inhabit with me. You must content yourself to sleep upon a mattress; and you will be like a State prisoner. You must only walk with me at midnight, for fear of discovery. My window commands a view of the lawn, where you will frequently see the object of your journey, — the object of my [i.e., your] fond affections. Time and opportunity must effect that in your favour with her which my entreaties cannot; indeed, I do not think it advisable to say too much on the subject; but more when we meet.[8]

Timothy Shelley, then, was not to be informed of the visit; nor apparently was Mrs. Shelley. But when Hogg arrived, as the above draft letter indicates, the plan must have been changed to take Mrs. Shelley into the secret. She had known that Hogg was at Field Place and apparently had met him: "I can never sufficiently express my gratitude for your kindness" (line 8); "I cannot refrain from presuming upon your kindness it was unusual unmerited" (line 64); "As you were so obliging as to be interested in my health" (line 3). Hogg would hardly have written in this way to Mrs. Shelley had he not met her, and the concept of her mind and character which underlies the letter seems to have been based upon personal observation.[9] Mrs. Shelley must have been let in on

---

7. Dowden, *Shelley*, I, 154: "Hogg did not travel from York to Horsham to enjoy imprisonment with an occasional view of Miss Shelley on the lawn; and his friend was not slow to perceive the unreasonable nature of his proposal." But see White, *Shelley*, I, 147, and F. L. Jones, "Hogg's Peep at Elizabeth Shelley."

8. Hogg printed "an object that will amply repay your journey" for "the object of your journey," "my favour" for "your favour," and omitted "my" before "entreaties." See Sotheby & Co., *Catalogue of The Correspondence of Thomas Jefferson Hogg* . . . , June 30, 1948, lot no. 26.

9. That Hogg met Mrs. Shelley is indicated also by Shelley's later comment (sc 170, line 9) that Hogg (at Field Place) had "made no secret" of their plan to go to York. Hogg had certainly talked

SC 168  the conspiracy, had probably met Hogg, and considered him not unfavorably as a suitor for her daughter.

The above draft is undated but an approximate date can be assigned. In the first place, it clearly follows the visit to Field Place. After he left Field Place, Hogg spent a few days in London, and can hardly have returned to York before July 6.[10] He could conceivably have written the above draft in London immediately after his visit, but the paper of the draft is the same as that of SC 177 (August 22, 1811), which was written at York.

As we noted above, by July 21 Shelley had received the letter for his mother of which the above was a draft. As Shelley was then at Cwm Elan and Hogg at York and as mail took about three days between Cwm Elan and York, the draft must have been written at least by July 18. Hence, the probable date span is July 6 to July 18.

to some member of the family. He would hardly discuss such plans with the servants, and he did not meet Elizabeth. In spite of Shelley's intentions it is not clear whether Hogg lodged at Field Place or at Horsham (with a visit to Field Place).

10. See "Prelude to Shelley's Elopement," below, p. 831.

# The Carl H. Pforzheimer Library

## PRELUDE TO SHELLEY'S ELOPEMENT:
### THE LETTERS TO HOGG FROM CWM ELAN

SHELLEY'S proposed visit to the Westbrooks in Aberystwyth having failed to materialize, he ended up at "Cwm Elan," the estate of his cousin, Thomas Grove, near the village of Rhayader in south Wales. While at Cwm Elan he was in correspondence with Harriet Westbrook and when he left Cwm Elan it was to elope with her.

During his stay there he wrote a series of letters to Hogg of considerable biographical interest. In order to understand them properly, however, we have first to try to untangle Shelley's rather mysterious movements between leaving Field Place and arriving at Cwm Elan, and then to see if we can put the letters in sequence and date them.[1]

Shelley's last letter from Field Place was dated June 25; his next clearly datable letters were both written at Cwm Elan on July 12 or 13.[2] What had happened in the intervening period?

It was on the morning of Sunday, June 23, that Shelley heard from Hogg that he intended to come to Field Place to see Elizabeth. Shelley answered on the same day: "The mail will convey you from York to London, whence the Horsham coach will bring you to Horsham; (news!) there I will meet you at midnight, whence you will be conveyed to your apartment." As this letter was dated at Field Place on June 23, it would not reach London until June 24 and would not get to York before June 26. If Hogg left York on June 26 he would not get to Horsham until June 28 or 29 (Friday and Saturday).

1. Ingpen in his editions of Shelley's letters and in Shelley, *Complete Works*, supplies tentative dates — sometimes on the month only — without comment. These seem to be largely guesses and are sometimes far from the mark.

2. The letters were to Elizabeth Hitchener and Edward Fergus Graham. Ingpen (Shelley, *Complete Works*, VIII, 124) notes that the postmark on the Elizabeth Hitchener letter was July 15 (a Monday). As it bears a date it must be a London postmark. The postmark on the Graham letter we derive from a photostat of the manuscript. It, too, is July 15 and is a morning duty inland mail stamp. And this must also be the type of stamp on the Elizabeth Hitchener letter.

To this information let us add that on post speeds and times. Paterson's *Roads*, 1811, gives the mail coach departure time from Rhayader as 3:00 p.m. A mail coach averaged seven to eight miles an hour. If a letter left Rhayader (181 miles from London) at 3:00 p.m. on a Saturday it would probably arrive in London on the Sunday evening and be given a morning duty stamp on Monday; so that the letters to Elizabeth Hitchener and Graham were probably posted from Rhayader on Saturday, July 13. (See also fn. 12.) As Cwm Elan was some four miles away, Shelley sometimes wrote letters the day before the post left. (See sc 171.) Hence, the assigned date for these letters — July 12–13.

# Shelley and his Circle : Manuscripts

*Letters from Cwm Elan*

On Tuesday, June 25, Shelley wrote to his schoolteacher friend, Elizabeth Hitchener, that he intended to be in London "on Monday" (July 1). As he wrote this letter after he knew that Hogg was coming, he cannot have intended to stay long with Hogg at Field Place, and so it is reasonable to assume that he did go to London on July 1. Hogg, then, must have got his "peep" at Elizabeth in Warnham Church on Sunday, June 30. He left Field Place "immediately" thereafter, apparently also for London.[3]

Shelley, as he had informed Hogg,[4] intended to spend a week in London with the Westbrooks and then leave for York to join Hogg there. When Hogg came to Field Place this arrangement was apparently changed to one in which Shelley, after his week in London, would "accompany" Hogg to York. But this plan miscarried. In a letter from Rhayader, Shelley wrote that as Hogg had "made no secret" of the plan (presumably when he was at Field Place), Shelley had told his father of it in a letter "from London" and his father put a stop to it: "he returned for answer on the Thursday that I might go but I should have no money from him if I did . . the case therefore became one of extreme necessity, I was forced to submit & now I am here."[5]

Shelley and Hogg, then, had planned to leave London together for York in the week of June 30–July 6. Hogg presumably accompanied Shelley from Field Place to London on Monday, June 30, but, if so, he does not seem to have been staying at the same place in London as Shelley.[6] He expected to leave London with Shelley but found after the "Thursday" ultimatum that Shelley had gone. "Thursday" must have been Thursday, July 4.

Shelley, then, was in London as late as July 4 and had been there since June 30. What was he doing there? Professor Hughes has suggested that he was involved with the Westbrooks: "In all probability the trouble arose in Chapel Street . . ."[7] There seems, in fact, to be no doubt that

3. sc 168 (July ?6–18), line 57.     4. sc 167 (June 20, 1811).

5. sc 170 (July ?18, 1811).

6. Shelley was probably staying with John Grove or Edward Fergus Graham. Grove forwarded his mail to Cwm Elan. See sc 169 (July ?15, 1811). He intended to stay with Graham in London on his return from Cwm Elan (sc 174, Aug. 3, 1811) and apparently did (sc 176, Aug. 15, 1811).

7. Hughes, *Nascent Mind*, p. 96.

# The Carl H. Pforzheimer Library

### Prelude to Elopement

he was in London mainly because of his interest in Harriet and that he
was spending a good part of his time with her.

Let us consider his activities. He rushed Hogg off to London after
only a two-day visit to Field Place, and apparently kept him in the dark
about his movements in London. He failed to see Elizabeth Hitchener
in London as he had promised,[8] an omission which can only be explained
by the presence of a strong counterattraction. When he arrived at Cwm
Elan he wrote to her in apology:

Your letter has just reached me, or rather has been just given to me after my
recovery from a short but violent nervous illness. It was occasioned by several
nights of sleeplessness, and days of pressing and urgent business; nothing else
could have prevented my calling on you in town, but my occupation was of
such a nature as would neither admit of delay or rest, and Stoic as I profess
myself, whilst yet this chain of clay fetters our nobler energies, it will at times
subdue them, it will at times remind us, and that forcibly, how mutually dependent on each other are mind and body. . . .[9]

What was the "urgent business" which demonstrated the power of the
body over the mind and resulted in "sleeplessness" and a "violent
nervous illness"? The answer must be Harriet Westbrook.

The Cwm Elan visit, then, not only ended with Harriet but began
with her also.

That the Cwm Elan letters to Hogg present a special problem in
dating Hogg himself was aware: "He [Shelley] too often omitted, in his
overwhelming, everlasting hurry, to date his letters. Not one of those
sent to me from South Wales has a date, the postmark being only
'Rhayader' [the post town]. Unless a letter passed through London and
the General Post Office, the date was not impressed upon it."[10]

As one might gather from these comments of Hogg the problem
has something of a floating-island air to it. There is no basic point of
reference for all the letters; each has to be dated in relation to the others.
The situation, however, is not quite so difficult as it first appears. At
least two other aids can be brought in to supplement the internal evidence:
we have some London postmarked letters from Cwm Elan (to corre-

8. To Elizabeth Hitchener, June 25, 1811; to Elizabeth Hitchener, July 15, 1811 (on date, see fn. 2).
(Shelley, *Complete Works*, VIII, 116, 124.)

9. July 15 (postmark), 1811.   10. Hogg, *Shelley*, I, 245.

spondents other than Hogg); we can ascertain the days on which the post left Rhayader and its time of departure. Furthermore, some points in the internal evidence are quite solid; and by putting all the evidence together we can get at least one exact date, several close approximations, and a fairly reliable general sequence for the series.

Shelley's first communication from Wales is an unsigned note to Hogg:

> I am just arrived. I have only time to say that I am most sincerely yours, and I will explain on Wednesday why I could not come to York. No post here but three times a-week.[11]

The post days from Rhayader were Monday, Thursday, and Saturday.[12] Cwm Elan was a little more than four miles west of Rhayader.[13] The unsigned note seems to have been written at Rhayader rather than at Cwm Elan: "no post *here* . . ." And this is what one would expect. Shelley would drop a note to Hogg as soon as he got off the coach at Rhayader and before being taken in the Groves' carriage to Cwm Elan. But when he next expected to write he would give himself more time —

11. Shelley, *Complete Works*, VIII, 123.

12. In a List of the Principal Post and Sub-post Towns appended to Cary's *New and Correct English Atlas* (London, 1793), the days of the arrival of mail at the two towns (Aberystwyth and New Radnor) which flanked Rhayader (374 inhabitants in 1811) on the road to London can be established as Monday, Thursday, Saturday. This schedule must also have applied to Rhayader as the same mail coach serviced the whole route. Shelley informs us that the mail went out the same day as it arrived (sc 169, July ?15, 1811; sc 173, ?July 27–29, 1811); and this is confirmed in Paterson's *Roads*, 1811, p. 533. Shelley states that the mail went out two hours after it came in; Paterson gives the time of arrival as 5 a.m. and that of departure as 3 p.m. Shelley may have been speaking of the times of arrival and departure at Cwm Elan for although sc 169 speaks of Rhayader, sc 173 seems to refer to Cwm Elan (see also sc 171, line 2).

That the Monday-Thursday-Saturday schedule given by Cary for 1793 was still in force in 1811 is indicated in Shelley's letters. The London postmarks on the letters to Elizabeth Hitchener are July 15 (Monday), July 27 (Saturday), July 29 (Monday); that on the letter to Graham is July 15 (Monday). As the mail from Rhayader was apparently stamped two days later in London (see fn. 2) this gives Thursday and Saturday as post days in Rhayader. The only letter from Cwm Elan that Shelley dated was one to Stockdale and this is dated August 1, which was a Thursday, and this letter seems to have been written directly upon his receiving Stockdale's. Shelley twice informs Hogg that he will write on "Thursday" (sc 169, line 11, sc 173, line 19).

In another letter (sc 171), clearly written on a Sunday, Shelley says that he expects a letter from Hogg "tomorrow." When Shelley left Rhayader he left on a Monday coach (sc 174).

13. Cary's *Roads*, 1819, p. 214. White (*Shelley*, I, 145) mistakenly places it "five miles south-east of Rhayader."

# The Carl H. Pforzheimer Library

## *Prelude to Elopement*

perhaps contemplating a letter of explanation — and write a day before the post day. Hence, the "Wednesday."

The reference to next writing on Wednesday shows also that the note on arrival was written to catch either the Saturday or the Monday mail preceding that Wednesday. Of these the Monday mail is the more likely, because Shelley would normally plan to write to Hogg by the first mail for which he had time to pen a letter, and if he had arrived on a Saturday he would have told Hogg that he would next write to catch the Monday and not the Wednesday mail. (If the note had been written on a Tuesday Shelley would have said that he would next write "tomorrow" and not "on Wednesday.") The note, therefore, was almost certainly written to catch a Monday mail; which means that Shelley arrived in Rhayader between the time the mail left on a Saturday and before it left on a Monday. What Saturday-to-Monday, however, was this? We know that it was later than July 4 because, as we have seen, Shelley was still in London on that date; and we know that it was earlier than July 13 because it was on July 13 that Shelley wrote the letter to Elizabeth Hitchener (quoted above) in which he implied that he had been at Cwm Elan for a day or more. And July 13 was a Saturday in 1811. Hence, the Saturday-to-Monday date range of the note on arrival cannot have been Saturday, July 13, to Monday, July 15. It must, therefore, have been Saturday, July 6, to Monday, July 8.

Following this note to Hogg of July 6–8 comes the main group of six letters, all without dates or dated postmarks. Of these, the last can, as we shall see, be dated fairly surely as August 3. The remaining five can be broken into two groups: three (sc 169, sc 170, sc 171) written before Shelley received a letter from Hogg directly addressed to Cwm Elan or Rhayader, two (sc 172 and sc 173) after he received such a letter.

Of the letters written before he heard from Hogg, let us first consider sc 169:

John Grove has sent *one* of yʳ letters . . I fancy the last. I am now at Rhayader . . the post comes in here but 3 times a week & goes out two hours after its' arrival; Cwm Elan is five miles thence, & I have ridden to R. & now write in the post office . . Pray write . . . confide in me . . believe that I am yours most sincerely what have you to say . . . What secret? . – – write: you know that every thing which you confide will be forever held in the inviolable

# Shelley and his Circle : Manuscripts

confidence of friendship You did me injustice by supposing that my own will detained me from York . . . Nothing but absolute & positive necessity could have superceded my determined intention . . . you will hear from me on Thursday . . . . at least I shall write then . .

The indications are that this was the first letter in the sequence (after the note on arrival). Hogg himself so placed it, and he may have had a special recollection of which letter came to him first. It informs Hogg of the location of Cwm Elan and the times of the mail. Hogg had either sent a letter to Shelley at John Grove's in London or had given Grove a letter to forward to him. This forwarded letter Shelley has now received. Hogg was doubtless angry at being left stranded in London without explanation, but Shelley seems to have expected a letter from him at Rhayader and is disappointed at not finding one. He seems, then, to have expected Hogg to have his address. But how could he have expected this? Hogg did not seem to know where Shelley was after he disappeared in London, for his letters to Shelley were not being sent to him directly but left for John Grove to forward.[14] The first intimation of Shelley's address in Wales presumably came from the note sent on arriving, which, like the other letters, must have been postmarked "RHAYADER" (a sufficient indication for "general delivery" mailing).[15] Shelley, then, must have assumed that there was time for this note to get to York and for Hogg to reply. If so, Shelley changed his intention of "explaining" to Hogg "on Wednesday," that is to say, on the very next post day, because it would take this note two or three days to get from Rhayader to York (not a main post route) and another two or three days for Hogg's reply to arrive, supposing him to have replied immediately. One can imagine that Shelley, when it came to the point, shrank somewhat from his task of explaining why he had changed his plans and decided to wait first for a letter from Hogg. When no letter came, he was worried that Hogg's anger was preventing him from replying. The indication, then, is that this letter was written about a week after the note on arrival (July 6–8).

14. sc 169 (July ?15, 1811), line 2. That Shelley's address was unfamiliar to Hogg is shown also in his misspellings of it in his annotations on this letter (lines 23 and 25). See Plates XXVI–XXVII.

15. Shelley had sent two letters to Hogg in April (sc 154, sc 155) to York simply marked "to be left until called for."

# The Carl H. Pforzheimer Library

## *Prelude to Elopement*

Let us consider one other point: the mail went out on Saturday, Monday, and Thursday; Shelley informs Hogg that he will next write on a Thursday. Because of his desire to mollify Hogg he would wish him to feel that he would write again at the earliest possible date. This makes it more likely that sc 169 was being written to catch a Monday than a Saturday mail. Furthermore, if it had been written on a Saturday, Shelley would have told Hogg that he would write next "on Monday" and not "on Thursday." As Shelley states that he is actually writing in the post office at Rhayader — had perhaps ridden there in his anxiety to hear from Hogg — the letter must have been written on a post day. The indication is, therefore, that it was written on Monday, July 15.

The probable sequence of events and letters, so far, is as follows: Shelley arrived in Rhayader Saturday-Monday, July 6–8, wrote a brief note to Hogg, proceeded to Cwm Elan, and was ill for a day or two. He wrote to Elizabeth Hitchener (and to Edward Fergus Graham) on the following Friday or Saturday (July 12 and 13), rode to Rhayader on Monday (July 15), hoping to find a letter from Hogg, and, finding none, wrote sc 169.

The two other letters written before Shelley got a reply from Hogg were sc 170 and sc 171. If our reasoning on sc 169 is correct, then, these two letters must follow it. And that they do is indicated by their content. For instance, in sc 170 Shelley gives a long explanation for his failure to meet Hogg at York but in sc 169 he simply mentions that he was unable to go there. There would be little point in his making the statement if he had already given the explanation.

sc 171 begins as follows:

Tomorrow I shall hear from you but cannot be able to answer your letter . . The post is here what the waves in Hell were to Tantalus. — I have heard from the Westbrooks & from my Mother. — The latter cannot yet have receved your's, as epistolary communications take some time in going to ~~York~~ Sussex from York via Rhayader. I have been to church today. they perach partly in Welsh.

From this letter we can gather (a) the letter was written on a Sunday; (b) although Shelley has not himself had a letter from Hogg he has received a letter for his mother which Hogg apparently wished him to read and forward. If Shelley had received this letter for his mother prior to writing sc 170 he would surely have mentioned it in that letter. But he does not, so that of these two letters sc 171 must follow sc 170.

On what Sunday was sc 171 written? We cannot exactly tell but the most likely is Sunday, July 21, because Shelley's feelings of guilt and anxiety are now driving him to write to Hogg with almost each post. And if sc 171 was written on Sunday, July 21, then sc 170 was probably written only a few days before, namely for the post of either Thursday (July 18) or Saturday (July 20). Of these two, the Thursday date is the more likely because of the comment in sc 169 (*circa* Monday, July 15) that Hogg would hear "on Thursday."

We can, therefore, assign approximate dates, for Shelley's arrival note and first three letters from Cwm Elan, as follows: the arrival note, July 6–8; sc 169, July 15; sc 170, July 18; sc 171, July 21.

From its tone and contents sc 172 is clearly the first letter written after Shelley received a reply from Hogg. Moreover, it contains a reference to sc 169 (*circa* July 15) which enables us to give it an approximate date. In sc 169 Shelley mentions that Harriet Westbrook had sent him a copy of Amelia Opie's novel *Adeline Mowbray*. In sc 172 he writes "I have not read Adeline . . ." in a context that indicates that Hogg had commented on the novel and asked whether he had read it.[16] sc 172, then, must be at least five to six days later than sc 169 (the time of the mail to and fro), which would place it about July 20 or 21. Shelley also informs us that he is writing on the afternoon or evening of a post day: "your animadversions of this morning." As July 15 was a Monday, Hogg's reply to sc 169 must have arrived either on Saturday, July 20, or Monday, July 22. If we are correct in dating sc 171 as Sunday, July 21, then of these alternatives Monday, July 22, is indicated.

The final letter in the series, sc 174, can be dated fairly securely as August 3. In it Shelley writes that he has had a letter from Harriet Westbrook: "she wrote to say that . . . she would fly with me, & threw herself on my protection." Consequently, "I set off for London on Monday."[17] On Thursday, August 1, Shelley was still at Cwm Elan, for on that day he wrote a dated letter from there to his publisher, J. J.

16. See sc 172 (July ?22, 1811) and Commentary.

17. See also Shelley to Elizabeth Hitchener, Oct. 27, 1811: "Her letters became more and more g[loomy] at length one assumed a tone of such despair, as induced me to quit Wales precipitately."

### Prelude to Elopement

Stockdale.[18] On Saturday, August 10, he was in London, for he wrote a dated letter there on that day to Elizabeth Hitchener.[19] Hence, the "Monday" of sc 174 can only be Monday, August 5. Shelley intended, therefore, to "set off for London" on that date.

In the excitement of the moment he believed that Harriet might "fly" with him immediately. The letter begins dramatically: "You will perhaps see me before I can answer this." Hogg changes "I" to "you" and this seems justified. Shelley in his confused haste must have written "I" for "you." He apparently meant that he and Harriet might arrive in York at about the same time as the letter. But if he arrived in London on August 6 he could not have got to York until at least August 7 or 8 even if he had experienced no delays. He cannot, then, have expected his letter to leave Rhayader until Monday, August 5. But it was not written on Sunday, August 4, or he would not have said that he was setting off for London "on Monday" but "tomorrow." The letter must, then, have been written on Saturday, August 3.

When had Harriet's letter arrived? The probability is that it came to Rhayader with the Saturday mail, and was then taken (perhaps by one of the Groves' servants) to Cwm Elan. The letter to Stockdale on Thursday, August 1, shows no sign of excitement. But on Saturday came Harriet's letter, and Shelley, as we would expect, sat down immediately to tell Hogg the good news. By that time, however, the exit mail had already left Rhayader and he knew that Hogg could not receive the letter until Wednesday, August 7, at the earliest.

The probable sequence and dating of Shelley's letters to Hogg from Cwm Elan is as follows:

1. Saturday-Monday, July 6–8. Note on arrival, quoted above.
2. Monday, July 15 (sc 169).
3. Thursday, July 18 (sc 170).
4. Sunday, July 21 (sc 171).
5. Monday, July 22 (sc 172).
6. Saturday-Monday, July 27–29 (sc 173).
7. Saturday, August 3 (sc 174).

K.N.C.

18. Shelley, *Complete Works*, VIII, 137.

19. *Ibid.*, p. 139. A photostat shows that the letter was dated by Shelley.

SC 169   P. B. SHELLEY TO T. J. HOGG, JULY ?15, 1811

AL signed *PBS*, 2½ pages. Double sheet, 4^to (8.8 x 7.3 inches).
Wove paper. Watermark: W TURNER & SON|.
Seal: wafer, blue.
Postmark: (provincial stamp): RHAY[ADER]|.
Notations, in the hand of T. J. Hogg.   (See Plates XXVI–XXVII.)

PROVENANCE: Thomas Jefferson Hogg; Major R. J. Jefferson Hogg (Sotheby,
June 30, 1948, lot 34); Dr. Silvain Brunschwig (Nicholas Rauch, Geneva, Nov.
22, 1955, lot 240). *De Ricci 82* (p. 126).


*My dear friend*

    *John Grove has sent* <u>one</u> *of y^r letters . . I fancy the last. I am now at*
*Rhayader . . the post comes in here but 3 times a week & goes out two hours*
*after its' arrival; Cwm Elan is five miles thence, & I have ridden to R. &*
5  *now write in the post office . . Pray write . . . confide in me . . believe that*
*I am yours most sincerely what have you to say . . . What secret? . – – write:*
*you know that every thing which you confide will be forever held in the*
*inviolable confidence of friendship You did me injustice by supposing that*
*my own will detained me from York . . .     Nothing but absolute & positive*
10  *necessity could have superceded my determined intention . . . you will hear*
*from me on Thursday . . . . at least I shall write then . . Adeiu*
                         *your* <u>eternally</u> *faithful*
                              *PBS*
             *Cwm Elan*
15                  *Rhayader Radnorshire*

[Page 3]
*Miss Westbrook Harriet has advised me to read M^rs Opie's Mother &*
*Daughter . . . she has sent it hither, she has desired my opinion with*
*earnestness      what is this tal< > but I shall read it tonight.*

[Address, page 4]
*T. Jefferson Hogg Esq^re——*
20  *M^rs Doughty's*
*Coney Street*
*York*

**Shelley to Hogg**                                    **July ?15, 1811**

SC 169   [Notations in the hand of T. J. Hogg, page 2]

*Crom Elan*

*Cuckfield*

25                                                    *Rayader*

*Cuckfield*

*RadnorShire*

*cwel*

*P I Injury*

30                                                    *CAPEL*

*Paris*             *PARIS*                           *CERIG*

*NORTH WAL.*

line 6. Shelley makes use of the fact that *sincerely* is the last word on a line as a stop; so, also, with *friendship*.

line 10. *superceded* (sic)

line 11. *Adeiu* (sic)

line 13. *PBS*: probable reading; the letters are compressed and unclear.

line 16. Lines 16–18, on page 3, form a kind of postscript. The blottings may indicate that Shelley wrote the return address (lines 14 and

15), folded the pages, and then opened the letter again to add first the complimentary close (lines 12 and 13) and then these lines on Harriet. See Plates XXVI–XXVII.

line 23. *Crom Elan*, *Cuckfield*, and *Rayader* are in script with unjoined letters.

line 28. Lines 28–32 are written vertically in the lower left margin. The second *PARIS* and *CAPEL| CERIG| NORTH WAL.|* are written in block capitals.

THE novel (line 16) which Harriet recommended[1] to Shelley (Amelia Opie's *Adeline Mowbray, or the Mother and Daughter*) turns out upon investigation to be of special biographical interest. It is less a narrative than a treatise against free love, specifically directed at William Godwin and Mary Wollstonecraft. The heroine, Adeline Mowbray (Mary Wollstonecraft), comes under the influence of Frederic Glenmurray (William Godwin), a learned author famous for his condemnation of marriage, and runs away with him to Lisbon. Glenmurray argues persuasively: "'Then, in defiance of the world's opinion, that opinion which I, you see, had not resolution to brave, you will be mine — not according

1. In Shelley's letter to Hogg of July ?22 (sc 172) he comments (line 3) "I have not read Adeline but shall as soon as I can get it." This appears to contradict his statements in the above letter (lines 16–18). It may be that he had received a letter from Harriet stating that she had sent the book but that he had not received it or perhaps one of the Groves had borrowed it.

SC 169   to the ties of marriage, but with no other ties or sanction than those of love and reason?'"[2]

Adeline proves an apt pupil. When Glenmurray later wishes to marry her she refutes him with his own arguments:

"Then, if you still are convinced your theory is good, why let your practice be bad? It is incumbent on you to act up to the principles that you profess, in order to give them their proper weight in society — else you give the lie to your own declarations."

"But it is better for me to do that, than for you to be the sacrifice to my reputation."

"I," replied Adeline, "am entirely out of the question: you are to be governed by no other law but your desire to promote general utility, and are not to think at all of the interest of an individual."[3]

In time, however, the horrors of retribution descend. Adeline finds that she has become an outcast from society, looked down upon as a "mistress" and snubbed by "respectable" women, even by her own servants.

Glenmurray on his (untimely) deathbed condemns himself bitterly for "having been the means of blasting all your fair fame and prospects in life." "Who led you to a train of reasoning, so alluring in theory, so pernicious in practice? Had not I, with the heedless vanity of youth, given to the world the crude conceptions of four-and-twenty, you might at this moment have been the idol of a respectable society; and I, equally respected, have been the husband of your heart."[4]

Why did Harriet (doubtless in concert with Eliza) recommend such a novel to Shelley? The answer must be that Shelley had discussed his own (and Godwin's) free-love doctrines with Harriet,[5] had perhaps asked

2. Amelia Opie, *Adeline Mowbray, or the Mother and Daughter, A Tale, in Three Volumes* (London, 1805), I, 100.

3. *Ibid.*, p. 186.

4. *Ibid.*, II, 190–191. After Glenmurray's death Adeline marries a rich relative of his who falls in love with her. He later taunts her with having been the mistress of Glenmurray, is unfaithful to her, and finally deserts her. At the end Adeline is converted to the soundness of marriage as an institution (III, 207 ff.) and pens a letter to her mother in deathbed repentance (she is dying of a "decline" accompanied by "languors"; III, 159).

5. Shelley's expression of his own views on these subjects in his letter to Hogg on May 8 (sc 157) were attributed to Godwin in Hogg's changed version of the letter (Collation, line 53). Shelley must have talked a good deal about Godwin's views on these matters at the time.

SC 169    her to run away with him, and the book was intended as a warning. Shelley was probably more active in his pursuit of Harriet — and less the passive victim of a trap — than his biographers have supposed.[6]

The author of the novel, Amelia Opie (Amelia Alderson before her marriage to John Opie, the portrait painter who painted both Godwin and Mary Wollstonecraft), had been admired by Godwin and had rejected his proposal of marriage.[7] She was opposed to Godwin's moral philosophy, but, to judge by *Adeline Mowbray*, really had little understanding of it — as even the above-quoted passages suffice to show. If Shelley read the book it certainly failed to have any effect on him. The Note on love and marriage in *Queen Mab*, published in the summer of 1813, reflects Godwin's views.

The notations by Hogg on page 2 of the manuscript seem almost like doodling with letters, some in a kind of copybook hand, some in block capitals.[8] The "Crom Elan" for instance is apparently an attempt to copy Shelley's "Cwm Elan" above it. "Cwel" seems to be an idle copying of the first two letters of Cwm and Elan. As to "Cuckfield" and "RadnorShire" we might note the following comment by Hogg in his life of Shelley: "Whilst I was stationary and tranquil, my friend was restless and uneasy; at one time he was in London, then at Field Place, now at Cuckfield, backwards and forwards; he even paid a visit to a cousin in Radnorshire. I received many letters from him . . . ."[9]

6. See Commentaries to sc 174 (Aug. 3, 1811) and sc 176 (Aug. 15, 1811).

7. See also sc 20 (June 26, 1797), fns. 5 and 6.

8. See also sc 129 (Jan. 6, 1811), line 1, and sc 131 (Jan. 10, 1811), line 70.

9. Hogg, *Shelley*, 244–245. Hogg was at this time, as he tells us, making plans for an approaching six-weeks' vacation. "The alternative was either to go home for a little partridge shooting, or to plan a tour; the latter was the more attractive, and it possessed the additional recommendation, that if my friend chose, he might join me and share in my excursion." It may be that Capel Cerrig (in North Wales) and Paris (line 31) were considered in Hogg's speculations.


SC 170    P. B. SHELLEY TO T. J. HOGG, JULY ?18, 1811

AL signed *P B Shelley.*, 2½ pages. Double sheet, 4$^{to}$ (8.8 x 7.2 inches). Wove paper. Gilt edges.
Seal: wafer, red.
Postmark: (provincial stamp): RHAYADER|.

**Shelley to Hogg**                                    **July ?18, 1811**

SC 170   PROVENANCE: Thomas Jefferson Hogg; Major R. J. Jefferson Hogg (Sotheby, June 30, 1948, lot 31). *De Ricci 80* (p. 126).

*My dearest friend*
         *I had a letter from my Father . . . all is found out about your journey*
*to Horsham, & mine to York, thereby for a while prevented   God send he*
*does not write to yʳ father . . . I thew cool water on the rage of the old buck.*
5     *I question whether he has let the Family into the secret of his discovery,*
*which must have been* <u>*magically effected*</u>*. I had previously to my intention*
*of coming to York accepted an invitation of a Cousin of mine here to say a*
*week or two whence I intended to procceed to Aberistwyth about thirty miles*
*off . . I then changed my mind in order to accompany you to York . . as*
10    *you made no secret of this I mentioned in a letter to my Father from London*
*that such was my intention he returned for answer on the Thursday that I*
*might go but I should have no money from him if I did . . the case therefore*
*became one of extreme necessity, I was forced to submit & now I am here . . .*
*Do not think however but that I shall come to see you long before you can*
15    *come to London . . but open warfare will never do, & Mʳ Peyton which will*
*be my nom de guerre will easily swallow up Mʳ Shelley. I shall keep quiet*
*here for a few weeks . . I have heard of the miscarriage of one of my letters*
*to you by the pillage of the Rhayader Mail. I shall write very often & enclose*
*Eliza's letters when I have them. — This is most divine scenery but all very*
20    *dull stale flat & unprofitable . . indeed this place is a very great bore . .*
*I shall see the Miss Westbrooks again soon, they were very well in Condowell*
*when I heard last . . they then proceed to Aberystwith where I shall meet*
*them . . The Post here is only 3 times a week & that very uncertain irregular*
*& unsafe . .*
25    *Let me here soon from you. I will write every Post day*
                         *Your most affect –*
                         *P B Shelley.*

*Cwm Elan*
         *Rhayader*
30                *Radnorshire*
[Address, page 4]

**Shelley to Hogg**                                        *July ?18, 1811*

SC 170  *T. Jefferson Hogg Esq^{re}——*
*M^{rs} Doughty's*
*Coney Street*
*York*

line 3. *prevented* comes at the end of a line and Shelley, as he often does, uses its position there as a stop.

line 4. *thew* (sic)

line 7. *say* (sic)

line 8. *procceed* (sic)

line 21. *Condowell:* probable reading; so, too, in Hogg, *Shelley*, I, 225. A possible reading is *londowell*, a hasty combining of *London* and *well*.

line 25. *here* (sic)

COLLATION (selected passages).
T. J. HOGG, *THE LIFE OF PERCY BYSSHE SHELLEY*, I, 385. (Hogg's changes indicated by italics.)

line 2. all is found out about *my inviting you* to Horsham, and *my proposed journey* to York,

line 4. father; *it would annoy him.*

THE Groves' estate at which Shelley was staying (with its "divine" scenery, line 19, on which he comments) was a celebrated tourist sight in south Wales. We find the following contemporary account in George Nicholson's *The Cambrian Traveller's Guide in Every Direction* in 1813:

The principal house in *Cwnland* belongs to Thomas Groves, esq. a Wiltshire gentleman, who purchased 10,000 almost worthless acres, which he is now converting into a paradise. This estate is called Cwn Elian, distant from Rhaiadyr 5 m., and is the summer residence of the proprietor. The approach to the house is over a handsome wooden bridge, leading to a fine verdant lawn, which stretches from the house, and forms a curve with the river Elian, uniting a singular combination of natural and artificial beauties, of wild scenery and elegant ornament; a foaming river, rugged rocks, precipices, and lofty mountains, contrasted with rich meadows, neat enclosures, and elegant buildings. In pursuing the Elian through mr. Groves's estate, it's various beauties are very striking, particularly at the distance of a mile from the house, where the pedestrian crosses a rude alpine bridge, formed of the branches of trees, thrown from rock to rock, under which the Elian dashes at the depth of 30 feet. This spot is well described by mr. Bowles in his poem of "Coombe Elian."[1]

The boredom which Shelley expresses with the "divine scenery" (line 19)[2] is echoed also in a letter to Graham: "Here are rocks, cataracts,

1. Nicholson (London, 1813), pp. 1140–1141.

2. The "dull stale flat & unprofitable" existence that went along with the scenery incorrectly echoes Hamlet — "dull" for "weary." The Variorum Shakespeare does not record "dull."

# Shelley and his Circle : Manuscripts

SC 170   woods and Groves."³ Why the boredom? Shelley hints at the answer in the next letter (sc 171): "I am more astonished at the grandeur of this scenery than I expected. I do not *now* much regard it. I have other things to think of ——" This can only mean that he was absorbed in Harriet Westbrook and restless to be with her although he does not want to say so to Hogg. Unfortunately we do not have Shelley's letters to Harriet from Cwm Elan. If we had we could better judge the degree of his feelings. For in his letters to Hogg he is hiding these feelings, sensing Hogg's jealousy and fearing his sarcasm. It was for this reason presumably that he kept Hogg in the dark about his movements in London and then suddenly left without informing him. His guilt feelings toward Hogg because of these actions appear in the above letter both in the jumpiness of its style and in its curious misspellings and other errors. Shelley, we may note, had a lot to explain. Not only had he left Hogg high and dry in London but he had told him a variety of stories (that he would visit the Westbrooks in London and then go on to York with Hogg, that he would go to York and forget about the Westbrooks). And after all of them he turned up in Wales on his cousin's estate, this time with a new story: he would go from Cwm Elan to Aberystwyth and then on to York.

The mystification is increased by the reference to the Westbrooks' being at "Condowell." We find no trace of a Condowell in the atlases or road guides of the early nineteenth century,⁴ and as some of these list even the smallest village we can assume that there was no such place. Perhaps Shelley is simply inventing a Welsh-sounding name to cover up his previous tales about the Westbrooks and Aberystwyth. There is no evidence of the Westbrooks' having actually been at Aberystwyth.

---

3. [July 13, 1811], Shelley, *Complete Works*, VIII, 123. On the dating of this letter see "Prelude to Shelley's Elopement," fn. 2.

4. For instance, Smith's *English Atlas* (1808); W. C. Oulton's *The Traveller's Guide* (1805), 2 vols.; G. B. Kearsley's *Traveller's Entertaining Guide* (1803); Paterson's *Roads* (1811); Cary's *Roads* (1819). Nor does Condowell appear in the *Oxford Dictionary of Place Names*. (We have also, we might note, checked for *Londawell* and *Llandowell* in these various books.) In addition to the story on the Westbrooks and Aberystwyth or "Condowell" one might also entertain suspicions on the pillaging (line 18) of the Rhayader mail. If our arguments on dating are correct, Shelley had previously only written twice: the note on arrival and sc 169. Neither of these items was "pillaged" (as the Provenance shows). Shelley, in trying to reassure Hogg of his friendship, perhaps exaggerated some rumor about the mail into a suggestion that he had written more frequently than in fact he had.

**Shelley to Hogg**                                         *July ?21, 1811*

sc 170 On the contrary, the indication is that they were in London all the time.
Harriet's letter to Shelley of about August 1 (see sc 174) seems to have
come from London, and Shelley's later comments to Elizabeth Hitchener
imply that all her letters came from London: "The frequency of her
letters became greater during my stay in Wales ... at length one
assumed a tone of such despair, as induced me to quit Wales precipitately.
— I arrived in London."[5]

5. "October 27, 1811.?", Shelley, *Complete Works*, VIII, 169.

sc 171 P. B. SHELLEY TO T. J. HOGG, JULY ?21, 1811

AL signed[?] *Percy*, 4¾ pages. Double sheet and single sheet, folio (12.2 x 7.2
inches).
Laid paper. Watermark, double sheet: [royal coat of arms, quartered, in
crowned shield]|; countermark, double sheet: 1810|; watermark, single sheet:
[royal coat of arms, quartered, in crowned shield]|.   (See Plate xxv.)
Seal: wax, black: [round grill with large centered circle]|.
Postmark: (provincial stamp): RHAYADER|.

PROVENANCE: Thomas Jefferson Hogg; Major R. J. Jefferson Hogg (Sotheby,
June 30, 1948, lot 32). *De Ricci 85* (p. 126).

*My dear friend*
*    Tomorrow I shall hear from you but cannot be able to answer your*
*letter . . The post is here what the waves in Hell were to Tantalus. — I have*
*heard from the Westbrooks & from my Mother. — The latter cannot yet*
5 *have receved your's, as epistolary communications take some time in going*
*to ~~York~~ Sussex from York via Rhayader. I have been to church today. they*
*perach partly in Welsh, which sounds most singularly — A Xting was*
*performed out of an old broken slop-bason . . This country is highly romantic*
*here are rocks of immense height, & picturesque waterfalls. I am more*
10 *astonished at the grandeur of this scenery than I expected. I do not now*
*much regard it. I have other things to think of —*
*    I have had no cause to alter my opinion, I do not think that I am at*
*liberty to give you any hopes . . I suppose whilst Warnham Church exists*
*that you will take them for yourself. — It is now far from being my wish*

SC 171   *that you should think more of Eliza . . I forsee that all hopes encouraged in that quarter will end in dissapointment. I do not say despair for I have too good an opinion of your firmness to suppose that you would yield to despair. Besides <u>wherefore</u> should you love her? . A disinterested appreciation of what is in itself excellent. this is good if it is so . . but what you feel*

20   *is a <u>passion</u> it is I <u>suppose</u> involuntary . . passion can evidently be neither interested or its opposite. Is it not then the business of reason to conquer passion, – particularly when you receive <u>all</u> the evidence of her loveliness from the latter, & <u>none</u> from the former . . . Ought you not to doubt the worthiness of what depends on the mere impulses of the latter, for what could*

25   *reason have to do with peeping in at Warnham Church I don't know on considering however, if you did not display <u>more</u> reason then, than at any other period of your passion, since for <u>once</u> you consented to refer to the evidence of your senses . . .*

  *Now there is Miss F. D. Browne, (certainly a tyger;) yet she surpasses my*

30   *sister in poetical talents, this your dispassionate criticism <u>must</u> allow . . that lovely extract of her poems <u>certainly</u> surpasses any of Eliza's . . and it was E's poetry that first attracted your attention, charmed, & now has bewitched you! . . unless you were influenced by the vague unconnected*

                                         *with*

35   *prejudiced praises which <u>I would</u> at times speak of E. . . .   let me <u>hope</u> that you will be dispassionate . . <u>Your</u> happiness & that of my sister has now for some months been my aim, do not <u>execrate</u> when I say that <u>now</u> < > see no chance of their being united . . . <u>She</u> is not what she was . . you continue the same; and ever may you be so! . I am <u>here</u> for the present*

40   *absolutely because I have no money to come to York, & because I <u>must</u> come there incog. —— I am what the sailors call banyaning. I do not see a soul. all is gloomy & desolate. I amuse myself however with reading Darwin, climbing rocks, & exploring this scenery . . amusement? I have seen the papers, & Burdons poem. It is certainly admirable as an architectural Poem,*

45   *but do not let <u>me</u> be considered <u>envious</u> when I say that it appears to me to want energy, since the very idea of <u>my</u> being able to write like it, is eminently ludicrous . . I wonder whether Burdon is a fool or an hypocrite. he <u>must</u> be*

**Shelley to Hogg**                                    *July ?21, 1811*

SC 171   *the latter.* —— *Have you read the Missionary it is a beautiful thing. It is here & I cd. not help reading it again – . or do you not read Novels.* ——

50                                                    *Adieu Your sincere*
                                                        *Percy*


         *Cwm Elan   Rh —— d –*
              *Radn —— hire*

         [Address, page 6]
         *T. Jefferson Hogg Esq^r*
55       *M^rs Doughty's*
         *Coney S^t — York –*

line 5. *receved* (sic)
line 7. *perach* (sic)
line 7. *Xting* (i.e., christening)
line 8. *slop-bason: bason* is given as an alternative form in the *NED*; see sc 131 (Jan. 10, 1811), line 32.
line 16. *dissapointment* (sic)
line 37. ⟨*I*⟩ *see*

line 51. *Percy* (probable reading). The initial *P* resembles an *F* and the *y* ends in a flourish. Shelley's signatures on these letters show great variations. He seems to be deliberately trying to sign each one somewhat differently.
line 52. *Rh⟨aya⟩d⟨er⟩ Radn⟨ors⟩hire:* The address goes off into a scrawl.

COLLATION (selected passages).
T. J. HOGG, *THE LIFE OF PERCY BYSSHE SHELLEY*, I, 390–391. (Hogg's changes indicated by italics.)

line 12. at liberty *to entertain* any hopes. I suppose, whilst *York Minster* exists, that you will *indulge* them *yourself on my account.* Now, there is Miss F. D. Browne (certainly a *tigress*), yet she surpasses my sister in poetical talents — this *every* dispassionate criticism

line 14. *For the rest,* it is now far from being my wish that you should think more *of the past.* I forsee that all *regrets cherished on that head* will end in *aggravating* disappointment;

line 17. an opinion of *my* firmness to suppose that *I* would yield to despair. Besides, wherefore should *I* love her?

line 19. but what *I felt was* a passion. It *was,* I suppose, involuntary:

line 22. particularly when *I received* all the evidences of her loveliness from the latter,

line 23. Ought *I* not to doubt

line 24. for what could reason have to do *with it any more than* with peeping *at a lady through a window.* I do not know, on considering, however, if *the lover would* not display more reason than at any other period of *his* passion, since for once *he* consented to refer to the evidence of *his* senses.

line 31. and it was *Elizabeth's* poetry that first *so strongly* attracted *my* attention, charmed, and, *as you were pleased to say,* bewitched *me; and which you admired,* unless you were influenced

line 35. Let me hope that *I shall* be dispassionate; *I did* execrate *my existence once,* when *I first discovered that there was* no chance of *our* being united. *To enjoy your society* and that of my sister has now for some months been my aim. She is not what she was; you continue the same, and ever may you be so!

[In this letter Hogg has changed the position of some sentences.]

# Shelley and his Circle : Manuscripts

SC 171      Hogg's picture of himself in his biography of Shelley as the dispassionate young sophisticate gently guiding the erring footsteps of the
impetuous "divine poet"[1] is not borne out by what we can deduce about
his end of this correspondence. Shelley here is apparently trying to knock
some sense into Hogg, whose "*passion*" (line 20) has gone beyond reason
or the "evidence" of the "senses" (line 28) and who when advised
execrates (line 37) his adviser. After the "peeping in at Warnham Church"
(line 25 — eliminated in Hogg's text), Shelley had clearly advised Hogg
to desist, and he has since "had no cause to alter [his] opinion." As he
had done before, he urges Hogg to give up the whole affair: "Is it not
then the business of reason to conquer passion" (line 21).

Hogg was first attracted by Elizabeth Shelley's intellectual qualities
as revealed in her poetry, and this, Shelley implies, is the only basis for
any further relationship. Otherwise it is just involuntary passion (line
20). Once there might have been a possibility for a deep relationship,
but now — the old refrain — Elizabeth "is not what she was" (line 38),
but is corrupted by the world.

"Miss F. D. Browne" (line 29) was Felicia Dorothea Browne, who
married Captain Alfred Hemans in 1812 and was better known thereafter
as Felicia Hemans, author of *Casabianca* ("The boy stood on the burning
deck"). In 1808, when only thirteen, she produced the volume here
referred to by Shelley. Shelley was first introduced to her poetry by
Medwin (who had met her) in 1808 or 1809. "He desired to become acquainted with the young authoress, and using my name, wrote to her . . . .
This letter produced an answer, and a correspondence of some length
passed between them."[2] Shelley, however — as with Harriet Grove —
discussed antireligious subjects and Miss Browne's mother wrote to Medwin's father asking him to use his influence to stop the correspondence.[3]

1. As Humbert Wolfe points out, Hogg "refers to Shelley as 'the divine poet', but in the same way
as Antony referred to Brutus as 'an honorable man'. The more he exhibited the ridiculous aspects of
Shelley, the more fervently he asserted his belief in his divinity." Hogg, *Shelley*, I, ix.

2. Medwin, *Shelley*, pp. 58–59.

3. Shelley's sister Hellen also remembered that Shelley wrote to Miss Browne but her impression
was that there was only one letter and a reply which was "to an effect which gave no encourage-
ment to farther correspondence." But whether there was one letter or more there must have been
a letter of the nature that Hellen remembered, for there is certainly nothing tigerish (line 29) about
the poems. (Hellen Shelley to Lady Jane Shelley, n. d., Hogg, *Shelley*, I, 26.)

# The Carl H. Pforzheimer Library

SC 171      Medwin states also that Miss Browne's poems "made a powerful impression on Shelley." A reading of the poems, however, discloses only occasional possible echoes, for example:

> The perfume stays, altho' the rose be dead;
> So virtue lives, when every grace is fled.[4]

Shelley, as we have seen,[5] intended to submit a poem for the Sir Roger Newdigate Prize at Oxford. These intentions, however, were upset by his expulsion. The 1811 prize was won by Richard Burdon (lines 44, 47), later fellow of Oriel and theological scholar, with the poem, *Parthenon*.[6]

"Darwin" (line 42) is Erasmus Darwin, grandfather of Charles Darwin. His views on science, as expressed in his *Temple of Nature* and other poems, had a considerable influence on Shelley. The results of this early reading are apparent in *Queen Mab*.[7]

Banyan days (line 41), according to the *New English Dictionary*, were days on which no meat was served in the British Navy. And Charles Lamb is quoted (1823): "We had three banyan to four meat days in the week." Shelley's biographers have missed the implication in the comment: it is Shelley's first reference to his vegetarianism. It has been assumed that he did not begin a vegetable diet until the spring of 1812.[8]

4. "On a Rose," *Poems*, Liverpool, 1808, p. 4. Cf. Shelley's "To ————":
   Music, when soft voices die,
   Vibrates in the memory —
   Odours, when sweet violets sicken,
   Live within the sense they quicken.

   Rose leaves, when the rose is dead,
   Are heaped for the belovèd's bed.

5. sc 140 (Feb. 17, 1811).

6. Burdon matriculated in 1808 and graduated in 1812 with a first class in classics. In 1814 he won the English Essay prize at Oxford with his essay *A Comparative Estimate of the English Literature of the 17th and 18th Century* (*Alumni Oxonienses; Oxford University Historical Register*, 1888, pp. 146, 252). The British Museum catalogue lists, in addition to *Parthenon* and the essay (1814), a number of theological works.

7. For the influence of Erasmus Darwin on Shelley see Carl Grabo, *A Newton Among Poets* (University of North Carolina Press, 1930).

8. On March 14, 1812, Harriet Shelley wrote to Elizabeth Hitchener from Dublin: "You do not know that we have forsworn meat and adopted the Pythagorean system. About a fortnight has elapsed since the change. . . ." (Shelley, *Complete Works*, viii, 295–296. See also Hogg, I, 146; II, 81–82.)

PLATE XXXVII

I shall be at 18 Sackville St.
At least direct there
My dear friend You will perhaps see me
before I can answer this, perhaps not
Heaven knows! I shall certainly come
to York, but Harriet Westbrook
will decide: whether or not in 3
weeks. — Her father has persecuted
her in a most horrible way, by endeavoring
to compel her to go to school... She
asked my advice: —assistance. own.
the answer at the same time that
I sprayed to mortify S'd to.. in vain!
& in consequence of my advice she
has thrown herself upon my protection.
I set off for London on Monday
How flattering a distinction;— I
___ am thinking of ten million
things at once... What have I said

*P. B. Shelley to T. J. Hogg, August 3, 1811 (SC 174), page 1*

PLATE XXXVIII

I declare quite hideous — I advised
her to resist. she wrote to say
that resistance was useless, but
that she would fly with me, &
throw herself on my protection: —
we shall have 200£ a year, when
we find it run short we must
live I suppose upon love.. Gratitude
& admiration all demand that
I should love her forever., we.
shall see you at York. I will
hear your arguments for matrimonialism by which I am now
almost convinced... I can get
lodgings at York I suppose.
direct to me at Grahams 18
Sackville st Piccadilly...
your enclosure of 10£ has arrived
I now am indebted to you 30£

*P. B. Shelley to T. J. Hogg, August 3, 1811 (SC 174), page 2*

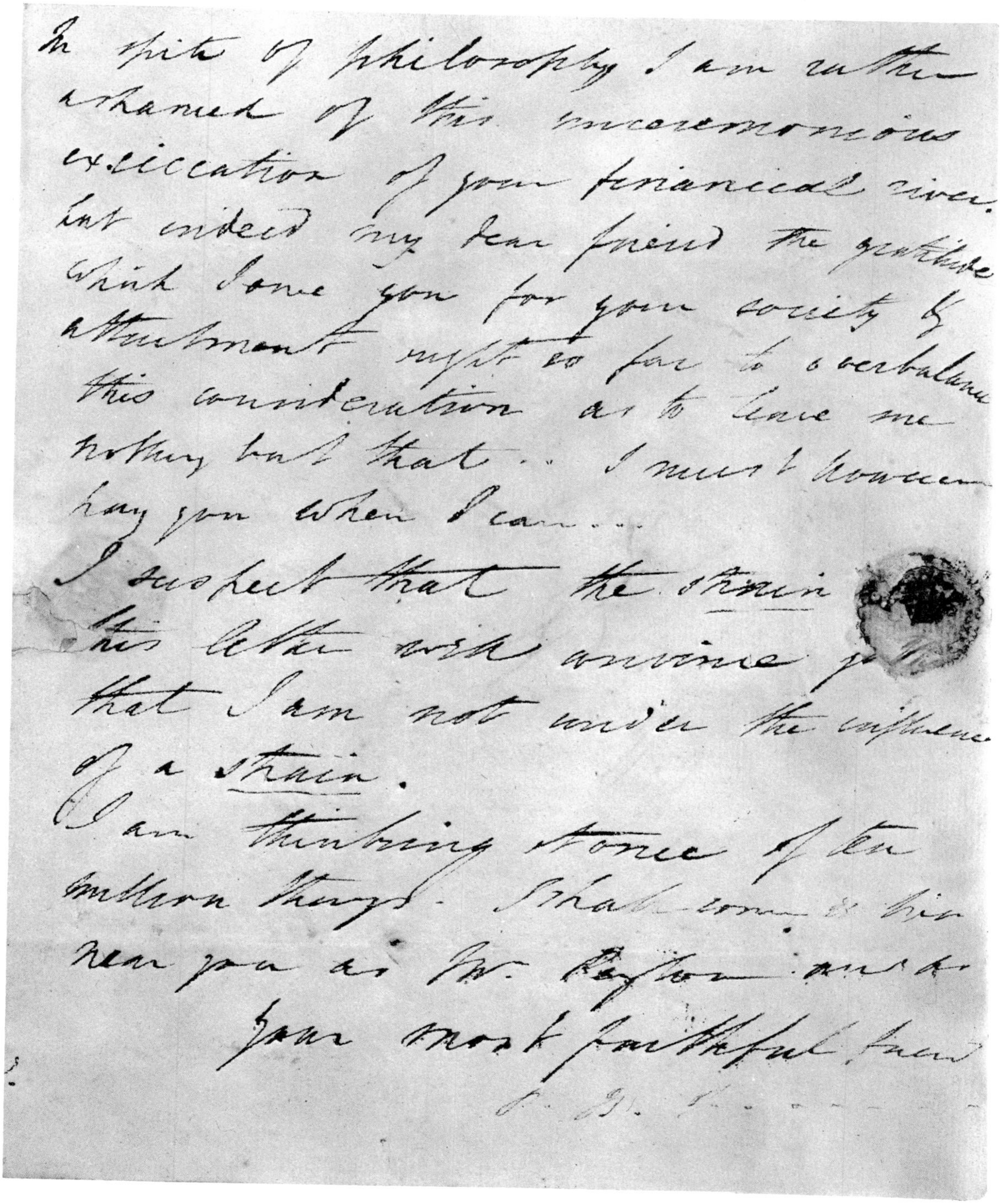

PLATE XXXIX

In spite of philosophy I am rather
ashamed of this unceremonious
exsiccation of your tyrannical river.
but indeed my dear friend the gratitude
which I owe you for your society &
attachment ought so far to overbalance
this consideration as to leave me
nothing but that. . I must however
pay you when I can. . . .

I suspect that the strain
of this letter will convince you
that I am not under the influence
of a strain.
I am thinking & once of ten
million things. I shall soon & be
near you as Mr Peyton and be
    your most faithful friend
        P. B. S————

*P. B. Shelley to T. J. Hogg, August 3, 1811 (SC 174), page 3*

PLATE XL

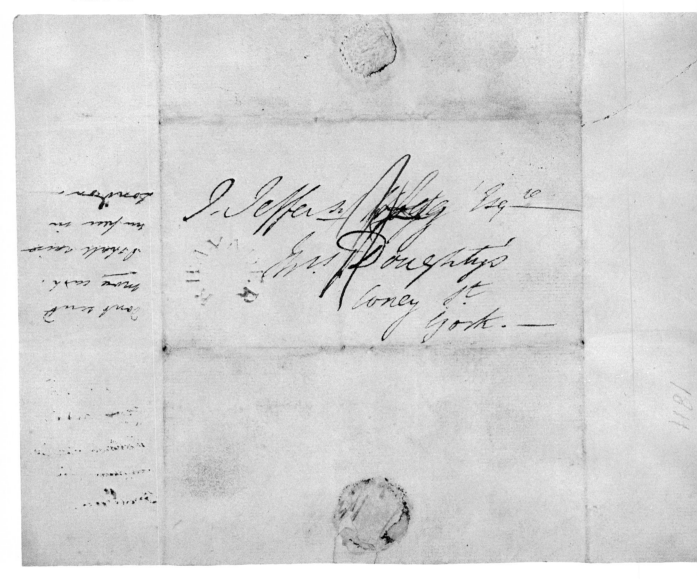

*P. B. Shelley to T. J. Hogg, August 3, 1811 (SC 174), address page*

**Shelley to Hogg**                                                     **July ?22, 1811**

SC 172   P. B. SHELLEY TO T. J. HOGG, JULY ?22, 1811

AL unsigned, 3½ pages. Double sheet, folio (12.9 x 8.1 inches).
Laid paper. Watermark: [Britannia in crowned oval]| P [outside oval, lower left],
B [outside oval, lower right]|; countermark: *P & B* [in circle]| *1807*|.
Seal: wafer, red.
Postmark: (provincial stamp): RHAYADER|.

PROVENANCE: Thomas Jefferson Hogg; Major R. J. Jefferson Hogg (Sotheby,
June 30, 1948, lot 33). *De Ricci 81* (p. 126).

*My dearest friend*

    *I do not accuse you of temporising, or if I did I retract that accusation . .*
*I have not read Adeline but shall as soon as I can get it; here one is as remote*
*from the communications of friendship, as the boriness of stupidity     it is*
5   *a price very high to pay for the exemption from the latter, for which reason*
*it is my intention as soon as financial strength will permit me to evacuate*
*these solitudes to come to York. When I come, I will not come under my own*
*name, it were to irritate my father needlessly, this is entirely a philautian*
*argument, but without the stream of which he is the fountain head I could*
10   *not get on . . We must live if we intend to live that is we must eat drink &*
*sleep, & money is the necessary procurer of these things ——*
*Your letter was sent to my Mother last post day, I am well assured that she*
*will do nothing prejudicial to our interests, she is a good worthy woman, and*
*altho she may in some cases resemble the fish & pheasant ladies honored with*
15   *your animadversions of this morning, yet there is one altitude which they*
*have attained, to which I think she cannot soar.     Intolerance. I have heard*
*frequently from her since my arrival here; she is of opinion that my father*
*could not by ordinary means have become acquainted with your visit to*
*Horsham . . I regard the whole as a finesse to which I had supposed the*
20   *Honb^le Members head piece unequal . . But the servants may . . No. they*
*did not know your name. ——     I have heard from my sister since I came*
*here, but her letter merely contains an account of a thunder storm, which*
*demolished a cottage of my father's . . I will not therefore send it you.*
*I find you still obstinate in what I call your error; as I am in what you must*
25   *consider a damnable Heterodoxy. I am truly surprised! The peep at Warn-*
*ham Church cannot have influenced you one way or the other but it may; for*

SC 172   *it is the only sensual intelligence that you have received of this fair one. I cannot call it intellectual, as even in the short view of her face which you had, you cannot pretend to guess her moral qualities; unless you intend to*

30   *support that the countenance is the index of the soul, which I cannot suppose you admit. Will you now cooly, if <u>possible</u> dispassionately examine your own soul, & that which now seems almost necessarily annexed to its <u>essence</u> your love for Eliza . . trace the grounds on which you love her; the origin of this passion, the things which strengthened & the things which have*

35   *weakened it. If you will do this without either ridiculing my difference of opinion from you, or employing any kind of declamation over-slurring or sophistry, you will <u>then</u> perhaps convince me of what you regard as truth founded on proof of resistless cogency: or . . . . you will come to ~~what I~~ ~~to~~ a knowledge of the incorrectness of your own ideas . . .   Either of these*

40   *is to be desired, since if you or I be wrong this error wherever it lies will necessarily terminate in dissapointment.*

      *Adeiu . .*       *Each Post day until we meet will carry a letter.*

                        *Yours sincerely ————*

*[Address, page 4]*
*T. Jeff^n Hogg Esq^r*

45   *M^rs Doughty's*
*Coney S^t*
*York. ——*

line 2. *not:* The underlinings here and for *live,* line 10, and *may,* line 26, are exceptionally heavy.

line 4. *boriness* (sic)

line 30. *index: d* and *e* are combined and written through some other letter.

line 32. *& that:* partly on the paper adhering to the seal

line 36. *slurring . . . dissapointment* is written in the top quarter of page 4 (the portion which was to be folded under when the letter was folded and sealed).

line 39. *to:* Following *o* is apparently the initial loop for an *n;* Shelley perhaps intended to write *consider.*

line 41. *dissapointment* (sic)

line 42. *Adeiu* (sic) . . . *sincerely* is written in the bottom quarter of page 4 (again on a portion which was to be folded under). It is in lighter ink than the rest of the letter and was perhaps added later.

COLLATION (selected passages).

T. J. HOGG, *THE LIFE OF PERCY BYSSHE SHELLEY,* I, 381–382. (Hogg's changes indicated by italics.)

**Shelley to Hogg**                                   *July ?27–29, 1811*

SC 172  line 12. Your letter was sent to my mother last post-day; *she feels a warm interest in you, as every woman must, and* I am well assured line 18. *proposed* visit.
line 24. These lines (24–41) Hogg puts in a post-script as though they were part of a novel,

changing "Eliza" to "Sophia" and introducing the passage with the added sentence: *The progress of our novel is but slow; however, I have written one more letter; it is for you to answer it:* line 25. The peep at *church*

APPARENTLY when Shelley finally did receive a letter from Hogg, it was not mainly concerned with his treatment of Hogg in London but with Elizabeth. Hogg's interest in Elizabeth seems to have developed into an obsession after his "peep" in Warnham Church (line 25) and he seems to be seeking help rather desperately. Something of the intensity of his reactions can be gathered from Shelley's comments on the declamations (line 36) and ridicule (line 35) with which he had met whatever advice had been previously offered. Shelley, however, it is only fair to add, was not having any notable success in following his own precepts of reason in regard to Harriet Westbrook.

Hogg's addition on line 12 — "she feels a warm interest in you, as every woman must" — is rather curious, for although Hogg deletes and changes he seldom adds a whole new phrase. The object of the addition is, of course, to obscure the fact that the letter concerned Elizabeth, but it may also contain a reflection of a genuine interest in Hogg by Mrs. Shelley.[1]

The span in this and the following letter (sc 173) of four years and in sc 166 of five years between the date of composition of the letter and the date of watermark on the paper is unusual. Shelley was presumably using paper that the Groves had stocked up in their country estate.

By "*philautian* argument" (line 8), Shelley means one motivated by self-centered interests.[2]

1. See sc 168 (July ?6–18), Commentary.          2. See sc 156 (May 8, 1811), fn. 5.

SC 173  P. B. SHELLEY TO T. J. HOGG, JULY ?27–29, 1811

AL unsigned, 2½ pages. Double sheet, 4$^{to}$ (8.7 x 7.3 inches). Wove paper. Watermark: J WHATMAN| 1807|. Gilt edges. Seal: wafer, black. Postmark: (provincial stamp): RHAYADER|.

# The Carl H. Pforzheimer Library

**Shelley to Hogg**                                    **July ?27-29, 1811**

PROVENANCE: Thomas Jefferson Hogg; Major R. J. Jefferson Hogg (Sotheby, June 30, 1948, lot 35). *De Ricci 86* (p. 126).

*My dear friend*
    *Only 2 hours elapse between the entrance & exit of the Post. Your letter is sent to my Mother, who is very much interested for you . .   I have at this moment no money, as Philipps & the other debt have drained me, You*
5  *will see me when I can get some . .   Altho I am not so degraded as to talk to you of pecuniary obligations, but is it not almost too bad to subsist on you . .   No, I must stay here for a short time ~pe~ because to contend against impossibilities may do for a lover but will not for a mortal. In the mean time believe that I am not inattentive to your interests . . .   As things*
10  *have been so quiet, I rather acquiesce in y<sup>r</sup> opinion that artifice may have been resorted to . . . as I returned no answer <u>my</u> indiscretion of which I have given two or three specimens cannot either substantiate or invalidate his guesses. —— I am all solitude, as I cannot call the society here ~either~ an alterative of it. I must stay here however to recruit my finances.   compelled*
15  *<u>now</u> to acknowledge Poverty an evil. —— Y<sup>r</sup>. jokes on H. Westbrook amuse me. it is a common error for people to fancy others' in their situation but if I know any thing about <u>Love</u> I am <u>not</u> in love . .   I have heard from the Westbrooks both of whom I highly esteem. Adeiu. I am going to ~wri~ ride with M<sup>rs</sup> G. to Rhayader. I will write on Thursd*
                                                         *Yours sincerely*
20

[Address, page 4]
*T. Jeff<sup>n</sup> Hogg Esq<sup>r</sup>*
*M<sup>rs</sup> Doughty's*
*Coney S<sup>t</sup>*
*York*

line 12. *invalidate:* The initial *i* is written through *d*.

line 13. *call:* looks like *cale*. Often in writing two *l*'s at the end of a word Shelley will make the loop of the second *l* much shorter than that of the first.

line 13. *an:* Shelley apparently first wrote *her* and then wrote *an* through it.

line 14. *alterative* (sic)

line 16. *others'* (sic): The apostrophe, which is lighter than the letters of the line, has made an imprint on the opposite page (page 3) in the folding, whereas the letters have not. Hence, Shelley must have read the letter through after writing it.

line 18. *Adeiu* (sic)

**Shelley to Hogg**                                    *July ?27–29, 1811*

SC 173   line 18. ~~wri:~~ Following the *i* is a stroke which   perhaps jumped ahead to his next sentence
could be the beginning of a *t*. Shelley's mind   because of the similarity of *write* and *ride*.

COLLATION (selected passages).
T. J. HOGG, *THE LIFE OF PERCY BYSSHE SHELLEY*, I, 386. (Hogg's changes indicated by italics.)

line 3. very much interested *in* you.

ONCE again, as in the preceding letter, we have indication of Mrs. Shelley's interest in Hogg's pursuit of Elizabeth (obscured in Hogg's change of "for you" into "in you").

"Philipps" debt (line 4) was presumably a debt owed to C. and W. Phillips of Worthing for printing *The Necessity of Atheism*.[1] If so, the fact that Shelley here assumes sole responsibility for it is additional evidence that, although the writing was a joint product of Shelley and Hogg, the actual printing was done on Shelley's initiative alone.

Shelley was a good deal more interested in Harriet Westbrook than he wished Hogg to know. He may not have been "in love" with her at this time but he was certainly not lagging in pursuit. He had apparently spent most of his time with her in London before leaving for Cwm Elan, and he was not, as one would gather from his comments to Hogg, receiving only occasional letters from her. On the contrary a brisk, perhaps almost daily, correspondence was going on:

I called on her, requested to correspond with her, designing that her advancement should keep pace with, and possibly accelerate, that of my sister. Her ready and frank acceptance of my proposal pleased me, and, tho' with ideas the remotest to those which have led to this conclusion of our intimacy, [I] continued to correspond with her for some time. The frequency of her letters became greater during my stay in Wales, I answered them; they became interesting.[2]

1. Ingpen suggests that "Philipps" may refer to Janetta Philipps, pointing out that the spelling is that of her name and not that of the printers. But Shelley was not meticulous in matters of spelling; nor would he have referred to Miss Philipps as "Philipps." (In SC 171, July ?21, he refers to Felicia Browne as "Miss F. D. Browne.") Furthermore, although Shelley offered to pay for Miss Philipps' volume of poems, the offer was once refused (Shelley to Janetta Philipps, May 16, 1811) and the indication is that it was never accepted. The volume was published with a list of subscribers ten pages long.
   The debt to C. and W. Phillips may also have included the printing bill on *Original Poetry* by Victor and Cazire, printed in September 1810.

2. Shelley, *Complete Works*, VIII, 168–169. Presumably neither Harriet's nor Shelley's letters in this correspondence have been preserved.

SC 174  P. B. SHELLEY TO T. J. HOGG, AUGUST 3, 1811

AL signed *P. B. S— — — — —*, 3¼ pages. Double sheet, 4^to (9.2 x 7.4 inches). (See Plates XXXVII–XL.)
Laid paper. Watermark: PORTAL & C°| 1[81] 1|.
Seal: wafer, red.
Postmark: (provincial stamp): RHAYADER|.

PROVENANCE: Thomas Jefferson Hogg; Major R. J. Jefferson Hogg (Sotheby, June 30, 1948, lot 36). *De Ricci 88* (p. 127).

> *I shall be at 18 Sackville S^t*
> *at least direct there*

*My Dear friend*

   *You will perhaps see me before I can answer this, perhaps not Heaven*
5  *knows! I shall certainly come to York, but Harriet Westbrook will decide*
*whether now or in 3 weeks. —— Her father has persecuted her in a most*
*horrible way, & endeavours to compel her to go to school . . . She asked my*
*advice: resistance was the answer at the same time that I essayed to mollify*
*old W . . in vain! & in consequence of my advice she has thrown herself*
10 *upon my protection! I set off for London on Monday How flattering a*
*distinction: – I ̶h̶a̶v̶e̶ am thinking of ten million things at once . . What*
*have I said I declare quite ludicrous – I advised her to resist . . she wrote*
*to say that resistance was useless, but that she would fly with me, & threw*
*herself on my protection. —— We shall have 200 £ a year, when we find*
15 *it run short we must live I suppose upon love . . Gratitude & admiration*
*all demand that I should love her forever . . We shall see you at York. I will*
*hear your arguments for matrimonialism by which I am now almost con-*
*vinced . . .     I can get lodgings at York I suppose. Direct to me at Graham's*
*18 Sackville S^t Piccadilly . .*
20 *Your inclosure of 10£ has arrived. I now am indebted to you 30£     In spite*
*of philosophy I am rather ashamed of this unceremonious exsiccation of your*
*financial river. but indeed my dear friend the gratitude which I owe you*
*for your society & attachment ought so far to overbalance this consideration*
*as to leave me nothing but that . . I must however pay you when I can . . .*
25     *I suspect that the strain < > this letter will convince yo< > that I*
*am not under the influence of a strain.*

**Shelley to Hogg**                                    **August 3, 1811**

SC 174  *I am thinking at once of ten million things. I shall come & live near you as*
        *M$^r$ Peyton and as*

                                    *Your most faithful friend*
                                         *P. B. S— — — — —*

30

        *Dont send*
        *more cash.*
        *I shall raise*
        *un peu in*
35      *London —*

        [Address, page 4]
        *T. Jeffer$^n$ Hogg Esq$^{re}$*
        *M$^{rs}$ Doughty's*
        *Coney S$^t$*
        *York. —*

line 1. The first two lines have blotted in folding.

line 4. *I* (sic)

line 9. *she:* heavily underlined

line 11. *at once* is run together as is *I suppose* on line 15. Running words together is often a sign of excited writing in Shelley.

line 11. *am:* written through *be*

line 25. < *?in, ?of* > : under the seal

line 30. The signature is very faint.

line 31. Lines 31–35 are written on the side of the address page that was turned under as a narrow flap when the letter was folded. They are in a small scrawling hand and have blotted in the folding.

SHELLEY's sudden departure from Cwm Elan, the above letter informs us, was motivated by a letter from Harriet Westbrook stating that because of her father's efforts to compel her to return to school (where she was being persecuted as a friend of the atheistic Shelley), she had thrown herself upon his "protection" (line 10) and would "fly" with him. And this story is verified by Charles Grove's recollection of a similar letter to himself (probably written on the same day): "He corresponded with me also during this period, and wrote me a letter concerning what he termed his summons to link his fate with another, closing his communication thus: 'Hear it not, Percy, for it is a knell, which summons

# The Carl H. Pforzheimer Library

SC 174 thee to heaven or to hell.'"[1] We get further information from the letter to Elizabeth Hitchener of October 27:

> The frequency of her letters became greater during my stay in Wales, I answered them; they became interesting. They contained complaints of the irrational conduct of her relations, and the misery of living where she could *love* no one. Suicide was with her a favorite theme, her total uselessness was urged as its defence. [This I] admitted, supposing she could *prove* her inutility, [and that she] was powerless. Her letters became more and more g[loomy] at length one assumed a tone of such despair, as induced me to quit Wales precipitately.

This final letter of "despair" must be the same as that referred to in the above letter. Putting the two descriptions together it appears that Harriet not only threw herself on Shelley's "protection" but threatened suicide[2] if the protection was not forthcoming.

As Shelley would normally write to Hogg immediately after receiving Harriet's letter and as Harriet was in London her letter was probably written on August 1 (mail taking two days from London to Cwm Elan). And August 1, 1811, it is interesting to note, was Harriet's sixteenth birthday.[3] Perhaps she had used the occasion to resist being sent back to school.

If Harriet was agitated, so, too, was Shelley. This is obvious from the appearance of the above manuscript, with its scrawlings, repetitions, blottings, run-on words, faint and incomplete signature, the last-minute hasty addition of his London address (line 1), which he had already given (line 18), and so on.

Shelley had previously proposed that he take "Peyton" (line 28) as a "nom de guerre" — i.e., in the war with his father — when he came to visit Hogg at York.[4]

1. Charles Grove to Hellen Shelley, Feb. 16, 1857, Hogg, *Shelley*, II, 156. Toward the end of Macbeth's "Is this a Dagger, which I see before me" speech (*Macbeth*, II.i. 46–78) the castle-gate bell rings and he concludes:
   Heare it not, *Duncan*, for it is a Knell
   That summons thee to Heaven or to Hell.
Shelley substituted his own name for that of Duncan. The fact that the passage came to his mind implies a mood of rather desperate adventurousness.

2. "She told me that at school . . . she had conceived and contrived sundry attempts and purposes of destroying herself." (Hogg, *Shelley*, I, 280. See also II, 12, 133.)

3. She was born on August 1, 1795. (Ingpen, *Shelley in England*, p. 265 fn. Ingpen misstates her age in January 1811 as "nearly sixteen and a half"; this should be "nearly fifteen and a half.")

4. See sc 170 (July ?18, 1811).

**Shelley to Hogg**                                    **August ?8–9, 1811**

SC 174      Shelley's friend, Edward Fergus Graham, apparently moved from
Vine Street to Sackville Street (line 18) between the middle of May
and early July.[5]

5. A letter to Graham just after Shelley's return to Field Place on about May 11 is addressed to
Vine Street; a letter postmarked July 15 from Cwm Elan is addressed to Sackville Street.

SC 175   P. B. SHELLEY TO T. J. HOGG, AUGUST ?8–9, 1811

AL unsigned, 1¼ pages. Single sheet, 4$^{to}$ (8.8 x 7.3 inches).
Laid paper. Watermark: T EDM[O]NDS|.
Seal: wafer, green.
Postmarks: 1. (receiving house stamp, London): HOUGHT[O]N ST|; 2. (evening
duty stamp, London): C|·[     ]|.

PROVENANCE: Thomas Jefferson Hogg; Major R. J. Jefferson Hogg (Sotheby,
June 30, 1948, lot 37). *De Ricci 90* (p. 127).

*My dear Friend*

~~*I shall not conceal something from you this*~~ *My arguments have been*
*your's — they have been urged by the force of the gratitude which their*
*occasion excited .. but I yet remain in London, remain embarassed &*
5  *melancholy. I am now dining at Grove's. <     > letter has just been brought*
*in. I cannot forbear* <u>*just*</u> *writing this.* <u>*Your*</u> *noble & exalted friendship, the*
*prosecution of your happiness, can alone engross my impassioned interest ..*
*I never was so fit for calm argument as now . . . This I fear more resembles*
*exerted action than inspired passion . . .     I shall take another opportunity*
10  *.. tomorrow of answering your long interesting, and conclusive letter of*
*yesterday*

                              *Your friend*

[Address, verso]
*T. Jeffn. Hogg Esq$^{re}$*
*M$^s$ Doughty's*
15  *Coney Street*
*York*

line 2. Probable reading. Shelley has scored          cross lines as well as by his normal straight
out the words by a series of spirals and criss-       lines.

# The Carl H. Pforzheimer Library

**_Shelley to Hogg_**                         **_August ?8–9, 1811_**

SC 175   line 4. *remain embarassed* (sic): *re* can be made out on the paper adhering to the seal. There is no *I* in front of *remain*.

line 5. <*?Your*>: seal tear

line 8. *resembles . . . answering* (lines 8–10) are written in the top quarter of page 2 (the portion which was to be folded under when the letter was folded and sealed).

line 10. *your long . . . friend* (lines 10–12) are written in the bottom quarter of page 2 (again on a portion which was to be folded over).

line 12: *f* seems to have been written through *P*.

SHELLEY, we learn from the above letter, is now in London. Hogg has received his letter of August 3 and has replied to it. If, as we have argued, the August 3 letter left Rhayader by the August 5 post Hogg cannot have received it until August 7. That his reply only took one day in transit between York and London is shown by Shelley's reference to it as a letter of "yesterday" (line 11) which had "just been brought in." As Shelley apparently replied immediately his letter must have been written late in the day; and the day must have been either August 8 or August 9.

Since he had given Graham's address to Hogg, Hogg's letter must have been brought from Graham's, most likely by Graham himself. Shelley's letter was posted at the receiving house at Houghton Street. Houghton Street was in the vicinity of John Grove's residence in Lincoln's Inn Fields, and between it and Graham's house on Sackville Street.[1] Shelley may have given the letter to Graham to post on his way home.

The difference in tone between this letter and that of August 3 is striking. On August 3 Shelley is preparing to leave Cwm Elan in a state of happy excitement. Harriet has agreed to "fly" with him; they will elope to York and live there near Hogg; perhaps they will be there even before the letter arrives.

On August 8 or 9, however, he is still in London. Harriet has not flown with him or thrown herself under his protection. On the contrary, he is "embarassed & melancholy" (line 4). He no longer believes, as he apparently did on August 3, that he was motivated by "inspired passion" but by "exerted action" — i.e., he believed that he was forcing himself in a mechanical way to keep up his interest. (We have, however, to keep in mind that Shelley did not wish Hogg to know how great his interest in Harriet was because he sensed Hogg's jealousy. He tends to play down his feelings in writing to Hogg.)

1. Plan of London, Front Endpapers, C1, C2, B2.

SC 176   P. B. SHELLEY TO T. J. HOGG, AUGUST 15, 1811

AL (incomplete) unsigned, 4 pages. Double sheet, 4$^{to}$ (8.7 x 7.1 inches). Laid paper. Watermark: C WILMOTT| 1810|.

PROVENANCE: Thomas Jefferson Hogg; Major R. J. Jefferson Hogg (Sotheby, June 30, 1948, lot 38). *De Ricci 91* (p. 127).

*My dear Friend*

    *The late perplexing occurrence which called me to Town, occupies my time engrosses my thoughts: . I shall tell you more of it when we meet . . which I hope will be soon . . It does not however so wholly occupy my*

5  *thoughts, but that you & your interest still is predominant ¬.¬.— You have a rival . . do not tremble for it is not one whom you have occasion to dread, if you fear merely those who are likely to be successful . . His chances of success are equal to your own . . .  he has the opportunity of frequently seeing, & conversing with Elizabeth, yet his conversation is not such as is*

10  *likely to produce any alteration in the resolve which she has taken not to encourage his addresses. —— It is John Grove. — she knows him well & has known him long —— Charles informed me of it, and I left London Yesterday, tho' now returned purposely to converse with my sister on the subject . . .  John Grove is certainly not a favored lover, nor ever will*

15  *be . . .  I thought she appeared rather chagrined at the intelligence. she fears that she will lose an entertaining acquaintance who sometimes enlivens her solitude, by his conversion into the more serious character of a lover . . I do not think she will, as his attachment is that of a cool unimpassioned selector of a companion for life . . I do not think the better of my cousin for*

20  *this unex-pected affair. I could tell you some thing & will, you will then coincide with me . .  This however is an object of secondary importance . . . I know from what I tell you that you will be elavated by hope . . yet beware, for altho' her rejection of the bare idea of Grove was full & unequivocal, I have no reason to suppose that it proceeded from any augmented*

25  *leniency for you . . I know how deep is the gulph of despair   I will not then increase your height, but must still think how unfortunate it is that I ever mentioned her very name to you, still must I long for the time when you will forget her, but which now you say can never come! . . —— I am now returned to London, direct to me as usual at Grahams . .  my father is here*

# The Carl H. Pforzheimer Library

SC 176   *wondering possibly at my London business —— He will be more surprised soon possibly! —— My unfortunate friend Harriet is yet undecided – . not with respect to me but herself . . how much my dear friend have I to tell you! – In my liesure moments for thought which since I wrote have been few . . I have considered the important point on which you reprobated my*

35   *hasty decision —— The ties of love and honor are doubtless ~~th~~ of sufficient strength to bind congenial souls, they are doubtless indissoluble but by the brutish force of power. they are delicate & satisfactory. – yet the arguments of impracticability, and what is even worse the disproportionate sacrifice which the female is called upon to make, these arguments which you have*

40   *urged in a manner immediately irrestibile I cannot withstand . . . Not that I suppose*

line 5. *is:* written through *are*

line 5. Shelley first put three dots, then apparently feeling that this was not sufficient to dramatize the importance of the new subject begun in *You have a rival*, placed a long black line above the dots.

line 13. *Yesterday:* The *Y* has been constructed from *Th* by adding a long loop.

line 20. *unex-pected* (sic)

line 22. *elavated* (sic)

line 25. *despair* comes at the end of a line.

line 33. *liesure* (sic)

line 38. *disproportionate: dis* is written through *sac.*

line 40. *irrestibile* (sic)

COLLATION (selected passages).

T. J. HOGG, *THE LIFE OF PERCY BYSSHE SHELLEY*, I, 416–417. (Hogg's changes indicated by italics.)

line 5. I have a rival *in my sister's affection;* do not tremble, for it is not one whom *I* have occasion to dread, if *I* fear merely those who are likely to be successful. His chances of success are equal to *my* own.

line 22. that *others might* . . . hope; *but I would say to them,* — Beware;

line 24. I have no reason to suppose that it pro-

ceeded from any augmented leniency for *another.*

line 25. I will not *therefore* increase *any one's* height;

line 26. but must still think how unfortunate it is *for any wooer that he ever heard* her very name; *he* must long for the time when *he* will forget her, but which *he* now *will* say can never come!

THE above manuscript ends on the last line of page 4 of a double sheet. Hogg, in his life of Shelley, gives the concluding portion as follows:

Not that I suppose it to be likely that *I* shall directly be called upon to evince my attachment to either theory. I am become a perfect convert to matrimony, not from temporizing, but from *your* arguments; nor, much as I wish to emulate

SC 176    your virtues and liken myself to you, do I regret the prejudices of anti-matri-monialism from your example or assertion. No. The *one* argument, which you have urged so often with so much energy: the sacrifice made by the woman, so disproportioned to any which the man can give, — this alone may exculpate me, were it a fault, from uninquiring submission to your superior intellect.

Write to Graham's: you will hear from me again soon. All that I have told you here is in *confidence*. Adieu!

Yours eternally affectionate,
PERCY B. S.

As this letter was among those borrowed by Lady Shelley from the Hogg family[1] presumably she forgot to return the second sheet, which contained the conclusion and the address.

Hogg dates the letter "August 15, 1811," a date which he probably took from the London postmark. As the letter was written in London (line 13) this is probably also the date of composition. We might also note Shelley's change in line 13 from "Th" to "Y"; apparently he intended to write "Thursday" and changed to "Yesterday." August 15 was a Thursday in 1811. Shelley, not untypically, may have been unclear on the date or day.

The account of the events immediately preceding the elopement given as they were occurring in these letters to Hogg needs to be supplemented by an account later (on October 27) to Elizabeth Hitchener:

I arrived in London. I was shocked at observing the alteration of her looks. Little did I divine its cause; she had become violently attached to *me*, and feared that I should not return her attachment . . . prejudice made the confession painful. It was impossible to avoid being much affected, I promised to unite my fate with hers. I staid in London several days [before leaving for Field Place], during which she recovered her spirits. I had promised at her bidding to come again to London. They endeavoured to compel her to return to a school where malice and pride embittered every hour; she wrote to me. I came to London [from Field Place]. I proposed marriage for the reasons which I have given you, and she complied.

If this account to Elizabeth Hitchener is correct, Harriet's letter from London of about August 1 did not contain a confession of love. It apparently stressed her "persecution" at school, her unhappiness, her desire for death, and concluded that to escape from this situation she

1. Koszul, *Jeunesse*, pp. xvi–xvii, 406, 416–418.

SC 176   would "fly" with Shelley. Only after his arrival in London from Wales did she confess ("painfully") her "violent attachment." Shelley then promised "to unite my fate with hers."

This "uniting" did not, however, he seems to imply, include marriage. The succession of events as related to Elizabeth Hitchener was as follows. After the "uniting" promise Shelley stayed in town for several days, during which Harriet "recovered her spirits." Then he left London for Field Place. The Westbrooks tried to send Harriet back to school. He returned to London. This time he did propose marriage; and Harriet "complied."

This account, however, cannot be quite accurate. For one thing it is extremely compressed; for another it is written under the embarrassing necessity of explaining to Elizabeth Hitchener how he — one of the anti-matrimonial enlightened — came to marry.

The compression obscures the fact that Shelley was in and out of London at least twice. From the above letter we gather that he left London on August 14 for Field Place (line 12) and returned to London (line 13) the next day. (That he had, indeed, been at Field Place is shown by the fact that the above letter is written on Wilmott paper, which, as we have seen, was stocked at Field Place, and some of which he must have brought back to London with him.[2]) But this one-day trip is not that intended in the comment to Elizabeth Hitchener "she wrote to me. I came to London. I proposed . . ." This letter from Harriet must have come later in the month and been sent to Cuckfield, for Shelley had arranged to have letters from the Westbrooks sent to his uncle's house there and not to Field Place.[3]

The embarrassment in regard to marriage obscures the fact that he actually proposed to Harriet shortly after his arrival in London from Wales. As he left Rhayader on August 5, he must have arrived in London on August 7. "My arguments have been *your's*," he informed Hogg on August 8–9 (sc 175). And Hogg's arguments, as both the letter of August 3 (sc 174) and the above letter[4] show, were for matrimony. "They [Hogg's arguments]," he continued, "have been urged by the

2. On Wilmott paper see sc 123, "The Wandering Jew," Commentary.

3. See sc 158 (May 9, 1811), Commentary.

4. Plus the conclusion (published by Hogg), quoted above.

SC 176 force of the gratitude which their occasion excited." If we put this together with the account to Elizabeth Hitchener it appears that the source of the "gratitude" was Harriet's "painful" declaration of love. And this declaration came immediately after Shelley's arrival from Wales and instigated Shelley's proposal. Harriet, as we have seen, had hinted at marriage in her recommendation of the anti-free-love novel, *Adeline Mowbray* (sc 169).

The above letter, one might conjecture from its tone, was written after the "recovery" of Harriet's "spirits" was already under way. The proposal has been made but Harriet has not yet "complied." She "is yet undecided –. not with respect to me but herself" (line 31). Harriet, that is to say, felt certain of her love for Shelley but — for she was just turned sixteen[5] and a schoolgirl — having some doubts about her own capabilities as a wife. But, in spite of those doubts, she must even by August 15 have hinted at a pending favorable decision: "I shall tell you more of it when we meet .. which I hope will be soon" (line 3); "He will be more surprised soon possibly!" (line 30). The melancholy of the August 8–9 letter has gone and something of the verve of the August 3 letter has returned.

The scale finally was tilted, one would gather from the letter to Elizabeth Hitchener, by the decision of Mr. Westbrook to send Harriet back to school. And it may be that in this we have the explanation for Shelley's comment in his August 3 letter: "I shall certainly come to York, but *Harriet Westbrook* will decide whether now or in three weeks . . . We shall see you at York." The elopement took place almost three weeks to the day after the penning of these lines, August 3–August 25. Harriet's August 1 letter to Wales had apparently stressed her dread at returning to school. Perhaps a decision on whether or not she returned had to be made by August 24 or 25.

Such, then, is the picture as we can gather it from Shelley's letters. It cannot, however, be the whole picture. Shelley emphasizes Harriet's interest in him and plays down his interest in Harriet. He had, as we have seen, almost certainly been with her during the week in London preceding his journey to Cwm Elan and his emotional state is probably reflected

5. Her sixteenth birthday was on August 1, 1811. Shelley's nineteenth birthday was on August 4, 1811.

# The Carl H. Pforzheimer Library

SC 176   in the "short but violent nervous illness" which struck him just after his arrival and which he told Elizabeth Hitchener was the result of "several nights of sleeplessness, and days of pressing and urgent business . . . in town"[6] (i.e., London). Shelley plays down his own feelings because he does not want Hogg to feel that he is being displaced in his affections by Harriet: "you & your interest still is predominant" (line 5).

Furthermore, Shelley and Harriet were not the only people involved. There were also the Shelleys and the Westbrooks. Timothy, we would gather from the above letter (line 29), was already getting suspicious. Indeed, he may have known more than his son thought; for, as we note in our discussion of provenance, the letter from Eliza Westbrook quoted below was found among the Whitton papers.[7] Hence, it must have been in Timothy Shelley's possession. And of Timothy's attitude there can be no doubt. He did not wish his son to marry John Westbrook's daughter.

The reason for this attitude is rather more complex than is generally thought.

John Westbrook was not simply "a tavern keeper" but a London businessman of considerable wealth and stature. At his death he left between £60,000 and £70,000.[8] We find him listed in *Boyle's Court Guide* for 1813 at 23 Chapel Street, South Audley Street, as John Westbrook, Esquire; and there are very few London businessmen in the *Court Guide*, which is a selected list of London society. (Tradesmen are given in the *Post Office Directory*, *Kent's Directory*, and similar special directories.)

Chapel Street was a fashionable address. In 1813, the *Court Guide* lists, for example, at No. 2, Viscountess Sydney (the widow of Thomas Townshend, Viscount Sydney, who was Home Secretary under Pitt and after whom Sydney, Australia, was named), the Honorable Miss Townshend, and the Honorable W. A. Townshend, M. P.; at No. 13 George Brummell ("Beau" Brummell); at No. 15 the Countess Dowager of Lismore; at No. 21, General Fitzroy (Lord Charles Fitzroy, Member of Parliament and aide-de-camp to George III); at No. 24, Mrs. Hoare (presumably connected with the well-known banking family of Fleet

6. Postmarked July 15, 1811.

7. See "The Provenance of Shelley and his Circle Manuscripts," below, page 903.

8. Ingpen, *Shelley in England*, p. 516; "Harriet Shelley's Brother-in-Law," *TLS*, Nov. 11, 1955.

SC 176   Street).[9] Of Brummell's residence on Chapel Street, Wheatley writes that he "lived here when in the height of his splendour, and here princes and nobles attended his levee."[10]

John Westbrook owned a coffee house, "The Mount," at 78–79 Lower Grosvenor Street. It must have been a well-conducted establishment, for it, too, was in the same neighborhood. The *Court Guide* gives the following for the houses preceding "The Mount": No. 69, the Dowager Duchess of Leeds; No. 71, the Dowager Marchioness of Bath; No. 72, Dr. Matthew Baillie;[11] No. 73, Sir John Shelley (Member of Parliament and head of the Michelgrove Shelleys).[12] In 1818 No. 28 was occupied by Sir Humphry Davy.[13]

Both Westbrook's daughter Eliza and his granddaughter Ianthe married very wealthy men, the granddaughter marrying into a leading banking family of Lombard Street, the Esdailes.[14] His daughter Harriet attended the same private school for young ladies as Timothy Shelley's daughters.

John Westbrook was, therefore, a prosperous representative of the new London business class of the early days of the Industrial Revolution. Timothy Shelley's opposition to the marriage must have been based largely on the general attitude of the landed gentry towards those "in trade." And to this was added the additional stigma of Westbrook's wealth — considerable though it was — having come from the hotel and liquor business, for by the late eighteenth century coffee houses and taverns were practically indistinguishable.[15] Furthermore, in pursuing

9. See Area of the Elopement of Shelley and Harriet, page 871.

10. Wheatley, *London*, I, 349. For a description of Brummell's extravagant way of life in Chapel Street, see Willard Connely, *The Reign of Beau Brummel* (London, [1940]), pp. 110–112.

11. Baillie (a famed anatomist and the brother of Joanna Baillie) is in the *DNB*. He once attempted to cure Byron's lameness.

12. Shelley tried to raise money from Sir John Shelley in 1814. (White, *Shelley*, I, 386, 390.) Sir John Shelley is sometimes confused with Shelley's uncle, Sir John Shelley-Sidney (who was not made a baronet until 1818).

13. Wheatley, *London*, II, 165.

14. See William Esdaile, *DNB*. Eliza Westbrook married Robert Farthing Beauchamp, whose property was later estimated at £190,000. ("Harriet Shelley's Brother-in-Law," *TLS*, Nov. 11, 1955.)

15. The London guides of the time customarily give them in one list headed "Coffee Houses and Taverns." For some account of them see Leopold Wagner, *London Inns and Taverns* (London, 1924); John Timbs, *Clubs and Club Life in London* (London, 1899).

SC 176   this question we find that "The Mount," located in the vicinity of Grosvenor Square, was not the only tavern owned by John Westbrook. Pigot's commercial directories in the 1820's record John Westbrook as proprietor of "The Poulterers' Arms Tavern," Freeman's Court, 103 Cheapside,[16] a district then notorious for its rough taverns and open-air markets.

If Timothy Shelley objected to the marriage, Westbrook apparently did not. He would naturally be expected to approve a marriage with a young aristocrat, heir to a £300,000 estate. Later in the month when Timothy had Whitton make some investigations, he reported that Mr. Westbrook was "at least passive if not aiding in the intercourse between the young persons."[17] Certainly Harriet's sister Eliza (fourteen years older than Harriet) was active in the cause. On June 11 she wrote to Shelley at Cuckfield:

> I am obliged to you for your proposition in regard to Harriett, but I am in hopes she will leave school for good — there has been another little misunderstanding between the friends at Clapham, which has rendered the situation of my sister so completely uncomfortable my Father has now determined upon

16. Pigot's *Commercial Directory* for 1822–23 and for 1823–24 give the address simply as Cheapside and the proprietor as J. Westbrook. Pigot's *Metropolitan Directory* for 1828–29 gives the address as Freeman's Court (which ran from 103 Cheapside) and the proprietor as John Westbrook. This directory also lists "Poulterers' Arms Public House," Trump Street, Cheapside. As the map of Freeman's Court, here reproduced, shows, the tavern and the public house were probably the same establishment with one door on Freeman's Court (opening into the yard), the other on Trump Street. J. Westbrook is doubtless also John Westbrook, Pigot using the J. in order to get the entry into one line. (Public House is contracted, as usual, to P. H.) The J. Westbrook of the earlier directories is clearly the John Westbrook — the *tavern* owner — of the 1829 entry. John Westbrook, then, owned a tavern and public house in Cheapside. And this John Westbrook is almost certainly the John Westbrook who owned "The Mount." Westbrook is a very rare name in the directories, and that there were two John Westbrooks, both tavern owners, is unlikely.

When Westbrook purchased "The Poulterers' Arms" tavern and public house we do not know. Pigot's *Commercial Directory* for 1822–23 lists "The Mount Hotel," 78–79 Lower Grosvenor Street, as owned by Tryce W. Birch; and the same directory lists Ann Birch, 30 Chapel Street, owner of a "riding school and livery stable." Westbrook, then, had apparently sold "The Mount" by 1822 to a relative of his Chapel Street neighbor. Perhaps he bought "The Poulterers' Arms" only after he had sold "The Mount." If so, he may have owned his new property *in absentia*. On his death in 1835 his residence was given as that of his son-in-law, Robert Farthing Beauchamp, near Taunton in Somerset. When he left London does not appear to be known. His address was given as Chapel Street in the trial for the custody of Shelley's children in January, 1817. (Medwin, *Shelley*, p. 463.) *Boyle's Court Guide* for 1813, as we noted, lists him, but he is not listed in the 1820 edition; nor is 23 Chapel Street listed in the street section. He may, therefore, have left London between 1817 and 1820.

17. Aug. 26, Ingpen, *Shelley in England*, pp. 301, 302.

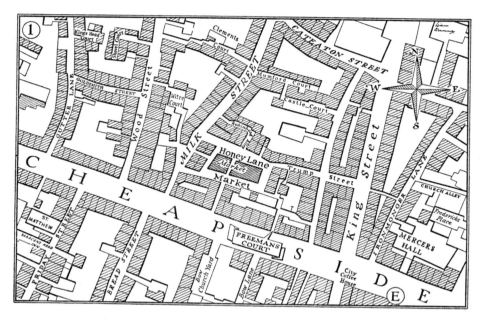

SC 176  her not returning there again; he talks of wholly retiring into the country, but not to any distant part. It is so much my wish to leave this busy scene that I shall do all in my power to expedite his plan.

You will not take any notice to your sister Mary, or indeed any of your family, of your intimacy with us; for particular reasons which I will explain to you when next I have the pleasure of seeing you.[18]

Eliza was clearly trying to arouse Shelley's interest in Harriet and was conscious of the importance of keeping knowledge of the affair from the Shelley family.

One final indication of Westbrook acquiescence is to be found in the circumstances of the elopement itself. Shelley had spent the preceding night with his cousin, Charles Grove. The next morning (according to Dowden's account, which is apparently derived from Charles Grove):

Mr. Grove's servant called a coach, into which entered the cousins Bysshe and Charles; at the Mount Street coffee-house, some time before the hour appointed for Harriet's arrival, the coach drew up. A breakfast was ordered and was ended, and Harriet did not yet appear. While the bridegroom-designate waited at the door he beguiled the time by flinging the shells of the oysters on which they had

18. *Ibid.*, pp. 276–277.

[ 869 ]

SC 176 breakfasted across the street, with the words, "Grove, this is a *Shelley* business!" Presently Harriet was seen tripping round the corner from Chapel Street, and the coach-wheels rattled towards the city inn from which the northern mails departed.[19]

The lovers, then, were to meet at a tavern in Mount Street — the next street to Chapel Street, where the Westbrooks lived. We cannot tell exactly where the coffee house was on Mount Street but the probability is that it was in the block parallel to the Westbrooks' house.[20] When Harriet came "tripping round the corner from Chapel Street" perhaps she came up Portugal Street (as the accompanying map of the elopement area shows). Next to Mount Street was Lower Grosvenor Street where Mr. Westbrook's tavern was located. Shelley would hardly have agreed to a rendezvous with the daughter of a well-known businessman of the neighborhood, just around the corner from his house and a block or so from his place of business, unless he had been sure that there would be no interference from the Westbrooks. And this is indicated also in the leisurely and conspicuous nature of the proceedings. The two young gentlemen drove up in a coach and had breakfast at the coffee house (during which time the coach was presumably drawn up outside); then they went out openly into the street to wait. What, one might ask, would have happened if Harriet had appeared while they were breakfasting? Would they all have had breakfast together?

19. Dowden, *Shelley*, I, 173. The account, the source of which puzzled Newman I. White (*Shelley*, I, 610), was apparently based on a letter of Charles Grove's of the year 1860. Dowden in his footnote refers to two letters of Grove's, one of 1857 and one of 1860. That of 1857 appears in Hogg's life of Shelley (II, 157) but that of 1860 is unpublished and its present location apparently unknown.

20. A letter from Mr. W. O. Hart, Clerk of the London County Council, informs us that the "Classified Directories give no mention of coffee houses, taverns or inns in Mount Street in 1811." This confirmed our own investigations. Mr. Hart, however, kindly supplied us with a list of names of the residents of Mount Street "taken from the Sewer Rate return for 1811." This list contains three "wine merchants"; and we find that what are listed in one part of a directory as wine shops will be listed in another part as taverns or coffee houses. Furthermore, Mr. Hart informs us that these wine shops are shown on Horwood's map of London for 1813 as having "stable yards or entrances," and this, as he suggests, may indicate an inn site. The three wine merchants are as follows: Charles Le Tavernier, No. 33; Selby Co., No. 60; Thomas Penn, No. 108. One of these three was probably the place of meeting of Harriet and Shelley. Of the three Penn's seems the least likely, for Dowden (following Grove's account) stated that the meeting took place at a "small" coffee house, whereas Penn's establishment appears from the map to have been large (and back from the street). The nearest of the three to the Westbrooks' house was Selby's at No. 60, and it would seem best to fit Grove's description (Dowden, *Shelley*, I, 173) of Harriet "tripping round the corner from Chapel Street." (Area of the Elopement of Shelley and Harriet, page 871.)

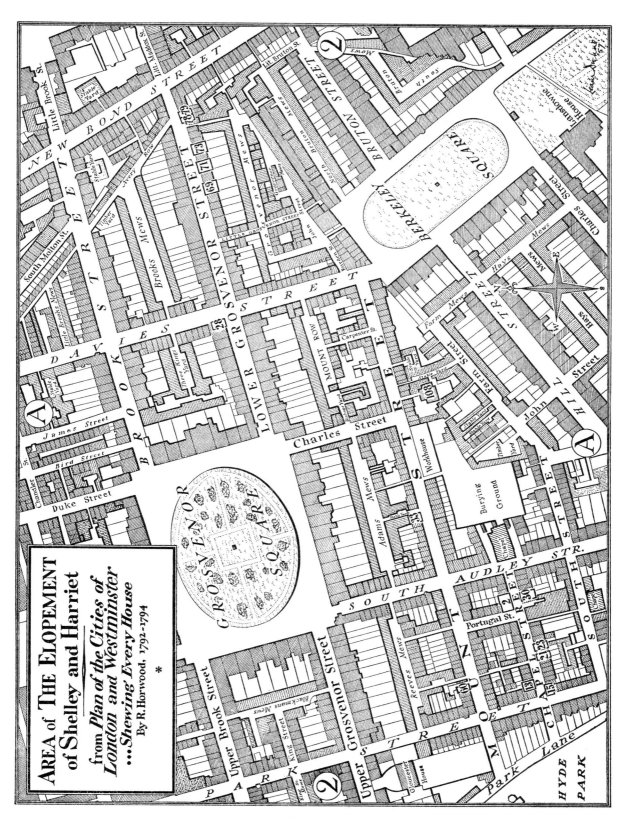

AREA of THE ELOPEMENT
of Shelley and Harriet

from *Plan of the Cities of
London and Westminster*
*...Shewing Every House*
By R. Horwood, 1792–1794

*

SC 176     The most likely explanation is that as the attitude of the Shelley family made a normal wedding impossible, the Westbrooks permitted an arranged elopement.

One other aspect of the above letter should be noted, namely Shelley's continued teasing of Hogg in regard to Elizabeth. In the pursuit of his interest in Hogg's welfare he has made a special trip to Field Place on hearing of John Grove's interest in Elizabeth. At first this is played up as something serious: "His chances of success are equal to your own" (line 7). But it becomes apparent that Elizabeth has no particular interest in Grove: "she appeared rather chagrined at the intelligence" (line 15). The result of this teasing is seen in Hogg's letter of August 22 (SC 177).

SC 177  T. J. HOGG TO MRS. TIMOTHY SHELLEY, AUGUST 22, 1811

AL (draft) signed *T. Jefferson*, 4½ pages. Double sheet, 4$^{to}$ (9.7 x 7.8 inches). Laid paper. Watermark: [posthorn in shield]| *TW&BB*| 1808|.

PROVENANCE: Thomas Jefferson Hogg; Major R. J. Jefferson Hogg (Sotheby, July 26, 1948, lot 270).

*York August 22$^{nd}$ 1811*

> *I again take the liberty of addressing you & I am convinced your*
> *goodness will again pardon me. – Perhaps my conduct appears strange*
> *It certainly must when considered abstractedly but* ~~whe~~ *– if attention is paid*
>                                                                                *by*
> 5   *to the circumstances w$^{ch}$ it was governed I think the wonder will cease* ~~not~~
>                                                                                            *almost*
> ~~only cease but~~ *To have acted thus will* ~~be~~ *appear not only natural but necessary*
> *– To adore a female without having seen her — This* ~~per~~ *when first stated*
> 10  *appears mysterious — An idea worthy of a madman. But upon a little*
> *examination the mystery will vanish . . Because the power of vision is the*
> *source of so many pleasures so many pains so powerfully excites the feelings*
> *& causes so many such varied emotions shall we in infer that* ~~the~~ *reason can*
> *be influenced by that sense alone . that every* ~~passion~~ *affection derived from*
> 15  *other sources is fancy & folly. Let us hope not: —— Is the narrative* ~~of the~~
> *spontaneous offspring of* ~~of~~ *admiring affection wholly inefficient a tale true*

[ 873 ]

*Hogg to Shelley*                                           *August 22,* 1811

SC 177  *because disinterested true because told by one who knows not falsehood a*
*tale where ~~the~~ a brother discusses the amiable qualities of a sister ~~to his friend~~*
*must always afford pleasure & command attention – In the wilderness of*
20      *this life the weeds are so numerous that when we find a flower we value it*
     *how often do*
*ₐwe return to visit it in this we act wisely the sorrows are numerous ~~we~~ we*
*seek the alleviation of pleasure & what has once pleased us we gladly repeat*
*And does conversation differ in this respect from all other human pursuits! –*
25      *No surely not – we repeat a thousand ~~tim~~ & a thousand times a topic w^{ch}*
*is agreable ~~It is or~~ We are formed by nature to worship female amiability*
*the morose Cynic says it is a weakness the Lover terms it virtue Who shall*
*decide? – but it is our nature. Then must he be a madman or a Sophister*
*who is ~~sens~~ deeply affected by a similar narrative? I trust not but if it must*
30      *be so may I ever remain insane & sophisticated. —— Then are the artless*
*yet melting strains of poetry to be considered incapable of exciting one*
*gentle emotion? —— Heaven defend me from the man who is insensible to*
*the graces of native goodness & native genius ~~cloathed~~ clad in a poetic dress*
*I cannot describe the effects of elegant poetry upon the mind I know not how*
35      *I know not why ~~yet~~ but I feel God knows how fervently that it pleases .*
*Am I then quite ~~mad~~ deranged because I know the Rose by its flowers or the*
*Vine by its cluster.? ——. Such are the causes independent of sight, w^{ch}*
       *wh had*
*can inspire passion   yet such a passion is foolish imaginary. ~~Had~~ it been*
40      *caused by the ceremony & restrained conversation of a ball w^d have been*
     *confess I*
*termed rational I will refrain from comparisons but Iₐcannot subscribe*
*to this doctrine neither can I suppose that ~~these~~ are your sentiments.    Was*
       *inestimable*
45      *it then strange to attempt in every possible manner to procure the ~~fav~~ favor*
*of an interview with the fair amiable. — It was presumptuous — but yet*
*after having once ~~atte~~ presumed to <u>love</u> what can be additional presumption*
*surely not to hope. — When hope is essential to existence when despair is*
*Death — I have often been disappointed every disappointmt has afforded*
50      *the keenest anguish. What now can I do where can I turn for assistance.*
*I have been singularly unfortunate this prevents my acting in the manner*

SC 177 *w^ch is most correct & w^ch is most ~~to be~~ congenial with my wishes —— Thus*

           *often*
 *am I situated my mind is overcome by sorrow when I reflect upon the diffi-*
55 *culties of my situation. Yet I cannot despair. to die is base is weak unworthy*
 *cowardice. —— The kind attentions the affectionate sympathy of my dear*
 *friend prevent ~~be~~ my being quite vanquished by grief. —— I venture to apply*
 *to you & I frankly own with the most sanguine hopes that your penetration*
 *will discover that my passion is not irrational that your kindness will pardon*

                   *& assist*
60 *the liberty I take in addressing you will perhaps pity me & will believe ~~that~~*
 *my hopes tho' presumptuous are correct & honorable that necessity alone*

           *the*
 *c^d have ~~i~~ driven to a breach even of strictest decorum. I venture to solicit your*

                 *a few minute conversation*
65 *advice to learn if it is possible by any means to procure an interview_∧with*
 *the fair amiable. If it were possible to procure her permission all the rest*
 *w^d be easy —— I can never hope to repay the obligation I must ever remain*
 *your debtor — you can conceive my misery you can conceive my gratitude I*
70 *will never attempt to describe it. Whatever may be your determination*

 [Written crosswise on page 1]

 *I am much indebted to you If you read to the end of this long letter*
 *accept my thanks for attending to me so far Any the most trifling attention*
 *if shewn ~~to one~~ from a motive of kindness & compassion is amiable &*
 *commands the most lively gratitude I shd be most ungrateful indeed if I did*
75 *not feel myself*

         *yours most*
         *sincerely*

        *T. Jefferson*

line 6. Hogg began to write *wonders* but changed the *s* to an upstroke flourish.

line 12. *pains so: so* is written through *such*.

line 13. *in infer* (sic)

line 26. *agreable* (sic)

line 37. Hogg wrote *causes w^ch can inspire passion*

*independent of sight;* then he inserted a looped line to indicate that *independent of sight* was to follow *causes.*

line 47. ~~*atte*~~: probable reading. *atte*[?mpted]

line 64. ~~*i*~~: Following ~~*i*~~ is what may be an upstroke for an *n*.

# The Carl H. Pforzheimer Library

SC 177    IF WE take the above letter (in Hogg's autograph) in conjunction with that to Mrs. Shelley in July (sc 168) it becomes apparent that this letter is also to Mrs. Shelley.[1]

Hogg had clearly received no reply to either his May 25 letter to Elizabeth or his July letter to Mrs. Shelley.[2] His visit to Field Place on the last weekend in June had been a failure. Elizabeth had refused to see him and he had had to content himself with the "peep" at her in Warnham Church. If, in spite of these rebuffs, Hogg once again wrote, it may be that he was alarmed by Shelley's news (sc 176) that John Grove was a possible rival for Elizabeth's affections. He perhaps felt that he might get further via Mrs. Shelley than directly with Elizabeth. But if he did actually mail a letter taken from the above draft it is not likely to have received much attention. It could not have arrived at Field Place until August 24; and on August 24 Shelley left Field Place for London to elope with Harriet Westbrook the next day. A brief note to Hogg as the honeymooners passed through York contains no mention of a letter to Mrs. Shelley.

Hogg, we may note, again places the responsibility for his infatuation on Shelley, one "who knows not falsehood" (line 17 — a different note from that struck in his biography) and who had inflamed him with his discussion of the "amiable qualities of a sister."

1. W. S. Scott (*New Shelley Letters*, p. 36) describes it as "Draft of letter from P. B. Shelley to a friend" and suggests Elizabeth Hitchener as the friend (p. [v]). But the letter is clearly in Hogg's hand (which does not at all resemble Shelley's). Frederick L. Jones correctly attributes it to Hogg but mistakenly identifies the intended recipient as Elizabeth Shelley. ("Hogg's Peep at Elizabeth Shelley," *Philological Quarterly*, XXIX, October 1950, p. 424.)

2. sc 162 (May 25, 1811); sc 168 (July ?6–18).

# EPILOGUE: ANOTHER SHELLEY FAMILY ELOPEMENT

WE HAVE already encountered Shelley's efforts to liberalize his sisters' views: "My Mo$^{th}$ fancies me in the High road to Pandemonium, she fancies I want to make a deistical coterie of all my little sisters."[1] It has been assumed by Shelley's biographers that these efforts fell on arid ground, and the general impression conveyed is that of aging maidenly virtue at Field Place. One seed, however, seems to have taken root.

Three of Shelley's sisters, Elizabeth (the object of Hogg's affection), Hellen, and Margaret, remained unmarried. A fourth sister, Mary, however, married and left Field Place. It was Mary who in December 1811 had provided her brother with an introduction to her schoolmate, Harriet Westbrook. In spite of Mary's tender years — in 1811 she was but twelve years of age — Shelley thought she showed promise. He sent her books[2] and hoped to "add her to the list of the good, the disinterested, the free."[3]

With this comment, Mary drops from Shelley biography. Shelley doubtless saw her along with his other sisters on his later visits to Field Place — the last in 1815 — but we hear nothing particular about her. When she married, in June 1819, her brother, then in Italy and out of touch with his family, apparently heard nothing of it. At least we find no comment in his letters or in his wife's letters or journals.

But if Mary drops rather early from Shelley's biography, she did not drop out of sight. In 1829 — as apparently has not previously been known to Shelley's biographers or editors — she was the center of divorce proceedings in the House of Lords, having left her husband and eloped with another man, thus following in the footsteps of her brother and grandfather in what, as Shelley remarked on another occasion, was something of a "Shelley business."

1. sc 132 (Jan. 11, 1811), line 45.

2. "Will you write to Mary under cover to Miss Pigeon, Clapham Common, Surrey, where I wish you to send the books, also for Mary." (Shelley to Edward Fergus Graham, May 29, 1810, Shelley, *Complete Works*, VIII, 13.)

3. Shelley to Elizabeth Hitchener, "October 27, 1811.?", *ibid.*, p. 168.

# The Carl H. Pforzheimer Library

## Epilogue

This elopement and its aftermath are interesting for several reasons, but perhaps most of all for the light which they indirectly shed upon the marital problems of Shelley himself. Today the marriage of Shelley and Harriet would have ended in the divorce court, and not in abandonment, social ostracism, and suicide. But when we see the barbed entanglements of divorce in early nineteenth-century England and specifically the hounding down and public pillorying that Shelley's sister had to go through we can appreciate more fully the dilemma that Shelley himself had faced.

The first we knew of Shelley's sister's elopement came when The Carl H. Pforzheimer Library purchased a copy of a parliamentary document entitled "An ACT to Dissolve the Marriage of *Daniel Franco Haynes*, Esquire, with *Mary*, his now Wife, and to enable him to marry again; and for other Purposes therein mentioned." Mary Haynes, the document informed us, was Mary Shelley. It was dated 1829 (the watermark bears the date 1828).

Why an Act of Parliament? The answer is that until the Matrimonial Causes Act of 1857 a marriage could be dissolved in England only by a special Act of Parliament. Such acts, as one can imagine, were exceedingly rare for Parliament was hardly equipped to handle a volume of divorce business. Until the accession of the House of Hanover, in fact, there were but five such acts. In the year 1829 there were seven.[4]

Following the introductory sentence given above the act proceeds as follows:

HUMBLY sheweth and complaineth unto Your most Excellent Majesty, Your true and faithful Subject, *Daniel Franco Haynes*, late of *Ashstead*, in the County of *Surry*, but now of *Barnfield*, in the County of *Southampton*, Esquire;

That on the Ninth Day of *June*, in the Year of our Lord One thousand eight hundred and nineteen, Your said Subject was married in *England*, to *Mary Shelley*, the Daughter of Sir *Timothy Shelley* Baronet:

That Your said Subject, and the said *Mary*, lived and cohabited together as Husband and Wife from the Time of their said Marriage, until the Time of her Elopement, as hereinafter mentioned, and there is Issue of their said Marriage One Son and Two Daughters:

4. *Encyclopædia Britannica*, 11th ed. (1910), "Divorce," "England."

[ 880 ]

# Shelley and his Circle : Manuscripts

That in the Month of *May*, in the Year of our Lord One thousand eight hundred and twenty-seven, the said *Mary* eloped from the said late Residence of Your said Subject at *Ashtead*, aforesaid, with *James O'Hara Trevor*, then or then late of *Millbrooke*, in the said County of *Southampton*, Esquire, and has since cohabited with and carried on an unlawful and adulterous Intercourse and criminal Conversation with him:

That Your said Subject hath not, since the said Elopement of the said *Mary* his Wife, lived, cohabited, or had any Intercourse with or Access to the said *Mary:*

That Your said Subject was unable to discover to what Place the said *Mary* and the said *James O'Hara Trevor* had gone after such her Elopement with him, until the latter End of the Month of *August*, in the Year of our Lord One thousand eight hundred and twenty-eight, when he discovered the Residence of the said *Mary*, and *James O'Hara Trevor:*

That Your said Subject in the latter End of the Month of *August*, in the Year of our Lord One thousand eight hundred and twenty-eight, brought an Action in His Majesty's Court of Common Pleas against the said *James O'Hara Trevor*, for such adulterous Intercourse and criminal Conversation with the said Wife of Your said Subject, and obtained Judgment by Default, and Two thousand Pounds have been assessed to Your said Subject, on a Writ of Inquiry, executed before the Sheriff of the County of *Surry*, and final Judgment has been entered up for that Sum and Costs, of *Hilary Term* last:

That Your said Subject has not been able to discover any Effects of the said *James O'Hara Trevor*, out of which Your said Subject could yet levy the said Damages by Writ of *Fieri Facias*, nor has Your said Subject been able to take the said *James O'Hara Trevor* himself in Execution, inasmuch as the said *James O'Hara Trevor* has, since the obtaining of the Judgment by Your said Subject against him, gone away from his Residence, near *Dover*, to some Place unknown to Your said Subject:

That Your said Subject exhibited a Libel in the Arches Court of *Canterbury* against the said *Mary* his Wife, and on or about the Fifth Day of *February*, in the Year of our Lord One thousand eight hundred and twenty-nine, obtained a Definitive Sentence of Divorce from Bed and Board, and mutual Cohabitation against her, the said *Mary*, for Adultery committed by her with the said *James O'Hara Trevor.*

That the said *Mary*, Your Subject's said Wife, has by her adulterous Conduct dissolved the Bond of Marriage on her Part, and Your said Subject stands deprived of the Comforts of Matrimony, and is liable to have a spurious Issue imposed upon him to succeed to his Estates and Fortune, unless the said Marriage be declared void and annulled by the Authority of Parliament.

# The Carl H. Pforzheimer Library

## *Epilogue*

From this we can gather, among other things, that Mary Shelley was married to Daniel Franco Haynes, had three children by him, a son and two daughters, and in May 1827 eloped with one James O'Hara Trevor, that her husband then instituted a search for the lovers and finally caught up with them at Dover in August of the following year.

Who was Daniel Franco Haynes? Little information is available in the standard biographical sources. He was presumably the author of a novel by "D. F. Haynes Esq." published in 1814 — the only work recorded by him — *Pierre and Adeline, or, The Romance of the Castle*.[5] But except for this one venture into literature, his life was apparently that of the country gentleman. He is noted in the act as coming from Ashstead, Surrey. Ashstead is about eighteen miles from the Shelley estate near Horsham, Sussex, and on the main road to London. In other sources we find Haynes listed also as the master of "Lonesome Lodge" near Wooton Hatch, Surrey, which is about twelve miles from Horsham. Both estates are recorded in Cary's *Roads* for 1819 as among the seats of the gentry. The Hayneses, therefore, were a landowning family in the same vicinity as the Shelleys.[6]

As the marriage was dissolved by an Act of Parliament, this indicated that some record of proceedings should exist among the parliamentary papers. In the *Journals of the House of Lords* for 1829 there was found, among other matter, the transcript of the divorce hearings before the Lords.

On March 3, 1829, the House heard a Petition by Haynes

praying their Lordships, "That he may have Leave to bring in a Bill to dissolve his Marriage with *Mary* his Wife, and to enable him to marry again; and to illegitimatise the Female Child born of the said *Mary Haynes* and *James O'Hara*

---

5. The novel was reprinted (as *The Romance of the Castle*) by William Hazlitt the younger in The Romancist and Novelists' Library in 1841. A cursory reading suggests that it was the work of a very young man. That Daniel Franco Haynes was indeed its author is almost certain because we find him referred to in other places as "D. F. Haynes, Esq.," for instance, in the note on his marriage in *The Gentleman's Magazine*, LXXXIX (June 1819), 578. We find no other work by him listed and no record of any other D. F. Haynes.

6. They cannot, however, have been landowners on the same scale as the Shelleys. We do not find them in *Burke's Landed Gentry*, and Daniel Franco Haynes does not appear in the alumni lists of Eton, Harrow, Oxford, or Cambridge.

## *Epilogue*

*Trevor* in the Month of *September* last; and for other Purposes therein mentioned."[7]

One John Jennings, representing Haynes, was then called in and delivered to their lordships a copy of the divorce proceedings and "the Definitive Sentence of Divorce, in the *Arches Court* of The Archbishop of *Canterbury*, intituled, '*Haynes* against *Haynes*.'" (The reference to the Arches Court brings up an interesting point: although a marriage could be legally dissolved only by an Act of Parliament, divorce hearings could take place in courts and divorces be recommended, not, however, in civil courts but only in ecclesiastical courts, of which the Arches Court of the Archbishop of Canterbury was one.)

After presenting his documents, Jennings left and the Earl of Shaftesbury arose to present a bill to the House for the dissolution of the marriage.

The hearings on the bill took place on March 19[8] at a regular session of the House of Lords. A copy of the marriage register from the church at Warnham (where in an earlier day Thomas Jefferson Hogg had had his "peep" at Elizabeth Shelley) was produced in evidence and showed that the marriage had taken place on June 9, 1819. The officiating minister was Charles Henry Grove (who, some eight years previously, as a young medical student, had accompanied Shelley to his elopement rendezvous with Harriet Westbrook). These legal facts were confirmed by David Haynes, brother of Daniel Franco, and himself a clergyman. Their sister, Mrs. Catherine Bligh ("married to Captain *Bligh* of the Navy"),[9] was

---

7. *Journals of the House of Lords Beginning Anno Decimo Georgii Quarti*, LXI (1829), 100.

8. On March 5 it was moved that the bill be read a second time on March 19. On March 12 it was "*Ordered*, That *William Whitton, Thomas Aviolet*, The Reverend *William Samuel Parr Wilder, Catherine Arthur, Aaron Jones, William Sankey* the younger, *Samuel Sutton* and *Richard Gill*, do attend this House on *Thursday* the 19th of this instant *March*, in order to their being examined as Witnesses upon the Second Reading of the Bill, intituled, 'An ACT to Dissolve the Marriage of *Daniel Franco Haynes*, Esquire, with *Mary*, his now Wife, and to enable him to marry again; and for other Purposes therein mentioned.'" Whitton, the Shelley family lawyer, did not, however, actually appear as a witness.

9. Not Captain William Bligh of *The Bounty*. In the Navy Lists for 1829 we find Captain George Miller Bligh, and in the *DNB* Admiral Sir Richard Rodney Bligh (1737–1821), who had "a son George Miller Bligh, who was a Lieutenant of the Victory of Trafalgar, where he was severely wounded, and died a captain in 1835." Cary's *Roads* (1819) informs us that Admiral Bligh had a house near Southampton.

[ 883 ]

# The Carl H. Pforzheimer Library

## *Epilogue*

next called in. She testified that the Hayneses used to visit her mother (Mary's mother-in-law) near Millbrook, Southampton, for two or three months every year and that they appeared to her to be happily married ("I never heard an angry word").

Following her testimony Haynes's counsel announced that he wished to "call Evidence" to support the illegitimizing clause. He was, however, informed that such a clause had "not of late been introduced into Bills of this Nature, there being no Person in Attendance to watch the Interests of the Child." The clause does not appear in the act (as quoted above).

The next witness was Elizabeth Rice, servant in the Haynes family, who remembered the circumstances of Mary's leaving home.

"Do you remember Mrs. *Haynes* leaving *Ashstead Lodge; Ashstead Cottage?*"
"Yes."
"Did Mr. *Haynes* go from Home that Morning?"
"Yes; the Morning before."
"Did you hear from Mrs. *Haynes,* or in her Presence, where Mr. *Haynes* was going?"
"Yes."
"Where was Mr. *Haynes* going?"
"To *Southampton;* to his Mother's."
"For what Purpose was that stated?"
"It was to see his Daughter."
"On what Day do you recollect that Mr. *Haynes* went away?"
"On *Friday.*"
"Do you remember the Month?"
"No I do not; it was in *May.*"
"Towards the Beginning or the End of *May?*"
"Near the End."
"Mr. *Haynes* went away on the *Friday;* did Mrs. *Haynes* go any where about that Time?"
"Yes; they went on the same Day, both."
"Where did Mrs. *Haynes* go?"
"She went down to *Dorking* to meet her Mamma."
"Did Mrs. *Haynes* tell you that she was going to *Dorking* to meet her Mamma?"
"Yes."
"Did you see her leave the House?"
"Yes."

[ 884 ]

# Shelley and his Circle : Manuscripts

"What did she leave it in?"

"In her own Carriage."

"Did the Carriage come back empty?"

"Yes."

"Have you ever seen Mrs. *Haynes* since?"

"No."

"Are you acquainted with Mr. *Trevor;* with his Person?"

"No, I am not, very much; I have seen him."

"Did you ever see him near *Ashstead?*"

"No."[10]

The Hayneses, then, were in the habit of spending two to three months a year with Haynes' mother near Millbrook. And it was at Millbrook that James O'Hara Trevor lived. Trevor, we gather from later testimony, used to visit the Hayneses there;[11] and it was doubtless out of these visits that the romance between him and Mary sprang up. We learn from Elizabeth Rice's testimony that the elopement adventure began one May morning in 1827 with Mary's simply getting into her carriage and never coming back (after stating that she was going to meet her mother at Dorking — some six miles from Ashstead, on the road to Horsham). What happened after she reached Dorking, we do not know. But in June she was seen by the Reverend Samuel Parr Wilder of Millbrook walking "arm in arm" with Trevor in a "public street" in Paris. Haynes, it appears, had information of their whereabouts and had sent Wilder to Paris.[12] After that, however, he must have lost the trail, for he did not find them until August of the following year. Part, at least, of the intervening fourteen months were spent in a kind of hare-and-hounds chase, with Mary and Trevor moving from place to place and lodging to lodging.

Early in 1828 they were in London living at Portman Place near the Edgeware Road.[13] In July they were in lodgings in Hereford (near the Welsh border).[14] How long they had been there we do not know, but they made the mistake of hiring a servant, Martha Pember, with a relentless memory for the minutiae of bed-making. From Hereford they went back to London, and Martha went with them. Here again they

10. *Journals of the House of Lords*, LXI, 217–218.  11. *Ibid.*, p. 221.

12. *Ibid.*, p. 218.  13. *Ibid.*, p. 221.

14. *Ibid.*, p. 219.

## *Epilogue*

sought lodgings in the Edgeware Road area (at Connaught Terrace, where they had five rooms).

But apparently they felt no security in London, for within a few weeks they left for Dover. After a month in lodgings they decided to take a house of their own in the country (as Mr. and Mrs. Trevor). It was there that the law (in the person of John Hovell Triston of Gray's Inn Square)[15] caught up with them, and it was there that a child was born to them (delivered by Mr. William Sankie, surgeon, of Snargate Street, Dover).[16]

The final major witness was one Thomas Powell.

Then *Thomas Powell* was called in; and having been sworn, was examined as follows:

(*By Counsel.*) "Were you Servant to Mr. *Trevor* at any Time?"

"Yes."

"How long did you live in his Service?"

"Between Nine and Ten Years."

"Where was he living at that Time?"

"At the *Hummums* Hotel."

"What was he; was he an Officer?"

"He was represented so to me."

"Did you live with him at *Milbrooke* near *Southampton?*"

"Yes."

"When you were living at *Milbrooke* near *Southampton*, did you see Mrs. *Daniel Haynes?*"

"Yes."

"How long did you live with Mr. *Trevor* at *Milbrooke?*"

"About Four Months."

"Did Mr. *Trevor* break up his Establishment at *Milbrooke?*"

"No, not quite."

"Did you leave Mr. *Trevor?*"

"I did."

"Why did you leave Mr. *Trevor?*"

"He told me he was going to *America*."

"Did he give you any Directions what to do after he should be gone to *America*, about yourself?"

"To write to him, if I had no Situation, in a few Months."

15. *Ibid.*, p. 217; *Clarke's New Law List*, 1825.

16. *Journals of the House of Lords*, LXI, 221; Pigot's *Commercial Directory*, 1823–24.

# Shelley and his Circle : Manuscripts

Trevor, then, lived at the Hummums Hotel; and the Hummums Hotel was not — as one might at first think — in the Southampton region, where Trevor had his house, but in London. It was, in fact, a large and well-known hotel (commented on by Samuel Johnson and Leigh Hunt).[17] It would seem, from Powell's testimony, that Trevor kept up two residences, one in London, where he had been for "between Nine and Ten Years" and one at Millbrook, which is described as an "establishment," i.e., a house with servants. Trevor, therefore, must have been moderately well off, although what he did for a living is not clear. He was not, as Counsel is apparently hinting, an "Officer" in either the regular Army or the Navy, for a search of the Army and Navy Lists for the period fails to disclose him. He could, however, have been an officer in a county militia.

How long he had been at Millbrook is not clear. Powell had been there with him for only a few months prior to the elopement and it may be that Trevor was a fairly recent resident.[18] If so, his romance with Mary may have been of rather sudden development; for they seem to have first met at Millbrook. Trevor had apparently never been at Ashstead.[19]

We gather also from Powell's testimony that Trevor and Mary intended at first to elope to America. And it is possible that they were there between their sojourn in Paris in July 1827 and their residence in London in the early months of 1828, during which period we have no record of their whereabouts. Trevor had told Powell to write to him in America, and Powell does not indicate that this plan was changed.

Powell, in continuing his testimony, stated that he had returned to Trevor's service in London (apparently about eight months after the elopement) and lived with him and Mary in their various lodgings

17. Henry C. Shelley, *Inns and Taverns of Old London* (Boston, 1909), pp. 128–131. The hotel, which featured hot baths "in the Oriental manner," was said to have enjoyed a "lively reputation." (*Ibid.*, p. 127.) It was situated near Covent Garden, on the east side of the Piazza south of Russell Street. (Plan of London, C2, Front Endpapers.)

18. The Reverend Samuel Parr Wilder (see fn. 8, above) testified that he had known Trevor "about a Twelve-month" and had lived "within Three or Four Miles of him." (*Journals of the House of Lords*, LXI, 218.)

19. As we have noted above, Elizabeth Rice, the Hayneses' servant at Ashstead, testified that she had never seen Trevor there.

# The Carl H. Pforzheimer Library

## *Epilogue*

(joined in July by Martha Pember), ending up with them at their house near Dover. He left them there in May or June 1828. The child was born in September.

The testimony concluded, it was *"Ordered*, That the further Consideration and Second Reading of the said Bill be put off 'till To-morrow; and that the Lords be summoned." On March 20, Haynes, through his attorneys, agreed to withdraw the illegitimizing clause (which, consequently, does not appear in the act). On March 25, a message having been received that the House of Commons had approved the bill, it was passed by the House of Lords. On April 13 the act was given "Royal Assent" and the marriage was officially dissolved.

This action in the House of Lords, however, was not the only one. As the act (quoted above) noted, Haynes had also brought action against Trevor in the Court of Common Pleas on the charge of "criminal Conversation with the said Wife of Your said subject" and had been awarded £2000 damages. But, as the act goes on to state, the "said Subject" had not been able to collect because James O'Hara Trevor was not to be found. (He had "gone away from his Residence, near *Dover*, to some Place unknown to Your said Subject.") Furthermore, the "said Subject" was unable to find any "Effects of the absent Trevor upon which he could "levy the said Damages."

Whether Haynes ever caught up with Trevor and got his pound of flesh we do not know; but financially Mary did not come out too badly. According to the divorce act Haynes was prevented from touching any of her effects or her possible inheritance from her father:

And be it further enacted, That the said *Daniel Franco Haynes*, and all Persons claiming or to claim by, from, or under him, is and are and shall be for ever barred and excluded of and from all Rights, Claims, Titles, and Interests of, in, to, or out of any Manors, Messuages, Lands, Tenements, and Hereditaments, and other Estates, Real, Freehold, Personal, and Mixed, and all Goods, Chattels, Personal Estate, and Effects whatsoever which the same *Mary* shall or may at any Time or Times hereafter acquire or become seised or possessed of, or entitled to by Descent, Gift, Devise, Purchase, or otherwise howsoever, during the Estate and Interest of the said *Mary*, her Heirs, Executors, Administrators, and Assigns therein respectively; and that the said *Mary*, her Heirs, Executors, and Administrators, shall and may hold and enjoy the same and every of them for all her and their Estate and Interest therein, for her and their

# Shelley and his Circle : Manuscripts

## *Epilogue*

own Use, Benefit, and Advantage, exclusive of the said *Daniel Franco Haynes*, his Heirs, Executors, and Administrators, and all and every other Person and Persons whomsoever claiming or to claim by, from, or under him.

What kind of settlement was actually made we can gather from some notations in ink on the outer leaf of our copy of the act. According to these, Haynes and Sir Timothy Shelley deposited jointly the sum of £10,000 with the trustees of the Shelley estate.[20] In his will, Sir Timothy left with the trustees a total of £10,000, the interest of which was for Mary's use, and, in addition left her £700 in cash.[21]

Both the divorce settlement and the will, one may remark, help to demolish the picture of Sir Timothy as a tyrannical father. His — and the trusty Whitton's — hands seem discernible in the protection given his daughter in the divorce settlement and he treated her in his will about as he did his other daughters. Whatever his intellectual limitations Sir Timothy was fundamentally honest and always attempted to be just. In his earlier dealings with his son he had been driven to distraction by that son's inflexible adherence to principles, moral and intellectual, which were beyond his comprehension.

What was the aftermath? We have also in our library an unpublished letter from Mary's sister Hellen, written after Sir Timothy Shelley's death in April 1844,[22] which provides part of the answer. It is to "Peggy and Flora:" and is signed "Your ever afte Aunt":

This a time of year that every one ought to hear of their friends even if they do not expect it & I should not have left my dear little girls so long in the dark concerning all our doings but that I know your Mama can tell you all that may interest you. . . . & now do you think you two can keep a little Secret? if I tell you that we propose before you leave Bath to pay it a visit if your Papas sojourn there Should be prolonged beyond that of the inhabitants of 12 Queen

20. Haynes put up £9425, Sir Timothy £575; a following notation records that Sir Timothy loaned £5000 "to M$^r$ Haynes on his Bond to the Trustees" (i.e., the trustees of the Shelley estate).

21. Photostatic copy of Sir Timothy Shelley's will (dated Apr. 26, 1834), pp. 3, 4, 18 (codicil, May 13, 1843), 19 (codicil). Prior to her marriage Mary had been assigned £2000 (p. 2), perhaps her dowry.

22. The letter bears only the date "Dec — 27$^{th}$" without a year, and the envelope is missing, but the watermark bears the date 1844 and the paper has a black border. As the date of the writing of letters is usually within two or three years of that of the watermark, and as two years was a customary span for a black border following the death of a close relative, the probability is that the letter was written on December 27 in either 1844, 1845, or 1846. See also fn. 23.

# The Carl H. Pforzheimer Library

## *Epilogue*

Square – for my Mama begins to think that She will not perhaps be able to take the long journey to Teignmouth, but I see no reason for the fear at present although yʳ grandmama's health & strength varies very much – I hear that Florry is knitting Something in concert with her Mama and you may be Sure that we Shall value very much whatever you do. . . . I was called away in the midst of my letter to place the China on the old Oak Chest because so much consultation is required upon all these grave affairs Your Grandmama was half inclined not to send this parcel but I thought the old Sussex Fowls might taste very sweet although they are but poor Speciments of feudal tenure Do you not See My dear Children that I might run on for ever but I will conclude by wishing you increased happiness every Succeeding year as well as yʳ dear Papa & Mama – Your grand mama & Margᵗ unite too in every Kind wish and Eternal love.

Who were Peggy and Flora? Who was "Papa"? We find in *Burke's Peerage* for 1857 that Mary had a daughter named Flora-Brenda;[23] we find in a codicil to Sir Timothy Shelley's will a reference to "my Daughter Mary Trevor."[24] Mary, therefore, married Trevor and had two daughters by him, the first of them presumably the child born near Dover in 1828.

From the tone of Hellen's letter, with its references to "yʳ dear Papa" and knitting "in concert" and so on, one gets the impression of a

---

23. As Flora-Brenda was married on December 5, 1848, and as she is clearly unmarried at the time of Hellen Shelley's letter, this sets an absolute terminal date on the letter of December 27, 1847.

24. Photostatic copy of will and codicils, p. 18 (May 13, 1843). In the will (Apr. 26, 1834) Sir Timothy refers to "her present or any future Husband"; hence, Mary and Trevor were married at least by April 26, 1834. The marriage, however, does not seem to have been publicized. *Burke's Peerage* in 1857 still refers to her as Mrs. Haynes. And the divorce proceedings seem to have been kept secret. We find no reference to them in the letters or journals of Shelley's wife, Mary Shelley, or in the letters of Leigh Hunt or Thomas Love Peacock. They are not mentioned by any of Shelley's biographers or editors; but perhaps Roger Ingpen knew something about the case, for, in his pedigree of the Shelley family at the back of his *Shelley in England* he lists Mary Shelley as having been married twice, first (mistakenly) to "David Francis Haynes" (Daniel Franco Haynes' brother was called David) and then to James O'Hara Trevor. He gives the date of her death as April 20, 1884.

The only other later references to Mary Trevor that we find in Shelleyian literature are by Trelawny. On June 19, 1869, William Michael Rossetti called on Trelawny and noted among other matters: "He dislikes Shelley's maiden sisters but likes Mrs. Haynes." (W. M. Rossetti, *Rossetti Papers, 1862 to 1870*, New York, 1903, p. 399.) We have in our library an autograph letter from Trelawny to Claire Clairmont, November 27, 1869, which contains the following sentence: "Your last letters were excedingly interesting to me every thing regarding S — is so — for I loved him from the first on the death of his son the present Percy the family will be extinct his three sisters are living; two unmarried the 3 married but no children and long seperated from her husband her name Mary Trevor." From this we can gather that Claire Clairmont did not know of the elopement and divorce, and that Trelawny himself did not know very much. Apparently, however, he called Mary "Mrs. Haynes" when speaking to Rossetti.

*Epilogue*

happy family circle. Furthermore, the relationship between the Trevors and the Shelleys seems amiable.

One cannot avoid a final conjecture. What would Percy Bysshe have thought? Was there perhaps a wisp of ironical laughter in the air as Florry and her Mama knitted?

K.N.C.

# THE PROVENANCE OF SHELLEY AND
# HIS CIRCLE MANUSCRIPTS

On FIRST seeing the original manuscripts of a great writer of a past
century library visitors usually first ask "where did they come
from?" and "how did they happen to be preserved?" The present essay
is an attempt to answer these questions so far as Shelley is concerned and
sketch in some of the facts for other members of the "circle" as well.
Curiously enough, so far as we can ascertain, no similar study exists for
the other major English poets.

In general the answer to both questions in regard to Shelley manuscripts is that they came from two main sources, his immediate family
(his widow and his son), and from friends or business associates (publishers, lawyers, and so on). His literary manuscripts mainly stayed in the
family; some letters stayed in the family but as we would expect, others
were widely scattered. The family preserved manuscripts and letters
because of their literary value and from a sense of family affection and
loyalty. Others, as we shall see, preserved them for various reasons.

Let us consider the family material first. On the death of Mary
Shelley in 1851 the family manuscripts passed to her son, Sir Percy
Florence Shelley, then living at Boscombe Manor, near Bournemouth.
Sometime following Sir Percy's death in 1889, the manuscripts were
divided into three parts. One part his widow, Lady Jane Shelley, presented to the Bodleian Library at Oxford in 1893; one part went to the
Shelley-Rolls family (descended from Shelley's younger brother John);
and one part went to the Abinger family (the fifth Baron Abinger was the
son of Sir Percy Florence Shelley's adopted daughter, Mrs. Bessie
Florence Scarlett). As Sir John C. E. Shelley-Rolls presented his part to
the Bodleian in 1946, two of the original three parts are now in that
library. The third part is in the possession of the present Lord Abinger.[1]

By noting the main contents of these three parts we can see the
extent of the family holdings.

The core of Lady Jane Shelley's gift to the Bodleian in 1893 was

1. For the Shelley-Rolls branch of the family see *Burke's Peerage*, "Shelley of Castle Goring," and
the pedigree at the end of Ingpen's *Shelley in England*. For Abinger see *Burke's Peerage*. Mrs. Scarlett
(née Gibson) was a niece of Lady Shelley (née Gibson).

# Shelley and his Circle : Manuscripts

made up of Shelley's literary manuscripts, including those of *Prometheus Unbound* and *A Defence of Poetry*. It contained also a number of letters by Shelley and Mary Shelley. Not all of these are letters within the family (for example, Mary and Shelley to each other); some, also secured by the family, are to such close friends as Leigh Hunt, Thomas Love Peacock, John and Maria Gisborne, and Thomas Hookham.[2]

Sir John Shelley-Rolls' gift also contained letters by Shelley and by Mary but its most important section consisted of 14 of Shelley's notebooks, 3 of which contain the manuscript of *Laon and Cythna* (*The Revolt of Islam*), and 1 of which contains parts of *Adonais*.[3] Shelley often did his first drafts in notebooks. As Lady Shelley's gift had contained 6 notebooks the Bodleian thus secured a total of 20.

The Abinger material, unlike the Lady Shelley (Bodleian) and Shelley-Rolls portions, contains little Shelley autograph material (5 letters and some journal entries), but represents that portion of the family papers which concerns William Godwin, Mary Wollstonecraft, and Mary Shelley. It contains the daily journal of William Godwin kept over a period of some forty-seven years, some of his literary manuscripts, a large number of letters to him (including some by Coleridge and Lamb), some of his own letters (partly copies made by Godwin for his own use); about 100 letters and notes by Mary Wollstonecraft; the diary of Mary Shelley (with a few entries by Shelley) from the time of her elopement with Shelley until after his death; the manuscript of part of Mary Shelley's *Frankenstein* and other literary manuscripts by her; a

---

2. For information on Lady Shelley's gift see *The Shelley Correspondence in the Bodleian Library*, ed. R. H. Hill (Oxford, 1926); C. D. Locock, *An Examination of the Shelley Manuscripts in the Bodleian Library* (Oxford, 1903); A. H. Koszul, *Shelley's Prose in the Bodleian Manuscripts* (London, 1910); Seymour de Ricci, *A Bibliography of Shelley's Letters* (Privately Printed, 1927); Shelley, *Complete Works*, X, 424–425 and *passim*. Hill lists the letters and prints some of them, lists the literary manuscripts (p. 46), and also notes the "Manuscripts Previously in the Library or Added Since the Shelley Donation" (p. 47). Locock examines the poetry, Koszul the prose. See de Ricci's entries for the Gisbornes, Henry Reveley (Mrs. Gisborne's son), Hookham, Hunt, Peacock, and Mary Shelley.

3. For information on Sir John Shelley-Rolls' gift see *The Bodleian Library Record*, II (July 1946), 144–145; *Verse and Prose from the Manuscripts of Percy Bysshe Shelley*, ed. Sir John C. E. Shelley-Rolls and Roger Ingpen (London, 1934); Ingpen, *Shelley in England*, pp. 659–691 (transcripts and facsimiles from the *Adonais* notebook); Neville Rogers in *The Times Literary Supplement*, London, July 27, Aug. 3, Aug. 10, 1951; July 24, 1953; Feb. 12, Nov. 5, 1954; Neville Rogers, *Shelley at Work* (Oxford, 1956).

# The Carl H. Pforzheimer Library

## *Provenance*

large number of letters to Mary Shelley (including some from Thomas Moore).[4]

The literary manuscripts of Mary Wollstonecraft do not seem to have survived. Many, if not most, of them appear to have gone to her publisher, Joseph Johnson.[5] If they are still extant their present location is unknown.

Of the literary manuscripts outside the family the most considerable group consists of the works of Godwin. Although the Abinger collection contains some of Godwin's literary manuscripts, most of them were sold along with his library following his death in 1836[6] (many of them bought by the great Norfolk collector Dawson Turner[7]), and these manuscripts are now in various libraries. Three of them, *The Lives of the Necromancers* and the novels *Fleetwood* and *Cloudesley*, are in The Carl H. Pforzheimer Library (as are also the manuscripts of an *Enquirer* essay and a historical essay on Sir William Davenant, both published in the present volumes).

A number of Shelley's literary manuscripts are also outside the family collections. Shelley himself gave away some manuscripts — usually of shorter poems — and left others with publishers; Mary Shelley gave some away, and so, too, later in the century, did Lady Jane Shelley.

Shelley, for instance, gave away some manuscripts to Hogg and some to Miss Sophia Stacey, the ward of his uncle, Robert Parker.[8] Those to Hogg included the poem "Death! where is thy victory!" and

---

4. This information was gathered by an examination and tabulation of Lord Abinger's manuscripts made in the spring of 1954 in preparing these manuscripts for exhibition at The New York Public Library, and from a microfilm subsequent to that time. For a detailed survey see Lewis Patton, "The Shelley-Godwin Collection of Lord Abinger," *Library Notes*, No. 27 (April 1953), pp. 11-17, Duke University Library, North Carolina.

5. See sc 19 (April 1797), fn. 7.

6. Sotheby and Sons, *Catalogue of the Curious Library of that Eminent and Distinguished Author, William Godwin, Esq., to which are added the Very Interesting and Original Autograph Manuscripts of his Highly Esteemed Publications*, June 17-18, 1838.

7. Puttick and Simpson, *Catalogue of the Important Manuscript Library of the late Dawson Turner, Esq.*, June 6 and following days, 1859, pp. 85-86. For Turner (1775-1858) see the *DNB*.

8. Edward John Trelawny also possessed some of Shelley's manuscripts. These were mainly copies of poems written to Jane Williams. How or when they came into Trelawny's possession does not seem to be known. W. M. Rossetti describes one of them — "With a Guitar, to Jane" — as "written out by Shelley with exquisite neatness." (*The Complete Poetical Works of Percy Bysshe Shelley*, London, 1881, III, 410. For a list of these poems, see H. J. Massingham, *The Friend of Shelley*, London, 1930, Appendix IV.)

# Shelley and his Circle : Manuscripts

the prose piece "The Wandering Jew," both published in the present volumes. Those given to Sophia Stacey comprised the lyrics partly written for her in Florence in 1819, including "The Indian Serenade."[9] Of the manuscripts of the poems left with publishers and subsequently placed on the market, the best known is that of *Julian and Maddalo*, a fair copy of which Shelley sent from Italy to Leigh Hunt for publication by his publishers, Charles and James Ollier. This manuscript remained in Hunt's possession and was discovered after his death by his friend, Samuel Ralph Townshend Mayer, and is now in The Pierpont Morgan Library.[10] (The Olliers, we might note here, had the manuscript of Shelley's prose work *A Proposal for Putting Reform to the Vote*, which was sold by their heirs in 1879.[11]) It is also possible that Hunt had at one time the manuscript of *Laon and Cythna* which was sent to the printers, for parts of this manuscript were among his papers. Some of these are at present in The Carl H. Pforzheimer Library, along with other Shelley manuscripts also once owned by Hunt.[12]

9. Shelley, *Complete Works*, III, 349; *The Poetical Works of Percy Bysshe Shelley*, ed. H. Buxton Forman (London, 1882), IV, 10–11; Helen Rossetti Angeli, *Shelley and his Friends in Italy* (London, 1911); pp. 98–99.

10. Forman, *Poetical Works of Shelley*, III, 102 (plus facsimile); Shelley, *Complete Works*, III, 332–333; George K. Boyce, "Modern Literary Manuscripts in the Morgan Library," *PMLA*, LXVII (February 1952), 21.

11. Shelley, *Complete Works*, VI, 351. This manuscript — a perfectly genuine manuscript — was declared a forgery in *The Shelley Legend*, by Robert Metcalf Smith, Theodore G. Ehrsam, *et al.* (New York, 1945), on grounds which were subsequently described by the bibliographical specialist of that work as follows: "The handwriting expert of *The Shelley Legend*, having designated the December 16 letter a forgery, used this letter as a touchstone to determine other forgeries. Such a procedure might have been perfectly proper had the touchstone actually been forged, but since the Wise letter, but for the signature, is a genuine Shelley manuscript, it cannot, obviously, be used as a sample of forgery. Thus the verdict that the manuscript of *A Proposal for Putting Reform to the Vote Throughout the Kingdom* is spurious must definitely be reversed." (Theodore G. Ehrsam, *Major Byron, The Incredible Career of a Literary Forger*, New York and London, 1951, p. 137.) On *The Shelley Legend* see Newman I. White, Frederick L. Jones, Kenneth N. Cameron, *An Examination of The Shelley Legend* (University of Pennsylvania Press, 1951).

12. That the *Laon and Cythna* fragments were part of a complete manuscript is indicated by their pagination. They were not, however, part of the first draft, for that draft, as we have noted, is in the Bodleian notebooks. Hence, they were probably part of the copy sent to the printer. The other Shelley manuscripts originating with Hunt include a draft of the dedication of *The Cenci* to Hunt, fragments of *Prometheus Unbound* and *The Masque of Anarchy* (all of which appear to have come from a notebook), and Shelley's translation of part of Moschus' "Elegy on the Death of Bion" (which is echoed in *Adonais*).

# The Carl H. Pforzheimer Library

## *Provenance*

Mary Shelley gave away at least 2 major manuscripts, that of *The Masque of Anarchy* (to John Bowring in 1826) and that of the first part of *Prince Athanase* (to John Chalk Claris in 1824).[13] The manuscript of *The Masque of Anarchy* came into the possession of Thomas J. Wise and passed with his library (The Ashley Library) into the British Museum. The present location of the *Prince Athanase* manuscript does not appear to be known.

Sir Percy Florence and Lady Shelley gave 4 of Shelley's notebooks to Richard Garnett. Three of these are at present in the Henry E. Hunt-

---

13. On *The Masque of Anarchy* see Mary Shelley to John Bowring, Feb. 25, 1826, *Letters*, I, 342; Thomas J. Wise, *A Shelley Library*, p. 72 (with photograph). Our information on the *Prince Athanase* manuscript comes from a sales catalogue of Sotheby, Wilkinson & Hodge, sale of July 22–25, 1918, lot no. 701, which runs as follows:

> SHELLEY (P. B.) ATHANASE, a fragment, 8½ pp. 8vo, THE MOST IMPORTANT POETICAL MS. OF SHELLEY SOLD BY AUCTION OF RECENT YEARS
>
> At the back of the last page is the following, written in pencil and traced over in ink: "This Poem of Shelley's was given me by his widow, June 7th, 1824, Speldhurst St., Brunswick Sq., A. Brooke." The poem is in *terza rima*, like the unfinished Triumph of Life, and was dated by Mrs. Shelley 1817. At the beginning is the following autograph note: "The Author was pursuing a further development of the ideal character of Athanase when it struck him that, in an attempt at extreme refinement and analysis, his conception might be betrayed into the assuming a morbid character — the reader will judge whether he is a loser or a gainer by this diffidence."
>
> The poem begins:
>
> > There was a Youth who, as with toil and travel
> > Had grown quite weak and grey before his time,
> > Nor any could the restless griefs unravel
> > Which burned within him, withering up his prime
> > And goading him, like fiends from land to land.
> > Not his the load of any secret crime, etc.
>
> This MS. includes the whole of Part I, the only consecutive passage of any length which was written.

"Arthur Brooke" was the pseudonym of John Chalk Claris (1797?–1866), editor of the *Kent Herald* and author of poems on Shelley. (*DNB*; White, *Shelley*, II, 302, 356, 392–393.) In 1824 Mary Shelley was living at 14 Speldhurst Street, Brunswick Square, London.

A manuscript of *Prince Athanase* was among those given to the Bodleian by Lady Jane Shelley in 1893. C. D. Locock in *An Examination of the Shelley Manuscripts in the Bodleian Library*, pp. 50–51, wrote of it as follows: "From MS. evidence I am inclined to think that Shelley must have made another copy of the earlier Part; so that the numerous MS. variations in that Part will have no authority, except in one or two instances, and a simple categorical list of them will be sufficient." The manuscript given to Claris, then, must have been this other copy. Locock's deduction is of interest in view of the fact that he presumably did not know of the Claris manuscript. This manuscript has not, so far as we know, been used by Shelley's editors (except insofar as it may have been embodied in Mary Shelley's text in 1824).

# Shelley and his Circle : Manuscripts

ington Library[14] and one in the Library of Congress.[15] To another friend and Shelley enthusiast, the Reverend Stopford Brooke, Lady Shelley gave a manuscript book containing *A Philosophical View of Reform* and the short essay *On Life*. Brooke cut out the *On Love* section (now in The Pierpont Morgan Library) and sold it to aid the British Red Cross during World War I.[16] The manuscript of *A Philosophical View of Reform* is at present in The Carl H. Pforzheimer Library. There are thus, we might note, 25 of Shelley's notebooks extant, 20 in England and 5 in the United States. And in addition there is a manuscript book of poems, copied partly by Shelley and partly by Mary Shelley, in the Harvard University Library.[17]

14. Sotheby, Wilkinson & Hodge, *Catalogue of the Library of the late Dr. Richard Garnett*, December 6, 1906, lots no. 232, 233, 234, with the introductory notation: "These Note Books were given by Shelley's widow to her son Sir Percy Shelley, he and Lady Shelley gave them to Dr. Garnett." These notebooks passed into the library of W. K. Bixby in St. Louis and were published by him in 1911 (edited by H. B. Forman).

15. Frederick L. Jones, "Unpublished Fragments by Shelley and Mary," *Studies in Philology*, XLV (July 1948), 472–476; Parke-Bernet Galleries, *The Renowned Library of the Late John A. Spoor*, May 3–5, 1939, lot no. 745. Garnett gave the book to Miss V. E. Neale in 1904.

16. The manuscript of *A Philosophical View of Reform*, then owned by Sir Percy Florence and Lady Jane Shelley, was described by Dowden in *The Fortnightly Review*, November 1886: "The manuscript occupies upward of two hundred pages in a small vellum-bound Italian note-book. On the outer side of one of the covers is a pen-and-ink drawing by Shelley . . . At one end of the little volume is the fragment 'On Life' . . ." Dowden's comments were repeated the following year in his *Transcripts and Studies* (London, 1887), p. 42. In an autograph letter dated February 21, 1916, now with the manuscript of *On Life* in the Morgan Library, Stopford Brooke writes: "It may interest you to know that I have sent to Gosse's Red Cross Sale at Christies Shelley's MS of the Essay "On Life," published in Mary's *Essays & Letters*. Vol. I, p. 223. It is the first draft of this, taken out of one his Note Books, & given to me in 1894 by Lady Shelley." We have made a comparative examination of the manuscripts of *On Life* and *A Philosophical View of Reform*, placing the two manuscripts side by side, and it is apparent that the two were originally together in the notebook which now houses the latter only (paper, stitching holes, etc., are identical).

Brooke's comment, we might note, is ambiguous in one respect. He does not make it clear whether he or Lady Shelley divided the notebook. Brooke's son-in-law, T. W. Rolleston, however, informs us that the manuscript of *A Philosophical View of Reform* — "contained in about 200 pages of a small vellum-covered note-book" — was presented to Brooke by Lady Shelley. (P. B. Shelley, *A Philosophical View of Reform*, ed. T. W. Rolleston, Oxford, 1920, p. iii.) As Brooke later had the manuscript of *On Life* in his possession and as Rolleston makes no separate mention of it as part of Lady Shelley's gift, we can presume that she gave Brooke a whole notebook — as she did to Garnett — and not an incomplete notebook plus a separate manuscript cut out of it. Brooke's ambiguity is doubtless deliberate; he did not want to admit that he had cut up the book (for the Red Cross). On Brooke's death in March 1916, the notebook passed to his daughter, Mrs. T. W. Rolleston.

17. For the provenance of this book see below, p. 911. The book was edited in 1929 by George Edward Woodberry under the title *The Shelley Notebook in the Harvard College Library*. It is not,

# The Carl H. Pforzheimer Library

## *Provenance*

The curious thing about Shelley's literary manuscripts is not the number which have survived but the number which have disappeared. It seems almost incredible, for instance, that there should be no manuscript of his play *The Cenci* or of *Alastor* and but partial manuscripts for such other of his major works as *Adonais*, *Epipsychidion*, and *Hellas*.[18] Not that one would expect Shelley to keep such manuscripts for he seldom kept anything, including letters; but Mary Shelley seems to have inherited the hoarding instincts of her father, who methodically filed everything away, and as she kept so many manuscripts the loss of the rest seems strange.

Particularly is there a lack of Shelley's early manuscripts. None of these was preserved in the family papers because the family papers, so far as Shelley was concerned, began with Mary Shelley. Harriet seems to have had as little interest in preserving literary manuscripts as Shelley himself. The only exception, so far as is known, is a manuscript book of poems, which contained a dedication to Harriet herself and was presumably given to her by Shelley. The book has been preserved in her family and is at present in the possession of the heirs of Shelley's great-grandson, William C. H. Esdaile.[19] The only other major early manuscript is one of a revised version of *Queen Mab* (made in a copy of the first edition). This manuscript (at present in The Carl H. Pforzheimer Library) was among some papers which Shelley left behind in England

however, a regular Shelley notebook, in which Shelley jotted down ideas and drafts for poems, but is a book of fair copies.

Woodberry made some errors in the ascription of the handwriting which have been corrected by Helen Darbishire and Marcel Kessel. For a summary of these see Smith, *The Shelley Legend*, pp. 39–40.

18. For *Adonais* see Ingpen, *Shelley in England*, pp. 671–687; Shelley-Rolls and Ingpen, *Verse and Prose*, pp. 36–48. For *Epipsychidion*, see Locock, *An Examination of the Shelley Manuscripts in the Bodleian Library*, pp. 3–13, and Shelley, *Complete Works*, II, 428. A transcript of *Hellas* in the hand of Edward Ellerker Williams is at present in the Huntington Library and was previously in Frederick Locker-Lampson's *The Rowfant Library* (which also contained other Shelley material). Some *Hellas* fragments in Shelley's hand are in the Shelley-Rolls notebooks (*Verse and Prose*, pp. 47–52).

19. Ianthe, the daughter of Shelley and Harriet, married Edward Jeffries Esdaile of Cothelstone House, Somerset, who was connected with the well-known banking firm, Esdaile, Hammet & Co. of Lombard Street, and they had seven children. (See *Burke's Landed Gentry*.) Shelley's other child by Harriet, Charles, died in 1826 at the age of eleven (whereupon his son by Mary, Percy Florence, became heir to the Shelley estates). (See *Burke's Peerage*.)

# Shelley and his Circle : Manuscripts

when he went to Italy in 1818. It was taken over with these papers by his landlord at Marlow, Robert Maddocks, and its transmission can then be traced in unbroken sequence.

Such, in brief, is the story of Shelley's major literary manuscripts. When we turn to the letters — with which we are mainly concerned here — the story is somewhat different, for whereas most of the manuscripts were in the possession of the family, most of the letters were in the hands of nonfamily correspondents. A few of these correspondents sold the letters themselves but usually they were either sold or given to an institution by heirs or legal executors.

Although there seems to be a common opinion to the contrary, there is probably no major difference in the patterns of letter preservation between the early nineteenth century and the present (although the telephone has cut down on the total number of letters). Letters sent to business or legal firms, for instance, are normally filed and often preserved for a long period. Some of Shelley's letters, as we shall see, were thus filed and preserved. In regard to personal correspondence, people tend to preserve the letters of authors and other prominent individuals, either for their intrinsic value or in the thought of eventually selling them.

Individual differences also play a part. Some people are natural hoarders, some are not. Some keep almost all letters; most keep some (from friends, lovers, or relatives); very few keep none.

If we put all these tendencies together we can see that there are certain general selective factors. There is, for instance, apt to be a larger proportion of business letters preserved than of personal letters; and among personal letters, a larger proportion of intimate than of nonintimate letters, a larger proportion of later letters (when an author is well known) than of earlier letters, a larger proportion of letters to some correspondents than to others. Some of these tendencies can, of course, be offset in individual cases by particular factors. For instance, as Shelley's genius became apparent early and he quickly developed intimate friendships, we have an unusually large number of his youthful letters.

It is important if one is using letters for biographical or critical purposes to see what particular selective factors are at work and to what degree they have rendered the existing body of correspondence unrepre-

# The Carl H. Pforzheimer Library

## *Provenance*

sentative of the total life. A person, for instance, writes differently to different correspondents, revealing different facets of his personality or thinking to each. Hence, a great number of letters to one person may reveal certain aspects of the writer and only a few letters show other aspects, but both may be equally important in attempting to get a balanced picture.

One does not work long with the letters and other manuscripts of Shelley and his circle without perceiving the constant recurrence of a small number of major sources. No matter how devious the later course of a letter through collections and sales rooms, the ultimate source is usually traceable to one of these.

Some groups of letters were early removed from circulation, for instance, the 46 letters which Shelley wrote to his friend, the Sussex schoolteacher, Elizabeth Hitchener, between June 1811 and June 1812. These were given to her solicitor, Henry J. Slack, when she left England for the Continent. On her death in 1822, Slack retained the letters. They later passed to his widow and from her to her nephew, who deposited them in the British Museum.[20]

Two other large groups of Shelley letters, also early removed from circulation, were those to Shelley's friends in Italy, the Gisbornes (and Mrs. Gisborne's son, Henry Reveley), and those to Shelley's publisher friend, Thomas Hookham. Most of the Gisborne-Reveley letters and apparently all of Shelley's to Hookham were given to the Shelley family and have now joined the letters in the Bodleian Library.[21]

Of sources for the letters of Shelley or those associated with him which have appeared on the open market, four great treasure-troves should first be noted: the Clairmont; the Whitton; the Byron-Murray; the Hogg family. Of these, all but the Byron-Murray contained extensive material by the Shelley circle as well as by Shelley.

When Claire Clairmont, stepsister to Mary Shelley, died in Florence in 1879 at the age of ninety-one, the letters and other manuscripts in her possession passed to her niece, Paola Clairmont. There then ensued the

20. De Ricci, pp. 105–106; *Letters about Shelley*, pp. 30–31 and *passim*.

21. De Ricci, pp. 57, 140, 221; Hill, *The Shelley Correspondence in the Bodleian Library*, pp. vii–xv. Three letters from Shelley to the Gisbornes and part of one to Reveley have come on the market. Many of John Gisborne's journals and notebooks are among the Abinger Manuscripts.

# Shelley and his Circle : Manuscripts

seesaw battle for possession between the English Shelley scholar, H. Buxton Forman, and the New England sea captain, Edward Silsbee, which formed the basis for Henry James's ironical novelette *The Aspern Papers*.[22] With one or two minor exceptions — for example, the Harvard copybook previously mentioned — the material was purchased by Forman. This material included 23 letters from Shelley to Claire Clairmont, 23 letters from Shelley to Godwin, 1 third-person note from Shelley to "Mr. Pike" (a lawyer associated with Godwin), 111 letters by Mary Shelley (5 of them "of old date"), "Shelley's will," 4 of Claire's notebooks, 1818–1820, her journal ("from 1825"), 8 or more letters by William Godwin, Godwin's "will, sermons, testimonial and other manuscripts," more than 50 letters from Edward J. Trelawny to Claire Clairmont, and 1 literary manuscript by Shelley, namely a section of *Notes on Sculptures in Rome and Florence*.[23] Part of this material was found in a box formerly belonging to William Godwin "with his name and address written in his own hand on the outside."[24]

Most of the letters by Shelley to Claire and Godwin Forman sold on the open market. (A number of them went into the great Shelley collection of Charles W. Frederickson in Brooklyn.[25]) Four letters to

22. See Leon Edel, "*The Aspern Papers:* Great-aunt Wyckoff and Juliana Bordereau," *Modern Language Notes*, LXVII (June 1952), 392–395.

23. See Appendix, below. A general account of Forman's purchases will be found in the introduction to his edition of the letters of Trelawny, pp. x–xi.

24. Paola Clairmont to H. B. Forman, Jan. 31, 1886 [misdated "1885"], The Berg Collection, The New York Public Library.

25. For Frederickson's holdings see Bangs & Co., *Catalogue of the Library of the late Charles W. Frederickson Sold by Order of the Administrator*, New York, May 24–28, 1897. Lots no. 2308 to 2370 consist of Shelley letters. As lot no. 2370 comprises 2 letters, this makes a total of 63. But one of the 2 letters in lot no. 2370 is a forgery and the other a copy. The first of them is one of the copies of Shelley's letter to Mary Shelley of December 16, 1816, the original of which is in the British Museum. The second is noted by de Ricci (p. 85; Shelley to Godwin, Nov. 13, 1816). It has now been safely removed from circulation. The Frederickson catalogue suggests that nos. 2339, 2341, and 2344 (to Ollier, Jan. 11, 1818; Dec. 22, 1817; Jan. 25, 1818) are in Shelley's hand. All of these letters are now in The Carl H. Pforzheimer Library; two are in Shelley's hand; one, December 22, 1817, is in Mary's hand; Mary wrote it for Shelley at the time. The catalogue states that lot no. 2342 (to Ollier, Jan. 22, 1818) is written by Mary. The present location of this letter does not appear to be known; but the probability is that the notation — which is unequivocal — is correct. In addition to these there is one letter (lot no. 2315, Shelley to Hogg, September 1815) which must be a copy (perhaps that in Mary Shelley's hand now in the Henry E. Huntington Library), whose history is traced by de Ricci (p. 131, no. 257) under the impression that it is a Shelley autograph, because the original is among the Abinger Manuscripts. Thus Frederickson had a total of 59 autograph Shelley letters. (There

# The Carl H. Pforzheimer Library

## *Provenance*

Claire and 2 to Godwin were retained by Forman, and they were sold
with his library in 1920 in New York.

Many of these letters thus preserved by Claire over the years —
Shelley to Claire and Godwin, Mary to Claire, Trelawny to Claire, etc.
— have come, by various routes, into The Carl H. Pforzheimer Library.
The first item in these volumes, in fact, the testimonial for William
Godwin, came from this source.

The story of the Whitton papers was told by Roger Ingpen in 1916:

It is now some years since an important discovery relating to Shelley was made
by Mr. Charles Withall, of Messrs. Withall & Withall, the successors to
Mr. William Whitton, who was entrusted more than a century ago with the
legal business of Sir Bysshe and Sir Timothy Shelley. Mr. Charles Withall
happened to find, among the papers preserved in his offices, some letters of
Percy Bysshe Shelley, and also some pamphlets, including copies of *A Necessity
of Atheism* and *An Address to the Irish People*. This discovery encouraged
Mr. Withall to make a further search, which resulted in bringing to light other
letters of the poet, besides a mass of correspondence, including numerous
letters from various members of the Shelley family, as well as a large number
of legal documents, pedigrees, Mr. Whitton's letter book and diaries and other
papers.[26]

The papers were sold at Sotheby's two years later, and the sales
catalogue shows their main contents as follows: 29 letters and 2 receipts
by Percy Bysshe Shelley; 67 letters by Shelley's father, Timothy (from
1815 on, Sir Timothy) Shelley; 66 letters by Mary Shelley (4 of them
signed jointly with Thomas Love Peacock).[27]

were no Shelley autographs sold at the earlier sales of his library — 1871, 1877, 1886, 1893. For
some account of the 1897 sale see Harry B. Smith, *First Nights and First Editions*, Boston, 1931,
p. 167.) We might note that lot no. 2335 ("Marlow, Dec. 3, 1817. No address") is to Charles Ollier
and lot no. 2369 ("no address and no date") is to Claire Clairmont, dated in *Complete Works* as
April 13, 1821.

Lots no. 2371–2394, 2399 contain Shelleyana, including letters by William Godwin, Mary
Shelley, Horace Smith, Trelawny, and Peacock.

In addition to Frederickson the American collectors Harry B. Smith, Jerome Kern, Edward A.
Newton, John A. Spoor, and W. Van R. Whitall had notable Shelley collections, all of which have
been sold on the open market.

26. Ingpen, *Shelley in England*, p. v.

27. Sotheby, Wilkinson & Hodge, *Catalogue of Fine Books . . . Autograph Letters, MSS. &c. By or
Relating to P. B. Shelley, discovered by and in the possession of the Solicitors to members of the Shelley
family, Sold by direction of Sir John Shelley-Rolls, Bart.*, London, July 22–25, 1918, lots no. 712–756.

# Shelley and his Circle : Manuscripts

*Provenance*

Of the 29 Shelley letters, 16 were to his father. Except for 2 letters from Oxford — apparently the only ones extant that Shelley wrote to his father from the university — these deal, in the main, with the two crises of the year 1811; the expulsion from Oxford and the elopement with Harriet Westbrook. These letters Timothy turned over to Whitton, whom he had appointed as his representative to deal with his son; and Whitton duly filed them in his office files where they lay undisturbed for a century. When he turned these letters over, Timothy also turned over the 2 earlier letters from Oxford, presumably because they discussed the philosophical views which had resulted in the expulsion. Other letters also dealt with these crises, for example, 2 from Shelley to his grandfather, Sir Bysshe Shelley; 6 from Shelley to William Whitton; 4 from John Hogg, father of Thomas Jefferson Hogg, to Timothy Shelley. Of particular interest is the presence among these papers of the letter from Eliza Westbrook to Shelley, June 11, 1811. (See sc 176, August 15, 1811, Commentary.) It is in the new light shed on these events of the year 1811 that the main biographical importance of the Whitton papers lies. But the later letters tell us much that we did not know of the lives of Sir Timothy and of Mary Shelley following the death of Shelley.

Once these papers were sold, they were dispersed. Some are now at Yale, some at the Huntington, some — including Shelley's two letters from Oxford — are in The Carl H. Pforzheimer Library.

Shelley first met Byron in Switzerland in the summer of 1816 and the two poets made a trip around the Lake of Geneva; they came together again in the fall of 1818 at Venice, their meeting there being described in *Julian and Maddalo*; in the fall of 1821 when Byron's mistress, the Countess Guiccioli, and her family were being persecuted at Ravenna and Byron himself was under fire for his assistance to the Italian nationalists, he asked Shelley to visit him; shortly afterwards he joined Shelley at Pisa. These and other happenings are discussed in Shelley's letters to Byron, which are rich also in philosophical, literary, and political comments.

On Byron's death in 1824 a large portion of his correspondence — including 21 letters from Shelley to Byron — passed on to his literary executor, John Cam Hobhouse, later, Lord Broughton; on Lord Broughton's death in 1869 it went to his daughter, Lady Dorchester; on

# The Carl H. Pforzheimer Library

## *Provenance*

the death of Lady Dorchester in 1914 it went to John Murray, descendant of Byron's publisher. In 1926 all 21 of the letters from Shelley to Byron were purchased from Murray for this library. In addition to these 21, only 8 other letters from Shelley to Byron are known to exist, and these are now in various libraries and collections (one of them in this library).

Shelley met Thomas Jefferson Hogg at Oxford in the fall of 1810 (a meeting memorably described in Hogg's life of Shelley). When the two students parted for the Christmas vacation a vigorous (almost daily) correspondence ensued, dealing with personal matters, philosophy, and poetry. When Shelley was expelled, Hogg was expelled with him; when he eloped with Harriet Westbrook to Edinburgh, Hogg joined them. In the fall of 1811, as a result of Hogg's attentions to Harriet, they quarreled and parted; and again correspondence (of a somewhat agonized character) ensued. The following year, the quarrel was made up, and, although the two never became as intimate as formerly, they remained friends, and Hogg was a frequent visitor at Shelley's various homes until the departure for Italy in 1818. And from Italy the correspondence continued, the last letter being dated October 22, 1821.

Through Shelley, Hogg came to know Mary Shelley, Thomas Love Peacock, and Leigh Hunt. With Mary he had a curious epistolary "affair" in 1815; and after Shelley's death the two remained friends. When Jane Williams, widow of Edward Ellerker Williams, who was drowned with Shelley, returned from Italy to England in 1822, she bore a letter of introduction from Mary to Hogg. The acquaintance resulted in her marriage to Hogg, who thus achieved a new entry into the later Shelley circle, one further extended by the marriage of Jane's daughter Dina to Leigh Hunt's son Henry.

When Hogg died in 1862, the vast mass of letters and other documents resulting from these connections passed on to his younger brother John; on John's death in 1869 it continued in the family and later became the property of John's son, John Ewer Jefferson Hogg, who was born late in his father's life (1860).[28] In 1922 John Ewer Jefferson Hogg sold 7 letters from Shelley to Hogg and 3 literary manuscripts by

28. See "Hogg of Norton" in *Burke's Landed Gentry;* and John Ewer Hogg in *Walford's County Families of the United Kingdom* (London, 1920).

# Shelley and his Circle : Manuscripts

Shelley (all of which were acquired by this library).[29] On his death the rest of the material passed to his son, Major Richard John Jefferson Hogg, who sold it in 1948 at two sales. The Hogg family, we might note, had during all this time occupied the same house, at Norton-on-Tees, County Durham, and the material had remained in the house, except for a few of Shelley's letters to Hogg lent to Lady Jane Shelley, some of which remained in her possession and are now among the Abinger Manuscripts.[30] In addition we should note one letter from Shelley to Hogg which somehow came early into the open market,[31] a poem that Hogg himself gave in 1834 to Dawson Turner,[32] and a few letters the location of which we have been unable to trace.[33] Otherwise, apparently

29. Sotheby, Wilkinson & Hodge, *Catalogue of Valuable Printed Books and Manuscripts Comprising . . . Important Letters & Manuscripts of P. B. Shelley, the Property of John Ewer Jefferson Hogg, Esq.,* July 27–28, 1922, lots no. 326–335.

30. We know that Lady Shelley had at least the following letters in her possession because she corrected them in the margin of a copy of Hogg's *Life of Shelley:* Dec. 20, 1810; Jan. 2, 1811; Jan. 17, 1811; Apr. 26, 1811; June 2, 1811; Aug. 15, 1811 (Koszul, *Jeunesse,* Appendice II, pp. 405–418). Two of these letters, that of December 20, 1810, and most of that of June 2, 1811, are now among the Abinger Manuscripts (which, as we have noted, came from Lady Shelley). The final page of the June 2 letter was not among the Hogg family papers sold in 1948, nor, so far as we could discover, is now among the Abinger Manuscripts (although the whole letter was corrected by Lady Shelley). In addition there are among the Abinger Manuscripts a letter from Shelley to Hogg from Bishopsgate in September 1815 (the postmark appears to be September 23), the first four pages of a letter dated in Shelley, *Complete Works,* "[? November 14–18, 1811]," and a letter of May 8, 1817. Hence, Lady Shelley must have had other Shelley to Hogg letters in her possession than those which she corrected (as noted by Koszul). The letters of January 2, January 17, April 26, and August 15 were returned to the Hogg family and are at present in this library. (The only other Shelley letter that we have noted in the Abinger Manuscripts is one to T. L. Peacock, March 21, 1821.)

31. De Ricci, p. 134, No. 379, April 30, 1818, from Milan. This letter first came into the market in 1870. It is at present in this library.

32. T. J. Hogg to Dawson Turner, May 30, 1834, Hogg, *Shelley,* I, 123–124. In the catalogue of the sale of Turner's library in 1859 (see fn. 7 above), we find the following among the autographs (p. 268): "Shelley, P. B., A.L.s., and an unpublished poem, partly in his autograph, 4 pages 8vo." The poem was presumably that given by Hogg for it is described by Hogg in his letter as "unpublished." (This poem, "A Dialogue," is also in the Esdaile copybook; Shelley, *Complete Works,* III, 315.)

33. The following letters were not among those sold by the Hogg family either in 1922 or 1948; nor are they, so far as we have discovered, among the Abinger Manuscripts. They were all, except for the last noted (No. 415), published in Hogg's *Life of Shelley* in 1858, so Hogg once had either them or copies of them in his possession. We give the de Ricci numbers (which are the same as in Shelley, *Complete Works*): No. 20, Dec. 26, 1810; No. 29, Jan. 16, 1811; No. 62, May 19, 1811; No. 64, May 26, 1811; No. 215, Apr. 5, 1813; No. 225, July 9, 1813; No. 415, July 25, 1819. No. 415 apparently exists only in transcript (one by Mary Shelley).

# The Carl H. Pforzheimer Library

## *Provenance*

everything Hogg received from Shelley remained in the hands of the Hogg family until sold in the present century.

Of the two sales in 1948 the first (in June) was the larger and more important.[34] At this sale were sold 64 letters from Shelley to Hogg and 1 translation by Shelley, making, with the 1922 sale, a total of 71 letters, 3 literary manuscripts, and 1 translation. In addition there were 23 letters by Mary Shelley, 11 of them dealing with her relationship with Hogg in 1815; 6 letters from Timothy Shelley, 1 of them to Thomas Jefferson Hogg, 1 to P. B. Shelley, 3 to John Hogg, father of Thomas Jefferson Hogg, and 2 to John Hogg's legal adviser, Robert Clarke; 1 letter from Robert Clarke to John Hogg; 3 letters from Thomas Love Peacock to Thomas Jefferson Hogg. The Timothy Shelley, John Hogg, Robert Clarke letters and some of Shelley's own letters deal with the expulsion and elopement crises of 1811. Thus our most important sources of information on these two events are derived from letters which none of the correspondents expected to be preserved, those retained in his legal files by Whitton and those kept by Thomas Jefferson Hogg.

The letters of Shelley to Hogg sold at this sale cover the whole range of their friendship. The earliest of them is the second letter Shelley wrote to Hogg — December 23, 1810. (The first letter to Hogg — December 20 — was retained by Lady Jane Shelley.) The final letter is the last letter that Shelley wrote to Hogg, that of October 22, 1821, mentioned above.

In the second sale of the Hogg family material in 1948[35] there were sold 16 letters by Thomas Jefferson Hogg (2 to Shelley's mother;[36] 1 to Shelley's sister Elizabeth;[37] 1 to Shelley; 1 to John Frank Newton; 11 to Thomas Love Peacock); 5 letters from Peacock to Hogg and 7 from Leigh Hunt to Hogg; a group of letters from members of the Hogg family; 3 short literary manuscripts by Peacock and some Greek epigrams by Hogg.

---

34. Sotheby & Co., *Catalogue of the Correspondence of Thomas Jefferson Hogg (1792–1862) Consisting Principally of Letters from Percy and Mary Shelley, sold by order of his Great-Nephew, Major R. J. Jefferson Hogg*, June 30, 1948.

35. Sotheby & Co., *Catalogue of Valuable Printed Books and a Few Manuscripts, Autograph Letters . . . The Final Portion of the Correspondence to Thomas Jefferson Hogg (Sold by Order of Major R. J. Jefferson Hogg, M.C.)*, July 26–27, 1948.

36. sc 168 (July ?6–18, 1811) and sc 177 (Aug. 22, 1811).     37. sc 162 (May 25, 1811).

# Shelley and his Circle : Manuscripts

Most of the material from these 1948 sales is at present in this library, which includes among its holdings more than 60 letters from Shelley to Hogg.

In addition to these four major sources, two other groups of Shelley letters should be noted, letters to his intimate friends, Thomas Love Peacock and Leigh Hunt, and to his publishers, Charles and James Ollier.

Some of Shelley's letters to Peacock were, as we have seen, acquired by the Shelley family; at least 15 are now in the Bodleian Library.[38] Seventeen were put on sale with Peacock's library following his death in 1866.[39] Thereafter wending their way through various collections (including that of Charles W. Frederickson) and sales rooms they are now scattered. Six are in this library.

Shortly before his death, Leigh Hunt gave several letters by Shelley and Mary Shelley to their son, Sir Percy Florence Shelley.[40] The 7 letters from Shelley to Leigh Hunt now in the Bodleian[41] presumably all came from the Shelley family. There was not, however, as there was for Peacock, any one sale at which the rest were put on the market. Some were retained by Leigh Hunt's son, Thornton Hunt;[42] at least 10 were in the possession of Leigh Hunt's grandson, Walter Leigh Hunt, as late as 1886, and some of these had been sold by 1890.[43] Some found their way into the Frederickson collection; some went to Thomas J. Wise. They are now scattered: the British Museum (via Wise), the Henry E. Huntington Library, the Stark Collection of the University of Texas, Texas Christian University, The Pierpont Morgan Library, The Berg Collection of The New York Public Library; 8 are in this library.

The Olliers became Shelley's publishers in 1817. Shelley's letters to them (addressed either to Charles or to the firm) extend from February of that year until April 1822, some two months before his death. Of Shelley's prose volumes the Olliers published *A Proposal for Putting*

---

38. Hill, *The Shelley Correspondence in the Bodleian Library*, pp. vii–xv.

39. Sotheby, Wilkinson & Hodge, *Catalogue of the Library of the Late Thos. Love Peacock . . . Some Highly Interesting Original Letters in the Autograph of P. B. Shelley*, June 11–12, 1866.

40. De Ricci, p. 146.

41. Hill, *The Shelley Correspondence in the Bodleian Library*, pp. vii–xv; Shelley, *Complete Works*, X, 424.

42. Hunt, *Correspondence*, I, vi.       43. De Ricci, pp. 146–158.

# The Carl H. Pforzheimer Library

## *Provenance*

*Reform to the Vote* and *History of a Six Weeks' Tour*, both in 1817; and the following volumes of poetry: *Laon and Cythna* (*The Revolt of Islam*), 1818; *Rosalind and Helen*, 1819; *The Cenci*, 1819; *Prometheus Unbound*, 1820; *Epipsychidion*, 1821; *Hellas*, 1822. Shelley's letters to them deal largely with these works, sometimes in business terms, sometimes in literary, for Charles Ollier was himself an author.

Ollier disposed of at least one letter before his death in 1859; a total of 43 others were preserved in his family and sold at two sales, one in 1877 and one in 1878.[44] Twenty-two of these letters went into the Frederickson collection and were dispersed at its sale in 1897. They are all now widely scattered. Nineteen are in this library, 8 at the Henry E. Huntington Library, 3 at the University of Texas, 2 at Harvard, and 1 each at other libraries.

Of Shelley's remaining correspondents, three should be noted in particular, as Shelley wrote a good many letters and other items to them and these continue to appear in the market. These are Brookes and Company, Shelley's bankers from the fall of 1815 until his death; his early friend and protégé of Timothy Shelley, Edward Fergus Graham; and the publisher of some of his juvenile novels and poems, John Joseph Stockdale.

Shelley wrote some 35 letters and notes to Brookes and Company (of Chancery Lane, one of the leading banking houses of the period), as well as about 130 signed checks.[45] Brookes and Company later became amalgamated with the Union of London Bank. Early in the present century these Shelley items were found in papers that had been preserved in the files of this latter firm. They were sold in 1916.

Shelley wrote some 30 letters to Graham, including one in verse, between April 1810 and July 1811. At least 12 of these were placed on sale as early as 1851 while Graham was perhaps still living.[46]

Shelley's 11 letters to Stockdale (also 1810 and 1811) were apparently kept in one group until 1872.[47] The earliest recorded sale is

44. *Ibid.*, p. 185.

45. *Ibid.*, pp. 20–25; Peck, *Shelley*, II, Appendix P, pp. 436–439 (list of checks); Walter T. Spencer, *Forty Years in My Bookshop* (Boston and New York, 1923), pp. 182–185.

46. De Ricci, p. 86. Graham seems to have died in 1852.

47. De Ricci, p. 261; *Stockdale's Budget of "all that is Good, and Noble and Amiable, in the Country,"* 1826–1827; Richard Garnett, "Shelley in Pall Mall," *Macmillan's Magazine*, II (1860), 100–110.

# Shelley and his Circle : Manuscripts

1877, which is for one letter only, but they may all have been sold privately by that date. The present whereabouts of most of them does not seem to be known.

As perhaps even the above brief summary may suffice to demonstrate, the history of the letters of few people is so well known as that of Shelley's. Almost every letter of the more than 600 extant can be traced back to its point of origin and usually from that point through an unbroken sequence into the present.[48]

A good deal of the provenance of the "circle" letters and manuscripts we have already noted in discussing Shelley: the great mass of Godwin and other material among the Abinger Manuscripts; the large number of the letters of Mary Shelley and Trelawny preserved by Claire Clairmont; the letters of Timothy Shelley and Mary Shelley in the Whitton papers; the letters of Peacock, Hunt, Mary Shelley, and others in the Hogg papers; the letters of Peacock, the Gisbornes, and

---

48. As Newman I. White pointed out, this fact affords "a protection against forgers enjoyed by the biographers of no other important English poet." (*An Examination of the Shelley Legend*, p. 14.) Yet, curiously enough, there has been in recent years a good deal of writing on forgeries of Shelley's letters. (Smith, *The Shelley Legend;* Theodore G. Ehrsam, *Major Byron;* Blunden, *Shelley*, pp. x, 162; Sylva Norman, *Flight of the Skylark, The Development of Shelley's Reputation,* University of Oklahoma Press, 1954, pp. 189–204; Edmund Blunden, *Selected Poems, Percy Bysshe Shelley,* London and Glasgow, 1954, p. 27; White, Jones, Cameron, *An Examination of The Shelley Legend;* Andreas Mayor, "A Suspected Shelley Letter," *The Library,* IV, September 1949, 144–145.) Now that the smoke of battle has cleared somewhat, however, one can see that there was not much to write about. As Professor White also pointed out, there has been a considerable deployment of the same letters repeatedly "like a stage army." (*An Examination of the Shelley Legend,* p. 7.) Actually only three Shelley letters were questioned: (a) the British Museum manuscript of Shelley's letter to Mary Shelley, Dec. 16, 1816, in which he tells of Harriet's suicide; (b) the Shelley-Rolls manuscript of Shelley to Mary, Jan. 11, 1817; (c) the John Murray manuscript of Shelley to Byron, Jan. 17, 1817. The questioning of these letters, we should note, was made without examining the manuscripts. Such examination has shown that they are all three genuine, as White, Frederick L. Jones, and other Shelley scholars had previously contended. (Mayor, "A Suspected Shelley Letter"; Ehrsam, *Major Byron.*)

The forgery discussion was partly set off by a curious circumstance, namely that Shelley's letter to Mary of December 16, 1816, was somehow remailed in 1859. We might note its subsequent history. In 1867 the Secretary of the Post Office sent it to Spencer Shelley, son of Sir John Shelley of Michelgrove. The letter then remained with this branch of the family until the year 1908 when Mrs. Spencer Shelley wrote to H. Buxton Forman about it. Forman, who was a post office official as well as a Shelley specialist, replied, offering to buy the letter. (ALs, draft, May 23, 1908; ALs, draft, June 1, 1908; both in The Carl H. Pforzheimer Library.) The negotiations were completed by Mrs. Shelley's daughter, Mrs. Dent. (June 19, 1908; ALs in The Berg Collection of The New York Public Library.) From Forman's library the letter passed to Thomas J. Wise and thence into the British Museum with Wise's library. (Wise, *A Shelley Library,* pp. 4–5, with photoduplicate.)

# The Carl H. Pforzheimer Library

## *Provenance*

Hookham preserved with the Shelley family papers and now in the Bodleian. In addition to these the following major sources should be mentioned: (a) letters from Mary Shelley to Leigh and Marianne Hunt preserved in the Hunt family and sold in 1922;[49] (b) letters from Leigh Hunt to Shelley and others (presumably secured from Mary Shelley) preserved in the Hunt family and sold in 1935 with the estate of Mrs. Beryl Dodgson, daughter of Leigh Hunt's grandson, Colonel C. Shelley Leigh Hunt;[50] (c) letters from Trelawny to Augusta White, who emigrated to Canada and married William Henry Draper, sold by her descendants in Montreal; (d) letters and manuscripts of Thomas Love Peacock, preserved in the family and sold in 1949 by Mrs. K. Hall Thorpe, Peacock's great-great-granddaughter.

K.N.C.

## APPENDIX

### *The Clairmont Papers*

The actual battle for possession of the Clairmont papers, although fought with less psychological finesse than in *The Aspern Papers*, has, nevertheless, a certain rugged interest of its own. It can be reconstructed from a series of autograph letters by Forman and others, partly in The Berg Collection of The New York Public Library and partly in The Carl H. Pforzheimer Library. The following brief summary makes use of materials from both collections, designating them respectively as "Berg Ms." and "CHP Ms." The Berg letters are quoted by permission of The Henry W. and Albert A. Berg Collection of The New York Public Library.

Claire Clairmont died on March 19, 1879, in Florence (in *The Aspern Papers* the locale is shifted to Venice.) But before that date Captain Edward Silsbee had moved into the house with her and Paola. Silsbee fully expected to be able to purchase the letters and papers which she had left. But while the estate was still unsettled Forman moved into action, using two friends, Henry Roderick Newman and Charles Fairfax Murray, to negotiate in his behalf. On May 26 Paola Clairmont wrote, in answer to an inquiry by Forman, to describe the Shelley letters. By July 2 matters had gone so far that Silsbee saw the prize slipping from his grasp and wrote in mingled indignation and alarm to Murray (CHP Ms.):

---

49. Mary Shelley, *Letters*, II, 346.    50. Sold at Sotheby's, April 8, 1935.

# Shelley and his Circle : Manuscripts

Dear Sir,

    I have been in treaty for the Shelly [*sic*] letters with Miss Clairmont the elder & her niece, & have always understood I should have the refusal of them if I would give more than any one else offered.

    The matter has been delayed owing to the absence of the executor & could not be decided until within a few days.

    I think the refusal belongs in honor to me & I will give more than has yet been offered for them or probably will be, & it would not be for Miss Clairmonts interest to sell them till they are offered to me.

I am vy truly<br>Your's E. A. Silsbee

P. S. It has been by a great misunderstanding they have been offered to another

By July 10 it looked as though Forman had the letters, for Paola had offered them for £150 and Forman was willing to meet this. Whereupon Murray (Berg Ms.) "locked the box and carried off the key which I have here with me (this that our friend Silsbee shouldn't go poking over them again as he was still in the house)." Paola still hesitated. On July 20 she informed Murray (CHP Ms.) that she did not feel herself "irrevocably bound to sell the letters to your friend." In the end, however, Forman won out, as he noted in his Introduction to *Letters of Edward John Trelawny* (Oxford, 1910), pp. x–xi: "An American who had been residing in the same house at Florence with the Clairmonts had been bidding against me for the collection; but, as his rather free bids turned out to be only in bills at long date, the executrix decided to accept my cash rather than his paper, in which she lacked confidence."

As a result Silsbee ended up with only the Harvard copybook (see fn. 17, above), a second smaller copybook, and a letter from Shelley to Claire (both now also at Harvard). (For some account of this second copybook, see Peck, *Shelley*, I, 477, and Smith, *The Shelley Legend*, pp. 43–44. On the letter — wrongly dated in Shelley, *Complete Works* — see Marion Kingston, "Notes on Three Shelley Letters," *Keats-Shelley Memorial Bulletin*, Rome, 1955, No. VI, pp. 16–17.) According to a letter from T. J. Wise (CHP Ms.) Silsbee secured the Harvard copybook manuscript by promising to marry Paola: "He recounted to us with glee how he had cheated Paola Clairmont out of the Manuscript."

On July 30 Paola sent to Newman (Berg Ms.) an inventory of the Shelley letters plus the 5 Mary Shelley letters of "old date," 106 other Mary Shelley letters, 11 letters from Sir Percy Florence Shelley, 4 notebooks by Claire, and "notes on Art etc." Paola also had letters by Trelawny to Claire but, in regard to these, Murray informed Forman on July 10 (Berg Ms.): "Trelawny wishes to have them himself & destroy them — He ret$^d$ all miss Clairmont's letters just before her death & she burnt them he now wants his own ret$^d$ (which is reasonable) to do the like." In April 1880, after the transaction was completed,

# The Carl H. Pforzheimer Library

## *Provenance*

Paola discovered that she had made some mistakes. On April 17 she wrote to Forman that she had apparently given him only 56 Mary Shelley letters instead of 106 and had given him a package of 8 Godwin letters in their place. "I have furthermore been told that among the papers I sent you by Mr Newman a MSS. of Shelleys was discovered containing his opinions of the Florence & other picture gallery which of course is of the greatest value." This, one might presume, was the "notes on Art etc." of the inventory, which Paola did not recognize as by Shelley, but Forman in reply (CHP Ms.) denied that this was so: "There was no manuscript of Shelley's but the 47 letters named in the list: I wish there had been." (Forman's edition of Shelley, *Prose Works*, the following year, gave new readings — III, 42 — in the "Notes and Sculptures in Rome and Florence" from "a MS. Notebook," but this may not have been in Shelley's hand.)

Forman replied to Paola also on the Mary Shelley letters: "Of course, I may be short in the number of Mrs Shelley's letters; but whether you choose to send me those you name I must leave to your sense of justice." The Godwin letters enclosed by error he airily dismissed as "unconsidered trifles" that no one would buy. (As 90 Mary-to-Claire letters were sold with Forman's library, presumably the appeal to Paola's "sense of justice" bore fruit and he received the extra 50.)

In May 1880 Newman wrote further to Forman (CHP Ms.) on the Trelawny letters and other matters: "Ellis is to come in a day or two & will probably carry off the rest of the plunder    Do you know the Trelawny letters were written while he was in Greece with Byron?" The reference to Ellis — of Ellis and White, booksellers — produced a letter to him from Forman attempting to stave him off, an effort which was successful. Trelawny's letters were not, as he had requested, returned to him for burning. On October 22, 1881, Paola offered them to Forman (Berg Ms.): "Trelawny is no more as you are aware. Would his letters of old date that you once wished to have, & that I was then not at liberty to give, be of any use to you?" On the blank pages of this letter Forman has drafted his reply, stating that he was interested in Trelawny's letters "early and late." In 1910 he published them (with some omissions).

In 1886 Paola offered a final lot of material for sale. Writing to Forman on January 10 (Berg Ms.), she listed the main "Contents of the box" as follows: 4 letters from Mary Shelley (3 of them to Claire Clairmont), "Godwin's will, sermons, testimonials & other MSS," "Claire Clairmont's Journal 1825," a "little Greek volume of Sophocles" and Shelley's inkstand. The story of the inkstand and the Sophocles Paola relates as follows: "When the news of Shelley's death became certain to Mrs Shelley, Mrs Williams & Claire who were then staying at Lerici, Mrs Shelley asked my aunt what souvenir she wd wish to have — & my Aunt begged for the inkstand & a little Greek book which Shelley always carried in his pocket & which was found — either in the boat or in his coat — after his death. These two things Mrs Shelley gave my Aunt. This little

# Shelley and his Circle : Manuscripts

volume of Sophocles is from the year 1809 English edition. It is in my possession my Aunt wrote on the first leaf 'P. B. Shelley. This book was always in his pocket.' Signed Cl. Cl." This volume Forman must have purchased along with the manuscripts for it was sold with his library in 1920 (lot no. 719, p. 170).

In this connection we might note that Trelawny gave a water-stained Sophocles to Shelley's son, Sir Percy Florence Shelley, which he said had been found on Shelley's body. This volume was seen by Dowden in Sir Percy's possession in 1886 and was presented to the Bodleian by Lady Shelley in 1893. It is noted in Hill, *The Shelley Correspondence in the Bodleian Library*, p. 46, as follows: "Sophoclis Tragoediae septem. Two volumes in one. Oxon., 1809. The copy found in Shelley's hand at his death." (Mr. L. W. Hanson, Keeper of the Printed Books at the Bodleian Library has very kindly verified for us the correctness of this description.) The copy purchased from Paola is listed in the sales catalogue of Forman's library as follows: "Sophoclis Tragoedae Septem. Ex editione R. F. P. Brunck. Vol. II 32 mo, old half calf. Oxonii, 1809." And it notes the inscription by Claire. Leslie Marchand (in "Trelawny on the Death of Shelley," *Keats-Shelley Memorial Bulletin*, Rome, 1952, No. IV, p. 17) speculated that the Bodleian copy might be a "bogus relic" constructed by Trelawny. That the Forman copy cannot be bogus is attested by Claire's inscription and Paola's comments. Shelley certainly carried this book with him; and it was found after his death either in the boat or in his "coat." Marchand apparently did not know of this copy; and its existence further complicates matters. Perhaps Shelley had two sets of the 1809 Sophocles, one in two separate volumes and one bound in one volume. Mary's journals and letters show that Sophocles was a favorite author both with her and with Shelley.

# POSTMARKS AND THE DATING
# OF MANUSCRIPTS

ALTHOUGH every literary scholar who has worked with the letters of the era prior to the envelope and the adhesive stamp (both introduced in 1840) has come up against the problems of British postmarks, few seem to have done much about them. The reason is perhaps that behind the postmark looms the endless maze of the early British postal system.

In preparing this book we have had so inescapably to face the postmark that we have also been forced to penetrate, at least a little way, into the maze.[1] And the journey has proved to be quite profitable. Even an elementary knowledge of the postal system and its stamps[2] is valuable for dating letters and for other purposes. How often letters are undated or but partially dated editors soon become unhappily aware. And all forms of aid (the perpetual calendar, the watermark, internal evidence) are welcome. It may seem at first that the role of the postmark in this process is a simple one, that all one has to do is to look at the date on it. But matters are not always this simple. Sometimes postmarks have no date; a date on a postmark is not necessarily the date of composition of a letter or even of its posting; and some letters have two or more postmarks, each with a different date. It helps to

1. On the history and procedures of the post office we have found Howard Robinson, *The British Post Office, A History* (Princeton University Press, 1948), the most useful single work. But we have also made use of the following: Howard Robinson, *Britain's Post Office* (Oxford University Press, 1953); William Lewins, *Her Majesty's Mails: a History of the Post-Office* (London, 1865); Herbert Joyce, *The History of the Post Office* (London, 1893); C. F. Dendy Marshall, *The British Post Office* (Oxford University Press, 1926); Kenneth Ellis, *The Post Office in the Eighteenth Century* (Oxford University Press, 1958). We have also learned much from the succinct accounts of post-office organization and practice in such contemporary works as the post-office directories, *The London Calendar* for 1793, *The Court and City Register* for 1807, and Feltham's *Picture of London* for 1809. We have supplemented the information from these works with that on coach routes and times in Paterson's *Roads* (1811) and Cary's *Roads* (1819). On postmarks the standard work is R. C. Alcock and F. C. Holland, *The Postmarks of Great Britain and Ireland* (Cheltenham, [1940]).

2. The words postmark and stamp may be used interchangeably if we keep in mind that we are not dealing with an adhesive stamp but a stamp imprinted by a hand-stamping device (wood or metal before the days of rubber) and ink. (Alcock and Holland, pp. 17, 22, 23.) A post-office expert could stamp letters "with a speed and accuracy which rivals machinery." (Lewins, *Her Majesty's Mails*, p. 293.)

know, in such cases, the kind of postmark, at what point in the history of the letter each was put on, and the length of the post trip.

Sometimes postmarks are useful for general period dating. All postmarks have a life span, sometimes quite a brief one, and the period in which a particular postmark was used can sometimes be ascertained by consulting one of the standard works on postmarks or post-office history. Hence, even an undated postmark can supply at least a general date span. And so, too, with a fragmentary or blurred postmark if enough remains to enable one to reconstruct the whole (for postmarks are sometimes stamped part on and part off the edge of the letter or mutilated by the seal tear or blurred by a faulty imprint, and so on).

More frequently, of course, postmarks serve not for assisting with a general period date but in pinpointing a date within a period already known. This process, too, often requires a knowledge of stamps and postal procedures.

Sometimes a stamp or fragment of a stamp will give a clue to place as well as time even if it has no place name upon it. For instance, certain stamps put on in London have no indication of place but can soon be recognized as London stamps. Sometimes, too, a postmark will give a clue to an actual address or to the movements of persons.[3]

One other particular use of a knowledge of postmarks should be noted, namely as an aid to the detection of forgery. Forgers of letters occasionally attempt to forge postmarks and in so doing they often make the most elementary mistakes. For instance, in one forgery that we have seen, the postmark — although skillfully drawn — was the wrong shape for that kind of mark at that time.

The editor or biographer should, therefore, learn to know the different kinds of stamps, what each signifies, and in what sequence they were placed on a letter. Such knowledge can form an important supplementary tool for research.

In the present work we have, of course, touched on but one segment of British postmarks. Our remarks do not extend beyond this segment and we make no pretension to definitiveness even within it. But we record them on the assumption that what has proved useful to us may prove useful to others and may encourage further research.

3. As does the receiving house stamp on sc 156 (May 8, 1811).

# The Carl H. Pforzheimer Library

## *Postmarks*

### THE THREE SYSTEMS

The first thing that an editor has to recognize in approaching the British mails of the late eighteenth and early nineteenth centuries is that there was not one postal system but three. Unless he grasps this at the outset his path will indeed be thorny.

Within England there were the Inland Mail, the Penny Post, and the Foreign Letter Office. Although all three came under the jurisdiction of the General Post Office, each had its own offices, its own postmarks, its own staff, its own postal routes, and even its own letter carriers (often all servicing the same areas).

The Inland Mail "was the largest executive department, handling London, country, and colonial letters,"[4] whereas the Penny Post was a district post only. The London Penny Post serviced London and environs; Edinburgh and Dublin and other large towns were similarly serviced. The Foreign Letter Office handled foreign mail sent out in government packet boats or received from the Continent.[5]

(Nor was this, we might mention parenthetically, the end. Letters not sent abroad in government packet boats but in private ships came under the Ship Letter Office — except, of course, mail to India, which was handled by the East India Company! Then there were the Irish mails, which went through various shades of relationship to the British. And finally there were letters which did not go through the mails at all but were handled by private messenger. To judge from the letters in our collection, a large proportion of letters — at least within London — were handled in this way, the messenger often being a personal servant.)

Let us say that a person wished to send a letter from London to York. He would normally mail it at an Inland Mail "receiving house" (often in a shop); it would there be stamped with a receiving house stamp before being sent to the Inland Mail section of the General Post Office to be stamped with an Inland Mail outgoing stamp. The letter would then be sent by coach to York and delivered there by an Inland

---

4. Ellis, *The Post Office in the Eighteenth Century*, p. 29.

5. See Robinson, *The British Post Office*, pp. 163, 198, 203, 206. The Foreign Letter Office maintained its own postmen until the 1830's.

# Shelley and his Circle : Manuscripts

Mail carrier. But if the same person wished to send a letter from one part of London to another, he would normally post it at a Penny Post receiving house (distinct from those of the Inland Mail); it would there be stamped with the Penny Post receiving house stamp, sent to the Penny Post section of the General Post Office, there stamped with a Penny Post outgoing stamp, and delivered by a Penny Post carrier.

Thus, the first question to be asked about a letter is through which of the postal systems did it pass.

## THE INLAND MAIL

We might, for convenience in discussion, divide Inland Mail letters into four categories and then trace the vicissitudes of a typical letter in each: (1) letters mailed outside London and delivered in London; (2) letters mailed in London and delivered outside the London area; (3) letters passing through London; (4) letters not passing through London.

1. Let us take, as an example, a letter by Shelley sent from his home at Field Place near Horsham in Sussex to a friend in London. We have, as ever, to keep in mind that there were no envelopes and no adhesive stamps. Shelley, therefore, would fold the letter — with the flaps tucked in to make a kind of little package — seal it, and give it to a servant to take to the post office at Horsham. (He could, if he wished, have the servant pay the postage to the postmaster there. He would not, however, normally do this because it was considered impolite to prepay letters.) The postmaster at Horsham would inscribe by pen a postal fee upon the address face of the letter. The size of this fee depended not upon weight but only upon the number of sheets and the distance the letter was to travel. A "single" (one-sheet) letter in 1807, for instance, could travel between thirty and fifty miles for sixpence,[6] and this regardless of the size of the sheet. A large folio double sheet, for instance, cost the same as a small quarto single sheet. (Postmasters were sometimes suspicious of a too-bulky letter; we find Shelley writing on the address face of a letter to Elizabeth Hitchener, "This is *only* a

6. *The Court and City Register* for 1807, pp. 251–252.

# The Carl H. Pforzheimer Library

## Postmarks

large single sheet," and he advised her to "open it before them" if they tried to charge her double.[7])

In addition to putting the postal charge on Shelley's letter the postmaster would stamp it "Horsham| 41" with a black-ink straight line stamp.[8] This kind of stamp, known as a "mileage stamp," was in general use in the smaller post offices throughout England. Larger post offices, such as Oxford, used a round mileage stamp with the date.

**BRIGHTON**
**59**

Straight Line Mileage

Dated Mileage

The number below the place name in such stamps — as some editors seem not to know — designated the number of miles from London by the post roads. Hence, such a stamp on a letter informs us of the distance between London and the town or village in which the letter was posted.

The mail coach for London left Horsham at 7 o'clock in the evening.[9] In London it went to the Inland Mail department of the General Post Office. There the postal charge put on by the Horsham postmaster was checked (the letter being held before a lamp to make sure that it was a single sheet), and a postmark was stamped on it.[10] This postmark, unlike the Horsham postmark, was round in shape and contained a date.[11] It was known as a "morning duty" stamp and it can be detected

---

7. Shelley, *Complete Works*, VIII, 226. See also sc 5 (May 11–12, 1787), lines 91, 96; sc 156 (May 8, 1811), line 57. Shelley uses "single sheet" in the post-office sense of "single letter," namely a letter on but one sheet of paper folded or unfolded, no matter how large. Bibliographically speaking the letter to Elizabeth Hitchener was probably (like sc 5 and sc 156) a double sheet folio.

8. See sc 134 (Jan. 14, 1811), Plate XXXII.

9. Paterson's *Roads* (1811), p. 528.

10. If the letter was franked — as many of Shelley's were in these years because his father was a Member of Parliament — it went through one more process. It was checked "to see that the sender or receiver had no more than the number allowed by law." (Robinson, *The British Post Office*, p. 205.)

11. See sc 134 (Jan. 14, 1811), Plate XXXII. In addition to the date the stamp contained a letter of the alphabet which indicated the table in the post office at which the letter was processed. (Alcock and Holland, p. 21.)

as such by the fact that it has but a single rim ("evening duty" stamps have a double rim[12]). In addition to the rim or rims a franking stamp also contained a crown and the word "FREE."

Morning Duty

Franking

Evening Duty

A "morning duty" stamp usually signifies that a letter had been received at the post office between midnight and noon, for most mail coaches came into London in the morning. The coach left Horsham at 7 p.m. and as mail coaches averaged about seven and a half miles an hour[13] this meant that the Horsham mail got into London about 1 a.m. Hence, the morning duty stamp on the letter is one day later than the day of mailing at Horsham.[14]

A morning duty stamp on a letter, then, informs us that the letter was mailed outside London (beyond the Twopenny Post circuit) and that it probably came into London earlier rather than later in the day. The elementary fact about the morning duty stamp for the literary student to keep in mind is that the date on the stamp cannot be taken as the date of the posting or writing of the letter. The date on the stamp is the date of arrival in London. The date on which the letter was posted can be determined in one of two ways. If it was posted in one of the larger towns (Dublin, Edinburgh, York, Oxford, etc.) there is no problem for it will bear a dated postmark stamped on at that town. If it was

12. See, for instance, sc 26 (Dec. 16, 1799). At first single rim stamps were used for both morning and evening duty. The double rim for evening duty came in about 1795. (Alcock and Holland, pp. 20–21.)

13. Joyce, *History of the Post Office*, pp. 399–400. On some main routes as much as nine miles an hour was attained. (Robinson, *The British Post Office*, p. 238.)

14. See, for instance, sc 116 (Sept. 6, 1810), sc 126 (Dec. 28, 1810), sc 129 (Jan. 6, 1811), sc 132 (Jan. 11, 1811).

# The Carl H. Pforzheimer Library

posted in a small town and bears a straight line mileage stamp (which contains no date but only the place and distance from London) we can derive the date by checking the time of the mail-coach departure in the road guides of the period.

From this it follows that any dated postmark on a letter mailed outside the London area and deliverable in London must be a London (morning duty) postmark unless the letter came from one of the larger towns. If the letter bears two dated postmarks one will be that of the town in which it was mailed and the other the London morning duty stamp. There is, however, no difficulty in telling which is which. For one thing, a stamp of the town of origin will bear its name whereas the London stamp does not have the name "London" on it. In most cases, also, the dates will be different, the London stamp bearing the later date (later usually by one or two days). And in doubtful cases — for instance, if the stamps are blurred — the reproductions of postmarks in Alcock and Holland may be consulted.

To return to Shelley's letter from Horsham. After it received its London stamp it was placed in its "divisional box," from which it was removed by the postman for the division. As the postman delivered the letters he usually collected the postal fee from the recipient. The first "walk" for delivering Inland Mail letters in London began at 10 a.m.[15] and the letter mailed at Horsham before 7 p.m. would be delivered in London before noon on the next day. (Forty to sixty thousand letters a day were thus delivered.)[16]

2. Let us now consider the reverse process, that of a letter mailed in London and intended for delivery outside the London area. Such a letter could reach the General Post Office in one of three ways: it could be taken directly there by the sender or posted at a receiving house or given to a postman between 5 and 6.30 in the evening.

The receiving houses closed at 5 p.m. After that the postmen went on set routes, ringing a bell as they went, to collect mail through the streets. (As one of them put it: "After we have made our collections, we have to ring the bell at five o'clock."[17]) Hence, if an Inland Mail letter, posted in London, does not bear a receiving house stamp, it must

15. Robinson, *The British Post Office*, p. 205.       16. *Ibid*.
17. Quoted, *ibid*.

# Shelley and his Circle : Manuscripts

have gone to the General Post Office either directly or via a postman
between 5 and 6.30 p.m.[18]

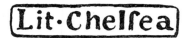

Lit·Chelfea

Inland Mail, Receiving House

King Street
Tower Hill

Inland Mail, Receiving House

There were only two establishments of the General Post Office in
London in the early nineteenth century, the "Chief Office" in Lombard
Street and the "Westminster Office" in Gerrard Street. When a letter
going out of London reached either of these offices it was stamped with
an "evening duty" stamp. And it is possible to tell from the postmark
at which of the two this was done: the Lombard Street postmark had
the month before the day, the Westminster had the day before the
month.[19]

After the letter was stamped and otherwise processed it was placed
in its bag for the mail coach leaving London.

Mail coaches might straggle into London at various times but they
did not straggle out. They all left together at 8.00 p.m. in a kind of
ceremonial procession. "The departure of the coaches at 8.00 P.M. was
regarded as one of the sights of London, as the gaily painted coaches,
drawn by freshly groomed horses, waited in double line for the mails
in the spacious yard of St. Martin's."[20] In the 1820's seventeen mail
coaches streamed out of London each evening.

From these procedures it follows that an evening duty stamp does
not necessarily mean that a letter was posted in the evening of the date
on the stamp. It means only that it went out of London on that evening.
It could have been posted anywhere between the previous evening —
too late to catch the last processing — and the early evening of the
stamped date. If it bears a receiving house stamp, it must have been

18. See, for instance, sc 151 (Apr. 18, 1811).

19. For a Lombard Street postmark see sc 29 (Aug. 31, 1799), and for a Westminster postmark see
sc 44 (Oct. 18, 1802).

20. Robinson, *The British Post Office*, p. 234.

# The Carl H. Pforzheimer Library

## Postmarks

mailed at least by 5 p.m. on the day of the date on the evening duty stamp.

The letter, then, left London at eight in the evening. When it arrived at the town to which it was addressed, it went to the local post office and was later delivered by the local postman (who at the same time collected the postal charge, if the letter was not prepaid). It was not, we should note, stamped at the local post office for such post offices stamped only outgoing mail and not incoming mail. Hence, there is no indication on the postmarks at what town the letter was received or when it was received, and, unless we know these facts from the text or address, we can tell only that the letter went through the London Post Office.

It follows from this also, as a kind of corollary, that if a letter bears a small town postmark the letter was posted from that town and not delivered in it. Hence, if there is no indication in a letter of its place of origin this can sometimes be ascertained by the postmark and may provide a clue to the identity of the writer.

3. We have considered letters coming into London and letters going out of London. Let us now consider letters which combined both procedures, namely those mailed outside of London and passing through London to be delivered in some other town.

As almost all the main coach roads in England converged upon London, a great volume of mail, much of it from towns far removed from London, passed through the General Post Office there. Such letters normally bear two postmarks, that of the town in which they originated and that of the Inland Mail office in London (and not, let us repeat, that of the town in which they were delivered). The question that naturally arises is which Inland Mail stamp did they bear, a "morning duty" stamp signifying that they had been received in London, or an "evening duty" stamp signifying that they were going out from London, or both? The answer is that they bore the "morning duty" stamp only.[21] A letter would normally come in in the morning and go out the same evening (with the eight o'clock cavalcade). Hence, a letter passing through London and bearing a morning duty stamp almost certainly left London on the evening of the date on the stamp.

4. Of letters that did not pass through London not much need be

21. See, for instance, sc 159 (May 14, 1811).

# Shelley and his Circle : Manuscripts

said. Usually their postmarks are of little help, for, unless they came from one of the larger towns, they bear no date. The letters that Shelley sent from Rhayader in Wales to Hogg in York are of this type; and as Shelley did not date them they pose a special problem. They do not bear a York postmark because they were going into and not coming out of York. (See sc 174, August 3, 1811, Plate XL.)

## THE PENNY POST

The Penny Post (or Twopenny Post as it was called after 1801) was a local or district post, handling the mail in and around the larger cities, London, Dublin, Edinburgh, and so on. By far the most important of these and the one most likely to be encountered by literary scholars is the London Penny Post.

The area of the London Penny Post was divided into an inner and an outer district, the inner comprising the city proper, the outer encompassing an area extending between ten and fifteen miles out (including Greenwich, Deptford, Dulwich, Wimbledon, Putney, Brentford, and Ealing).[22] For the inner circle the charge per letter was twopence, for the outer, threepence. The inner circle had six deliveries a day (the first at 8 a.m., the last at 7 p.m.), the outer, three. After 1794 letters could be either prepaid or paid on delivery. On their way back after each delivery the postmen collected the letters from the Penny Post receiving houses and took them to one of the two main Post Office buildings, the Chief Office or the Westminster Office, within each of which the Penny Post had its own separate establishment. The Penny Post postmen did not make a bell-through-the-streets collection after the closing of the receiving houses, however, as did the Inland Mail postmen. The Penny Post receiving houses, unlike those of the Inland Mail, closed at 8 p.m. and not 5 p.m. In addition "letters could be mailed after 8 p.m. at the receiving houses through a hole cut in the shutter."[23]

These procedures determined the nature of the Penny Post postmarks.

Each Penny Post letter would normally bear two stamps, that of

22. See the map in Robinson, *The British Post Office*, between pages 198 and 199.
23. Robinson, *The British Post Office*, p. 197.

# The Carl H. Pforzheimer Library

## *Postmarks*

the receiving house and that of the Penny Post main office. The first was stamped on when the letter was taken in at the receiving house; the second was stamped on when the letter was going out for delivery from one of the two main offices. There is no difficulty in telling which is which because the receiving house stamp contains the name and, if it is in London, the number of the receiving house, whereas a main office stamp contains no place name. If the letter has not been prepaid it will also contain a postal fee.

Penny Post, Main Office (delivery)

Penny Post, Receiving House
(with postal fee)

Nor is there any difficulty in telling the difference between Inland Mail and Penny Post stamps. The Penny Post receiving house stamp contains the designation "Penny Post" upon it in various forms (e.g., "Two-Penny Post," "2 Py Post," "2py P"); and the Penny Post main office (delivery) stamp contains the time of day.[24] Furthermore, as our illustrations show,[25] the stamps differ in design and type.

One final characteristic of Penny Post stamps should be noted. Both receiving house and main office stamps indicate whether or not the letter was prepaid.

The problem of postmarks, then, is somewhat more complex than

24. If one wishes to ascertain the general time of day on which a Penny Post letter was posted, one should keep the following facts in mind: if such a letter bears a receiving house stamp, it must have been mailed at least two hours prior to the time noted in the delivery stamp; if it bears no receiving house stamp, the letter must have been taken directly to one of the main post offices, and, hence, could have been mailed as little as one hour and fifteen minutes earlier.

25. Our illustrations are taken from J. H. Daniels, *A History of British Postmarks* (London, 1898). Daniels reproduces the original lettering of the postmarks. Alcock and Holland were unable to do this, as they state in the preface, because of "wartime costs."

at first appears, and while the editor of letters does not have to become an expert, he should have some knowledge of the main reference works in the field.

One cannot understand postmarks without understanding the rationale behind them and this, as we have indicated, means some knowledge of the history and practices of the post office. But usually books on postmarks do not give enough elementary information on the post office and books on the post office do not give sufficient attention to stamps. In the above brief remarks we have attempted some closing of the gap in a limited area.

K.N.C.

# POSTMARK LIST, SUPPLEMENTARY INFORMATION

IN THE Bibliographical Notes we give a transcription of the postmark and its general or functional designation (for example, mileage stamp, evening duty stamp). In the thought that additional information might be helpful to editors working with similar letters we indicate in the list below through which postal service each letter passed (Inland Mail, Penny Post, Irish Post Office) and give a brief description of each postmark with reference in parentheses to Alcock and Holland's figure number for a similar postmark. We include the color because different colored inks were used at different times and for different purposes. (See, for instance, Alcock and Holland, pages 22–24.)

The names of stamps and other terms we derive from the standard reference works. One term which seems useful and which we do not find elsewhere is "delivery stamp" which we use to designate the Penny Post postmark stamped on at the main office when the letter was to be delivered (in contradistinction to that stamped on at the receiving house).

SC 4
1. Irish Post Office: straight line stamp, unframed, black (575)
2. Irish Post Office: Bishop stamp, Dublin; circular, black (550)
3. Inland Mail: Bishop stamp, London; circular, black (3)

SC 5
1. Irish Post office: straight line stamp, unframed, black (574)
2. Irish Post Office: Bishop stamp, Dublin; circular, black (549)
3. Inland Mail: London; circular, single rim stamp, black (21)

SC 13
Penny Post: delivery stamp, London; oval, unframed, red (129)

SC 22
1. Inland Mail: evening duty stamp, London; circular, double rim, black (23)
2. Inland Mail: (trace)

SC 26
Inland Mail: black; see SC 22, stamp no. 1

SC 29
1. Inland Mail: provincial stamp; curved line, unframed, black (224)
2. Inland Mail: morning duty stamp, London; circular, single rim, red (26)

SC 33
1. Penny Post: receiving house stamp, London; oval, unframed, black (137)

# Shelley and his Circle : Manuscripts

2. Penny Post: delivery stamp, London; oval, framed, red (131)

sc 36
1. Inland Mail: receiving house stamp, London; rectangular, double frame, black (42)
2. Inland Mail: evening duty stamp, London; circular, double rim, black (29)

sc 40
1. Penny Post: receiving house stamp, London; oval, unframed, brown (163)
2. Penny Post: delivery stamp, London; indented frame, red (120)

sc 44
1. Penny Post: black; see sc 40, stamp no. 1
2. Penny Post: red; see sc 40, stamp no. 2

sc 46
1. Penny Post: receiving house stamp, London; straight line stamp, unframed, black
2. Penny Post: delivery stamp, London; oval frame, red (140)

sc 48
1. Penny Post: receiving house stamp, London; oval, unframed, black (165)
2. Penny Post: red; see sc 33, stamp no. 2

sc 49
1. Penny Post: black; see sc 48, stamp no. 1
2. Penny Post: red; see sc 33, stamp no. 2

sc 52
1. Inland Mail: black; see sc 116, stamp no. 1
2. Inland Mail: brownish red; see sc 29, stamp no. 2

sc 56
1. Penny Post: black; see sc 48, stamp no. 1
2. Penny Post: red; see sc 33, stamp no. 2

sc 67
1. Penny Post: (trace)
2. Penny Post: red; see sc 44, stamp no. 2

sc 76
1. Inland Mail: black; see sc 36, stamp no. 2
2. Irish Post Office: Dublin; circular, single rim stamp, black (552)

sc 77
1. Inland Mail: mileage stamp; straight line stamp with bar above and below the mileage number, black (249)
2. Inland Mail: brownish red; see sc 29, stamp no. 2

sc 91
1. Inland Mail: black; see sc 36, stamp no. 2
2. Irish Post Office: Dublin; mermaid stamp, red (553)

sc 105
1. Inland Mail: black; see sc 36, stamp no. 2
2. Inland Mail: morning duty stamp, Edinburgh; circular, single rim stamp, red (365)

# The Carl H. Pforzheimer Library

## Postmark List

SC 110

1. Penny Post: receiving house stamp, London; straight line, unframed, black (167)
2. Penny Post: red; see SC 46, stamp no. 2

SC 113

1. Inland Mail: black; see SC 77, stamp no. 1
2. Inland Mail: morning duty stamp, London; circular, single rim, brownish red (27)

SC 116

1. Inland Mail: mileage stamp; straight line stamp with mileage number in small rectangle, black (247)
2. Inland Mail: morning duty franking stamp, London; circular, single rim surmounted by crown, brownish red (841, 842)

SC 121

1. Inland Mail: dated mileage stamp, circular, brown (260)
2. Inland Mail: brownish red; see SC 113, stamp no. 2

SC 126

1. Inland Mail: black; see SC 116, stamp no. 1
2. Inland Mail: black; see SC 113, stamp no. 2

SC 127

1. Inland Mail: black; see SC 116, stamp no. 1
2. Inland Mail: black; see SC 113, stamp no. 2

SC 128

1. Inland Mail: black; see SC 116, stamp no. 1
2. Inland Mail: black; see SC 113, stamp no. 2

SC 129

1. Inland Mail: black; see SC 116, stamp no. 1
2. Inland Mail: brown; see SC 116, stamp no. 2 (841, 842)

SC 132

1. Inland Mail: black; see SC 116, stamp no. 1
2. Inland Mail: black; see SC 116, stamp no. 2

SC 133

1. Inland Mail: black; see SC 116, stamp no. 1
2. Inland Mail: black; see SC 113, stamp no. 2

SC 134

1. Inland Mail: black; see SC 116, stamp no. 1
2. Inland Mail: black; see SC 113, stamp no. 2

SC 135

1. Inland Mail: black; see SC 116, stamp no. 1
2. Inland Mail: black; see SC 113, stamp no. 2

SC 139

1. Inland Mail: black; see SC 121, stamp no. 1
2. Inland Mail: red; see SC 116, stamp no. 2

sc 140
1. Inland Mail: black; see sc 121, stamp no. 1
2. Inland Mail: red; see sc 116, stamp no. 2

sc 143
1. Inland Mail: black; see sc 116, stamp no. 1
2. Inland Mail: black; see sc 116, stamp no. 2
4. Inland Mail: black; see sc 121, stamp no. 1

sc 144
Inland Mail: evening duty franking stamp, London; circular, double rim surmounted by crown, brownish red (843)

sc 145
Inland Mail: brownish red; see sc 144

sc 146
Inland Mail: black; see sc 77, stamp no. 1

sc 148
1. Penny Post: black (trace)
2. Penny Post: red; see sc 40, stamp no. 2

sc 150
1. Inland Mail: black; see sc 116, stamp no. 1
2. Inland Mail: brownish red; see sc 116, stamp no. 2

sc 151
Inland Mail: black; see sc 36, stamp no. 2

sc 152
Inland Mail: black; see sc 36, stamp no. 2

sc 154
Inland Mail: black; see sc 36, stamp no. 2

sc 155
Inland Mail: black; see sc 36, stamp no. 1

sc 156
1. Inland Mail: black; see sc 36, stamp no. 1
2. Inland Mail: black; see sc 36, stamp no. 2
3. Inland Mail: red (1813)

sc 157
1. Illegible
2. Inland Mail: black; see sc 36, stamp no. 2

sc 158
Inland Mail: black; see sc 36, stamp no. 2

sc 159
1. Inland Mail: black; see sc 116, stamp no. 1
2. Inland Mail: red; see sc 116, stamp no. 2

sc 161
1. Inland Mail: black; see sc 116, stamp no. 1
2. Inland Mail: black; see sc 113, stamp no. 2

sc 163
1. Inland Mail: black; see sc 77, stamp no. 1
2. Inland Mail: black; see sc 113, stamp no. 2

# The Carl H. Pforzheimer Library

## *Postmark List*

sc 164
1. Inland Mail: black; see sc 116, stamp no. 1
2. Inland Mail: black; see sc 113, stamp no. 2

sc 165
1. Inland Mail: black; see sc 116, stamp no. 1
2. Inland Mail: brownish red; see sc 116, stamp no. 2

sc 167
1. Inland Mail: black; see sc 116, stamp no. 1
2. Inland Mail: black; see sc 113, stamp no. 2

sc 169
Inland Mail: provincial stamp; horseshoe, unframed, black (227)

sc 170
Inland Mail: black; see sc 169

sc 171
Inland Mail: black; see sc 169

sc 172
Inland Mail: black; see sc 169

sc 173
Inland Mail: black; see sc 169

sc 174
Inland Mail: black; see sc 169

sc 175
1. Inland Mail: black; see sc 36, stamp no. 1
2. Inland Mail: black (trace); see sc 36, stamp no. 2

# Appendix

## MANUSCRIPTS AND ESSAYS, 1773–?1783

"Unpublished Letters of Mary Wollstonecraft"

# "UNPUBLISHED LETTERS OF MARY WOLLSTONECRAFT"

VOLUME I of the present work was already in plate proof except for some of the front matter and most of Volume II was in page proof when The Carl H. Pforzheimer Library acquired a copybook bearing the title "Unpublished Letters of Mary Wollstonecraft." After a survey had shown that of the 15 letters in the book 14 had not previously been published and that they constituted, in fact, transcripts of letters long since thought to have been lost, it was decided to publish them immediately, even though our schedule allowed us insufficient time for full research.

The letters — addressed to a Miss Jane Arden — first appeared in 1900 and then disappeared again. On May 27 of that year Edward Dowden wrote excitedly to Richard Garnett that he had "got a few days ago a considerable number of Mary Wollstonecraft letters written before she went to Lisbon — transcribed by I know not whom — certainly genuine . . . addressed to a Miss Arden."[1] In 1951 Ralph M. Wardle in his biography of Mary Wollstonecraft published one letter from her to "a Miss Arden, probably a friend of her Beverley days" and commented that he had been unable to find the "considerable number" once possessed by Dowden: "Neither the letters nor the transcripts seem to have survived."[2] He noted also that "only two of Mary Wollstonecraft's letters written during the first twenty-one years of her life survive in the collection of Lord Abinger."[3] These two are also the only two so far published. Of the 14 unpublished letters in the copybook at least 10 were written before Mary Wollstonecraft's twenty-first birthday.

The copybook, as we note in our Bibliographical Description, is an ordinary notebook (9 x 7.4 in.) in brown boards. It bears no indication of the identity of either the owner or transcriber.[4] Nor is it dated. The front fly and first leaf, however, bear watermarks dated 1803 and other leaves, 1801; both ink and covers give an impression of considerable age. The probability is that the transcripts were made between 1803 and 1806, for we find that paper in this period was usually written on within three years of its date of manufacture.

1. *Letters about Shelley*, p. 215. Dowden had the letters as late as 1905. (*Ibid.*, p. 258.)
2. Wardle, *Wollstonecraft*, pp. 14, 343.  3. *Ibid.*, p. 342.
4. As Dowden also noted. (*Letters about Shelley*, p. 215.)

# The Carl H. Pforzheimer Library

*Wollstonecraft*                    *"Unpublished Letters"*

There seems to be a fair chance that the transcriber of the letters was Jane Arden herself. The autograph letter which is among the Abinger Manuscripts was addressed to her and must have been in her possession. As the Abinger Manuscripts consist largely of the Godwin family papers[5] there is some likelihood that this letter was given or sold to William Godwin or perhaps to Everina Wollstonecraft.[6] But if one letter went to the Godwin family papers it may be that all of them did, and that the others were later lost or destroyed.[7] It may be, then, that they were transcribed by Jane Arden (or someone close to her) and that she wished to make copies before giving them up.

One other interesting fact to emerge from a comparison of the Abinger autograph with the copybook version (sc 187) is that the copybook version is a reasonably careful transcription and was made directly from the original.[8] As the Collation shows, the transcriber changed the punctuation rather freely and tidied up the grammar — "if I were" for "if I was," "have written" for "have wrote" — but on the whole followed the original quite well. In other letters even Mary Wollstonecraft's cancellations are retained. The copybook, we might also note, is a school-type notebook and the transcriptions are done in a neat copying hand with margins faintly ruled in pencil and rigidly adhered to; in fact, when a line does not quite come to the margin it is filled out with a dash of the appropriate length (omitted in our transcripts). It is probable, then, that all the letters are fairly accurate reflections of the originals.

Professor Wardle was correct in assuming that Jane Arden was a friend from Mary Wollstonecraft's "Beverley days." Godwin in his *Memoirs of the Author of a Vindication of the Rights of Woman* (1798) describes these "days" as follows:

In Michaelmas, 1768, Mr. Wollstonecraft again removed to a farm near Beverley in Yorkshire. Here the family remained for six years, and consequently, Mary did not quit this residence, till she had attained the age of fifteen years and five months. The principal part of her school education passed during this period; but it was not to any advantage of infant literature, that she was

5. See above, "The Provenance of Shelley and his Circle Manuscripts," p. 893.

6. See above, Volume I, "Mary Wollstonecraft," p. 50.

7. Lady Shelley is thought to have destroyed material in 1870. (*Letters about Shelley*, pp. 36–37.)

8. See below, "Bath, 1778–?1779," and sc 187, Collation.

indebted for her subsequent eminence; her education in this respect was merely such, as was afforded by the day-schools of the place, in which she resided. To her recollections Beverley appeared a very handsome town, surrounded by genteel families, and with a brilliant assembly. She was surprized, when she visited it in 1795, upon her voyage to Norway, to find the reality so very much below the picture in her imagination.[9]

Until the present this was almost all we knew of the "Beverley days." Now we have an account of them — in the first seven letters — from Mary Wollstonecraft's own pen.

Daniel Paterson in his survey of English roads in 1811 stops to make a special note on Beverley (population 6000):

Beverley is one of the neatest towns in the county; it stands about two miles west of the river Hull, from which there is a navigable canal for small vessels to the town. The Minster is highly worthy of the traveller's attention; several genteel families reside in and near Beverley.[10]

Who some of the "genteel families" were will appear in the following Commentaries. Beverley, however, was famed not only for its neatness and its gentry. One would gather from Mary's letters that there was a good deal of literary, theatrical, and scientific interest in the town and it may have struck deeper intellectual roots in the young schoolgirl than Godwin seemed to think. Her early letters, in fact, show an almost avid interest in poetry and similar matters. One might assume also that the schools of Beverley were of a somewhat higher caliber than Godwin indicates.[11]

In addition to his comments on Jane Arden, Professor Wardle notes that while at Beverley Mary Wollstonecraft "corresponded with a Miss Massey, evidently one of her teachers, who later published eleven of

---

9. Godwin, *Memoirs*, pp. 14–15.                    10. Paterson's *Roads*, pp. 239–240.

11. In 1736 John Clarke became headmaster of the Grammar School at Beverley. Clarke was "a man of known ability" who inspired a biography: Thomas Zouch, *The Schoolmaster, Exemplified in the Life of John Clarke, M.A.* (London, 1798). According to K. A. MacMahon in *Beverley Corporation Minute Books (1707–1835)* (London, 1958), p. xvii, there is some evidence that although the Grammar School "appears to have been principally for boys," girls were admitted "at least in the middle years of the eighteenth century." In 1823 the "Free Schools of Beverley" included, in addition to the Grammar School, the National School and Grave's School, the latter founded in 1812. (Edward Baines, *History, Directory, and Gazetteer of the County of York*, 1823, II, xvii.) And there were other schools also. What school Mary attended we do not know, but Beverley appears to have been rather well off educationally.

# The Carl H. Pforzheimer Library

Mary's letters written between 1773 and 1882."[12] These letters were published "as a supplement to *English Exercises* at York in 1801 by Miss Massey under the pseudonym 'Jane Gardiner.'"[13] Both Wardle and Durant report searching in vain for a copy of *English Exercises*.

Such in brief is the information that has so far appeared in Mary Wollstonecraft biography regarding this correspondence and Jane Arden. We have been able to add somewhat to this information and to untangle the mystery of "Jane Gardiner."

Who was Jane Arden? Mary in one of her letters refers to Jane's father as a "Master" (sc 179, line 66) and in another (sc 184, line 7) as "the worthy philosopher" who has just given her "a lesson on the globes" (perhaps the instrument known as an orrery, with globes for the planets). From a third letter (sc 185) we learn that he gave "lectures" at Bath in 1778. When we turned to the British Museum catalogue we found an entry for a James Arden as author of a book entitled *Analysis of Mr. Arden's Course of Lectures on Natural and Experimental Philosophy*, 2nd edition, [?London], 1782. We then wrote to Mr. Peter Pagan, Director, Victoria Art Gallery and Municipal Libraries at Bath, and Mr. Pagan found advertisements for Arden's lectures on "Natural and Experimental Philosophy" in the *Bath Chronicle* for 1777.[14] The first of the notices concludes as follows: "Young Ladies and Gentlemen may be taught as usual, at home, or at his house, Geography, the Elements of Astronomy, Use of the Globes and Maps."

On Jane herself we learn from Mary's letters that after she left Beverley she was for a time a governess in the household of Sir Mortdant Martin of Burnham[15] in Norfolk[16] and later went to Bath.[17]

In the meantime we had learned from Mr. H. E. Whiteley, Librarian of the Beverley Public Library, that there were Ardens still living in that town. In reply to an inquiry we received a letter from Mr. C. A. Arden

---

12. Wardle, *Wollstonecraft*, p. 9.              13. *Ibid.*, p. 343.

14. Oct. 16, Nov. 13, Dec. 1, Dec. 25.

15. sc 187, Collation, Address, page 4. Wardle, *Wollstonecraft*, p. 14, misread "Burnham" as "Bronham."

16. See also Everilda Anne Gardiner, *Recollections of a Beloved Mother* (London, 1842), p. 3, and *Burke's Peerage* (1826).

17. See below, "Bath, 1778–?1779."

with enclosed biographical material "assembled from a little book 'Recollections of a Beloved Mother' written by Jane's daughter published (1400 copies were sold) in 1842,[18] and from a number of letters and other documents in my possession." This information we might summarize as follows:

Jane Arden, daughter of John Arden, was born in 1758 at Beverley and educated there by her father. In 1780 she left her position with Sir Mortdant Martin to become a governess in the family of Lord Ilchester, of Redlynch, Somerset. In 1784 she went back to Beverley and opened a boarding school there.[19] In 1797 she married a Mr. Gardiner but continued school teaching. She died in 1840. She published the following books: *The Young Ladies' English Grammar; English Exercises* (2 vols., 3 editions, 1801); *An Excursion from London to Dover* (2 vols., 1806); *A French Grammar* (1808).[20]

John Arden, Jane's father, was born in 1721 and died in 1792. He was first a schoolmaster at Heath, Yorkshire, but later settled in Beverley where he was described in the poll books as a "Philosopher."[21]

It is clear from this information that Jane Arden and Jane Gardiner were one and the same person and that there were probably not two but one set of letters written by Mary Wollstonecraft at Beverley.[22]

We might note also that Mr. Arden informs us in his letter that the Wollstonecraft farm was at Walkington "some three miles from Beverley."

The first three letters written at (or near) Beverley are happy, girlish letters (the next four reflect a temporary falling-out between the

18. See above, fn. 16.

19. Mr. Whiteley informs us that a Beverley directory for 1792 lists "Arden, J. & A., ladies boarding school, Eastgate."

20. The British Museum catalogue gives 1799 as the date for the *Young Ladies' English Grammar*, notes a second edition of *English Grammar* for 1808 and a third "improved" edition for 1809.

21. Information from Mr. C. A. Arden. The James Arden who wrote the *Analysis of Mr. Arden's Course on Natural and Experimental Philosophy* was apparently John Arden's son. We find in the *Alumni Oxonienses* a James Arden, son of John of Heath, Yorkshire, who entered Trinity College, Oxford, in 1774 at the age of nineteen; and he was at Oxford also in 1785 (*Recollections of a Beloved Mother*, p. 5).

22. According to "W.C.B." (Walter Consitt Boulter), writing in *Notes and Queries* in 1870 (4th series, VI, 341–342), there were but eleven letters by Mary Wollstonecraft in *English Exercises*. The copybook contains fourteen letters and one third-person note. If the two sets were the same, as seems almost certain, Jane Gardiner must have omitted four items from *English Exercises*.

friends). "I often think of the merry days we spent together at Beverley," Mary wrote later, "when we used to laugh from noon 'till night."[23] Even twenty years later the memories of her happy youth there still inspired her, twenty years in which she had gone through much, including the French Revolution and the vacillations of Gilbert Imlay: "They took me in their carriage to [Beverley], and I ran over my favourite walks, with a vivacity that would have astonished you."[24]

Late in 1774 the Wollstonecrafts left Beverley for Hoxton, to the north of London (Environs of London, page 47), Mr. Wollstonecraft, according to Godwin, having temporarily given up farming for "a commercial speculation of some sort."[25] Within some fifteen months this "speculation" had failed and he was back at farming, this time near the town of Laugharne in Wales (later to become known to literary history as the residence of Dylan Thomas). But failure came once more; and by the next summer (1777) the family was back in the vicinity of London, at the village of Walworth, about as far south of the city as Hoxton was north of it (Environs of London, page 47). Sometime later they moved back to the northern suburbs, to the town of Enfield.

These repeated business failures took their toll of Mr. Wollstonecraft. The consequent deterioration within the family was reflected by Mary in 1797 in her unfinished novel *The Wrongs of Woman: or Maria:*

His orders were not to be disputed; and the whole house was expected to fly, at the word of command. . . . He was to be instantaneously obeyed, especially by my mother, whom he very benevolently married for love; but took care to remind her of the obligation, when she dared, in the slightest instance, to question his absolute authority. My eldest brother, it is true, as he grew up, was treated with more respect by my father; and became in due form the deputy tyrant of the house.[26]

It was doubtless this breakdown of the family that decided Mary to leave home. "In the year 1778, she being nineteen years of age, a proposal was made to her of living as a companion with a Mrs. Dawson of Bath, a widow lady, with one son already adult."[27]

23. sc 191, line 15.
24. To Gilbert Imlay, June 14, [1795], Wollstonecraft, *Posthumous Works*, III, 137.
25. Godwin, *Memoirs*, p. 16.
26. Wollstonecraft, *Posthumous Works*, I, 142–143.
27. Godwin, *Memoirs*, p. 25.

# Shelley and his Circle : Manuscripts

During these four years of family wanderings, failures, and increasing domestic tensions Mary had not written to Jane Arden. The correspondence reopened at Bath:

> You will, my dear girl, be as much surprised at receiving a letter from me, as I was at hearing, that your family resided at Bath; – I have been at this place two months yet chance never threw your sisters in my way — and if I had not by accident been informed of your father's giving lectures, I might never have met with them. —— [28]

This second section of the correspondence is very different from the first. The experiences of 1775–1778 have brought Mary to a rapid maturity. The happy note of the earlier letters with their enclosed poetry and minor intrigues and girlish quarrels has gone, and a soberer Mary, now earning her living, and earning it, as she said, "among Strangers"[29] looks with questioning eyes at the world. Signs of both her later rebellion and humanitarianism begin to appear. She condemns the king as an "unfeeling mortal" whose "humanity" is "confined to a very narrow circle," for he has reportedly killed three horses by riding them too fast. "Indeed I carry my notions on this subject a great way: — I think it murder to put an end to any living thing unless it be necessary for food, or hurtful to us"[30] (an attitude with which her future son-in-law would have agreed — up to a point). The views of *A Vindication of the Rights of Woman* begin to show roots also. Mrs. Dawson's sister is condemned for bringing up her daughters to be "accomplished and fashionable [rather] than good and sensible, in the true sense of the word: — In this she follows the crowd, and it is much to be lamented, that the Stream runs so rapidly that way."[31]

These letters, like those from Beverley, give us a picture of Mary's life in her own words for a period about which we had previously been mainly dependent for our knowledge upon Godwin's comments and upon reflections in Mary's fiction. In the second letter from Bath, for instance (sc 186), Mary gives a running commentary on her life from Beverley to Bath, the period (1775–1778) during which she has not corresponded with Jane Arden. In the next two letters (sc 187 and sc 188) she

---

28. sc 185, line 1.      29. sc 188, line 12.

30. sc 190, line 28.      31. sc 190, line 15.

[ 939 ]

# The Carl H. Pforzheimer Library

describes her life at Bath with Mrs. Dawson. Then come two letters (sc 189 and sc 190) from Windsor. Mrs. Dawson has a house there, and she and Mary have moved from Bath to Windsor. They are planning still another move when Mary's career as companion is broken up by the illness of her mother. The final letters (sc 191 and sc 192), following her mother's death, were written at the village of Walham Green near London, where she was living with her friend Fanny Blood.

As the above and following comments indicate we have received most generous and often extensive outside assistance without which it would not have been possible to have edited these letters. We should like to express our sincerest thanks to the following: Mr. H. E. Whiteley, Borough Librarian and Curator of the Beverley Public Library, Art Gallery and Museum; Mr. K. A. MacMahon, Tutor in Yorkshire local history at Hull University; Miss Margaret Jowett of York; Mr. C. A. Arden; Mr. Peter Pagan, Director, Victoria Art Gallery and Municipal Libraries of Bath; Mr. A. H. Hall, Librarian, Guildhall Library, London; Mr. O. S. Tomlinson, Librarian, City Library, York; Professor Lewis Patton of the English Department of Duke University. We wish also to thank the Library and Art Gallery Committee, Bath, for permission to quote from the *Bath Chronicle*.

K.N.C.

## BEVERLEY, 1773-1774

As their context makes clear, the first three of the Beverley letters form a unit. The occasion for writing them was that Jane Arden had gone to Hull (some nine miles away), apparently to visit a "Miss C——" who was engaged to be married. The second letter enables us to give the sequence at least an approximate date. In it Mary mentions that she is "going to see the Macaroni if it be performed" (sc 179, line 71). *The Macaroni, a Comedy* by Robert Hitchcock, published anonymously at York in 1773,[1] was performed in Beverley on May 26 and June 3 of the same year. Miss Margaret Jowett of York, who secured this information on the Beverley performances for us by searching a

1. Halkett and Laing; *DNB*. The *DNB* notes that another play by Hitchcock, *The Coquette*, was acted at Hull. "Macaroni" was the term used at the time for a fop or dandy.

# Shelley and his Circle : Manuscripts

collection of the playbills of the York company in the York Minster Library, comments: "The Minster collection of play-bills is absolutely complete, so I feel certain that the performances listed here are the only ones."[2]

The second Beverley letter, then, was written between, say, May 20 and June 3, 1773. The context indicates that the first one came but shortly before (say, May 1–20) and the third shortly after (say, June 4–July 31). The general dating period (1773) is supported also by the reference to the "verses on the death of H. Bethell Esq." (sc 179, line 4). This must be the "Hugh Bethell, esq. of Rise, high-sheriff of Yorkshire in 1761, who died unmarried 8th May, 1772," as noted in *Burke's Landed Gentry* for 1837.[3]

Mary Wollstonecraft included three poems in these letters, "Sweet Beverley" in sc 178, a satire on "Sweet Beverley by "D^r Drake" in sc 179, and "Verses on the Beverley Beauties" by "M^r Rudd" in sc 180. Apparently neither the poem "Sweet Beverley" nor its author is now known at Beverley. The "Driffield Bards" of that poem (line 69), however, are identifiable as a group of poets who lived at Driffield (about ten miles north of Beverley), including William Mason,[4] who had two plays produced at Covent Garden and edited the poems of Thomas Gray. Mason was a minister at Driffield from 1762 until his death in 1797. "Dr. Drake" was either Dr. Francis Drake (1695–1771), historian of York (*Eboracum*, 1736), or, more likely, his son, also Dr. Francis Drake (1721–1795), who was a minister at Beverley.[5] "Mr. Rudd" was perhaps related to the "Miss R——" mentioned in these Beverley letters as Jane Arden's best friend; in the Abinger Manuscript version of sc 187 (line 50) the "Miss R——" of the copybook version is "Miss Rud."[6] We find a

---

2. Miss Jowett writes further: "'The Macaroni' appeared as a new play in York on April 3, 1773, and was played there again on April 24 and August 25. On December 10th, 1773 it appears at Hull. . . . Then it disappears, plainly not a success."

3. I, 452. The Bethells had an estate at Watton Abbey as well as at Rise. Watton Abbey was some fourteen miles from Beverley. See Paterson's *Roads*, pp. 239–240.

4. Information from K. A. MacMahon, tutor in local history at Hull University. Mr. MacMahon refers to F. Ross, *History of Driffield*, p. 139. "Ross also lists others who aspired to the composition of poetic effusions: see in his list, Anderson, Bell, Topham, Traves, and possibly Wrangham."

5. Both Drakes are in the *DNB*.

6. Wardle (*Wollstonecraft*, p. 15) mistakenly gives "Reed" for "Rud."

# The Carl H. Pforzheimer Library

Rudd family in the vicinity and one Rudd who married an Arden.[7] The family names of the various "Beverley Beauties" — Champion, Ward, Webb, Smelt, Clubley, Acklom, Stanhope — also appear in local history,[8] so that the poem deals with actual persons, all of them doubtless known to Mary Wollstonecraft.

As Mary Wollstonecraft and Jane Arden both lived in or near Beverley there had to be some special reason for them to communicate with each other. The first three letters were motivated by Jane's trip to Hull. The next three were motivated by a quarrel. The girls are not speaking to each other and so write letters back and forth. Following these three letters comes a third-person note and "Copy of a letter from D$^r$ Clegg to D$^r$ Lathan." The note is dated November 16, 1774. Allowing for the possibility that the last letter of our first sequence (sc 180) was written in June and not July 1773, the first three letters of this second group (sc 181, sc 182, sc 183) must have been written somewhere between June 4, 1773, and November 16, 1774. It does not seem possible to place them more exactly within this period but one gets the impression that they come nearer to the beginning of it than the end. The quarrel centers about the same Miss C—— whom Jane went to visit at Hull. Miss C—— has evidently returned the visit and during her stay at Beverley Mary felt that Jane was overly attentive to her and neglected Mary. Mary does not mind taking second place to "Miss Rud,"[9] whom she recognizes as Jane's best friend — but not to Miss C——. The quarrel is petering out in sc 183 — which begins "Dear Jenny" instead of "Miss A——" or "Miss Arden." By the time of the third-person note the quarrel is over.

The letter from Dr. Clegg to Dr. Latham (Lathan is doubtless a miscopying) seems to have been enclosed in the note (sc 184, line 10)[10]

---

7. Edward Baines, *History, Directory, and Gazetteer of the County of York* (Leeds, 1823), II, 602, 604; [Henry Drummond], *Histories of Noble British Families* (London, 1846), I, 7–8.

8. These family names can be found recurring in such guides as Baines, *History, Directory, and Gazetteer of the County of York*, and *Burke's Landed Gentry* for 1837.

9. See sc 187, line 50, and Collation.

10. sc 184, line 12. That it was enclosed may be indicated also by the line drawn across the center of the page. The copyist used a similar line in sc 178 and sc 180 to indicate that "Sweet Beverley" and the "Verses on the Beverley Beauties" were enclosed.

# Shelley and his Circle : Manuscripts

and to have been connected with the "globes" and the "problem."[11] Who or what the letters "I. B." at the end of the note stand for we do not know. Dr. Clegg was probably James Clegg (1679–1755), a Dissenting minister and physician, who published sermons and other works and was interested in science.[12] Latham was probably Ebenezer Latham (1688–1754), a Dissenting minister and educator.[13] Goldsmith's *Citizen of the World*, which Mary recommends to Jane in the note, was first published in book form in 1762. Goldsmith had died in the spring of the year in which this note was written.

Durant places the date of departure of the Wollstonecrafts from Beverley for Hoxton variously at July and September 1774,[14] but this note (sc 184) appears to have been written at Beverley, and Mary apparently intends to be there at least long enough for a second "lesson on the globes" (line 8). Possibly Mr. Wollstonecraft left ahead of his family.

As we noted, Mary returned to Beverley for a brief visit in 1795. Then, although her early memories stirred her, she had the usual experience of one returning to a place he or she has not seen since childhood, namely that it seemed "diminutive." And her own advance in thought made the "genteel families" that she had previously admired[15] seem ultraconservative:

They took me in their carriage to [Beverley], and I ran over my favourite walks, with a vivacity that would have astonished you. The town did not please me quite so well as formerly — It appeared so diminutive; and, when I found that many of the inhabitants had lived in the same houses ever since I left it, I could not help wondering how they could thus have vegetated, whilst I was running over a world of sorrow, snatching at pleasure, and throwing off prejudices. The place where I at present am, is much improved; but it is astonishing

---

11. The "globes," as Arden's advertisements in the *Bath Chronicle* indicate, were the planets, and perhaps the "problem" was on which planet did the ascending souls fix "their residence" (line 31). Such speculations were perhaps increasing at the time as the notion of "the plurality of worlds" began to spread. We find anticlerical writers such as Paine making use of them later in the century.

12. *DNB* and J. W. Ashley Smith, *The Birth of Modern Education: The Contributions of the Dissenting Academies 1660–1800* (London, 1954), pp. 17–20.

13. Smith, pp. 81–83.                    14. Durant, "Supplement," p. 138, "Preface," p. xv.

15. Godwin, *Memoirs*, p. 15.

what strides aristocracy and fanaticism have made, since I resided in this country.[16]

Mary Wollstonecraft's sojourn in Beverley was not forgotten. A history of the town published in 1829 contained the following comment:

Mary Godwin is said to have been born in Beverley; she is better known by the name of Wolstencroft [*sic*]. The fact is she was born in or near London, April 17th, 1759, of poor parents, who then resided at Epping, but afterwards removed to a farm near Beverley, where this daughter frequented a day school in the neighbourhood, from whence the story of Beverley being her birth place has arisen. She was a woman of extraordinary genius, but whose history and opinions are unhappily calculated to excite a mixture of admiration, pity, and scorn.[17]

16. To Gilbert Imlay, June 14, [1795], Wollstonecraft, *Posthumous Works*, III, 137–138. Mary Wollstonecraft was at Hull awaiting a boat to Sweden when she met the people (a physician and his wife) who took her on the nine-mile trip to Beverley (on a main coach road).

17. George Poulson, *Beverlac; or, The Antiquities and History of the Town of Beverley* (London, 1829), I, 487.

SC 178   MARY WOLLSTONECRAFT TO JANE ARDEN, ?MAY 1–?20, 1773

L (transcript) and copy of anonymous poem, 3¾ pages; pages [1, 3, 5, 7, 9] of COPYBOOK\* containing also SC 179–SC 192.

\*56 leaves, unnumbered, 4$^{to}$ (8.9 x 7.3 in.), bound in brown paper boards backed in orange (9 x 7.4 in.).
Wove paper. Watermarks: 1. (front fly and leaf 1): J WHATMAN| 1803; 2. (leaves 5, 45, 46, 50, 51, 52): 1801|; 3. (leaf 36): COBB & CO|; 4. (leaf 49): O & P| 1801|.
Contents: endpaper, front fly, 4 leaves, all blank; title page, leaf five (verso blank): *Unpublished letters| of| Mary Wollstonecraft.* —|; blank leaf; 46 leaves with writing on rectos only, containing transcripts of 14 letters and one third-person note by Mary Wollstonecraft, the first three letters accompanied by copies of poems, the note followed by a copy of a letter, leaf 30$^r$ (page [47]) with "23" written in pencil in upper right corner, leaf 43$^r$ (page [73]) with [?] "W" written in pencil in left margin; 4 leaves, back fly, endpaper, all blank.

*Dear Miss Arden /*
       *According to my promise I sit down to write to you*

"*My promise and my faith shall be so sure*
"*As neither age can change, nor art can cure*
5       "*Perform thy promise keep within faith's bounds*
"*Who breaks his word, his reputation wounds.*" —

SC 178     *Inclosed you will find "Sweet Beverley" for meeting with an old copy, and being in a hurry I thought you would excuse the badness of the writing. —*

10     *"True ease in writing comes from art not chance*
*as "As those move easiest who have learnt to dance".*

*I assure you I expect a complimentary letter in return for my staying from church to day. —*

*I should likewise beg pardon for not beginning sooner so agreeable a*
15 *correspondence as that I promise myself yours will prove, but from a lady of your singular good nature I promise myself indulgence. —*

*"Indulgence soon meets with a noble mind,*
*"Who can be harsh, that sees another kind?*
*"Goodnature & good sense must ever join;*
20     *"Mildness of Temper has a force divine.*

*When you write to Miss G —*     *pray present my compliments to her, and tell her I should be obliged to her if she would write to me, and inclose it in her letter to you, and I flatter myself you will excuse my asking you to inclose it in your answer to this. —*     *I thought Miss R. — behaved*
25 *rather oddly on Saturday but I believe I was in the wrong ——*

*"I see the right, and I approve it too —*
*"I blame the wrong and yet the wrong pursue."*
*— "To you good gods I make my last appeal*
*"Or clear my virtues or my crimes reveal*
30     *"If in the maze of fate I blindly run*
*"And backward tread those paths I ought to shun*
*"Impute my errors to your own decree,*
*"My hands are guilty, but my heart is free."*

*But however I think it very unpolite in Company if all present are*
35 *unacquainted with the Cause; —*     *you need not tell Miss R —— or Miss G —— what I have said, but I need not doubt your friendship. —*

## Wollstonecraft to Arden        *?May 1–?20, 1773*

SC 178

    *"A friend should always like a friend indite*
    *"Speak as she thinks, and as she thinks sho^d write."*

    *Pray make haste and translate the french Song as I have already made a*
40 *couple of ænigmas one on Beverley, the other on a friend, and the first time*
*I see you I will shew you them. —*
    *Pray tell Miss C —— that if she can get time to write she may inclose*
*it in your letter. —*
    *I wish you may not be as tired. with reading as I am with writing. ——*
45               *I am, your friend*
                  *& humble Servant*
                    *Mary Wollstonecraft*
*Sunday afternoon 4 o'Clock.*
    *P.S. Pray write soon — I have a hundred things to add, but can't get time*
50 *for my Mama is calling me, so shall reserve them for another letter.*

---

        *"Sweet Beverley."*
             *1.*
    *"What nymph so fair as Dolly,*
    *"Smart as Stanhope's polly,*
55     *"Should you be seen, with gout or spleen*
    *"They'll cure your melancholy.*
  *"Its Beverley, sweet Beverley, in thee I take delight*
  *"Its' Beverley, sweet Beverley, whose charms I now recite."*

            *2.*
60     *"Should you be fond of dancing,*
    *"With steps cotillon prancing*
    *"Our lasses bound,*
    *"In festal round,*
    *"The frolic joy enhancing,*
65             *Its Beverley &c —*

SC 178

3<sup>d</sup>

"*Should noble sports incite you*
"*The jovial chase invite you*
"*The Driffield Bards*
70 "*With Song and cards*
"*Will after chase requite you.*
                              *Its Beverley &c*

4<sup>th</sup>

"*Our grave Dons muse and ponder*
75 "*Take Snuff, read news and wonder*
"*And then dear souls —*
"*They play at Bowls*
"*Like Jove with all his Thunder*
                              *Its Beverley &c*

80 5<sup>th</sup>

"*The Dames of ancient Story*
"*In wisdom placed their glory*
"*Divine Quadrille*
"*Spadille manille*
85 "*Here banish all before you.*
                              *Its Beverley &c*

6<sup>th</sup>

"*If woman's wit can kill you*
"*With Sappho's numbers chill you*
90 "*But they were nought*
"*In tongue or thought*
"*To Lady Elizabeth Bielby.*
                              *Its Beverley &.*

7<sup>th</sup>

95 "*Newmarket boasts its ponies*
"*Thatch house macaroni's,*

[ 947 ]

SC 178
> *" But Thursday's Club*
> *" Would tightly drub*
> *" Such addle pated honies*

100
> *" It's Beverley &c*

> *8ᵗʰ —*

> *" But secrets to unlock it*
> *" Avoid my friend the mocket*
> *" Or else his grace*

105
> *" With every ace*
> *" Will jump into your pocket.*
> *" It's Beverley &.*

> *9ᵗʰ*

> *" Let Jacomb toast piano*

110
> *" Or squall Italiano*
> *" It would make one huff*
> *" To hear such stuff*
> *" Poor soul he's mad 'tis plaino.*
> *" It's Beverley &.*

SC 179   MARY WOLLSTONECRAFT TO JANE ARDEN, ?MAY 20–JUNE 3, 1773

L (transcript) and copy of poem by "Dʳ Drake," 3 pages, pages [9, 11, 13, 15] of COPYBOOK* containing also SC 178 and SC 180–SC 192.

*See SC 178, Bibliographical Description.

> *Dear Miss Arden/*
>            *As I think ingratitude worse than impertinence I take this*
> *opportunity to thank you for your agreeable letter, and likewise for your*
> *verses on the death of H. Bethell Esq. but you forgot part of your promise*
> 5 *which was to tell me who wrote them. —     The most adequate return I can*
> *make, is to send Dʳ Drake's Satire on " Sweet Beverley"; the Chorus same*
> *as the other.*

SC 179

*1.*

10
> *" Attend thou great mockpoet*
> *" Thy verses plainly shew it*
> *" While in metres rough as thine*
> *" I describe each hobbling line*
> *" That all the world may know it*
> > > *It's Beverley &c*

15
*2.*

> *" Slow hand and bold the duty*
> *" To sing of Dolly's beauty*
> *" When such folly and nonsense —*
> *" Cannot claim the least pretence*
20
> *" To the shadow of her shoe.*
> > > *It's Beverley &c*

*3.*

> *" Thy Sappho and thy Lyric*
> *" Disgrace all panegyric*
25
> *" For wit as thick as Tripes*
> *" It would give a man the gripes*
> *" And make the maids hysteric.*
> > > *It's Beverley &c*

*4.*

30
> *" Such rhymes so rough and teazing*
> *" As sour as Crabs when squeezing*
> *" Like Cleavers on Marrow bones —*
> *" Or rattling of millstones*
> *" Or cart Wheels that want greasing.*
35
> > > *It's Beverley &c*

*5.*

> *" At whist would you pick his pocket*
> *" His grace would sneer and mock it*

SC 179

*"For thy verses are as stale*

40 *"As the dregs of muddy ale*

*"Or candle end when in the Socket*

　　　　　　　　　　　*It's Beverley &c*

### 6.

*"At bowls on the green when bowling*

45 *"It's more music than thy squalling*

*"For thy singing and thy rhymes*

*"Are worse a thousand times —*

*"Than Cats, when catterwauling*

　　　　　　　　　　*"It's Beverley &c*

50 ### 7.

*"Then stick to thy fate piano*

*"And scream Italiano*

*"Such a Song is out of Season*

*"That has neither Rhyme nor reason*

55 *"Nor of mirth or sense one grain. —*

　　　　　　　　　　*"Its Beverley &c*

*It is so long since I wrote the first part of this letter that I don't know how to apologize for my negligence, but by being a more regular correspondent for the future. —　My Papa informs me that Miss R—　is gone to York*

60 *to day: —　I wish her an agreeable journey – For my part all animosities have ceased, but I was resolved not to make the first concession. —　I hope my not writing sooner, will not prevent your answering it when conven-ient; —　I should indeed then be punished for my neglect.　I have just glanced over this letter and find it so ill written that I fear you cannot make*

65 *out one line of this last page, but — you know, my dear, I have not the advantage of a Master as you have, and it is with great difficulty to get my brother to mend my pens: — I am at present in a dilemna, for I have not one pen that will make a stroke, but however I will try to sign myself*

　　　　　*Yours sincerely*

70 　　　　　*Mary WollstoneCraft*

SC 179 *P.S. I intend going to see the Macaroni if it be performed, and expect a great deal of pleasure*

*M.W.*

SC 180 MARY WOLLSTONECRAFT TO JANE ARDEN, ?JUNE 4–?JULY 31, 1773

L (transcript) and copy of poem by "Mᴿ Rudd," 5 pages, pages [15, 17, 19, 21, 23, 25] of COPYBOOK* containing also SC 178, SC 179, and SC 181–SC 192.

*See SC 178, Bibliographical Description.

*I have just read your account of the oddest mortal that ever existed, and can't help approving of Miss C — 's choice, as the contrast will be very entertaining, — her over-giddiness, and his over-graveness must be superlatively ridiculous; — in short you must allow me to*
5 *laugh. — I cannot help observing there is not that sympathy of which the poets speak, but you could not more oblige me than your description of Miss C— and her lover (lovers you know we are to call them) as it is my greatest pleasure to read odd characters; — – her dutifulness too I admire, to parents whose indulgence she has so long experienced; — I cannot*
10 *help pitying you; a girl of your delicacy must be disgusted with such nonsense; — you may give my compliments to her and inform her that I will go to Hull myself, and set my cap at him, but upon second thoughts the object is too despicable. — I shall inclose you a Copy of Verses which Mᴿ Rudd has made on the Beverley beauties — — I lament, —*
15 *I am sorry I am not older to have had my name inscribed in such divine poetry. —*

*I think I have answered all the parts of your letter, except your not dancing with the macaroni at the Concert. — I was in hopes you had left the prude at Beverley by the first part of your letter, but the latter reminds*
20 *me that you will mend in time. — I have no Beverley news, but that Miss N— s are in mourning for an uncle who has left them a great fortune; — report says that it is £300 a year between them, and a woman of any œconomy may live very genteelly on £150 a year, but report generally adds. —*

*Wollstonecraft to Arden*                    *?June 4–?July 31, 1773*

SC 180    *We had a very agreeable afternoon at M*ʳˢ *C— 's on Monday; —*
*all the world was there, but there was a want: — I could have been far*
*happier with two persons I could name; — don't be jealous, — the other*
*is not a lady, but more of that by and by. — I won't flatter you so much*
*as to inform you how severely I feel your absence, and beg as you love your*
30    *affectionate friend to return to Beverley as soon as possible. — I beg*
*you will write again. — I am afraid you cannot read this as all the*
*children are plaguing me.*

Your's sincerely
Mary Wollstonecraft

---

35                    *Verses on the Beverley Beauties.*

*"Ye tuneful nine and all Apollo's choir,*
*"With daring thoughts as suppliant bards inspire,*
*"Nor arms, nor arts employ your Votary's care*
*"His sole ambition's to oblige the fair*
40    *"To paint their virtues with the pen of truth*
*"The rare the best attendant upon youth.*
*"To shew their foibles in their truest light,*
*"Not swayed by prejudice, or Hellborn spite;*
*"What blooming nymph shall first adorn the lay,*
45    *"All knowing muse, divine Thalia say; ——*
*"Amongst the foremost be fair Champion placed*
*"Champion with sense, with every virtue graced;*
*"A form complete in each minutest part,*
*"A mind enlarged with every useful art;*
50    *"From ~~pride~~ all her sexes faults entirely free,*
*"From pride, ill nature, and coquetry;*
*"In Ward a second Champion we find*
*"A graceful person and a gen'rous mind*
*"In temper and in form tis rare to see*
55    *"Such perfect union and such Symmetry.*

[ 952 ]

SC 180
  " *To these a contrast, we will now produce*
  " *The hints perhaps may be of general use;*
  " *How lovely, how serene did Eve appear*
  " *Till that arch fiend the rebel power drew near*

60  " *Till then her mind ne'er knew th'effects of pride*
  " *E'er she had known, happy had she died;*
  " *A truly noble form in Webb is seen —*
  " *Such as might rival e'en the Cyprian queen,*
  " *But shall there dwell in such a form as this,*

65  " *Which seems externally the seat of bliss,*
  " *That fell destroyer —  Pride?*
  " *Beauty alas, a few short years will stay*
  " *And e'er you know its value fly away;*
  " *A proper pride's what all the sex should wear*

70  " *The badge and ornament of british fair; —*
  " *This guards their virtue from each rude assault*
        *horror at*
  " *Inspires their minds with<sub>∧</sub>each fault:*
  " *But self conceit, ill manners sure disgrace*

75  " *The finest person and the fairest face.*
  " *The growing charms of Helen next rehearse*
  " *Which well deserve the tribute of a verse,*
  " *But oh! fair nymph, your sister's pride avoid*
  " *That pride by which each virtue is destroyed*

80  " *Nature and sense in fairest Smelt you see*
  " *With virtue graced, from every foible free:*
  " *Her sister too, with blooming charms appears*
  " *Each charm encreasing with encreasing years;*
  " *Oh! happy parents of this lovely pair,*

85  " *Still happier he, decreed their love to share; —*
  " *My muse to Clubley now must take its flight*
  " *And paint each beauty in its proper light;*
  " *Happy the man, who shares her mutual love,*
  " *His time one series of true joy will prove;*

[ 953 ]

SC 180  *"Formed to delight she captivates each eye,*

           wish to
*"If scorned by her, the wretch must~~surely~~die!*
*"Graceful in form, see lovely Acklom move*
*"Attracting nymph, her look commanding love;*

95  *"Truth makes me speak, alas! I do't with pain*
*"Formed to delight, Oh! not to heal a swain: ——*
*"Sweet Stanhope last, not least in love,*
*"In temper gentle as the Turtle Dove;*
*"In beauty too no second part she bears,*

100  *"In every pleasing form she amply shares.*
*"Excuse ye fair ones this too faint essay,*
*"By truth attended, I've pursued my way.*
*"Beauties like powerful princes from their youth*
*"Are often strangers to the voice of truth;*

105  *"Some praise is his who dares to be sincere*
*"And wisdom their's who lend a candid ear."*

SC 181 MARY WOLLSTONECRAFT TO JANE ARDEN, ?JUNE 4, 1773–NOVEMBER 16, 1774

L (transcript), 1 page, pages [25, 27] of COPYBOOK* containing also SC 178–SC 180 and SC 182–SC 192.

*See SC 178, Bibliographical Description.

*Miss A. —  Your behaviour at Miss J— 's hurt me extremely, and your not answering my letter shews that you set little value on my friendship. — If you had sent to ask me, I should have gone to the play, but none of you seemed to want my company. — I have two favors to*

5 *beg, the one is that you will send me all my letters; — the other that you will never mention some things which I have told you. To avoid idle tell-tale, we may visit ceremoniously, and to keep up appearances, may whisper, when we have nothing to say: — The beaux whisper insignificantly, and nod without meaning. — I beg you will take the trouble to bring the letters*

SC 181    *yourself, or give them to my sister Betsy. — You never called yesterday;*
*if you wish to be on the least friendly footing, you will call this morning. —*
*If you think it worth while, send an answer by my sister.*

*M.W.*

SC 182    MARY WOLLSTONECRAFT TO JANE ARDEN, ?JUNE 4, 1773–NOVEM-
BER 16, 1774

     L (transcript), 2½ pages, pages [27, 29, 31] of COPYBOOK* containing also
sc 178–sc 181 and sc 183–sc 192.

     *See SC 178, Bibliographical Description.

*Miss Arden. —*     *Before I begin I beg pardon for the freedom of my*
*style. — If I did not love you I should not write so; — I have a heart that*
*scorns disguise, and a countenance which will not dissemble: —   I have*
*formed romantic notions of friendship. — I have been once disappointed: —*
5    *I think if I am a second time I shall only want some infidelity in a love*
*affair, to qualify me for an old maid, as then I shall have no idea of either*
*of them. —    I am a little singular in my thoughts of love and friend-*
*ship;    I must have the first place or none. —    I own your behaviour*
*is more according to the opinion of the world, but I would break such narrow*
10   *bounds. —    I will give you my reasons for what I say; — since Miss C—*
*has been here you have behaved in the coolest manner. — I once hoped our*
*friendship was built on a permanent foundation: — We have all our fail-*
*ings — I have more than usual, but I thought you might mildly have cor-*
*rected me as I always loved you with true sisterly affection. If I had found*
15   *any faults I should have told you but a lady possessed of so many accom-*
*plishments as Miss A—   cannot want for admirers, and who has so many*
*friends cannot find any loss in your humble Servant. —    I would not have*
*seen it, but your behaviour the other night I cannot pass over; — when I*
*spoke of sitting with you at Church you made an objection, because I and*
20   *your sister quarrelled; — I did not think a little raillery would have been*
*taken in such a manner, or that you would have insinuated, that I dared to*
*have prophaned so sacred a place with idle chit-chat.*

*Wollstonecraft to Arden*                    *?June 4, 1773–November 16, 1774*

SC 182       *I once thought myself worthy of your friendship; — I thank you for*
*bringing me to a right sense of myself. —     When I have been at your*

25       *house with Miss J—   the greatest respect has been paid to her; every thing*
*handed to her first; – in short, as if she were a superior being. — Your*
*Mama too behaved with more politeness to her.*

*I am much obliged to your Papa and Mama and desire you will give*
*them my complimentary thanks, and as I have spent many happy hours in*

30       *your company, shall always have the sincerest esteem for Miss A. — . —*
*There is no accounting for the imbecillity of human nature — I might*
*misconstrue your behaviour, but what I have written flows spontaneously*
*from my pen and this I am sure, I only desire to be done by as I do; — I*
*shall expect a written answer to this, —*

35                                    *and am yours*
                                    *M. W.*

*Don't tell C—     to you I have told all my failings; — I would not be*
*so mean as to shew only the bright side of the picture; — I have reason to*
*think you have not been so ingenuous to me. —     I cannot bear the reflec-*

40       *tion that when Miss R — comes I should have less of your company. —*
*After seeing you yesterday, I thought not to have sent this — (but you desire*
*it) for to see you and be angry, is not in my power. — I long for a walk in*
*my darling Westwood. Adieu.*
                    *Mary Wollstonecraft.*

SC 183    MARY WOLLSTONECRAFT TO JANE ARDEN, ?JUNE 4, 1773–NOVEM-
BER 16, 1774

L (transcript), 2¾ pages, pages [31, 33, 35, 37] of COPYBOOK* containing also
SC 178–SC 182 and SC 184–SC 192.

*See SC 178, Bibliographical Description.

*Dear Jenny/*
*I have read some where that vulgar minds will never own*
*they are in the wrong: — I am determined to be above such a prejudice, and*
*give the lie to the poet who says —*

**Wollstonecraft to Arden**          *?June 4, 1773–November 16, 1774*

SC 183          *"Forgiveness to the injured does belong*
*"But they ne'er pardon, who have done the wrong"*

*and hope my ingenuously owning myself partly in fault to a girl of your*
*good nature will cancel the offence —— I have a heart too susceptible for*
*my own peace: — Till Miss C — came, I had very little of my own;*
10   *I constantly felt for others; —*

*"I gave to misery all I had, a tear,*
*"I gained from heaven, "twas all I wished, a friend."*

*Love and Jealousy are twins. — I would allow Miss R — the first*
*place, but I could not bear the thought of C —— s rivalling me in your love.*
15   *As to the affair at Miss J —'s I am certain I can clear myself from*
*the imputation. — I spent part of the night in tears; (I would not meanly*
*make a merit of it.) — I have not time to write fully on the subject, but this*
*I am sure of, if I did not love you ~~so well~~, I should not be angry. — I cannot*
*bear a slight from those I love, . . — I mean no reflection on your Papa, I*
20   *shall always think myself under an obligation for his politeness to me. —*
*I should have called this morning but for a hint in your letter which made me*
*think you have told your Mama and sisters. — I shall take it as a*
*particular favor if you will call this morning, and be assured that however*
*more deserving Miss R — may be of your favor, she cannot love you better*
25   *than your humble Servant*
*Mary Wollstonecraft*
*P.S. I keep your letters as a Memorial that you once loved me, but it will be*
*of no consequence to keep mine as you have no regard for the writer. —*
*There is some part of your letter so cutting, I cannot comment upon it. —*
30   *I beg you will write another letter on this subject. — Pray send me word by*
*your sister, if you will call this morning. — I inclose the Essay upon*
*friendship which your Papa lent me the other day.*
*I have copied it for it is beautiful: Many thanks for it. — Friendship*
*founded upon virtue Truth and love; — it sweetens the cares, lessens the*
35   *sorrows, and adds to the joys of life. — It corrects our foibles and errors,*
*refines the pleasures of sense and improves the faculties of the mind. —*

[ 957 ]

SC 183   *It is adapted to all the various changes and exigencies of life, and by a kind of sympathy flowing from mutual sincerity, it bears a part of pain or pleasure as different events affect the mind. — Its pleasures are permanent and*
40   *increase by reflection, so that a view of the past adds to the enjoyment of the present, opening to the mind the prospect of endless bliss. —     Such was the friendship, intended by providence to adorn the most solemn sacred union, displaying itself in all the offices of true affection and esteem. — Happy beyond expression is that pair who are thus united; how rational are*
45   *their pleasures, how solid their joys, how certain their hopes: — dispositions so excellent are guardian angels to each other, and in a finite degree resemble the harmony above.*


SC 184   MARY WOLLSTONECRAFT TO JANE ARDEN, NOVEMBER 16, 1774

N (transcript), third person, and copy of letter from "Dʳ Clegg," 1¾ pages, pages [37, 39, 41] of COPYBOOK* containing also SC 178–SC 183 and SC 185–SC 192.

*See SC 178, Bibliographical Description.

*Miss Wollstonecraft presents her compliments to Miss J– A.— the book which she would recommend to her particular notice is the Citizen of the World, or letters from a Chinese Philosopher residing in London to to his friends in the East. ——*
5   *From my opinion of the Delicacy of your sentiments I am͜ sure̵ it* (certain)
*will meet with your approbation. — Pray tell the worthy Philosopher, the next time he is so obliging as to give me a lesson on the globes, I hope I shall convince him I am quicker than his daughter at finding out a puzzle, tho'*
10   *I can't equal her at solving a problem. —     I inclose it with my thanks.*
*Wednesday noon. Nov. 16ᵗʰ 1774.*

---

*Copy of a letter from Dʳ Clegg to Dʳ Lathan.*

---

*I know you are pleased with any thing curious and uncommon in nature, and if what follows shall appear such, I can assure you, from eye*
15   *witnesses, of the truth of every particular. —*

SC 184    *In a Church at about three miles distance from us, the indecent custom still prevails of burying the dead in the place set apart for the devotion of the living, yet the parish not being very populous, one would scarcely imagine the inhabitants of the grave could be straitened for room, yet it sho<sup>d</sup>*

20    *seem so, for on the last of August several hundred bodies, rose out of the grave in the open day in that Church, to the great astonishment and terror of several spectators; — they deserted the Coffin, and arising out of the grave immediately ascended towards heaven, singing in concert all along, as they mounted through the air: — They had no winding-sheets about them,*

25    *yet did not appear quite naked: — their vesture seemed streaked with gold interlaced with sable, skirted with white, yet thought to be exceedingly light; — by the agility of their motion and the swiftness of their ascent they left a most fragrant and delicious odour behind them, but were quickly out of sight, and*

30    *what is become of them, or in what distant region of this<sub>∧</sub>*<sup>vast</sup>*system, they have fixed their residence, no mortal can tell. —*

*I. B.*

### BATH, 1778–?1779

THE second series of the letters to Jane Arden begins with sc 185, the first of four letters written from Bath, following which come two from Windsor and two from Walham Green. Those from Bath and Windsor were written while Mary was companion to Mrs. Dawson. As with the Beverley letters (except for the third-person note) they are undated and the first task is to give them at least approximate dates. This, fortunately, it is possible to do.

Godwin, as we have noted, informs us that Mary Wollstonecraft entered the service of Mrs. Dawson in 1778 when she was nineteen years of age. As Godwin was usually precise about such matters, this probably means that she did not enter that service until after her nineteenth birthday, which was on April 27, 1778. "With Mrs. Dawson," Godwin continues, "she continued to reside for two years, and only left her, summoned by the melancholy circumstance of her mother's rapidly

# The Carl H. Pforzheimer Library

declining health."[1] She left Mrs. Dawson, then, in 1780. Thus the general period of the Bath and Windsor letters is 1778–1780.

To this let us add the evidence from the Bath letters themselves, leaving the Windsor ones until later. The third letter is undated in our copybook but it is the one for which the original exists among the Abinger Manuscripts. This original is dated "Oct[r] 17[th]." Is this October 17, 1778, or 1779? By working forward to this letter from the first two we can determine that it must have been 1778. In the first letter (sc 185) Mary states that she has been in Bath for two months (line 2). Then comes a second letter, which, as its contents show, followed closely on the first. Then came a reply from Jane. This reply, Mary informs us in the third letter (sc 187, line 4), arrived just as she was leaving Bath to spend the "summer" at Southampton, and she is now replying to it a few months later: "I put off writing till I returned to Bath." The three letters, therefore, follow in sequence, and as we know that Mary arrived in Bath in 1778, the date on the third one must be October 17, 1778, and the first two must come just before the "summer" of the same year, say, May to June. And this fits in with Godwin's comments.

Let us now consider the four letters from Bath (sc 185–sc 188) as a unit.

When Mary went to Bath in 1778 the town was in the height of its glory, its great hotels, squares, and assembly rooms crowded with the elite of British society. Mary's excitement must have been similar to that of Fanny Burney on arriving at Bath some two years later:

I shall now skip to our arrival at this beautiful city which I really admire more than I did, if possible, when I first saw it. The houses are so elegant, the streets are so beautiful, the prospects so enchanting. I could fill whole pages upon the general beauty of the place and country . . . Tuesday morning we spent in walking all over the town, viewing the beautiful Circus, the company-crowded Pump-room, and the exquisite Crescent, which, to all the excellence of architecture that adorns the Circus, adds all the delights of nature that beautify the Parades.[2]

Among the society ladies who flocked to Bath for "the season" was "Mrs. Dawson." So far "Mrs. Dawson" has not been identified;

1. Godwin, *Memoirs*, p. 26.
2. Diary entries, April 7 and 9, 1780, *Diary and Letters of Madame D'Arblay* (London, 1842), I, 304, 307.

# Shelley and his Circle : Manuscripts

sc 185, however, enables us to do so. Jane Arden is requested (line 17) to write to Mary at "W<sup>m</sup> Dawson's Esq. Milson Street, Bath." If we put this together with Godwin's information that Mrs. Dawson was a widow with "one son already adult," it appears that the name and address are those of this son. Turning now in *Burke's Landed Gentry* to "Dawson of Langcliffe Hall" and running our eye down the entries we find a William Dawson "of London and Bath, merchant, bapt. 3 June, 1723" who married Sarah Regis, daughter of Balthasar Regis, Canon of Windsor, and had a son also called William of "St. Leonard's Hill, Windsor, and Settle, York." When Mr. Dawson died is not recorded but Mrs. Dawson died in 1812. When we combine this information with the fact that Mrs. Dawson had a house in Windsor (sc 190, line 2), and that Godwin referred to Mr. Dawson as "an opulent tradesman of the city of London,"[3] there can be no doubt that this is the Mrs. Dawson whose companion Mary was.

Throughout these letters there are references to "franks." In sc 185, for example, Mary notes that Jane's sister is sending Mary's letter to her "in a frank." The Ardens, then, must have had a supply of franked address sheets.[4] The laws on franking were so lax and the abuses of the privilege so widespread at the time — more than half the mail in England was franked in the mid-eighteenth century[5] — that the frank could have come from any Member of Parliament to whom the Ardens were known or related.

The reference (sc 185, line 9) to Jane's being so well and agreeably situated refers to her position with the family of Sir Mortdant Martin in Norfolk.

In the second letter in the Bath sequence (sc 186) Mary gives a running commentary on her life since she left Beverley. She speaks first of the sojourn in Wales (line 30) and then of the return to the London area (line 32), to the village of Walworth. She then comes back to the

---

3. Godwin, *Memoirs* (Durant ed.), p. 22.

4. The original of sc 187 among the Abinger Manuscripts bears an address on its address page (page 4) but no postmarks. As it went from Bath to Burnham in Norfolk it can hardly have gone by private messenger. It must, therefore, have gone inside an address sheet which was postmarked and presumably franked.

5. Robinson, *British Post Office*, p. 116.

# The Carl H. Pforzheimer Library

period immediately before the removal to Wales, when the family was at Hoxton. The "Clergyman and his lady" (line 48) whom she met there and who tried to "cultivate my understanding" were the Clares; and the dear friend (line 53) whom she met at their house was Fanny Blood: "I could dwell for ever on her praises."[6] Mary then returns to the present, her father's house "near Town" (line 66), her sisters "at School at Chelsea,"[7] and her brother Edward "married some time."

It would seem from this letter that Mr. Wollstonecraft's economic "misconduct" and "ungovernable temper" (lines 44 and 33) — both to grow in the following years — had been a matter of gossip even at Beverley (line 26). We might note, too, in view of Mary's later concern with family "money matters,"[8] that she had given up her inheritance voluntarily in order to help her father (line 45).

The third letter (sc 187) tells of her summer at Southampton, where (line 10) she bathed in the sea on the advice of "one of the faculty" (i.e., the medical profession). She praises Mrs. Dawson (line 40) for her "good understanding." This gives a better impression of her than does Godwin's picture — "a woman of great peculiarity of temper" who had had "a variety of companions in succession"[9] — but it is clear that Mary felt her subordinate status "among Strangers" (sc 188, line 12) keenly. How keenly she later showed in *Thoughts on the Education of Daughters*, in the chapter titled "Unfortunate Situation of Females, Fashionably Educated, and Left Without a Fortune":

Few are the modes of earning a subsistence, and those very humiliating. Perhaps to be an humble companion to some rich old cousin, or what is still worse, to live with strangers, who are so intolerably tyrannical, that none of their own relations can bear to live with them, though they should even expect a fortune in reversion. It is impossible to enumerate the many hours of anguish such a person must spend. Above the servants, yet considered by them as a spy, and ever reminded of her inferiority when in conversation with the superiors. If she cannot condescend to mean flattery, she has not a chance of being a favorite;

---

6. See above, Volume I, "Mary Wollstonecraft," pp. 41–42.

7. Chelsea, according to Wheatley's *London* (I, 376), was "famous . . . for its Ladies Boarding Schools, for which it rivalled Hackney at the other end of London."

8. See above, Volume I, sc 5, Commentary, pp. 86–87.

9. Godwin, *Memoirs*, p. 25.

and should any of the visitors take notice of her, and she for a moment forget her subordinate state, she is sure to be reminded of it.

Painfully sensible of unkindness, she is alive to every thing, and many sarcasms reach her, which were perhaps directed another way. She is alone, shut out from equality and confidence, and the concealed anxiety impairs her constitution; for she must wear a cheerful face, or be dismissed. The being dependant on the caprice of a fellow-creature, though certainly very necessary in this state of discipline, is yet a very bitter corrective, which we would fain shrink from.[10]

We might note one point in the Collation of this third letter (sc 187) with the original manuscript. In line 21 Mary wrote "a very agreeable summer, S——n is a very pleasant place." The copyist has erased something following "summer," left a space, and then filled in "Southampton." The copyist evidently at first went mechanically ahead and began "S——n," then perceived that this meant Southampton, went back, erased the "S——n," and put in "Southampton." The interesting fact to be gathered from this procedure is that the copyist must have been working directly from the original manuscript.

The date of this third letter, as we have noted, is October 17, 1778. The fourth and final letter from Bath (sc 188) was evidently written about Christmas, for Mary (line 34) wishes Jane the "compliments of the season." We might date it, then, between about December 20, 1778, and January 5, 1779. Mary is unhappy at Bath — "a piece of still life" (line 25) — seldom going out to the assembly or ballrooms (line 24). She hopes to be able to leave sometime (line 19), but expects to stay there at least until spring (line 40).

10. *Thoughts on the Education of Daughters* (London, 1787), pp. 69–71.

SC 185   MARY WOLLSTONECRAFT TO JANE ARDEN, ?MAY–?JUNE 1778

L (transcript), 1 page, pages [41, 43] of COPYBOOK* containing also sc 178–sc 184 and sc 186–sc 192.

*See sc 178, Bibliographical Description.

*You will, my dear girl, be as much surprised at receiving a letter from me, as I was at hearing, that your family resided at Bath; — I have been at this place two months yet chance never threw your sisters in my way —*

*Wollstonecraft to Arden*                                        *?May–?June* **1778**

SC 185    *and if I had not by accident been informed of your father's giving lectures,*
    5    *I might never have met with them. ——*

      *As soon as I could enquire out their habitation I seized the first oppor-*
*tunity of paying my compliments to them: — my principal reason for so*
*doing, was the hopes of seeing you, tho' I rather wished than expected that*
*pleasure. —    I was happy however to hear that you were well and agree-*
   10    *ably situated. —    I often recollect with pleasure the many agreeable days*
*we spent together when we eagerly told every girlish secret of our hearts*
*—    Those were peaceful days; — your's since that period may have been as*
*tranquil, but mine have been far otherwise. — Your sister obligingly offered*
*to send you this in a frank; — and I write it by way of a prelude to a*
   15    *correspondence. ——*

      *I would not have you send your answer to this under cover to your own*
*family, but direct to me at W^m Dawson's Esq. Milson Street, Bath. —*

      *It would be needless again to say that a letter from you, will give*
*sincere pleasure to*

   20                *Your affectionate friend*
                      *Mary Wollstonecraft*


SC 186    MARY WOLLSTONECRAFT TO JANE ARDEN, ?MAY–?JUNE 1778

L (transcript), 5¼ pages, pages [43, 45, 47, 49, 51, 53] of COPYBOOK* containing
also SC 178–SC 185 and SC 187–SC 192

*See SC 178, Bibliographical Description.

      *I am happy, my dear girl, to find by your letter that you are so agreeably*
*situated; – your mild and amiable temper will always command the love*
*and esteem of those who have the happiness of being well acquainted with you,*
*and I am glad to hear that the family you are with, are of a kind to set a*
    5    *value on merit, for generally speaking to deserve and gain esteem, are two*
*very different things. —    I hinted to you in my last that I had not been*
*very happy — indeed, I have been far otherwise: — Pain and disappoint-*
*ment have constantly attended me since I left Beverley. I do not however*
*repine at the dispensations of Providence, for my philosophy, as well as my*

## Wollstonecraft to Arden          ?May–?June 1778

SC 186    *religion will ever teach me to look on misfortunes as blessings, which like a*
*bitter potion is disagreeable to the palate tho' 'tis grateful to the Stomach—*
— *I hope mine have not been thrown away on me, but that I am both the*
*wiser, and better for them. — Tho' I talk so philosophically now, yet I must*
*own, when under the pressure of afflictions, I did not think so rationally; my*

15    *feelings were then too acute, and it was not 'till the Storm was in some*
*measure blown over, that I could acknowledge the justness of it: —*
*Young people generally set out with romantic and sanguine hopes of happi-*
*ness, and must receive a great many stings before they are convinced of*
*their mistake, and that they are pursuing a mere phantom; an empty*

20    *name. — I think I have said enough by way of Preface to an account of*
*myself , tho' I do not intend to be very particular, as the less that is said on a*
*disagreeable subject the better —*

     *It is almost needless to tell you that my father's violent temper and*
*extravagant turn of mind, was the principal cause of my unhappiness and*

25    *that of the rest of the family. —*

     *The good folks of Beverley (like those of most Country towns) were very*
*ready to find out their Neighbours' faults, and to animadvert on them;*
*— Many people did not scruple to prognosticate the ruin of the whole family,*
*and the way he went on, justified them for so doing: — a pretended scheme*

30    *of œconomy induced my father to take us all into Wales, — a most expensive*
*and troublesome journey that answered no one good end. — Business or*
*pleasure took him often to London, and at last obliged him once more to fix*
*there. — I will not say much of his ungovernable temper, tho' that has*
*been the source of much* ~~*uneasiness*~~ *misery to me; — his passions were*

35    *seldom directed at me, yet I suffered more than any of them — my spirits*
*were weak — in short, a lingering sickness was the consequence of it, and*
*if my constitution had not been very strong, I must have fallen a sacrifice long*
*before this. — as it is, my health is ruined, my spirits broken, and I have a*
*constant pain in my side that is daily gaining ground on me: — My head*

40    *aches with holding it down, I wrote a long letter before I* <sub>began to</sub> *write to you:*
*— I am tired so good night.*

     *12ᵗʰ — I resume my pen and subject; I have only to add that my*

# The Carl H. Pforzheimer Library

## *Wollstonecraft to Arden* ?May– ?June **1778**

SC 186

45 *father's affairs were so embarrassed by his misconduct that he was obliged to take the fortune that was settled on us children; I very readily gave up my part; I have therefore nothing to expect, and what is worse depend on a stranger. — I must not forget to tell you that I spent some time with a Clergyman and his lady — a very amiable Couple: — They took some pains to cultivate my understanding (which had been too much neglected) they not*

50 *only recommended proper books to me, but made me read to them; — I should have lived very happily with them if it had not been for my domestic troubles, and some other painful circumstances, that I wish to bury in oblivion. —*

*At their house too, I enjoyed the society of a friend, whom I love better than all the world beside, a friend to whom I am bound by every tie of gratitude*

55 *and inclination: To live with this friend is the height of my ambition, and indeed it is the most rational wish I could make, as her conversation is not more agreeable than entertaining improving.*

*I could dwell for ever on her praises, and you wo$^d$ not wonder at it, if you knew the many favors she has conferred on me, and the many valuable*

60 *qualifications she possesses: — She has a masculine understanding, and sound judgment, yet she has every feminine virtue; – she is now in a bad state of health, and if she should recover, we shall soon be far separated from each other, for she will I believe be obliged to reside in a neighbouring Kingdom: — Tho' this change may probably restore her health, yet I cannot*

65 *help grieving at it, as I shall then be deprived of my only comfort — My father has a house near Town, and I hope he will see his error, and act more prudently in future, and then my mother may enjoy some comfort.*

*— My sisters are at School at Chelsea; — they are both fine girls and*

70 *Elizabeth in particular is very handsome: — My eldest Brother has been married some time to a very agreeable woman, and is now a father. — Now I think of it, let me congratulate you on a circumstance that I know must have given you great pleasure, I mean your brother's marriage: — I sincerely wish him and his agreeable wife joy, and all the other customary good*

75 *wishes. — Your sisters are I think very much improved: Elizabeth is exceedingly so, and will I dare say do some execution at Beverley. — As a correspondence will be dull without some swain to talk of, pray tell me*

**Wollstonecraft to Arden**                              *October 17, 1778*

SC 186   *when you write, if you have met with an agreeable Norfolk Swain to help to*
*render the Country so delightful: — you had I am sure a little spice of*
80      *romance in your composition and must before this time have had a pre-*
        *in favor of*
*dilection, for some happy man; — tell me all about it, it will be kind in you,*
*as I want something to divert my mind — Joking apart — I should be glad to*
*hear that you had met with a sensible worthy man, tho' they are hard to be found*
85      *— — You never mention your old friend Miss R — — Send me some account*
*of her — — You see I am full of my enquiries, and as I would not wish to*
*confine you to one Sheet of paper, if you have a frank to M^r A — you may*
*inclose your answer to him or your sister, only desire her to keep it, till I*
*call for it. —     I have written a vast deal, and shall now only assure you*
90      *that my best wishes will ever attend you, and that I am yours affectionately*
                                             *Mary Wollstonecraft.*


SC 187   MARY WOLLSTONECRAFT TO JANE ARDEN, OCTOBER 17, 1778

L (transcript), 3¼ pages, pages [53, 55, 57, 59] of COPYBOOK* containing also
SC 178–SC 186 and SC 188–SC 192.

*See SC 178, Bibliographical Description.

*It is so long since I received your letter — that I am half ashamed to*
*acknowledge the receipt of it; — the only thing that I can say by way of excuse*
                                                     *of writing: —*
*is, that I was just going to Southampton, and had no opportunity, after*
5      *my arrival at that place, I had sufficient leisure, but as I had nothing of*
*consequence to say to you, I put off writing till I returned to Bath, that I*
*might not put you to the expence of postage. — So much by way of apology.——*
*As you kindly interest yourself about me I know it will give you pleasure*
*to hear that I have received great benefit from my summer excursion. I was*
10     *advised by one of the faculty to bathe in the Sea, and it has been of signal*
*service to me. —     As to the vivacity you talk of, 'tis gone for ever, and*
*all I wish for is a cheerful settled frame of mind, which I use all my*
*endeavours to attain, and hope in time I shall.*
*I never let imaginary troubles disturb me, indeed so many real ones have*
15     *occurred to harrass my mind and body, that it will require time to bring them*

[ 967 ]

SC 187  into tune again: — Tho I mention this I would not have you imagine that I
repine at what has befallen me. — Reason as well as religion convinces me
all has happened for the best — — This is an old worn-out maxim, but
it is not the less true for, I am persuaded misfortunes are of the greatest
20  service, as they set things in the light they ought to be viewed in and give
those who are tried by them a kind of early old age. —    I have spent a very
agreeable summer.    Southampton is a very pleasant place in every sense of
the word; — the situation is delightful, and the Inhabitants polite, and
hospitable: —    I received so much civility that I left it with regret. — I am
25  apt to get attached to places, and tho' backward & reserved in forming
friendships, yet I get sometimes so interested in the happiness of mere
acquaintances that it is the source of much pain to me. —
    I quite agree with you in admiring Bath: — It is a most delightful
                                                        in the manner
30  place, yet I imagine the prospects did not strike me ˄as they did you, and
I will tell you why I think so. — You came out of Yorkshire, and out of
a part not very beautiful, while on the contrary I had very lately visited
Wales, where nature appears in the most romantic dress; — tho' with respect
to its natural beauties, I think Bath much inferior, — yet as to the embellish-
35  ments of art they are not to be compared, for I think the buildings here, are
the most regular and elegant I have ever seen. — I cannot say that I sho^d
choose a large Town for my constant residence, if I was my own mistress,
as I am fond of the Country, but if I were obliged to fix in one, in point of
situation Bath would be as agreeable to me as any. — The family I am with
40  here is a very worthy one: — M^rs Dawson has a very good understanding,
and she has seen a great deal of the world; I hope to improve myself by her
conversation, and I endeavour to render a circumstance (which was at first
disagreeable) useful to me. —    Write to me soon and tell me you are
merry and well, and I then will laugh and sing: — the keen blast of adversity
45  has not frozen my heart, so far from it that I cannot be quite miserable, while
one of my fellow creatures enjoys some portion of content; — that your's
may not be a scanty share is the sincere wish of
                                        Your affectionate friend
                                        Mary Wollstonecraft.

**Wollstonecraft to Arden**                                    *October 17, 1778*

SC 187          *Pray send me some account of your old friend Miss R —— when you*
*write — make my compliments to her: —      I am so unwilling to bid you*
*adieu that I have written to the bottom of my paper tho' the watch has long*
*since informed me tis past twelve o'Clock.*

                                                                    *M.W.*

## COLLATION

AUTOGRAPH LETTER SIGNED MARY WOLLSTONECRAFT (ABINGER MANUSCRIPTS, PFORZHEIMER MICRO-
FILM, REEL IX).

Large "X" in top margin of letter; possibly
copyist's mark.

line 2. it. The
    excuse,

line 4. opportunity of writing. After

line 5. leisure;

line 6. return'd

line 8. me,

line 9. hear,

line 10. the Faculty
    the sea, and,

line 11. Has to
    of — 'tis
    ever —

line 12. for,
    chearful
    , which,

line 13. endeavors

line 14. me — indeed

line 16. again.
    this,

line 17. befalen me —

line 18. happen'd
    best. This
    maxim; but 'tis

line 19. true — for

line 20. view'd in;
    gives those that ᴀ$^{are}$

line 21. them,
    [¶] I have spent

line 22. summer, S——n
    place,

line 23. word —
    delightful; and,
    inhabitants

line 24. hospitable. I
    regret.

line 25. attach'd
    places —
    and reserved

line 26. , yet,
    ᴀ$^{the}$happiness

line 27. acquaintances,

line 28. I am quite agree
    Bath, it is

line 30. place — yet,
    me in the manner they did you. And

line 31. so:

line 32. beautiful:

line 33. Wales — where Nature
    dress ——

line 34. beauties I
    inferior, yet,

line 35. art,
    not be compared
    here are

line 36. seen.
    should chuse

line 37. town
    Mistress

line 38. country; but if I was obliged$_ᴧ$$^{to}$
    one —

line 39. any. [¶] The

line 40. one,
    Dawson —
    understanding —

line 41. has$_ᴧ$$^{seen}$
    World,

line 42. (that at first was disagreeable,)

*Wollstonecraft to Arden*       *?December 20, 1778–?January 5, 1779*

SC 187  line 43. me. [¶] Write
line 44. well —
    sing. — The
line 45. heart — so
    miserable while
line 46. fellow —— [ends line]
    -creatures [begins new line]
    content, that
line 48. Friend
line 49. Bath Oct$^r$ 17$^{th}$ [to left of signature]
line 50. Miss Rud [*sic*],

line 51. write make
    her. =
line 52. have wrote
    paper, tho
line 53. inform'd$_\wedge$ $^{me}$
    o'clock
[Address, page 4]
    Miss Arden
Sir Mordant Martin's bart.
Burnham
Norfock [*sic*]

SC 188  MARY WOLLSTONECRAFT TO JANE ARDEN, ?DECEMBER 20, 1778–
?JANUARY 5, 1779

L (transcript), 2½ pages, pages [59, 61, 63, 65] of COPYBOOK* containing also
SC 178–SC 187 and SC 189–SC 192.

*See SC 178, Bibliographical Description.

*I am happy, my dear girl, to hear from you and should sooner have
acknowledged the receipt of your friendly Epistle, if your sister had not told
me that her franks were out: — indeed she very obligingly offered to inclose a
note, if I could write by the next day; —    I accordingly did, but the weather*
5 *proved so unfavorable, that I was not able to take it to her; — — I am
exceedingly flattered by your kind remembrance of me ; and be assured it
will ever give me the sincerest pleasure to be informed of your welfare.
There is no prospect of my quitting this place in a hurry, necessity not
choice ties me to it, (not but that I feel receive the greatest civility from this*
10 *family) — yet, I am detained here only by prudential motives, if I was to
follow the bent of my inclination I sho$^d$ haste away. —    You will not
wonder at this, — when you consider I am among Strangers, far from all
my former connexions: — The more I see of the world, the more anxious I
am to preserve my old friends, for I am now slower than ever in forming*
15 *friendships; — I would wish to cherish a universal love to all mankind,
but the principal part of my heart must be occupied by those who have for
years had a place there.*

SC 188    *As I ever endeavour to be uniform and constant in my regards, it will*
          *not, I assure you be my fault, if our correspondence drops on my leaving*
     20   *Bath, for when that much wished for moment arrives, I shall take care to*
          *inform you how you may direct for me, so that it will remain with yourself*
          *whether you choose to continue it or not*
          *—— Bath is remarkably full at present, and nothing is going forward, but*
          *Balls & plays without end or number. — I seldom go into public; — I have*
     25   *been but twice at the rooms; — I am quite a piece of still life, not but that I*
          *am a friend to mirth and cheerfulness; but I would move in a small circle; —*
          *I am fond of domestic pleasures and have not spirit sufficient to bustle*
          *about. —*
          *— I wish I could write any thing that would entertain you, but I mix so*
     30   *little with the world, that I am at a loss for news, however I shall always be*
          *glad to hear about my old School-fellows and acquaintances at Beverley, and*
          *any account you occasionally send me will be very acceptable.*
          *— Pray send me the promised description of the family you are with, and*
          *let me hear from you soon. —     To the accustomary compliments of the*
     35   *Season, permit me to add my good wishes, and believe me to be*
                        *Your most affectionate friend,*
                        *Mary Wollstonecraft.*
          *P. S. — My compliments attend your Brother and Sister. — I am sorry for*
          *the Miss R ——s but I never had a perfect account of their misfortunes. —*
     40   *Tell me, is there any hope of your visiting Bath this spring, for I should*
          *not so much regret my being detained here, if I had any prospect of seeing*
          *you. — Once more adieu. —*

### WINDSOR, 1780

IT might at first seem that sc 189 was written at Bath but examination
indicates that it was written at Windsor. For instance, in the next
letter (sc 190), which was definitely written at Windsor, Mary implies
that she had written previously from Windsor (line 4). The comment
(sc 189, line 14) "this is the gayest of all gay places; — nothing but dress

# The Carl H. Pforzheimer Library

and amusements are going forward" is equally applicable to Windsor (seat of the royal family) as to Bath and is apparently echoed in the next letter, in which Windsor is described (line 9) as "too gay" a place where the people dress "amazingly" (line 18). Mary tells Jane that she is going to write to the sister who supplies the franks (line 51); this sister was at Bath and Mary while there had gone to her personally.[1]

In sc 188 Mary had expressed the hope that Jane might visit Bath "this spring." From the opening sentence of sc 189, with its reference to the friends' parting, we presumed that this hope had materialized. This speculation was confirmed by Mr. C. A. Arden's information that Jane took a position at Redlynch, Somerset, in 1780, for Redlynch is but 15 miles from Bath and Jane doubtless visited her parents from there. A further search through the *Bath Chronicle* turned up the following:

A New ACADEMY of FEMALE EDUCATION, CATHARINE–PLACE, BATH.

Miss Arden and Sisters intend to open a Boarding-School for Young Ladies on Monday the 9th of April, 1781; and respectfully offer their terms to those Ladies and Gentlemen who may be induced to entrust them with the care and education of their Daughters; and hope their united endeavours to discharge the duties of that important charge will meet with the countenance and support of their friends and the public.

Board; English, and French, by the rules of grammar; Writing, Arithmetic, and Needle-work, Twenty-five Guineas per year, and one guinea entrance. The Elements of Astronomy, Geography, use of the Globes and Maps, Four Guineas per year, and one guinea entrance.

This notice explains the implications in sc 189 (lines 28 and 36) that Jane and her sister were planning to open a school in Bath.

Since parting from Jane at Bath, Mary has had a week's visit with Fanny Blood at Walham Green (just south of London). One would gather that she went directly from Bath to London and then to Walham Green for she begins the theme abruptly, "I had a very pleasant journey to Town" ("Town," so used, normally referred to London) as though Jane knew all about it. Jane, in fact, may have seen her off at Bath. Mary then presumably went from Walham Green to Windsor.

There is no mention of Mrs. Dawson. Perhaps she and Mary went

1. See, for instance, sc 185, line 13, and sc 188, line 2.

# Shelley and his Circle : Manuscripts

from Bath to Windsor together and Mary continued on to London (the Bath-to-London coach passed through Windsor).

When, however, did Jane come to Bath, and when did Mary leave Bath for Windsor? Let us turn once more to Godwin's account: "With Mrs. Dawson she continued to reside for two years, and only left her, summoned by the melancholy circumstance of her mother's rapidly declining health."[2] Mary, as we have seen, probably did not enter Mrs. Dawson's employment until the spring or early summer of 1778. She must, then, have left Mrs. Dawson in the spring or summer of 1780. We know also that Mrs. Wollstonecraft died in 1780 but we do not know in what month. The sequence of events and letters, however, indicates that she died later rather than earlier in the year. In sc 191 Mary tells Jane of her mother's death; and the letter was evidently written not very long after that death.[3] A reference in it (line 9) to Jane's sister's writing to Mary "last year" places it in 1781, and the indication is that it was written within the first six months of that year. Another comment in it informs us that Mary had heard from Jane "some months ago" and at a time when she was still nursing her mother (line 2). The letter from Jane must have been a reply to sc 190. The indication is, then, that Mary left Windsor for Enfield[4] to nurse her mother shortly after writing sc 190.[5] As she evidently nursed her mother for several weeks or months, the mother's death probably took place in the last three or four months of 1780. And this places Mary's time of departure from Windsor in the summer or fall of that year. If we are to assume that Godwin's span of "two years" is not too stretchable, the summer seems more likely than the fall. This, then, would indicate that sc 190 was written in the summer, say, June to August. And sc 189 was evidently written within a few weeks or months previously (sc 190,

---

2. Godwin, *Memoirs*, p. 26.       3. See, for instance, lines 7 and 13.

4. It has previously been assumed incorrectly that Mary went to Enfield from Bath. (Wardle, *Wollstonecraft*, p. 18.)

5. Godwin states that Mary was "summoned" to her mother's side; but in sc 190 (line 46) she states that she intends to visit her family "the latter end of this month," and it may be that on the occasion of this visit she found out how ill her mother was. In a letter to her sister from Windsor she inquires, with perhaps an undertone of anxiety, about her mother's health: "You don't say a word of my mother. I take it for granted she is well. . . ." (Wardle, *Wollstonecraft*, pp. 17–18.) Perhaps the family had kept the news from her.

# The Carl H. Pforzheimer Library

line 4), say, April to June. This general dating period for both letters receives some support also from Mary's comments in sc 189 (line 43) about her "pleasant" journey from Bath to London and her comments in sc 190 (line 7) on the pleasures of the countryside around Windsor. Mary, then, probably left Bath in the spring or early summer of 1780, and wrote to Jane shortly after she arrived at Windsor.

The gap in the correspondence between the last Bath letter in the Christmas season of 1778-1779 and the first Windsor letter in the spring or early summer of 1780 was doubtless due to Jane's presence in or near Bath.

In sc 189 Mary is in a gloomy mood (at least before "Noon" — line 43). Presumably some of this gloom was due to her recent parting with Fanny Blood, but some of it was also due to her continuing dissatisfaction with her position of companion. Even though she respected Mrs. Dawson's "understanding" and knowledge, she again indicates that she felt her inferior status very bitterly, and as at Bath, so, too, at Windsor she is retreating from social life into herself.

In the next letter (sc 190) Mary has cheered up considerably. She has the "whole" of Mrs. Dawson's house (perhaps formerly the canon's residence[6]) to herself as Mrs. Dawson is off somewhere visiting. She gives an interesting running commentary on life at Windsor. Her remarks (line 37) on the prince — then a somewhat younger "Adonis" and about a year away from his affair with "Perdita" — are done in a new and amusingly lively vein.

Mary's comments on her family (line 46) are expanded in an undated letter she wrote to her sister Elizabeth from Windsor: "You don't do me justice in supposing that I seldom think of you – the happiness of my family is nearer my heart than you imagine – perhaps too near for my own health or peace – For my anxiety preys on me, and is of no use to you."[7] The family had evidently already moved from Walworth to Enfield, for if they had still been at Walworth Mary could hardly have avoided visiting them when she was staying with Fanny Blood at nearby Walham Green.[8]

6. See above, p. 961. The canon, according to *The Gentleman's Magazine*, died in 1757.

7. Wardle, *Wollstonecraft*, p. 17.

8. The letter to Elizabeth from Windsor is addressed to Enfield. (*Ibid.*, p. 18.)

## *Wollstonecraft to Arden* *?April–?June* 1780

SC 189  MARY WOLLSTONECRAFT TO JANE ARDEN, ?APRIL–?JUNE 1780

L (transcript), 4 pages, pages [65, 67, 69, 71, 73] of COPYBOOK* containing also SC 178–SC 188 and SC 190–SC 192.

*See SC 178, Bibliographical Description.

> *Such a variety of things have taken up my attention since I parted with you, that I have not been able to write so soon as I intended.*
>
> *I cannot lay it all to the charge of my engagements, but I fear I have a kind of indolence growing upon me, that I must endeavour to shake off. —*
> 5 *Ceremony you know has long been banished from our correspondence, I shall not therefore multiply apologies, but in a few words assure you, that I have your interest very much at heart, and among the small number of friends in whose memory I wish to live, you hold one of the first places. —    To say the truth, I am very indifferent to the opinion of the world in general; — I*
> 10 *wish to retire as much from it as possible — I am particularly sick of genteel life, as it is called; — the unmeaning civilities that I see every day practiced don't agree with my temper; — I long for a little sincerity, and look forward with pleasure to the time when I shall lay aside all restraint. —*
> *This is the gayest of all gay places; — nothing but dress and amuse-*
> 15 *ments are going forward; — I am only a spectator — I have lost all my relish for them: — early in life, before misfortune had broken my spirits, I had not the power of partaking of them, and now I am both from habit and inclination averse to them. — My wishes and expectations are very moderate. — I don't know which is the worst — to think too little or too much. —*
> 20 *'tis a difficult matter to draw the line, and keep clear of melancholy and thoughtlessness; — I really think it is best sometimes to be deceived — and to expect what we are never likely to meet with; — deluded by false hopes, the time would seem shorter, while we are hastening to a better world, where the follies and weaknesses that disturb us in this, will be no more: —    In*
> 25 *that abode of peace I hope to meet you, and there our early friendship will be perfected; —·    You'll think me in a very dull mood, but I am persuaded your goodnature will excuse what arises from ill health & lowness of spirits. —    Write me soon, my dearest girl, and tell me how your sister's school goes on. — I want to know, if you have heard of any eligible situation*

SC 189 *in the country, for I think you would be much more comfortable in a small Town, than as such a large one as Bath: — I have ever approved of your plan, and it would give me great pleasure to find that you and your sister could contrive to live together; — let not some small difficulties intimidate you, I beseech you; — struggle with any obstacles rather than go into a state*

35 *of dependance: — I speak feelingly. — I have felt the weight, and wo<sup>d</sup> have you by all means avoid it. — Your employm<sup>t</sup> tho a troublesome one, is very necessary, and you have an opportunity of doing much good, by instilling good principles into the good young and ignorant, and at the close of life you'll have the pleasure to think that you have not lived in vain, and, believe*

40 *me, this reflection is worth a life of care. —*

  *I must now go to breakfast, — when I return to finish this, I may have roused up more spirits. —*

*(Noon). — I had a very pleasant journey to Town the post Coach, is very convenient, and the passengers happened to be agreeable: — They consisted*

45 *of a Physician and his Son, whose character I was acquaint<sup>d</sup> with, and whose conversation was very rational & entertaining: — he has published several things that have been much approved of, and he has travelled thro' the old and new Continent. — We had likewise a civil young woman, — and altogether I should have been very well pleased, if my impatience to*

50 *reach London had not increased, as I draw nearer to it. — To my great satisfaction, I found Miss Blood in better health than I expected from the accounts I have had of her. — She received me as she ever has done in the most friendly manner, and we passed a comfortable week together, which knew no other alloy than what arose from the thoughts of parting so soon.*

55 *— The next time we meet, it will be for a longer continuance, and to that period I look, as to the most important one of my life: — this connexion must give the colour to my future days, for I have now given up every expectation and dependance that wo<sup>d</sup> interfere with my determination of spending my time with her. —  I know this resolution may appear a*

60 *little extraordinary, but in forming it I follow the dictates of reason as well as the bent of my inclination; for tho' I am willing to do what good I can in my generation, yet on many accounts I am averse to any matri-*

*Wollstonecraft to Arden*                    *?June–?August* **1780**

SC 189   *monial tie: — If ever you should venture may success attend you; — be*
*not too sanguine in your expectations, and you will have less reason to fear a*
65   *disappointment; — however it don't much signify what part in life we bear,*
*so as we act with propriety. —    Remember me in the kindest manner to*
*your sister, and tell her I would write to her, but I am not willing to put her to*
*the expence of postage: — when I get franks, I shall certainly do myself that*
*pleasure. — My paper admonishes me to bid you adieu, and let me assure*
70   *you that tho' you may not find the most regular correspondent, you may be*
*sure of the most constant friend in yours &ᶜ.*

*Mary Wollstonecraft.*

SC 190   MARY WOLLSTONECRAFT TO JANE ARDEN, ?JUNE–?AUGUST 1780

L (transcript), 4 pages, pages [73, 75, 77, 79, 81] of COPYBOOK* containing also
SC 178–SC 189 and SC 191 and SC 192.

*See SC 178, Bibliographical Description.

*Here I am, quite alone. —— Mʳˢ Dawson is gone to pay a visit, and*
*I have the whole house to range in. — I cannot now I have so much time put*
*off answering your last epistle which was truly welcome to me. —    I*
*indeed began to wonder at your silence, tho' I hardly deserved a speedy reply,*
5   *but you used me better than I merited, and I am determined to let you see*
*that I intend to be a regular correspondent. —*
*Windsor is a most del/ightful place; — the country about it is charming,*
*and I long to live in the forest every time we ride through it. — The only*
*fault I find is that it is too gay; — I should like a more retired situa-*
10   *tion. —    I go constantly to the Cathedral: — I am very fond of the Service.*
*— I have beside made some visits. — Mʳˢ Dawson has a sister who lives near*
*here; — she is a most pleasant and entertaining woman and behaves to me*
*in the politest manner. — She is rather too fond of dissipation and brings*
*up her daughters in a stile I dont approve of — that is, she seems to wish*
15   *rather to make them accomplished and fashionable than good and sensible,*
*in the true sense of the word: — In this she follows the crowd, and it is*

[ 977 ]

# The Carl H. Pforzheimer Library

SC 190 *much to be lamented, that the Stream runs so rapidly that way. —    You cannot imagine how amazingly they dress here; — It is the important business that takes up great part of the time of both old and young. — I believe*

20 *I am thought a very poor creature, but to dress violently neither suits my inclination, nor ~~power~~ purse. —    I told you before, I fancy, that the royal family reside almost constantly here: — The King is quite a domestic ~~character~~ man and it is pleasing to see him surrounded by his children: — he is a most affectionate father, but his love seems to be confined to a very*

25 *narrow circle, at least I am sure his humanity is: — to tell you the truth, he is out of favor with me, and you will not wonder at it when I inform you that he killed three horses the other day riding in a hurry to pay a visit; this has lost him my warm heart; — I cannot bear an unfeeling mortal: — Indeed I carry my notions on this subject a great way: — I think it murder to put an end to*

30 *any living thing unless it be necessary for food, or hurtful to us. — If it has pleased the beneficent creator of all to call them into being, we ought to let them enjoy the common blessings of nature, and I declare no thing gives me so much pleasure as to contribute to the happiness of the most insignificant creature: —    bound as my power of doing good is, I have sometimes saved*

35 *the life of a fly, and thought myself of consequence:*
*— I am running on in a romantic way —— to change the subject, let me tell you, that the Prince of Wales is the principal beau here; — all the damsels set their caps at him, and you would smile to hear how the poor girls he condescends to take notice of are pulled to pieces: — the withered old maids*

40 *sagaciously hint their fears, and kindly remark that they always thought them forward things: you would suppose a smile or a look of his had something fatal in it, and that a maid co$^d$ not look at him, and remain pure: — joking apart — you can have no idea of the commotion he throws the good ladies into; he certainly keeps both envy & vanity alive, — but enough of him. — I*

45 *beg your pardon for not mentioning my family, and thank you for remembering them; — they are all well, and I intend going to them the latter end of this month, and I shall spend as much time with them as I possibly can: — I dont like to think of parting, — it will be a severe trial, but I must submit to it. — We shall leave Windsor very soon and where we next bend our course,*

SC 190   *is not yet determined: — I shall not therefore expect to hear from you till*
*I write to your sister, and that I intend doing as soon as I am fixed to any*
*place for a time; —— Pray make my best compliments to her, or use a more*
*meaning phrase and assure her of my love and good wishes, — the same*
*awaits all your family — What shall I now say to you but that I am your*
55   *ever affectionate friend*

*Mary Wollstonecraft.*

    *I have put so much water in my ink, I am afraid you will not be able*
*to read my faint characters, and besides my candle gives such a dreadful*
*light. —    I am just going to sup <u>solus</u> on a bunch of grapes, and a bread*
60   *crust; — I'll drink your health in pure water. —    I take up my pen*
*again to tell you I have not for a long time been so well as I am at present. —*
*The roses will bloom when there's peace in the breast, and the prospect of*
*living with my ffanny gladdens my heart: — You know not how I love*
*her. —    I can hardly bid you adieu, till I come to the bottom of my paper.*
65     *To hear often from you will give me great pleasure. — God bless you. —*

*M. W.*

## WALHAM GREEN, 1781–?1783

**B**OTH SC 191 and SC 192 were written at the Bloods' house in the
village of Walham Green[1] in Middlesex just outside London.
The first tells of the death of Mary's mother, the second announces
the marriage of her sister Elizabeth.

The death of her mother and the "disagreeable circumstances"
(SC 191, line 7) that attended it Mary described in her last work, the
fragmentary novel *The Wrongs of Woman: or, Maria*:

> During my mother's illness, I was obliged to manage my father's temper,
> who, from the lingering nature of her malady, began to imagine that it was
> merely fancy. At this period, an artful kind of upper servant attracted my
> father's attention, and the neighbours made many remarks on the finery, not
> honestly got, exhibited at evening service. But I was too much occupied with
> my mother to observe any change in her dress or behaviour, or to listen to the
> whisper of scandal.

1. "Waltham" (SC 191, line 43) is presumably a copyist's error.

[ 979 ]

# The Carl H. Pforzheimer Library

I shall not dwell on the death-bed scene, lively as is the remembrance, or on the emotion produced by the last grasp of my mother's cold hand; when blessing me, she added, "A little patience, and all will be over!" . . . My father was violently affected by her death, recollected instances of his unkindness, and wept like a child.

My mother had solemnly recommended my sisters to my care, and bid me be a mother to them. They, indeed, became more dear to me as they became more forlorn; for, during my mother's illness, I discovered the ruined state of my father's circumstances, and that he had only been able to keep up appearances, by the sums which he borrowed of my uncle.[2]

The father's grief was short-lived. Within a short time of his wife's death his mistress was in charge in the house. "The house-keeper, as she was now termed, was the vulgar despot of the family." Consequently Mary again left home, this time to live with the Bloods at Walham Green.

There she apparently stayed for two years and left only when she was confronted with another domestic tragedy, namely the childbed psychosis of her sister Elizabeth following the birth of her first child.[3]

According to the records in the Guildhall Library, London, Elizabeth Wollstonecraft married Meredith Bishop on October 20, 1782.[4] By November the child had been born, so evidently the marriage was made under some pressure (which may have contributed to Elizabeth's breakdown).[5] By January 6 Mary had turned violently against Bishop and later in the month took Elizabeth away from him.[6]

2. Wollstonecraft, *Posthumous Works*, I, 173–174.

3. See above, Volume I, "Mary Wollstonecraft," pp. 43–45; Godwin, *Memoirs*, pp. 17–18; Paul, *Godwin*, I, 166–170.

4. Letter from Mr. A. H. Hall, F.L.A., Librarian, Guildhall Library, London: "the following is a transcript of an entry in the register of marriages of the church of St. Katherine by the Tower (*Guildhall Library MS. 9671*):

'Meredith Bishop Batchelor of the Parish of St. Mary Magdalene Bermondsey and Elizabeth Wollstonecraft Spister [*sic*] were married in this Church by Licence this twentieth day of October in the Year One Thousand seven Hundred and Eighty two by me George Baxter Minister in the Presence of Ed. Wollstonecraft [and] William Davis.'"

See also Eleanor L. Nicholes, ed., Mary Wollstonecraft, *A Vindication of the Rights of Men* (Gainesville, Florida, 1960), p. x.

5. It was perhaps to obscure the rapid sequence of the marriage and the birth that someone, possibly Lady Shelley, penciled in "1783" dates on these letters. (See above, Volume I, "Mary Wollstonecraft," p. 43.)                     6. *Ibid.*, p. 44.

SC 192, then, which both announces the marriage and praises Bishop (line 18)— "My sister however has done well, and married a worthy man, whose situation in life is truly eligible" — must have been written between October 20, 1782, and January 6, 1783. If so there is a span of about a year between SC 191 and SC 192. Jane apparently did not write to Mary until she had a special announcement to make, namely her "Sister's wedding." But Mary had also taken her time (line 4) — "I find by the date of your letter that the honey moon, and the next moon too must be almost over" — and perhaps did not reply until she, too, had some announcement to make, namely her own sister's marriage and her plans to leave for Lisbon.[7]

With SC 192 the correspondence comes to a close. Immediately after writing it Mary went into hiding with Elizabeth and Jane probably did not know how to reach her. At any rate the two seem to have lost contact. Jane may have heard no more of her friend until her years of fame in the 1790's.

---

7. Fanny Blood was engaged to Hugh Skeys, an Irish merchant with business connections in Portugal. In February 1785 Fanny went to Lisbon and married him there. Toward the end of the year Mary joined them. This trip had evidently been planned for some two years and was held up by Skeys' dilatory tactics. (Godwin, *Memoirs*, pp. 36–41; Wardle, *Wollstonecraft*, pp. 31, 38.)

SC 191    MARY WOLLSTONECRAFT TO JANE ARDEN, ?JANUARY–?MAY 1781

L (transcript), 2½ pages, pages [81, 83, 85] of COPYBOOK* containing also SC 178–SC 190 and SC 192.

*See SC 178, Bibliographical Description.

*I should be quite ashamed, my dear Jane to own that I received your obliging letter some months ago, if I could not give sufficient reason for my silence; but at the time it arrived, I was employed in the most melancholy way; — my poor mother was confined to her room, and had been so a long*

5    *while: — her disorder was a dropsy attended with many other disagreeable complaints, which at last ended in her death. — I was so fatigued with*

# The Carl H. Pforzheimer Library

SC 191 *nursing her, & the many disagreeable circumstances that occurred, that I could not think of writing to you, till I got a little better spirits. — Your sister was so polite as to write to me, I believe it was last year, but I have not*
10 *as yet answered it, and I have put it off so long, that I don't know how to set about it.*

  *— To say the truth I begin to hate writing, it is grown quite a task to me. — I was some time before I could rouse myself enough to tell you that I am alive, for I send this merely to convince you that I am in the land of the*
15 *living, and still remember you. — I often think of the merry days we spent together at Beverley, when we used to laugh from noon 'till night; — You are a laugher still, but I am a stupid creature, and you would be tired to death of me, if you were to be with me a week.*

  *I am glad to hear, that you are in every respect so pleasantly situated: —*
20 *I wish you may continue in it, and that it may be as advantageous as it is agreeable. — I assure you I envy* ~~you~~ *your trip; — of all places in the world, I long to visit Ireland and in particular the dear County of Clare. — The women are all handsome, and the men agreeable; — I honor their hospitality and doat on their freedom and ease, in short they are the people after my own*
25 *heart ——— I like their warmth of Temper, and if I was my own mistress I would spend my life with them: — However, as a friend, I would give you a caution, the men are dreadful flirts, so take care of your heart, and don't leave it in one of the Bogs. — Preserve your cheerful temper, and laugh & dance when a fiddle comes in your way, but beware of the sly collectors; ——*
30 *admire the pretty girls as much as you will, but dont so critically remark the beauty of the men: — You are a good girl — I would therefore have you grow fat, and your good nature, and obliging temper will always ensure you admirers that will have sense enough to prefer such good qualities to a baby face: — For my part — I have already got the wrinkles of old age, and so,*
35 *like a true woman, rail at what I don't possess. —*

      letter
  *The inclosed is to a friend, I should take it as a favor, if you would forward it to the next post; and I should be happy to hear soon from you. —  My stay in England is very uncertain, and I wish to hear from you*

[ 982 ]

SC 191    *before I leave it. — Tell me all about your family, and every thing else that gives you pleasure, and believe me to be Yours &ᵉᶜ —*

> *Mary Wollstonecraft.*
> *Mʳ Bloods, Waltham Green,*
> *Fulham, Middlesex. —*

45    *If you can procure a frank of the inclosed, — you would much oblige me. —*

SC 192    MARY WOLLSTONECRAFT TO JANE ARDEN, OCTOBER 20, 1782–JANUARY 6, 1783

L (transcript), 1½ pages, pages [85, 87, 89] of COPYBOOK* containing also SC 178–SC 191.

*See SC 178, Bibliographical Description.

*I congratulate you, my dear Jane, on account of your Sister's wedding, and am happy to find that she is settled to her satisfaction. — I was just going to desire you to wish her joy (to use the common phrase) but I am afraid my good wishes might be unseasonable, as I find by the date of your letter that*
5    *the honey moon, and the next moon too must be almost over — — The joy, and all that, sort of thing is certainly over by this time, and all the raptures have subsided, and the dear hurry of visiting and figuring away as a bride, and all the rest of the delights of matrimony are past and gone and have left no traces behind them, except disgust: — I hope I am mistaken, but this is the*
10    *fate of most married pairs. — Solomon says "there is nothing new under the sun" for which reason I will not marry, for I dont want to be tied to this nasty world, and old maids are of so little consequence — that "let them live or die, nobody will laugh or cry." — It is a happy thing to be a mere blank, and to be able to pursue one's own whims, where they lead, without having a*
15    *husband and half a hundred children at hand to teaze and controul a poor woman who wishes to be free. —    Some may follow Sᵗ Paul's advice "in doing well," but I, like a true born Englishwoman, will endeavour to do better. — My sister however has done well, and married a worthy man,*

SC 192  *whose situation in life is truly eligible. — You remember Bess; she was a*
20  *mere child when we were together, and it would have hurt our dignity to have*
*admitted her into our Parties, but she must now take place of us, being of the*
*most honorable order of matrons. — I am still in England, and likely to*
*remain here sometime longer, as some unexpected delays have retarded our*
*journey, but I believe we shall certainly go to Lisbon next spring. —     I*
25  *shall expect to hear from you soon; tell me all about your Beverley friends,*
*and tell me you are well and happy. ——*

*Make my good wishes acceptable to your Sister and assure yourself*
*of the love and esteem of*

*Your ever affectionate*
*Mary Wollstonecraft.*
30

# REFERENCE SOURCES, ABRIDGED
# TITLE LIST

Abinger Manuscripts — The manuscripts and letters of William Godwin, Mary Wollstonecraft, and others in the possession of Lord Abinger (Pforzheimer Microfilm).

Alcock and Holland — R. C. Alcock and F. C. Holland. *The Postmarks of Great Britain and Ireland, Being a Survey of British Postmarks from 1660 to 1940.* Cheltenham, England [1940].

Allibone — S. Austin Allibone. *A Critical Dictionary of English Literature and British and American Authors.* Philadelphia and London, 1884–1891.

*Alumni Cantabrigienses* — *Alumni Cantabrigienses*, ed. John Venn and J. A. Venn. Cambridge University Press, 1922 —

*Alumni Oxonienses* — *Alumni Oxonienses*, ed. Joseph Foster. Oxford, 1887–1891.

Blunden, *Leigh Hunt* — Edmund Blunden. *Leigh Hunt, a Biography.* London, 1930.

Blunden, *Shelley* — Edmund Blunden. *Shelley, a Life Story.* New York, 1947.

Boaden, *Inchbald* — *Memoirs of Mrs. Inchbald*, ed. James Boaden. London, 1833.

Boase — Frederic Boase. *Modern English Biography.* Truro, England, 1892–1921.

British Army List — *A List of the Officers of the Army and Royal Marines on Full and Half-Pay.* War Office, [London], 1754–1851.

Brown, *Godwin* — Ford K. Brown. *The Life of William Godwin.* London, Toronto, and New York, 1926.

*Burke's Landed Gentry* — *Genealogical and Heraldic History of the Landed Gentry*, ed. John Burke, Bernard Burke, *et al.* London, [various dates].

*Burke's Peerage* — *Genealogical and Heraldic History of the Peerage Baronetage and Knightage*, ed. John Burke, Bernard Burke, *et al.* London, [various dates].

# The Carl H. Pforzheimer Library

## Reference Sources

| | |
|---|---|
| Burr, *Correspondence* | *Correspondence of Aaron Burr and His Daughter Theodosia*, ed. Mark Van Doren. New York, 1929. |
| Burr, *Journal* | *The Private Journal of Aaron Burr, Reprinted in Full from the Original Manuscript . . .*, [ed. W. H. Sampson]. Rochester, N.Y., 1903. |
| Byron, *Letters and Journals* | *The Works of Lord Byron, Letters and Journals*, ed. Rowland E. Prothero. London and New York, 1898. |
| Cameron, *The Young Shelley* | Kenneth Neill Cameron. *The Young Shelley, Genesis of a Radical*. New York, 1950. |
| Cary's *Roads* | *Cary's New Itinerary or an Accurate Delineation of the Great Roads, Both Direct and Cross throughout England and Wales*. London, [various dates]. |
| *CBEL* | *Cambridge Bibliography of English Literature*. Cambridge University Press, 1940–1957. |
| Coleridge, *Letters* | *Collected Letters of Samuel Taylor Coleridge*, ed. Earl Leslie Griggs. Oxford, 1956–1959. |
| *Complete Peerage* | *The Complete Peerage*, ed. George E. Cokayne and Vicary Gibbs. London, 1910 —. |
| *DAB* | *Dictionary of American Biography*, ed. Allen Johnson and Dumas Malone. New York, 1928 —. |
| De Ricci | Seymour de Ricci. *A Bibliography of Shelley's Letters, Published and Unpublished*. [Bois-Colombes, France], Privately Printed, 1927. |
| *DNB* | *Dictionary of National Biography*, ed. Leslie Stephens and Sidney Lee. New York, 1908–1909. |
| Dowden, *Shelley* | Edward Dowden. *The Life of Percy Bysshe Shelley*. London, 1886. |
| Durant, "Preface" "Supplement" | *Memoirs of Mary Wollstonecraft Written by William Godwin . . . with a Preface, a Supplement*, ed. W. Clark Durant. London and New York, 1927. |

# Shelley and his Circle : Manuscripts

**Reference Sources**

Feltham, *Picture of London*  
The Picture of London for 1809, Being a Correct Guide to All the Curiosities, Amusements, Exhibitions, Public Establishments and Remarkable Objects in and near London . . . London, [1809].

Forman, *Shelley Library*  
H. Buxton Forman. *The Shelley Library, an Essay in Bibliography*. London, 1886.

Gisborne, *Journals and Letters*  
Maria Gisborne & Edward E. Williams, Shelley's Friends, Their Journals and Letters, ed. Frederick L. Jones. University of Oklahoma Press, 1951.

Godwin, Journal  
The manuscript journal of William Godwin (from 1788 to 1836) in the possession of Lord Abinger (Pforzheimer Microfilm).

Godwin, *Memoirs*  
William Godwin. *Memoirs of the Author of a Vindication of the Rights of Woman*. London, 1798. (The first edition used unless otherwise noted.)

Godwin, *Political Justice*  
(Priestley ed.)  
William Godwin. *Enquiry Concerning Political Justice and Its Influence on Morals and Happiness*, ed. F. E. L. Priestley. University of Toronto Press, 1946.

Grabo, *The Magic Plant*  
Carl Grabo. *The Magic Plant, the Growth of Shelley's Thought*. University of North Carolina Press, 1936.

Grylls, *Clairmont*  
R. Glynn Grylls. *Claire Clairmont, Mother of Byron's Allegra*. London, 1939.

Halkett and Laing  
Samuel Halkett and James Laing. *Dictionary of Anonymous and Pseudonymous English Literature*. Edinburgh and London, 1926–1956.

Harben, *Dictionary of London*  
Henry A. Harben. *A Dictionary of London. Being Notes Topographical and Historical Relating to the Streets and Principal Buildings in the City of London*. London, 1918.

Haydon, *Autobiography*  
*Life of Benjamin Robert Haydon, Historical Painter, from His Autobiography and Journals*, ed. Tom Taylor. London, 1853.

Hazlitt, *Complete Works*  
*The Complete Works of William Hazlitt*, ed. P. P. Howe. London, 1930–1934.

# The Carl H. Pforzheimer Library

## *Reference Sources*

Hogg, *Shelley*

Thomas Jefferson Hogg. *The Life of Percy Bysshe Shelley*, in *The Life of Percy Bysshe Shelley . . .*, ed. Humbert Wolfe. London, 1933.

Hogg, T. J., *The Life of Percy Bysshe Shelley*

Thomas Jefferson Hogg, *The Life of Percy Bysshe Shelley*. London, 1858 (first edition, used for Collations).

Horwood, *Plan of London*

R. Horwood. *Plan of the Cities of London and Westminster the Borough of Southwark, and Parts Adjoining Shewing Every House*. London, 1792–1799.

Hughes, *Nascent Mind*

A. M. D. Hughes. *The Nascent Mind of Shelley*. Oxford University Press, 1947.

Hunt, *Autobiography*

*The Autobiography of Leigh Hunt*, ed. Roger Ingpen. Westminster, 1903.

Hunt, *Correspondence*

*The Correspondence of Leigh Hunt*, ed. [Thornton Hunt]. London, 1862.

Hunt, *First Editions*

*My Leigh Hunt Library, the First Editions*, ed. Luther A. Brewer. Cedar Rapids, Iowa, 1932.

Hunt, *Letters*

*My Leigh Hunt Library, the Holograph Letters*, ed. Luther A. Brewer. Cedar Rapids, Iowa, 1938.

Ingpen, *Shelley in England*

Roger Ingpen. *Shelley in England: New Facts and Letters from the Shelley-Whitton Papers*. London, 1917.

Kippis, *Biographia Britannica*

*Biographia Britannica: or, the Lives of the Most Eminent Persons Who Have Flourished in Great Britain and Ireland*. 2nd edition, ed. Andrew Kippis. London, 1778–1793.

Koszul, *Jeunesse*

André Koszul. *La Jeunesse de Shelley*. Paris, 1910.

Lamb, *Letters*

*The Letters of Charles Lamb to Which Are Added Those of His Sister Mary Lamb*, ed. E. V. Lucas. London, 1935.

Lamb, *Works*

*The Works of Charles and Mary Lamb*, ed. E. V. Lucas. London, 1903–1905.

Landré, *Hunt*

Louis Landré. *Leigh Hunt*. Paris, 1935–1936.

## Reference Sources

*Letters about Shelley*

*Letters about Shelley Interchanged by Three Friends — Edward Dowden, Richard Garnett and Wm. Michael Rossetti*, ed. R. S. Garnett. London, 1917.

Lowndes

William Thomas Lowndes. *The Bibliographer's Manual of English Literature*. London, 1865.

MacCarthy, *Shelley*

Denis Florence MacCarthy. *Shelley's Early Life*. London, 1872.

Mary Shelley, *Letters*

*The Letters of Mary Shelley*, ed. Frederick L. Jones. University of Oklahoma Press, 1944.

*Mary Shelley's Journal*

*Mary Shelley's Journal*, ed. Frederick L. Jones. University of Oklahoma Press, 1947.

Marshall, *Mary Shelley*

Mrs. Julian Marshall. *The Life and Letters of Mary Wollstonecraft Shelley*. London, 1889.

Medwin, *Shelley*

Thomas Medwin. *The Life of Percy Bysshe Shelley*, ed. H. Buxton Forman. Oxford University Press, 1913.

*NED*

*New English Dictionary on Historical Principles*. Oxford University Press, 1888–1933.

*New Shelley Letters*

*New Shelley Letters*, ed. W. S. Scott. Yale University Press, 1949.

Notopoulos, *Platonism*

James A. Notopoulos. *The Platonism of Shelley*. Duke University Press, 1949.

Paterson's *Roads*

[Daniel] Paterson. *A New and Accurate Description of All the Direct and Principal Cross Roads in England and Wales and Part of Scotland*. London, [various dates].

Paul, *Godwin*

C. Kegan Paul. *William Godwin, His Friends and Contemporaries*. London, 1876.

Paul, *Wollstonecraft*

C. Kegan Paul. *Mary Wollstonecraft, Letters to Imlay, with Prefatory Memoir*. London, 1879.

Peacock, *Memoirs*

"Memoirs of Percy Bysshe Shelley," *The Works of Thomas Love Peacock*, Vol. VIII, ed. H. F. B. Brett-Smith and C. E. Jones (Halliford Edition). London, 1934.

# The Carl H. Pforzheimer Library

## Reference Sources

| | |
|---|---|
| Peacock, *Works* | *The Works of Thomas Love Peacock*, ed. H. F. B. Brett-Smith and C. E. Jones (Halliford Edition). London, 1924–1934. |
| Peacock, *Works* (1875) | *The Works of Thomas Love Peacock*, ed. Henry Cole. London, 1875. |
| Peck, *Shelley* | Walter Edwin Peck. *Shelley, His Life and Work*. Boston and New York, 1927. |
| Robinson, *British Post Office* | Howard Robinson. *The British Post Office, a History*. Princeton University Press, 1948. |
| Robinson, *Diary* | *Diary, Reminiscences, and Correspondence of Henry Crabb Robinson*, ed. Thomas Sadler. London, 1869. |
| Robinson, *On Books* | Henry Crabb Robinson. *On Books and Their Writers*, ed. Edith J. Morley. London, 1938. |
| Scott, *Hogg* | Winifred Scott. *Jefferson Hogg*. London, 1951. |
| *Shelley and Mary* | *Shelley and Mary*. For Private Circulation Only [London, 1882]. |
| Shelley, *Complete Works* | *The Complete Works of Percy Bysshe Shelley*, ed. Roger Ingpen and Walter E. Peck (Julian Edition). London, New York, 1926–1930. |
| *Shelley-Leigh Hunt* | *Shelley-Leigh Hunt: How Friendship Made History and Extended the Bounds of Human Freedom and Thought*, ed. R. Brimley Johnson. London, 1928. |
| Thieme-Becker | U. Thieme and Felix Becker. *Allgemeiner Lexikon der Bildenden Kunstler* . . . Leipzig, 1911–1947. |
| *TLS* | *Times Literary Supplement* (London). |
| Van Doren, *Peacock* | Carl Van Doren. *The Life of Thomas Love Peacock*. London, 1911. |
| Wardle, *Wollstonecraft* | Ralph M. Wardle. *Mary Wollstonecraft, a Critical Biography*. University of Kansas Press, 1951. |
| Wheatley, *London* | Henry B. Wheatley. *London Past and Present, Its History, Association, and Traditions*. London, 1891. |

# Shelley and his Circle : Manuscripts

*Reference Sources*

White, *Shelley*              Newman I. White. *Shelley*. New York, 1940.

Wise, *Shelley Library*      Thomas James Wise. *A Shelley Library, a Catalogue of Printed Books, Manuscripts and Autograph Letters by Percy Bysshe Shelley, Harriet Shelley and Mary Wollstonecraft Shelley*. London, 1924.

Wollstonecraft, *New Letters*      *New Letters of Mary Wollstonecraft and Helen Maria Williams*, ed. Benjamin P. Kurtz and Carrie C. Autry. University of California Press, 1937.

Wollstonecraft, *Posthumous Works*      Mary Wollstonecraft. *Posthumous Works of the Author of a Vindication of the Rights of Woman*, ed. William Godwin. London, 1798.

# INDEX OF NAMES

The spelling of English place-names follows that in *The Concise Oxford Dictionary of English Place-Names* (Oxford, 1960). Boldface type is used to designate authors whose manuscripts are in The Carl H. Pforzheimer Library and are transcribed in the present volumes.

# Index of Names

Baldwin, Edward, *pseud.*, *see* Godwin, William, WORKS
Barbauld, Anna Letitia, I:63, 66, 67, 69, 72, 161, 197, 198
Barbauld, Rev. Rochemont, I:72 fn.-73 fn.
Barclay, James, I:413, 415, 416
Barclay, Tritton and Bevan, I:428
Barking, Essex, I:41
Barlow, Joel, I:69, 125, 142
Barlow, Ruth, I:69, 125, 186
Barnes, Mr., II:520
Barnes, Thomas, I:187, 200
Barnfield, Southampton, II:880
Barry, Mr., I:194, 196 fn.
Barton, Mrs., II:484, 577
Barwell, Charles, I:92-93, 95, 138
Barwell, Richard, I:93 fn.
Barwell, Roger, I:93 fn.
Barwell, William, I:93
Bassett, Thomas, II:602
Bastard, Rev. and Mrs., II:596
Bath, Somerset, I:42-43, 46, 230-231; II:479, 480, 486, 496, 513, 522, 526 fn., 539, 567, 569, 579, 580, 581, 595, 889, 936, 938, 939, 940, 959-961, 963-964, 967, 968, 971, 972, 973, 974, 976
Baxter, Christina, II:558, 559
Baxter, Elizabeth, II:559
Baxter, George, II:980 fn.
Baxter, Isabella (Doig), II:559
Baxter, Jessie, II:559
Baxter, John Cowley, II:559
Baxter, Mary Ann (Scott), II:559
Baxter, Robert, II:559
Baxter, William Thomas, I:322; II:542, 558-559
Bayers, Lady, II:579
Bays, N., I:382
Bazire & Haddan, I:386
Beaconsfield, Buckinghamshire, I:33
Beard, Mary, I:60
Bearwood, Dr., II:486, 581 fn., 582
Beauchamp, Eliza, II:751, 752, 754, 760, 770, 773, 777, 779, 781-782, 791, 816, 819, 841, 866, 867, 868-869, 903
Beauchamp, Robert Farthing, II:867 fn., 868 fn.
Beckford, William, I:160

Beckford, William Horace, II:589
Bedford, Duke of, *see* Russell, Lord John
Bennet, Mrs., I:232, 234 fn.
Bennett, Catherine, II:490, 503, 516, 522, 529, 533, 537, 569, 572, 573, 580, 581, 588, 589, 590, 593, 596
Bennett, Charles (Lyme Regis, Dorset), II:572
Bennett, Charles (Pitt House), II:503, 509, 510, 520, 528, 530, 569, 580, 591, 592
Bennett, Mrs. Charles (Pitt House), II:511, 512, 514, 521, 524, 527, 580, 587, 591, 592
Bennett, Frances, II:490, 503, 516, 522, 588, 590, 593
Bennett, John, II:572 fn.
Bennett, Miss P., II:518
Bennett, Sarah Burlton, II:572
Bennett, William, II:503, 510 fn., 516 fn., 517, 518, 529, 582
Bennett, Mrs. William, II:580
Bensley, T., I:96
Benson, Miss, II:594
Bentham, Jeremy, I:103, 112, 181 fn., 442, 443
Berkeley, Bishop George, I:206, 208
Bernbaum, Ernest, I:270
Berry, Mr., II:541, 543, 544
Berwick, St. John, Wiltshire, II:503, 537, 538, 593
Berwick St. Leonard, Wiltshire, II:494, 495
Bethell, Hugh, II:941, 948
Bethlehem Hospital, I:37, 38
Beverley, Yorkshire, I:41; II:933-938, 939, 940-954, 959, 961, 962, 964, 965, 966, 971, 982, 984
Bielby, Lady Elizabeth, II:947
Billington, Elizabeth, II:547, 550 fn.
Binfield, Berkshire, I:327; II:546 fn.
Bingham, Mr. and Mrs., II:533, 572, 590
Bishop, Elizabeth (Wollstonecraft), I:40, 43-45, 49, 85, 87, 124, 125, 127, 132; II:953, 962, 966, 974, 979, 980-981, 983-984
Bishop, Meredith, I:43-45; II:980-981, 983
Bishopsgate, London, I:40, 101
Blackfriars, London, I:247 fn.

# Index of Names

Blake, William, I:51, 69, 129; II:620
Blandford, Dorset, II:478, 498, 506, 509, 535, 566, 595
Blenkinsop, Mrs., I:186, 188, 189, 192, 193
Bligh, Capt., II:883
Bligh, Mrs. Catherine, II:883–884
Blood, Mr., I:49
Blood, Mrs., I:43, 49
Blood, Frances, *see* Skeys, Frances (Blood)
Blood, George, I:49, 75, 78, 86
Bloomsbury, London, II:546
Boccaccio, Giovanni, I:302
Boinville, Cornelia, *see* Turner, Cornelia (Boinville)
Boinville, Mrs. Harriet, I:112; II:551
Bonaparte, Joseph, I:441
Bonaparte, Napoleon, *see* Napoleon I
Boningale, Shropshire, I:223
Bonnycastle, John, I:69
Booth, ——, I:188
Booth, David, II:540–544, 557–560, 603
Booth, Isabella (Baxter), II:559
Booth, Margaret (Baxter), II:542, 559
Bowles, Mr., II:591
Bowring, John, II:896
Boy, Mr. and Mrs., II:505, 523, 528, 538
Bracknell, Berkshire, I:98–99, 106
Braham, John, II:547, 550 fn.
Brailsford, H. N., I:22, 52
Brant, John, I:420
Brashier, William, I:380–381, 394, 421
Bregantz, Aline, *see* Fillettaz, Aline (Bregantz)
Brentford, Buckinghamshire, II:923
Brentford, Middlesex, II:477
Brereton, Col., II:514, 521, 579
Brereton, Mrs., II:533
Brett-Smith, H. F. B., I:113
Brewster, John, II:737, 738
Brewster, Rev. John, II:738, 756
Bridgewater, Earl of (7th Earl), I:738, 744, 753
Brighton, Sussex, I:419
Brissot, Jacques Pierre, I:51, 123 fn., 126
Bristol Hot Wells, Gloucestershire, I:46
Bromley family, II:483, 517, 520, 574
Brooke, Rev. Stopford, II:897
Brooks, Son and Dixon, II:546, 908
Brotherton, Mr., II:531

Brown, Barrett, *Great Democrats*, I:22
Brown, Charles Brockden, I:20
Brown, Ford K., *The Life of William Godwin*, I:296, 447
Brown, John, II:727–729
Browne, Felicia Dorothea, *see* Hemans, Felicia Dorothea (Browne)
Browne, John, I:24, 26, 32; II:562
Buchanan, Robert, I:104
Bull, G., I:128
Bulwer-Lytton, Edward (1st Baron Lytton), I:20
Burdett, Sir Francis, I:14, 263
Burdon, Richard, II:726 fn., 847, 850
Burgh, James, I:49 fn., 56, 58
Burgh, Mrs. James, I:45, 46, 59, 85–86
Burke, Edmund, I:9, 57, 65, 206, 324
Burlton, Mrs. and Miss, II:528
Burlton, William, II:572 fn.
Burney, Charles, Sr., II:564
Burney, Rev. Charles, Jr., II:563–564, 598–600
Burney, Fanny, I:238, 241; II:564, 960
Burnham, Norfolk, II:936, 961 fn.
Burr, Aaron, I:34, 185, 297, 299, 324, 326, 327, 328, 329, 330, 331, 441–443
Burr, Theodosia, I:328, 330
Burrell, Peter, 1st Baron Gwydir, I:310, 311, 312
Burton, Mrs., II:591
Bury, Miss Lucy, II:585, 596
Bury St. Edmunds, Suffolk, I:222
Busby, Thomas, II:547, 550 fn.
Bute, 3rd Earl, *see* Stuart, John
Butler, Mr., II:529
Buttenshaw, Edward, I:430
Button, Miss, II:528
Button, S. J., II:694–695
Button and Whitaker, II:695
Buttson, Mrs., II:523
Byles, John Barnard, I:378–379, 434
Byron, Anne Isabella (Milbanke), Lady Byron, I:392 fn.
Byron, Lord George Gordon (6th Baron), I:12, 15, 107, 109, 218, 242, 265, 266, 292; II:610, 653, 903

Cadiz, I:289
Calais, I:125

# Index of Names

Comfort, James, I:429
Compton, Wiltshire, II:483, 531, 574
Condorcet, Marquis de, II:614
Constable, Archibald, I:312, 342
Cook, Mr., II:586
Cooke, Mrs. and Miss, II:490, 505, 517,
    518, 523, 524, 525, 527, 528, 529, 530,
    531, 532, 535, 536, 580, 588, 589,
    590, 591, 592, 593, 594, 595
Cooke, L., II:529
Coolanowle, Ireland, I:73 fn.
Cooper, Thomas, I:21, 123 fn., 152, 207,
    227, 228, 313–314
Cotton, Mrs., I:197, 198
Coulson, Walter, I:103
Courtenay, Lord, 3rd Viscount, II:770,
    774
Courtney, Mr., II:534
Covent Garden Theatre, London, I:240;
    II:543 fn., 649, 939
Coward, William, I:23, 24–25
Cowley, Abraham, I:458, 460
Cowper, William, I:70
Cramer, Franz, II:547, 550 fn.
Cramer, Johann Baptist, II:547, 550 fn.
Cranbourn, Dorset, II:567, 590, 591
Croome, Miss, II:523, 528
Crosdill, John, II:547, 550 fn.
Crow Street Theatre, Dublin, I:81
Cuckfield, Sussex, II:477, 484, 487, 494–
    495, 517, 576, 579, 586 fn., 590 fn.,
    782–784, 787, 793, 800, 842, 864, 868
Curran, Amelia, I:410
Curran, John Philpot, I:210, 214, 229, 239,
    317, 407–412, 432, 438–441; II:601,
    603
Cuthy and Cuthy, I:421
Cwm Elan, Radnorshire, II:486, 489, 497,
    498, 525, 581, 819, 824, 829, 830, 832–
    838, 842, 844, 845, 855, 857, 865

Dallaway, Rev. Edward, II:725, 726 fn.
Daly, Richard, I:81
Dance, William, II:547, 550 fn.
Daniel, Peter Austin, I:104
Dante, II:616
D'Arblay, Mme., *see* Burney, Fanny
Darwin, Erasmus, II:847, 850
Davenant, Sir William, I:448–467

Daventry Academy, Northamptonshire,
    II:562
Davis, William, II:980 fn.
Davy, Sir Humphry, I:250; II:867
Dawe, Elizabeth, I:391, 392
Dawe, George, I:383–385, 389–392, 442
Dawe, Henry Edward, I:384 fn.
Dawe, Philip, I:384 fn.
Dawson, Sarah (Regis), II:938, 939, 940,
    959, 960, 961, 962, 968, 972–974, 977
Dawson, William, Sr., II:961, 964
Dawson, William, Jr., II:938, 961
Dawson, Brooks, Son and Dixon, *see*
    Brooks, Son and Dixon
Dayrell, Rev. John, II:707, 709
Deal, Kent, I:97
Dealty, ——, I:145
Debenham, Suffolk, I:24
Delaney, Mary Granville, I:80
Demosthenes, II:662
Denham, John, I:449
Denham, Dr. Thomas, I:194–195
Dent, Rosamond Blanche Isabel, II:909 fn.
Deptford, Kent, II:923
De Ricci, Seymour, II:778, 802, 813
Devereux, Andrew Peter, I:296
Devereux, Mary Jane, *see* Godwin, Mary
    Jane
Devizes, Wiltshire, II:581 fn., 582
Devon, Mrs., II:519
D'Holbach, Paul Henri Thiry, Baron,
    II:686
Dickens, Charles, I:20
Dickson, Elizabeth, *see* Wollstonecraft,
    Elizabeth (Dickson)
Dickson, Lucy, I:85
Diderot, Denis, II:686
Dimmer, Mary, II:509, 529, 531, 533, 539,
    566, 569, 571, 579, 583, 586, 595, 597
Dinton, Buckinghamshire, II:487, 592
Dionysius of Halicarnassus, I:206
Dobson, Mrs. and Miss, II:592
Doddridge, Philip, I:24, 72 fn.; II:562 fn.
Dodgson, Mrs. Beryl, II:910
Doig, Isabella, *see* Baxter, Isabella (Doig)
Doig, Robert, II:559
Donalson, Capt., II:588
Donhead St. Andrew, Wiltshire, II:480,
    481, 503, 522, 523, 532, 536, 566, 580,
    590, 593

# Index of Names

# Index of Names

# Index of Names

# Index of Names

# Index of Names

# Index of Names

# Index of Names

# Index of Names

# Index of Names

# Index of Names

# Index of Names

# Index of Names

Shacklewell, Middlesex, I:73 fn., 96, 316

Shaftesbury, Dorset, II:476, 505, 539, 598, 682

Sharp, Richard, I:431–432

Sharp, William, I:433

Sharpe, Charles Kirkpatrick, II:739 fn.

Shaw, George Bernard, II:611, 621

Shelley, Sir Bysshe, I:410; II:604, 605, 726 fn., 746, 752, 768

Shelley, Charles, II:610, 629 fn., 898 fn.

Shelley, Clara, II:610

**Shelley, Elizabeth**, II:879

and Harriet Grove, II:481, 482, 483, 484, 485, 486, 487, 492, 501, 510 fn., 524, 526, 528, 529, 530, 531, 533, 534, 535, 539, 540, 566, 567, 568, 569, 570, 571, 573, 576, 577, 579, 585

and John Grove, II:861, 873, 876

and T. J. Hogg, II:609, 628–631, 668–678, 686, 687–688, 692, 699, 700–706, 708, 761, 766, 768, 779, 784, 786, 789–790, 793, 794–829, 830, 831, 847, 851–855, 861, 873, 876

death, II:629

WORKS:

"Cold cold is the blast," II:625–627, 629–631

*Original Poetry* (by "Victor and Cazire"), II:486, 487, 493, 590, 607, 625 fn., 628–631, 634–635, 640, 645, 647, 674, 855 fn.

[?] "Yes! The Arms of Britannia," II:701–703

Shelley, Harriet (Westbrook):

and Charles Grove, II:717, 883

and Thomas Grove, II:498, 525 fn.

and T. L. Peacock, I:98–99, 108

and Mary Shelley, II:879

and P. B. Shelley, I:98–99, 265; II:490, 494, 525 fn., 609, 668, 709, 717, 751–752, 754–762, 766, 770, 773, 777, 778, 782, 783, 784, 791, 810, 816, 819–820, 830–873, 876, 879, 880, 883, 898, 903

and Sir Timothy Shelley, II:866–868

death, I:265; II:606

family, II:866–868

Shelley, Hellen, II:479, 490, 501, 517, 538, 609, 628, 758, 759, 849 fn., 858 fn., 879, 889–890

Shelley, Ianthe, I:389 fn.; 610, 867, 898 fn.

Shelley, Lady Jane, I:50; II:668, 671, 805 fn., 892, 893, 894, 896, 897 fn., 905

Shelley, John, II:892

Shelley, Sir John, II:867, 909 fn.

Shelley, Margaret, II:879

Shelley, Mary, *see* Trevor, Mary (Shelley)

Shelley, Mary W.:

and T. J. Hogg, II:904, 906

and T. L. Peacock, I:102–103, 108

and P. B. Shelley, I:15, 16, 99–102; II:610

early years, I:12, 50, 186, 193, 196, 199, 293, 322

Journal, I:100; II:628 fn., 913

provenance, II:893, 901–902, 907, 909, 910, 911–912, 913

WORKS:

*Frankenstein*, II:893

"The Trial of Love," I:180 fn.

**Shelley, Percy Bysshe:**

and Bishop George Berkeley, I:208

and David Booth, II:542

and Lord Byron, I:266, 267; II:653–654, 903

and William Godwin, I:14, 15, 21, 207, 208, 218, 385, 464; II:610, 614, 678, 779, 780, 842

and Harriet Grove, II:475, 477–493, 501, 510, 511, 512, 513, 514, 516, 517, 518, 519, 520, 522, 523, 524, 525, 526, 527, 528, 529, 568, 569, 570, 571 fn., 572, 573, 576 fn., 577, 585, 588, 607, 609, 625, 630, 647, 668, 669, 674, 675, 681–682, 686, 692, 693, 699, 704, 708, 709, 713, 761, 766, 793, 815

and Elizabeth Hitchener, II:645, 678 fn., 815, 830 fn., 831, 832, 834, 836, 838, 846, 858, 863, 864, 865, 866, 900, 917–918

and T. J. Hogg, I:36; II:488, 607–609, 611, 629–631, 634, 640, 644, 658–659, 663, 665–666, 668–694, 699–716, 723, 724, 731–741, 743–876, 894, 904, 906–907

# Index of Names

and William Whitton, II:730, 734, 739,
741, 745, 903
franking privileges, II:635, 709–710,
788, 918 fn.
*Letters by, to:*
Robert Clarke, II:749–750
John Hogg, II:734–735
T. J. Hogg, II:730
P. B. Shelley, II:739–740
*Letter to, from:*
P. B. Shelley, II:719–721, 724–725
provenance, II:902, 909
will, II:889, 890

Shelley, William, II:610
Shelley-Rolls, Sir John C. E., II:892, 893
Shelley-Sidney, Henrietta Frances, II:724,
726 fn.
Shelley-Sidney, John, II:726 fn.
Shenley, Capt., I:266
Shepherd, Richard Herne, II:633–634
Sheppard, Ed., I:429
Sheppard, William, I:429
Shere, Thomas, II:566, 587
Sheridan, R. B., I:12, 209, 236–242, 260,
301
Sherwill, James Lind, II:639 fn.
Sherwill, Lucy (Lind), II:636, 639 fn.
Sherwill, M. E., II:635–636, 638
Sherwill, Markham, II:639 fn.
Shield, William, II:547–550
Shifnal, Shropshire, I:219, 223
Shrewsbury, Shropshire, I:223
Sidmouth, Lord (1st Viscount Sidmouth),
I:37; II:600
Siddons, Sarah, I:240, 241
Silsbee, Edward, II:910–911
Skeys, Frances (Blood), I:42, 43, 44, 45,
46; II:940, 962, 966, 972, 974, 976,
979, 980, 981 fn.
Skeys, Hugh, II:981 fn.
Skifington, Mr., II:574
Skinner, Miss, II:572
Skinner, Mr., II:567
Skinner Street, London, I:215, 411, 431,
437
Slack, Henry J., II:900
Slatter, Henry, II:605, 678, 727–729
Slatter, John, II:727–729
Smelt, ——, II:942, 953

Smets, Alexander A., I:170 fn.
Smith, Adam, II:720
Smith, Ashley, I:55–56
Smith, Charlotte, I:64, 67, 71
Smith, Horace, I:103, 276
Smith, James, I:276
Smith, John, I:121
Smith, William, I:431, 433
Smock Alley Theatre, Dublin, I:81
Smollet, Lt. Col. Alexander, II:636, 639 fn.
Snow, George, II:532, 566, 567, 596
Snow Hill, London, I:215; II:600, 678 fn.
Somers Town, Middlesex, I:185 fn., 215,
297, 437
Sophocles, II:912–913
Sothren, Mrs., I:446
Soulaire, Jean Louis, I:295, 300
Southampton, Hampshire, I:42; II:483,
574, 586, 960, 962, 963, 967, 968
Southey, Robert, I:10, 12, 13, 107, 221,
234, 257, 262, 271, 330, 433; II:761
Spettisbury, Dorset, II:596
Speyer, James, I:324, 331
Spezzia, Bay of, II:610
Spinoza, II:707, 709 fn.
Spital Square, London, I:40
Spitalfields, Northumberland, I:39 fn.
Stacey, Benjamin, I:428–429
Stacey, Sophia, II:894, 895
Staines, Rev. Samuel, II:498
Stanhope, ——, II:942, 954
Stanhope, Mr., II:575
Steele, Sir Richard, I:312
Steers, F., I:388
Stephen, Sir Leslie, I:21
Stephens, Mrs. Ann S., I:331
Stephens, Frederic G., I:392
Stephenson, M., I:420
Sterne, Laurence, I:302; II:706; *Sermons*, II:580; *Tristram Shandy*, I:158,
160
Stevenson, Sir John, II:696
Stewart, Lady, II:585
Still, John, II:505, 532, 537
Still, Mrs. John, II:532
Still, Mrs. Peter, II:518, 519, 592
Stillwell, John Edwin, *The History of the
Burr Portraits*, I:331
Stockdale, John Joseph, II:487, 590 fn.,
631, 632–635, 677, 701, 707, 709, 711,

# Index of Names

# Index of Names

# Index of Names

# Index of Names

# DATE DUE

| | | | |
|---|---|---|---|
| | | | |
| | | | |
| | | | |
| | | | |
| | | | |
| | | | |
| | | | |
| | | | |
| | | | |
| | | | |
| | | | |
| | | | |
| | | | |
| | | | |
| | | | |
| | | | |
| | | | |
| | | | |
| | | | |
| | | | |
| | | | |

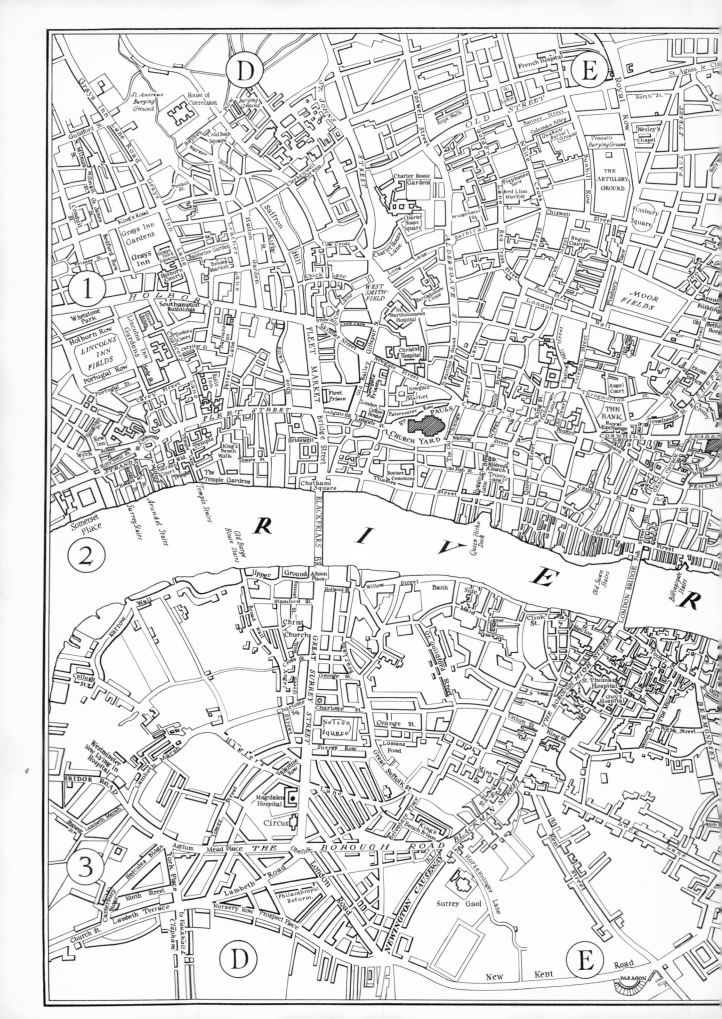